Handbook of Posttraumatic Stress

The *Handbook of Posttraumatic Stress* provides a comprehensive review of post-traumatic stress in its multiple dimensions, analyzing causation and epidemiology through prevention and treatment.

Written by a diverse group of scholars, practitioners, and advocates, the chapters in this book seek to understand the history, the politics, and the biological, psychological, and social processes underlying posttraumatic stress disorder (PTSD). Featuring studies that focus on some of the most seriously affected occupational groups, the text examines topics such as how individuals experience PTSD in different work settings and the complexities of diagnosis, treatment, and recovery for those workers and their families. Together, the contributions provide an in-depth examination of the currently understood causes, impacts and treatments of and for posttraumatic stress, mobilizing academic, administrative, and clinical knowledge, and lived experience to inform ongoing and future work in the field.

Drawing from a range of different topics, fields of study, and research methods, this text will appeal to readers across medical, mental health, and academic disciplines.

Rosemary Ricciardelli, PhD, is professor of sociology and criminology at Memorial University Newfoundland, Canada. Elected to the Royal Society of Canada, her research centres on evolving understandings of gender, vulnerabilities, risk, and experiences and issues within different facets of the criminal justice system.

Stephen Bornstein, PhD, is a political scientist and is the director of the Newfoundland and Labrador Centre for Applied Health Research at Memorial University Newfoundland, Canada. He has served as the co-director of the SafetyNet Centre for Occupational Health and Safety Research at Memorial and as assistant deputy minister of Intergovernmental Affairs in the government of the province of Ontario, Canada.

Alan Hall, PhD, retired from his full-time position in the sociology department at Memorial University Newfoundland, Canada in 2019. He now has an honorary research professorship at Memorial and is currently involved in research on the role of worker participation in workplace COVID-19 safety plans.

R. Nicholas Carleton, PhD, is a professor of psychology and scientific director for the Canadian Institute for Public Safety Research and Treatment. He is well published with several prestigious awards and substantial research funding.

Handbook of Posttraumatic Stress

Psychosocial, Cultural, and Biological Perspectives

Edited by
Rosemary Ricciardelli,
Stephen Bornstein, Alan Hall,
and R. Nicholas Carleton

First published 2022
by Routledge
605 Third Avenue, New York, NY 10158

and by Routledge
2 Park Square, Milton Park, Abingdon, Oxon OX14 4RN

Routledge is an imprint of the Taylor & Francis Group, an informa business

© 2022 selection and editorial matter, Rosemary Ricciardelli, Stephen Bornstein, Alan Hall, and R. Nicholas Carleton; individual chapters, the contributors

The right of Rosemary Ricciardelli, Stephen Bornstein, Alan Hall, and R. Nicholas Carleton to be identified as the authors of the editorial material, and of the authors for their individual chapters, has been asserted in accordance with sections 77 and 78 of the Copyright, Designs and Patents Act 1988.

All rights reserved. No part of this book may be reprinted or reproduced or utilised in any form or by any electronic, mechanical, or other means, now known or hereafter invented, including photocopying and recording, or in any information storage or retrieval system, without permission in writing from the publishers.

Trademark notice: Product or corporate names may be trademarks or registered trademarks, and are used only for identification and explanation without intent to infringe.

Library of Congress Cataloging-in-Publication Data
Names: Ricciardelli, Rose, 1979– editor.
Title: Handbook of posttraumatic stress: psychosocial, cultural, and biological perspectives / edited by Rosemary Ricciardelli [and three others].
Description: New York, NY: Routledge, 2022. |
Includes bibliographical references and index. |
Identifiers: LCCN 2021011520 (print) | LCCN 2021011521 (ebook) |
ISBN 9780815375722 (hardback) | ISBN 9780815375777 (paperback) |
ISBN 9780815375777 (ebook)
Subjects: LCSH: Post-traumatic stress disorder. |
Post-traumatic stress disorder–Treatment.
Classification: LCC RC552.P67 .H348 2022 (print) |
LCC RC552.P67 (ebook) DDC 616.85/21–dc23
LC record available at https://lccn.loc.gov/2021011520
LC ebook record available at https://lccn.loc.gov/2021011521

ISBN: 978-0-8153-7572-2 (hbk)
ISBN: 978-0-8153-7577-7 (pbk)
ISBN: 978-1-3511-3463-7 (ebk)

DOI: 10.4324/9781351134637

Typeset in Times New Roman
by Newgen Publishing UK

Contents

List of Illustrations	viii
List of Contributors	x
Acknowledgements	xvi

Introduction	1

ROSEMARY RICCIARDELLI, STEPHEN BORNSTEIN, ALAN HALL, AND R. NICHOLAS CARLETON

PART 1
Foundational   13

1   Changes in Our Understanding of Trauma and the
Human Psyche as a Consequence of War: A Brief History   15
SAMANTHA C. HORSWILL AND R. NICHOLAS CARLETON

2   A Systematic Review of the Prevalence of
Posttraumatic Stress Disorder Reported in
Canadian Studies   38
MURRAY WEEKS, SU-BIN PARK, SAMANTHA GHANEM,
SIEARA PLEBON-HUFF, ANNE-MARIE ROBERT, HARRY MACKAY,
AND ALLANA G. LEBLANC

3   Posttraumatic Stress Disorder and the Limits of
Presumptive Legislation   109
THERESA SZYMANSKI AND ALAN HALL

4   Recognizing Posttraumatic Stress Disorder in
Primary Care   131
JAMES M. THOMPSON, ALEXANDRA HEBER, JON DAVINE,
RYAN MURRAY, AND DONALD R. MCCREARY

vi *Contents*

5 The Epidemiology of PTSD in Canada 157
DANIEL MARRELLO, BETH PATTERSON, JASMINE TURNA,
JASMINE ZHANG, AND MICHAEL VAN AMERINGEN

PART 2
Perspectives and Populations 175

6 Psychology of Men and Masculinities: Implications for
Men's Experiences of Posttraumatic Stress Disorder 177
DONALD R. MCCREARY

7 Implications of PTSD for Military Veteran Families 198
HEIDI CRAMM, DEBORAH NORRIS, CHLOÉ HOULTON,
MOLLY FLINDALL-HANNA, AND LINNA TAM-SETO

8 Posttraumatic Stress Symptoms in Workers within
the Homeless Serving Sector: The Impact of
Organizational Factors 221
JEANNETTE WAEGEMAKERS SCHIFF AND ANNETTE M. LANE

9 Emotional Labour, Police, and the Investigation of Sex
Crimes Perpetrated Against Children: Posttraumatic
Stress and the Toll of Dirty Work 247
DALE SPENCER, ALEXA DODGE, ROSEMARY RICCIARDELLI,
AND DALE BALLUCCI

10 Firefighters and Posttraumatic Stress Disorder:
A Scoping Review 264
HEIDI CRAMM, LINNA TAM-SETO, ALYSON MAHAR,
LUCIA RÜHLAND, AND R. NICHOLAS CARLETON

11 Correctional Officers: Experiences of Potentially
Psychologically Traumatic Events and Mental Health
Injuries 296
ROSEMARY RICCIARDELLI, NICOLE GERARDA POWER, AND
DANIELLA SIMAS MEDEIROS

12 Posttraumatic Growth among Prisoners: Findings,
Controversies, and Implications 318
ESTHER F. J. C. VAN GINNEKEN AND SIEBRECHT VANHOOREN

Contents vii

PART 3
Biology, Understanding, and Treatment 341

13 The Use, Validity, and Translational Utility of Animal
Models of Posttraumatic Stress Disorder 343
ERIC D. EISENMANN, CHELSEA E. CADLE,
AND PHILLIP R. ZOLADZ

14 Developing a Reliable Animal Model of PTSD in
Order to Test Potential Pharmacological Treatments:
Predator Stress and the Mechanistic Target of
Rapamycin 373
PHILLIP MACCALLUM, JESSE WHITEMAN, THERESE KENNY,
KATELYN FALLON, SRIYA BHATTACHARYA, JAMES DROVER,
AND JACQUELINE BLUNDELL

15 Severing the Trauma—PTSD Connection with Public
Safety Personnel: The Role of Personal Social Support
Networks 403
GRACE B. EWLES, PETER A. HAUSDORF, TERRY A. BEEHR,
AND M. GLORIA GONZÁLEZ-MORALES

16 Group Cognitive Processing Therapy for PTSD:
Preliminary Outcomes, Group Cohesion, Therapeutic
Alliance, and Participant Satisfaction in Current
and Former Members of the Canadian Military and
Federal Police Force 429
SARAH J. CHAULK AND DAVID J. PODNAR

17 Eye Movement Desensitization and Reprocessing in
PTSD: Neurobiology and its Applications in Other
Mental Disorders 457
CRISTINA TRENTINI, SARA CARLETTO, AND MARCO PAGANI

Conclusion: Towards a Better Future 482
ALAN HALL, ROSEMARY RICCIARDELLI, STEPHEN BORNSTEIN,
AND R. NICHOLAS CARLETON

Index 490

Illustrations

Figures

2.1 PRISMA flow diagram of included studies on the prevalence of PTSD in Canada   42

2.2 Descriptive analyses of the prevalence (%) of PTSD for: (a) lifetime prevalence; (b) current prevalence—clinical diagnosis; (c) current prevalence—self-reported, occupation-related; and (d) current prevalence—self-reported, non-occupation-related   44

10.1 Prisma chart   267

14.1 mTOR activation in control and stressed groups across subregions of the hippocampus in each hemisphere. C. mTOR activation by subregion of the periaqueductal grey   384

14.2 mTOR activation in control and stressed groups across subregions of the hippocampus in each hemisphere. C. mTOR activation by subregion of the periaqueductal grey   385

14.3 mTOR activation by subregion of the periaqueductal grey   385

14.4 Exposure freezing for control and stressed animals during the rat-exposure test   388

14.5 Re-exposure freezing for control and stressed animals following the rat-exposure test   388

14.6 Time spent on open arms of elevated plus maze for control and stressed animals following the rat-exposure test   389

14.7 Number of entries into light side of light–dark box for control and stressed animals following the rat-exposure test   389

14.8 Freezing for the four Experiment 2B groups during re-exposure to the rat-exposure test context   390

14.9 Ratio time (time in open arms/time in all arms) in the elevated plus maze for the four groups in Experiment 2B   390

16.1 Participant mean ratings on the group climate questionnaire on the subscales of engaged, conflict, and avoiding at pre-, mid-, and post-treatment   443

List of Illustrations ix

16.2 Participant mean scores on Therapeutic Alliance subscale of the Alert Signal Client questionnaire at pre-, mid-, and post-treatment 444

16.3 Participant mean ratings on the Session Rating Scale by session 445

Tables

2.1 Summary of all included studies 47

2.A1 Database search strategies used in the current systematic review 63

2.A2 Lifetime prevalence: Details of included clinical diagnosis and self-report studies 65

2.A3 Current prevalence: Details of included clinical diagnosis and self-report studies 73

2.A4 Modified Newcastle–Ottawa Quality Assessment 105

4.A1 Some of the many faces of adult PTSD. These fictitious cases demonstrate principles of trauma-informed primary care 151

6.1 General overview of reviewed masculinity constructs 179

7.1 Complete list of search terms across databases—PTSD and Secondary Trauma 200

8.1 Participant demographics 227

8.2 Regression analysis of burnout, secondary traumatic stress, and trauma symptoms 230

8.3 Correlational analysis of organizational factors 231

15.1 Social support dimensions summary 419

16.1 Demographic variables 439

16.2 Data collection schedule 440

16.3 Means and standard deviations for the primary symptom variables (PCL-5, PHQ-9, GAD-7, and OQ-45) at pre-, post-, and three-month follow-up 442

17.1 Overview of EMDR treatment 459

Boxes

4.1 PC-PTSD (Primary Care PTSD) screening tool, DSM-5 version (National Center for PTSD) 138

4.2 A knowledge transfer tool summarizing principles of recognizing PTSD in primary care 143

10.1 Search terms for each database 266

Contributors

Editors

Rosemary Ricciardelli is professor of Sociology and Criminology at Memorial University. Elected to the Royal Society of Canada, her research centres on evolving understandings of gender, vulnerabilities, risk, and experiences and issues within different facets of the criminal justice system.

Stephen Bornstein is a political scientist by training. His graduate degrees are from Harvard University. He is the director of the Newfoundland and Labrador Centre for Applied Health Research at Memorial. From 2001 through 2020, he was the co-director of the SafetyNet Centre for Occupational Health and Safety Research at Memorial. From 1991 through 1995 he served as assistant deputy minister of Intergovernmental Affairs in the government of the province of Ontario.

Alan Hall retired from his full-time position in the Sociology Department at Memorial University in 2019 with research focused on occupational health and safety. He now has an honorary research professor position with Memorial and is currently involved in research on the role of worker participation in workplace COVID-19 safety plans. His most recent publication is *The Objectivities and Politics of Occupational Risk* (Routledge, 2021).

R. Nicholas Carleton, professor of Psychology, is scientific director for the Canadian Institute for Public Safety Research and Treatment. He is well-published with several prestigious awards and substantial research funding.

Contributors

Dale Ballucci is an assistant professor in the Department of Sociology at Western University. She is a criminologist who investigates policing, administration of criminal justice, and theories of governance.

Terry A. Beehr is a professor emeritus of Psychology at Central Michigan University. His research interests include careers, employee survey research, leadership, occupational stress, and retirement.

List of Contributors xi

Sriya Bhattacharya completed her PhD from Memorial University and is currently completing a postdoctoral fellowship at Penn State University. Her research interests include identifying the long-term consequences of drug use.

Jacqueline Blundell is a professor of Psychology at Memorial University of Newfoundland. Her research interests lie in understanding the behavioural and neuroplastic changes that are involved in affective and cognitive disorders.

Chelsea E. Cadle earned her bachelor's degree in psychology from Ohio Northern University in 2015. Her research has focused on examining PTSD-related behaviours in human participants.

Sara Carletto, PhD in Neuroscience, is a Research fellow at the Department of Neuroscience, University of Torino, Italy and Clinical psychologist at the Clinical Psychology Unit of University Hospital Città della Salute e della Scienza of Turin, Italy.

Sarah J. Chaulk is a clinical psychologist and assistant professor in the Department of Clinical Health Psychology, University of Manitoba.

Heidi Cramm, PhD, OT Reg. (Ont.) is associate professor in the School of Rehabilitation Therapy, Queen's University. She has a particular interest in the mental health and well-being of public safety personnel and their families.

Jon Davine, MD, CCFP, FRCP(C) is an associate clinical professor in the Department of Psychiatry at McMaster University. His clinical work focuses on liaising with primary care practitioners in the collaborative care model.

Alexa Dodge is the Hill Postdoctoral Fellow in Technology and Society at Dalhousie University. Her research analyses the impact of digital technology on crime, law, and society.

James Drover is an associate professor at Memorial University of Newfoundland with interests are visual development, cognitive development, and the development of PTSD.

Eric D. Eisenmann earned a bachelor's degree in psychology and a doctor of pharmacy degree from Ohio Northern University in 2016. He is now completing his PhD at The Ohio State University.

Grace B. Ewles completed her MA and PhD in Industrial-Organizational Psychology at the University of Guelph. Her research interests include employee health and well-being, work stress, coping, and social support.

Katelyn Fallon holds a BSc (Honors) from Carleton University in Ottawa and an MSc from Memorial University of Newfoundland. She is currently a senior policy analyst for Health Canada.

xii *List of Contributors*

Molly Flindall-Hanna is an occupational therapist passionate about advocating for diversity and inclusion. This career path has taken her to Tanzania, Northern Alberta, and to Vancouver supporting Indigenous families with early intervention.

Samantha Ghanem holds a MSc in Public Health and is a policy analyst in the Centre for Chronic Disease Prevention and Health Equity, Public Health Agency of Canada.

M. Gloria González-Morales is an associate professor of Psychology at Claremont Graduate University and associate editor of *Work & Stress*. She studies work stress, victimization, and positive organizational interventions.

Peter A. Hausdorf is a professor of Industrial-Organizational Psychology who specializes in employee health and well-being, organizational selection systems, and the research–practice gap.

Alexandra Heber, MD, FRCP(C), CCPE is the chief of Psychiatry at Veterans Affairs Canada and assistant professor of Psychiatry at the University of Ottawa.

Samantha C. Horswill is a registered psychologist who primarily treats PTSD in Public Safety and Healthcare workers. Alongside her practice, she remains active in research through publications and peer-review activities.

Chloé Houlton is an occupational therapist working in outpatient geriatrics and rehabilitation in Ottawa. She is devoted to supporting the independence and well-being of older adults in their communities.

Therese Kenny is a PhD student in the Clinical Child and Adolescent Psychology Program at the University of Guelph. Her research primarily focuses on lived experience perspectives of recovery from mental illness.

Annette M. Lane is an associate professor in the Faculty of Health Disciplines at Athabasca University. Her research involves older adults and transitions, and mental health in the homeless serving sector.

Allana G. Leblanc completed her PhD at the University of Ottawa and her MSc at Queen's University. She works as an epidemiologist at the Public Health Agency of Canada.

Phillip MacCallum is a PhD candidate in Experimental Psychology at Memorial University. While his primary focus is behavioural neuroscience, Phillip's research projects have ranged from predator–prey ecology to clinical rehabilitation trials in humans.

Harry MacKay completed his PhD in Neuroscience at Carleton University. He currently works as a postdoctoral associate in the Department of Pediatrics at Baylor College of Medicine.

List of Contributors xiii

Alyson Mahar is a research scientist with the Manitoba Centre for Health Policy, an assistant professor in the Department of Community Health Sciences at the University of Manitoba and an adjunct scientist with the Research Institute in Oncology and Hematology at CancerCare Manitoba.

Daniel Marrello is currently a Neuroscience MSc student at McMaster University, in Hamilton, Ontario, Canada. He is currently investigating the association between Problematic Internet Use and Attention Deficit Hyperactivity Disorder.

Donald R. McCreary is an independent consultant and adjunct professor of Psychology. He studies the psychology of men, masculinity, and men's health, as well as workplace stress and health.

Ryan Murray, BSc, MAHSR (Master of Applied Health Services Research) is in medical school at Memorial University.

Deborah Norris, PhD, is professor, Department of Family Studies and Gerontology, Mount Saint Vincent University, Halifax, Nova Scotia. Dr Norris's military and Veteran family health research program focuses on the impact of operational stress injuries on the mental health and well-being of families.

Marco Pagani, MD PhD in Brain Neurophysiology, is a senior researcher at the Institute of Cognitive Sciences and Technologies-CNR, Italy, and associate researcher at the Karolinska University Hospital of Stockholm and at the UMCG, Groningen.

Su-Bin Park completed her MSc in Neuroscience at Carleton University and works as an Epidemiologist in the Centre for Surveillance and Applied Research at the Public Health Agency of Canada.

Beth Patterson is a senior researcher at the MacAnxiety Research Centre in Hamilton, Ontario, Canada. She is also a registered psychotherapist.

Sieara Plebon-Huff is an MSc student at Queen's University and works as an epidemiologist in the Center for Surveillance and Applied Research at the Public Health Agency of Canada.

David J. Podnar is an assistant professor within the Department of Clinical Health Psychology at the University of Manitoba, in Winnipeg, Manitoba, Canada.

Nicole Gerarda Power (she/her) is professor in the Sociology Department at Memorial University. Her research has examined the gendered health and safety of a range of workers including fisheries workers, young workers, and skilled trades workers, correctional officers, and academics.

xiv *List of Contributors*

Anne-Marie Robert completed her MSc in Statistics at Université de Montréal and is a manager in the Centre for Surveillance and Applied Research at the Public Health Agency of Canada.

Lucia Rühland, MSc, is a research project manager at the School of Rehabilitation Therapy at Queen's University. Ms Rühland has an interest in research methods.

Daniella Simas Medeiros is a Master of Arts (Sociology) candidate at Memorial University of Newfoundland.

Dale Spencer is associate professor in the Department of Law and Legal Studies at Carleton University. An Ontario Early Research Award recipient, his main research interests are violence, sport, victimization, policing, and youth.

Theresa Szymanski is a Health and Safety Officer at the Ontario Public Service Employees Union (OPSEU). She completed her Masters in McMaster University's Work & Society program.

Linna Tam-Seto holds a PhD in Rehabilitation Science and an occupational therapist. Linna's research interests include understanding the health and well-being of Canada's military members, veterans, public safety personnel, and their families with a focus on life transitions and changes.

James M. Thompson, MD, FCFP(EM) is a family physician and research medical consultant at the Canadian Institute for Military and Veteran Health Research. He studies the well-being of military veterans.

Cristina Trentini, PhD in Dynamic, Clinical, and Developmental Psychology, is Associate professor at the Department of Dynamic and Clinical Psychology, and Health Studies, Sapienza University of Rome, Italy.

Jasmine Turna, received her PhD in Neuroscience from McMaster University and completed a postdoctoral fellowship at the Michael G DeGroote Centre for Medicinal Cannabis Research in the Department of Psychiatry and Behavioral Neuroscience at McMaster University, Hamilton, Ontario, Canada.

Michael Van Ameringen, is a professor in the Department of Psychiatry and Behavioural Neurosciences at McMaster University and is the director of the MacAnxiety Research Centre, in Hamilton, Ontario, Canada.

Esther F. J. C. Van Ginneken, PhD, works as an assistant professor in criminology at the Institute for Criminal Law and Criminology at Leiden University (the Netherlands).

Siebrecht Vanhooren, PhD, works as a professor at the Faculty of Psychology and Educational Sciences at KU Leuven (Belgium), Research Group Clinical Psychology and Meaning & Existence.

Jeannette Waegemakers Schiff is a professor in the Faculty of Social Work, University of Calgary. Her current research includes the psychosocial needs of staff in frontline staff in services for homeless people, especially in the context of the COVID-19 pandemic.

Murray Weeks completed his PhD in Psychology at Carleton University and works as an epidemiologist in the Centre for Surveillance and Applied Research at the Public Health Agency of Canada.

Jesse Whiteman received his BA from the University of British Columbia and MSc from Memorial University of Newfoundland. He is with the psychology department at the University of Toronto.

Jasmine Zhang is currently completing her MA/PhD studies in clinical psychology at the University of Waterloo in Ontario, Canada.

Phillip R. Zoladz is a professor of psychology at Ohio Northern University. He oversees two federally funded research laboratories that examine the impact of psychological stress on cognition and PTSD-like behaviours.

Acknowledgements

We would like to thank Amanda Butt for her efforts coordinating the publication of the current collection as well as the SafetyNet Centre for Occupational Health & Safety Research at Memorial University. Thanks and appreciation are given to all those involved in the Posttraumatic Stress Disorder conference held at Memorial University in 2016, which was the impetus for the current collection. We also want to thank our families for their support during the processes of editing, writing, and creating the handbook.

Introduction

Rosemary Ricciardelli, Stephen Bornstein,
Alan Hall, and R. Nicholas Carleton

There is no shortage of recent compilations and monographs focusing on posttraumatic stress disorder (PTSD) and examining the complexities of definition, diagnosis, and treatment from a wide range of disciplinary perspectives – epidemiological, neurological, psychiatric, and psychological (e.g., Breslau, 2009; Galea, Nandi, & Vlahov, 2005; Gurvits et al., 1993; Vasterling & Brewin, 2005; Wilson, Friedman, & Lindy, 2012). In our handbook we take a different approach. We combine diverse study types with an added focus on understanding PTSD through the lens of occupational and employment perspectives. We also draw on historical, political, and sociological viewpoints. Our contributors address the impact of PTSD on a wide range of people serving in various professions including military personnel, public safety personnel, and health care personnel. Many of our contributors examine how individuals experience PTSD in different work settings, as well as the complexities of diagnosis, treatment, and recovery for those workers. In doing so, we mobilize academic expertise, administrative and clinical knowledge, and lived experience to inform ongoing work in the area of PTSD, while bringing together leading scholars from a wide range of disciplines spanning the sciences, medicine, the social sciences, and the humanities.

Our collection was designed to move beyond the existing literature in three ways. First, we try to add a present and future orientation to the largely historical approach used by much of the extant PTSD scholarship. Studies on the identification and formal psychiatric categorization of PTSD along with development in treatments, research, and classification, have largely been done historically, first with a focus on personnel experiences from the armed forces in the two World Wars, the Korean War, and the Vietnam War, to the formalization of PTSD being formalized in 1980. Many of our chapters, while reflecting on the knowledge developed by these historical studies, focus on more recent and current situations and issues related to PTSD (Haas & Hendin, 1985; Koenen et al., 2007).

Second, some contributors to the current collection examine PTSD among military personnel and veterans in line with much of the literature (Haas & Hendin, 1985; Koenen et al., 2007); however, many contributors

DOI: 10.4324/9781351134637-1

consider other occupational groups, including firefighters, paramedics, police, correctional workers, and other public safety personnel, all of whom have recently become an increasing focus of PTSD research (see Carleton et al., 2018a, 2018b; Ricciardelli et al., 2018; Ricciardelli et al., 2018). Other contributors focus on occupations where even less PTSD research has occurred, such as nursing, social work retail employment, hospital staff, and prison employees (see Bride, 2007; Hilton, Ham, & Dretzkat, 2017; MacDonald et al., 2003; Ricciardelli & Power, 2020; Ricciardelli et al., 2019).

Third, the current collection takes a deliberately multi-disciplinary and inter-disciplinary approach in an effort to foster innovation. Our contributors incorporate insights developed by researchers in the fields of psychiatry, clinical psychology, and neurobiology, as well as disciplines such as sociology, social work, and the humanities, focusing on military and non-military personnel. The multi-disciplinary nature of the compilation helps to highlight controversial issues concerning definitions, knowledge, and interventions for PTSD (Purtle, 2016; Wise & Beck, 2015; Scott, 1990, 1992), all of which may support innovative solutions to the complex challenges associated with PTSD. For example, employment legislation, institutional policies, and government policies related to PTSD compensation, treatment, and prevention have been developed and shaped as responses to occupational and organizational pressures. The current collection showcases how developments in legislation and policy have been informed by continued research from psychiatry, clinical psychology, and neuro-biology. Our collection acknowledges the enormous progress made regarding PTSD within and across disciplines and highlights the continuing controversies and limitations in current knowledge. Our collection highlights several current controversies including 1) the terminology associated with PTSD (e.g., posttraumatic stress symptom, posttraumatic stress injuries, occupational stress injuries, operational stress injuries); 2) disagreements about what constitutes a potentially psychologically traumatic event (Canadian Institute for Public Safety Research and Treatment [CIPSRT], 2019); and 3) which symptoms warrant inclusion for a diagnosis.

We have structured the introduction to begin with the controversies, starting with language and definitions, and then to move to diagnostic shifts for PTSD across versions of the Diagnostic and Statistical Manual for Mental Disorders (DSM). We then present our intent for, our collection and its followed by a structural overview of the collection and contents.

Regarding Terminology

Posttraumatic Stress Disorder?

Throughout the current collection we use the term "disorder". We recognize the word disorder can be perceived as involving negative valence;

however, in the current collection the word intentionally reflects a process of construct interpretation that accounts for different disciplinary understandings. The word is not intended to be used punitively and does not preclude the notion of an injurious causal mechanism producing symptoms that meet criteria consistent with one or more "disorders".

The American Psychological Association (APA, 2019) defines a mental disorder as:

> Any condition characterized by cognitive and emotional disturbances, abnormal behaviors, impaired functioning, or any combination of these. Such disorders cannot be accounted for solely by environmental circumstances and may involve physiological, genetic, chemical, social, and other factors. Specific classifications of mental disorders are elaborated in the American Psychiatric Association's Diagnostic and Statistical Manual of Mental Disorders (see DSM–IV–TR; DSM–5) and the World Health Organization's International Classification of Diseases.
>
> Also called mental illness; psychiatric disorder; psychiatric illness; psychological disorder. See also psychopathology.
>
> (APA, 2019, np)

The American Psychiatric Association (APA, 2018) collectively refers to all diagnosable mental disorders as mental illness, defined as:

> Mental illnesses are health conditions involving changes in emotion, thinking or behavior (or a combination of these). Mental illnesses are associated with distress and/or problems functioning in social, work or family activities… Serious mental illness is a mental, behavioral or emotional disorder (excluding developmental and substance use disorders) resulting in serious functional impairment, which substantially interferes with or limits one or more major life activities. Examples of serious mental illness include major depressive disorder, schizophrenia and bipolar disorder.
>
> (APA, 2018, np)

In the fifth version of the DSM, DSM-5, mental disorder is defined as:

> A mental disorder is a syndrome characterized by clinically significant disturbance in an individual's cognition, emotion regulation, or behavior that reflects a dysfunction in the psychological, biological, or developmental processes underlying mental functioning. Mental disorders are usually associated with significant distress in social, occupational, or other important activities. An expectable or culturally approved response to a common stressor or loss, such as the death of a loved one, is not a mental disorder. Socially deviant behavior (e.g., political, religious, or sexual) and conflicts that are primarily between

the individual and society are not mental disorders unless the deviance or conflict results from a dysfunction in the individual, as described above.

(APA, 2013, p. 20)

The three definitions overlap in that disorders are defined as conditions that impact individuals, are internal to an individual, and can be responses to factors external to an individual (e.g., stressors). A cluster of pre-specified symptoms are required for a person to meet criteria consistent with any given mental disorder.

We recognize significant benefits and challenges have been raised as being associated with the term "mental disorder" and the inherent labelling (Link & Phelan, 1999). For example, a mental disorder label allows people to access necessary resources for recovery and to receive evidence-based treatment specific to the disorder. In contrast, a mental disorder label can induce stigma and negative social reactions resulting in social debilitation, as well as facilitating internationalization of negative self-perspectives (Angermeyer & Matschinger, 2005; Link & Phelan, 1999; Link, 1987, Moses, 2009). For example, there is evidence that people often inaccurately perceive persons diagnosed with schizophrenia as particularly dangerous and unpredictable, resulting in social distancing (Angermeyer & Matschinger, 2005). Thus, while a mental disorder label may increase understanding, treatment access, and treatment utility, the label can also perpetuate stigma and isolation.

Historically, the stigma associated with mental disorders may stem, in part, from the medicalization of human conditions (Conrad, 1992). Identifying specific states of being as disordered (i.e., abnormal) allows for reframing behaviours as part of a "condition", propagating divisive othering, and for better or worse justifying requirements for medical control and oversight (Conrad, 2007). A full discussion of the complexities associated with the mental disorder diagnostic discourse is beyond the scope of the current collection; nevertheless, we hope the current preface to the term helps explain our intended use and highlights our respect for the ongoing controversy. We use mental disorder to describe a cluster of symptoms causing distress or impairment that may be reduced from additional supports, including professional supports. We hope the content of the current collection will help to support the continuous development and proliferation of effective and empirically supported activities that help change how PTSD, the mental disorder, is experienced—socially, psychologically, and physically.

Defining (and Differentiating) Posttraumatic Stress: PTSD, PTSS, PTSIs, C-PTSD?

PTSD is a mental disorder included in the DSM-5 and the tenth edition of the International Classification of Diseases (ICD); however, many terms or phrases have problematically become colloquially related to, or used interchangeably with, PTSD. There are a myriad of consequences associated with diagnosis labelling, which underscore the importance of clear language when describing human experiences. Here, we help to define several terms and phrases associate with PTSD and clarify how the terms and phrases are being (mis)used; specifically, "Posttraumatic Stress", "Posttraumatic Stress Injury", "Posttraumatic Stress Syndrome", none of which appear as diagnoses in the DSM-5 of the ICD-10. We draw our definitions from a newly created "Glossary of Terms" designed by numerous experts from several disciplines to provide "a shared understanding of the common terms used to describe psychological trauma" (CIPSRT, 2019).[1]

"Posttraumatic Stress" is too often used interchangeably with PTSD, referring to stress and/or compromised mental health resulting from exposure to a potentially psychologically traumatic event that consequentially impedes participation in activities of daily living (CIPSRT, 2019). The phrase "Posttraumatic Stress Injury" is increasingly used in reference to public safety personnel or members of the armed forces (active or retired) who experience a mental health challenge that may be consistent with one or more mental disorders after being exposed to one or more potentially psychologically traumatic event. The shift from PTSD to posttraumatic stress injuries was based on efforts initiated by Canadian Lieutenant Colonel (Retired) Stéphane Grenier to destigmatize the need for mental health care among military members and increase their willingness to seek treatment. Grenier proposed referring to mental health challenges subsequent to service as "Operational Stress Injuries" to better reflect the causal mechanisms, undermine the associated stigma, and support more equal impression of physical and mental harm. The term operational stress injuries has been conflated with two related but distinct constructs, Organizational Stress Injuries and Occupational Stress Injuries (McCreary & Thompson, 2006). Organizational Stress Injuries refer to mental health challenges resulting from various stressors such as staff shortages or inconsistent leadership styles; in contrast, Occupational Stress Injuries subsume Operational and Organizational Stress Injuries. The Glossary recommends reserving the acronym OSI only for Operational Stress Injuries in order to reduce confusion. "Posttraumatic Stress Syndrome" has also been used, in part because of conflation with other disorders, and in part because syndrome may be perceived as less stigmatizing than disorder.

From *Diagnostic and Statistical Manual of Mental Disorders III* to the *Diagnostic and Statistical Manual of Mental Disorders 5*

The first DSM was published in 1952 and has since undergone considerable revision. The latest edition is DSM-5 and was published in 2013 (APA, 2013). PTSD was first introduced in the third edition (i.e., DSM-III; APA, 1980) and contextualized as an "anxiety disorder" (Reynolds, 1997). The introduction of PTSD involved significant controversy, but was considered necessary to account for evidence that potentially psychologically traumatic event exposure was causing symptoms, rather than symptoms signifying inherent individual "weakness" (Waldram, 2004). PTSD potentiated a shift in responsibility for symptoms following exposure to a "traumatic" event away from the individual (i.e., the idea of a person having a traumatic neurosis); however, there was substantial controversy regarding what would constitute a traumatic event. Initially, events considered valid causal mechanisms potentially consistent with a diagnosis of PTSD were limited to events that "would evoke significant symptoms of distress in most people" and would be" generally outside the range of such common experiences as simple bereavement, chronic illness, business losses, or marital conflict" (p. 236, APA, 1980). Eligible events included, but were not limited to, war (e.g., deployment experiences), being victimized (i.e., torture, rape), natural disasters (e.g., volcanos) and manmade disasters (e.g., plane crashes) (Green, 1990; Spitzer, First, & Wakefield, 2007). Qualifying traumatic events did not include potentially painful and debilitating stressors such as divorce, serious illness, and financial strain. A DSM-III diagnosis of PTSD required distressing or impairing symptoms of re-experiencing the traumatic event (e.g., recurrent recollections or dreams), numbed responsiveness to the world (e.g., diminished interest in activities), and symptoms or hyperalertness or avoidance. In DSM-III-R (APA, 1987), the trauma experience needed to include a threat to physical integrity, and could be experienced directly or indirectly (e.g., vicariously through a loved one), or witnessed.

In the DSM-IV (APA, 1994) and DSM-IV-TR (APA, 2000), the PTSD diagnostic criteria included exposure to the traumatic event (as defined in the DSM III), but involving actual or threatened death or serious injury as well as intense fear, helplessness, or horror. The symptoms of PTSD were reorganized in DSM-IV (APA, 1994) and DSM-IV-TR (APA, 2000) to include re-experiencing the traumatic event, avoidance of the traumatic event or numbing, and hyperarousal. The experience of symptoms needed to last longer than one month.

In the DSM-5 (APA, 2013), PTSD was shifted out of the anxiety disorders category and into a new category titled "trauma- and stress-related disorders". The diagnosis still required exposure to a traumatic event as defined in DSM-IV-TR, revised to read, "exposure to actual or threatened death, serious injury, or sexual violence" (APA, 2013, p. 271). The requirement for the experience to incite intense fear, helplessness, or horror was removed, and the methods of exposure now included repeated exposures, such as may be experienced by public safety personnel (PSP) (APA, 2013). The symptoms were regrouped into four clusters, each required for a diagnosis of PTSD: 1) intrusions related to the traumatic event (e.g., distressing memories or dreams); 2) avoidance of stimuli associated with the traumatic event; 3) negative cognitions and mood (e.g., persistent negative emotional state, reduced interest in activities); and 4) hyper-arousal symptoms (e.g., irritable behaviour, exaggerated startle response; APA, 2013).

Introduction 7

The debate and developments regarding qualifying stressors continued through to DSM-5, but what remains unique to PTSD is the emphasis on a required etiological agent (e.g., exposure to a traumatic event) for diagnosing the disorder. Researchers and clinicians (CIPSRT, 2019) have recently begun distinguishing physical traumas (e.g., injury to living tissue) and psychological traumas (e.g., psychological stressors that are emotionally overwhelming). Relatedly, researchers and clinicians recognize that not all people will experience an event the same way, even if the event involves actual or threatened death, serious injury, or sexual violence (APA, 2013). A psychological stressor is not necessarily traumatic for all people at all times, which means the most appropriate phrase should be potentially psychologically traumatic events (CIPSRT, 2019).

Most of the North American general population (i.e., 50–90%) are exposed to one or more potentially psychologically traumatic event during their lifetime (Kilpatrick et al., 2013; Perrin et al., 2014). Despite the prevalence of exposure to potentially psychologically traumatic events most people will not develop symptoms of PTSD and most will not meet the diagnostic criteria for PTSD (Kilpatrick et al., 2013). Increasing public awareness and acceptance of PTSD is laudable, but using PTSD to frame how we address potentially psychologically traumatic events has shortcomings (Comack, 2018); for example, PTSD as a diagnosis has the potential to individualize social problems, pathologizing persons exposed to potentially psychologically traumatic events and ignoring potentially critical concomitant social factors (see also Cormack, 2018; Waldram, 2004). The global reality is that there are natural and human-made events that shape individual experiences. People exposed to potentially psychologically traumatic events (PPTE) will have diverse reactions, some benign and some that are compromising. An individual may have limited control over their exposures to PPTE and may similarly have limited control over their reaction at any given moment; as such, the consequences, including the implications for mental health and wellbeing, can never be solely the responsibility of the individual. Ideally, scholars, clinicians, policy makers, activists, and corporate officials will continue to advance supports for evidence-based PTSD programming and treatments alongside developing efforts to address the systemic variables associated with potentially psychologically traumatic event exposures – the causal variables driving the mental health injuries.

Scope and Intentions

In the current collection, we bring together a diverse group of scholars, practitioners, and clinicians in a shared effort towards understanding the multiple dimensions of PTSD. Our intention was to provide a comprehensive examination of PTSD from varying perspectives and contribute to the ongoing debates about causes, impacts, and treatments in Canada and internationally. We take a multi-disciplinary and multi-sectoral approach,

8 Ricciardelli, Bornstein, Hall, and Carleton

where each contribution in the collection provides engaged discovery and scholarship about PTSD from the WWI battlefield soldiers to a significant and broadly shared modern health concern. By unpacking historical and contemporary insights about PTSD, we hope to advance our collective understanding, allowing us to respond more effectively to the important societal challenges associated with potentially psychologically traumatic event exposures. We hope the broad framework and discourse in the current collection helps readers reconceptualize PTSD as a pervasive and pernicious challenge that warrants innovative individual and collective actions, proactive and responsive, at the individual, group, and societal levels.

We intended the collection to serve as a bridging point for diverse academic communities to showcase similarities (and differences) in research on the causes, consequences, and responses associated with PTSD. As such, the collection includes a diverse range of expertise from psychologists, sociologists, neurobiologists, historians, physicians, and psychiatrists among others, organized into subsections to juxtapose and blend their perspectives and insights. Given the diversity in perspectives offered, we cannot say we all agree with the contexts, propositions, suppositions, or conclusions of every chapter. We also underscore that any and all clinical commentary is the sole responsibility of the individual authors from each independently peer-reviewed contribution; as such, the editors offer no warranty regarding any specific clinical commentary. We respect the diverse positions and are deeply indebted to the team of anonymous peer reviewers who helped evaluate quality and empirical soundness of the submitted chapters, particularly when the approach to the subject matter extended beyond our individual or collective expertise as editors.

Overview of Chapters

The collection is subdivided into three sections. The first five chapters comprise the *Foundational* section and provide a historical and theoretical groundwork for contemporary frameworks regarding PTSD. In Chapter 1, Horswill and Carleton provide an overview of the history of how our understanding of the relationship between combat and psychological trauma has evolved over past millennia. The authors emphasize the role of twentieth-century wars, particularly the First World War, in transforming our understanding of potentially psychologically traumatic event exposure sequala and the associated discourse from psychiatry, clinical psychology, and the public. In Chapter 2, Weeks and colleagues provide a systematic review of scientific studies examining the prevalence of PTSD in Canada. In Chapter 3, Szymanski and Hall consider recent developments in compensation legislation and policy for PTSD in Canada, focusing on the country's largest province, Ontario. The chapter begins with the introduction of presumptive legislation for PTSD, examines the positive contributions, and describes how legislation is limited with respect to efforts at prevention. In Chapter 4, Thompson and colleagues examine

Introduction 9

the multiple and complex challenges that diagnosing and treating PTSD poses for family physicians. The chapter offers recommendations to help family physicians manage PTSD as an important and growing component of their practices. In Chapter 5, Marrello, Patterson, Turna, Zhang, and Van Ameringen unpack the epidemiology of PTSD in Canada. The authors discuss PTSD as evidenced in diverse populations and across diverse samples in Canada.

The second section, *Perspectives and Populations*, consists of seven chapters, each focusing on how PTSD impacts a specific population. In Chapter 6, McCreary examines how gender impacts the way men experience various forms of mental stress, including PTSD. McCreary provides an overview of theories of masculinities, examines the ways in which masculinities can compromise men's mental health, and reviews existing research on the links between masculinities and the way men experience PTSD. In Chapter 7, Cramm and colleagues call on scholars and policy makers to focus on how PTSD experienced by military veterans also impacts their families. The authors review the available literature and provide recommendations for future research, theory, and practice. In Chapter 8, Waegermakers Schiff and Lange examine PTSD in workers who serve homeless individuals. The authors, review study data derived from workers who serve homeless individuals, highlighting evidence that PTSD symptoms are extremely prevalent. In Chapter 9, Spencer and colleagues discuss the impact of the "dirty work" performed by police officers who investigate internet sex crimes perpetrated against children. They unpack how the realities of doing child sex crime investigations affects police officers to varying degrees over time. In Chapter 10, Cramm and colleagues provide a scoping review of the limited, but growing, literature on PTSD among firefighters. The authors report on what is currently known and highlight critical gaps in the existing literature. In Chapter 11, Ricciardelli and colleagues consider how potentially psychologically traumatic event and operational stress injuries affect Canadian provincial and territorial correctional officers. They draw from interviews with correctional officers to illuminate the multiple and varying stressors interlacing the working lives of correctional workers, as well as the importance of protecting correctional workers from, and compensating them for, workplace exposures to potentially psychologically traumatic events. In Chapter 12, van Ginneken and Vanhooren examine PTSD among a population that is typically overlooked—prisoners. The authors showcase what is known about the prevalence and nature of PTSD in prisoner populations, and discuss the significance of "posttraumatic growth" in correctional institutional contexts.

The third section, *Biology, Understanding, and Treatment* consists of five chapters, two that focus on the biological bases of PTSD and three that focus on a range of innovative treatment methods. In Chapter 13, Eisenmann and colleagues examine how research using animal models, rather than clinical research involving human participants, can provide valuable insights into the etiology and biological mechanisms associated with PTSD. In Chapter 14, McCallum and colleagues discuss the use of a specific animal model involving predator stress to enhance our understanding of how fear memories develop in the brain. The research offers insights into potentially effective pharmacological treatments for PTSD. In Chapter 15, Ewles and her colleagues consider the role of personal support networks in helping public safety personnel—particularly first responders—and their families to deal with repeated exposures to potentially psychologically traumatic events and PTSD. In Chapter 16, Chalk and Podnar provide a preliminary evaluation of group-based cognitive processing therapy for PTSD, outlining advantages and limitations relative to individual cognitive therapies. The authors also identify factors that can enhance the effectiveness of group therapy. In Chapter 17, Trentini and colleagues examine the historical and contemporary research on Eye Movement Desensitization and Reprocessing.

In the final chapter, we conclude the collection by drawing together the overlapping themes and the implications from each section of the book, highlighting some of the important empirical and theoretical insights from our chapters. We also identify some remaining knowledge gaps for future researchers to address as we collectively work towards ever-better solutions for potentially psychologically traumatic event exposures and PTSD.

Note

1 The glossary is publicly available at: www.cipsrt-icrtsp.ca/glossary-of-terms/

References

American Psychiatric Association. (1980). *Diagnostic and statistical manual of mental disorders* (3rd edn). Arlington, VA: American Psychiatric Association.
American Psychiatric Association. (1987). *Diagnostic and statistical manual of mental disorders* (3rd edn, Revision). Arlington, VA: American Psychiatric Association.
American Psychiatric Association. (1994). *Diagnostic and statistical manual of mental disorders* (4th edn). Arlington, VA: American Psychiatric Association.
American Psychiatric Association. (2000). *Diagnostic and statistical manual of mental disorders* (4th edn, Text Revision). Arlington, VA: American Psychiatric Association.
American Psychiatric Association. (2013). *Diagnostic and statistical manual of mental disorders* (5th edn). Arlington, VA: American Psychiatric Association.
American Psychiatric Association (2018). What is mental illness.? Retrieved from www.psychiatry.org/patients-families/what-is-mental-illness.
American Psychological Association. (2019). Dictionary. Retrieved from https://dictionary.apa.org/mental-disorder.
Angermeyer, M. C., & Matschinger, H. (2005). Labeling—stereotype—discrimination. *Social Psychiatry and Psychiatric Epidemiology*, 40(5), 391–395.
Breslau, N. (2009). The epidemiology of trauma, PTSD, and other posttrauma disorders. *Trauma, Violence, & Abuse*, 10(3), 198–210.

Introduction 11

Bride, B. E. (2007). Prevalence of secondary traumatic stress among social workers. *Social Work, 52*(1), 63–70.

Canadian Institute for Public Safety Research and Treatment (CIPSRT). (2019). *Glossary of terms: A shared understanding of the common terms used to describe psychological trauma (version 2.0)*. Regina, SK: Author. http://hdl.handle.net/10294/9055

Carleton, R. N., Afifi, T. O., Tailieu, T., Turner, S., Duranceau, S., LeBouthillier, D. M., ... Asmundson, G. J. G. (2018a). Mental disorder symptoms among Canadian first responder and other public safety personnel. *Canadian Journal of Psychiatry, 63*(1), 54–64. https://doi.org/10.1177/0706743717723825

Carleton, R.N., Afifi, T.O., Tailieu, T., Turner, S., Krakauer, R., Anderson, G.S., ... McCreary, D. (2018b). Exposures to potentially traumatic events among public safety personnel in Canada. *Canadian Journal of Behavioural Sciences, 51*(1), 37–52. https://doi.org/10.1037/cbs0000115.

Comack, E. (2018). *Coming back to jail: Women, trauma, and criminalization*. Black Point, NS: Fernwood Publishing.

Conrad, P. (1992). Medicalization and social control. *Annual Review of Sociology, 18*(1), 209–232.

Conrad, P. (2007). *The medicalization of society*. Baltimore, MD: Johns Hopkins University Press.

Galea, S., Nandi, A., & Vlahov, D. (2005). The epidemiology of post-traumatic stress disorder after disasters. *Epidemiologic Reviews, 27*(1), 78–91.

Green, B. L. (1990). Defining trauma: Terminology and generic stressor dimensions 1. *Journal of Applied Social Psychology, 20*(20), 1632–1642.

Gurvits, T. V., Lasko, N. B., Schachter, S. C., Kuhne, A. A., Orr, S. P., & Pitman, R. K. (1993). Neurological status of Vietnam veterans with chronic posttraumatic stress disorder. *The Journal of Neuropsychiatry and Clinical Neurosciences, 5*(2), 183–188.

Haas, A. P., & Hendin, H. (1985). *Wounds of war: The psychological aftermath of combat in Vietnam*. New York: Basic Books, Inc., Publishers.

Hilton, N. Z., Ham, E., & Dretzkat, A. (2017). Psychiatric hospital workers' exposure to disturbing patient behavior and its relation to post-traumatic stress disorder symptoms. *Canadian Journal of Nursing Research, 49*(3), 118–126.

Kilpatrick, D. G., Resnick, H. S., Milanak, M. E., Miller, M. W., Keyes, K. M., & Friedman, M. J. (2013). National estimates of exposure to traumatic events and PTSD prevalence using DSM-IV and DSM-5 criteria. *Journal of Traumatic Stress, 26*, 537–547. https://doi.org/10.1002/jts.21848

Koenen, K. C., Stellman, S. D., Dohrenwend, B. P., Sommer Jr, J. F., & Stellman, J. M. (2007). The consistency of combat exposure reporting and course of PTSD in Vietnam War veterans. *Journal of Traumatic Stress, 20*(1), 3–13.

Link, B. G. (1987). Understanding labeling effects in the area of mental disorders: An assessment of the effects of expectations of rejection. *American Sociological Review, 52*(1), 96–112.

Link, B. G., & Phelan, J. C. (1999). The labeling theory of mental disorder (II): The consequences of labeling. In A. V. Horwitz & T. L. Scheid (eds), *A handbook for the study of mental health: Social contexts, theories, and systems* (pp. 361–376). Cambridge: Cambridge University Press.

MacDonald, H. A., Colotla, V., Flamer, S., & Karlinsky, H. (2003). Posttraumatic stress disorder (PTSD) in the workplace: A descriptive study of workers experiencing PTSD resulting from work injury. *Journal of Occupational Rehabilitation, 13*(2), 63–77.

McCreary, D. R., & Thompson, M. M. (2006). Development of two reliable and valid measures of stressors in policing: The operational and organizational police stress questionnaires. *International Journal of Stress Management, 13*, 494–518.

Moses, T. (2009). Self-labeling and its effects among adolescents diagnosed with mental disorders. *Social Science & Medicine, 68*(3), 570–578.

Perrin, M., Vandeleur, C. L., Castelao, E., Rothen, S., Glaus, J., Vollenweider, P., & Preisig, M. (2014). Determinants of the development of post-traumatic stress disorder in the general population. *Social Psychiatry and Psychiatric Epidemiology, 49*, 447–457. https://doi.org/10.1007/s00127-013-0762-3

Purtle, J. (2016). "Heroes' invisible wounds of war:" Constructions of posttraumatic stress disorder in the text of US federal legislation. *Social Science & Medicine, 149*, 9–16.

Reynolds, J. L. (1997). Post-traumatic stress disorder after childbirth: The phenomenon of traumatic birth. *CMAJ, 156*(6), 831–835.

Ricciardelli, R., Carleton, R. N., Cramm, H., & Groll, D. (2018). Qualitatively unpacking Canadian public safety personnel trauma experiences and their wellbeing. *Canadian Journal of Criminology and Criminal Justice, 60*(4), 566–577. https://doi.org/10.3138/cjccj.2017-0053.r2

Ricciardelli, R., Carleton, R. N., Mooney, T., & Cramm, H. (2018). "Playing the system": Structural factors potentiating mental health stigma, challenging awareness, and creating barriers to care for Canadian Public Safety Personnel. *Health: An Interdisciplinary Journal for the Social Study of Health, Illness and Medicine, 24*(3), 259–278.

Ricciardelli, R. & Power, N. (2020). How "conditions of confinement" impact "conditions of employment": The work-related wellbeing of provincial correctional officers in Atlantic Canada. *Victims and Violence, 35*(1), 88–107. https://doi.org/10.1891/0886-6708.VV-D-18-00081

Ricciardelli, R., Taillieu, T., Carleton, R.N., Afifi, T. O., Mitchell, M.M., Barnim, N., Bahji, A., & Groll, D. (2019). Correctional work, wellbeing and mental health disorders. *Advancing Corrections Journal, 8*, 53–69.

Scott, W. J. (1990). PTSD in DSM-III: A case in the politics of diagnosis and disease. *Social Problems, 37*(3), 294–310.

Scott, W. J. (1992). PTSD and Agent Orange: Implications for a sociology of veterans' issues. *Armed Forces & Society, 18*(4), 592–612.

Spitzer, R. L., First, M. B., & Wakefield, J. C. (2007). Saving PTSD from itself in DSM-V. *Journal of Anxiety Disorders, 21*(2), 233–241.

Waldram, J. B. (2004). *Revenge of the Windigo: The construction of the mind and mental health of North American Aboriginal people.* Toronto, ON: University of Toronto Press.

Wilson, J. P., Friedman, M. J., & Lindy, J. D. (eds). (2012). *Treating psychological trauma and PTSD.* New York: Guilford Press.

Wise, E. A., & Beck, J. G. (2015). Work-related trauma, PTSD, and workers compensation legislation: Implications for practice and policy. *Psychological Trauma: Theory, Research, Practice, and Policy, 7*(5), 500.

Vasterling, J. J., & Brewin, C. (eds). (2005). *Neuropsychology of PTSD: Biological, cognitive, and clinical perspectives.* New York: Guilford Press.

Part 1
Foundational

1 Changes in Our Understanding of Trauma and the Human Psyche as a Consequence of War

A Brief History

Samantha C. Horswill and R. Nicholas Carleton

Introduction

Posttraumatic stress disorder (PTSD) requires exposure to one or more potentially psychologically traumatic events (PPTEs; Canadian Institute for Public Safety Research and Treatment, 2019), coupled with symptoms of intrusive thoughts and memories, avoidance behaviours, negative changes to cognition and mood, and changes in arousal and reactivity (American Psychiatric Association, 2013). The contemporary psychological community views PTSD as a relatively common and treatable disorder, but the current view has not always been the prevalent perspective. PTSD has a complex history, particularly during the twentieth century. Understanding symptoms sequalae to potentially psychologically traumatic events was developed with necessary speed in conjunction with total warfare. Exposure to potentially psychologically traumatic events as a function of war became the norm for military services around the globe; cohorts of soldiers began to display ill-understood, but unquestionably severe, physical and psychological symptoms. In the context of World War I (WWI), medical and mental health professionals struggled to understand the adverse consequences of warfare, while also navigating the heavily politicized stigmatization of men who were no longer fit to serve. Prior to WWI the dominant discourse on mental health regarded individuals with disorders as being deficient in some fashion that left them vulnerable. The presumed deficiencies were thought to be the responsibility of the individual, rather than corporations or governments, and were thought to be generally unresolvable. A critical understanding of the immense impact of WWI on mental health requires an understanding of the context; specifically, the available research on psychology and mental health at the time of WWI, the cultural considerations surrounding mental health, and the historical use of technologies.

DOI: 10.4324/9781351134637-2

Before the Great War: The Historical Context

Historical and literary records have long documented human exposure to potentially psychologically traumatic events and the changes that can occur in people as a result. Reports of sequelae from witnessing physical traumas occurred as early as *The Iliad*, where the effects of battle dramatically changed the proverbial "heart" of Achilles. Modern documentation of the symptoms eventually classified as PTSD first appeared in 1667; Samuel Pepys wrote of sleepless nights more than six months after the great fire of London, lamenting that "to this very day I cannot sleep a-night without great terrors of fire" (Pepys, 1667, as quoted by Daly, 1983).

The booming development of the railway system in the 1800s occurred alongside the industrial revolution and expedited everything, including construction-related injuries due to a variety of disasters. Railway construction workers exposed to such disasters began reporting symptoms associated with hysteria, with nerve damage suggested as a possible cause (Erichsen, 1866). The causal mechanisms of hysteria became critical points of contention, as railway corporations confronted new liabilities they had no desire to cover and some medical practitioners protested that publicizing such a disorder would lead to a rise in men taking advantage of corporations for financial benefit (Caplan, 1998).

The idea that the mind could be medicalized did not emerge formally until the term *psychiatry* was coined in 1808 (Marneros, 2008). At the turn of the nineteenth century the field of psychology was growing roots in the medical profession. Kierkegaard completed the first full exposition on anxiety in 1844, followed shortly by the first formal text by Lotze addressing mental health as part of efforts by the medical community to resolve mental disorders. The year 1861 brought about a monumental achievement for mental health; specifically, Paul Broca identified an area of the brain dedicated to articulated speech (Broca, 1861) and, in doing so, undermined Cartesian dualism by providing a tangible link between the material and mental worlds. The link provided demonstrable evidence of a physical and measurable mind that could be intentionally impacted, suggesting that all mental disorders could have physical bases with potential for physical treatments.

The American Civil War also began in the same year, followed shortly by the Boer War. As a result of these prominent wars, many nations found themselves actively engaging in extremely violent combat or coping with the casualties and infirmities of war veterans or both. During both wars, an increasing number of soldiers reported a common cluster of physiological symptoms, with no readily identifiable physical abnormalities to explain them that could result in total exhaustion and physical debilitation (Holdorff & Dening, 2011). Unexplained heart palpitations were observed in a small number of soldiers following the American Civil War. The cardiac symptoms appeared to arise after protracted exposure to combat combined with overexertion, deficient rest, and deficient nourishment

Trauma and the Human Psyche 17

(DiMauro et al., 2014). The number of soldier suicides doubled following the end of the Civil War; however, at the time, the increase in suicides was not conceptualized as a psychological consequence of exposure to war (McNally, 2012). Other international accounts of war-related distress also typically featured cardiovascular arousal, fatigue, and tremors. Several terms were employed for this cluster of symptoms, including soldier's heart, irritable heart, effort syndrome, and DaCosta's syndrome (Lasiuk & Hegadoren, 2006).

Early efforts to provide a comprehensive account of this unexplained cluster of symptoms (i.e., cardiovascular arousal, fatigue, tremors) involved labelling the cluster *traumatic neurosis*, a term coined by German medical professional Hermann Oppenheim in the 1880s to describe symptoms experienced as a consequence of fear (for review, see Holdorff & Dening, 2011). Oppenheim defined traumatic neurosis as visual field and sensory deficits occurring as a direct result of psychological traumatisation. The most dramatic symptoms involved conversion disorder, in which various paralyses would occur in the absence of neurological damage. Beard had classified the cluster of symptoms as *neurasthenia*, which he described as overlapping with hysteria (Beard, 1869).

Wundt opened his pioneering laboratory for conducting experiments to study psychology with scientific methods in 1879 (Lilienfeld et al., 2015). Only three years later, the French Academy of Science approved Charcot's hypnosis therapy for treating hysteria. Charcot's therapy was the first sanctioned treatment that did not include a biological focus (e.g., electroshock therapy; narcotics) for treating hysteria, which was becoming increasingly pervasive (Geotz, 1995). Freud would study hypnosis under Charcot and, during that time, developed the "talking cure" as an alternative treatment for hysteria (Lilienfeld et al., 2015; Munger, 2003). The talking cure, based on his famous work with patient Anna O, included a premise that repression of traumatic memories results in the generation of symptoms of hysteria. Freud's talking cure initially involved allowing the patient to speak freely about whatever came to mind while the therapist asked probing questions to uncover the repressed traumatic memories (Munger, 2003).

The American Psychological Association was established in 1892 and led to increasingly broad interest in neuroses following significant fear-inducing events, particularly exposures to potentially psychologically traumatic events. Prior to the onset of WWI, the causal mechanisms for neuroses and associated mental disorders focused on individual deficiencies and were largely considered a consequence of weak constitution or femininity. Hysteria and neurasthenia were the prevailing diagnoses in the early 1900s, with the former involving tearfully emotional patients and the latter involving the almost lifelessly depressed (Shephard, 2000). Hysteria was more often the diagnosis provided to women and was considered a psychological function of poor genetics and frailty. In contrast, neurasthenia was more often the diagnosis provided to wealthy and heroic men, attributed to the biomechanical function of the nerves being overwhelmed to the point of exhaustion. Importantly, hysteria carried immense social stigma, while neurasthenia did not. Later conceptualizations of hysteria by Charcot allowed for the diagnosis of hysteria in men who had suffered trauma (Shephard, 2000). The diagnosis of war-related neurasthenia was broadly assigned to soldiers displaying any otherwise unexplained physiological or emotional symptoms following a combat experience (DiMauro et al., 2014). By the early 1910s, a variety of treatments were being employed for hysteria and neurasthenia. The treatments included indulgent rest, changes in diet, narcotics, alcohol, medicines with dubious scientific bases, and psychotherapy (Shephard, 2000). Indeed, psychotherapy was a rapidly growing profession in the years prior to the First World War and was defended by the American Medical Association as being useful for treating genuine (i.e., non-malingering) nervous disorders (Lutz, 2001). In 1914, the British Medical Association publicly denounced various forms of treatment as pseudoscience and raised the bar for medicines and treatments, including those for hysteria and neurasthenia.

The Onset of WWI and Psychological Consequences

Warfare has been ubiquitous in human history, yet prior wars paled in comparison to the totality and ruthlessness of WWI (Dyer, 2004). The magnitude of the fighting was unprecedented, with 1,485,000 German soldiers prepared to fight by August 1914. Canada mobilized quickly, developing an army of 31,000 people from almost none in the span of a few months (Bench, 1918). As militaries were formed and deployed, men began to die in staggering numbers. Death was reported as being perceived as always imminent, from exploding shells, shrapnel, hidden mines, long distance snipers, aerial bombings, and chemical toxins. More than a million soldiers died between August 1914 and Christmas (Dyer, 2004). Trench-based combat became the norm and with that new norm came a host of new brutalities. Soldiers were regularly lying in ditches that were very close to their enemies (Dyer, 2004); the trenches were cramped, hostile environments filled with mud, rats, lice, and the bodies of fallen soldiers. The unique nature of WWI was recognized by all sides in the war, with one German naval leader commenting that "modern warfare is total warfare" and that to win a modern war required devastating tactics (Lawson & Lawson, 1996, p. 79). Retrospective accounts noted that such extreme experiences very commonly resulted in fear and anxiety, with most men experiencing distress at some point (MacPhail, 1925).

Despite the new and varied methods of killing, and despite the immense number of deaths on both sides of the trenches, advances in medicines and health technologies allowed unprecedented numbers of combatants to survive. That said, men who experienced and survived the atrocities of WWI soon began to display unfamiliar and unpredictable symptoms beyond the exhaustion and irregular heartbeats seen as consequences of prior wars. As the symptoms were so disparate and confusing, physicians in the field took until late 1914 and early 1915 to begin describing the symptoms in medical journals (Copp & Osborne Humphries, 2010). As Forsyth (1915) wrote in the prominent medical journal, *The Lancet*:

> To enumerate the commonest [symptoms], the patients may appear obviously shaken in nerves, jumpy, and easily alarmed, with a tense, worried, or harassed expression; or they are dazed or stunned, or even stuporose. They probably feel physically exhausted; almost certainly they sleep badly, starting up, perhaps several times in a night, from fearful dreams of the horrors they have witnessed or undergone. They may be emotional, depressed, reserved, or irritable, and many of them are sexually impotent. They commonly complain of headache, perhaps of dyspepsia and other pains, giddiness, buzzing in the head, palpitations, memories fail them repeatedly, especially over proper nouns, and their power of concentration of attention is feeble. They may present some functional disturbances of common sensation, or may be deaf or blind. Most of them are tremulous; many twitch involuntarily, especially in the face. Some stutter; some are aphonic; mutism is the condition of others.
>
> (p. 1400)

With the effects of the Great War thus becoming apparent, the medical profession scrambled to synthesize the symptoms into comprehensible syndromes. The physical damage many soldiers sustained due to shrapnel from exploding shells seemed a likely candidate for causing such symptoms, and British military psychiatrist Myers encapsulated this idea in the term *Shell Shock* (Myers, 1915). Myers focused his attention on the physiological symptoms, which he suspected were caused by concussions and ruptures in neural blood vessels. He did, however, describe some psychological symptoms such as waking up crying, feeling "nervy," and having unclear memories of the moment when shells exploded. He later suspected that those individuals who developed Shell Shock in WWI were the same men who would likely develop hysteria or neurasthenia in civilian life (Myers, 1916, as cited in Copp & Osborne Humphries, 2010). Mott (1916) also agreed that the cluster of symptoms labelled Shell Shock were occurring after proximity to explosions, though he suspected the explosions were causing compression and decompression in the brain rather than neurological lesions.

Oppenheim, the researcher who coined the phrase *traumatic neurosis*, served as an advising neurologist in Berlin at the onset of WWI. Oppenheim's work with patients in a military hospital supported his understanding of *traumatic neurosis* (Holdorff & Dening, 2011). He began to classify muscle cramps and tremors as the typical symptoms rather than visual field and somatosensory deficits, but otherwise his original conceptualization was preserved. Despite Oppenheim's frequent attempts to establish *traumatic neurosis* as the diagnostic phrase of choice in papers and conferences, Myers' term Shell Shock proved more popular and became widespread in medical discourse early in WWI (DiMauro et al., 2014).

As the diagnosis of Shell Shock became better recognized, several proponents began to assert that the causal mechanisms and symptom sequalae were purely psychological—a first in the literature on psychology and stress related to physical trauma (Micale & Lerner, 2001). That said, certainly not all medical professionals agreed that exposure to physical trauma was causing Shell Shock symptoms. For example, most German professionals were providing a diagnosis of hysteria rather than Shell Shock based on the predominant view in Germany that such symptoms were the result of individual deficiencies producing vulnerabilities rather than of exposure to war (Linden, Hess, & Jones, 2012). Irrespective of the disagreements regarding causation, a cure was eagerly sought in order to return the thousands of men afflicted by the strange cluster of symptoms to the front line.

Despite challenges and controversies, Shell Shock became a diagnosis used by British military medical professionals. There were two diagnostic subtypes created for Shell Shock: *Shell Shock W* and *Shell Shock S* (Shephard, 2000). Persons with symptoms that could be directly and easily tied to enemy exposure were designated with a "W" and given a "wounded stripe", which was a badge of honour. In all other cases, persons exhibiting such symptoms were designated with an "S", which was dishonourable, and excluded them from accessing care or pensions (Shorter, 1992). Unfortunately, British physicians of the day reported significant difficulties in definitively determining who should receive a W and who should receive an S, and there was tremendous pressure from military and government leadership to avoid assigning a W. In their personal medical journals, physicians clearly revealed their own difficulties as first responders interacting with suffering patients: "Even now I am haunted by the touching look of the young, bright, anxious eyes, as we passed along the rows of sufferers" (Somervell, 1936).

The magnitude of post-war mental health challenges led to initial attempts in the recruitment process to screen out persons thought likely to develop Shell Shock symptoms. Researchers began exploring personality as a possible predictor of who would develop Shell Shock symptoms. The Woodworth test was designed expressly to screen out persons more likely to develop mental health symptoms from exposure to war. The Woodworth test was not developed in time for use during WWI, but was accepted afterwards by the Surgeon General of the UK for future use, even though the test was unable to discriminate between persons who would and would not develop Shell Shock symptoms (Gibby & Zickar, 2008). Perhaps ironically, the indiscriminate Woodworth test would form the basis for almost all later personality tests, with some of the original items still in use today (Kaplan & Saccuzzo, 2012).

The early 1900s also brought the rapid development of research into human intelligence in order to identify persons most suited for advancement and additional training and those most suited for front line service (Yoakum & Yerkes, 1920). Researchers worked to build structured tests that could be widely and quickly administered in order to objectively rank-order people based on their intellect (Binet & Simon, 1905). Human intelligence research forced the development of tools that could be administered *en masse* and had either verbal content (e.g., completing word problems) or non-verbal content (e.g., identifying the missing part of incomplete drawings of objects). The first such test, called Army Alpha, involved verbal content such as language and problem-solving skills; the second, called Army Beta, involved non-verbal content for those who were illiterate or did not speak English fluently. Army Alpha and Army Beta were used in ranking and classifying soldiers but also included recommendations for discharging men deemed inferior or deficient based on their performance (Yoakum & Yerkes, 1920). There were also notions that intelligence deficiencies indicated other mental deficiencies that would increase an individual's vulnerability for developing symptoms after potentially psychologically traumatic event exposures.

Ultimately, as with the Woodworth tests, attempts to use Army Alpha and Army Beta to screen out men based on potential susceptibility to mental health challenges after potentially psychologically traumatic event exposures proved fruitless and the development of treatments became imperative. Despite their inability to predict incidence of mental health diagnoses, the fate of Army Alpha and Army Beta paralleled that of the Woodworth test and personality assessments: Army Alpha and Army Beta were widely used and the content and style of their questions became foundational for subsequent intelligence tests. Indeed, several of the questions are identical to items found on modern intelligence tests.

Initial Treatments

Despite difficulties with assessment and screening, the diagnosis of Shell Shock increasingly replaced the diagnoses of traumatic neurosis and war neurasthenia. Thousands of soldiers were declared unfit for duty based on this diagnosis, producing substantial enthusiasm for developing novel treatments for this novel disorder and driving a huge increase in research on treating war-related stress. The ongoing war effort and demand for additional soldiers meant that treatments for Shell Shock needed to be able to move large numbers of men quickly out of hospital beds and back to the front line. Shell Shock was still not clearly understood (Shepard, 2000); as a result, treatments for Shell Shock were also incoherent. The treatments that were developed over the course of the WWI varied dramatically in both intensity and effectiveness, with some physicians relying on physiological treatments, such as anaesthesia and electricity, while others tried new psychodynamic therapies (McKenzie, 2012). In retrospect, soldiers who were able to recover appear to have done so independently of what passed for medical care at the time (Winter, 2011).

Despite the limited initial understanding of Shell Shock, the medical profession pressed on in an effort to develop treatment options. Shell Shock was initially purported to be a disease with physical and physiological origins, a theory harkening back to the shift away from Cartesian dualism driven by Broca's research (1861); accordingly, the shift towards psychological origins was slow and many initial treatments focused on physiological interventions. For example, given the assumption that Shell Shock was considered a disorder of the nerves, galvanic stimulation of the nerves (i.e., electroshock therapy) was attempted. A prominent clinician claimed most Shell Shock cases could be cured by galvanic shock after a treatment course of no longer than three months (Garton, 1916); however, soldiers were not allowed to linger in hospitals so that the long-term effects of electroshock therapy could be observed, which precluded assessments of sustained symptom reduction and side effects. Claims by Garton (1916) of immediate success with electroshock therapy also contrasted suspiciously with outcomes described at other hospitals. For instance, in Germany, electroshock therapy (labelled "the Kaufmann cure" after its most zealous proponent) was used with vigour, not infrequently resulting in death and rendering most patients unsuitable for further duty (Shephard, 2000). By 1917, Kaufmann and other practitioners had abandoned electroshock therapy in favour of hypnosis and other psychoanalytic treatments, in part because the electroshock therapy was perceived as brutal and in part because the evidence did not support electroshock therapy as effective (Shephard, 2000).

Perhaps the most important development in treatment methods during WWI was coined "forward psychiatry" which asserted that optimal care required proximity to battle, immediacy, and the patient's expectation of recovery. The principles of forward psychiatry (i.e., Proximity, Immediacy, Expectation) are now more commonly referred to with the acronym PIE (Jones & Wessely, 2003), but the work originated in French neurological hospitals as part of efforts to systematically treat Shell Shock and rapidly return soldiers to the front line. The French hospitals initially used psychotherapy in conjunction with electric shock to treat Shell Shock and claimed a more than 90% success rate in return to duty; however, the same hospitals were later criticized for sending still-traumatized men back to the front lines with little or no evidence indicating that the treatments had produced actual symptom reduction (Jones & Wessely, 2003). The British and Canadian armies also established hospitals for neurological symptoms in 1915 (Jones & Wessely, 2003; Russel, 1919). The British and Canadian forward psychiatric hospitals focused on occupational therapy through skills training rather than on psychological treatments to reduce symptoms, but the hospitals had a comfortable environment and "the morale among the patients was very much improved" (Russel, 1919, p. 30). The predominant view in the special hospitals designed for neurological symptoms was that "all functional nervous disorders are curable—provided that the desire for cure is present in the patient" (p. 33). Nevertheless, successful return to duty was significantly lower among the British and Canadian hospitals compared to the French hospitals, with some UK hospitals sending only 4–5% of men back to the front lines (Jones & Wessely, 2003). Along with developing hospitals based on PIE principles, the British were also issuing formal instructions to medical officers on how to handle cases of Shell Shock (Russel, 1919). British officers were instructed to never diagnose a solider with Shell Shock, verbally or in writing, but instead to use the British acronym NYDN (Not Yet Diagnosed Nervous).

British medical officer W. H. Rivers presented a paper in 1918 to the Royal Society of Medicine discussing soldiers' repression of war-related memories of trauma (Rivers, 1918). According to Rivers, soldiers were trained to react calmly to war, but some soldiers attempted to keep calm by repressing the memories of their experience. The active repression of war memories was posited as a potential trigger for war neuroses. Rivers counselled his patients not to repress their memories, but instead to recall them and try to make them tolerable. The treatment involved three mechanisms of change: 1) catharsis, or relief due to integration of the memory into the self; 2) re-education, or adopting a new view of old memories; and 3) faith or suggestion, or the importance of the doctor communicating effectiveness to the patient. Rivers noted that his treatment was not effective for all patients, particularly those with dissociation symptoms; nevertheless, Rivers expected his treatment would be effective for most men affected by Shell Shock. Rivers' paper foreshadowed contemporary exposure-based treatments for PTSD that would not be introduced until 65 years later, during which patients intentionally and repeatedly re-engage with and reprocess psychologically traumatic memories (e.g., Foa & Kozak, 1986; Keane et al., 1989).

Psychodynamic interventions were well known in some medical circles; that said, even doctors with no training in psychoanalysis or psychodynamic therapy were noticing the benefit of what might now be called talk therapy. For example, an army physician noted in a letter to the *British Medical Journal* that most of his patients with Shell Shock displayed impaired memory of the psychological trauma and "the revival of the memory of those experiences is followed by the disappearance of the symptoms" (Culpin, 1919, p. 501). Culpin's work made him a prominent neurologist and medical psychologist in the years following WWI (Loughran, 2009).

Stigma and the Brand of Cowardice

The concept of mental health malingering would have been almost unheard of prior to 1914 because mental disorders were so severely stigmatized. Indeed, mental health was persecuted in Canadian communities, with sufferers and their families being ostracized as well as saddled with huge expenses for inadequate treatment options. In an annual report from British Columbia's first hospital for the mentally ill, Medical Superintendent C. E. Doherty remarked on the widespread and problematic denial that mental illness could be hereditary, despite what Doherty felt was growing evidence for a genetic predisposition to mental disorders; he wrote that "it is a common sight to see a relative strenuously denying the fact that there is a family predisposition, while he himself has neurosis writ large on his forehead" (B.C. Legislative Assembly, 1905, p. G7). Accordingly, displaying mental health symptoms offered nothing for an individual to gain and everything to lose.

After the onset of WWI, perceptions surrounding mental health began to change. The medical field also developed a growing curiosity and openness about mental disorders, which helped to begin reducing the stigma of mental health in the general community, with one exception: a soldier with Shell Shock remained surrounded by an aura of suspicion and shame. The Canadian War Office recognized hysteria, neurasthenia, and Shell Shock as valid diagnoses resulting from the war, but people who developed any of the three diagnoses were still considered to have had a natural proclivity to emotionality (Duguid, 1938). Furthermore, there was a persistent idea that the soldiers who developed any one of hysteria, neurasthenia, or Shell Shock during wartime were also men who would crumble under the stressors of civilian life (Duguid, 1938); accordingly, ideas were perpetuated that mental disorders, particularly hysteria, neurasthenia, and Shell Shock, were based on inherent deficiencies rather than on exposure to potentially psychologically traumatic events, such as war.

The military leaders of the day took a strong and early stance against recognizing Shell Shock as being anything but an inherent deficiency, weakness, cowardice, and a failure of manhood. Lord Moran, a prominent physician in the British military during WWI, wrote in his seminal text on the psychological effects of warfare that four categories of men existed: "men who did not feel fear; men who felt fear but did not show it; men who felt fear and showed it but did their job; men who felt fear, showed it, and shirked" (Moran, 1945, p. 3). His experiences as a physician led him to conclude that men who were psychologically healthy before the war and undamaged physically during the war would not experience adjustment difficulties after the war. Only those with "real" physical injuries and not "imagined" injuries could claim to be distressed. All others were cowards to be condemned and shamed. Lord Moran expressed a strong belief that men who showed psychological damage in the absence of prior weakness or physical trauma were cowards (Coleman, 2006). The label of cowardice carried strong social and professional consequences. Malingering, often considered the consequence of cowardice, was not a matter that sat lightly with medical officers whom the Canadian army required to attend the executions of soldiers branded malingerers (MacPhail, 1925).

Despite the prevalent scorn for cowardice and malingering, identification of malingering proved difficult, if not impossible, paralleling the earlier failures of personality and intelligence tests to predict mental challenges (Gibby & Zickar, 2008; Yoakum & Yerkes, 1920). Medical professionals Yealland and Buzzard (1918) proposed that malingering seemed mostly to

Trauma and the Human Psyche 25

do with faked paralysis. Based on their hypothesis, hospitals were advised to illuminate malingering by either 1) applying strong electrical current to the supposedly paralyzed limb to see if the limb reacted as would be expected without paralysis, or 2) startling the patient into acting normally, both of which resulted in a soldier's dismissal from the hospital. The concept of malingering carried an unusual new flavour in WWI: not only could a man be a coward and a malingerer based on his pre-war character, seeking refuge in a new diagnosis to avoid the front line, but he could also become a coward and malingerer as a direct consequence of a diagnosis. Medical personnel were strongly advised that a person diagnosed with hysteria could "develop the habits of an invalid" (Yealland & Buzzard, 1918, p. 244), whereby the soldier would "cling to his disorder, and after he has been cured may feign the symptoms of the disorder" (p. 245). Given that men who displayed symptoms of Shell Shock for long periods of time were suspected to be malingerers by default, medical personnel were further advised to discourage long hospital stays to reduce the appeal of malingering. Newly trained medical personnel were taught never to tell a soldier he had Shell Shock for fear that he would become complacent in that diagnosis (Coleman, 2006).

> It is advisable [...] to tell him it is impossible to discriminate between a functional disease and malingering before treatment, and that if there is a recurrence of the condition after treatment, it is undoubtedly due to malingering. The genuineness of the condition is only proved in the fact of the cure being permanent.
>
> (Yealland & Buzzard, 1918, p. 56)

Alongside the potential of malingering, widespread diagnosis of Shell Shock was feared for economic reasons, with medical professionals cautioning that a generation of soldiers returning from war with trauma-related diagnoses would cripple national productivity (Micale & Lerner, 2001). The term "pension hysterics" was used as early as 1914 to delegitimize the use of posttraumatic diagnoses, particularly to prevent men from stopping work because of such a diagnosis. By 1916, the protracted nature of the war had become clear. Strengthening national armies became of utmost importance and doctors were pressured to send soldiers without physical disabilities back to fight (Loughran, 2009). Conceptualizations of Shell Shock diverged in 1917, with one stream espousing physiological causes and the other espousing psychological causes, yet both streams essentially claimed that Shell Shock resulted from individual weakness and pathology (Loughran, 2009). A few medical professionals relayed case studies of men who were truly psychologically healthy and resilient but developed Shell Shock, which undermined prevailing views that mental illness was based purely on heredity and weakness; however, even those cases were quickly dismissed in favour of theories of faulty predisposition (Shephard, 2000).

The End of WWI

The Great War ended, but symptoms lingered and the reasons why exposure to war-related trauma resulted in symptoms such as war neurosis and hysteria remained unclear (Lasiuk & Hegadoren, 2006). The original hypothesis—that proximity to explosions was causing physical neurological damage—was demonstrably untrue, as no anatomical lesions could be found (Russel, 1919). A conference of German physicians was held in 1916 in Munich and a discussion was held on the topic of posttrauma nervous disorders. At the conference, Oppenheim's concept of traumatic neurosis was formally rejected by most of his peers in favour of pursuing a diagnosis such as neurasthenia or Shell Shock (Holdorff & Dening, 2011); however, the diagnosis of neurasthenia also lost popularity in the years following WWI, as medical professionals resisted the broad application of the diagnosis to dozens of medical conditions, including diseases later understood to be tuberculosis and appendicitis (Lutz, 2001). WWI-era treatments also came under fire, with electroshock therapy in particular being criticized as brutal (Shephard, 2000).

The term Shell Shock persisted briefly, but the stigma associated with Shell Shock remained pervasive among military and government leaders, medical professionals, and the general public. One strongly worded account in an official government history of the Canadian medical services stated that "'shell-shock' was a manifestation of childishness and femininity. Against such there is no remedy" (MacPhail, 1925, p. 273). In Germany, patients with Shell Shock were identified by visible symptoms such as trembling, and then ridiculed as malingerers (Shephard, 2000). The only cases of Shell Shock that were publicly accepted by the British government were those soldiers who had become crippled by Shell Shock and yet prevailed, recovering fully to become heroes on the front line.

The predominant professional post-WWI opinion on responses to potentially psychologically traumatic event exposures was to close neurological hospitals and send veterans back home (Barham, 2004). Providing pensions to soldiers who were discharged from the neurological hospitals was nonetheless considered ill-advised (Russel, 1919), reflecting the popular notion that men who did not recover from their neurological symptoms did not want to get better. Ultimately, the politicized nature of Shell Shock would lead to dramatic changes in global attitudes towards the "right to care" for injured veterans of wars, especially with regard to financial compensation (Winter, 2011). Prior to WWI, veterans were given financial compensation as "a matter of charity, of grace and favour" (p. 29). As a result of WWI, the rise of stigma towards soldiers with Shell Shock brought a new, grudging attitude towards postwar compensation. In a painful irony, war pension offices were particularly unsympathetic to veterans with Shell Shock.

The political environment remained largely unforgiving of mental health challenges resulting from the war; however, societies and families were focused on rehabilitating their damaged veterans (Barham, 2004). In an early qualitative study conducted by Canadian clergymen, 100 returned soldiers and their families were surveyed to assess the effect of war on their sense of responsibility to their family and their trust in government (Bench, 1918). Most of the participating soldiers were considered to be adjusting to civilian life quite well; unfortunately, a number of soldiers returned from the war full of bitterness towards the government and even towards their own families and loved ones, indicating they did not receive the gratitude they had expected and instead felt condescended to for their service and their maladies. As married men returned to their families, Bench (1918) wrote that the returned veteran "may be absent all day at work, and may show small interest in family affairs when he returns" (p. 476). The familial disconnect Bench described in men with Shell Shock was a dramatic foreshadowing of the well-known consequences of PTSD in veterans following subsequent wars, including the Vietnam War. Psychiatric social work grew roots in this era, with the Red Cross training case workers to help American families suffering in the aftermath of WWI (Black Jr., 1991).

After WWI, detailed stories of the events and the struggles of veterans became increasingly available to the public. British autobiographical literature described in vivid detail the harsh life of the WWI trenches. Great literary figures used the written word in attempts to convey the reality of wartime; for example, Ernest Hemingway's short stories about WWI are now interpreted as an attempt to make meaning of his time as a soldier in the Great War (Seiden & Seiden, 2013). Literature produced in the period after the war also included accounts of civilian traumatisation as a result of hearing about the war (Tate, 2013), including for the first time the experiences of women who were not allowed to serve on the front lines but who nonetheless experienced symptoms akin to Shell Shock. Despite the abundance of WWI literary accounts, most of the public remained largely fearful of mental illness and unsympathetic to veterans; autobiographical literature was gradually replaced with unflattering portrayals of Shell Shock in stories and plays (Shephard, 2000). Nevertheless, reliance on literary devices to communicate the total devastation of war persisted, with poets attempting to give retrospective voice to patients with Shell Shock (Loughran, 2012) in spite of the prevailing stigma.

Beyond the Great War

Most medical professionals had expected Shell Shock and related mental disorders to fade rapidly upon the end of the war; however, their expectations never materialized. Even though many patients remained affected by the war and the associated mental health challenges, the medical field gradually lost interest in Shell Shock, stalling advances in screening, assessment, and treatment. The lessons learned from WWI would not be meaningfully applied until the onset of new European battles a few decades later (Lasiuk & Hegadoren, 2006).

The Return to Global War

In late 1939, Canada declared war less than two weeks after Germany began invading Poland—the start of what is now known as World War II (WWII). Recruitment began in earnest and the air force and navy were rapidly expanded. By the end, approximately 1.1 million of the 11 million Canadian citizens had served in the Canadian Forces during WWII. "Combat neurosis" replaced Shell Shock as the label for similar symptoms and the rates of diagnoses varied by exposure level from 10 to 100% (DiMauro et al., 2014). Having recalled the lessons from WWI, American war leaders tried to identify common timelines of symptom onset; specifically, leaders of the day believed that, based on available evidence, every soldier would become symptomatic after 240 days of combat exposure (Dyer, 2004). In the Canadian military, combat neurosis would comprise the largest proportion of medical discharges, with 15% having the diagnosis of "psychoneurosis" and a further 15% having other unexplained psychiatric symptoms (Griffin et al., 1945).

In the middle of WWII, Abram Kardiner released what was perhaps the first comprehensive text on treating "those neurotic disturbances which are incidental to war" (1941, p. vi). Kardiner had studied the lingering symptoms suffered by WWI Veterans in the 1920s, and endeavoured to apply his understanding of wartime symptoms to help those injured by the new war. He surmised that most people would develop similar neuroses from exposure to the horror of war as they would in response to non-war trauma, but suspected that war would strip away any natural resiliencies found in peacetime (e.g., the security of home) —leaving an individual afflicted by neuroses with no easy path to recovery. Kardiner identified consistent features across all possible presentations of traumatic neurosis: fixation on the trauma; "perseverative" dreams of the trauma which prove challenging to analyse (an important treatment tool in this era); irritability and physiological hypersensitivity; and a tendency to become aggressive when angered. For treatment, Kardiner recommended rest and alleviation of discomfort, hypnosis and electroshock therapy, and encouraging the patient to talk about his experience to ultimately "free him of the idea that the world is hostile and his powers to control it are gone" (p. 220).

Alongside psychotherapeutic approaches to treating an affliction of the psyche, there was an ongoing, but mostly futile, effort to find causal physical damage (e.g., Heppenstall, Hill, & Slater, 1945; Kupper, 1945). Subsequent biological research would eventually clarify the search as valid, but limited in the 1940s by the available methods: the most obvious impact of potentially psychologically traumatic event exposures would be found not in structural brain damage but rather in changes to the production of hormones by the endocrine system. Indeed, the post-WWII research culminated in Hans Selye elucidating his now-famous General Adaptation Syndrome, or the impact of significant stress on hormone production (Selye, 1950, 1955).

Many accounts of combat neurosis continued to carry prejudice during and after WWII. Stress from the war was blamed on pre-existing personality neurosis, "nervous" mothers, poor maternal relationships, and a lifetime of poor coping with pre-war stress such as automobile accidents (Henderson & Moore, 1944). During the post-WWII era, afflicted individuals were described as complaintive and focused on escaping their wartime duties (Henderson & Moore, 1944). Studies distinguished "the neurotics" from "the normals" (e.g., Tanner & Jones, 1948); soldiers who broke down in the early days of their deployment were held to be qualitatively different from, and weaker than, soldiers who broke down after prolonged exposure to war (Swank & Merchand, 1946). Soldiers with combat neurosis were described as having "tantrums and immature projections" like children (Goldfarb & Kiene, 1945, p. 564).

Despite stigmatization and scientific confusion, the medical community of the 1940s began to recognize the validity of the symptoms. The Canadian military implemented psychiatric treatment centres during WWII so that many soldiers with combat neurosis were provided early and prolonged treatment (Billings, Chalke, & Shortt, 1947). Canadian soldiers discharged for combat neurosis were generally able to secure favourable employment upon their return to Canada, except when they believed themselves to be physically injured; as such, physicians were advised to explain to all soldiers why they were being discharged (i.e., for psychological reasons) so that they did not have false impressions of being physically disabled (Griffin et al., 1945). Importantly, medical personnel began to understand that the symptoms were not as transient as previously believed. The cluster of symptoms displayed by WWII veterans continued to match Kardiner's (1941) description of startle responses, nightmares, and irritability, and persisted for decades following the end of WWII (Archibald & Tuddenham, 1965). The experience of WWII consolidated lessons of traumatic stress from WWI, setting the dramatic consequences of war exposure within a growing understanding of typical responses to potentially psychologically traumatic event (DiMauro et al., 2014).

The Influence of the Korean and Vietnam Wars

The concept of combat neurosis continued to be refined during the Korean and Vietnam wars, as did our understanding of war-related stress and its consequences. The first fully formalized and broadly accepted recognition of the psychological impact of potentially psychologically traumatic event exposures came in 1952 when the first edition of the Diagnostic and Statistical Manual of Mental Disorders (DSM) included *Gross Stress Reaction* as a diagnosis (American Psychiatric Association, 1952). Behavioural descriptions of "ineffective combat performance" were outlined in the Korean War, including withdrawing from the fight, social isolation, malingering, defensively overreacting, and becoming "hysterically incapacitated" (Kern, 1966, p. 5). The stress-related overproduction of adrenal hormones was confirmed in frontline soldiers (Howard et al., 1955). Researchers were beginning to conceptualize traumatic neurosis as a product of internal dispositional factors (e.g., despair), internal physiological factors (e.g., hormone response), and the severity of external potentially psychologically traumatic event stimuli (Kern, 1966).

The Vietnam War presented an entirely new experience of trauma. The Vietnamese did not use European rules of conduct for warfare and the war was not publicly supported in the United States to the same degree as previous wars (Drew, 1988). Furthermore, soldiers were faced with difficulty distinguishing friend from enemy, as many South Vietnamese would be "ally by day and Vietcong by night" (Laufer et al., 1984, p. 67). The distinctive nature of the Vietnam War led to escalated symptoms following potentially psychologically traumatic event exposures. WWII and Vietnam veterans tended to report similar types of symptoms, but the latter presented as more severely symptomatic than the former (Davidson et al., 1990). Vietnam veterans displayed greater depression, guilt and survivor's guilt, impairment in work and recreational interests, avoiding reminders of war-related events, social detachment, and suicidality than their WWII counterparts. WWII veterans were most concerned about physical injury and being captured, whereas Vietnam veterans were more often upset by the death of friends, witnessing extreme brutality, and exposure to mutilated and dismembered bodies.

The diagnosis of Gross Stress Reaction was removed from the second edition of the DSM published in 1968 (American Psychiatric Association, 1968), possibly because of insufficient advocacy by medical professionals and a pressure to minimize combat-specific diagnoses, and perhaps to decrease the financial liabilities of Veteran's Affairs (Scott, 1990). Veterans were discouraged by the public from speaking about their experiences and their symptoms; medical professionals often opted not to provide a diagnosis, which prevented veterans from accessing government-funded treatment (Blank, 1985). Canadian veterans who had served with the American Military in Vietnam had even higher rates of combat-related symptoms, likely on account of poor access to treatment and limited recognition of their experience by the Canadian public (Stretch, 1991).

By the late 1970s, military and civilian leaders, as well as the medical community, had acknowledged that soldiers returning from Vietnam were not integrating back into society as expected and that their need for treatment was overwhelming the existing American system (Blank, 1985). Nevertheless, getting a diagnosis focused on potentially psychologically traumatic event exposure included in the DSM required vigorous advocacy from grassroots organizations including psychologists, psychiatrists, veterans, and public supporters of veterans (Scott, 1990). A snowballing series of meetings, fundraising efforts, radio broadcast campaigns, and presentations at American psychology conferences culminated in the formation of the Vietnam Veterans Working Group. The Working Group spent more than a year collecting hundreds of Vietnam veterans' stories for a report presented to the DSM-III taskforce (Scott, 1990). In 1980, the third edition of the DSM officially provided a diagnosis for symptoms resulting from potentially psychologically traumatic event exposure using the label Posttraumatic Stress Disorder (American Psychiatric Association, 1980). Symptoms that had been identified as early as WWI and WWII were preserved in the diagnosis of PTSD within the symptom clusters of re-experiencing, avoidance and numbing, and physiological arousal. The DSM-III clarified that symptoms could occur regardless of pre-existing personality neurosis or life stress and stated that the severity of the stressor was the best predictor of the severity of the symptoms. At the same time as the new edition was published, the American Veterans' Affairs system established a series of counselling centres for veterans (Blank, 1985). The diagnosis of PTSD was thus legitimized by the American government and medical profession, and improved public awareness and acceptance followed.

The effort required to have PTSD recognized and included underscores the critical sociopolitical nature of mental health and the long history of biases against recognizing the potential causal influences of potentially psychologically traumatic event exposures on the development of mental health challenges. The biases stemmed from underdeveloped understandings of mental health; the same biases were likely reinforced by some leaders who were concerned about the economic and personnel costs associated with mental health-related disability (Linker, 2011; Loughran, 2009). Nevertheless, the Vietnam War may be considered the war that brought the impact of potentially psychologically traumatic event exposures on mental health to the forefront.

The Contemporary Understanding of PTSD

The details of the PTSD diagnosis continued to change after 1980 (American Psychiatric Association, 1987, 1994, 2000), largely focusing on what kinds of potentially psychologically traumatic event and which associated responses or symptoms would be recognized as sufficient to warrant a diagnosis, coupled with relatively minor changes to the description of specific symptom patterns.

Adam Montgomery (2017) recently explored how the Canadian peacekeeping missions of the 1990s—including Somalia, Croatia, and Rwanda—could be just as psychologically traumatic as combat exposure. Montgomery noted that stigma against PTSD within the military meant that peacekeeping personnel relied on peer support or "suffered in silence" (p. 133). The Canadian experience of PTSD was brought to public attention with General Roméo Dallaire's personal account of exposure to atrocities in Rwanda and his subsequent struggle with his mental health (2003). There is now a significant modern literature on the effects of war exposure on soldiers and veterans, including consideration of the ongoing mental health challenges of aging war veterans (e.g., Spiro, Schnurr, & Aldwin,

32 *Samantha C. Horswill and R. Nicholas Carleton*

1994; Sutker & Allain, 1996) and investigations into the effects of recent war activity, such as in Iraq and Afghanistan (e.g., Fulton et al., 2015; Schnurr et al., 2009). The focus of researchers has shifted from critiquing the validity of war-related symptoms to exploring what prevents soldiers with PTSD from seeking treatment and how better to help them do so (Fikretoglu et al., 2007). Notably, recent research has evidenced that mild traumatic brain injury from exposure to explosive blasts results in symptoms similar to, but nevertheless distinct from, the symptoms of PTSD (e.g., Ling et al., 2009), which likely explains why early medical professionals often consolidated brain trauma and mental health challenges into a single diagnosis.

Changes to the most recent edition of the DSM (American Psychiatric Association, 2013) reflect the ongoing discussions of what constitutes a potentially psychologically traumatic event exposure. The symptom clusters have been thoroughly clarified and refined. Many of the initially suspected factors (e.g., personality traits, family support, prior potentially psychologically traumatic event exposure) continue to be seen as influencing PTSD susceptibility (American Psychiatric Association, 2013). The susceptibilities may no longer involve the same pejorative perceptions, but the stigma surrounding mental health appears ongoing (Clement et al., 2015). The research base and social support for the diagnosis have made the removal of PTSD from any future DSM increasingly unlikely.

Conclusion

The impact of war on our understanding of mental health has been profound. The economic demands of the WWI and WWII forced mental health injuries to be dismissed or downplayed, which carried negative repercussions for individuals struggling with poor mental health. At the same time, however, the economic demands spurred advances in assessment and treatment to meet the growing mental health needs of embattled generations. The two world wars also produced a tremendous surge in research. The pressure of heavy demand also led investments in the development of new ways to assess and treat mental health, while exponentially expanding our understanding of the impact of stress on behaviour and physiology. By the time of the Korean and Vietnam wars, early forms of modern PTSD treatment (e.g., reframing the impact of potentially psychologically traumatic event exposures) were being considered alongside more classic approaches such as hypnotherapy and electroshock therapy. The search for effective protective programming and accessible treatments continues with particular urgency, as Canadian military members are now more likely to die at their own hand than they are in service (National Defence and the Canadian Armed Forces, 2013; National Defence (Canada), 2019).

Advances in our understanding of PTSD have recently facilitated positive changes in policy on mental health challenges associated with

Trauma and the Human Psyche 33

potentially psychologically traumatic event exposures. For example, the impact of potentially psychologically traumatic event exposures on first responders (e.g., firefighters, paramedics, police officers) and other public safety personnel (e.g., border services officers, correctional workers, public safety communications officials [e.g., 911 operators, dispatchers]), is increasingly recognized. In 2012, Alberta became the first province in Canada to recognize PTSD as a presumptive injury for first responders in the provincial Workers' Compensation Act. There is now increasing advocacy for awareness, education, and the reduction of stigma for mental health. The recent social and political advances in PTSD and mental health (e.g., Canada's 2019 National Action Plan on Post-Traumatic Stress Injuries; Public Safety Canada, 2019) have largely been the result of persistent advocacy coupled with increases in our willingness and ability to communicate about our own psyche.

We thought we knew in 1919. We were more certain in 1945. We are much more certain now. As we continue to move forward in our understanding of the causes and consequences of potentially psychologically traumatic event exposures, and as we improve our ability to effectively protect against and treat PTSD and related disorders, we must remember and build on the lessons from the great wars of the twentieth century.

References

American Psychiatric Association. (1952). *Diagnostic and statistical manual of mental disorders.* Washington, DC: American Psychiatric Association.

American Psychiatric Association. (1968). *Diagnostic and statistical manual of mental disorders* (2nd edn). Washington, DC: American Psychiatric Association.

American Psychiatric Association. (1980). *Diagnostic and statistical manual of mental disorders* (3rd edn). Washington, DC: American Psychiatric Association.

American Psychiatric Association. (1987). *Diagnostic and statistical manual of mental disorders* (3rd edn, Revision). Washington, DC: American Psychiatric Association.

American Psychiatric Association. (1994). *Diagnostic and statistical manual of mental disorders* (4th edn). Washington, DC: American Psychiatric Association.

American Psychiatric Association. (2000). *Diagnostic and statistical manual of mental disorders* (4th edn, Text Revision). Washington, DC: American Psychiatric Association.

American Psychiatric Association. (2013). *Diagnostic and statistical manual of mental disorders* (5th edn). Washington, DC: American Psychiatric Association.

Archibald, H. C., & Tuddenham, R. D. (1965). Persistent stress reaction after combat: A 20-year follow-up. *Archives of General Psychiatry, 12*(5), 475–481.

B.C. Legislative Assembly. (1905). *Annual report on the public hospital for the insane of the province of British Columbia for the year 1905.* Victoria, BC: Public Hospital for the Insane.

Barham, P. (2004). *Forgotten lunatics of the Great War.* Bury St Edmunds: St. Edmundsbury Press.

Beard, G. (1869). Neurasthenia, or nervous exhaustion. *The Boston Medical and Surgical Journal, 80*(13), 217–221.

Bench, P. J. (1918). Canadian war experience. *The Public Health Journal, 9*(10), 473–477.

Billings, R. M., Chalke, F. C. R., & Shortt, L. (1947). Battle exhaustion. *Canadian Medical Association Journal, 57*(2), 152–155.

Binet, A., & Simon, T. (1905). Méthodes nouvelles pour le diagnostic du niveau intellectual des anormaux. *L'Année psychologique, 11*, 191–336.

Black Jr., W. G. (1991). Social work in World War I: A method lost. *Social Service Review, 65*(3), 379–402.

Blank, A. S. (1985). Irrational reactions to post-traumatic stress disorder and Viet Nam veterans. In S. M. Sonnenberg, A. S. Blank, Jr., & J. A. Talbott (eds), *Trauma of war: Stress and recovery in Viet Nam veterans* (pp. 69–98). Washington, DC: American Psychiatric Press, Inc.

Broca, P. (1861). Nouvelle observation d'aphémie produite par une lésion de la troisième circonvolution frontale. *Bulletins de la Société d'Anatomie (Paris), 6*, 398–407.

Canadian Institute for Public Safety Research and Treatment (CIPSRT). (2019). *Glossary of terms: A shared understanding of the common terms used to describe psychological trauma (version 2.0).* Regina, SK: CIPSSRT.

Caplan, E. (1998). *Mind games: American culture and the birth of psychotherapy.* Berkeley, CA: University of California Press.

Clement, S., Schauman, O., Graham, T., Maggioni, F., Evans-Lacko, S., DBezborodovs, N., ... Thornicroft, G. (2015). What is the impact of mental health-related stigma on help-seeking? A systematic review of quantitative and qualitative studies. *Psychological Medicine, 45*, 11–27. https://doi.org/10.1017/S0033291714000129

Coleman, P. (2006). *Flashback: Posttraumatic Stress Disorder, suicide, and the lessons of war.* Boston, MA: Beacon Press.

Copp, T., & Osborne Humphries, M. (2010). *Combat stress in the 20th century: The Commonwealth perspective.* Kingston, ON: Canadian Defence Academy Press.

Culpin, M. (1919). Correspondence: The discussion on war neuroses. *The British Medical Journal, 1*, 501.

Daly, R. J. (1983). Samuel Pepys and post-traumatic stress disorder. *British Journal of Psychiatry, 143*, 64–68.

Dallaire, R. (2003). *Shake hands with the devil: The failure of humanity in Rwanda.* Toronto, ON: Random House Canada.

Davidson, J. R. T., Kudler, H. S., Saunders, W. B., & Smith, R. D. (1990). Symptom and comorbidity patterns in World War II and Vietnam veterans with Posttraumatic Stress Disorder. *Comprehensive Psychiatry, 31*(2), 162–170.

DiMauro, J., Carter, S., Folk, J. B., & Kashdan, T. B. (2014). A historical review of trauma-related diagnoses to reconsider the heterogeneity of PTSD. *Journal of Anxiety Disorders, 28*(8), 774–786.

Drew, D. M. (1988). *The eagle's talons: The American experience at war.* Darby, PA: DIANE Publishing.

Duguid, A. F. (1938). *Official history of the Canadian Forces in the Great War 1914-1919.* Ottawa, ON: The Minister of National Defence.

Dyer, G. (2004). *War: The new edition.* Toronto, ON: Random House Canada.

Erichsen, J. E. (1866). *On railway and other injuries of the nervous system.* London: Walton and Maberly.

Fikretoglu, D., Brunet, A., Guay, S., & Pedlar, D. (2007). Mental health treatment seeking by military members with Posttraumatic Stress Disorder: Findings on rates, characteristics, and predictors from a nationally representative Canadian military sample. *The Canadian Journal of Psychiatry, 52*(2), 103–110.

Foa, E. B., & Kozak, M. J. (1986). Emotional processing model of fear: Exposure to corrective information. *Psychological Bulletin, 99*, 20–35.

Forsyth, D. (1915). Functional nerve disease and the shock of battle: A study of the so-called traumatic neuroses arising in connexion with the War. *The Lancet, 186*(4817), 1399–1403.

Fulton, J. J., Calhoun, P. S., Wagner, H. R., Schry, A. R., Hair, L. P., Feeling, N., & Beckham, J. C. (2015). The prevalence of Posttraumatic Stress Disorder in Operation Enduring Freedom/Operation Iraqi Freedom (OEF/OIF) veterans: A meta-analysis. *Journal of Anxiety Disorders, 31*, 98–107.

Garton, W. (1916). Shell-shock and its treatment by cerebro-spinal galvanism. *The British Medical Journal, 2*, 584–586.

Geotz, C. G. (1995). *Charcot*. New York: Oxford University Press.

Gibby, R. E., & Zickar, M. J. (2008). A history of the early days of personality testing in American industry: An obsession with adjustment. *History of Psychology, 11*(3), 164–184.

Goldfarb, W., & Kiene, H. E. (1945). The treatment of the psychotic-like regressions of the combat soldier. *Psychiatric Quarterly, 19*(4), 555–565.

Griffin, J. D., Ross, W. D., Josie, G. H., & Henderson, M. F. (1945). Psychoneurotics discharged from the Canadian Army. *Canadian Medical Association Journal, 52*(4), 330–341.

Henderson, J. L., & Moore, M. (1944). The psychoneuroses of war. *New England Journal of Medicine, 230*(10), 273–278.

Heppenstall, M. E., Hill D., & Slater, E. (1945). The E.E.G. in the prognosis of war neurosis. *Brain, 68*(1), 17–22.

Holdorff, B., & Dening, T. (2011). The fight for "traumatic neurosis", 1889–1916: Hermann Oppenheim and his opponents in Berlin. *History of Psychiatry, 22*(4), 465–476.

Howard, J. M., Olney, J. M., Frawley, J. P., Peterson, R. E., Smith, L. H., Davis, J. H., & Dibrell, W. H. (1955). Studies of adrenal function in combat and wounded soldiers: A study in the Korean theatre. *Annals of Surgery, 141*(3), 314–320.

Jones, E., & Wessely, S. (2003)."Forward psychiatry" in the military: Its origins and effectiveness. *Journal of Traumatic Stress, 16*(4), 411–419.

Kaplan, R., & Saccuzzo, D. (2012). *Psychological testing: Principles, applications, and issues*. Belmont, CA: Cengage Learning.

Kardiner, A. (1941). *The traumatic neuroses of war*. Washington, DC: National Research Council.

Keane, T. M., Fairbank, J. A., Caddell, J. M., & Zimering, R. T. (1989). Implosive (Flooding) Therapy reduces symptoms of PTSD in Vietnam combat veterans. *Behavior Therapy, 20*(2), 245–260.

Kern, R. P. (1966). *A conceptual model of behavior under stress, with implications for combat training* (No. HUMRRO-TR-66-12). Alexandria, VA: George Washington University.

Kupper, H. I. (1945). Psychic concomitants in wartime injuries. *Psychosomatic Medicine, 7*(1), 15.

Lasiuk, G. C., & Hegadoren, K. M. (2006). Posttraumatic Stress Disorder Part I: Historical development of the concept. *Perspectives in Psychiatric Care, 42*(1), 13–20.

Laufer, R. S., Gallops, M. S., & Frey-Wouters, E. (1984). War stress and trauma: The Vietnam veteran experience. *Journal of Health and Social Behavior, 25*(1), 68.

Lawson, E., & Lawson, J. (1996). *The First Air Campaign, August 1914-November 1918*. Cambridge, MA: Da Capo Press.

Lilienfeld, S. O., Lynn, S. J., Namy, L. L., Woolf, N. J., Cramer, K. M., & Schmaltz, R. (2015). *Psychology: From inquiry to understanding*. Toronto, ON: Pearson.

Linden, S. C., Hess, V., & Jones, E. (2012). The neurological manifestations of trauma: Lessons from World War I. *European Archives of Psychiatry and Clinical Neuroscience, 262*(3), 253–264.

Ling, G., Bandak, F., Armonda, R., Grant, G., & Ecklund, J. (2009). Explosive blast neurotrauma. *Journal of Neurotrauma, 26*(6), 815–825.

Linker, B. (2011). *War's waste: Rehabilitation in World War I America*. Chicago, IL: The University of Chicago Press.

Loughran, T. (2009). Shell-shock and psychological medicine in First World War Britain. *Social History of Medicine, 22*(1), 79–95.

Loughran, T. (2012). Shell shock, trauma, and the First World War: The making of a diagnosis and its histories. *Journal of the History of Medicine and Allied Sciences, 67*(1), 94–119.

Lutz, T. (2001). Varieties of medical experience: Doctors and patients, psyche and soma in America. In Gijswijt-Hofstra, M. & Porter, R. (eds), *Cultures of neurasthenia: From Beard to the First World War* (pp. 51–76). New York: Brill Rodopi.

MacPhail, A. (1925). *Official history of the Canadian forces in the Great War: The medical services*. Ottawa, ON: King's Printer.

Marneros, A. (2008). Psychiatry's 200th birthday. *British Journal of Psychiatry, 193*(1), 1–3.

McKenzie, A. G. (2012). Anaesthetic and other treatments of shell shock: World War I and beyond. *Journal of the Royal Army Medical Corps, 158*(1), 29–33.

McNally, R. J. (2012). Psychiatric disorder and suicide in the military, then and now: Commentary on Frueh and Smith. *Journal of Anxiety Disorders, 26*(7), 776–778.

Micale, M., & Lerner, P. (2001). *Traumatic pasts, history, psychiatry and trauma in the modern age 1860–1930*. Cambridge: Cambridge University Press.

Montgomery, A. (2017). *The invisible injured: Psychological trauma in the Canadian military from the First World War to Afghanistan*. Montréal, QC: McGill-Queen's University Press.

Moran, C. M. W. (1945). *The anatomy of courage*. Edinburgh: Constable.

Mott, F. W. (1916). The effects of high explosives upon the central nervous system. *The Lancet, 1*(12), 331–338.

Munger, M. P. (2003). *The history of psychology*. New York: Oxford University Press.

Myers, C. S. (1915). A contribution to the study of shell shock. *The Lancet, 185*(4772), 316–330.

National Defence and the Canadian Armed Forces. (2013). Canadian forces' casualty statistics (Afghanistan). Retrieved from www.forces.gc.ca/en/news/article.page?doc=canadian-forces-casualty-statistics-afghanistan/hie8w9c9.

National Defence (Canada). (2019). Suicide and suicide prevention in the Canadian Armed Forces. Retrieved from www.canada.ca/en/department-national-defence/news/2017/05/suicide_and_suicidepreventioninthecanadianarmedforces.html

Public Safety Canada. (2019). *Supporting Canada's public safety personnel: An action plan on post-traumatic stress injuries*. Ottawa, ON: Government of Canada. Retrieved from www.publicsafety.gc.ca/cnt/rsrcs/pblctns/2019-ctn-pln-ptsi/index-en.aspx.

Rivers, W. H. (1918). The repression of war experience. *Proceedings of the Royal Society of Medicine*, *11*, 1–20.

Russel, C. (1919). The management of psycho-neuroses in the Canadian Army. *Journal of Abnormal Psychology*, *14*(1–2), 27–33.

Schnurr, P. P., Lunney, C. A., Bovin, M. J., & Marx, B. P. (2009). Posttraumatic Stress Disorder and quality of life: Extension of findings to veterans of the wars in Iraq and Afghanistan. *Clinical Psychology Review*, *29*(8), 727–735.

Scott, W. J. (1990). PTSD in DSM–III: A case of the politics of diagnosis and disease. *Social Problems*, *37*, 294–310.

Seiden, H. M., & Seiden, M. (2013). Ernest Hemingway's World War I short stories: PTSD, the writer as witness, and the creation of intersubjective community. *Psychoanalytic Psychology*, *30*(1), 92–101.

Selye, H. (1950). Stress and the General Adaptation Syndrome. *British Medical Journal*, *1*(4667), 1383–1392.

Selye, H. (1955). Stress and disease. *The Laryngoscope*, *65*(7), 500–514.

Shephard, B. (2000). *A war of nerves: Soldiers and psychiatrists in the twentieth century*. Cambridge, MA: Harvard University Press.

Shorter, E. (1992). *From paralysis to fatigue*. New York: The Free Press.

Somervell, T. H. (1936). *After Everest: The experiences of a mountaineer and medical missionary*. London: Hodder & Stoughton.

Spiro, A., Schnurr, P. P., &. Aldwin, C. M. (1994). Combat-related Posttraumatic Stress Disorder symptoms in older men. *Psychology and Aging*, *9*(1), 17–26.

Stretch, R. H. (1991). Psychosocial readjustment of Canadian Vietnam veterans. *Journal of Consulting and Clinical Psychology*, *59*(1), 188.

Sutker, P. B., & Allain, A. N. (1996). Assessment of PTSD and other mental disorders in World War II and Korean conflict POW survivors and combat veterans. *Psychological Assessment*, *8*(1), 18–25.

Swank, R. L., & Marchand, W. E. (1946). Combat neuroses: Development of combat exhaustion. *Archives of Neurology & Psychiatry*, *55*(3), 236–247.

Tate, T. (2013). *Modernism, history, and the First World War*. Penrith: Humanities-Ebooks, LLP.

Tanner, J. M., & Jones, M. (1948). The psychological symptoms and the physiological response to exercise of repatriated prisoners of war with neurosis. *Journal of Neurology, Neurosurgery, and Psychiatry*, *11*(1), 61–71.

Winter, J. (2011). Shell shock and the lives of the lost generation. In Stewart, E., & Ekins, A. (eds), *War wounds: Medicine and the trauma of conflict* (pp. 28–40). Dunedin: Exisle Publishing Limited.

Yealland, L. R., & Buzzard, E. F. (1918). *Hysterical disorders of warfare*. London: Macmillan.

Yoakum, C. S., & Yerkes, R. M. (1920). *Army mental tests*. New York: H. Holt and Company.

2 A Systematic Review of the Prevalence of Posttraumatic Stress Disorder Reported in Canadian Studies

Murray Weeks, Su-Bin Park, Samantha Ghanem, Sieara Plebon-Huff, Anne-Marie Robert, Harry MacKay, and Allana G. LeBlanc

Many Canadians (76.1%) have been exposed to at least one significant potentially psychologically traumatic event (Canadian Institute for Public Safety Research and Treatment, 2019) in their lifetime (e.g., been in a serious accident, been a victim of assault or of rape, participated in combat) (Van Ameringen et al., 2008). Most individuals who are directly or indirectly exposed to such events will not develop any long lasting negative effects; however, some will go on to develop posttraumatic stress disorder (PTSD), a mental disorder characterized by the persistent re-experiencing of the traumatic event, frequent avoidance of event reminders, and negative changes to thoughts and mood (American Psychiatric Association [APA], 2013).

PTSD is a highly burdensome condition associated with overall disability (Weeks, Garber, & Zamorski, 2016), work stress and unemployment (Nandi et al., 2004), attempted death by suicide (Sareen, Cox, Stein, et al., 2007), physical health problems such as cardiovascular and metabolic disease (Ryder, Azcarate, & Cohen, 2018), and high comorbidity with other mental disorders (e.g., alcohol and substance use disorder and major depression) (Kessler et al., 1995; Van Ameringen et al., 2008). Based on existing estimates of the economic burden of mental disorders in Canada (Lim et al., 2008), the economic burden of PTSD (lost productivity, attributable healthcare costs, reductions in health-related quality of life) may be as high as billions of dollars per year.

Risk factors for developing PTSD include events that occur pre-exposure (e.g., previous potentially psychologically traumatic event exposures, history of mental disorders), those that are exposure-related (e.g., severity and type of potentially psychologically traumatic event), and those that occur post-exposure (e.g., low social support) (Brewin, Andrews, & Valentine, 2000; Ozer et al., 2003). Finally, the prevalence of PTSD is higher among certain populations. For example, Canadian women have roughly twice the risk of developing PTSD as compared to men (Statistics Canada, 2013; Van Ameringen et al., 2008). The sex difference is likely due to several

DOI: 10.4324/9781351134637-3

factors, including sex differences in the types of trauma experienced (Tolin & Foa, 2006) and use of health services for mental disorders (Canadian Chronic Disease Surveillance System, 2018). Certain occupational groups are also at increased risk for developing PTSD, likely due to an increased risk of potentially psychologically traumatic event exposures; for example, active military personnel (Weeks et al., 2016), military veterans (Van Til et al., 2017), and public safety personnel (e.g., firefighters, police officers, paramedics) (Carleton et al., 2018).

A recent meta-analysis across 24 countries reported a lifetime prevalence of PTSD of 3.9% (Koenen et al., 2017). High-income countries reported PTSD prevalence (5%) that was more than twice that of upper-middle-income (2.3%) and lower-low middle-income (2.1%) countries. Canada was not included in the recent meta-analysis, which limits our ability to directly compare the prevalence of PTSD in Canada with other high-income countries.

In June of 2018, the Government of Canada enacted the *Federal Framework on Post-Traumatic Stress Disorder Act* (Government of Canada, 2018). The legislation called for the creation of a Federal Framework on PTSD (Public Health Agency of Canada [PHAC], 2020) that includes the improved tracking of PTSD and its associated economic and social costs as a priority. The legislation focuses on occupational groups known to have an increased risk of PTSD, while also recognizing all Canadians (Government of Canada, 2018).

To date, there has been no large review of the existing research reporting the prevalence of PTSD in Canadian studies. As such, the scope of available data is unclear, and evaluating the available evidence by following an orderly approach in a systematic way is essential. Accordingly, in support of the development of the Federal Framework on PTSD (PHAC, 2020) and to address the stated priorities of the PTSD Act (Government of Canada, 2018), we sought to systematically review the literature reporting on the prevalence of PTSD in Canadian studies to provide a broad overview of the available evidence. The scope of our review covers all populations in Canada, and includes clinical and self-reported assessments of both current and lifetime rates of PTSD.

Methods

We registered the review through the International Prospective Register of Systematic Reviews (PROSPERO; CRD42019126190). We also followed the population, interventions, comparisons, outcomes, and study design framework (PICO) (Schardt et al., 2007), and reported following the Meta-analysis of Observational Studies in Epidemiology (MOOSE) guidelines (Stroup et al., 2000), and the Preferred Reporting Items for Systematic Reviews and Meta-Analyses (PRISMA) guidelines (Moher et al., 2009).

Eligibility Criteria

All study designs were eligible to be included in the review, but only baseline results were retained for analysis (i.e., in the case of experimental, intervention, or longitudinal studies). We included studies that reported current prevalence (e.g., 12-month prevalence, 30-day prevalence), lifetime prevalence, or incidence of PTSD, as well as studies that reported on posttraumatic stress injury (PTSI) or operational stress injury (OSI). Furthermore, we considered all age groups for inclusion. Participants did not need to be Canadian citizens but needed to be living in Canada during the study period. We excluded studies presenting data exclusively on clinical PTSD populations (i.e., all participants were considered to have PTSD), studies with populations from outside of Canada, grey literature (e.g., conference proceedings, unpublished studies, conference abstracts, non-indexed reports), and studies published in languages other than English or French.

Search Strategy

We developed the search strategy in partnership with a research librarian (LG). We systematically searched Medline, Embase, the Cochrane Evidence-Based Medicine Reviews, and PsychInfo from inception to February 20, 2018 to identify studies on the prevalence (e.g., lifetime prevalence, 12-month prevalence, 30-day prevalence) and incidence of PTSD in Canada. In all databases, we searched using terms related to three concepts: i) PTSD, ii) occupation, and iii) Canada. We identified additional articles by a hand search and through consultation with experts. We provide full details regarding the search strategy in Appendix 2A. We saved all records as text files and imported each to RefWorks version 2.0 (Refworks, 2001). We also used the software to remove any duplicate articles.

Study Selection

After training, two independent reviewers (AGL and SG) screened the titles and abstracts of all records identified through the search using RefWorks version 2.0 (Refworks, 2001). For all studies identified as potentially relevant by at least one reviewer, we conducted a full-text evaluation. Two independent reviewers (AGL and SG) assessed all full-texts, keeping track of the primary reason for exclusion. We resolved disagreements by consensus or, if necessary, by a third reviewer (SBP). We managed full-text evaluation using Excel software (Microsoft Corporation, 2010).

Data Extraction

Two independent reviewers (SG and SPH) extracted data using a standardized and pilot-tested data collection form. Discrepancies were

Prevalence of Posttraumatic Stress Disorder 41

resolved by consensus or by a third reviewer (SBP). Reviewers were not blind to study details (e.g., author, journal) during extraction. Data extracted included study author, publication date, location, sample size, study population (e.g., occupation, sex, age), study design, data source, diagnostic classification tool, prevalence (lifetime prevalence, 12-month prevalence, 30-day prevalence), incidence, and diagnosis type (self-reported, clinical diagnosis). We examined rates of PTSD by type of rate (i.e., lifetime versus current), type of assessment (i.e., clinical assessment versus self-report), and population (i.e., occupation related versus non-occupational related). Current prevalence here refers to timeframes of one year and more recent, and occupation related studies included those focusing on any occupational group.

Due to an overall lack of homogeneity in study populations and assessment tools used, we judged that a meta-analysis with calculation of pooled estimates was not appropriate for the current study (systematic reviews are not always accompanied by a meta-analysis; Egger & Smith, 1997). Moreover, even in the absence of pooled data, following a systematic approach to sorting data by making use of meta-analytic techniques is nevertheless helpful in highlighting the overall structure of the existing literature (Egger, Smith, & Phillips, 1997). In order to enhance the presentation of results, we calculated non-weighted median rates along with rates reported in individual studies, although median rates should not be used to estimate differences across groups. We completed all analyses using Excel software (Microsoft Corporation, 2010) and RStudio 1.1.463 (R statistical computing, 2018).

Quality Assessment

Two independent reviewers (SG and SPH) performed the quality assessment using a modified version (Mata et al., 2015) of the Newcastle–Ottawa Scale (Wells et al., 2018). The scale assesses study quality in the following domains: sample representativeness and size, comparability between respondents and non-respondents, ascertainment of PTSD, and statistical quality. We provide full details regarding scoring in Appendix 2B. The reviewers gave a point score from 0 to 5 (0 points=lowest quality; 5 points=highest quality) to each study. We resolved disagreements by consensus or, if necessary, by a third reviewer (SBP). Scores of 3 points or greater indicate high quality and scores of fewer than 3 points indicate low quality.

Results

Search Results

We identified 1,650 potentially relevant publications through our search (Figure 2.1). After de-duplication, 1,034 records remained. After screening

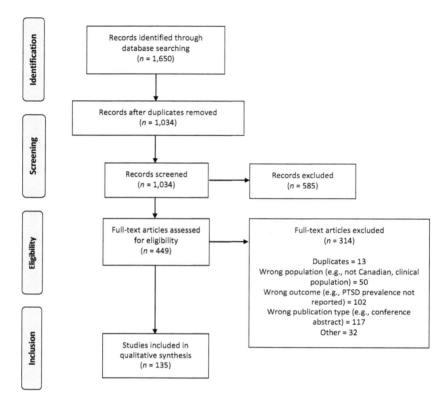

Figure 2.1 PRISMA flow diagram of included studies on the prevalence of PTSD in Canada.

of titles and abstracts, we retrieved 449 records for full-text review, and 135 met inclusion criteria and were included in the final review. The most common reason for full-text exclusion was wrong publication type (e.g., conference abstract; $n = 117$) followed by wrong outcome (e.g., PTSD prevalence or incidence not reported; $n = 102$).

Study Characteristics

In total, data for the current review came from 517,564 unique participants across 129 unique studies (135 total papers). Several papers reported on the same study, or used the same dataset. To avoid double counting participants, when there was a lack of clarity between two (or more) papers reporting on the same population, we counted the population only once, and used the largest reported sample size for analysis. If two authors used the exact same dataset but reported slightly different estimates, we calculated the average (mean) estimate between the studies. Details on

Prevalence of Posttraumatic Stress Disorder   43

all studies can be found in Appendix 2C. Sample sizes ranged from 13 to 16,193 participants. However, because several studies reported weighted sample sizes, we included a mix of weighted and unweighted samples in study descriptions. Most studies (n = 114) reported on current prevalence and/or lifetime prevalence (n = 24); very few (3) reported on incidence (data not shown).

PTSD Prevalence

The overall prevalence of PTSD ranged from 0% to 87.1% and the median rate across all included studies was 17.8% (95% CI: 8.6, 19.3). Figures 2.2a–d show results for individual studies. Also, Table 2.1 and Figures 2.2a–d show summary statistics for studies by type of rate, type of assessment, and population. Prevalence rates were right-skewed, with higher rates located in the upper tail of the distribution (i.e., very high rates are further from the median than are very low rates). Median lifetime prevalence ranged from 4.1% using a clinical assessment in non-occupation related studies, to 10.4% using self-reported assessment among occupation related studies. Median current prevalence ranged from 10.1% using a clinical diagnosis among non-occupation related studies, to 44.1% using a clinical diagnosis among occupation related studies.

The few studies reporting the prevalence of PTSD using a representative sample of a large population are worth noting. Nationally representative estimates of the prevalence of PTSD in the general Canadian population were limited to two sources of data. First, two studies using data from the 2002 Canadian Community Health Survey (Statistics Canada, 2003) reported a current prevalence of 1.3% (Goodwin et al., 2010; Sareen, Cox, Stein, et al., 2007). More recently, Statistics Canada reported a current prevalence of 1.7% from the 2012 Canadian Community Health Survey (Statistics Canada, 2013), although this latter estimate did not meet criteria for our review based on publication type. Canadian Community Health Survey estimates from 2002 and 2012 were based on a question about current diagnosis of PTSD by a health professional (Statistics Canada, 2003, 2013). The second source was a study using data from 2002 (Van Ameringen et al., 2008) in which PTSD was assessed with a symptom-based questionnaire that yields a probable diagnosis (Kessler et al., 1995). Results indicated that lifetime and current prevalence rates of PTSD were 9.2% and 2.4%, respectively (Van Ameringen et al., 2008).

There were two data sources involving a representative sample of Canadian Armed Forces regular force personnel. First, using data from the 2002 Canadian Community Health Survey Canadian Forces Supplement, four studies reported a current prevalence of 2.4% (Nelson et al., 2011; Sareen, Cox, Afifi, et al., 2007; Sareen et al., 2008; Zamorski et al., 2016) and another two reported a lifetime prevalence of 6.5% (Brunet et al., 2015; Fikretoglu & Liu, 2012). More recent estimates came from the 2013 Canadian Forces Mental Health Survey, which mirrored the 2012 Canadian

44 *Murray Weeks et al.*

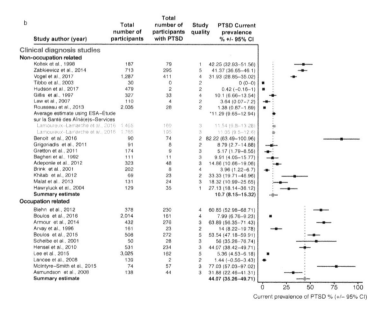

Figure 2.2 Descriptive analyses of the prevalence (%) of PTSD for: (a) lifetime prevalence; (b) current prevalence—clinical diagnosis; (c) current prevalence—self-reported, occupation-related; and (d) current prevalence—self-reported, non-occupation-related.

Note: Summary estimate = median prevalence. CI = Confidence Interval. Studies in grey used the same data source; in these cases, we used an average estimate for the summary estimate calculation.

Prevalence of Posttraumatic Stress Disorder 45

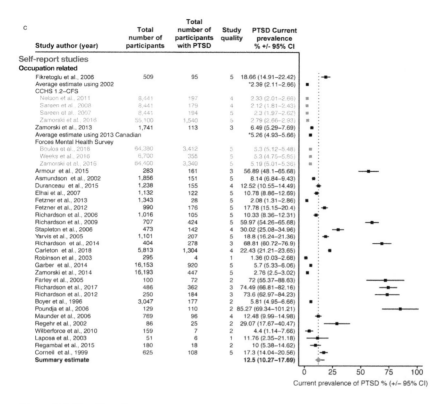

Figure 2.2 Continued

Community Health Survey. There were three studies that reported current prevalence of 5.3% (Boulos & Zamorski, 2016; Weeks et al., 2016; Zamorski et al., 2016), and one study reported lifetime prevalence of 11.1% (Weeks et al., 2016). The military personnel studies all reported prevalence based on a symptom-based questionnaire that yields a probable diagnosis (Kessler et al., 1995). Additionally, a Veterans Affairs Canada technical report (Van Til et al., 2017) included PTSD prevalence from three cycles of a large representative survey of Canadian Armed Forces regular force veterans (the Life After Service Survey). The report did not meet inclusion criteria for the current review based on publication type, but the results are worth mentioning. According to the report, the prevalence of PTSD among veterans was 12.8% in 2010, 15.2% in 2013, and 16.4% in 2016 (Van Til et al., 2017). Prevalence was based on a question about current diagnosis of PTSD by a health professional.

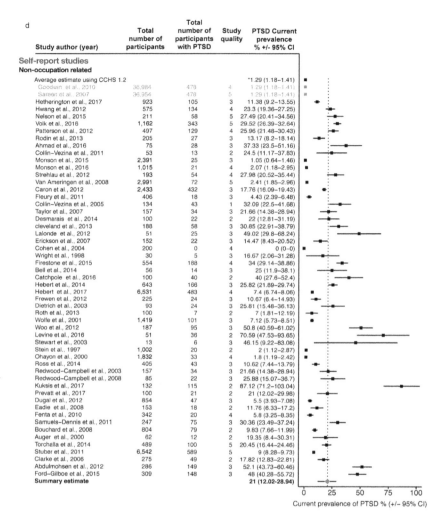

Figure 2.2 Continued

Quality Assessment

We present study quality scores in Table 2.1 by subgroup and in Figures 2.2a–d for each study individually. Detailed scores are presented for each study in Appendix 2D. We judged that the majority of studies (75.7%) had overall high quality (i.e., scores of 3 to 5). However, less than half of studies had scores of 4 (17.8%) or 5 (18.5%), whereas 40% had a score of 3. A further 20.7% and 3.7% had scores of 2 and 1, respectively, indicating low quality. The most common issues were lack of representativeness (only 34.1% of studies included populations from at least three

Prevalence of Posttraumatic Stress Disorder 47

Table 2.1 Summary of all included studies

Population		Number of papers	Number of unique studies	Total number of participants	Age (years)	Prevalence of PTSD (% range)	Summary estimate (median, 95% CI)	Risk of bias (range)
Current prevalence								
Clinical	Non-occupational	19	18	8,253	3+	0–82.22	10.7 (8.15–15.32)	1–5
	Occupational	11	11	7,450	18+	1.44–77.03	44.07 (35.26–49.71)	2–5
Self-reported	Non-occupational	54	53	75,174	2+	0–87.12	21 (12.02–28.94)	1–5
	Occupational	35	32	136,437	16+	1.36–85.27	12.5 (10.27–17.69)	1–5
Lifetime prevalence								
Clinical	Non-occupational	5	5	11,488	18+	0–19.33	4.13 (2.04–6.22)	2–4
	Occupational	4	4	1,088	18+	2.88–69.6	10.15 (6.47–13.82)	2–3
Self-reported	Non-occupational	9	9	17,302	15+	2.51–50	4.63 (3.44–5.95)	3–5
	Occupational	7	6	18,959	16+	6.52–65.24	10.38 (8.55–12.42)	2–5

Note: some studies reported on both current and lifetime prevalence. In such cases, both results are presented. If more than one paper reported on the same population, the mean of the two prevalence rates was calculated. To account for skewness in the data, summary estimates are the median of all included studies. CI = Confidence Interval.

48 *Murray Weeks et al.*

provinces/territories), lack of information on non-respondents (40.7% of studies had a response rate that was unsatisfactory, had unsatisfactory comparability between respondents and non-respondents, or had no description of the response rate or the characteristics of the responders and the non-responders), and small sample size (37.8% of studies included a sample size of fewer than 200 participants, and more than half of studies had fewer than 500 participants).

Discussion

To our knowledge, the current study is the first systematic review of rates of PTSD in studies from Canada. We included 129 unique studies (135 total studies) representing more than 500,000 participants. Most studies reported on prevalence and very few studies reported on incidence. The prevalence of PTSD ranged considerably across studies. Overall, median prevalence was 17.8%, with lifetime prevalence ranging from about 4% to about 10%, and current prevalence ranging from about 10% to about 44%. We deemed most studies to have high quality, but the largest group of studies had what could be argued to be a "medium" score on the quality scale (i.e., a score of 3). Also most studies were also limited to small or unrepresentative samples, or represented small geographic regions.

There is a tacit understanding that the prevalence of PTSD is variable, particularly due to the variability that exists in the population studied, sample size, type of study, timing of assessments, and assessment tool used to capture cases of PTSD. In our main descriptive analyses, we categorized studies by prevalence type (lifetime versus current), type of assessment (clinical diagnosis versus self-reported), and population type (occupation related versus non-occupation related). Non-occupation related studies included (but were not limited to) victims of abuse, individuals with problematic substance use, survivors of a disaster, as well as the Canadian general population. Occupation related studies included (but were not limited to) military personnel, veterans, public safety personnel, bus drivers, and sex workers. Clinical diagnosis studies varied in length and detail, involving long-form interviews, short screening tools, or administrative data indicating a diagnosis. Diagnostic criteria for PTSD have also changed over time, leading to variability in clinical diagnosis studies in terms of the time period during which PTSD was assessed. Similarly, self-report studies used a broad range of PTSD case finding assessment tools (e.g., questionnaires on current diagnosis, brief screening tools, and long questionnaires based on diagnostic criteria). The within-group variability should be kept in mind when considering the results of our descriptive analyses, which must be interpreted with caution.

Studies of lifetime prevalence reported lower rates of PTSD than studies of current prevalence. Typically, we would expect lifetime prevalence to be higher than current prevalence. Scholars of studies that reported both types of rates with the same dataset reported higher lifetime prevalence

Prevalence of Posttraumatic Stress Disorder 49

than current prevalence (e.g., Van Ameringen et al., 2008; Weeks et al., 2016). Nevertheless, median current prevalence in our review was about two to four times higher than lifetime prevalence in all clinical studies as well as self-reported non-occupation related studies. The above-mentioned issues related to variability likely impacted the current results, but the proportion of lifetime prevalence estimates in our review was relatively small (about 17%). The range of estimates among studies of current prevalence (0 to 87.1%) was also larger than among studies of lifetime prevalence (0 to 69.6%). Furthermore, studies of current prevalence tended to have lower quality; about 28% of current prevalence studies had scores of 1 or 2 (i.e., low quality) and lifetime prevalence studies included no studies with a score of 1 and only two studies with a score of 2.

For studies of lifetime prevalence, the median rates in clinical diagnosis studies and self-reported studies were similar. Among studies of current prevalence, clinical diagnosis rates were similar to self-reported rates for non-occupation related studies, but were almost four times higher in the case of occupation related studies. As mentioned, most of the prevalence estimates in our review were of current prevalence and a larger portion of these studies were of low quality as compared to lifetime prevalence studies.

Among studies of lifetime prevalence, occupation related studies reported higher median prevalence than non-occupation related studies. For studies of current prevalence, higher median prevalence was observed among clinical diagnosis studies, but rates in occupation versus non-occupation related studies were similar among self-reported studies. As mentioned, we grouped studies based on occupational or non-occupational groups in a general way and not all subgroups within or across these two categories are necessarily comparable, including in terms of the potential risk of potentially psychologically traumatic event exposures.

The few estimates based on representative samples of large populations (Canadian general population, military personnel, veterans) provide an important contrast to the often much higher estimates from studies using smaller and non-representative samples (e.g., clinical samples, victims of trauma) that appear to have inflated the overall prevalence across studies. In particular, the lifetime prevalence of 9.2% reported by Van Ameringen et al. (2008) is more in line with findings from other high-income countries using similar assessment methods (Koenen et al., 2017). Nevertheless, the existing estimates from representative samples of large populations are based on limited data.

Estimates from the 2002 and 2012 Canadian Community Health Survey were based on a single question asking whether respondents currently had a diagnosis of PTSD by a health care professional (Statistics Canada, 2003, 2013). The prevalence from the 2012 Canadian Community Health Survey represents the most recent estimate of PTSD prevalence in the Canadian general population; nevertheless, the data is several years out of date. The question regarding current diagnosis would not have captured individuals

50   Murray Weeks et al.

with PTSD who did not want to divulge their condition, as well as individuals who never received a diagnosis as a result of misdiagnosis, alternate diagnosis, or lack of treatment-seeking. In contrast, Van Ameringen et al. (2008) used a symptom-based questionnaire that was not conditional upon care seeking; however, respondents may nevertheless have been reluctant to divulge details of mental health-related experiences. The symptom-based method may capture cases of undiagnosed PTSD that are missed when asking about diagnoses, but likely underestimate true PTSD prevalence. The estimates reported by Van Ameringen et al. (2008) are dated; the estimates are based on data collected in 2002. Existing nationally representative estimates being out of date means the results are not representative of the *current* Canadian population and are based on an earlier version of the Diagnostic and Statistical Manual of Mental Disorders—the latest edition of the manual was published in 2013 (APA, 2013).

Other estimates from large representative samples were also limited to a few surveys of Canadian Armed Forces personnel and veterans using methods with the same strengths and limitations as the surveys of the general population. Direct comparisons between occupational and other groups and the general population are inherently difficult due to characteristics of groups such as military personnel, including demographics, employment status, health status, and pre-career (i.e., baseline) differences such as childhood experiences, as compared to civilians. If comparable surveys are used (e.g., Rusu et al., 2016), differences in group characteristics can be partially accounted for by restriction of the civilian population and adjustment for available variables. Important differences remain between the general population and specific occupational groups that are more difficult to control for, including differences in healthcare delivery and access as well as the perceived career consequences of divulging mental disorders. Nevertheless, the current estimates provide the best available points of comparison to those from the Canadian general population.

Strengths and Limitations

The current study has several strengths. We created a comprehensive search strategy with help from an expert in systematic review, we followed best practices in systematic review methodology, and we registered our review with PROSPERO. We also conferred with PTSD experts from across Canada on the systematic review, including participants at a national working meeting on PTSD (PHAC, 2020). There are also several limitations to the current study. First, we limited the current review to studies covering individuals living in Canada. For example, new immigrants, refugees, or expatriates may have been impacted by events outside of Canada that may have influenced their PTSD diagnosis. Second, we did not include grey literature (e.g., non-indexed reports) in our search criteria, meaning that we may have missed additional information from some organizations. We are aware of two important data sources (Statistics Canada, 2012; Van Til et al., 2017) that did not meet criteria for our review, although the relevant results were noted above. Third, we did not assess the quality of assessments used to derive rates of PTSD. For example, assessment tools (whether clinician-rated or self-reported) may produce different estimates due to differences in case definitions, including different cut-offs for screening tools and different versions of standard clinical criteria. Such differences may be exacerbated by the quality of individual assessment tools. We encourage future researchers to look to provide information on best practices in PTSD assessment.

Conclusion

In conclusion, the current study is the first to systematically review and report on the rates of PTSD in Canada. Across 129 unique studies and half a million participants, the prevalence of PTSD varied widely. Our results indicate that existing information on the prevalence of PTSD in Canada is out of date, including representative estimates of the Canadian general population and other populations such as Canadian military personnel. Based on our review, up-to-date prevalence estimates from nationally representative surveys appears needed. In addition to the lack of representative estimates, our results suggest there is room for quality improvement in many of the studies reviewed. Up-to-date, high-quality prevalence estimates in the Canadian general population and key sub-populations will further our understanding of the scope of the PTSD challenge and may have important implications for health policies. The current results may be used to inform future decisions regarding public health surveillance activities that will increase our understanding of the burden of PTSD in Canada.

Acknowledgements

We would like to thank Lisa Glandon, Master's in Information Science, Health Canada Library, for her assistance in the development of the search strategy for this work.

References

American Psychiatric Association (APA). (2013). Diagnostic and statistical manual of mental disorders (5th edn). *BMC Med*, *17*, 133–137.

Boulos, D., & Zamorski, M. A. (2016). Contribution of the mission in Afghanistan to the burden of past-year mental disorders in Canadian Armed Forces personnel, 2013. *Canadian Journal of Psychiatry*, *61*(1), 64S–76S.

Brewin, C. R., Andrews, B., & Valentine, J. D. (2000). Meta-analysis of risk factors for posttraumatic stress disorder in trauma-exposed adults. *Journal of Consulting and Clinical Psychology*, *68*(5), 748–766.

Brunet, A., Monson, E., Liu, A., & Fikretoglu, D. (2015). Trauma exposure and posttraumatic stress disorder in the Canadian military. *Canadian Journal of Psychiatry*, *60*(11), 488–496.

Canadian Chronic Disease Surveillance System (CCDSS). (2018). Data Tool 2000–2016. Public Health Infobase, Public Health Agency of Canada. Retrieved from https://health-infobase.canada.ca/ccdss/data-tool/.

Canadian Institute for Public Safety Research and Treatment (CIPSRT). (2019). Glossary of terms: A shared understanding of the common terms used to describe psychological trauma (version 2.0). Regina, SK: Author. http://hdl.handle.net/10294/9055.

Carleton, R. N., Afifi, T. O., Turner, S., Taillieu, T., Duranceau S., LeBouthillier, D. M., ... Asmundson, G. J. G. (2018). Mental disorder symptoms among public safety personnel in Canada. *Canadian Journal of Psychiatry*, *63*(1), 54–64.

Egger, M., & Smith, G. D. (1997). Meta-analysis. Potentials and promise. *BMJ* (Clinical Research edn), *315*(7119), 1371–1374.

Egger, M., Smith, G. D., & Phillips, A. N. (1997). Meta-analysis: Principles and procedures. *BMJ* (Clinical Research edn), *315*(7121), 1533–1537.

Fikretoglu, D., & Liu, A. (2012). Prevalence, correlates, and clinical features of delayed-onset posttraumatic stress disorder in a nationally representative military sample. *Social Psychiatry and Psychiatric Epidemiology*, *47*(8), 1359–1366.

Goodwin, R. D., Pagura, J., Cox, B., & Sareen, J. (2010). Asthma and mental disorders in Canada: Impact on functional impairment and mental health service use. *Journal of Psychosomatic Research*, *68*(2), 165–173.

Government of Canada. (2018). Federal framework on Post-Traumatic Stress Disorder Act. Retrieved from https://laws-lois.justice.gc.ca/eng/acts/F-7.38/page-1.html.

Government of Canada. (2019, April). The national conference on PTSD: Working together to inform Canada's Federal Framework on PTSD. Ottawa, ON: Government of Canada.

Kessler, R. C., Sonnega, A., Bromet, E., Hughes, M., & Nelson, C. B. (1995). Posttraumatic stress disorder in the National Comorbidity Survey. *Archives of General Psychiatry*, *52*(12), 1048–1060.

Koenen, K., Ratanatharathorn, A., Ng, L., McLaughlin, K., Bromet, E., Stein, D., ... Scott, K. (2017). Posttraumatic stress disorder in the world mental health surveys. *Psychological Medicine*, *47*(13), 2260–2274.

Lim, K. L., Jacobs, P., Ohinmaa, A., Schopflocher, D., & Dewa, C. S. (2008). A new population-based measure of the economic burden of mental illness in Canada. *Chronic Diseases in Canada*, *28*(3), 92–98.

Mata, D. A., Ramos, M. A., Bansal, N., Khan, R., Guille, C., Di Angelantonio, E., & Sen, S. (2015). Prevalence of depression and depressive symptoms among resident physicians: A systematic review and meta-analysis. *Journal of the American Medical Association*, *314*(22), 2373–2383.

Microsoft Corporation. (2010). Microsoft Excel software (v.14.0) (Excel 2010). Retrieved from www.microsoft.com/en-ca/.

Moher, D., Liberati, A., Tetzlaff, J., & Altman, D. G. (2009). Preferred reporting items for systematic reviews and meta-analyses: The PRISMA statement. *Annals of Internal Medicine*, *151*(4), 264–269.

Nandi, A., Galea, S., Tracy, M., Ahern, J., Resnick, H., Gershon, R., & Vlahov, D. (2004). Job loss, unemployment, work stress, job satisfaction, and the persistence of posttraumatic stress disorder one year after the September 11 attacks. *Journal of Occupational and Environmental Medicine*, *46*(10), 1057–1064.

Nelson, C., Cyr, K. S., Corbett, B., Hurley, E., Gifford, S., Elhai, J. D., & Donald, R. J. (2011). Predictors of posttraumatic stress disorder, depression, and suicidal ideation among Canadian forces personnel in a national Canadian military health survey. *Journal of Psychiatric Research, 45*(11), 1483–1488.

Ozer, E. J., Best, S. R., Lipsey, T. L., & Weiss, D. S. (2003). Predictors of post-traumatic stress disorder and symptoms in adults: A meta-analysis. *Psychological Bulletin, 129*(1), 52–73.

Public Health Agency of Canada (PHAC). (2020). Federal framework on post-traumatic stress disorder: Recognition, collaboration and support. Ottawa (ON): Government of Canada. Retrieved from www.canada.ca/en/public-health/services/publications/healthy-living/federal-framework-post-traumatic-stress-disorder.html.

R Statistical Computing. (2018). The R project for statistical computing. Retrieved from www.R-project.org/.

Refworks. (2001). Refworks reference data manager. Retrieved from www.refworks.com/refshare/help/Welcome.htm.

Rusu, C., Zamorski, M. A., Boulos, D., & Garber, B. G. (2016). Prevalence comparison of past-year mental disorders and suicidal behaviour in the Canadian Armed Forces and the Canadian general population. *Canadian Journal of Psychiatry, 61*(1 Suppl), 46S–55S.

Ryder, A. L., Azcarate, P. M., & Cohen, B. E. (2018). PTSD and physical health. *Current Psychiatry Reports, 20*(12), 116.

Sareen, J., Belik, S.-L., Afifi, T. O., Asmundson, G. J. G., Cox, B. J., & Stein, M. B. (2008). Canadian military personnel's population attributable fractions of mental disorders and mental health service use associated with combat and peacekeeping operations. *American Journal of Public Health, 98*(12), 2191–2198.

Sareen, J., Cox, B. J., Afifi, T. O., Stein, M. B., Belik, S.-L., Meadows, G., & Asmundson, G. J. G. (2007). Combat and peacekeeping operations in relation to prevalence of mental disorders and perceived need for mental health care: Findings from a large representative sample of military personnel. *Archives of General Psychiatry, 64*(7), 843–852.

Sareen, J., Cox, B. J., Stein, M. B., Afifi, T. O., Fleet, C., & Asmundson G. J. G. (2007). Physical and mental comorbidity, disability, and suicidal behavior associated with posttraumatic stress disorder in a large community sample. *Psychosomatic Medicine, 69*(3), 242–248.

Schardt, C., Adams, M. B., Owens, T., Keitz, S., & Fontelo, P. (2007). Utilization of the PICO framework to improve searching PubMed for clinical questions. *BMC Medical Informatics and Decision Making, 7*(1), 16.

Statistics Canada. (2003). Canadian Community Health Survey – Mental health and well-being. Retrieved from www23.statcan.gc.ca/imdb/p2SV.pl?Function=getSurvey&Id=5285.

Statistics Canada. (2012). Table 13-10-0465-01: Mental health indicators. Retrieved from www150.statcan.gc.ca/t1/tbl1/en/tv.action?pid=1310046501.

Statistics Canada. (2013). Canadian Community Health Survey – Mental health (CCHS-MH). Retrieved from www23.statcan.gc.ca/imdb/p2SV.pl?Function=getSurvey&SDDS=5015.

Stroup, D. F., Berlin, J. A., Morton, S. C., Olkin, I., Williamson, G. D., Rennie, D., ... Thacker, S. B. (2000). Meta-analysis of observational studies in epidemiology: A proposal for reporting. *JAMA, 283*(15), 2008–2012.

Tolin, D. F., & Foa, E. B. (2006). Sex differences in trauma and posttraumatic stress disorder: A quantitative review of 25 years of research. *Psychological Bulletin, 132*(6), 959–992.

Van Ameringen, M., Mancini, C., Patterson, B., & Boyle, M. H. (2008). Post-traumatic stress disorder in Canada. *CNS Neuroscience & Therapeutics*, *14*(3), 171–181.

Van Til, L., Sweet, J., Poirier, A., McKinnon, K., Sudom, K., Dursun, S., & Pedlar, D. (2017). Well-being of Canadian regular force veterans. Findings from LASS 2016 Survey (Research Directorate Technical Report). Charlottetown, PE: Veterans Affairs Canada. Retrieved from www.veterans.gc.ca/eng/about-vac/research/research-directorate/publications/reports/lass-2016.

Weeks, M., Garber, B. G., & Zamorski, M. A. (2016). Disability and mental disorders in the Canadian Armed Forces. *Canadian Journal of Psychiatry*, *61*(1 Suppl), 56S–63S.

Wells, G., Shea, B., O'Connell, D., Peterson, J., Welch, V., & Losos, M. (2018). The Newcastle–Ottawa Scale (NOS) for assessing the quality of nonrandomized studies in meta-analyses. Retrieved from www.ohri.ca/programs/clinical_epi-demiology/oxford.asp.

Zamorski, M. A., Bennett, R. E., Rusu, C., Weeks, M., Boulos, D., & Garber, B. G. (2016). Prevalence of past-year mental disorders in the Canadian Armed Forces, 2002–2013. *The Canadian Journal of Psychiatry*, *61*(1_suppl), 26S–35S.

References (Included Studies in the Systematic Review Analyses)

Abdulmohsen, A. E., Ford-Gilboe M., Kerr M., & Davies L. (2012). Identifying factors that predict women's inability to maintain separation from an abusive partner. *Issues in Mental Health Nursing*, *33*(12), 838–850.

Adeponle, A. B., Thombs, B. D., Groleau, D., Jarvis, E., & Kirmayer, L. J. (2012). Using the cultural formulation to resolve uncertainty in diagnoses of psychosis among ethnoculturally diverse patients. *Psychiatric Services*, *63*(2), 147–153.

Ahmad, F., Shakya Y., Ginsburg L., Lou W., Ng P.T., Rashid M., … McKenzie K. (2016). Burden of common mental disorders in a community health centre sample. *Canadian Family Physician*, *62*(12), e758–e766.

Armour, C., Karstoft, K.-I., & Richardson, J. D. (2014). The co-occurrence of PTSD and dissociation: Differentiating severe PTSD from dissociative-PTSD. *Social Psychiatry and Psychiatric Epidemiology*, *49*(8), 1297–1306.

Armour, C., Contractor, A., Elhai, J. D., Stringer, M., Lyle, G., Forbes, D., & Richardson, J. D. (2015). Identifying latent profiles of posttraumatic stress and major depression symptoms in Canadian veterans: Exploring differences across profiles in health related functioning. *Psychiatry Research*, *228*(1), 1–7.

Arvay, M. J., & Uhlemann, M. R. (1996). Counsellor stress in the field of trauma: A preliminary study. *Canadian Journal of Counselling*, *30*(3), 193–210.

Asmundson, G. J. G., Stein, M. B., & McCreary, D. R. (2002). Posttraumatic stress disorder symptoms influence health status of deployed peacekeepers and nondeployed military personnel. *The Journal of Nervous and Mental Disease*, *190*(12), 807–815.

Asmundson, G. J. G., & Stapleton, J. A. (2008). Associations between dimensions of anxiety sensitivity and PTSD symptom clusters in active-duty police officers. *Cognitive Behaviour Therapy*, *37*(2), 66–75.

Auger, C., Latour, S., Trudel, M., & Fortin, M. (2000). Post-traumatic stress disorder after the flood in Saguenay. *Canadian Family Physician*, *46*, 2420–2427.

Bagheri, A. (1992). Psychiatric problems among Iranian immigrants in Canada. *Canadian Journal of Psychiatry*, *37*(1), 7–11.

Beal, A. L. (1995). Post-traumatic stress disorder in prisoners of war and combat veterans of the Dieppe raid: A 50-year follow-up. *Canadian Journal of Psychiatry*, *40*(4), 177–184.

Beiser, M., Simich, L., Pandalangat, N., Nowakowski, M., & Tian, F. (2011). Stresses of passage, balms of resettlement, and Posttraumatic Stress Disorder among Sri Lankan Tamils in Canada. *Canadian Journal of Psychiatry*, *56*(6), 333–340.

Bell, N., Sobolev, B., Anderson, S., Hewko, R., & Simons, R. K. (2014). Routine versus ad hoc screening for acute stress following injury: Who would benefit and what are the opportunities for prevention. *Journal of Trauma Management & Outcomes*, *8*(1), 5.

Benoit, A. C., Cotnam, J., Raboud, J., Greene, S., Beaver, K., Zoccole, A., ... Loutfy, M. (2016). Experiences of chronic stress and mental health concerns among urban indigenous women. *Archives of Women's Mental Health*, *19*(5), 809–823.

Biehn, T. L., Elhai, J. D., Fine, T. H., Seligman, L. D., & Richardson, J. D. (2012). PTSD factor structure differences between veterans with and without a PTSD diagnosis. *Journal of Anxiety Disorders*, *26*(3), 480–485.

Bouchard, E.-M., Tourigny, M., Joly, J., Hebert, M., & Cyr, M. (2008). Psychological and health sequelae of childhood sexual, physical and psychological abuse. *Revue d'épidémiologie et de santé publique*, *56*(5), 333–344.

Boulos, D., & Zamorski, M. A. (2015). Do shorter delays to care and mental health system renewal translate into better occupational outcome after mental disorder diagnosis in a cohort of Canadian military personnel who returned from an Afghanistan deployment? *BMJ Open*, *5*(12), e008591.

Boulos, D., & Zamorski, M. A. (2016). Contribution of the mission in Afghanistan to the burden of past-year mental disorders in Canadian Armed Forces personnel, 2013. *Canadian Journal of Psychiatry*, *61*(1), 64S–76S.

Boulos, D., & Zamorski, M. A. (2016). Military occupational outcomes in Canadian Armed Forces personnel with and without deployment-related mental disorders. *Canadian Journal of Psychiatry*, *61*(6), 348–357.

Boyer, R., & Brunet, A. (1996). Prevalence of post-traumatic stress disorder in bus drivers. *Santé mentale au Québec*, *21*(1), 189–208.

Brink, J. H., Doherty, D., & Boer, A. (2001). Mental disorder in federal offenders: A Canadian prevalence study. *International Journal of Law and Psychiatry*, *24*(4–5), 339–356.

Brunet, A., Monson, E., Liu, A., & Fikretoglu, D. (2015). Trauma exposure and posttraumatic stress disorder in the Canadian military. *Canadian Journal of Psychiatry*, *60*(11), 488–496.

Carleton, R. N., Afifi, T. O., Turner, S., Taillieu, T., Duranceau, S., LeBouthillier, D. M., ... Asmundson, G. J. G. (2018). Mental disorder symptoms among public safety personnel in Canada. *Canadian Journal of Psychiatry*, *63*(1), 54–64.

Caron, J., Fleury, M.-J., Perreault, M., Crocker, A., Tremblay, J., Tousignant, M., ... Daniel, M. (2012). Prevalence of psychological distress and mental disorders, and use of mental health services in the epidemiological catchment area of Montreal South-West. *BMC Psychiatry*, *12*, 183.

Catchpole, R. E. H., & Brownlie, E. B. (2016). Characteristics of youth presenting to a Canadian youth concurrent disorders program: Clinical complexity, trauma, adaptive functioning and treatment priorities. *Journal of the Canadian Academy of Child and Adolescent Psychiatry*, *25*(2), 106–115.

Clarke, D. E., Colantonio, A., Rhodes, A., Conn, D., Heslegrave, R., Links, P., & van Reekum, R. (2006). Differential experiences during the holocaust and suicidal ideation in older adults in treatment for depression. *Journal of Traumatic Stress, 19*(3), 417–423.

Cleveland, J., & Rousseau, C. (2013). Psychiatric symptoms associated with brief detention of adult asylum seekers in Canada. *Canadian Journal of Psychiatry, 58*(7), 409–416.

Cohen, M. M., Ansara, D., Schei, B., Stuckless, N., & Stewart, D. E. (2004). Posttraumatic stress disorder after pregnancy labor, and delivery. *Journal of Women's Health, 13*(3), 315–324.

Collin-Vezina, D., & Hebert, M. (2005). Comparing dissociation and PTSD in sexually abused school-aged girls. *The Journal of Nervous and Mental Disease, 193*(1), 47–52.

Collin-Vezina, D., Coleman, K., Milne, L., Sell, J., & Daigneault, I. (2011). Trauma experiences, maltreatment-related impairments, and resilience among child welfare youth in residential care. *International Journal of Mental Health and Addiction, 9*(5), 577–589.

Corneil, W., Beaton, R., Murphy, S., Johnson, C., & Pike, K. (1999). Exposure to traumatic incidents and prevalence of posttraumatic stress symptomatology in urban firefighters in two countries. *Journal of Occupational Health Psychology, 4*(2), 131–141.

Desmarais, S. L., Pritchard, A., Lowder, E. M., & Janssen, P. A. (2014). Intimate partner abuse before and during pregnancy as risk factors for postpartum mental health problems. *BMC Pregnancy and Childbirth, 14*(1), 132.

Dietrich, A. (2003). Characteristics of child maltreatment, psychological dissociation, and somatoform dissociation of Canadian inmates. *Journal of Trauma and Dissociation, 4*(1), 81–100.

Du Fort, G. G., Bland, R., Newman, S., & Boothroyd, L. (1998). Spouse similarity for lifetime psychiatric history in the general population. *Psychological Medicine, 28*(4), 789–802.

Dugal, N., Guay, S., Boyer, R., Lesage, A., Seguin, M., & Bleau, P. (2012). Alcohol and drug consumption of students following the Dawson shooting: A gender-differentiated analysis. *Canadian Journal of Psychiatry, 57*(4), 245–253.

Duranceau, S., Fetzner, M. G., & Carleton, R. N. (2015). The home front: Operational stress injuries and veteran perceptions of their children's functioning. *Traumatology, 21*(2), 98–105.

Eadie, E. M., Runtz, M. G., & Spencer-Rodgers, J. (2008). Posttraumatic stress symptoms as a mediator between sexual assault and adverse health outcomes in undergraduate women. *Journal of Traumatic Stress, 21*(6), 540–547.

Elhai, J. D., Don, R. J., & Pedlar, D.J. (2007). Predictors of general medical and psychological treatment use among a national sample of peacekeeping veterans with health problems. *Journal of Anxiety Disorders, 21*(4), 580–589.

Erickson, D. H., Janeck, A. S., & Tallman, K. (2007). A cognitive-behavioral group for patients with various anxiety disorders. *Psychiatric Services, 58*(9), 1205–1211.

Farley, M., Lynne, J., & Cotton, A. J. (2005). Prostitution in Vancouver: Violence and the colonization of first nations women. *Transcultural Psychiatry, 42*(2), 242–271.

Fenta, H., Hyman, I., Rourke, S. B., Moon, M., & Noh, S. (2010). Somatic symptoms in a community sample of Ethiopian immigrants in Toronto, Canada. *International Journal of Culture and Mental Health, 3*(1), 1–15.

Prevalence of Posttraumatic Stress Disorder 57

Fetzner, M. G., Mcmillan, K. A., & Asmundson, G. J. G. (2012). Similarities in specific physical health disorder prevalence among formerly deployed Canadian forces veterans with full and subsyndromal PTSD. *Depression and Anxiety, 29*(11), 958–965.

Fetzner, M. G., Abrams, M. P., & Asmundson, G. J. G. (2013). Symptoms of posttraumatic stress disorder and depression in relation to alcohol-use and alcohol-related problems among Canadian forces veterans. *Canadian Journal of Psychiatry, 58*(7), 417–425.

Fikretoglu, D., Brunet, A., Schmitz, N., Guay, S., & Pedlar, D. (2006). Posttraumatic stress disorder and treatment seeking in a nationally representative Canadian military sample. *Journal of Traumatic Stress, 19*(6), 847–858.

Fikretoglu, D., & Liu, A. (2012). Prevalence, correlates, and clinical features of delayed-onset posttraumatic stress disorder in a nationally representative military sample. *Social Psychiatry and Psychiatric Epidemiology, 47*(8), 1359–1366.

Firestone, M., Smylie, J., Maracle, S., McKnight, C., Spiller, M., & O'Campo, P. (2015). Mental health and substance use in an urban first nations population in Hamilton, Ontario. *Canadian Journal of Public Health, 106*(6), e375–e381.

Fleury, M. J., Grenier, G., Bamvita, J. M., & Perreault, M. (2011). Typology of adults diagnosed with mental disorders based on socio-demographics and clinical and service use characteristics. *BMC Psychiatry, 11*(1), 67.

Ford-Gilboe, M., Varcoe, C., Noh, M., Wuest, J., Hammerton, J., Alhalal, E., & Burnett, C. (2015). Patterns and predictors of service use among women who have separated from an abusive partner. *Journal of Family Violence, 30*(4), 419–431.

Frewen, P. A., Allen, S. L., Lanius, R. A., & Neufeld, R. W. J. (2012). Perceived causal relations: Novel methodology for assessing client attributions about causal associations between variables including symptoms and functional impairment. *Assessment, 19*(4), 480–493.

Frise, S., Steingard, A., Sloan, M., Cotterchio, M., Kreiger, N. (2002). Psychiatric disorders and use of mental health services by Ontario women. *The Canadian Journal of Psychiatry, 47*(9), 849–856.

Garber, B. G., Rusu, C., & Zamorski, M. A. (2014). Deployment-related mild traumatic brain injury, mental health problems, and post-concussive symptoms in Canadian Armed Forces personnel. *BMC Psychiatry, 14*(1), 325.

Gillis, K., Russell, V. R., & Busby, K. (1997). Factors associated with unplanned discharge from psychiatric day treatment programs: A multicenter study. *General Hospital Psychiatry, 19*(5), 355–361.

Goodwin, R. D., Pagura, J., Cox, B., & Sareen, J. (2010). Asthma and mental disorders in Canada: Impact on functional impairment and mental health service use. *Journal of Psychosomatic Research, 68*(2), 165–173.

Gretton, H. M., & Clift, R. J. W. (2011). The mental health needs of incarcerated youth in British Columbia, Canada. *International Journal of Law and Psychiatry, 34*(2), 109–115.

Grigoriadis, S., De Camps, M. D., Barrons, E., Bradley, L., Eady, A., Fishell, A., ... Ross, L.E. (2011). Mood and anxiety disorders in a sample of Canadian perinatal women referred for psychiatric care. *Archives of Women's Mental Health, 14*(4), 325–333.

Guglietti, C., Rosen, B., Laframboise, S., Murphy, J., Dodge, J., Ferguson, S., ... Ritvo, P. (2009). Prevalence and predictors of post-traumatic stress in women undergoing an ovarian cancer investigation. *Psycho-Oncology, 18*, S40–S41.

Hawryluck, L., Gold, W. L., Robinson, S., Pogorski, S., Galea, S., & Styra, R. (2004). SARS control and psychological effects of quarantine, Toronto, Canada. *Emerging Infectious Diseases, 10*(7), 1206–1212.

Hebert, M., Lavoie, F., & Blais, M. (2014). Post traumatic stress disorder/PTSD in adolescent victims of sexual abuse: Resilience and social support as protection factors. *Ciência & Saúde Coletiva, 19*(3), 685–694.

Hebert, M., Daspe, M., Blais, M., Lavoie, F., & Guerrier, M. (2017). *Criminologie, 50*(1), 157–179.

Hensel, J., Bender, A., Bacchiochi, J., Pelletier, M., & Dewa, C. S. (2010). A descriptive study of a specialized worker's psychological trauma program. *Occupational Medicine, 60*(8), 654–657.

Hensel, J., Selvadurai, M., Anvari, M., & Taylor, V. (2016). Mental illness and psychotropic medication use among people assessed for bariatric surgery in Ontario, Canada. *Obesity Surgery, 26*(7), 1531–1536.

Hetherington, E., McDonald, S., Wu, M., & Tough, S. (2017). Risk and protective factors for mental health and community cohesion after the 2013 Calgary flood. *Disaster Medicine and Public Health Preparedness, 12*(4), 470–477.

Hudson, A., Al, Y. S., Samargandi, O. A., & Paletz, J. (2017). Pre-existing psychiatric disorder in the burn patient is associated with worse outcomes. *Burns, 43*(5), 973–982.

Hwang, S. W., Stergiopoulos, V., O'Campo, P., & Gozdzik, A. (2012). Ending homelessness among people with mental illness: The at Home/Chez soi randomized trial of a housing first intervention in Toronto. *BMC Public Health, 12*, 787.

Khitab, A., Reid, J., Bennett, V., Adams, G. C., & Balbuena, L. (2013). Late onset and persistence of post-traumatic stress disorder symptoms in survivors of critical care. *Canadian Respiratory Journal, 20*(6), 429–433.

Koltek, M., Wilkes, T. C. R., & Atkinson, M. (1998). The prevalence of post-traumatic stress disorder in an adolescent inpatient unit. *The Canadian Journal of Psychiatry, 43*(1), 64–68.

Kuksis, M., Di, P. C., Hawken, E. R., & Finch, S. (2017). The correlation between trauma, PTSD, and substance abuse in a community sample seeking outpatient treatment for addiction. *Canadian Journal of Addiction, 8*(1), 18–24.

Lalonde, F., & Nadeau, L. (2012). Risk and protective factors for comorbid posttraumatic stress disorder among homeless individuals in treatment for substance-related problems. *Journal of Aggression, Maltreatment and Trauma, 21*(6), 626–645.

Lamoureux-Lamarche, C., Vasiliadis, H.-M., Preville, M., & Berbiche, D. (2016). Healthcare use and costs associated with post-traumatic stress syndrome in a community sample of older adults: Results from the ESA-services study. *International Psychogeriatrics, 28*(6), 903–911.

Lamoureux-Lamarche, C., Vasiliadis, H.-M., Preville, M., & Berbiche, D. (2016). Post-traumatic stress syndrome in a large sample of older adults: Determinants and quality of life. *Aging & Mental Health, 20*(4), 401–406.

Lancee, W. J., Maunder, R. G., & Goldbloom, D. S. (2008). Prevalence of psychiatric disorders among Toronto hospital workers one to two years after the SARS outbreak. *Psychiatric Services, 59*(1), 91–95.

Laposa, J. M., Alden, L. E., & Fullerton, L. M. (2003). Work stress and post-traumatic stress disorder in ED nurses/personnel. *Journal of Emergency Nursing, 29*(1), 23–28.

Prevalence of Posttraumatic Stress Disorder   59

Law, S. F., & Hutton, E. M. (2007). Community psychiatry in the Canadian Arctic – Reflections from a 1-year continuous consultation series in Iqaluit, Nunavut. *Canadian Journal of Community Mental Health*, *26*(2), 123–140.

Ledgerwood, D. M., & Milosevic, A. (2015). Clinical and personality characteristics associated with post traumatic stress disorder in problem and pathological gamblers recruited from the community. *Journal of Gambling Studies*, *31*(2), 501–512.

Lee, J. E. C., Garber, B., & Zamorski, M. A. (2015). Prospective analysis of premilitary mental health, somatic symptoms, and postdeployment post-concussive symptoms. *Psychosomatic Medicine*, *77*(9), 1006–1017.

Levine, A. R., & Fritz, P. A. T. (2016). Coercive control, posttraumatic stress disorder, and depression among homeless women. *Partner Abuse*, *7*(1), 26–43.

Malat, J., & Turner, N. E. (2013). Characteristics of outpatients in an addictions clinic for co-occurring disorders. *American Journal on Addictions*, *22*(3), 297–301.

Martin, M., Marchand, A., Boyer, R., & Martin, N. (2009). Predictors of the development of posttraumatic stress disorder among police officers. *Journal of Trauma and Dissociation*, *10*(4), 451–468.

Maunder, R. G., Lancee, W. J., Balderson, K. E., Bennett, J. P., Borgundvaag, B., Evans, S., … Wasylenki, D. A. (2006). Long-term psychological and occupational effects of providing hospital healthcare during SARS outbreak. *Emerging Infectious Diseases*, *12*(12), 1924–1932.

McIntyre-Smith, A., St. Cyr, K., & King, L. (2015). Sexual functioning among a cohort of treatment-seeking Canadian military personnel and veterans with psychiatric conditions. *Military Medicine*, *180*(7), 817–824.

McLean, L. M., Toner, B., Jackson, J., Desrocher, M., & Stuckless, N. (2006). The relationship between childhood sexual abuse, complex post-traumatic stress disorder and alexithymia in two outpatient samples: Examination of women treated in community and institutional clinics. *Journal of Child Sexual Abuse*, *15*(3), 1–17.

Monson, E., Brunet, A., & Caron, J. (2015). Domains of quality of life and social support across the trauma spectrum. *Social Psychiatry and Psychiatric Epidemiology*, *50*(8), 1243–1248.

Monson, E., Lonergan, M., Caron, J., & Brunet, A. (2016). Assessing trauma and posttraumatic stress disorder: Single, open-ended question versus list-based inventory. *Psychological Assessment*, *28*(8), 1001–1008.

Nelson, C., Cyr, K. S., Corbett, B., Hurley, E., Gifford, S., Elhai, J. D., & Donald, R. J. (2011). Predictors of posttraumatic stress disorder, depression, and suicidal ideation among Canadian forces personnel in a national Canadian military health survey. *Journal of Psychiatric Research*, *45*(11), 1483–1488.

Nelson, G., Patterson, M., Kirst, M., Macnaughton, E., Isaak, C. A., Nolin, D., … Goering, P. N. (2015). Life changes among homeless persons with mental illness: A longitudinal study of housing first and usual treatment. *Psychiatric Services*, *66*(6), 592–597.

Newman, S. C., & Bland, R. C. (2006). A population-based family study of DSM-III generalized anxiety disorder. *Psychological Medicine*, *36*(9), 1275–1281.

Ohayon, M. M., & Shapiro, C. M. (2000). Sleep disturbances and psychiatric disorders associated with posttraumatic stress disorder in the general population. *Comprehensive Psychiatry*, *41*(6), 469–478.

Patterson, M. L., Moniruzzaman, A., Frankish, C. J., & Somers, J. M. (2012). Missed opportunities: Childhood learning disabilities as early indicators of risk among homeless adults with mental illness in Vancouver, British Columbia. *BMJ Open, 2*(6), e001586.

Poundja, J., Fikretoglu, D., & Brunet, A. (2006). The co-occurrence of post-traumatic stress disorder symptoms and pain: Is depression a mediator? *Journal of Traumatic Stress, 19*(5), 747–751.

Prevatt, B.-S., Desmarais, S. L., & Janssen, P. A. (2017). Lifetime substance use as a predictor of postpartum mental health. *Archives of Women's Mental Health, 20*(1), 189–199.

Puri, N., Shannon, K., Nguyen, P., & Goldenberg, S. M. (2017). Burden and correlates of mental health diagnoses among sex workers in an urban setting. *BMC Women's Health, 17*(1), 133.

Redwood-Campbell, L., Fowler, N., Kaczorowski, J., Molinaro, E., Robinson, S., Howard, M., & Jafarpour, M. (2003). How are new refugees doing in Canada? Comparison of the health and settlement of the Kosovars and Czech Roma. *Canadian Journal of Public Health, 94*(5), 381–385.

Redwood-Campbell, L., Thind, H., Howard, M., Koteles, J., Fowler, N., & Kaczorowski, J. (2008). Understanding the health of refugee women in host countries: Lessons from the Kosovar re-settlement in Canada. *Prehospital and Disaster Medicine, 23*(4), 322–327.

Regambal, M. J., Alden, L. E., Wagner, S. L., Harder, H. G., Koch, W. J., Fung, K., & Parsons, C. (2015). Characteristics of the traumatic stressors experienced by rural first responders. *Journal of Anxiety Disorders, 34*, 86–93.

Regehr, C., Goldberg, G., Glancy, G. D., & Knott, T. (2002). Posttraumatic symptoms and disability in paramedics. *Canadian Journal of Psychiatry, 47*(10), 953–8.

Robinson, J. R., Clements, K., & Land, C. (2003). Workplace stress among psychiatric nurses. *Journal of Psychosocial Nursing and Mental Health Services, 41*(4), 32–41.

Richardson, J. D., Cyr, K. S., Nelson, C., Elhai, J. D., & Sareen, J. (2014). Sleep disturbances and suicidal ideation in a sample of treatment-seeking Canadian forces members and veterans. *Psychiatry Research, 218*(1–2), 118–123.

Richardson, J. D., Elhai, J. D., & Pedlar, D. J. (2006). Association of PTSD and depression with medical and specialist care utilization in modern peacekeeping veterans in Canada with health-related disabilities. *Journal of Clinical Psychiatry, 67*(8), 1240–1245.

Richardson, J. D., Ketcheson, F., King, L., Shnaider, P., Marlborough, M., Thompson, A., & Elhai, J. D. (2017). Psychiatric comorbidity pattern in treatment-seeking veterans. *Psychiatry Research, 258*, 488–493.

Richardson, J. D., Long, M. E., Pedlar, D., & Elhai, J .D. (2008). Posttraumatic stress disorder and health-related quality of life among a sample of treatment- and pension-seeking deployed Canadian forces peacekeeping veterans. *Canadian Journal of Psychiatry, 53*(9), 594–600.

Richardson, J. D., Pekevski, J., & Elhai, J. (2009). Post-traumatic stress disorder and health problems among medically ill Canadian peacekeeping veterans. *Australian and New Zealand Journal of Psychiatry, 43*(4), 366–372.

Richardson, J. D., St Cyr, K. C., McIntyre-Smith, A. M., Haslam, D., Elhai, J. D., & Sareen, J. (2012). Examining the association between psychiatric illness and suicidal ideation in a sample of treatment-seeking Canadian peacekeeping and combat veterans with posttraumatic stress disorder. *The Canadian Journal of Psychiatry, 57*(8), 496–504.

Prevalence of Posttraumatic Stress Disorder   61

Rodin, G., Yuen, D., Mischitelle,A., Minden, M. D., Brandwein, J., Schimmer, A., ... Zimmermann, C. (2013). Traumatic stress in acute leukemia. *Psycho-Oncology*, *22*(2), 299–307.

Ross, L. E., Bauer, G. R., MacLeod, M. A., Robinson, M., MacKay, J., & Dobinson, C. (2014). Mental health and substance use among bisexual youth and non-youth in Ontario, Canada. *PLoS One*, *9*(8), e101604.

Roth, M. L., Cyr, K. S., Harle, I., & Katz, J. D. (2013). Relationship between pain and post-traumatic stress symptoms in palliative care. *Journal of Pain and Symptom Management*, *46*(2), 182–191.

Rousseau, C., Laurin-Lamothe, A., Anneke, R. J., Meloni, F., Steinmetz, N., & Alvarez, F. (2013). Uninsured immigrant and refugee children presenting to Canadian paediatric emergency departments: Disparities in help-seeking and service delivery. *Paediatrics and Child Health (Canada)*, *18*(9), 465–469.

Samuels-Dennis, J. A., Ford-Gilboe, M., & Ray, S. (2011). Single mother's adverse and traumatic experiences and post-traumatic stress symptoms. *Journal of Family Violence*, *26*, 9–20.

Sareen, J., Belik, S.-L., Afifi, T. O., Asmundson, G. J. G., Cox, B. J., & Stein, M. B. (2008). Canadian military personnel's population attributable fractions of mental disorders and mental health service use associated with combat and peacekeeping operations. *American Journal of Public Health*, *98*(12), 2191–2198.

Sareen, J., Cox, B. J., Afifi, T. O., Stein, M. B., Belik, S.-L., Meadows, G., & Asmundson, G. J. G. (2007). Combat and peacekeeping operations in relation to prevalence of mental disorders and perceived need for mental health care: Findings from a large representative sample of military personnel. *Archives of General Psychiatry*, *64*(7), 843–852.

Sareen, J., Cox, B. J., Stein, M. B., Afifi, T. O., Fleet, C., & Asmundson, G. J. G. (2007). Physical and mental comorbidity, disability, and suicidal behavior associated with posttraumatic stress disorder in a large community sample. *Psychosomatic Medicine*, *69*(3), 242–248.

Sareen, J., Stein, M. B., Cox, B. J., & Hassard, S. T. (2004). Understanding comorbidity of anxiety disorders with antisocial behavior: Findings from two large community surveys. *Journal of Nervous and Mental Disease*, *192*(3), 178–186.

Scheibe, S., Bagby, R. M., Miller, L. S., & Dorian, B. J. (2001). Assessing post-traumatic stress disorder with the MMPI-2 in a sample of workplace accident victims. *Psychological Assessment*, *13*(3), 369–374.

Sockalingam, S., Cassin, S., Crawford, S. A., Pitzul, K., Khan, A., Hawa, R., ... Okrainec, A. (2013). Psychiatric predictors of surgery non-completion following suitability assessment for bariatric surgery. *Obesity Surgery*, *23*(2), 205–211.

Stapleton, J. A., Asmundson, G. J. G., Woods, M., Taylor, S., & Stein, M. B. (2006). Health care utilization by united nations peacekeeping veterans with co-occurring, self-reported, post-traumatic stress disorder and depression symptoms versus those without. *Military Medicine*, *171*(6), 562–566.

Stein, M. B., Walker, J. R., Hazen, A. L., & Forde, D. R. (1997). Full and partial posttraumatic stress disorder: Findings from a community survey. *American Journal of Psychiatry*, *154*(8), 1114–1119.

Stewart, S. H., Mitchell, T. L., Wright, K. D., & Loba, P. (2004). The relations of PTSD symptoms to alcohol use and coping drinking in volunteers who responded to the Swissair Flight 111 airline disaster. *Journal of Anxiety Disorders*, *18*(1), 51–68.

Strehlau, V., Torchalla, I., Kathy, L., Schuetz, C., & Krausz, M. (2012). Mental health, concurrent disorders, and health care utilization in homeless women. *Journal of Psychiatric Practice, 18*(5), 349–360.

Stretch, R. H. (1991). Psychosocial readjustment of Canadian Vietnam veterans. *Journal of Consulting and Clinical Psychology, 59*(1), 188–189.

Stuber, M. L., Meeske, K. A., Leisenring, W., Stratton, K., Zeltzer, L. K., Dawson, K., ... Krull, K. R. (2011). Defining medical posttraumatic stress among young adult survivors in the childhood cancer survivor study. *General Hospital Psychiatry, 33*(4), 347–53.

Taylor, S., Asmundson, G. J., Carleton, R. N., & Brundin, P. (2007). Acute posttraumatic stress symptoms and depression after exposure to the 2005 Saskatchewan centennial air show disaster: Prevalence and predictors. *American Journal of Disaster Medicine, 2*(5), 217–230.

Tibbo, P., Swainson, J., Chue, P., & LeMelledo, J.-M. (2003). Prevalence and relationship to delusions and hallucinations of anxiety disorders in schizophrenia. *Depression and Anxiety, 17*(2), 65–72.

Torchalla, I., Strehlau, V., Li, K., Linden, I. A., Noel, F., & Krausz, M. (2014). Posttraumatic stress disorder and substance use disorder comorbidity in homeless adults: Prevalence, correlates, and sex differences. *Psychology of Addictive Behaviors, 28*(2), 443–452.

Van Ameringen, A. M., Mancini C., Patterson B., & Boyle M.H. (2008). Posttraumatic stress disorder in Canada. *CNS Neuroscience and Therapeutics, 14*(3), 171–181.

Vasiliadis, H.-M., Lamoureux-Lamarche, C., & Preville, M. (2016). Benzodiazepine use associated with co-morbid post-traumatic stress syndrome and depression in older adults seeking services in general medical settings. *International Psychogeriatrics, 28*(6), 913–920.

Vedantham, K., Brunet, A., Boyer, R., Weiss, D. S., Metzler, T. J., & Marmar, C. R. (2001). Posttraumatic stress disorder, trauma exposure, and the current health of Canadian bus drivers. *Canadian Journal of Psychiatry, 46*(2), 149–155.

Vogel, M., Frank, A., Choi, F., Strehlau, V., Nikoo, N., Nikoo, M., ... Schutz, C. G. (2017). Chronic pain among homeless persons with mental illness. *Pain Medicine, 18*(12), 2280–2288.

Volk, J. S., Aubry, T., Goering, P., Adair, C. E., Distasio, J., Jette, J., ... Tsemberis, S. (2016). Tenants with additional needs: When housing first does not solve homelessness. *Journal of Mental Health, 25*(2), 169–175.

Weeks, M., Garber, B. G., & Zamorski, M. A. (2016). Disability and mental disorders in the Canadian Armed Forces. *Canadian Journal of Psychiatry, 61*(1 Suppl), 56S–63S.

Wilberforce, N., Wilberforce, K., & Aubrey-Bassler, F. K. (2010). Post-traumatic stress disorder in physicians from an underserviced area. *Family Practice, 27*(3), 339–343.

Wolfe, D. A., Scott, K., Wekerle, C., & Pittman, A.-L. (2001). Child maltreatment: Risk of adjustment problems and dating violence in adolescence. *Journal of the American Academy of Child and Adolescent Psychiatry, 40*(3), 282–289.

Woo, W. L., & Vedelago, H. R. (2012). Trauma exposure and PTSD among individuals seeking residential treatment in a Canadian treatment centre for a substance use disorder. *Canadian Journal of Addiction Medicine, 3*(1), 4–8.

Wright, J., Friedrich, W. N., Cyr, M., Theriault, C., Perron, A., Lussier, Y., & Sabourin, S. (1998). The evaluation of Franco-Quebec victims of child sexual

Prevalence of Posttraumatic Stress Disorder 63

abuse and their mothers: The implementation of a standard assessment protocol. *Child Abuse and Neglect, 22*(1), 9–23.

Yarvis, J. S., Bordnick, P. S., Spivey, C. A., & Pedlar, D. (2007). Subthreshold PTSD: A comparison of alcohol, depression, and health problems in Canadian peacekeepers with different levels of traumatic stress. *Stress, Trauma, and Crisis, 8*(2–3), 195–213.

Zabkiewicz, D. M., Patterson, M., & Wright, A. (2014). A cross-sectional examination of the mental health of homeless mothers: Does the relationship between mothering and mental health vary by duration of homelessness? *BMJ Open, 4*(12), e006174.

Zamorski, M. A., & Wiens-Kinkaid, M. E. (2013). Cross-sectional prevalence survey of intimate partner violence perpetration and victimization in Canadian military personnel. *BMC Public Health, 13*(1), 1019.

Zamorski, M. A., Bennett, R. E., Rusu, C., Weeks, M., Boulos, D., & Garber, B. G. (2016). Prevalence of past-year mental disorders in the Canadian Armed Forces, 2002–2013. *Canadian Journal of Psychiatry/Revue canadienne de psychiatrie, 61*(1), 26S–35S.

Zamorski, M. A., Rusu, C., & Garber, B. G. (2014). Prevalence and correlates of mental health problems in Canadian forces personnel who deployed in support of the mission in Afghanistan: Findings from postdeployment screenings, 2009–2012. *Canadian Journal of Psychiatry, 59*(6), 319–326.

Appendix 2A

Table 2.A1 Database search strategies used in the current systematic review

#	Searches	Results
1	Stress Disorders, Post-Traumatic/	27,373
2	(PTSD* or CPTSD* or PTSI* or ((posttrauma* or post trauma*) adj4 (disorder* or stress* or neurosis or neuroses or injur* or syndrome* or psychosis)) or (moral adj2 injur*)).tw,kf.	32,694
3	Combat Disorders/	2,934
4	(((combat* or deployment* or war) adj4 (disorder* or stress* or neurosis or neuroses or psychosis)) or shell shock*).tw,kf.	3,507
5	((operational stress* or occupational stress*) adj3 (injur* or disorder*)).tw,kf.	34
6	1 or 2 or 3 or 4 or 5	43,130
7	exp Canada/ or (Canad* or Ottawa* or British Columbia* or Colombie Britannique* or Vancouver* or Alberta* or Edmonton* or Calgar* or Saskatchewan* or Regina* or Saskatoon* or Manitoba* or Winnipeg* or Ontari* or Toronto* or Quebec* or Montreal* or New Brunswick* or Nouveau Brunswick* or Fredericton* or Nova Scotia* or Nouvelle Ecosse* or Halifax* or Haligonian* or Prince Edward Island* or ile du Prince Edouard* or Pei or Charlottetown* or Newfoundland* or Terre Neuve* or Labrador* or nfld or Yukon* or Whitehorse* or Northwest Territor* or Territoires du Nord Ouest* or nwt or Yellowknife* or Nunavut* or Iqaluit* or Mississauga* or Brampton* or Laval or Surrey* or Gatineau* or Burlington* or Kitchener* or Waterloo* or "St. Catharines*" or Niagara* or Oshawa* or Whitby* or	235,840

(continued)

64 *Murray Weeks et al.*

Table 2.A1 Cont.

#	Searches	Results
	Windsor* or Sherbrooke* or "St. John's" or Barrie or Kelowna* or Abbotsford* or Sudbury* or Kingston* or Saguenay* or Trois-Rivieres* or Guelph* or Moncton* or Brantford* or Saint John* or Peterborough* or Thunder Bay* or Lethbridge* or Nanaimo* or Kamloops* or Belleville* or Fredericton* or Petawawa* or Gagetown* or Shilo* or Suffield* or Valcartier* or Wainwright* or Meaford* or Aldershot* or Esquimalt* or Bagotville* or Borden* or Comox* or Cold Lake* or Gander* or Goose Bay* or Greenwood* or Moose Jaw* or North Bay* or Trenton* or Dundurn* or Leitrim*).tw,kf.	
8	6 and 7	522
9	limit 8 to (English or French)	519

Note: Database: Ovid MEDLINE(R) Epub Ahead of Print, In-Process & Other Non-Indexed Citations, Ovid MEDLINE(R) Daily, Ovid MEDLINE and Versions(R) 1946 to February 14, 2018.

Appendix 2B

Modified Newcastle–Ottawa Scale scoring guide

(1) **Representativeness of the sample:**
   1 point: Population was Canada-wide (≥3 provinces/territories).
   0 point: Population was limited to fewer than 3 provinces/territories.
(2) **Sample size:**
   1 point: Sample size was ≥200 participants.
   0 point: Sample size was <200 participants.
(3) **Non-respondents:**
   1 point: Comparability between respondent and non-respondent characteristics was established, and the response rate was satisfactory.
   0 point: The response rate was unsatisfactory, the comparability between respondents and non-respondents was unsatisfactory, or there was no description of the response rate or the characteristics of the responders and the non-responders.
(4) **Ascertainment of PTSD:**
   1 point: Validated measuring tool using a validated cut-off score.
   0 point: Non-validated measuring tool, or validated measuring tool with non-validated cut off score.
(5) **Quality of descriptive statistics reporting:**
   1 point: Reported descriptive statistics to describe the population (e.g., age, sex) with proper measures of dispersion (e.g., standard deviation, standard error, range).
   0 point: Descriptive statistics were not reported, were incomplete, or did not include proper measures of dispersion.

Appendix 2C

Table 2.A2 Lifetime prevalence: Details of included clinical diagnosis and self-report studies

First author	Publication year	Data source	Location	Population	Number of participants	Age	Sex	Rate	Diagnostic tool	Additional note/ Observation
Clinical diagnosis studies										
Non-occupation related										
Ledgerwood	2015	In-person interview	Windsor, Ontario, Canada	Adults who met the criteria for pathological gambling based on DSM-IV screen for gambling problems	150	18+	T	19.33	Structured Clinical Interview for DSM-IV (SCID)	
Guglietti	2010	Interview	Toronto, Ontario, Canada	Cancer patients – women	75	54.75 (mean)	F	0	PTSD – Civilian Version (PCL-C) and the Structured Clinical Interview for DSM–IV Non Patient-PTSD (SCID-NP-PTSD)	
Hensel	2016	Ontario Bariatric Registry (2010–2015)	Ontario, Canada	Patients referred for bariatric surgery	10,698	NA	T	3.21	Clinical interview by health care worker	

(continued)

Table 2.A2 Cont.

First author	Publication year	Data source	Location	Population	Number of participants	Age	Sex	Rate	Diagnostic tool	Additional note/ Observation
Clinical diagnosis studies										
Non-occupation related										
Brink	2001	Interviews at Regional Reception and Assessment Centre in BC, 1999	Canada	Male Prisoners	202	17–72	M	4.95	Structured Clinical Interview for DSM-IV (SCID)	
Sockalingam	2013	Psychiatric assessment	Toronto, Ontario, Canada	Patients in referred to the Toronto Western Hospital Bariatric Surgery Program	363	18–65	T	4.13	Mini-International Neuropsychiatric Interview 6.0 (MINI 6.0) supplemented with modules to assess various disorders, including PTSD, based upon criteria from DSM-IV-TR	
Occupation related										
Puri	2017	An Evaluation of Sex Workers Health Access (AESHA). Self-administered questionnaires	Vancouver, British Columbia, Canada	Sex workers	692	28–42	F	12.72	Self-report of previous clinical mental health diagnoses	

Author	Year	Methodology	Location	Sample	N	Age			Instrument	Notes
Richardson	2008	Data was obtained via files from Veterans Affairs Canada pertaining to comprehensive psychiatric assessments (2000–2006)	Canada	Consecutive male deployed Canadian Forces peacekeeping veterans referred by way of their medical providers or through Veterans Affairs Canada	125	41.49 (mean)	M	69.6	Clinician-Administered PTSD Scale (CAPS)	Authors reported the rate of 77.6%; however, the rate was adjusted based on reported sample of 87 (n) and 125 (N) number of participants
Martin	2009	Interviews with police officers contacted through human resources	Quebec, Canada	French speaking police officers exposed to at least one duty related traumatic event	132	18+	T	7.58	Structured Clinical Interview for DSM-IV (SCID)	
Lancee	2008	Secondary analysis of Impact of SARS Study (health care workers in Toronto and Hamilton)	Toronto, Ontario, Canada	Health care workers from hospitals in Toronto that treated SARS patients	139	18+	T	2.88	Structured Clinical Interview for DSM-IV (SCID), with Clinician-Administered PTSD Scale (CAPS) replacing the PTSD module	

(continued)

Table 2.A2 Cont.

First author	Publication year	Data source	Location	Population	Number of participants	Age	Sex	Rate	Diagnostic tool	Additional note/ Observation
Self-report studies										
Non-occupation related										
Monson	2015	Data captured from a previous longitudinal study on the general population regarding mental health and mental health service use in an epidemiological catchment area (ECA) in Montreal	Montreal, Quebec, Canada	Respondents newly recruited for the third cycle of the ECA	2,391	15–65	T	3.85	World Health Organization Composite International Diagnostic Interview (WHO-CIDI) version 2.1	
Monson	2016	Data captured from a previous longitudinal study on the general population regarding mental health and mental health	Montreal, Quebec, Canada	Respondents newly recruited for the third cycle of the ECA	1,015	15–65	T	4.63	World Health Organization Composite International Diagnostic Interview (WHO-CIDI) version 2.1	

		service use in an epidemiological catchment area (ECA) in Montreal						
Newman	2006	Data obtained from a previous follow-up of a community sample originally recruited for a prevalence study	Edmonton, Alberta, Canada	First degree relatives of individuals completing a re-interview from the original community sample	2,386	18+	T	2.51	Diagnostic Interview Schedule (DIS) version III
Van Ameringen	2008	Telephone interview using random digit dialling by ASDE software	Canada	Canadian individuals, age 18+ years, owning a telephone	2,991	18+	T	9.19	World Health Organization Composite International Diagnostic Interview (WHO-CIDI) version 2.1 from the Canadian Community Health Survey (CCHS) 1.2 module. Additional questions were added to the CCHS module to elicit symptoms of current PTSD
Dufort	1998	Family Study of Mental Disorders	Edmonton, Alberta, Canada	Spouses from the Family Study of Mental Disorders	2,328	18+	T	2.53	Diagnostic Interview Schedule (DIS)/ DSM-III diagnosis

(*continued*)

Table 2.A2 Cont.

First author	Publication year	Data source	Location	Population	Number of participants	Age	Sex	Rate	Diagnostic tool	Additional note/ Observation
Self-report studies										
Non-occupation related										
McLean	2006	In-person interview in clinics	Toronto, Ontario, Canada	English speaking women with early onset sexual abuse that are currently in outpatient therapy or are from the community	70	18+	F	50	Structured Interview for Disorders of Extreme Stress (SIDES) included in the Trauma Assessment Package	
Beiser	2011	Mental Health Survey	Toronto, Ontario, Canada	Sri Lankan Tamils in Toronto	1,603	18+	T	5.8	World Health Organization Composite International Diagnostic Interview (WHO-CIDI) version 2.1	
Frise	2002	Women's Health Study (ON)	Ontario, Canada	Ontario women	3,062	25–74	F	10.68	DSM-IV, the Structured Clinical Interview for DSM-III-R, and the Diagnostic Interview Schedule (DIS)	

Occupation related

Brunet	2015	2002 Canadian Community Health Survey 1.2 – Canadian Forces Supplement	Canada	Canadian Forces members	8,441	16+	T	6.53	World Health Organization Composite International Diagnostic Interview (WHO-CIDI) version 2.1	Same data source. Average estimate of the reported rate was used for Figures 2a–2b
Fikretoglu	2012	2002 Canadian Community Health Survey 1.2 – Canadian Forces Supplement	Canada	Canadian Forces members	8,441	18+	T	6.5	World Health Organization Composite International Diagnostic Interview (WHO-CIDI) version 2.1	
Weeks	2016	2013 Canadian Forces Mental Health Survey (CFMHS)	Canada	Canadian Forces regular force members	6,700	17+	T	11.1	World Health Organization Composite International Diagnostic Interview (WHO-CIDI) version 3.0	
Stretch	1991	Mailed questionnaires	Canada	Members of the Canadian Vietnam Veterans Coalition	164	42 (mean)	M	65.24	Vietnam-Era Veterans Adjustment Survey (VEVAS)	
Boyer	1996	Questionnaire using PTSD-I in French	Montreal, Quebec, Canada	Bus drivers	3,047	18+	T	7.78	PTSD Interview (PTSD-I) DSM-III-R	

(continued)

Table 2.A2 Cont.

First author	Publication year	Data source	Location	Population	Number of participants	Age	Sex	Rate	Diagnostic tool	Additional note/ Observation
Self-report studies *Occupation related*										
Vedantham	2001	Questionnaires with urban bus drivers	Montreal, Quebec, Canada	Canadian urban bus drivers employed by the Société des Transports de la Communauté Urbaine de Montréal	342	42.1 (mean)	T	9.65	PTSD Interview (PTSD-I) DSM-III-R	
Beal	1995	The Dieppe Veterans and Prisoners of War Association provided the names and addresses of potential subjects	Canada	Military veterans	265	18+	M	43.77	Questionnaire with 17 individual DSM-III-R criteria for PTSD as separate questions	

Note: M, male; F, female; T, transgender.

Table 2.A3 Current prevalence: Details of included clinical diagnosis and self-report studies

First author	Publication year	Data source	Location	Population	Number of participants	Age	Sex	Rate	Diagnostic tool	Additional note/ Observation
Clinical diagnosis studies										
Non-occupation related										
Koltek	1998	Inpatient discharge diagnoses	Calgary, Alberta, Canada	Adolescents with inpatient discharge diagnoses, with ICD-9 codes, from Foothills Hospital	187	13–19	T	42.25	Clinical judgement based on DSM-III-R and DSM-IV	
Zabkiewicz	2014	At Home/Chez Soi project (subsample of homeless mothers)	Five Canadian cities (Vancouver, Toronto, Winnipeg, Moncton, Montreal)	Homeless/ precariously housed women with a mental illness	713	18+	F	41.37	Mini-International Neuropsychiatric Interview (MINI)	
Vogel	2017	At Home/Chez Soi project (largest sample)	Canada (Winnipeg Toronto, Vancouver)	Legal adults with a current mental disorder who are absolutely homeless or precariously housed	1,287	18+ (19+ in Vancouver)	T	31.93	Mini-International Neuropsychiatric Interview (MINI)	

(*continued*)

Table 2.A3 Cont.

Clinical diagnosis studies

Non-occupation related

First author	Publication year	Data source	Location	Population	Number of participants	Age	Sex	Rate	Diagnostic tool	Additional note/ Observation
Tibbo	2003	Caseworker/ psychiatrist interviews	Edmonton, Alberta, Canada	Individuals with a DSM-IV diagnosis of schizophrenia from an outpatient population at the University of Alberta Schizophrenia Clinic as well as a downtown based Community Living Program (CIP)	30	NA	T	0	Clinician-Administered PTSD Scale (CAPS) was used assess PTSD severity when the DSM-IV criteria was met for an anxiety disorder upon administration of the Mini-International Neuropsychiatric Interview Plus (MINI-Plus) version 4.4	
Hudson	2017	Chart data (burn unit, Halifax, 1995–2013)	Halifax, Nova Scotia, Canada	Patients recovering from a burn	479	18+	T	.42	.	
Gillis	1997	Chart Data – psychiatric treatment programs in Ottawa, 1990–1992	Ottawa, Ontario, Canada	Patients who attended three psychiatric day treatment programs	327	NA	T	10.1	Clinical variables in chart	

Law	2007	Chart data obtained from a one-year continuous psychiatric consultation series	Baffin Island & Iqaluit, Nunavut, Canada	Inuit community members	110	3–58	T	3.64	DSM-IV diagnosis from chart review	
Rousseau	2013	EMR data of children from three paediatric hospitals (refugee, undocumented, etc.)	Montreal, Quebec & Toronto, Ontario, Canada	Immigrant, refugee, and undocumented children without provincial health care coverage who sought care at three major paediatric hospitals	2,035	≤ 18	T	1.38		
Lamoureux-Lamarche	2016	ESA – Étude sur la Santé des Aîné(e)s-Services	Quebec, Canada	Community dwelling older adults waiting for health services in primary care clinics	1,465	65+	T	11.54	PTSS Scale	Same data source. Average estimate of the reported rate was used for Figures 2a–2b
Lamoureux-Lamarche	2016	ESA – Étude sur la Santé des Aîné(e)s-Services	Quebec, Canada	Community dwelling older adults waiting for health services in primary care clinics	1,765	65+	T	11.05	PTSS Scale	

(*continued*)

Table 2.A3 Cont.

Clinical diagnosis studies

Non-occupation related

First author	Publication year	Data source	Location	Population	Number of participants	Age	Sex	Rate	Diagnostic tool	Additional note/Observation
Benoit	2016	Indigenous Women's Stress Study (IWSS)	Toronto and Thunder Bay, Ontario, Canada	Indigenous women (First Nation, Inuit, or Metis)	90	18+	F	82.22	PTSD Checklist – Civilian Version (PCL-C)	
Grigoriadis	2011	Interviews	Toronto, Ontario, Canada	Pregnant and postpartum with mood and anxiety disorders (RLS program)	91	18–55	F	8.79	Mini-International Neuropsychiatric Interview (MINI) version 5	
Gretton	2011	Interviews in BC, 2006–2009	Burnaby, Prince George, and Victoria, British Columbia, Canada	Incarcerated male and female youth	174	NA	T	5.17	Massachusetts Youth Screening Instrument Version 2 (MAYSI-2), the Diagnostic Interview Schedule for Children Version IV (DISC-IV), review of youth's forensic psychiatric file records	

Prevalence of Posttraumatic Stress Disorder 77

Author	Year	Source/Method	Location	Sample	N	Age	M/T	%	Assessment	Notes
Bagheri	1992	Referrals for consultation and treatment either by family doctor or a social agency between July 1985–March 1988	Canada	Iranian immigrants	111	13–67	T	9.91	Psychiatric interview with DSM-III-R criteria	
Adeponle	2012	Medical records of patients seen at the cultural consultation service of the Jewish General Hospital	Montreal, Quebec, Canada	Patients of the Cultural Consultation Service (CCS) at a Montreal Hospital	323	16+	T	14.86	Hospital intake diagnosis using DSM-IV-TR criteria	
Brink	2001	Interviews at Regional Reception and Assessment Centre in BC, 1999	Canada	Male prisoners	202	17–72	M	3.96	Structured Clinical Interview for DSM-IV (SCID)	
Khitab	2012	Questionnaires	Saskatoon, Saskatchewan, Canada	Post-ICU admission patients	37	18+	T	33.33	Davidson Trauma Scale (DTS), the Impact of Event Scale (IES) and the Post-Traumatic Symptom Scale (PTSS-10)	Study reported different rates using multiple PTSD assessment instrument. Only PTSD

(*continued*)

Table 2.A3 Cont.

First author	Publication year	Data source	Location	Population	Number of participants	Age	Sex	Rate	Diagnostic tool	Additional notel Observation
Clinical diagnosis studies										
Non-occupation related										
										cases assessed using Davidson Trauma Scale was included, as it had most argument for validity
Malat	2013	Questionnaires	Toronto, Ontario, Canada	Treatment-seeking outpatients with a co-occurring substance use disorder and mental illness who were referred to the clinic	131	43.8 (mean)	T	18.32	Psychiatrist diagnosis using DSM-IV-TR criteria	
Hawryluck	2004	Web-based questionnaire	Toronto, Ontario, Canada	Voluntarily quarantined patients during SARS epidemic	129	18+	T	27.13	Impact of Event Scale – Revised (IES-R)	

Occupation related

Biehn	2012	Veterans referred by Veterans Affairs Canada for either a pension examination or for community mental health treatment, between 2000–2008	Canada	Military veterans	378	18+	T	60.85	Clinician-Administered PTSD Scale (CAPS)
Boulos	2016	CAF medical records over the period from June 22, 2010–May 30, 2011	Canada	Canadian Forces members deployed to Afghanistan from 2001–2008	2,014	18+	T	7.99	.
Armour	2014	Data gathered in the context of a clinical assessment	Canada	Military veterans who were referred to Veterans Affairs Canada or to a community mental health clinic for a comprehensive psychiatric assessment	471	24–93	T	63.89	Clinician-Administered PTSD Scale (CAPS)

(*continued*)

Table 2.A3 Cont.

First author	Publication year	Data source	Location	Population	Number of participants	Age	Sex	Rate	Diagnostic tool	Additional note/ Observation
Clinical diagnosis studies										
Non-occupation related										
Arvay	1996	Mail survey	British Columbia, Canada	Counsellors dealing with trauma patients	161	18+	T	14	Impact of Event Scale (IES)	
Boulos	2015	Medical records of stratified random sample	Canada	Canadian Forces members who were deployed to Afghanistan 2000–2008 and had a mental disorder diagnosis	508	18+	T	53.54	DSM-IV-TR axis, excluding axis IV	Authors reported weighted rate of 49.1% but provided no weighted sample size. Based on the unweighted sample (*n*) of 272, and unweighted total participants (*N*) of 508, rate of PTSD was re-calculated

(continued)

Scheibe	2001	Psychological evaluations	Ontario, Canada	Men with workplace accidents referred by the Workplace Safety and Insurance Board (WSIB) of Ontario	50	39.08 (mean)	M	56	Structured Clinical Interview for DSM-IV (SCID)
Hensel	2010	Psychological Trauma Program referrals from 1999–2006	Toronto, Ontario, Canada	Workers who had experienced work place trauma	531	18+	T	44.07	Structured Clinical Interview for DSM-IV (SCID)
Lee	2015	Recruit Health Questionnaire (RHQ) and Enhanced Post Deployment Screening (EPDS)	Canada	Canadian Forces regular force members	3,319	18+	T	5.36	PTSD Checklist – Civilian Version (PCL-C)
Lancee	2008	Secondary analysis of Impact of SARS Study	Toronto, Ontario, Canada	Health care workers from hospitals in Toronto that treated SARS patients	139	18+	T	1.44	Structured Clinical Interview for DSM-IV (SCID), with Clinician-Administered PTSD Scale (CAPS) replacing the PTSD module

Table 2.A3 Cont.

First author	Publication year	Data source	Location	Population	Number of participants	Age	Sex	Rate	Diagnostic tool	Additional note/ Observation
Clinical diagnosis studies										
Non-occupation related										
McIntyre-Smith	2015	Survey	London, Ontario, Canada	Male Canadian Forces members and veterans attending the Parkwood Hospital Operational Stress Injury clinic for treatment	74	21–85	M	77.03	PTSD Checklist – Military Version (PCL-M), a self-administered 17-item scale used to assess self-reported PTSD symptom severity related to military specific traumatic experiences. Past-month PTSD prevalence	
Asmundson	2008	Web-based questionnaire	Regina, Saskatchewan, Canada	Active-duty police officers	138	18+	T	31.88	PTSD Checklist – Civilian Version (PCL-C)	
Self-report studies										
Non-occupation related										
Goodwin	2010	2002 Canadian Community Health Survey 1.2	Canada	Canadians living in the ten provinces and three territories, excluding those	36,984	15+	T	1.29	Single question regarding diagnosis of PTSD by a	Same data source. Average estimate of the reported

Author	Year	Study	Location	Sample	N	Age	T	Rate (%)	Measure	Note
				on reserves, full-time Canadian Forces members, and institutionalized					health care professional in the past six months	rate was used for Figures 2a–2b
Sareen	2007	2002 Canadian Community Health Survey 1.2	Canada	Canadians living in the ten provinces and three territories, excluding those on reserves, full-time Canadian Forces members, and institutionalized	36,954	15+	T	1.29	Single question regarding diagnosis of PTSD by a health care professional in the past six months	
Hetherington	2017	All Our Families Study (Calgary)	Calgary, Alberta, Canada	People following the flood	923	18+	T	11.38	Perceived Post-Disaster Community Cohesion Scale (PDCC)	
Hwang	2012	At Home/Chez Soi project (Toronto only)	Toronto, Ontario, Canada	Homeless individuals	575	18+	T	23.3	Mini-International Neuropsychiatric Interview (MINI)	
Nelson	2015	At Home/Chez Soi project	Vancouver, Toronto, Winnipeg, Moncton, Montreal, Canada	Legal adults with a currently mental disorder who are absolutely homeless or precariously housed	211	18+ (19+ in Vancouver)	T	27.49	Mini-International Neuropsychiatric Interview (MINI)	
Volk	2016	At Home/Chez Soi project	Vancouver, Toronto, Winnipeg, Moncton, Montreal, Canada	Homeless/precariously housed women with a mental illness	1,162	18+	T	29.52	Mini-International Neuropsychiatric Interview (MINI)	

(continued)

Table 2.A3 Cont.

First author	Publication year	Data source	Location	Population	Number of participants	Age	Sex	Rate	Diagnostic tool	Additional note/ Observation
Clinical diagnosis studies										
Non-occupation related										
Patterson	2012	At Home/Chez Soi project (Vancouver sub-project)	Vancouver, British Columbia, Canada	Legal adults with a current mental disorder who are absolutely homeless or precariously housed	497	19+	T	25.96	Mini-International Neuropsychiatric Interview (MINI)	
Rodin	2013	Chart data	Toronto, Ontario, Canada	Patients with acute myeloid, lymphocytic, and promyelocytic leukemia who were newly diagnosed, recently relapsed, or had treatment failures	205	18+	T	13.17	PTS symptoms were assessed using the 30-item Stanford Acute Stress Reaction Questionnaire (SASRQ), a DSM-IV correspondent scale that assessed symptoms of Acute Stress Disorder	

Ahmad	2016	Computer-assisted survey	Toronto, Ontario, Canada	Patients from three Access Alliance Community Health Centres in Toronto, which primarily serve refugees, marginalized immigrants, and low income populations	75	18+	T	37.33	Existing diagnosis or, in the absence of an existing diagnosis, the Primary Care PTSD Screen (PC-PTSD)
Collin-Vezina	2011	Questionnaire	Montreal, Quebec, Canada	Youth in residential care facilities	53	14–17	T	24.5	Trauma Symptom Checklist for Children (TSCC)
Monson	2015	Data captured from previous Epidemiological Catchment Area (ECA) study in Montreal	Montreal, Quebec, Canada	Respondents newly recruited for the third cycle of the ECA	2,391	15–65	T	1.05	World Health Organization Composite International Diagnostic Interview (WHO-CIDI) version 2.1
Monson	2016	Data captured from previous Epidemiological Catchment Area (ECA) study in Montreal	Montreal, Quebec, Canada	Respondents newly recruited for the third cycle of the ECA	1,015	15–65	T	2.07	World Health Organization Composite International Diagnostic Interview (WHO-CIDI) version 2.1

(*continued*)

Table 2.A3 Cont.

First author	Publication year	Data source	Location	Population	Number of participants	Age	Sex	Rate	Diagnostic tool	Additional note/ Observation
Clinical diagnosis studies										
Non-occupation related										
Strehlau	2012	BC Health of the Homeless Survey (BCHOHS)	Three BC cities (Vancouver, Victoria, Prince George), Canada	Homeless women	193	19+	F	27.98	Mini-International Neuropsychiatric Interview Plus (MINI-Plus) version 5.0	
Van Ameringen	2008	Telephone interview using the random digit dialling by ASDE software	Canada	Canadian individuals, age 18+ years, owning a telephone	2,991		T	2.41	World Health Organization Composite International Diagnostic Interview (WHO-CIDI) version 2.1 from the Canadian Community Health Survey (CCHS) 1.2 module. Additional questions were added to the CCHS module to elicit symptoms of current PTSD	

Prevalence of Posttraumatic Stress Disorder

(continued)

Caron	2012	Epidemiological Catchment Area Study	Montreal, Quebec, Canada	People from five neighbourhoods in the South-West Sector on Montreal	2,433	15–65	T	17.76	World Health Organization Composite International Diagnostic Interview (WHO-CIDI)
Fleury	2011	Epidemiological Catchment Area Study	Montreal, Quebec, Canada	Montreal Residents	406	15–65	T	4.43	World Health Organization Composite International Diagnostic Interview (WHO-CIDI)
Collin-Vezina	2005	Girls referred for evaluation	Montreal, Quebec, Canada	Sexually abused French-speaking girls	134	7–12	F	32.09	Children's Impact of Traumatic Events Scale – Revised (IES-R) and DSM-IV criteria
Taylor	2007	Internet-based assessment of people at Moose Jaw Air Show tragedy	Moose Jaw, Saskatchewan, Canada	2005 Air Show attendees	157	16–71	T	21.66	PTSD Checklist – Civilian Version (PCL-C)
Desmarais	2014	Interviews of mothers in Western Canada	Vancouver, British Columbia, Canada	Women (before and during pregnancy)	100	18+	F	22	Posttraumatic Stress Disorder Symptom Scale (PSS-SR)
Cleveland	2013	Interviews with Community partners	Montreal, Quebec, and Toronto, Ontario, Canada	Asylum Seekers in Canada	188	18+	T	30.85	16-item PTSD scale of the Harvard Trauma Questionnaire (HTQ)

Table 2.A3 Cont.

First author	Publication year	Data source	Location	Population	Number of participants	Age	Sex	Rate	Diagnostic tool	Additional note/ Observation
Clinical diagnosis studies										
Non-occupation related										
Lalonde	2012	Interviews	Montreal, Quebec, Canada	Homeless individuals seeking treatment for substance use dependence	51	18+	T	49.02	Modified PTSD Symptom Scale, Self-Report (MPSS-SR)	
Erickson	2007	Interviews	Vancouver, British Columbia, Canada	Outpatients with an anxiety disorder	152	18+	T	14.47	Structured Clinical Interview for DSM-IV (SCID)	
Cohen	2004	Interviews	Montreal, Quebec, Canada	New mothers	200	18+	F	0	Structured Clinical Interview for DSM-III-R (SCID)	
Wright	1998	Interviews with child sexual abuse victims	Quebec, Canada	Sexually abused children with abuse occurring no more than one year before disclosure	30	2–12	T	16.67	Trauma Symptom Checklist for Children (TSCC)	
Firestone	2015	Our Health Counts	Hamilton, Ontario, Canada	First Nations	554	18+	T	34	Primary Care PTSD Screen (PC-PTSD)	

Author	Year	Method	Location	Sample	N	Age	Statistic	Prevalence	Measure
Bell	2014	Participants referred or admitted to Trauma Services at Vancouver General Hospital	British Columbia and Yukon, Canada	People referred or admitted directly to trauma services at Vancouver General Hospital following injury	56	19+	T	25	Posttraumatic Stress Disorder Checklist Scale (PCL-S) (Specific) (contains 17 DSM-IV symptoms of PTSD)
Catchpole	2016	Questionnaires	Vancouver, British Columbia, Canada	Youth with mental health and substance use disorders presenting for service at a Canadian youth concurrent mental health and substance use disorders program	100	15–25	T	40	Child PTSD Symptom Scale and Posttraumatic Stress Diagnostic Scale
Hebert	2014	Quebec Youths' Romantic Relationships survey (cluster sampling of 34 Quebec high schools)	Quebec, Canada	Sexual abuse victims	643	14–18	T	25.82	Abbreviated UCLA PTSD Reaction Index (A-UCLA-PTSD-RI)
Hebert	2017	Quebec Youths' Romantic Relationships survey (cluster sampling of 34 Quebec high schools)	Quebec, Canada	Secondary students in Quebec	6,531	14–18	T	7.4	UCLA PTSD Index

(continued)

Table 2.A3 Cont.

Clinical diagnosis studies

Non-occupation related

First author	Publication year	Data source	Location	Population	Number of participants	Age	Sex	Rate	Diagnostic tool	Additional note/ Observation
Frewen	2012	Questionnaires	London, Ontario, Canada	Undergraduate students at the University of Western Ontario (UWO)	225	18+	T	10.67	Posttraumatic Diagnostic Scale (PDS) combined with use of DSM-IV-TR criteria	
Dietrich	2003	Questionnaires	Canada	Inmates with child maltreatment histories	93	18+	T	25.81	Detailed Assessment of Posttraumatic States (DAPS) assesses for the full DSM-IV-TR	Author reported rate of 38.7%, however the rate was adjusted based on reported sample of 24 (n) and 93 (N) numbers of participants
Roth	2013	Questionnaires at London Regional Cancer Program and London Health Sciences Centre	London, Ontario, Canada	Patients with a cancer diagnosis receiving palliative care	100	18+ (19–87)	T	7	PTSD Checklist – Civilian Version (PCL-C)	

Wolfe	2001	Questionnaires	South-western Ontario, Canada	Adolescents – high school students	1,419	14–19	T	7.12	Trauma Symptom Checklist for Children (TSCC)
Woo	2012	Questionnaires	Guelph, Ontario, Canada	Recruits from a five-week, residential program for treatment of substance dependence	187	19+ (20–71)	T	50.8	PTSD Checklist – Civilian Version (PCL-C)
Levine	2016	Questionnaires	Windsor, Ontario, Canada	Women residing in a short-term shelter for homeless women having experienced at least one act of (self-defined) physical abuse by a romantic partner during their lifetime	51	18+ (19–58)	F	70.59	PTSD Checklist – Civilian Version (PCL-C)
Stewart	2003	Questionnaires/ Interviews	Margaret's Bay, Nova Scotia, Canada	Recovery and instrumental volunteers responding to the Swissair Flight 111 crash	13	27–60	T	46.15	Modified PTSD Symptom Scale (MPSS)
Stein	1997	Random-digit sampling, interviews with community sample, 1994	Winnipeg, Manitoba, Canada	General public	1,002	18+	T	2	Modified PTSD Symptom Scale (MPSS)

(*continued*)

Table 2.A3 Cont.

First author	Publication year	Data source	Location	Population	Number of participants	Age	Sex	Rate	Diagnostic tool	Additional note/ Observation
Clinical diagnosis studies										
Non-occupation related										
Ohayon	2000	Representative random sample using random telephone numbers in metro Toronto (1996–1997)	Toronto, Ontario, Canada	General public	1,832	15–90	T	1.8	Sleep-EVAL software	
Ross	2014	Risk & Resilience Survey of Bisexual Mental Health	Ontario, Canada	Bisexual individuals, age 16+ residing in Ontario	405	16+	T	10.62	PTSD Checklist – Civilian Version (PCL-C)	
Redwood-Campbell	2003	Self-administered questionnaires in 2001	Hamilton, Ontario, Canada	Refugees from Kosovar, a part of the Settlement and Integration Services Organization in Ontario	157	18+	T	21.66	Translated version of the Harvard Trauma Questionnaire (HTQ) for PTSD	
Redwood-Campbell	2008	Self-administered questionnaires. Data previously collected as part of a larger project (2003 study, same author)	Hamilton, Ontario, Canada	Kosovar and Czech Roma women refugees in Southern Ontario	85	18+	F	25.88	Translated version of the Harvard Trauma Questionnaire (HTQ) for PTSD	

Kuksis	2017	Self-report questionnaires of Canadians seeking outpatient addiction treatment	Kingston, Ontario, Canada	People with a history of drug or alcohol addiction	132	43.7 (mean)	T	87.12	PTSD Checklist – Civilian Version (PCL-C)
Prevatt	2017	Semi-structured interviews; participants recruited in 2009–2010	Vancouver, British Columbia, Canada	Mothers who were within three months postpartum	100	18+	F	21	Posttraumatic Stress Disorder Symptom Scale (PSS-SR)
Dugal	2012	Survey	Montreal, Quebec, Canada	College Students (following trauma – shooting)	854	18+	T	5.5	Posttraumatic Stress Disorder Checklist Scale (PCL-S)
Eadie	2008	Survey	Victoria, British Columbia, Canada	Female Undergraduate Students who had experienced sexual assault	153	17–39	F	11.76	Posttraumatic Diagnostic Scale (PDS) DSM- IV
Fenta	2010	Survey of random sample	Toronto, Ontario, Canada	Ethiopian immigrants	342	18+	T	5.8	Scale developed in a study of Cambodian refugees
Samuels-Dennis	2011	Survey	Ontario, Canada	Single mothers receiving social assistance for at least six months with at least one dependent child living at home	247	18+	F	30.36	Davidson Trauma Scale (DTS)

(*continued*)

Table 2.A3 Cont.

First author	Publication year	Data source	Location	Population	Number of participants	Age	Sex	Rate	Diagnostic tool	Additional note/ Observation
Clinical diagnosis studies										
Non-occupation related										
Bouchard	2008	Telephone survey in 2006	Quebec, Canada	Childhood sexual assault victims	804	18+	T	9.83	Primary Care PTSD Screen (PC-PTSD)	Combined analysis of PTSD rate of sexual, physical, and psychological abuse victims
Auger	2000	Telephone survey	Chicoutimi, Quebec, Canada	Victims of Saguenay flood	62	18+	T	19.35	Post-Traumatic Stress Disorder Reaction Index	
Torchalla	2014	The BC Health of the Homeless Survey (BCHOHS)	Three BC cities (Vancouver, Victoria, Prince George)	Self-identified homeless adults able to communicate in English and give informed consent	489	19–66	T	20.45	Mini-International Neuropsychiatric Interview Plus (MINI-Plus) version 5.0	
Stuber	2011	The Childhood Cancer Survivor Study (CCSS) and follow-up survey	USA and Canada	Long-term survivors of childhood cancer	6,542	18+	T	9	Posttraumatic Diagnostic Scale (PDS)	
Clarke	2006	Questionnaires	Toronto, Ontario, Canada	Jewish individuals in a geriatric psychiatry day hospital program 1986–2000	275	50+	T	17.82	Psychiatrist diagnosis using DSM-III, DSM-III-R, DSM-IV criteria	

Prevalence of Posttraumatic Stress Disorder 95

				N	Age	Sex	%	Measure	Notes
Abdulmohsen 2012	Women's Health Effects Study (WHES) – Waves 1 and 2	Canada (three provinces)	Adult, English-speaking Canadian women	286	18+ (19–63)	F	52.1	Davidson Trauma Scale (DTS)	
Ford-Gilboe 2015	Women's Health Effects Study (WHES), ON, NB, BC	New Brunswick, Ontario, British Columbia, Canada	English-speaking women who had been separated from an abusive partner	309	18+	F	48	Davidson Trauma Scale (DTS)	
Occupation related									
Fikretoglu 2006	2002 Canadian Community Health Survey 1.2 – Canadian Forces Supplement	Canada	Canadian Forces members	509	18+	T	18.66	World Health Organization Composite International Diagnostic Interview (WHO-CIDI) version 2.1	
Nelson 2011	2002 Canadian Community Health Survey 1.2 – Canadian Forces Supplement	Canada	Canadian Forces members	8,441	16–64	T	2.33	World Health Organization Composite International Diagnostic Interview (WHO-CIDI) version 2.1	Same data source and sample extraction. Average estimate of the reported rate was used for Figures 2a–2b

(continued)

Table 2.A3 Cont.

First author	Publication year	Data source	Location	Population	Number of participants	Age	Sex	Rate	Diagnostic tool	Additional note/ Observation
Clinical diagnosis studies										
Non-occupation related										
Sareen	2008	2002 Canadian Community Health Survey 1.2 – Canadian Forces Supplement	Canada	Canadian Forces members (regular force and reserve)	8,441	16–54	T	2.12	World Health Organization Composite International Diagnostic Interview (WHO-CIDI) version 2.1	
Sareen	2007	2002 Canadian Community Health Survey 1.2 – Canadian Forces Supplement	Canada	Canadian Forces members (regular force and reserve)	8,441	16–54	T	2.3	World Health Organization Composite International Diagnostic Interview (WHO-CIDI) version 2.1	
Zamorski	2016	2002 Canadian Community Health Survey 1.2 – Canadian Forces Supplement	Canada	Canadian Forces regular force members	55,100	17+	T	2.79	World Health Organization Composite International Diagnostic Interview (WHO-CIDI) version 2.1	

Prevalence of Posttraumatic Stress Disorder 97

Zamorski	2013	2008/2009 Health and Lifestyle Information Survey	Canada	Canadian Forces members	18+	T	6.49	Four-item Primary Care PTSD Screen with a cut-off of three or more positive responses to the four yes/no items	Same data source and sample extraction. Average estimate of the reported rate was used for Figures 2a–2b
Boulos	2016	2013 Canadian Forces Mental Health Survey (CFMHS)	Canada	Canadian Forces members	17–60	T	5.3	World Health Organization Composite International Diagnostic Interview (WHO-CIDI) version 3.0	
Weeks	2016	2013 Canadian Forces Mental Health Survey (CFMHS)	Canada	Canadian Forces regular force members	17+	T	5.3	World Health Organization Composite International Diagnostic Interview (WHO-CIDI) version 3.0	Note: For Zamorski et al., 2016, the authors reported 5.3% but this was based on weighted sample size 3,340 (n) and weighted total participants 64,400 (N); the rate was recalculated

(continued)

Table 2.A3 Cont.

First author	Publication year	Data source	Location	Population	Number of participants	Age		Sex	Rate	Diagnostic tool	Additional note/ Observation
Clinical diagnosis studies											
Non-occupation related											
Zamorski	2016	2013 Canadian Forces Mental Health Survey (CFMHS)	Canada	Canadian Forces regular force members	64,400	17+		T	5.19	World Health Organization Composite International Diagnostic Interview (WHO-CIDI) version 2.1 (CCHS-CFS) and version 3.0 (CFMHS)	
Armour	2015	Archival data from Parkwood Hospital Operational Stress Injury (OSI) clinic	Canada	Treatment-seeking Canadian Forces members and veterans referred to the OSI clinic between January 2002 – May 2012	283	18+		T	56.89	PTSD Checklist – Military Version (PCL-M)	
Asmundson	2002	Canadian Forces Veterans – Health Status Assessment 1999	Canada	Former peacekeepers deployed from Canada on various United Nations missions	1,856	18+		M	8.14	PTSD Checklist – Military Version (PCL-M)	

Author	Year	Data Source	Country	Population	N	Age	Type	Prevalence	Measure	Notes
Duranceau	2015	Canadian Forces Veterans – Health Status Assessment 1999	Canada	Canadian Forces members	1,238	18+	T	12.52	PTSD Checklist – Military Version (PCL-M)	Same data source; however, each study extracted unique sub-population to examine
Elhai	2007	Canadian Forces Veterans – Health Status Assessment 1999	Canada	Male Peacekeeping Veterans (who are Canadian Forces Veterans)	1,132	18–65	M	10.78	PTSD Checklist – Military Version (PCL-M)	
Fetzner	2013	Canadian Forces Veterans – Health Status Assessment 1999	Canada	Military Veterans	1,343	18+	T	2.08	PTSD Checklist – Military Version (PCL-M)	
Fetzner	2012	Canadian Forces Veterans – Health Status Assessment 1999	Canada	Military Veterans	990	18+	T	17.78	PTSD Checklist – Military Version (PCL-M)	
Richardson	2006	Canadian Forces Veterans – Health Status Assessment 1999	Canada	Male veterans serving in the Canadian Forces from 1990–1999	1,016	<65	M	10.33	PTSD Checklist – Military Version (PCL-M)	
Richardson	2009	Canadian Forces Veterans – Health Status Assessment 1999	Canada	Peacekeeping veterans with service-related disabilities	707	20–65	T	59.97	PTSD Checklist – Military Version (PCL-M)	

(continued)

Table 2.A3 Cont.

Clinical diagnosis studies
Non-occupation related

First author	Publication year	Data source	Location	Population	Number of participants	Age	Sex	Rate	Diagnostic tool	Additional note/ Observation
Stapleton	2006	Canadian Forces Veterans – Health Status Assessment 1999	Canada	UN Peacekeeping veterans from Canadian military sample	473	NA	T	30.02	PTSD Checklist – Military Version (PCL-M)	
Yarvis	2005	Canadian Forces Veterans – Health Status Assessment 1999	Canada	Previously deployed male, Canadian Peacekeepers	1,101	20–66	M	18.8	PTSD Checklist – Military Version (PCL-M)	
Richardson	2014	Archival data from Parkwood Hospital Operational Stress Injury (OSI) clinic	Canada	Canadian Forces members and Veterans referred to the OSI Clinic, 2002–2012	404	18+	T	68.81	PTSD Checklist – Military Version (PCL-M)	
Carleton	2018	Web-based self-report survey in English or French	Canada	Public Safety Personnel (PSP; e.g., correctional workers, dispatchers, firefighters, paramedics, police officers)	5,813	19+	T	22.43	PTSD Checklist 5 (PCL-5)	Authors reported 72.8% but did not provide total participants (N) who completed the assessment with no missing data

										Rate was adjusted using the reported total participants (404)
Robinson	2003	Self-administered survey	Manitoba, Canada	Practicing registered psychiatric nurses	295	18+	T	1.36	PTSD symptoms measured using a checklist of symptoms based on the DSM-IV criteria for PTSD and included in the survey	Authors reported the rate of 23.2%, however the rate was adjusted based on reported sample of 1,304 (*n*) and 5,813 (*N*) participants who completed survey
Garber	2014	Enhanced Post Deployment Screening (EPDS)	Canada	Canadian Forces members	16,153	18+	T	5.7	PTSD Checklist – Civilian Version, two-item version	
Zamorski	2014	Enhanced Post Deployment Screening (EPDS)	Canada	Canadian Forces members returning from deployment in support of the mission in Afghanistan completing an EPDS	16,193	18+	T	2.76	Patient Health Questionnaire (PHQ) and PTSD Checklist – Civilian Version (PCL-C)	Same data source, however each study extracted a unique sub-population to examine

(*continued*)

Table 2.A3 Cont.

First author	Publication year	Data source	Location	Population	Number of participants	Age	Sex	Rate	Diagnostic tool	Additional note/ Observation
Clinical diagnosis studies										
Non-occupation related										
Farley	2005	Interview with prostituting women in Vancouver	Vancouver, British Columbia, Canada	Female sex workers	100	18+	F	72	PTSD Checklist (PCL) (DSM-IV)	
Richardson	2017	Archival data	Ontario, Canada	Canadian Forces and RCMP members and veterans seeking treatment at the Parkwood Hospital Operational Stress and Injury Clinic	486	<65	T	74.49	PTSD Checklist – Military Version (PCL-M)	
Richardson	2012	Archival data	Ontario, Canada	Canadian Forces and RCMP members and veterans seeking treatment at the Parkwood Hospital Operational Stress and Injury Clinic	250	<65	T	73.6	PTSD Checklist – Military Version (PCL-M)	

Author	Year	Method	Location	Sample	N	Age		Value	Measure	Notes
Boyer	1996	Questionnaire using PTSD-I in French	Montreal, Quebec, Canada	Bus drivers	3,047	18+	T	5.81	PTSD Interview (PTSD-I) DSM-III-R	
Poundja	2006	Questionnaires	Montreal, Quebec, Canada	French-Canadian male veterans having been assessed or treated at Ste. Anne's National Centre of Operational Stress Injury	129	NA	M	85.27	PTSD Checklist (PCL) (DSM-IV)	
Maunder	2006	Questionnaires (after SARS 2004-2005)	Toronto, Ontario, Canada	Health care workers from hospitals in Toronto that treated SARS patients and Hamilton, where SARS patients were not treated	769	18+	T	12.48	Impact of Event Scale (IES)	
Regehr	2002	Questionnaires with paramedics in Toronto	Toronto, Ontario, Canada	Paramedics	86	39.68 (mean)	T	29.07	Impact of Event Scale (IES)	Total number (N) of participants was calculated by combining Toronto and Hamilton regions. Based on this, the rate was readjusted (continued)

Table 2.A3 Cont.

104

Murray Weeks et al.

First author	Publication year	Data source	Location	Population	Number of participants	Age	Sex	Rate	Diagnostic tool	Additional note/ Observation
Clinical diagnosis studies										
Non-occupation related										
Wilberforce	2010	Questionnaires	North-western Ontario, Canada	Physicians practicing in a predominantly rural and remote and medically underserviced region of Canada	159	21+	T	4.4	PTSD Checklist – Civilian Version (PCL-C)	
Laposa	2003	Secondary analysis of data previously reported	Vancouver, British Columbia, Canada	Emergency department personnel	51	23–51	T	11.76	Posttraumatic Diagnostic Scale (PDS)	
Regambal	2015	Survey of active first responders	British Columbia, Canada	First responders (RCMP, volunteer firefighters, and British Columbia Ambulance Service personnel) from rural settings	180	NA	T	10	Posttraumatic Diagnostic Scale (PDS)	
Corneil	1999	Survey of Canadian and US firefighters	Canada	Firefighters	625	18+	M	17.3	Impact of Event Scale (IES)	

Appendix 2D

Table 2.A4 Modified Newcastle–Ottawa Quality Assessment

	Representa-tiveness	Size	Comparability	Outcome	Statistics	Total
Abdulmohsen 2012	1	0	0	1	1	3
Adeponle 2012	0	1	0	1	1	3
Ahmad 2016	0	0	1	1	1	3
Armour 2014	1	1	0	1	0	3
Armour 2015	1	1	0	1	0	3
Asmundson 2002	1	1	1	1	1	5
Asmundson 2008	0	0	1	1	1	3
Auger 2000	0	0	0	1	1	2
Avary 1996	0	0	0	1	1	2
Bagheri 1992	1	1	0	1	0	3
Beal 1995	1	1	0	1	0	3
Beiser 2011	0	1	1	1	0	3
Bell 2014	0	0	1	1	1	3
Benoit 2016	0	0	0	1	1	2
Biehn 2012	1	1	1	1	0	4
Bouchard 2008	0	1	0	1	0	2
Boulos 2015	1	1	1	1	1	5
Boulos 2016a	1	1	1	0	1	4
Boulos 2016b	1	1	1	1	1	5
Boyer 1996	0	1	0	1	0	2
Brink 2001	1	1	1	1	0	4
Brunet 2015	1	1	1	1	1	5
Carleton 2018	1	1	0	1	1	4
Caron 2012	0	1	0	1	1	3
Catchpole 2016	0	0	1	1	0	2
Clarke 2006	0	0	1	1	0	2
Cleveland 2013	0	0	1	1	1	3
Cohen 2004	0	1	1	1	1	4
Collin-Vezina 2005	0	0	0	1	0	1
Collin-Vezina 2011	0	0	0	1	1	2
Corneil 1999	1	1	1	1	1	5
Desmarais 2014	0	0	0	1	1	2
Dietrich 2003	0	0	1	1	1	3
Dufort 1998	0	1	1	1	0	3
Dugal 2012	0	1	0	1	1	3
Duranceau 2015	1	1	1	1	0	4
Eadie 2008	0	0	1	1	0	2
Elhai 2007	1	1	1	1	1	5
Erickson 2007	0	0	1	1	1	3
Farley 2005	0	0	0	1	1	2
Fenta 2010	0	1	1	1	1	4
Fetzner 2012	1	1	1	1	1	5
Fetzner 2013	1	1	1	1	1	5

(continued)

106   Murray Weeks et al.

Table 2.A4 Cont.

	Representativeness	Size	Comparability	Outcome	Statistics	Total
Firestone 2015	0	1	1	1	1	4
Fikretoglu 2006	1	1	1	1	1	5
Fikretoglu 2012	1	1	1	1	1	5
Fleury 2011	0	1	0	1	1	3
Ford-Gilboe 2015	0	1	0	1	1	3
Frewen 2012	0	1	0	1	1	3
Frise 2002	0	1	1	1	0	3
Garber 2014	1	1	1	1	1	5
Gillis 1997	0	1	1	1	1	4
Goodwin 2010	1	1	1	0	1	4
Gretton 2011	0	0	1	1	1	3
Grigoriadis 2011	0	0	0	1	1	2
Guglietti 2010	0	0	1	1	1	3
Hawryluck 2004	0	0	0	1	0	1
Hebert 2014	0	1	1	1	0	3
Hebert 2017	0	1	1	1	1	4
Hensel 2010	0	1	0	1	1	3
Hensel 2016	0	1	0	1	0	2
Hetherington 2017	0	1	0	1	1	3
Hudson 2017	0	1	0	0	1	2
Hwang 2012	0	1	1	1	1	4
Khitab 2012	0	0	0	1	1	2
Koltek 1998	0	0	0	1	0	1
Kuksis 2017	0	0	1	1	0	2
Lalonde 2012	0	0	1	1	1	3
Lamoureux-Lamarche 2016	0	1	1	1	0	3
Lamoureux-Lamarche 2016	0	1	1	1	0	3
Lancee 2008	0	0	0	1	1	2
Laposa 2003	0	0	0	1	0	1
Law 2007	0	0	0	1	1	2
Ledgerwood 2015	0	0	1	1	1	3
Lee 2015	1	1	1	1	1	5
Levine 2016	0	0	1	1	0	2
Malat 2013	0	0	1	1	1	3
Martin 2009	0	0	1	1	1	3
Maunder 2006	0	1	1	1	1	4
McIntyre-Smith 2015	0	0	1	1	1	3
McLean 2006	0	0	1	1	1	3
Monson 2015	0	1	0	1	1	3
Monson 2016	0	1	1	1	1	4
Nelson 2011	1	1	1	1	0	4
Nelson 2015	1	1	1	1	1	5
Newman 2006	0	1	1	1	1	4
Ohayon 2000	0	1	1	1	1	4

Prevalence of Posttraumatic Stress Disorder 107

	Representa-tiveness	Size	Comparability	Outcome	Statistics	Total
Patterson 2012	0	1	1	1	1	4
Poundja 2006	0	0	0	1	1	2
Prevatt 2017	0	0	0	1	1	2
Puri 2017	0	1	0	1	1	3
Redwood-Campbell 2003	0	0	1	1	1	3
Redwood-Campbell 2008	0	0	1	1	1	3
Regambal 2015	0	0	1	1	0	2
Regehr 2002	0	0	0	1	1	2
Richardson 2006	1	1	1	1	1	5
Richardson 2008	1	0	0	1	1	3
Richardson 2009	1	1	1	1	1	5
Richardson 2012	0	1	0	1	1	3
Richardson 2014	1	1	0	1	0	3
Richardson 2017	0	1	0	1	1	3
Robinson 2003	0	1	0	0	0	1
Rodin 2013	0	1	0	1	1	3
Ross 2014	0	1	0	1	1	3
Roth 2013	0	0	0	1	1	2
Rousseau 2013	0	1	0	1	0	2
Samuels-Dennis 2010	0	1	0	1	1	3
Sareen 2007	1	1	1	1	1	5
Sareen 2007	1	1	1	1	1	5
Sareen 2008	1	1	1	1	0	4
Scheibe 2001	0	0	1	1	1	3
Sockalingam 2013	0	1	1	1	1	4
Stapleton 2006	1	1	0	1	1	4
Stein 1997	0	1	0	1	0	2
Stewart 2003	0	0	1	1	1	3
Strehlau 2012	1	0	1	1	1	4
Stretch 1991	1	0	0	1	1	3
Stuber 2011	1	1	1	1	1	5
Taylor 2007	0	0	1	1	1	3
Tibbo 2003	0	0	1	1	0	2
Torchalla 2014	1	1	1	1	1	5
Van Ameringen 2008	1	1	1	1	1	5
Vasiliadis 2016	0	1	1	1	0	3
Vedantham 2001	0	1	0	1	1	3
Vogel 2017	1	1	0	1	1	4
Volk 2016	1	1	1	1	1	5
Weeks 2016	1	1	1	1	1	5
Wilberforce 2010	0	0	0	1	1	2
Wolfe 2001	0	1	0	1	1	3
Woo 2012	0	0	1	1	1	3
Wright 1998	0	0	1	1	1	3

(continued)

108 Murray Weeks et al.

Table 2.A4 Cont.

	Representa-tiveness	Size	Comparability	Outcome	Statistics	Total
Yarvis 2007	1	1	1	1	1	5
Zabiewicz 2014	1	1	1	1	1	5
Zamorski 2013	1	1	0	1	0	3
Zamorski 2014	1	1	1	1	0	4
Zamorski 2016	1	1	1	1	1	5

3   Posttraumatic Stress Disorder and the Limits of Presumptive Legislation

Theresa Szymanski and Alan Hall

Introduction

Posttraumatic Stress Disorder (PTSD) has historically been tied to military conflicts, its terminology changing during various wars – shellshock in World War I, battle fatigue in World War II, and operational exhaustion in the Korean War. The current term, PTSD, was coined after the Vietnam conflict and institutionalized as a formal diagnostic category in the American Psychiatric Association's Diagnostic and Statistical Manual of Mental Disorders (DSM-III; American Psychiatric Association, 1980). PTSD continued to be a major topic of controversy surrounding the psychological impacts of the Gulf War and the more recent Iraq and Afghanistan Wars (Houston, Spialek, & Perrault, 2016; Marin, 2012). Research by Purdle (2016) and others (Houston et al., 2016) suggests that the media discourse and legislative actions on PTSD continue to be focused mainly on the military. Nevertheless, recent developments in the reform of compensation legislation in Canada, Australia, Britain, and the United States suggest a shift in public and legislative attention to PTSD within non-military occupations and workers more generally. The reform have been happening at the same time that worker and mental health advocates have been pushing employers, governments, the courts, and worker compensation boards to shift more attention from physical health and occupational injuries to mental health injuries (Lockwood, Henderson, & Stansfield, 2015; Shain, 2010, 2016a).

One key development in the recent shifts involves governments introducing "presumptive legislation", which requires compensation boards or commissions to presume a causal link between work-related exposures to potentially psychologically traumatic events and a PTSD diagnosis unless the link can be disproved by the employer. Presumptive coverage does not ensure compensation for workers in every case but is a significant policy development because workers no longer have to prove a workplace cause for their PTSD diagnosis.

In the current chapter, we outline the development of presumptive legislation in Canada and, in particular, in Canada's largest province, Ontario. We frame the development within a broader analysis of the development of

DOI: 10.4324/9781351134637-4

110   *Theresa Szymanski and Alan Hall*

compensation and other legislation on psychological injuries. Recognizing the positive aspects of presumptive legislation, we argue that unions, workers, employers, and mental health advocates need to look beyond both PTSD and presumptive legislation to discern a more comprehensive approach to workplace mental health that emphasizes the full range of workplace injuries and causes, an approach that includes primary prevention as well as early intervention and treatment. We conclude by describing a primary prevention strategy developed by the union movement in Ontario that is intended to identify, assess, and control organizational factors that may cause or contribute to diagnosed or undiagnosed mental health challenges including PTSD.

PTSD and Presumptive Legislation in Canada

In Canada, provincial jurisdictions govern compensation law which means that 14 different compensation laws and compensation boards or commissions exist (covering ten provinces, three territories and the federal jurisdiction that covers federal government workers and workers in federally controlled industries such as banking and transportation). Mental health claims, as documented by Lippel and Sikka (2010), were not formally recognized in Canadian law or policy until the late 1980s and early 1990s. As appeal tribunals increasingly began to approve both acute and chronic stress claims involving issues such as harassment and workload, several provincial governments responded by explicitly excluding chronic stress as compensable while, at the same time, highlighting and recognizing potentially psychologically traumatic events-related stress, and PTSD specifically, as the sole manifestation of workplace stress recognized for compensation. As Lippel & Sikka (2010) and others argue, these exclusions took place in the context of growing concerns about rising compensation costs and the potential for "opening the floodgates" on mental stress claims (p. s17; See also Gnam, 1998; Samra, 2017; Shortt, 1995). During this period, considerable inconsistency and inequity began to emerge in occupational mental stress compensation across Canada. Many jurisdictions (e.g., Ontario and all the Atlantic provinces) moved to exclude chronic stress, while Quebec (the country's second largest province), Alberta, Saskatchewan, the three territories and the Federal Government did not do so and, instead, continued to accept chronic stress claims including those involving harassment, workload, and labour relations complaints.

Canadian jurisdictions began to diverge around the question of chronic stress, but all jurisdictions had compensation policies that made it difficult for workers to get their claims accepted, whether acute or chronic (Hall et al., 2019; Lippel, 1990; Shain, 2010; Gnam, 1998). A principal constraint in both chronic and acute mental stress claims was that the worker bore the burden of proving work-relatedness. Coverage for acute potentially psychologically traumatic events exposures required proof that the condition had resulted from a physical injury (so-called "physical-mental" claims) or

The Limits of Presumptive Legislation   111

from an acute response to a potentially psychologically traumatic event. Many jurisdictions required proof that a single "anchor" event was the principle cause, and the potentially psychologically traumatic events had to be unusual or atypical for the occupation in question. Compensation was difficult to obtain if the condition resulted from a series of potentially psychologically traumatic event exposures designated as less-serious events— despite research evidence that these effects can be cumulative and lead to both PTSD and other mental disorders (Carleton et al., 2020; Corneil et al., 1999; Gnam, 1998). Many compensation boards' practices also required workers to release several years of clinical records before decision-makers would even consider approving other kinds of psychological claims.

Perhaps in part because of the many constraints added by several jurisdictions, the much-feared explosion of mental stress claims never materialized in Canada even in those provinces that permitted chronic stress claims (Samra, 2017; Lippel & Sikka, 2010). This contrasts with the United States which had experienced some significant increases in the 1980s when court cases had opened up the possibility of chronic stress claims, most notably in California where stress claims doubled between 1980 and 1987 (Gnam, 1998). In Quebec for example, Lippel and Sikka (2010) report that in 2007, after decades of allowing chronic stress claims, the percentage of claims compensated for stress injuries represented only 1.1% of total claims (p. S19). It is not clear whether the limited claim experiences were instrumental in allaying some of the concerns of government or business about stress-related compensation, but in the last decade several provinces have loosened their restrictions by introducing presumptive legislation for PTSD.

In 2012, Alberta introduced presumptive legislation covering police officers, firefighters, and paramedics (Workers' Compensation Board [WCB]—Alberta, 2017). The Alberta legislation was similar to laws emerging in countries such as the United States and Australia, emphasizing coverage for so-called "first-responder" occupations on the grounds that these professionals had higher rates of potentially psychologically traumatic events exposures and PTSD, although the evidence for higher rates was perceived as somewhat mixed (Marin, 2012). Manitoba was next, introducing presumptive legislation in 2015. Despite the ongoing debates about whether certain professions involved special risk, Manitoba's law extended PTSD presumption to all workers. As long as any worker was exposed to certain types of potentially psychologically traumatic events and able to demonstrate a clinical PTSD diagnosis, the link would be presumed unless proved otherwise by the employer (Workers Compensation Board of Manitoba [WCB Manitoba], 2012; 2016). Manitoba had reviewed its compensation statistics prior to their legislation and found that 89% of disallowed PTSD claims between 2000 and 2014 were from occupations other than police, firefighters, or paramedics. Specifically, the province noted that PTSD claims had been filed by child protection workers, social workers, nurses, correctional services employees (including institutional and community), and mental health workers. Manitoba included its PTSD legislation strategy as part of *a Five-Year Plan for Workplace Injury and Illness Prevention* initiative, launched in 2013, that included mental health as one of its ten action areas. In an effort to reduce work-related PTSD, the plan committed the Manitoba government to improve supports, resources and coverage for workers who routinely face potentially psychologically traumatic events as part of their work (Manitoba Family Services and Labour, 2013).

A year later, on April 5, 2016, rather than taking Manitoba's lead, Ontario's Minister of Labour Kevin Flynn announced the passage of Bill 163, the *Supporting Ontario's First Responders Act*, which provided presumption coverage but limited the coverage to first responders only (Ontario Ministry of Labour, 2016). When the Minister announced the law, the government made it very clear that it considered "first responders" as a special category of workers that warranted presumptive coverage. As Minister Flynn put it, "They [first-responders] put themselves in harm's way each and every day to ensure our safety, and we need to be sure they have the resources and treatment they need to heal and return to work safely" (Ontario Ministry of Labour, 2016). The Ontario legislation covered a few more occupations than Alberta by including not only firefighters, police officers, and paramedics, but also correctional officers, youth service workers, and certain other workers in correctional or secure youth facilities; however, Ontario excluding other occupations quickly became a significant point of criticism. Unions representing excluded groups, most notably nurses, criticized the legislation for failing to follow the example set by Manitoba and include all workers in the legislation. Considerable research evidence supported arguments that occupations other than police, paramedics, and firefighters can have high rates of potentially psychologically traumatic events exposures and PTSD (Skogstad et al., 2013). Workers in health care, social services, retail, child protection, and other sectors who interact with the public can be regularly exposed to disturbing situations and materials, while also facing the risk of workplace violence (O'Brien, 1998). There was mounting pressure and a considerable campaign by unions and professional associations representing several groups of excluded Ontario workers to have the legislative protections extended to them or to all workers. Ultimately, the pressure led Ontario to extend the presumption coverage to probation and parole officers, bailiffs, nurses, and other regulated health professionals (Ontario Public Service Employees Union [OPSEU], 2016; Registered Nurses Association of Ontario, 2017). In addition to seeking to extend the occupational coverage of the legislation, some Ontario unions have criticized the law's exclusive focus on PTSD. The criticism was based on the argument that by ignoring other mental disorders that can be sequalae to potentially psychologically traumatic events exposure (e.g., anxiety and depressive disorders), the Ontario presumptive legislation perpetuated the incorrect assumption that potentially psychologically traumatic events exposures lead to only one diagnostic outcome – PTSD (OPSEU, 2016). The Ontario Public Services Employees Union highlighted a considerable body of research evidence that potentially psychologically traumatic events exposures can lead to a variety of mental health challenges other than PTSD (McCann & Pearlman, 1990).

As the debates continued in Ontario, the province of Saskatchewan addressed both criticisms in its presumptive legislation passed in December, 2016 by including all workers and all potentially psychologically traumatic events-related psychological injuries including anxiety and depressive disorders (Saskatchewan Government, 2016). It is noteworthy that the inclusion of all workers was actually the product of a Conservative government amendment to a private members' bill introduced by the NDP that initially had been limited to PTSD and first responder populations. The Saskatchewan Minister of Labour indicated that, although most of cases involving potentially psychologically traumatic events exposures are expected to be experienced by first responders, the province, after looking at other jurisdictions and the evidence, could not justify defining potentially psychologically traumatic events exposures around one particular set of occupations. The Minister also insisted that the amendment would not require any increases in employer contributions (Canadian Press, 2016). Public statements by the government also emphasized that a key rationale of the legislation was to reduce the stigma of reporting trauma-related mental illness so that more people would report and seek help:

> While the majority of workers experiencing such injuries are first responders such as police officers, firefighters and medical professionals, the legislation applies to all workers in Saskatchewan. The government recognizes that anyone can be exposed to traumatic situations at work and that seeking help for psychological injuries can be daunting. The legislation was changed to reduce barriers and expand coverage.
> (Saskatchewan Government, 2016)

Saskatchewan's move suggested a trend towards including all workers, but more recent developments in all four Atlantic Provinces have gone in the opposite direction. New Brunswick and Prince Edward Island introduced amendments in 2016 covering only first responders, while parties campaigning in Nova Scotia and Newfoundland and Labrador announced plans to provide presumptive legislation but again for first responders only (Laroche & Willick, 2017). Most recently, in Newfoundland and Labrador, presumptive legislation was proclaimed to come into effect in July of 2019, covering all workers, but only for PTSD diagnoses (Executive Council, Service NL, 2018). However, as in Ontario, labour unions in Atlantic Canada called for broader coverage for all workers and all psychological disorders (Registered Nurses Union Newfoundland and Labrador, 2018; Ricciardelli & Hall, 2018).

The Exclusion of Chronic Stress

As Shain (2010) points out, several court and labour arbitration decisions since 2001 challenge the legal validity of compensation board policies and compensation laws that refuse to acknowledge chronic stress injuries. One case of particular importance was Plesner in British Columbia (*Plesner v. British Columbia Hydro and Power Authority, 2009*), a court appeal of a Workers' Compensation Appeals Tribunal decision to deny a BC Hydro worker compensation on the grounds that the mental stress involved was caused by chronic rather than acute stress from one or more potentially psychologically traumatic events exposures. The court found that the restriction to potentially psychologically traumatic events violated section 15 of the *Canadian Charter of Rights and Freedoms* by requiring a higher standard of proof (Shain, 2010, p. 9). Shain also points to a number of appeal tribunal cases in which increasingly significant damages have been paid to workers based on employer responsibility to create psychologically safe and healthy workplaces. Shain's work helped lead to the creation and the 2013 launch of the Canadian Standard Association's *Psychological Health and Safety in the Workplace* (Standards Council of Canada, 2013). As a member of the working committee that developed the Standard, Shain was optimistic that Canada was moving to make major changes in developing prevention efforts for mental disorders and hoped the impact on employee health and morale would spill over to society at large to lessen the burdens on the health care system and social institutions. Later, in supporting the Standard, Shain argued that the Standard outlines how employers could create and sustain "careful workplaces" that would satisfy their duty to prevent psychological harm (Shain, 2013). However, as Shain (2016a) argues more recently in his book, *The Careful Workplace*, the Standard did not have the effect he had hoped for because it was voluntary rather than compulsory and not specifically related to occupational health and safety; accordingly, human resources (HR) departments took the lead rather than occupational health and safety departments. "It went in the wrong door," says Shain (2016b). We agree with Shain's point but add that if the Standard had been made compulsory, substantive changes in compensation laws to recognize chronic stress would have had to occur to help establish a clearer economic interest in preventing harm. Unfortunately, the changes taking place in the compensation of chronic stress are slow and fragmented. British Columbia, the first province of the seven that had previously excluded chronic stress from its legislation, was the first to add coverage for some forms of chronic stress, with particular reference to harassment. In June, 2012 BC passed the following amendment to its Workers Compensation Act:

> 5.1 (1) Subject to subsection (2), a worker is entitled to compensation for a mental disorder that does not result from an injury for which the worker is otherwise entitled to compensation, only if the mental disorder either

(i) is a reaction to one or more traumatic events arising out of and in the course of the worker's employment, or

(ii) is predominantly caused by a significant work-related stressor, including bullying or harassment, or a cumulative series of significant work-related stressors, arising out of and in the course of the worker's employment.

Several provinces introduced new health and safety legislation between 2009 and 2014 to define and address workplace violence and harassment (Lippel, 2011), but so far none has moved to recognize more explicitly other workplace sources of stress. Between 2009 and 2014, compensation law changes in most provinces were limited to the introduction of presumption provisions. Ontario's Bill 127 came into effect at the beginning of 2018 to finally recognize compensation for chronic stressors (Ontario Workplace Safety and Insurance Board [WSIB], 2018). As in the BC legislation, the Ontario legislation excludes any chronic stressor claims arising from labour relations issues such as disciplinary actions or changes in an employee's work; instead, the Ontario legislation focuses on compensating workers who experience bullying and harassment. The narrow focus is seen in communications from the Ontario Workplace Safety and Insurance Board where bullying and harassment are repeatedly used to illustrate their definition of chronic stressors, while specifically listing the following exclusions:

> An employer's decisions or actions that are part of the managerial function would not be considered causes of traumatic or chronic mental stress. For example:
> * terminations
> * demotions
> * transfers
> * discipline
> * changes in working hours, or changes in productivity expectations.
> (Ontario WSIB, 2018)

Also, as in the British Columbia provisions, the new Ontario law requires that workers prove that the workplace stressors were "the cause or significantly contributed to" the chronic mental health injury. As in British Columbia, this requirement likely means that an employee's entire life and history can be subject to Board scrutiny (Health Sciences Association of British Columbia, 2012). Meanwhile, Manitoba and all the Atlantic provinces continue to exclude chronic stress entirely (WCB Manitoba, 2016; WorkplaceNL, 2018).

To better understand the development of compensation legislation for potentially psychologically traumatic events exposures and chronic stress, in the next section we delve more deeply into the case of Ontario, drawing particular attention to the government's recent efforts to narrowly limit

116   *Theresa Szymanski and Alan Hall*

presumptive coverage for potentially psychologically traumatic events exposures to certain occupations, while continuing to restrict compensation coverage for chronic stress.

Ontario's Focus on PTSD and First Responders

Although Ontario firefighters and paramedics had been actively lobbying for PTSD presumptive legislation for several years (Cohn, 2016), perhaps the most significant push towards presumptive legislation in Ontario came in 2012 when the Office of the Ontario Ombudsman released its investigation report, *In the Line of Duty*, that addressed complaints from current and retired police officers (Marin, 2012). The investigation into PTSD began in response to a 2010 complaint from a retired Ontario Provincial Police officer, and then several other police officers who had alleged that police services were failing to address the work-related traumas of their officers. After an initial review of the Ontario Provincial Police member complaint and 50 other complaints from past and present provincial and municipal police officers, the *Report* concluded that Ontario Police Services (that operate under the Ontario Ministry of Safety and Correctional Services) were failing to provide adequate information, training and support to their personnel. The Ombudsman noted a lack of effective professional mental health services for police, and found that information and training was "*ad hoc*" and coordinated with "little or no organizational planning and programming" (Marin, 2012, p. 8). The *Report* also found that a police culture of toughness and silence prevents officers from seeking early intervention and treatment (Marin, 2012, p. 83). While the need for "prevention" was frequently noted in the 2012 Ombudsman Report (Marin, 2012), the high risk of potentially psychologically traumatic events exposures and associated injuries was largely accepted as a fact of life in policing, paralleling historical discourse involving other first responders (Marin, 2012; Haslam & Marin, 2003). Accordingly, the principal focus for prevention within the *Report* was on early identification and treatment, or what in preventive terminology is understood as secondary and tertiary prevention. *Report* recommendations emphasized enhanced training and support services so officers and supervisors would be able to identify symptoms of mental health injuries in themselves and others, and act accordingly and quickly to seek professional treatment (Marin, 2012, p. 138). Possibilities to prevent or minimize the impact of potentially psychologically traumatic events exposure by engaging in primary prevention measures were not considered in any substantial way. For example, the Ombudsman's report describes reducing police exposure to potentially psychologically traumatic events through job rotation, however the idea did not make it into the recommendations. Completely absent from the *Report* and its recommendations was any attention to changing management structures and practices, despite the significant literature on the connections between stress, police culture, and other work organizational characteristics such as military hierarchy, supervisory practices, and lines of authority (Carleton et al., 2018, 2020; Murphy & McKenna, 2007; Padyab, Backteman-Erlanson, & Brulin, 2014).

The government emphasis on early identification and treatment and the exclusion of primary prevention measures was also evident in other policy forums leading up to the presumptive legislation. On September 12, 2012, and a month earlier than the anticipated the release of the Ombudsman's Report, the Ontario Minister of Labour announced the formation of a "Roundtable on Traumatic Mental Stress" (Ontario Ministry of Labour, News Release, September 28, 2012). Reflecting its policy emphasis on first responders, membership of the Roundtable was focused on first responders and consisted of management and front-line associations in firefighters, paramedic services, police, municipality associations, transit, the Ontario Federation of Labour and a small number of unions that represented some first responders. Other unions and organizations with no first responders were essentially excluded. Led by the Ontario Minister of Labour, the group met six times over a year, with the final meeting on September 25, 2013. Meetings consisted of group discussions and Ontario Minister of Labour-arranged speakers. An Ontario Public Service Employees Union request to present its "beyond-trauma approach" (which advocated the inclusion of chronic stress in future legislation and policy), was not accepted by the Ministry.

The Ontario Ministry of Labour released the final report on November 2014. The "Roundtable on Traumatic Mental Stress: Ideas Generated" describes the discussions and provides a list of ideas for moving forward, such as engaging cultural change, peer-oriented approaches, organizational leadership, government and policy leadership, access to knowledge, and training and support (Ontario Ministry of Labour, 2014). The Roundtable Report recognized the significance of cultural and organizational contributions to individual and institutional responses to potentially psychologically traumatic events exposures, but no attention focused on primary prevention goals of reducing or eliminating such exposures. The Report failed to mention expanding the discussion beyond PTSD to chronic stress and failed to commit to any specific government actions. Nevertheless, the Roundtable process communicated a government policy emphasis on potentially psychologically traumatic events discourse focused on helping first responders cope and survive with "operational injuries" that are accepted as the inevitable consequence of potentially psychologically traumatic events exposures for these professionals. As such, it was less than surprising that when the government finally introduced its presumptive legislation, Bill 163 in 2016, presumptive compensation access was limited to first responders diagnosed with PTSD (*Ontario Bill 163*, 2016).

The government's narrow focus on first responders and PTSD limited the discussion of potentially psychologically traumatic events and prevention in the Roundtable, but contesting viewpoints still emerged. For example, one of the ideas for moving forward proposed by the Ontario

118   *Theresa Szymanski and Alan Hall*

Minister of Labour Roundtable was that the Ontario Minister of Labour host an annual Traumatic Mental Health Summit. While the one-day "invitation only" conferences continued the focus on high risk occupations, the Ministry invited attendees beyond first responder occupations, such as from social services, mental health advocates, mental health agencies, and researchers. Over two years of summits, several speakers urged that the event focus should be broader than potentially psychologically traumatic events and the overall government approach broader than providing support after harm. For example, the keynote speaker in 2015, the Honourable Romeo Dallaire, a member of the Senate, retired Canadian military leader and PTSD sufferer, argued that the workplace approach ought to care for the well-being of every individual arguing that "True leadership is prevention". Dr. Rakesh Jetly, Senior Psychiatrist of the Canadian Forces also criticized a narrow approach, contending "it is a mental health strategy, not a PTSD strategy. It is about the everyday toll of work" (Ontario Ministry of Labour, 2015). Jetly's 2015 remarks were largely echoed in 2017 by retired Royal Canadian Mounted Police Assistant Commissioner, former Commanding Officer for New Brunswick, Roger Brown who suggested, "we don't have control over the work but we have control over our department. We have control over our procedures and policies. We have control over how supportive our organizations are" (Ontario Ministry of Labour, 2015). In 2015, Eric Jolliffe and Beth Milliard of the York Regional Police discussed the police service's peer support unit, describing the unit as driven from the bottom yet supported by the top and dedicated to the overall psychological well-being of employees and not just potentially psychologically traumatic events-related responses (Jolliffe and Milliard, 2015). Another 2015 speaker, Robert Maunder from Mount Sinai Hospital in Toronto reinforced the idea that workplaces ought to build both individual resilience and organizational resilience (Maunder, 2015). Maunder defined organizational resilience to include training, leadership and communication, organizational character (justice), decentralized decision-making, and unit-level self-government. For Maunder, the goal was to "create a fair place to work".

At and beyond the annual Ontario summits, unions engaged several arguments in efforts to get the government to alter the Ontario PTSD legislation, Bill 163. For example, in an effort to direct more attention to workplace change, the Ontario Public Service Employees Union's submission to Bill 163 proposed that the government "add employer and supervisor obligations in the *Occupational Health and Safety Act* that could be enforced by Ministry of Labour inspectors" (OPSEU, 2016) The union added that,

> incorporating prevention of PTSD in the *Occupational Health and Safety Act* also empowers the internal responsibility system to "action" the issue. Employers and workers on joint health and safety committees and health and safety representatives who have the most

The Limits of Presumptive Legislation 119

workplace expertise can engage in activities, make recommendations, and implement measures to prevent PTSD.

(OPSEU, 2016)

The Ontario Public Service Employees Union intended to bring mental health prevention into the regular operations and responsibilities of health and safety representatives and committees, which researchers suggest had been largely absent (Hall et al., 2016), not withstanding the previous changes in Ontario's *Occupational Health and Safety Act* requiring management to develop and implement policies on harassment and violence.

Despite the efforts of individuals and certain unions to shift the attention in Ontario beyond first responders and PTSD to other occupations and other stressors, the Ontario government passed its narrowly crafted Bill 163 for PTSD presumption for first responders on February 1, 2016. While the unions welcomed the Bill as a step forward, the Ontario Nurses' Association (ONA), the Ontario Public Service Employees Union, and the Ontario Federation of Labour (OFL) continued to raise concerns that Bill 163 failed to cover all workers or the full range of medical conditions that arise from potentially psychologically traumatic events exposures (OPSEU, 2016; ONA, 2018). The unions cited many difficulties with the current compensation (Ontario Workplace Safety and Insurance Board) system that could affect the success of the changes, starting with the fact that a third of Ontario's workers were still not covered by the Ontario Workplace Safety and Insurance Board. Secondly, the unions pointed out that Ontario had long wait-lists to see psychologists and psychiatrists to get any diagnosis, which was argued as problematic because the Workplace Safety and Insurance Board would not accept PTSD diagnoses from a family physician.

The unions argued that Ontario should have followed Manitoba's lead regarding presumption legislation and allowed primary care physicians to diagnose PTSD and then, once a claim is filed, the compensation system arranges for consultation by a psychologist or psychiatrist to assess the claimant. Unfortunately, as noted, most debate since the passage of Bill 163 has involved who should be covered for presumption, with little or no discussion on the issue of what should be covered (e.g., chronic or acute stress, potentially psychologically traumatic events, other stressors).

Ontario's Bill 163 contained some requirements for prevention when introduced as part of a broader strategy to prevent and address potentially psychologically traumatic events exposures. However, the approach followed the established line of narrowly construing prevention in terms of post-potentially psychologically traumatic events and individual-level interventions. Bill 163 amended the *Ministry of Labour Act* to require employers of first responders to provide the Ministry with a PTSD prevention plan that still did not address issues related to preventing potentially psychologically traumatic events exposures. For example, an online Ministry guide for employers developing a prevention plan concentrates

120   *Theresa Szymanski and Alan Hall*

entirely on ensuring that managers and staff know the symptoms of PTSD and that there are policies in place to ensure potentially psychologically traumatic events are reported and that affected staff are supported and treated if necessary (Ontario Ministry of Labour, Training and Skills Development, 2019; see also www.firstrespondersfirst.ca/prevention-2/page-3#mechanisms-ptsd).

In an attempt to introduce primary prevention and expand secondary prevention planning to chronic stress in occupational health and safety and compensation legislation, the Ontario Public Service Employees Union and other unions argued for a European approach which not only required more extensive primary prevention planning for chronic and acute stress but which also included enforcement of plan implementation. For example, in 2012, European Union health and safety inspectors blitzed over 22 countries in Europe focusing on how employers were addressing psychosocial hazards. Inspectors visited workplaces and asked employers which psychosocial hazards had been identified in their workplace, with whom the employers had consulted to develop the list, and what steps the employer had taken to address the identified hazards (Swedish Work Environment Authority, 2012).

Contrary to the Ontario Public Service Employees Union's recommendations, no provisions were added to Ontario's *Occupational Health and Safety Act* to require that an employer be subject to enforcement by the Ministry of Labour's occupational health and safety inspectors. Instead, implementation of any activities for primary, secondary, or tertiary prevention of PTSD was left entirely up to employers. At the 2017 annual PTSD Summit, Minister Kevin Flynn spoke only of the launch of a new PTSD website (www.firstrespondersfirst.ca), and reported that over 450 employers had sent PTSD plans to the Ontario Minister of Labour, all of which he indicated were posted on the Ontario Ministry of Labour website for information-sharing purposes. The Ministry's main response to the call for a greater recognition of injuries related to potentially psychologically traumatic events exposures involved pointing to 1) three summits on PTSD prevention; 2) the creation of the new website developed by system partners (www.firstrespondersfirst.ca); and 3) the sharing via the web of employers' PTSD plans (Ontario Ministry of Labour, 2016). None of the Ministry's deliverables involved expanding the narrow focus on PTSD, supporting primary prevention, developing support groups, or ensuring access to evidence-based treatments. There was no meaningful attention to workplace organization, workload, protocols for investigation and response, supervisory practices, or workplace culture as sources of stress and significant impediments to reporting a mental health injury.

There was little evidence from Ontario government communications to suggest that any major initiatives were forthcoming on chronic stress compensation or on primary prevention; nevertheless, the Ontario government, somewhat surprisingly, moved to its new chronic stress compensation policy within a large budget bill (Bill 127) introduced in 2017.

The Limits of Presumptive Legislation   121

Perhaps Shain (2010) was correct that a "perfect legal storm" of court and labour arbitration challenges had finally pushed the Ontario government to recognize arbitrary exclusion of chronic stress from compensation was unsustainable. The Ontario government legislative revisions still imposed significant policy restrictions on chronic stress compensation, which in our estimation, will continue to limit access and undermine the dynamics needed to push for more comprehensive primary and secondary prevention policies. The lack of any changes within the *Occupational Health and Safety Act* is particularly indicative of the government's failure to take PTSD prevention seriously. The problem from a labour standpoint is not just the need to recognize employer responsibility for the PTSD challenge, but also our collective failure to push beyond diagnostic categories such as PTSD and the limited notions of prevention which surround the discussion of PTSD. In an effort to present an alternative vision, in the final section of the current chapter, we describe a union initiative in Ontario that seeks to focus attention on chronic stress and primary prevention through organizational change that we argue can also transform the approach to PTSD prevention.

Union Response to Bill 163: A Comprehensive Mental Health and Safety Approach

In response to the limits of the Ontario government's approach, some unions and workers began developing their own strategies for change in the workplace. In 2009, a group of unions, worker health and safety representatives, and worker organizations formed a committee called the "Mental Injury Tool Group", following a research conference at the Occupational Health Clinics for Ontario Workers to develop "workplace tools" for stress prevention. Occupational Health Clinics for Ontario Workers is an independent ministry-funded organization made up of interdisciplinary health professionals (occupational hygienists, ergonomists, occupational doctors and nurses) that provides assistance to joint health and safety committees. Occupational Health Clinics for Ontario Workers also offers occupational health services for workers to evaluate toxic work exposures. The Mental Injury Tool Group included representatives from Occupational Health Clinics for Ontario Workers, the Office of the Worker Advisor, researchers, and representatives from almost all provincial, and some federal, unions and associations (e.g., Ontario Public Service Employees Union, Canadian Union of Public Employees, Ontario Nurses Association, Ontario Secondary Schools Teachers Federation, Unifor, Service Employees International Union, Elementary Teachers Federation of Ontario, United Steelworkers, United Food and Commercial Workers, Canadian Association of University Teachers, Workers United Union). The Mental Injury Tool Group decided to develop an online workplace stress toolkit that workplaces could use to develop strategies for intervention and action to prevent workplace stress. Their vision was that the toolkit would be used as a "one-stop shop" for workers to learn about the issue and take action in their workplaces to identify and help combat organizational sources of workplace stress. The group launched the Mental Injury Toolkit in November 2012 (Occupational Health Clinics for Ontario Workers, 2012), just prior to the January 2013 launch of Canadian Standard, Psychological Health and Safety in the Workplace (Standards Council of Canada, 2013).

Central to the Mental Injury Toolkit approach is an attempt to combine interventions designed to support individuals with interventions designed to change how organizations function. Accordingly, the online Guide to the Mental Injury Toolkit begins by identifying a number of key workplace stressors that may need to be addressed: excessive demands at work, workplace bullying/harassment, threats of violence, lack of control over work processes, insecure job arrangements, technological changes that interfere with tasks, lack of recognition and rewards, and inadequate resources and support (Mental Injury Toolkit, Introduction, p. 3). The Mental Injury Toolkit recommends that unions and workers should engage their health and safety representatives and joint committees as opportunities to identify, assess, and recommend controls for workplace stressors much the same as they do for traditional safety hazards. To help in identifying organizational stressors, the Mental Injury Toolkit recommends a survey instrument which workers and unions, hopefully in collaboration with management, can use to identify hazards and then proceed to develop prevention and action strategies. The instrument, the Copenhagen Psychosocial Questionnaire (Kristensen et al., 2005) identifies whether specific stressors are associated with survey participants' self-reported health outcomes. As such, the results enable workplaces to prioritize and address the most important issues in their workplace.

The Mental Injury Tool Group and Occupational Health Clinics for Ontario Workers piloted the medium-length Copenhagen Psychosocial Questionnaire survey in over 100 workplaces and added questions (such as physical safety, discrimination, and vicarious trauma) based on feedback they received. On January 25, 2018, Occupational Health Clinics for Ontario Workers and the Canadian Centre for Occupational Health and Safety announced the release of www.stressassess.ca, an online web wizard that enables workplaces to do the Copenhagen Psychosocial Questionnaire (with the Ontario additions) to identify psychosocial hazards that can lead to mental injury. The online toolkit provides suggestions to address the issues identified and how to act to prevent emotional or physical harm. Both the Mental Injury Tool Group and the online *Stress Assess* wizard provide recommendations on how to conduct the study and how to develop an intervention plan based on the results.

The "Social Epidemiological Model" used by the Mental Injury Toolkit recognizes that organizational factors are as central to understanding the causes of mental health injuries as they are to understanding physical injuries (Raphael, 2012; Veitch, 2011). Critically, the work environment is

The Limits of Presumptive Legislation   123

also understood as reflecting and expressing differences in power and control, with significant consequences for individual employees' mental health and their capacity to respond to mental health challenges through organizational change. While most psychiatric perspectives acknowledge that cultural and social factors affect mental health, there is little or no analysis of the political, economic or cultural origins of those conditions, and consequently no capacity to theorize and/or recommend the changes needed in organizations and how they can be achieved. Ultimately, the central focus for intervention is to treat the individual while primary prevention is reduced essentially to education and building individual coping capacity (Schnall, 2009).

By focusing on the individual, the approach may lead to interventions aimed at changing or fixing the behaviour of the individual, rather than changing the unhealthy aspects of the work environment. Familiar to health and safety representatives, the Mental Injury Tool Group argued that a "Hierarchy of Controls" model can be used to develop and evaluate mental health interventions (Cottrell, 2001). Controlling a hazard "at the source", or primary prevention, means eliminating or minimizing the hazard itself. Secondary prevention, the second-best approach, is controlling the hazard "along the path", or taking steps to minimize the effects of the hazard, where efforts focus on screening and early detection of harm. The least effective method for addressing hazards is "at the worker", referred to as tertiary prevention, where addressing the hazard's effects relies on the worker's actions, proficiency, behaviour, or equipment. Tertiary prevention does not prevent or minimize the harm, it deals with the effects of the harm.

Mental Injury Tool Model to Intervene in Mental Health

In addressing mental health in a health and safety framework, the Mental Injury Tool Group sees a clear role for the government regulator, which in the case of Ontario, is the Ontario Ministry of Labour. As we outlined in the current chapter, the Ontario Ministry of Labour's current focus on PTSD presumption can be characterized as principally a tertiary approach, as it deals with the situation after significant harm is done. Secondly, focusing on first responders and potentially psychologically traumatic events frames Ontario's concern as focused on operational stressors, which have to do with potentially psychologically traumatic events experienced on the job, and not stressors unrelated to the occupational context, such as workload, work organization, or justice and respect. While the Ontario government promises that PTSD coverage for first responders is part of a broader strategy to encourage prevention and mitigation of workplace trauma, the failure to require mental health prevention planning to be enforceable under the *Occupational Health and Safety Act* effectively undermines any meaningful initiative in this direction, while the lack of effective compensation coverage for chronic stress limits employer interest in taking primary prevention through organizational change in any serious way. The failure to link mental health injury prevention to the health and safety legislation also leaves out the crucial role that health and safety committee and worker representatives can play in planning, implementing and monitoring a comprehensive plan. As researchers suggest, effective worker representation can lead to heightened employer action on violence and harassment issues and there is no reason to expect that this would not be the case for potentially psychologically traumatic event sequala such as PTSD and other mental health challenges (Hall et al., 2013; Hall et al., 2016).

A key principle underlying the Mental Injury Tool Group is that health and safety committees must have explicit powers under the current law to address mental health issues. The Tool Group is meant to help workers develop a three-level prevention plan through health and safety committees, which are mandated in both union and non-union workplaces. While the Mental Injury Tool Group and Occupational Health Clinics for Ontario Workers used the Copenhagen Psychosocial Questionnaire survey in over 100 workplaces, most have been unionized which points to the need for legislation to require action at the workplace level. However, even unionized workers often find that employers refuse to participate. As such, government protections and enforcement measures are critical in supporting the capacity of workers to raise stress-related issues, whether unionized or not.

Ontario unions have realized that, in the absence of better legislation, workers must seek to realize and expand legal rights in other ways. Many Ontario unions are beginning to pursue change through collective bargaining. For example, in 2013, the Ontario Public Service Employees Union negotiated collective agreement language to establish "Occupational Stress Injury" committees with two different employers, the Ministry of Community Safety and Correctional Services and the Ministry of Children, Community, and Social Services. Made up of three union representatives and three employer members, the committees have provincial scope and collaborate on ministry initiatives to identify and address psychosocial hazards, and provide mental health supports for all employees across the province. Since the committees' inception, both ministries have made some progress. The Ministry of Children, Community, and Social Services has introduced a peer support program, and the Ministry of Community Safety and Correctional Services has formed a dedicated unit in the Ministry to create and implement a strategic plan that includes collecting baseline data and investigating the effectiveness of various resilience training programs.

Ontario unions are also shifting their thinking about how they use their collective agreements, approaching the collective agreements as both labour relations documents and as health documents. Reflecting changes in arbitration law (Shain, 2010), unions in Ontario have come to understand that every clause in a collective agreement puts a term and condition of work in writing and can be relied upon to bring clarity and a sense of justice to how workers are treated at work. Unions and workers have increasingly realized

The Limits of Presumptive Legislation   125

that language that commits the employer and the union to collaborate and develop a strategic plan to identify, prevent, and address the full range of psychosocial hazards can make work less injurious.

Some unions have also participated in another initiative that took place at the federal level, that is, the development of a Canadian Standard for Psychological Health and Safety in the Workplace by the Canadian Standards Association, together with the Mental Health Commission of Canada and the Bureau de normalisation du Québec, which is Quebec's version of the Canadian Standards Association. The Standard, "Psychological Health and Safety in the Workplace", was released in January 2013, a couple of months after the Mental Injury Tool Group. While crafted more as a management policy tool, two members of the Mental Injury Tool Group with national reach (the UNIFOR and Canadian Association of University Teachers representatives) also participated in developing the Standard, and brought the tool groups' vision of psychological safety and prevention to the federal table.

Unions aim to bargain general language in their collective agreements on the adoption of the Standard. Of particular interest is recognition by employers that psychosocial hazards shall be identified and addressed (as safety hazards are), that employers shall consult with the union in identifying strategies to improve psychological health and safety at the workplace, and that employers will provide supports such as access to professionals with appropriate training in managing the potential sequalae of exposure to potentially psychologically traumatic events.

Finally, the Ontario Public Service Employees Union and other unions are actively mobilizing their members to forge ahead with or without legislation. Grounded in research on worker health and safety representatives (Hall et al., 2006; Hall et al., 2016), this involves an explicit effort to educate and mobilize worker representatives to take a proactive knowledge and prevention-based approach to all aspects of health and safety including the use of the Mental Injury Tool Group to address psychosocial stress. The preliminary evidence is that this approach to worker representation, what Hall and colleagues (2016) have referred to as "knowledge activism", can generate more attention to psychosocial issues and more efforts towards primary, secondary, and tertiary prevention (see also Hall et al., 2006; 2013). The absence of stronger compensation and health and safety legislation is a significant constraint on worker power, but more explicit strategic efforts by unions and workers to strengthen the wider recognition of mental health issues and programming needs within the workplace itself are, in our view, vital to both legislative and workplace change.

Rights and compensation can also be pursued through other means – Human Rights Codes, the Charter, and in some provinces, Employment Standards. Legal actions may have played a significant role in pushing governments to finally recognize and work towards mitigating chronic stress, but the broader history of health and safety and compensation legislation suggests that collective action is the key to substantive gains in

126 *Theresa Szymanski and Alan Hall*

policies and practices (Storey & Tucker, 2006), whether it is in advocating for further reforms in compensation and occupational health laws and policies, negotiating better collective agreements, or negotiating in health and safety committees. At the level of the workplace, the Mental Injury Tool Group has broader potential because it promotes worker action and is aimed at any type of workplace or group of workers, unionized or not. If the Mental Injury Tool Group project can succeed in joining workers, unions, worker organizations, and even employers, or anyone who supports taking a comprehensive approach to mental health at work, it can work towards legal change without being dependent on laws or system entitlements to make progress on an employer-by-employer basis.

References

American Psychiatric Association. (1980). *Diagnostic and statistical manual of mental disorders* (3rd edn). Washington, DC: APA.

Bill 163. An Act to amend the Workplace Safety and Insurance Act, 1997 and the Ministry of Labour Act with respect to posttraumatic stress disorder, 1st Session, 41st Legislature, Ontario, 2016. Retrieved from www.ola.org/sites/default/files/node-files/bill/document/pdf/2016/2016-04/bill---text-41-1-en-b163ra.pdf.

Canadian Press. (2016, October 2). Saskatchewan changes law to help workers with psychological injuries [News release]. Retrieved from http://regina.ctvnews.ca/saskatchewan-changes-law-to-help-workers-with-psychological-injuries-ptsd-1.3131229.

Carleton, R. N., Afifi, T. O., Taillieu, T., Turner, S., Mason, J. E., Ricciardelli, R., … & Donnelly, E. A. (2020). Assessing the relative impact of diverse stressors among public safety personnel. *International Journal of Environmental Research and Public Health*, *17*(4), 1234. https://doi.org/10.3390/ijerph17041234.

Carleton, R. N., Afifi, T. O., Turner, S., Taillieu, T., Duranceau, S., LeBouthillier, D. M., … & Hozempa, K. (2018). Mental disorder symptoms among public safety personnel in Canada. *The Canadian Journal of Psychiatry / La Revue canadienne de psychiatrie*, *63*(1), 54–64. https://doi.org/10.1177%2F0706743717723825.

Cohn, M. (2016, February 18). How firefighters beat politicians at their own game. *Toronto Star*. Retrieved from www.thestar.com/news/queenspark/2016/02/18/how-firefighters-beat-politicians-at-their-own-game-cohn.html.

Corneil, W., Beaton, R., Murphy, S., Johnson, C., & Pike, K. (1999). Exposure to traumatic incidents and prevalence of posttraumatic stress symptomatology in urban firefighters in two countries. *Journal of Occupational Health Psychology*, *4*(2), 131–141.

Cottrell, S. (2001). Occupational stress, job satisfaction in mental health nursing: Focused interventions through evidence-based assessment. *Journal of Psychiatry and Mental Health Nursing*, *8*(2), 157–164.

Executive Council, Service NL. (2018, December 4). Presumptive coverage for post-traumatic stress disorder for all workers covered by the Workplace Health, Safety and Compensation Act [News release]. St. John's, NL. Retrieved from www.releases.gov.nl.ca/releases/2018/exec/1204n04.aspx.

Gnam, W. (1998). Mental disorders, mental disability at work, and workers' compensation. Submission of the Institute for Work & Health to the Royal Commission

The Limits of Presumptive Legislation 127

on Workers' Compensation in British Columbia. Retrieved from https://pdfs.semanticscholar.org/1628/7fe25fc612d98bbf0399eebff418ad9b8ba5.pdf.

Hall, A., Forrest, A., Sears, A., & Carlan, N. (2006). Making a difference: Knowledge activism and worker representation in joint OHS committees. *Relations Industrielles/Industrial Relations, 61*(3), 408–436.

Hall, A., King, A., Lewchuk, W., Oudyk, J., & Naqvi, S. (2013). Making participation work in the new economy: Final report to RAC. Toronto, ON: Workplace Safety and Insurance Board. Retrieved from www.whsc.on.ca/Files/What-s-New/MakingParticipationWorkInTheNewEconomyFinalReport.aspx.

Hall, A., Oudyk, J., King, A., Lewchuk, W., & Naqvi, S. (2016). Identifying knowledge activism in worker health and safety representatives: A cluster analysis. *American Journal of Industrial Medicine, 59*, 42–56.

Hall, A., Ricciardelli, R., Sitter, K., & Simas Medeiros, D. (2019). Occupational stress injuries in two Atlantic provinces: A policy analysis. *Canadian Public Policy, 44*(4), 1–16.

Haslam, C., & Marin, K. (2003). A preliminary investigation of post-traumatic stress symptoms among firefighters. *Work and Stress, 17*(3), 277–285.

Health Sciences Association of British Columbia (BC). (2012). Worker Compensation Board changes won't help victims of mental stress. *Bulletin, 33*(3). New Westminster, BC. Retrieved from https://hsabc.org/news/wcb-changes-wont-help-victims-mental-stress.

Houston, J., Spialek, M., & Perrault, M. (2016). Coverage of post-traumatic stress disorders in the *New York Times*, 1950–2012. *Journal of Health Communications, 21*(2), 240–248.

Jolliffe, E., & Milliard, B. (2015, March 5). Mental health and changing the organizational culture, York Regional Police. PowerPoint presentation at Ontario Ministry of Labour Summit on Work Related Traumatic Stress, Toronto, ON, Canada.

Kristensen, T., Hannerz, H., Hogh, A., & Borg, V. (2005). The Copenhagen Psychosocial Questionnaire – A tool for the assessment and improvement of the psychosocial work environment. *Scandinavian Journal of Work, Environment and Health, 31*(6), 438–449.

Laroche, J., & Willick, F. (2017, April 28). PTSD coverage changes for first responders garners praise but also skepticism. *CBC*. Retrieved from www.cbc.ca/news/canada/nova-scotia/ptsd-workers-compensation-act-paramedics-nurses-police-jail-guards-nsgeu-1.4089823.

Lippel, K. (1990). Compensation for mental claims under Canadian law. *Behavioural Sciences and the Law, 8*, 375–398.

Lippel, K. (2011). Law, public policy and mental health in the workplace. *Healthcare Papers, 11*, Special Issue, 20–37.

Lippel, K., & Sikka, A. (2010). Access to workers' compensation benefits and other legal protections for work-related mental health problems: A Canadian overview. *Canadian Journal of Public Health, 101 (Supplement 1)*, 16–22.

Lockwood, G., Henderson, C., & Stansfeld, S. (2015). An assessment of employer liability for workplace stress. *International Journal of Law and Management, 59*(2), 202–216.

Manitoba Family Services and Labour (2013). Manitoba's five-year plan for workplace injury and illness prevention. Retrieved from http://digitalcollection.gov.mb.ca/awweb/pdfopener?smd=1&did=23078&md=1.

Marin, A. (2012). In the line of duty: Investigation into how the Ontario Provincial Police and the Ministry of Community Safety and Correctional Services have addressed operational stress injuries affecting police officers. Toronto, ON: Ombudsman Office. Retrieved from www.ombudsman.on.ca/Media/ombudsman/ombudsman/resources/Reports-on-Investigations/OPP-final-EN-accessible.pdf.

Maunder, R. (2015). Prevention of traumatic stress: Mount Sinai's approach to building staff resilience. Presentation at Ontario Ministry of Labour Summit on Work Related Traumatic Stress. Toronto, March 5.

McCann, L., & Pearlman, L. (1990). Vicarious traumatization: A framework for understanding the psychological effects of working with victims. *Journal of Traumatic Stress*, *3*(1), 131–149.

Murphy, C., & McKenna, P. (2007). Rethinking police governance, culture and management: A summary review of the literature. Prepared for the task force on Governance and Cultural Change in the RCMP, Public Safety Canada. Retrieved from www.publicsafety.gc.ca/cnt/cntrng-crm/tsk-frc-rcmp-grc/_fl/archive-rthnk-plc-eng.pdf.

O'Brien, L. (1998). *Traumatic Events and Mental Health.* Cambridge: Cambridge University Press.

Occupational Health Clinics for Ontario Workers (OHCOW). (2012). Mental Injury Toolkit. Retrieved from www.ohcow.on.ca/edit/files/mip/mit%20intro-duction.pdf

Ontario Ministry of Labour, Training and Skills Development. (2019). Post-traumatic stress disorder prevention plans. Retrieved from www.ontario.ca/page/post-traumatic-stress-disorder-prevention-plans.

Ontario Ministry of Labour (2012, September 28). Helping workers with job-related post-traumatic mental stress [Archived news release]. Retrieved from https://news.ontario.ca/mol/en/2012/09/helping-workers-with-job-related-post-traumatic-mental-stress.html.

Ontario Ministry of Labour. (2014). Roundtable on traumatic mental stress: Ideas generated. Health and Safety Policy Branch. Toronto, ON. Retrieved from www.labour.gov.on.ca/english/hs/pubs/tms/index.php.

Ontario Ministry of Labour. (2015). Summit on work-related traumatic mental stress: Summary report. Toronto, ON. Retrieved from www.labour.gov.on.ca/english/hs/pdf/tms_summit.pdf.

Ontario Ministry of Labour. (2016, April 5). *Ontario passes legislation to support first responders with PTSD* [News release]. Retrieved from https://news.ontario.ca/en/release/36382/ontario-passes-legislation-to-support-first-responders-with-ptsd.

Ontario Nurses Association (ONA). (2018). Send your message: Include nurses in PTSD presumptive legislation. Retrieved from www.ona.org/campaigns-actions/ptsd/.

Ontario Public Service Employees Union (OPSEU). (2016). Responding to PTSD by supporting Ontario's first responders: A submission to the Standing Committee on Social Policy from the Ontario Public Service Employees Union regarding Bill 163, the Supporting Ontario's First Responders Act. Submitted to the Ministry of Labour. Retrieved from https://opseu.org/news/responding-ptsd-opseus-take-bill-163.

Ontario Workplace Safety and Insurance Board (WSIB). (2018). Bill 127: Chronic mental stress FAQ. Toronto, ON. Retrieved from www.wsib.on.ca.

The Limits of Presumptive Legislation   129

Padyab, M., Backteman-Erlanson, S., & Brulin, C. (2014). Burnout, coping and stress of conscience and psychosocial work environment of patrolling police officers. *Journal of Police and Criminal Psychology, 31*, 229–237.

Purdle, J. (2016). "Heroes' invisible wounds of war": Constructions of post-traumatic stress disorder in the text of United States federal legislation. *Social Science and Medicine, 149*, 9–16.

Raphael, D. (2012). *Tackling health inequalities: Lessons from international experiences.* Toronto: Canadian Scholars Press.

Registered Nurses Association of Ontario. (2017, November 24). Do not exclude nurses from PTSD legislation: Sign action alert [News release]. Retrieved from https://rnao.ca/news/do-not-exclude-nurses-ptsd-legislation-sign-action-alert.

Registered Nurses Union Newfoundland and Labrador. (2018). Submission to the Workplace NL pertaining to post-traumatic stress disorder in the nursing profession. St. John, NL. Retrieved from http://rnunl.ca/app/uploads/2018/02/RNUNL_PTSD-Submission.pdf.

Ricciardelli, R., & Hall, A. (2018). A call for presumptive legislation: Post-traumatic stress disorder, occupational stress injuries and the wellbeing of the work force. Position Paper V.5 for NAPE submitted to NL Government. Retrieved from www.nape.ca/article/a-call-for-presumptive-legislation/.

Samra, J. (2017). The evolution of workplace mental health in Canada: Research report (2007-2017). Commissioned by Great West Life Centre for Mental Health in the Workplace, University of New Brunswick. Retrieved from www.hrpa.ca/Documents/Public/Thought-Leadership/The-Evolution-of-Workplace-Mental-Health-in-Canada.pdf.

Saskatchewan Government. (2016). Backgrounder – Amendments to the Workers' Compensation Act, 2013. Retrieved from www.saskatchewan.ca/~/media/news%20release%20backgrounders/2016/oct/amendment%20to%20workers%20compensation%20act%20backgrounder.pdf.

Schnall, P. (2009, March 31). Session # 1 – Part 1: Introduction to "Work and health, UCLA School of Public Health Environmental Safety and Health Class 270/CHS 278.

Shain, M. (2010). Tracking the perfect legal storm: Converging systems create mounting pressure to create the psychologically safe workplace. Mental Health Commission of Canada. Retrieved from www.mentalhealthcommission.ca/English/media/3051.

Shain, M. (2013, October 21). Presentation at Ontario Workplace Health Coalition (OWHC) Annual General Meeting. Mississauga, ON.

Shain, M. (2016a). The careful workplace: Seeking psychological safety at work in the era of Canada's national standard. Thomson Reuters. Toronto, ON.

Shain, M. (2016b). October 15 Presentation to Lancaster House Conference. Toronto, ON.

Shortt, S. (1995). The compensability of chronic stress: A policy dilemma for the Ontario Workers' Compensation Board. *Canadian Public Policy, 21*(2), 219–232.

Skogstad, M., Skorstad, M., Lie, A., Conradi, H.S., Heir, T., & Weisaeth, L. (2013). Work-related post traumatic stress disorder. *Occupational Medicine, 63*, 175–182.

Standards Council of Canada. (2013). Psychological health and safety in the workplace: Prevention, promotion and guidance to staged implementation. National

Standard CAN/CSA-Z1003-12/BNQ 9700-803/2013. Retrieved from www.csagroup.org/documents/codes-and-standards/publications/CAN_CSA-Z1003-13_BNQ_9700-803_2013_EN.pdf.

Storey, R., & Tucker, E. (2006). All that is solid melts into air: Worker participation and occupational health and safety regulation in Ontario – 1970–2000. In V. Mogensen (ed.), *Worker safety under siege: Labor, capital and the politics of workplace safety in a deregulated world* (pp. 157–186). New York: M.E. Sharpe.

Swedish Work Environment Authority. (2012). Inspektionskampanj SLIC 2012 – psykosociala riskbedömningar [website of the Swedish Work Environment Authority]. www.av.se/en/search/?qry=slic+2012.

Veitch, J. (2011). Workplace design contributions to mental health and wellbeing. *Health Care Papers*, *11*, Special Issue, 38–46.

Workers' Compensation Board (WCB)–Alberta. (2017). Post-traumatic stress disorder. Worker Compensation Board fact sheet. Retrieved from www.wcb.ab.ca/assets/pdfs/workers/WFS_PTSD.pdf.

Workers Compensation Board of Manitoba (WCB Manitoba). (2012). Benefits and administration: Adjudication and compensation of psychological injuries, Policy 44.05.30 Section 40. Retrieved from www.wcb.mb.ca/sites/default/files/44.05.30%20Adj%20of%20Psychological%20Injuries%20and%20Guidelines%20January%201%2C%202016.pdf.

Workers Compensation Board of Manitoba (WCB Manitoba). (2016). Post-traumatic stress disorder (PTSD) presumption FAQ. Retrieved from www.wcb.mb.ca/post-traumatic-stress-disorder-ptsd-presumption-faq.

WorkplaceNL. (2018). Client services policy manual: mental stress entitlement (Policy Number EN-18). Retrieved from www.workplacenl.ca/policiesandprocedures.whscc.

4 Recognizing Posttraumatic Stress Disorder in Primary Care

James M. Thompson, Alexandra Heber,
Jon Davine, Ryan Murray, and
Donald R. McCreary

Psychological trauma is a psychiatric injury that can occur in response to sufficiently stressful events and can become chronic if left untreated (Canadian Institute for Public Safety Research and Treatment [CIPSRT], 2019). Responses range from minor transient distress to acute adjustment reactions, subthreshold (partial) but distressing states that do not meet full diagnostic criteria for Posttraumatic Stress Disorder (PTSD), and full-criteria PTSD (American Psychiatric Association, 2013; McFarlane et al., 2017). PTSD is a syndrome of emotional, behavioural, thought, and somatic symptoms and signs that can occur following exposure to traumatic events perceived as a severe threat to self and others. PTSD is characterized by: (i) intrusive involuntary memories, flashbacks, nightmares, or distress on exposure to triggers of the traumatizing event; (ii) avoidance of reminders of the traumatizing event; (iii) persistent, event-related negative moods and thoughts like fear, mistrust, shame, or detachment; (iv) sleep disturbance, hypervigilance, startle response, irritability, or anger; and (v) sometimes significant dissociation, with amnesia or decreased responsiveness to external stimuli. Manifestations of PTSD lead to considerable social, occupational, and interpersonal dysfunction (Sareen, 2018). Some researchers propose to view PTSD and associated somatic (physical) symptoms and disorders together as a systemic condition (McFarlane, 2017).

Many types of potentially psychologically traumatic events (CIPSRT, 2019) have been associated with PTSD. Examples include adverse childhood experiences, motor vehicle accidents, sexual violence, interpersonal and community violence, unexpected death or threat of death witnessed or learned about in others, especially the death of a loved one; severe physical injury; iatrogenic experiences; military combat; natural disasters; and exposure to bodies or environmental hazards (American Psychiatric Association, 2013; Sareen, 2018; Fortier et al., 2019). The variety of mechanisms of injury in psychological trauma contributes to the challenge of recognizing PTSD in primary care. However, commonly there is an element of significant threat to the safety of the self or others.

Psychiatrists have long recognized the adverse effects of severe psychological stress, but psychological trauma research did not develop fully until

DOI: 10.4324/9781351134637-5

132   *James M. Thompson et al.*

the end of the Vietnam War in the 1970s. Much of the early focus of psychological trauma research was on military veterans. PTSD entered the third edition of the Diagnostic and Statistical Manual of Mental Disorders in 1980 (Reynolds, 1997); at that time, adjustment, mood, anxiety, psychotic, personality, and substance disorders topped the list of psychiatric disorders in primary care provider training. The significance of psychologically traumatic reactions to stress was only beginning to be widely appreciated. In the third and fourth editions of the Diagnostic and Statistical Manual of Mental Disorders, PTSD was bundled with anxiety disorders. In the fifth edition, published in 2013, PTSD was unbundled into a new chapter called, *"Trauma- and Stressor-Related Disorders"* along with acute stress disorder, adjustment disorders, reactive attachment disorder and disinhibited social engagement disorder (American Psychiatric Association, 2013).

Today, PTSD is considered one of the more common psychiatric disorders in civilian as well as military populations, along with mood and anxiety disorders (Cooper, Metcalf, & Phelps, 2014). PTSD and other types of psychological trauma therefore should be in the back of all primary care clinicians' minds when interacting with patients (Levine & Jain, 2002). Studies in several countries have shown that PTSD is common in primary care patient populations but tends to be underdiagnosed (Stein et al., 2000; Bruce et al., 2001; Taubman-Ben-Ari et al., 2001; Levine & Jaine, 2002; Munro, Freeman, & Law, 2004; Liebschutz et al., 2007; Greene, Neria, & Gross, 2016; Sareen, 2018).

There are many reasons why potentially psychologically traumatic events and PTSD often are unrecognized worldwide by health care providers (Brady, 1997; Levine & Jain, 2002; Sareen, 2018). First, most persons exposed to potentially psychologically traumatic events do not develop lasting psychiatric disorders, including PTSD (McQuaid et al., 2001; Levine & Jain, 2002). Second, presenting signs and symptoms can have broad differential diagnoses of conditions other than just PTSD. Alternative diagnoses that explain a patient's presenting symptoms can include physical health conditions, chronic pain, substance use disorders, addictions, other psychiatric disorders, and medically unexplained symptoms (Richardson et al., 2010; Sareen, 2018; Forbes et al., 2019). PTSD is also commonly comorbid with many physical health conditions, mental health conditions, chronic pain and medically unexplained symptoms (McFarlane et al., 2008; Edwards et al., 2010; Haller et al., 2015; Goodstein, 1985; Osório et al., 2012; Sareen, 2018; Thompson et al., 2016; Forbes et al., 2019). Third, mental health stigma is pervasive (Mackenzie et al., 2014). When asked, many patients are reluctant to disclose a history of potentially psychologically traumatic events. Delays in treatment-seeking for many years after the onset of mental health problems are typical (Wang et al., 2005). Fourth, individuals who develop PTSD vary in their symptom presentations, owing to age at exposure, gender, cultural differences and varying symptom severity (Lanius, Hopper, & Menon, 2003; Forbes et al., 2005; Galovski et al., 2010; McFarlane et al., 2017). Masculine gender role norms, for

Recognizing PTSD in Primary Care 133

example, can influence the ways that men present when they experience a mental health problem, often delaying treatment or minimizing symptoms (McCreary, 2020). Fifth, patients may present believing that they have PTSD when in fact some other physical, psychological, or social diagnosis explains their symptoms and signs. Social diagnoses include, for example, distress caused by marital distress or parenting challenges that can be resolved by addressing coping styles and social issues, usually relationships. Lastly, milder, subthreshold or partial forms of PTSD are more difficult to recognize than the fully developed syndrome. Partial PTSD refers to the presence of some PTSD symptoms but not enough to meet full criteria for PTSD.

Most primary care PTSD guidelines focus on Diagnostic and Statistical Manual of Mental Disorders criteria (e.g. Feliciano, 2009; Forbes, 2009; Cooper et al., 2014), but PTSD has many different presenting faces in clinical practice (Schumann & Miller, 2000; Classen & Heber, 2017). In the current chapter, we offer evidence-informed tips for efficiently recognizing psychological trauma in adults, specifically PTSD, as primary care clinicians work through their clinic lists, hospital rounds and home care visits. We begin by discussing the extent of PTSD and the advantages of recognizing psychological trauma in primary care practices. Then, we review principles of trauma-informed care, including engagement, stabilization, screening, and diagnosing PTSD, as well as initial treatment. Since much of primary care diagnosis begins with pattern recognition, we illustrate trauma-informed care through fictitious vignettes derived from published case reports and our clinical experiences. We focus on adults, but many of the principles discussed here apply also to paediatric psychological trauma (Dyregrov & Yule, 2006).

PTSD: A Common Psychiatric Disorder

Along with mood and anxiety disorders, PTSD is one of the more common psychiatric disorders among adults in the general population. Prevalence estimates vary owing to methodological and cultural differences. Most people will experience one or more potentially psychologically traumatic events in their lifetimes. In the United States and Canada, 60–73% of adult men and 51–65% of adult women have been exposed to at least one potentially psychologically traumatic event, and about 10–20% develop PTSD (Levine & Jain, 2002). Most people exposed to potentially psychologically traumatic events do not develop PTSD, but post-rape rates as high as 46% in women and 65% in men have been reported (Sareen, 2018). Children and adolescents also can develop PTSD (Dyregrov & Yule, 2006; Espinel & Shaw, 2018).

Lifetime PTSD prevalence ranges from 6–9%, and one-year prevalence from 2–5% in the general adult populations of the United States, Canada, and Australia (Cooper et al., 2014; Sareen, 2018). In Canada, current and lifetime prevalence of partial- and full-criteria PTSD in women are twice

134 *James M. Thompson et al.*

those in men (Van Ameringen et al., 2008). PTSD prevalence estimates in military veterans are comparable to, or higher than, civilian populations, and higher in those engaged in difficult deployments (Forbes et al., 2019). Carleton et al. (2018) published prevalence estimates for PTSD in Canadian public safety personnel (i.e., 23.2%) that are similar to those in military populations. Lower PTSD prevalence is reported among civilian adults outside of North America, Europe, and Australia. Paradoxically, lifetime PTSD prevalence appears lower in countries that have higher markers of socioeconomic vulnerability (coping and adaptive capacities) and a higher likelihood of potentially psychologically traumatic events exposure (war, genocide) than in countries like Canada, the United States, Australia, and New Zealand (Dückers, Alisic, & Brewin, 2016). These cultural differences are the subject of much debate and research, and reasons for them remain unclear.

Potentially psychologically traumatic event exposures and PTSD are common in primary care populations, but detection or documentation by clinicians is low. Estimates of adult PTSD prevalence in primary care populations range from 2–39% (Spottswood, Davydow, & Huang, 2017). In a United States community primary care clinic, 65% reported a history of potentially psychologically traumatic events exposures, and 12% went on to develop PTSD (Stein et al., 2000). In a study in the United States of 14 primary care waiting rooms, 83% of patients reported at least one lifetime traumatic event and 37% met PTSD criteria on a standardized diagnostic clinical interview (Bruce et al., 2001). PTSD prevalence is higher in patients with depression, anxiety, chronic pain, and various chronic physical health conditions (Stein et al., 2000; American Psychiatric Association, 2013; Sareen, 2018), so it is not surprising that PTSD is common in primary care.

Documented detection of PTSD by primary care physicians remains generally low, ranging from 0–52% of those meeting PTSD criteria (Greene, Neria, & Gross, 2016). In a large Israeli study of primary care settings 20 years ago, 23% of patients had experienced one or more potentially psychologically traumatic events, and 39% of those with potentially psychologically traumatic events exposures met PTSD criteria, but only 2% of those meeting PTSD criteria were given a PTSD diagnosis by physicians (Taubman-Ben-Ari et al., 2001). A study with United States data 12 years ago found that 23% of academic primary care waiting room patients had PTSD criteria, but PTSD was only noted in the medical record of about half of those patients (Liebschutz et al., 2007). There are many advantages to enhancing primary care PTSD detection and management for patients, their families, their communities, and primary care providers.

Advantages of Recognizing Psychological Trauma in Primary Care

Recognizing and engaging a psychologically traumatized patient for diagnosis and treatment is one of the most satisfying clinical experiences in

Recognizing PTSD in Primary Care   135

primary care, opening doors for both patient and provider. Recognition can deepen the clinician–patient relationship and unlock pathways to recovery. The diagnosis can explain behaviours that previously seemed difficult on both sides of the clinician–patient relationship, helping the provider to understand and accept the patient's reactions during clinical encounters (Purkey, Patel, & Phillips, 2018). Primary care clinicians can encourage patients to engage with care sooner than if they were left on their own, lessening the risk of long-term dysfunction, poor quality of life, and the worsening or onset of serious physical health problems (Cooper et al., 2014, Sareen, 2018). Engagement can improve compliance with treatment of PTSD and co-occurring physical and mental health conditions and can lead to more efficient use of health care resources (Harriet et al., 2000). Researchers have proposed that PTSD be viewed as a systemic illness, where treatment might improve co-occurring medically unexplained symptoms (McFarlane, 2017; McFarlane et al., 2017). Informed families can better understand their loved ones' emotions, behaviours and thinking (Cox et al., 2018). Most importantly, PTSD treatment can also improve the patient's functioning in work, home, and community and reduce risk of death by suicide in vulnerable persons.

"Trauma-Informed" Primary Care

"Trauma-informed" primary care practices routinely accommodate the needs of patients with psychological trauma, approaching all patients as if they could have been psychologically traumatized. Trauma-informed care begins with understanding how psychological trauma can change the ways that people feel, think, and behave. Harris and Fallot (2001) identified five principles of a trauma-informed approach in the therapeutic relationship: ensuring safety, trustworthiness, choice, collaboration, and empowerment (Levine & Jain, 2002; Forbes, 2009; Cooper at al., 2014; Classen & Heber, 2017). A team of family physicians recommended a 5-point approach to trauma-informed practice (Purkey et al., 2018). The points include: 1. *Bear witness to the patient's experience of psychological trauma,* which is often therapeutic, acknowledges the effects of psychological trauma on the patient's life, and allows physician to point out how their patient has developed coping strategies. 2. *Help patients to feel they are in a safe place,* which requires being mindful of verbal and nonverbal signals to the patient, being consistently available, and recognizing their need for safety. 3. *Include patients in their healing process,* by presenting positive and negative choices to promote patient engagement in recovery. 4. *Believe in the patient's strength and resilience,* here the physician views the patient, rather than as a victim with pathology, as a person with strength and resilience, breaking the cycle of learned helplessness. 5. *Use practices that are sensitive to the patient's culture, ethnicity, and identities,* which include demonstrating sensitivity to group marginalization and encouraging participation in social groups.

136   *James M. Thompson et al.*

Short courses are available for clinicians to develop the skills and knowledge necessary for identifying and working with psychologically traumatized patients. The recognition, diagnosis, and management of paediatric and adolescent psychological trauma require awareness of developmental nuances not discussed in this chapter (Dyregrov & Yule, 2006).

Could this be PTSD? Barriers and Facilitators to Recognition and Diagnosis

Awareness of barriers and facilitators can help recognition that patients might have been psychologically traumatized (Forbes, 2009, Cooper et al., 2014, Feliciano, 2009; Sareen, 2018; Possemato et al., 2018). Barriers include not seeking care owing to: stigma; negative treatment beliefs; past negative health care or institutional experiences; employment concerns; worry that clinicians will not understand their cultural or occupational contexts; lack of continuity of care; geographical barriers to care; and a lack of time or transportation to seek care. Patients can be reluctant to discuss past traumatic events because of guilt, embarrassment, or symptom exacerbation caused by recalling their traumatic memories, and can even be amnestic regarding the components of some events. Clinicians often are pressed for time in busy settings and might not be fully aware of psychological trauma-informed principles or might feel uncomfortable or unskilled in asking about psychological trauma. Finally, referral by primary care clinicians to providers specialized in psychological trauma care can be limited owing to geography, limited referral pathways, and limited supply.

Just as there are barriers, there also are facilitators that primary care clinicians can use to promote PTSD recognition and diagnosis (Dückers et al., 2016; Possemato et al., 2018). For example, primary care clinicians can assume that all patients have had psychologically stressful experiences. Even though most people exposed to potentially psychologically traumatic events do not become chronically traumatized, providers can ask routinely about psychological trauma, when there are reasons to ask. Several visits with the patient might be necessary to develop trust, which can be established by letting the patient know that their clinician understands about psychological trauma. Passive means include putting posters and pamphlets in waiting and examination rooms. Active means include listening and being prepared to show empathy. Providers need to remain flexible by tailoring approaches to individual patients rather than using the same approach for everyone, owing to the heterogeneity of potentially psychologically traumatic events, coping styles, and PTSD courses. Options for initiating the discussion include suggesting that stressful life events can have lifetime effects in some people, or that one possibility for their problems is a psychological injury that can be managed. In addition, keeping questions open-ended and probing about past or ongoing psychological trauma, give patients permission and a safe space to disclose, within their abilities to cope. Finally, primary care clinicians can engage

Recognizing PTSD in Primary Care 137

and inform families and supportive peers, since often they are instrumental in bringing patients to care in the first place.

Attention by clinicians to barriers and facilitators enables patients to feel more comfortable about addressing psychological trauma. Trauma patients might not have found a safe, respectful, and confidential environment to disclose. When trauma patients begin disclosing, convey compassion rather than judging or blaming, validate and normalize their feelings, and then ask how they feel. Reframing and reattribution are central in recovery from psychological trauma. Some patients respond well when told that their condition is an understandable and manageable response to psychological stressors, yet others might resist the "disorder" label and might prefer words like "injury".

Screening for PTSD

In screening for PTSD, the first step is recognizing that the patient might have a mental health problem, meaning an emotional, thought content or behavioural difficulty. Most mental health problems are mild, transient, and normal reactions to the stresses of daily life, influenced by personality and learned responses. However, when mental health problems are severe enough to significantly impair physical, mental, or social functioning, then clinicians need to consider psychiatric disorders. The key is to initiate discussion when the patient is ready and when the provider thinks that exploring psychological trauma will help. "No pain, no gain" means that beginning to talk about psychological trauma is often painful for patients, but that it is a necessary first step. The need for early intervention must be balanced with timing that first step appropriately. In other words, initiating discussions when the patient is ready to disclose and when the provider thinks that exploring psychological trauma will be most effective and helpful is an important part of providing care.

Current guidelines do not recommend formally screening all primary care patients for PTSD (Phoenix Australia, 2013; Katzman et al., 2014). Instead, guidelines support a targeted strategy, offering screening to patients with risk indicators including prior adverse childhood experiences, physical health problems, chronic pain, depressed mood, anxiety, suicidality, at-risk occupations, or other exposures to potentially traumatizing events (Brady, 1997; Sareen, 2018; Morgan et al., 2017)). We suggest, however, that screening be considered routinely following exposure to two common types of potentially psychologically traumatic events: the unexpected death of someone close or motor vehicle accidents. Full criteria for PTSD can emerge months to years after a potentially psychologically traumatic events exposure; accordingly, there is a need for periodic screening of at-risk patients as they age to confirm cases of late onset or late emergence PTSD (McFarlane, 2017).

Several brief PTSD screening tools have been evaluated in primary care settings. The four-question Primary Care PTSD DSM-5 (PC-PTSD-5)

138 *James M. Thompson et al.*

screener shown in Box 4.1 is easily administered and has performance characteristics as good as any other (Freedy et al., 2010; Prins et al., 2015; Spoont et al., 2013; Sareen, 2018). A positive screen can be used to aid a patient in considering the PTSD diagnosis. The 20-item PTSD Checklist for the DSM-5 (PCL-5) both screens for PTSD and monitors symptoms over time (Weathers et al., 2013).

Screening tools are not diagnostic: each tool can lead to false positives and false negatives. Researchers continue to evaluate PTSD screening tools in different occupations and cultures (Freedy et al., 2010; Spoont et al., 2013). Screening therefore must be coupled with access to high-quality mental health services to be effective and to provide a diagnosis (Sareen, 2018).

The United States Army's integrated collaborative care Re-Engineering Systems of Primary Care Treatment in the Military (RESPECT-Mil) program is a treatment model demonstrated to coordinate screening, assessment and treatment of active duty soldiers with depression or PTSD (Engel et al., 2016; Morgan et al., 2017). The program coordinates primary care providers, care facilitators, and behavioural health specialists serving soldiers with behavioural health needs. The RESPECT-Mil program enables Army commanders to ensure that members are screened in primary care settings that are embedded in trauma-informed mental health care systems.

BOX 4.1 PC-PTSD (Primary Care PTSD) screening tool, DSM-5 version (National Center for PTSD)

Sometimes things happen to people that are unusually or especially frightening, horrible, or traumatic. For example: A serious accident or fire, a physical or sexual assault or abuse, an earthquake or flood, a war, seeing someone be killed or seriously injured, or having a loved one die through homicide or suicide.

Have you ever experienced this kind of event? YES / NO

If no, screen total = 0. Please stop here.

If yes, please answer the questions below.

In the past month, have you...

1. Had nightmares about the event(s) or thought about the event(s) when you did not want to? YES / NO
2. Tried hard not to think about the event(s) or went out of your way to avoid situations that reminded you of the event(s)? YES / NO
3. Been constantly on guard, watchful, or easily startled? YES / NO
4. Felt numb or detached from people, activities, or your surroundings? YES / NO

> 5. Felt guilty or unable to stop blaming yourself or others for the event(s) or any problems the event(s) may have caused? YES / NO
>
> Interpretation: Answering yes to 3 or more of 5 suggests PTSD with maximum sensitivity, while a cut-point of 4 or more maximizes specificity.
>
> Note: Not to be used for diagnosis or to rule out PTSD.

PTSD Diagnosis

The Diagnostic and Statistical Manual of Mental Disorders provides diagnostic criteria for PTSD (American Psychiatric Association, 2013). Criteria categories include exposure to a traumatizing event, the presence of intrusion symptoms, persistent avoidance of stimuli associated with the event, negative thought or mood alterations associated with the event, and markedly altered arousal, duration of symptoms, a requirement for clinically significant distress or impairment, and a requirement that the symptoms are not attributable to another physical or mental health condition or addiction. The manual provides criteria for subtypes with dissociative symptoms, for delayed expression PTSD, and for PTSD in children aged six years and younger (see American Psychiatric Association, 2013 for a full discussion of the criteria).

The 30-item Clinician-Administered PTSD Scale (CAPS) is a structured interview for making a diagnosis and assessing symptom severity (Weathers et al., 2013; Sareen, 2018). When adults present within 30 days of stressor exposure and meet PTSD criteria with functional impairment for the first time, the primary care clinician would consider acute stress disorder (Bryant, Stein, & Hermann, 2019). When symptoms persist longer than a month, then the considered diagnosis could be Acute Stress Disorder or PTSD, and after three months as PTSD (American Psychiatric Association, 2013). Roughly a third of those diagnosed with PTSD recover in a year, a third over the next decade, and a third are still symptomatic more than ten years after the traumatizing event (Sareen, 2018). PTSD symptoms range in severity and can wax and wane over time. Patients with partial PTSD symptoms could have subthreshold PTSD stages (McFarlane et al. 2017). Delayed onset or expression can occur years or even decades following index events. "Complex PTSD" occurs in response to repeated, chronic stressor exposure, often during childhood or sexual violence. Researchers have described "posttraumatic growth" resulting from exposure to potentially psychologically traumatic events whereby the individual eventually becomes mentally healthier, as a result of PTSD therapy for example (Schubert, Schmidt, & Rosner, 2016).

140 *James M. Thompson et al.*

Diagnostic and Statistical Manual of Mental Disorders criterion "H" emphasizes the need to rule out a physical health condition that could explain the patient's presentation, meaning medical-social history and examination findings. Little has been published on the primary care differential diagnoses for symptoms in patients who might have psychological trauma. While clinical experience suggests that the full PTSD syndrome has a very narrow differential diagnosis, comorbidities and co-occurrences of other conditions are common. Therefore, clinicians must consider alternative, comorbid, or co-occurring diagnoses that would explain the symptoms, including another psychiatric disorder, a physical condition, chronic pain, or medically unexplained symptoms.

Medically unexplained symptoms account for more than a third of primary care presentations and often are comorbid with PTSD (McFarlane et al., 2008; Haller et al., 2015; Sareen, 2018). Principles for managing medically unexplained symptoms are similar to those for PTSD. The basis is a good provider–patient relationship, with attention to the patient's story and active listening to understand what matters to the patient. When no diagnosis is found to explain the symptoms, then non-judgmental attitude, identity sensitivity, cultural awareness, collaborative patient-centred care, social support, assisted reattribution, symptom treatment with medications and psychotherapy, and watchful management all play roles (Edwards et al., 2010; Kroenke, 2014). There is emerging evidence that medically unexplained symptoms could arise in vulnerable individuals from determinants common to PTSD as part of a common systemic response to severe psychological stress (McFarlane et al., 2017), which could explain why medical unexplained symptoms co-occurring with PTSD can respond to PTSD treatment.

PTSD Treatment

Owing to delays in help-seeking and long wait times for referrals, primary care clinicians play key roles in identifying traumatized patients and engaging them in treatment (Forbes, 2009; Cooper et al., 2014; Sareen, 2018). Primary care clinicians participate in all three stages of prevention: primary, secondary, and tertiary. Primary prevention includes mitigating psychological trauma in the first month after exposure; for example, by using psychological "first aid" (Forbes, 2009). Guidelines recommend individualized practical and emotional support, encouraging helpful coping strategies, engaging social supports, and providing trauma-informed psychotherapy (Forbes, 2009; Phoenix Australia, 2013). Secondary prevention to limit or reverse the progression of established PTSD begins with identifying and engaging patients. In practising trauma-informed primary care, clinicians can help patients to begin treatment sooner. PTSD treatment includes pharmacotherapy and psychotherapy for the PTSD (American Psychological Association, 2017, Forbes et al., 2019), as well as treatment for co-occurring physical and mental health problems, chronic pain and medically unexplained symptoms. Tertiary prevention in persistent PTSD aims to prevent the onset or worsening of physical, mental, and social health problems. Clinicians encourage compliance with treatment and assist patients to learn to live well using a recovery paradigm.

Primary care clinicians both initiate treatment and provide continuity of whole-person care while their patients receive specialized trauma therapy, ideally within collaborative teams tailored to meet individual needs. PTSD treatment is a three-phase process consisting of: (i) stabilizing psychological and physical symptoms, (ii) processing traumatic memories, and iii) integrating psychological trauma awareness into the patient's world- and self-views to enable reconnection with family, work, and community (Schumann & Miller, 2000). Individualized pharmacotherapy and psychotherapy both play roles in PTSD treatment. Primary care clinicians refer PTSD patients to psychiatrists and psychologists for severe functional problems, unclear diagnosis, long chronicity, complex presentations, and insufficient response to basic treatment (Levine & Jain, 2002). Pharmacotherapy and psychotherapy initiated by primary care clinicians stabilizes and encourages patients to engage in ongoing treatment, including referral for care by other providers.

Pharmacotherapy by primary care clinicians decreases intrusive thoughts and images, phobic avoidance, pathological hyperarousal, hypervigilance, irritability and anger, and depression (Stein, 2019). Selective serotonin reuptake inhibitors (SSRIs) and serotonin-norepinephrine reuptake inhibitors (SNRIs) can reduce the core symptoms as well as associated depression and impairment (Katzman et al., 2014; Stein, 2019). Used as first-line treatment, these medications help to stabilize symptoms in the first phase of PTSD treatment, reducing the risk of chronicity in this vulnerable population (Katzman et al., 2014). Trials for at least six to eight weeks are used in doses equivalent to those used in major depression. Patients with PTSD who respond to pharmacotherapy may need to remain on therapeutic doses for a year or more (Ipser & Stein, 2012). As in other psychiatric disorders, the search for effective pharmacological and psychotherapeutic treatments for PTSD is ongoing (Forbes et al., 2019).

Psychotherapy by primary care clinicians begins with trauma-informed counselling. Depending on training and comfort, primary physicians can use imaginal exposure, systematic desensitization for avoided activities, and cognitive reformulation, particularly for less complex forms of PTSD such as first onset following motor vehicle accidents or after the unexpected loss of a loved one (Classen & Heber, 2017; Hoge & Chard, 2018; Stein, 2019). While primary care providers should consider referring any patient with PTSD, patients with more complex PTSD (e.g., in the context of sexual violence) generally should be referred to specialized therapists. Disability, meaning work, family, and community role participation restriction can be identified simply by asking how PTSD affects their life, and then addressed with trauma-informed rehabilitation. Family and positive peer support engagement are important adjuncts to clinical treatment. The emotional,

142 *James M. Thompson et al.*

behavioural, and functional impacts of a disorder like PTSD challenge a person's personal and social identities (Thompson et al., 2017). Recovery includes encouraging membership in social groups and integrating new, positive social identities (Jetten, Haslam, & Haslam, 2012).

Experiences today can reactivate a patient's traumatic past through triggering, also referred to as re-experiencing (Sareen, 2018). Patients can be triggered by physical examinations and invasive procedures. Taking a trauma-informed approach includes asking permission and demonstrating before doing, while assessing the patient's reaction along the way. A triggered patient might suddenly freeze, display unexpected anger, pull away, or shut down. If the patient freezes and stops responding, use a "grounding" technique by reminding them in a clear voice where they are and who you are, avoiding touching them, and invite them to experience the sensations of their feet on the floor or their body on the chair (Classen & Heber, 2017).

Treatment dropout is common (Hoge & Chard, 2018). Patients and families may find it helpful to know that symptoms are normal responses to psychologically stressful events, and that everybody recovers on a different pathway. Effective clinical approaches include encouraging psychologically traumatized patients to focus on their coping strengths, encouraging collaboration, empowering the patient, and offering choice in treatment processes, including choice of provider gender; for example, a male patient traumatized by male rape might prefer a female provider. When patients are referred for care by other clinicians, the patient should be reassured that the primary care clinician will still be there for them. Social support can be promoted through education for the patient and family to help them understand the nature of the condition and shape a positive future.[1]

The Many Faces of Adult PTSD in Primary Care

Clinicians who connect well with patients are good listeners who understand that "the diagnosis lies in the patient's story" (Kroenke, 2014). In Table 4.A1, we demonstrate common presentations for some of the faces of PTSD and other sequelae of psychological trauma among adults in primary care practice. These vignettes demonstrate how primary care clinicians can see through the fog to identify and manage possible PTSD (Feliciano, 2009). In reading these stories, primary care clinicians are encouraged to think about the principles of trauma-informed primary care described above and consider what they might do in their practices. The vignettes are based on adult cases, but psychological trauma also occurs in children and adolescents, and needs to be recognized and treated in those age groups.

Summary

The principles we demonstrated in the current chapter can help primary care clinicians to reflect on their approach to psychologically traumatized patients. In Box 4.2, we summarize the basic principles for easy reference

BOX 4.2 A knowledge transfer tool summarizing principles of recognizing PTSD in primary care

Recognizing PTSD in PRIMARY CARE

Posttraumatic stress disorder (PTSD) is a syndrome of emotional, behavioural, thought, and bodily changes that can occur following exposure to traumatic events in all age groups.

Psychological trauma is...

A psychiatric injury that occurs in response to psychologically traumatic events characterized by threat to self.

Trauma-Aware primary care practices...

- Understand how psychological trauma can change people.
- Recognize and help psychologically traumatized patients.

Psychologically traumatic events and PTSD are common AMONG PRIMARY CARE PATIENTS

- Psychologically traumatic events include: adverse childhood experiences; motor vehicle accidents; physical or sexual assault or abuse; witnessing or experiencing threat, injury or death; war; natural disasters; physical health experiences; or unexpected death of a loved one.
- In the U.S. and Canada, about half to three-quarters of men and women have been exposed to potentially traumatizing events, and about 10–20% of those develop PTSD.

PTSD HAS MANY PRIMARY CARE PRESENTATIONS

- PTSD symptoms and signs variably include anger, irritability, fear, negative self- or world-view, self-harming, withdrawal, anxiety, hypervigilance, intrusive thoughts, sleep disturbances, flashbacks, avoidance or dissociation (depersonalization or derealization).
- PTSD often co-occurs with physical health conditions, chronic pain, sleep disturbance, medically unexplained symptoms, substance use disorders, and other psychiatric conditions.
- Risk indicators: Exposure to psychologically traumatic events, physical or mental health problems, suicidality, lack of social support, or occupations with a higher likelihood of exposure to such events.

PTSD Screening

- Screen using trauma-aware interviewing when the patient has risk indicators and is ready.

---

*Primary Care-PTSD Screener for DSM-5 (PC-PTSD-5)**

Sometimes things happen to people that are unusually or especially frightening, horrible, or traumatic. Have you ever experienced this kind of event? If yes, in the past month, have you…	Yes	No
Had nightmares about it or thought about it when you did not want to?	Yes	No
Tried hard not to think about it or went out of your way to avoid situations that reminded you of it?	Yes	No
Were constantly on guard, watchful, or easily startled?	Yes	No
Felt numb or detached from others, activities, or your surroundings?	Yes	No
Felt guilty or unable to stop blaming yourself or others for the event or any problems the event may have caused?	Yes	No

0 = Negative Screen 1–2/5 = Consider Subthreshold PTSD
3–5/5 = Possible PTSD

- Positive screens require diagnosis; negative screens do not rule out psychological trauma.
- Diagnose using DSM-5 criteria. Consider differential diagnoses and co-occurring conditions.

PTSD treatment in primary care

- Three phase therapy: Stabilize psychological and physical symptoms, process traumatic perceptions, and integrate psychological trauma awareness into world- and self-views.
- Initiate medication and psychotherapy depending on training and comfort. Provide continuity of care.
- Refer for: Unclear diagnosis, severe functional problems, chronicity, complex presentations, specialized psychotherapy, or insufficient response to basic treatment.

Source: Prins et al. (2015). Primary Care PTSD Screen for DSM-5 (PC-PTSD-5) [Measurement instrument]. Open source available from www.ptsd.va.gov.

for readers. In all walks of life, many people are exposed to potentially psychologically traumatic events and most do well. Some develop acute stress disorder, PTSD or other types of psychological trauma, and some experience delayed onset of PTSD later in life. PTSD is common in primary care populations, but under-detected. Trauma-informed clinicians are able to recognize and efficiently help traumatized patients while dealing with busy practices. Becoming a "trauma-informed" primary care provider starts by understanding how psychological trauma can change the ways that people feel, think, and behave. Recognizing that PTSD presents to primary care providers with many different faces and follows a variety of types of potentially psychologically traumatic events, it is important to develop efficient, trauma-informed interviewing skills that encourage patients to talk about the trauma when they are ready. The differential diagnoses for presenting symptoms can be broad in mild PTSD. Moreover, many PTSD patients have co-occurring or comorbid chronic physical health conditions, chronic pain, medically unexplained symptoms, and other mental health problems. Targeted and appropriate use of brief screening tools like the PC-PTSD can assist in recognizing possible subthreshold or full PTSD to engage patients in diagnosis and treatment. Prompt recognition and effective treatment mitigates the effects of diverse psychological traumas, improving participation in life roles and optimizing quality of life.

Note

1 A full discussion of PTSD treatment is beyond the scope of this chapter. Readers are encouraged to review current practice guidelines, for example the online resource by Stein (2019). Primary care clinicians can direct families to the growing availability of credible online information, for example the resource at www.uptodate.com/contents/search.

References

American Psychological Association. (2017). Clinical practice guideline for the treatment of posttraumatic stress disorder (PTSD) in adults. Guideline Development Panel for the Treatment of PTSD in Adults. Retrieved from. www. apa.org/ptsd-guideline/ptsd.pdf

American Psychiatric Association. (2013). *Diagnostic and statistical manual of mental disorders*, Fifth Edition. Arlington, VA: American Psychiatric Association.

Brady, K. T. (1997). Posttraumatic stress disorder and comorbidity: Recognizing the many faces of PTSD. *The Journal of Clinical Psychiatry*, *58* (Suppl 9), 12–15.

Bruce, S. E., Weisberg, R. B., Dolan, R. T., Machan, J. T. Kessler, R. C., Manchester, G., … Keller, M. B. (2001). Trauma and posttraumatic stress disorder in primary care patients. *Primary Care Companion Journal of Clinical Psychiatry*, *3*(5), 211–217. PMCID: PMC181217 PMID: 15014575

Bryant, R., Stein, M. B., & Hermann, R. (2019). Acute stress disorder in adults: Epidemiology, pathogenesis, clinical manifestations, course, and diagnosis.

Retrieved from www.uptodate.com/contents/acute-stress-disorder-in-adults-epidemiology-pathogenesis-clinical-manifestations-course-and-diagnosis.

Carleton, R. N., Afifi, T. O., Turner, S., Taillieu, T., Duranceau, S., LeBouthillier, D. M., ... Hozempa, K. (2018). Mental disorder symptoms among public safety personnel in Canada. *The Canadian Journal of Psychiatry*, *63*(1), 54–64.

Canadian Institute for Public Safety Research and Treatment (CIPSRT). (2019). Glossary of terms: A shared understanding of the common terms used to describe psychological trauma (version 2.0). Regina, SK.

Classen, C. C., & Heber, A. (2017). Posttraumatic Stress Disorder – A primer for primary care physicians. Retrieved from www.mdcme.ca.

Cooper, J., Metcalf, O., & Phelps, A. (2014). PTSD – An update for general practitioners. *Australian Family Physician*, *43*(11), 754–757.

Cox, D. W., Baugha, L. M., McCloskeya, K. D., & Iyar, M. (2018). Social causation or social erosion? Evaluating the association between social support and PTSD among Veterans in a transition program. *Journal of Military, Veteran and Family Health*, *5*(1), 71–79.

Dückers, M. L. A., Alisic, E., & Brewin, C. R. (2016). A vulnerability paradox in the cross-national prevalence of post-traumatic stress disorder. *The British Journal of Psychiatry*, *209*(4), 300–305. https://doi.org/10.1192/bjp.bp.115.176628

Dyregrov, A., & Yule, W. (2006). A review of PTSD in children. *Child and Adolescent Mental Health*, *11*(4), 176–184.

Edwards, T. M., Stern, A., Clarke, D. D., Ivbijaro, G., & Kasney, L. M. (2010). The treatment of patients with medically unexplained symptoms in primary care: A review of the literature. *Mental Health in Family Medicine*, *7*(4), 209–221.

Engel, C. C., Jaycox, L. H., Freed, M. C., Bray, R. M., Brambilla, D., Zatzick, D., ... Katon, W. J. (2016). Centrally assisted collaborative telecare for post-traumatic stress disorder and depression among military personnel attending primary care: A randomized clinical trial. *JAMA Internal Medicine*, *176*(7), 948–956. https://doi.org/10.1001/jamainternmed.2016.2402

Espinel, Z., & Shaw, J. A. (2018). PTSD in children. In: C. B. Nemeroff, & C. Marmar (eds), *Post-Traumatic Stress Disorder*. Chicago, IL: Oxford University Press.

Feliciano, M. (2009). An overview of PTSD for the adult primary care provider. *The Journal for Nurse Practitioners*, *5*(7), 516–522. https://doi.org/10.1016/j.nurpra.2008.12.009

Forbes D. (2009). Post-traumatic stress disorder best practice GP guidelines. *Australian Family Physician*, *38*(3), 106–111.

Forbes, D., Bennett, N., Biddle, D., Crompton, D., McHugh, T., Elliott, P., & Creamer, M. (2005). Clinical presentations and treatment outcomes of peacekeeper veterans with PTSD: Preliminary findings. *American Journal of Psychiatry*, *162*(11), 2188–2190. https://doi.org/10.1176/appi.ajp.162.11.2188

Forbes D., Pedlar D., Adler, A. B., Bennett, C., Bryant, R., Busuttil, W., ... Wessley, S. (2019). Treatment of military-related posttraumatic stress disorder: Challenges, innovations, and the way forward. *International Review of Psychiatry*, *31*(1), 95–110.

Fortier, J., Turner, S., Tailleau, T., Sareen, J., & Afifi, T. O. (2019). Positive functioning and emotional well-being among military personnel and the general population with and without a history of child abuse in Canada. *Journal of Military, Veteran and Family Health*, *5*(1), 105–114. https://doi.org/10.3138/jmvfh.2017-0039

Freedy, J. R., Steenkamp, M. M., Magruder, K. M., Yeager, D. E., Zoller, J. E., Hueston, W. J., & Carek, P. J. (2010). Post-traumatic stress disorder screening test performance in civilian primary care. *Family Practice*, *27*(6), 615–624. https://doi.org/10.1093/fampra/cmq049

Galovski, T. E., Mott, J. M., Young-Xu, Y., & Resick, P. A. (2010). Gender differences in the clinical presentation of PTSD and its concomitants in survivors of interpersonal assault. *Journal of Interpersonal Violence*, *26*(4), 789–806. https://doi.org/10.1177/0886260510365865

Goodstein, R. K. (1985). Common clinical problems in the elderly: Camouflaged by ageism and atypical presentation. *Psychiatric Annals*, 15(5), 299–312. https://doi.org/10.3928/0048-5713-19850501-05

Greene, T., Neria, Y., & Gross, R. (2016). Prevalence, detection and correlates of PTSD in the primary care setting: A systematic review. *Journal of Clinical Psychology in Medical Settings*, *23*(2), 160–180.

Griffin, B. J., Purcell, N., Burkman, K., Litz, B. T., Bryan, C. J., Schmitz, M., ... Maguen, S. (2019). Moral injury: An integrative review. *Journal of Traumatic Stress*, *32*(3), 350–362.

Haller, H., Cramer, H., Lauche, R., & Dobos, G. (2015). Somatoform disorders and medically unexplained symptoms in primary care: A systematic review and meta-analysis of prevalence. *Deutsches Ärzteblatt International*, *112*(16), 279–287.

Harriet J., Rosenberg, S. D., Wolford, G. L., Manganiello, P. D., Brunette, M. F., & Boynton, R. A. (2000). The relationship between trauma, PTSD and medical utilization in three high risk medical populations. *The International Journal of Psychiatry in Medicine*, *30*(3), 247–259. https://doi.org/10.2190/J8M8-YDTE-46CB-GYDK

Harris, M. E., & Fallot, R. D. (eds). (2001). *New directions for mental health services. Using trauma theory to design service systems.* San Francisco, CA: Jossey-Bass.

Hoge, C. W., & Chard, K. M. (2018). A window into the evolution of trauma-focused psychotherapies for posttraumatic stress disorder. *JAMA*, *319*(4), 343–345. https://doi.org/10.1001/jama.2017.21880

Ipser, J. C., & Stein, D. J. (2012). Evidence-based pharmacotherapy of post-traumatic stress disorder (PTSD). *International Journal of Neuropsychopharmacology*, *15*(6), 825–840. https://doi.org/10.1017/S1461145711001209

Jetten, J., Haslam, C., & Haslam, S. A. (eds). (2012). *The social cure: identity, health and well-being.* London: Psychology Press.

Katzman, M. A., Bleau, P., Blier, P., Chokka, P., Kjernisted, K., Van Ameringen, M., and the Canadian Anxiety Guidelines Initiative Group on behalf of the Anxiety Disorders Association of Canada. (2014). Canadian Anxiety Disorders Guidelines Initiative: Clinical practice guidelines for the management of anxiety, posttraumatic stress and obsessive-compulsive disorders. *BMC Psychiatry*, *14*(Suppl 1), S1. https://doi.org/10.1186/1471-244X-14-S1-S1

Kroenke, K. (2014). A practical and evidence-based approach to common symptoms: A narrative review. *Annals of Internal Medicine*, *161*(8), 579–586.

Lanius, R. A., Hopper, J. W., & Menon, R. S. (2003). Individual differences in a husband and wife who developed PTSD after a motor vehicle accident: A functional MRI case study. *American Journal of Psychiatry*, *160*(4), 667–669.

Levine, R. E., & Jain, S. (2002). Recognizing and treating posttraumatic stress disorder: A guide for the primary care physician. *Hospital Physician*, *38*(9), 28–37.

148 *James M. Thompson et al.*

Liebschutz, J., Saitz, R., Brower, V., Keane, T.M., Lloyd-Travaglini, C., Averbuch, T., & Samet, J. H. (2007). PTSD in urban primary care: High prevalence and low physician recognition. *Journal of General Internal Medicine*, 22(6), 719–726.

McFarlane, A. C. (2017). Post-traumatic stress disorder is a systemic illness, not a mental disorder: Is Cartesian dualism dead? *Medical Journal of Australia*, 206(6), 248–249.

McFarlane, A. C., Ellis, F. N., Barton, C., Browne, D., & Van Hooff, M. (2008). The conundrum of medically unexplained symptoms: Questions to consider. *Psychosomatics*, 49(5), 369–377.

McFarlane, A. C., Lawrence-Wood, E., Van Hooff, M., Malhi, G. S., & Yehuda, R. (2017). The need to take a staging approach to the biological mechanisms of PTSD and its treatment. *Current Psychiatry Reports*, 19(2), 10. https://doi.org/ 10.1007/s11920-017-0761-2

Mackenzie, C. S., Erickson, J., Deane, F. P., & Wright, M. (2014). Changes in attitudes toward seeking mental health services: A 40-year cross-temporal meta-analysis. *Clinical Psychology Review*, 34(2), 99–106. https://doi.org/10.1016/ j.cpr.2013.12.001

McQuaid, J. R., Pedrelli, P., McCahill, M. E., & Stein, M. B. (2001). Reported trauma, post-traumatic stress disorder and major depression among primary care patients. *Psychological Medicine*, 31(7), 1249–1257.

McCreary, D. (2020). Psychology of men and masculinities: Implications for men's experiences of post-traumatic stress disorder. In Ricciardelli, R., Bornstein, S., Hall, A., & Carleton, R. N. (eds), *Handbook of Post-Traumatic Stress: Psychosocial, cultural and biological perspectives*. New York: Informa.

Morgan, J .K., Olmsted, K. R., Bray, R. M., Williams, J., & Engel, C. C. (2017, August). Pain as a moderator of collaborative care treatment effects for PTSD and depression. Paper presented at Military Health System Research Symposium, Kissimmee, FL.

Munro, C. G., Freeman, C. P., & Law, R. (2004). General practitioners' knowledge of post-traumatic stress disorder: A controlled study. *British Journal of General Practice*, 54 (508), 843–847.

National Center for PTSD. Primary Care PTSD Screen for DSM-5 (PC-PTSD-5). Washington, DC: United States Department of Veterans Affairs. Retrieved from: www.ptsd.va.gov/professional/assessment/screens/pc-ptsd.asp.

Osório, C., Carvalho, C., Fertout, M., & Maia, Â. (2012). Prevalence of post-traumatic stress disorder and physical health complaints among Portuguese Army Special Operations Forces deployed in Afghanistan. *Military Medicine*, 177(8), 957–962. https://doi.org/10.7205/MILMED-D-12-00024

Phoenix Australia. (2013). *Australian guidelines for the treatment of Acute Stress Disorder and Posttraumatic Stress Disorder*. Melbourne, Vic: Phoenix Australia Centre for Posttraumatic Mental Health. www.phoenixaustralia.org/resources/ ptsd-guidelines/.

Possemato, K., Wray, L.O., Johnson, E., Webster, B., & Beehler, G. P. (2018). Facilitators and barriers to seeking mental health care among primary care veterans with posttraumatic stress disorder. *Journal of Traumatic Stress*, 31(5), 742–752. https://doi.org/10.1002/jts.22327

Prins, A., Bovin, M. J., Kimerling, R., Kaloupek, D. G., Marx, B. P., Pless Kaiser, A., & Schnurr, P. P. (2015). The Primary Care PTSD Screen for DSM-5 (PC-PTSD-5). *Journal of General Internal Medicine*, 31, 1206–1211. https://doi. org/10.1007/s11606-016-3703-5

Purkey, E., Patel, R., & Phillips, S. P. (2018). Trauma-informed care: Better care for everyone. *Canadian Family Physician*, *64*(3), 170–172.

Reynolds, J. J. (1997). Post-traumatic stress disorder after childbirth: The phenomenon of traumatic birth. *Canadian Medical Association Journal*, *156*(6), 831–835. www.cmaj.ca/content/156/6/831

Richardson, J. D., Thompson, J. M., Boswall, M., & Jetly, R. (2010). Horror comes home – Veterans with posttraumatic stress disorder. *Canadian Family Physician*, *56*, 430–433.

Sareen, J. (2018). Posttraumatic stress disorder in adults: Epidemiology, pathophysiology, clinical manifestations, course, assessment, and diagnosis. Retrieved from www.uptodate.com/contents/posttraumatic-stress-disorder-in-adults-epidemiology-pathophysiology-clinical-manifestations-course-assessment-and-diagnosis.

Schubert, C. F., Schmidt, U., & Rosner, R. (2016). Posttraumatic growth in populations with posttraumatic stress disorder – A systematic review on growth-related psychological constructs and biological variables. *Clinical Psychology & Psychotherapy*, *23*(6), 469–486.

Schumann, L., & Miller, J. L. (2000). Post-traumatic stress disorder in primary care practice. *Journal of the American Academy of Nurse Practitioners*, *12*(11), 475–482. https://doi.org/10.1111/j.1745-7599.2000.tb00159.x

Spoont, M., Arbisi, P., Fu, S., Greer, N., Kehle-Forbes, S., Meis, L., ... Wilt, T. J. (2013). Screening for post-traumatic stress disorder (PTSD) in primary care: A systematic review. (VA-ESP Project #09-009). Retrieved from www.usafp.org/wp-content/uploads/2013/12/ptsd-screening-2012-systematic-review.pdf.

Spottswood, M., Davydow, D. S., & Huang, H. (2017). The prevalence of Posttraumatic Stress Disorder in primary care: A systematic review. *Harvard Review of Psychiatry*, *25*(4), 159–169. https://doi.org/10.1097/HRP.0000000000000136

Stein, M. B. (2019). Approach to treating posttraumatic stress disorder in adults. Retrieved from www.uptodate.com/contents/approach-to-treating-posttraumatic-stress-disorder-in-adults?topicRef=501&source=see_link.

Stein, M. B., McQuaid, J. R., Pedrelli, P., Lenox, R., & McCahill, M. E. (2000). Posttraumatic Stress Disorder in the primary care medical setting. *General Hospital Psychiatry*, *22*(4), 261–269. https://doi.org/10.1016/S0163-8343(00)00080-3

Taubman-Ben-Ari, O., Rabinowitz, J., Feldman, D., & Vaturi, R. (2001). Post-traumatic Stress Disorder in primary-care settings: Prevalence and physicians' detection. *Psychological Medicine*, *31*(3), 555–560. https://doi.org/10.1017/S0033291701003658

Thompson, J. M., Lockhart, W., Roach, M. B., Atuel, H., Bélanger, S., Black, T., ... Truusa, T. T. (2017). Veterans' identities and well-being in transition to civilian life – A resource for policy analysts, program designers, service providers and researchers. Report of the Veterans' Identities Research Theme Working Group, Canadian Institute for Military and Veteran Health Research Forum 2016 (Cat. No. V32-279/2017E). Charlottetown, PE: Research Directorate, Veterans Affairs Canada. Retrieved from https://cimvhr.ca/documents/Thompson%20 2017%20veterans%20Identities%20Technical%20Report.pdf.

Thompson, J. M., Van Til, L. D., Zamorski, M. A., Garber, B., Dursun, S., Fikretoglu, D., ... Pedlar, D. (2016). Mental health of Canadian Armed Forces veterans – Review of population studies. *JMVFH*, *2*(1), 70–86. http://dx.doi.org/10.3138/jmvfh.3258

150 *James M. Thompson et al.*

Van Ameringen, M., Mancini, C., Patterson, B., & Boyle, M. H. (2008). Post-traumatic stress disorder in Canada. *CNS Neuroscience & Therapeutics, 14*(3), 171–181.

Wang, P. S., Berglund, P., Olfson, M., Pincus, H. A., Wells, K. B., & Kessler, R. C. (2005). Failure and delay in initial treatment contact after first onset of mental disorders in the national comorbidity survey replication. *Archives of General Psychiatry, 62*(6), 603–613. https://doi.org/10.1001/archpsyc.62.6.603

Weathers, F. W., Litz, B. T., Keane, T. M., Palmieri, P. A., Marx, B. P., & Schnurr, P. P. (2013). The PTSD Checklist for DSM-5 (PCL-5). Retrieved from www.ptsd.va.gov.

Appendix 4.1

Table 4.A1 Some of the many faces of adult PTSD. These fictitious cases demonstrate principles of trauma-informed primary care

Presentation	Comments
New mother with fatigue following a difficult delivery. She has poor sleep and nightmares about the delivery. Delivery was managed by an obstetrician she had never met, and complicated by foetal distress requiring a physically traumatic forceps procedure. She was sexually abused in childhood. Trauma-informed supportive mental health care was initiated.	Reynolds (1997) proposed a variant of PTSD that may occur following psychologically traumatic birth experiences. They recommended: a careful history to look for pre-pregnancy psychological trauma that could place the patient at risk for a traumatic birth experience; good communication and effective pain control during childbirth; careful postpartum care demonstrating understanding of the woman's birth experience; and ruling out postpartum depression.
Angry young man with stomach aches. Edgy and impatient from the outset. He gets angry at some of the questions and storms out of the clinic. The provider restores their relationship and gains his trust. No explanatory physical health diagnosis found. Physically abused by father in childhood. Referred to a mental health team, reassured that provider will care for him. Explores male gender-related coping styles.	Anger is normal, but disproportionate anger might be explained by depression or PTSD, particularly in men (Seidler et al., 2016; McCreary, 2020). Adverse childhood experiences can be associated with later life coping and mental health problems (Fortier et al., 2019). Gastrointestinal symptoms commonly can be associated with psychiatric disorders, leading to the hypothesis of a physiologically linked "gut-brain axis" (Carabotti et al., 2015). Since medically unexplained somatic symptoms are so common in PTSD, some researchers propose that PTSD is a systemic illness (McFarlane, 2017).
Young woman self-harming. The provider notices scars on her forearms when she presents with non-specific aches and pains. After careful engagement, the provider learns that she has self-harming behaviours including cutting, binge-drinking, and binge-eating with purging. She lives alone with no social support. She was sexually abused and cannot recall her life from age six to 12.	Traumatized patients often need to feel safer and more stable in life (Classen & Heber, 2017). One initial approach while ensuring that she is physically well and not suicidal is to point out that using self-harm was an effective way of coping in the past. Gradually, she can learn better coping strategies to deal with her emotions and recognize triggers that lead her to feel overwhelmed. She can learn that recovery is not linear and that mistakes are learning opportunities. Over time, her somatic symptoms should diminish if there is no co-occurring physical disorder requiring treatment.

(continued)

152 *James M. Thompson et al.*

Table 4.A1 Cont.

Presentation	Comments
Young wife, former military, anxious about foreigners. Husband says she avoids shopping trips, worried about foreigners. The clinician explores her anxiety and rules out explanatory physical health diagnoses. The young Veteran had been released voluntarily from the military. She eventually discloses her combat experiences, including rape while on deployment overseas.	Anxiety is common in PTSD and can be the patient's initial presenting symptom (Henslee et al., 2009). The patient had two potentially traumatic exposures. First, sexual assault is well-recognized cause of PTSD and other forms of psychological trauma (Sareen, 2018). She is referred to a psychotherapist specialized in sexual assault victims, and a peer support group. Second, women in military service increasingly are engaged in combat roles. The constant diligence required of soldiers in insurgency conflicts, where anybody on the street could be a threat, can play a role in the onset of psychological trauma (Forbes et al., 2019).
Elderly patient who wakes at night in distress. Daughter says he has just been moved from his home to a long-term care facility following his wife's death. He wakes at night confused, calling out. He had overseas military experience, but never spoke about it. Reports having nightmares about his service experiences. Clinician listens supportively, makes practical suggestions for the facility clinicians and refers him to a geriatric mental health care team for assessment.	Nightmares and other sleep pathology are common in PTSD (Germain, 2013). Delayed onset or manifestation of PTSD is well recognized, including elderly veterans stressed by institutionalization or the development of new physical health problems or mild cognitive impairment (Bonwick & Morris, 1996; Ruzich, Loo, & Robertson, 2005; Sareen, 2018). Elderly Veterans avoid reminders of war and experience restless sleep and chronic anxiety. PTSD symptoms complicate early dementia (Moye, 1997; Johnston, 2015; Hierholzer et al., 1992). It is important to identify mental health problems in the elderly, a heterogenous population less likely to acknowledge psychological difficulties and often seen as simply "getting old" (Goodstein, 1985).
Young man thinking about suicide. Presents with back pain from a car accident. He seems depressed and says his life is a mess. Recently fired from his job as a labourer, and his housemates are demanding rent. In collaboration with a psychologist and social worker, the team stabilizes his suicidal feelings, arranges financial support, and eventually learns that he had a difficult childhood.	Most persons with psychiatric disorders do not contemplate, attempt or complete suicide, but suicidal behaviour commonly is associated with psychiatric disorders, and both are associated with adverse childhood experiences (Sareen, 2018; Fortier et al., 2019). Depression is common in death by suicide and both are associated with PTSD. Multiple factors operate together to induce suicidality, including personal predisposition to suicidal thinking, the presence of an acute life stressor following chronic stressors, limited access to effective supports, impulsivity, and access to lethal means (Thompson et al., 2019).

Presentation	Comments

Complex patient avoiding health care. Diabetic man with chronic lung disease frequently misses follow-up appointments. He makes emergency department visits for urgent problems that could have been avoided with regular follow-up. He smokes and the provider suspects that he drinks. Provider discovers history of several lifetime potentially psychologically traumatic events.

Patients with PTSD can both over- and under-utilize health care and try to manage symptoms with alcohol and other addictive substances (Classen & Heber, 2017). Health care avoidance is typical in males (Seidler et al., 2016). The co-occurrence of physical and mental health conditions and addictions is common in PTSD. Substance withdrawal or PTSD triggering can cause acute anxiety in hospitalized patients. Recognition and treatment of psychological trauma can inform and potentially improve the care and recovery of such patients (Purkey et al., 2018).

Heart attack patient becomes socially withdrawn; high user of urgent health care. A prior healthy, known female patient in a primary care clinic has a myocardial infarction treated in hospital with invasive procedures after nearly dying at home. She makes more frequent clinic and emergency department visits than necessary. Family tell the provider that she rarely leaves the house and has withdrawn from social activities.

Receiving a life-threatening diagnosis and experiencing invasive medical procedures can be psychologically traumatic, particularly in persons traumatized earlier in life. There are many reasons why this patient could be socially withdrawn and excessively utilizing health care services, but PTSD is recognized as a potential iatrogenic complication of experiences with physical disorders and medical treatment (Kwekkeboom & Seng, 2002; Tedstone & Tarrier, 2003; Shalev et al., 1993).

Middle-aged man declines a rectal examination. Known patient presents with difficulty voiding. The clinician offers a rectal examination. The patient declines, offers no explanation, seems anxious, breaks off the appointment, and apologizes as he leaves. In trauma-informed interviewing, the patient discloses that he had been raped years earlier. He is barely holding things together at home and at work. The clinician suspects PTSD and initiates support and referrals.

Sexual assault is well-recognized as one of the types of psychological trauma that can precipitate PTSD. In a study discussed by Sareen (2018), 65% of raped men develop PTSD. Trauma-informed practice means understanding how psychologically traumatized patients react (Purkey et al., 2018). Eventually, the patient and clinician agree to find a way to complete the rectal examination in a psychologically safe way. Brief and online trauma-informed interviewing courses are available for practising primary care clinicians.

(continued)

154 *James M. Thompson et al.*

Table 4.A1 Cont.

Presentation	Comments
Police officer not sleeping and withdrawn from family life. Middle-aged husband says that his wife sleeps poorly and has been withdrawn from family and community life. Provider knows that she is a 15-year police officer. The provider eventually learns that she has been ruminating about an event where she had to shoot a suspect.	Sleep pathology has been linked to PTSD (Germain, 2013). Social withdrawal is common in PTSD. There is substantial evidence that public safety personnel in police, paramedic, correctional and fire services can acquire PTSD and other mental health problems through work experiences (Carleton et al., 2018). Although PTSD symptoms are not uncommon in police officers following shooting incidents (Gersons, 1989), other types of potentially psychological traumatizing exposures are more common in police service. The patient's differential diagnosis includes physical health conditions and the emerging concept of moral injury (Griffin et al., 2019).
Unemployed man with chronic pain. He had been driving a company truck that rolled off the highway a year ago, trapping him until rescued with jaws of life. Orthopaedic injuries left him with chronic pain for which he has been taking pain killers, and he has been drinking alcohol daily. He is on disability insurance and is not working.	Civilian workers can develop occupational PTSD following industrial accidents, interpersonal violence, disasters and motor vehicle accidents (Lanius et al., 2003). Chronic pain is associated with PTSD (Morgan et al., 2017). Since longer time off work reduces the likelihood of return to work, then early recognition and treatment of psychological trauma could prevent prolonged role participation disability (Morganstein, West, & Ursano, 2019).
Demanding patient wants cannabis for chronic pain. A new patient wants a form signed to access cannabis for chronic pain. The patient is impatient and quick to anger when asked questions. He feels frustrated from years of living with the pain, and simply wants to try cannabis. He was reluctant to disclose his psychologically traumatic past.	PTSD is more prevalent in patients with chronic pain (Sareen, 2018). Provider–patient communication can be difficult when unrecognized PTSD manifests as agitated behaviours during clinic visits (Purkey et al., 2018). Paradoxically, public interest and confidence in the use of cannabis for treating chronic pain and psychiatric disorders like PTSD are ahead of scientific evidence, creating confrontation opportunities (Ladouceur, 2018). Trauma-informed clinicians can manage conflict to find the best way forward.

Presentation	Comments
New Canadian struggling with childcare. A refugee wearing a mix of Canadian winter clothes and traditional clothing presents withdrawn, depressed, and anxious. A church volunteer says she escaped from her home country after her husband was killed in front of the family. She fears authorities.	Trauma-informed care includes cultural competency. A growing population of displaced persons have arrived in Canada after leaving home countries disrupted by war and socioeconomic upheaval. Cultural differences complicate mental health care, both within groups native to our own countries and among immigrants (Kooab et al., 2016, Sareen, 2018; Dückers et al., 2016).
New patient with diagnosed PTSD. A female patient moves to town and presents with a previous diagnosis of PTSD. The provider obtains prior records, confirms the diagnosis, arranges referral to a local trauma-informed psychologist for collaborative care, and starts building the provider–patient relationship by learning her story.	When PTSD is confirmed, it is important to attend to possible co-occurrence of other physical and psychiatric diagnoses, chronic pain, medically unexplained symptoms and suicidality. There are concerns that PTSD can be over-diagnosed for a variety of complex psychosocial reasons when other physical or psychological diagnoses might better explain the patient's condition (Gravely et al., 2011). PTSD might be viewed as preferred over other diagnosis owing to stigma or for socioeconomic reasons.

Table References

Bonwick, R. J., & Morris, P. L. P. (1996). Posttraumatic stress disorder in elderly war veterans. *Geriatric Psychiatry, 11*(2), 1071–1076.

Carabotti, M., Scirocco, A., Maselli, M. A., & Severi, C. (2015). The gut-brain axis: Interactions between enteric microbiota, central and enteric nervous systems. *Annals of Gastroenterology, 28*(2), 203.

Carleton, R. N., Afifi, T. O., Turner, S., Taillieu, T., Duranceau, S., LeBouthillier, D. M., … Hozempa, K. (2018). Mental disorder symptoms among public safety personnel in Canada. *The Canadian Journal of Psychiatry, 63*(1), 54–64.

Classen, C. C., & Heber, A. (2017). Posttraumatic Stress Disorder – A primer for primary care physicians. Retrieved from www.mdcme.ca.

Dückers, M. L. A., Alisic, E., & Brewin, C. R. (2016). A vulnerability paradox in the cross-national prevalence of post-traumatic stress disorder. *The British Journal of Psychiatry, 209*(4), 300–305.

Forbes D., Pedlar D., Adler, A. B., Bennett, C., Bryant, R., Busuttil, W., … Wessley, S. (2019). Treatment of military-related posttraumatic stress disorder: Challenges, innovations, and the way forward. *International Review of Psychiatry, 31*(1), 95–110.

Fortier, J., Turner, S., Tailleau, T., Sareen, J., & Afifi, T. O. (2019). Positive functioning and emotional well-being among military personnel and the general population with and without a history of child abuse in Canada. *Journal of Military, Veteran and Family Health, 5*(1), 105–114.

Germain, A. (2013). Sleep disturbances as the hallmark of PTSD: Where are we now? *American Journal of Psychiatry, 170*(4), 372–382.

Gersons, B. P. R. (1989). Patterns of PTSD among police officers following shooting incidents: A two-dimensional model and treatment implications. *Journal of Traumatic Stress, 2*(3), 247–257.

Goodstein, R. K. (1985). Common clinical problems in the elderly: Camouflaged by ageism and atypical presentation. *Psychiatric Annals, 15*(5), 299–312.

156 *James M. Thompson et al.*

Gravely, A. A., Cutting, A., Nugent, S., Grill, J., Carlson, K., & Spoont, M. (2011). Validity of PTSD diagnoses in VA administrative data: Comparison of VA administrative PTSD diagnoses to self-reported PTSD Checklist scores. *Journal of Rehabilitation Research & Development*, *48*(1), 21–31.

Griffin, B. J., Purcell, N., Burkman, K., Litz, B. T., Bryan, C. J., Schmitz, M., ... Maguen, S. (2019). Moral injury: An integrative review. *Journal of Traumatic Stress*, *32*(3), 350–362.

Henslee, A. M., Schumacher, J. A., Holloman, G., & Coffey, S. F. (2009). Unresolved PTSD in a Hispanic woman presenting with test anxiety. *Clinical Case Studies*, *8*(4), 340–350.

Hierholzer, R., Munson, J., Peabody, C., & Rosenberg, J. (1992). Clinical presentation of PTSD in World War II combat veterans. *Psychiatric Services*, *43*(8), 816–820.

Johnston, D. (2015). A series of cases of dementia presenting with PTSD symptoms in World War II combat veterans. *Journal of the American Geriatrics Society*, *48*, 70–72.

Kooab, K. H., Hebenstreitab, C. L., Maddena, E., & Maguenab, S. (2016). PTSD detection and symptom presentation: Racial/ethnic differences by gender among veterans with PTSD returning from Iraq and Afghanistan. *Journal of Affective Disorders*, *189*(1), 10–16.

Kwekkeboom, K. L. & Seng, J. S. (2002). Recognizing and responding to post-traumatic stress disorder in people with cancer. *Oncology Nursing Forum*, *29*(4), 643–650.

Ladouceur, R. (2018). The cannabis paradox. *Canadian Family Physician*, *64*(2), 86.

Lanius, R. A., Hopper, J. W., & Menon, R. S. (2003). Individual differences in a husband and wife who developed PTSD after a motor vehicle accident: A functional MRI case study. *American Journal of Psychiatry*, *160*(4), 667–669.

McFarlane, A. C. (2017). Post-traumatic stress disorder is a systemic illness, not a mental disorder: Is Cartesian dualism dead? *Medical Journal of Australia*, *206*(6), 248–249.

McCreary, D. (2020). Psychology of men and masculinities: Implications for men's experiences of post-traumatic stress disorder. In R. Ricciardelli, S. Bornstein, A. Hall, & N. Carleton (eds), *Handbook of Post-Traumatic Stress: Psychosocial, cultural and biological perspectives*. New York: Informa.

Morganstein, J. C., West, J. C., & Ursano, R. J. (2019). Work-associated trauma. In Riba, M. B., Parikh, S., & Greden, J. (eds), *Mental health in the workplace: Strategies and tools to optimize outcomes* (pp. 161–180). Cham: Springer Nature Publishing Company.

Moye, J. (1997). PTSD in long term care. *Clinical Gerontologist*, *18*(2), 84–88.

Purkey, E., Patel, R., & Phillips, S. P. (2018). Trauma-informed care: Better care for everyone. *Canadian Family Physician*, *64*(3), 170–172.

Reynolds, J. J. (1997). Post-traumatic stress disorder after childbirth: The phenomenon of traumatic birth. *Canadian Medical Association Journal*, *156*(6), 831–835. www.cmaj.ca/content/156/6/831

Ruzich, M. J., Loo, J.C.L., & Robertson, M. D. (2005). Delayed onset of posttraumatic stress disorder among male combat veterans: A case series. *American Journal of Geriatric Psychiatry*, *13*(5), 424–427.

Sareen, J. (2018). Posttraumatic stress disorder in adults: Epidemiology, pathophysiology, clinical manifestations, course, assessment, and diagnosis. Retrieved from www.uptodate.com/contents/posttraumatic-stress-disorder-in-adults-epidemiology-pathophysiology-clinical-manifestations-course-assessment-and-diagnosis.

Seidler, Z. E., Dawes, A. J., Rice, S. M., Oliffe, J. L., & Dhillon, H. M. (2016). The role of masculinity in men's help-seeking for depression: A systematic review. *Clinical Psychology Review*, 49, 106–118.

Shalev, A. Y., Schreiber, S., Galai, T., & Melmed, R. N. (1993). Posttraumatic stress disorder following medical events. *British Journal of Clinical Psychology*, *32*(2), 247–253.

Tedstone, J.E., & Tarrier, N. (2003). Posttraumatic stress disorder following medical illness and treatment. *Clinical Psychology Review*, *23*(3), 409–448.

Thompson, J. M., Heber, A., VanTil, L., Simkus, K., Carrese, L., Sareen, J., & Pedlar, D. (2019). Life course well-being framework for suicide prevention in Canadian Armed Forces veterans. *Journal of Military, Veteran and Family Health*, *5*(2), 176–194.

5 The Epidemiology of PTSD in Canada

Daniel Marrello, Beth Patterson, Jasmine Turna, Jasmine Zhang, and Michael Van Ameringen

Introduction

The scientific literature discussing prevalence rates of posttraumatic stress disorder (PTSD) in the general Canadian population is relatively sparse. With the exception of a 2008 cross-sectional study in Canadians (Van Ameringen et al., 2008), the epidemiological data has come largely from the United States (Breslau et al., 1991; Breslau et al., 1998; Davidson et al., 1991; Helzer, Robins, & McEvoy, 1987; Kessler et al., 1995; Kessler et al., 2005). Despite being neighbours, Canada and the United States differ in many ways including their health care systems. As such, rates of exposure to potentially psychologically traumatic events (PPTEs; Canadian Institute for Public Safety Research and Treatment [CIPSRT], 2019) and PTSD may not be experienced to the same degree in both countries. In the current chapter, we summarize what is known about current rates of PTSD in Canadian civilians. We also examine the Canadian literature on the armed forces, as well as those in active military service, because of the high risk of trauma associated with combat exposure (Breslau, 2001). Similarly, epidemiological studies examining rates of PTSD in other populations regularly exposed to violence, disaster, and death in their occupations are presented (Breslau, 2001; Bromet, Sonnega, & Kessler, 1998; Kessler et al., 2005; Norris, 1992).

Changes in PTSD Criteria: DSM IV to 5

Previous researchers describing the epidemiology of PTSD in Canada used criteria from the Diagnostic Statistical Manual of Mental Disorders-Fourth Edition (DSM-IV) or the text revision (DSM-IV-TR). In previous iterations of the DSM, PTSD was classified as an anxiety disorder (American Psychiatric Association [APA], 2000). The most recent iteration, the DSM-5 released in 2013, included several changes to the PTSD criteria, the most significant being that PTSD is no longer classified as an anxiety disorder, but in a new chapter called Trauma- and Stressor-Related Disorders (APA, 2013). In addition, the definition of what constitutes a

DOI: 10.4324/9781351134637-6

158 *Daniel Marrello et al.*

PPTE has been broadened, the requirement of a response with helplessness and horror has been omitted and there are now four diagnostic clusters (re-experiencing, avoidance, negative cognitions and mood, and arousal). The distinction between acute and chronic PTSD has also been omitted and two additional subtypes have been added: 1) PTSD in children under six years of age; and 2) PTSD with prominent dissociative symptoms (APA, 2013). There are currently no epidemiological reports on civilian PTSD using DSM-5 criteria.

Current Canadian PTSD Estimates

The first study to provide insight into rates of PTSD among Canadians examined the one-month prevalence rates of full and partial PTSD (n = 1,002; Stein et al., 1997). Phone interviews using a modified PTSD Symptom Scale for DSM-IV criteria revealed that the one-month prevalence rate of PTSD was approximately four times greater in women than men (6% vs. 1.5%, OR [95% CI] = 4.29 [2–9.19], p < .001; Stein et al., 1997). Overall, 2.7% and 3.4% of women and 1.2% and .3% of men met criteria for full and partial PTSD, respectively. Rates for men and women combined were 2% for full PTSD (all DSM-IV criteria) and 1.9% for partial PTSD (fewer than the required number of DSM-IV criterion C symptoms [avoidance/ numbing] or criterion D symptoms [increased arousal]) (Stein et al., 1997).

Ohayon and Shapiro (2000) analysed sleep disturbances and psychiatric disorders associated with PTSD in the Canadian population using a one-time phone interview evaluating DSM-IV criteria. The sample included 1,832 individuals, 15 to 90 years of age, living in the Metropolitan Toronto area, of whom 1.8% met full DSM-IV criteria for PTSD, with a higher prevalence noted among women than men (2.6% vs. .9%, OR [95% CI] = 2.8 [1.3–6.1]; Ohayon & Shapiro, 2000). There was a high level of comorbidity between PTSD and other mental disorders, with 75.7% of respondents with PTSD being diagnosed with at least one other mental disorder. The most commonly comorbid disorders were bipolar disorder (28.8%, OR [95% CI] = 14.1), depressive disorders (22.9%, OR [95% CI] = 8.4), and panic disorder (22.1%, OR [95% CI] = 9.7).

Sareen et al. (2007) investigated the prevalence of PTSD diagnosis among respondents to the Canadian Community Health Survey (n = 36,984). A multistage stratified cluster design was used to ensure the sample was representative of the general Canadian population. The results indicated current PTSD prevalence, as diagnosed by health professionals, was 1% with a higher prevalence noted among women than men (1.51% vs. 1.07%, p < .05) (Sareen et al., 2007). Participants on short- and long- term disability who reported poor well-being, high distress, and attempted death by suicide were significantly more likely to be diagnosed with PTSD. After adjusting for sociodemographic variables, all mental disorders remained significantly associated with PTSD, with the largest effects found for major depressive disorder (Adjusted OR [95% CI] = 10.45 [7.76–14.06]),

The Epidemiology of PTSD in Canada 159

social phobia (Adjusted OR [95% CI] = 7.06 [4.96–10.03]), and drug dependence (Adjusted OR [95% CI] = 6.37 [3.07–13.23]) (Sareen et al., 2007). Physical health problems were also associated with PTSD after adjustment, specifically respiratory diseases (asthma [Adjusted OR (95% CI) = 1.99 (1.38–2.88)], chronic bronchitis [Adjusted OR (95% CI) = 3.08 (2.01–4.72)]), cardiovascular diseases (heart disease [Adjusted OR (95% CI) = 1.69 (1.08–2.65)], hypertension [Adjusted OR (95% CI) = 1.55 (1.09–2.2)]), chronic pain conditions (arthritis [Adjusted OR (95% CI) = 3.46 (2.49–4.81)], back problems [Adjusted OR (95% CI) = 2.04 (1.51–2.74)], fibromyalgia [Adjusted OR (95% CI) = 2.59 (1.5–4.47)], chronic fatigue syndrome (Adjusted OR [95% CI] = 5.78 [3.47–9.65]), migraine headaches [Adjusted OR (95% CI) = 2.77 (1.99–2.88)]), gastrointestinal illnesses (ulcers [Adjusted OR (95% CI) = 1.93 (1.22–3.07)], Crohn's disease/ulcerative colitis [Adjusted OR (95% CI) = 1.85 (1.07–3.21)]), cancer (Adjusted OR [95% CI] = 2.69 [1.365.32]), and multiple chemical sensitivities (Adjusted OR [95% CI] = 3.95 [2.46–6.35]) (Sareen et al., 2007).

In a 2008 cross-sectional study, Canadian PTSD prevalence and comorbidity statistics were estimated in a nationally representative sample of men and women aged 18 or above (*n* = 2,991; Van Ameringen et al., 2008). Participants were recruited from across Canada, with each province and territory sampled proportionately to the population size (Van Ameringen et al., 2008). Using modified versions of the Composite International Diagnostic Interview (CIDI), the Mini International Neuropsychiatric Interview (MINI), and the Childhood Trauma Questionnaire (CTQ), each participant was screened for lifetime exposure to PPTE, lifetime and current (one-month) DSM-IV-TR PTSD, major depressive disorder, alcohol and substance abuse and dependence, and exposure to childhood maltreatment (Van Ameringen et al., 2008). Lifetime and current (one-month) PTSD in the Canadian general population was found to be 9.2% and 2.4% respectively (Van Ameringen et al., 2008). Most participants (76.1%) reported lifetime exposure to at least one PPTE, with the unexpected death of a loved one, sexual assault, and seeing someone badly injured or killed, most often leading to the development of PTSD (Van Ameringen et al., 2008). Most participants who screened positive for PTSD (68.5%; 58.7% of men, 71.9% of women) reported chronic PTSD symptoms presenting for more than one year (Van Ameringen et al., 2008). There were high rates of comorbidity with major depressive disorder (74%, OR [95% CI] = 6.36 [4.44–9.11], *p* < .001), alcohol (27.8%, OR [95% CI] = 1.83 [1.25–2.71], *p* < .01) and substance abuse/dependence (25.5%, OR [95% CI] = 4.43 [2.69–7.28], *p* < .001) (Van Ameringen et al., 2008). The strongest demographic correlate of PTSD was being divorced, separated, or widowed (OR [95% CI] = 3.26 [2.29–4.63], *p* < .001). Higher estimates of PTSD were identified for participants living in rural areas, Western Canada, and Ontario, and for participants who were never married and women (Van Ameringen et al., 2008). The subsequent Canadian PTSD literature has predominantly examined armed forces personnel as well as other at-risk

160 *Daniel Marrello et al.*

populations including first-responders or other public safety personnel (PSP; e.g., border services, communications officials, correctional workers, firefighters, paramedics, police; CIPSRT, 2019), inpatient and outpatient populations, immigrant and refugee populations, and the homeless and indigenous populations.

Canadian Armed Forces

Armed forces populations are the most represented in terms of the literature examining PTSD prevalence in Canada. A retrospective file review of Pension-Seeking Canadian World War II and Korean War Veterans (n = 120; Richardson et al., Elhai, 2010) examined PTSD and Health-Related Quality of Life using the Clinician-Administered PTSD Scale (CAPS). Most participants screened positive for current PTSD (61.7%), with the most common PPTE exposures being combat/war zones (96.4%), sudden death of a close loved one (77.5%), and life-threatening illness or injury (72.7%) (Richardson et al., 2010). The high rate of current PTSD may have been attributed to the relatively small sample size. Another retrospective study explored occupational outcomes following mild traumatic brain injury in Canadian military personnel deployed to Afghanistan (n = 16,193; Garber et al., 2016). Participants completed the Enhanced Post-Deployment Screening Questionnaire, which contained an abbreviated version of the PTSD checklist (PCL-2) (Garber et al., 2016), and resulted in 5.7% of participants reported symptoms consistent with current PTSD (cut-off ≥6 PCL-2) (Garber et al., 2016).

A Veterans Affairs Canada survey administered to Canadian veterans (n = 3,154) transitioning to civilian life indicated 11% of participants met criteria for current PTSD (Thompson et al., 2011). A 2014 study also indicated 8% of Class C Primary Reserve Force Personnel reported current symptoms of PTSD as did 13% of Regular Force (Thompson et al., 2014).

Researchers have also analysed data collected in the 2002 Canadian Community Health Survey-Canadian Forces Supplement (CCHS-CFS), which was designed to detect prevalence, correlates, and clinical features of PTSD (i.e., full, subsyndromal, delayed onset, and lifetime) in a nationally representative Canadian military sample (n = 8,441; Fetzner, McMillan, & Asmundson, 2012, Fikretoglu & Liu, 2012; Brunet et al., 2015). The first study used the PTSD Checklist – Military Version (PCL-M; Weathers et al., 1993) and reported that 17.8% of the sample met criteria for current full PTSD and 12.6% of participants met criteria for current subsyndromal PTSD (Fetzner et al., 2012); in contrast, a study using PTSD diagnostic status from the World Health Organization World Mental Health Composite International Diagnostic Interview (WHO WMH-CIDI, included in the Canadian Community Health Survey-Canadian Forces Supplement) reported the prevalence of delayed-onset PTSD (symptoms starting after six months following a PPTE) was less than 1% and accounted for approximately 8.5% of all PTSD cases (PTSD rate 6.5%) within the

The Epidemiology of PTSD in Canada   161

sample (Fikretoglu & Liu, 2012). PPTE exposure by age 12 (Adjusted OR [95% CI] = 2.57 [1.20–5.5], $p < .05$), repeated PPTE exposures (Adjusted OR [95% CI] = 3.28 [1.19–9.06], $p < .05$), and serving in the land troops during combat (Adjusted OR [95% CI] = 2.52 [1.08–5.86], $p < .05$), all increased the likelihood of delayed-onset PTSD (Fikretoglu & Liu, 2012). Lifetime prevalence of PTSD within the total sample has most recently been estimated at 6.6% (11.6% women; 5.7% men; Brunet et al., 2015), with higher prevalence rates for Regular Force Personnel than Reserve Force Personnel (7.3% vs. 4.8%), which is consistent with other research results (e.g., Thompson et al., 2014). A subsequent study compared data from the 2013 Canadian Forces Mental Health Survey (CFMHS) to that of the Canadian Community Health Survey-Canadian Forces Supplement to assess for changes in past-year medical disorders among Canadian Armed Forces personnel using PTSD criteria from the composite international diagnostic interview (Zamorski et al., 2016). The results indicated an increase in past-year PTSD prevalence from 2.8% in 2002 to 5.3% in 2013 (Zamorski et al., 2016).

Combat exposure has been associated with the worsening of PTSD severity. A cross-sectional survey indicated symptom severity was significantly greater for deployed than non-deployed veterans ($n = 1,066$; PCL-M scores: 30.8 [deployed] vs. 24.01 [non-deployed], $p < .001$) (Engdahl et al., 2011). Another study with Canadian military personnel deployed to Afghanistan indicated that combat exposure was significantly associated with poorer general mental health ($B = -1.56, p < .001$) and greater PTSD symptoms ($B = 2.92, p < .001$) (Watkins, Lee, & Zamorski, 2017). Marital status significantly moderated the relationship between combat exposure and all mental health outcomes, with the decrease in mental health associated with increased combat exposure being significantly greater in married participants ($R^2 = .16, F(12, 14,611) = 232.52, p < .001$ for PTSD). Married participants also reported significantly greater PTSD symptoms ($B = .34, p < .05$) (Watkins et al., 2017).

Other Careers With Frequent PPTE Exposures

There is a small body of research examining PTSD rates in civilian populations where work-related PPTE exposure is prevalent. First, a few studies have measured PTSD prevalence among medical professionals. A cross-sectional study of physicians from underserviced areas ($n = 159$; Wilberforce, Wilberforce, & Aubrey-Bassler, 2010) analysed "probable" PTSD using the PTSD Check List-Civilian version – PCL-C; Weather et al., 1993). The results indicated 4.4% screened positive for probable PTSD (PCL-C score ≥50) and 36.7% for "possible" PTSD (PCL-C score ≥30). Another study using the PCL-C evidenced 24% of psychiatric hospital workers ($n = 219$) screened positive for PTSD using a third cut-off score (PCL-C score ≥44) (Hilton, Ham, & Dretzkat, 2017). In the same sample, nursing staff were significantly more likely to screen positive for

162   *Daniel Marrello et al.*

PTSD relative to other hospital workers (31% vs. 11%, $p \leq .001$; Hilton et al., 2017). Second, Canadian PSP also appear important for PTSD epidemiology estimates. Canadian police officers ($n = 132$) screened for PTSD via the Structured Clinical Interview (SCID; First et al., 1996) for DSM–IV Axis I Disorders evidenced lifetime PTSD rates of 7.6% (full PTSD) and 6.8% (partial PTSD) (Martin et al., 2009). A large portion (31%) of police communications officials ($n = 113$) also screened for PTSD based on self-reported symptoms on Impact of Event Scale – Revised [IES] (score ≥ 33) (Regehr et al., 2013). A large proportion of participants (23.2%) from a national cross-sectional study of multiple PSP sectors (Carleton et al., 2018) also screened positive for PTSD using the PCL-5 self-report scale (PCL-5 cut-off score ≥ 33; Weathers et al., 2013). In the same study (Carleton et al., 2018), the Royal Canadian Mounted Police (30%), correctional workers (29.1%), and paramedics (24.5%) were significantly (all $p \leq .05$) more likely to screen positive for PTSD criteria than municipal/provincial police (19.5%) and firefighters (13.5%).

Medical Comorbidity

Prevalence rates of PTSD have also been assessed with Canadian patients who have medical comorbidities, particularly those with asthma, cardiovascular issues, or burns. A retrospective analysis of the Canadian Community Health Survey examined the association between asthma and various psychiatric disorders. In respondents with asthma, the rate of PTSD was more than twice that of subjects without asthma (2.35% vs. .89% AOR [95% CI] = 2.62 [1.89 – 3.63], $p \leq .001$) (Goodwin et al., 2010). In two additional studies, researchers have measured PTSD prevalence in patients with cardiovascular health problems. First, patients diagnosed with a myocardial infarction (MI) ($n = 477$) reported significant rates of full (4.1%), partial (12%), and past (2.8%) PTSD per the SCID-IV, one month after experiencing an MI (Roberge, Dupuis, & Marchand, 2010). Second, a retrospective chart review of unstructured interviews using DSM-5 diagnostic criteria indicated a significant percentage of patients with cardiovascular disease also had PTSD (i.e., 3% Long et al., 2018). Large portions of a burn clinic outpatient sample ($n = 132$) also a reported symptoms consistent with clinical (39.4%) or subclinical (35.6%) PTSD (Gardner et al., 2012). Many spouses and close relatives from a sample of burn survivors ($n = 56$) also reported symptoms consistent with PTSD at 2–5 days post-admission (23.2%) and again at discharge (8.3%; Bond et al., 2017).

Results from a cross-sectional study of a palliative care sample ($n = 100$) indicated 7% of patients screened positive for PTSD based on having PCL-C scores ≥ 44; Roth et al., 2013). A sample of critical care survivors ($n = 69$; Khitab et al. 2013) responded to surveys at three- and nine-months post-admission which included the Davidson Trauma Scale (DTS; Davidson et al., 1997), the Post-Traumatic Symptom Scale (PTSS-10; Raphael et al., 1989), and the Impact of Event Scale (IES; Weiss & Marmar, 1996).

The Epidemiology of PTSD in Canada 163

Participants scores at three-months post-admission indicated substantial portions screened positive for PTSD (i.e., DTS ≥40, 33%; PTSS ≥35, 25%; IES avoidance ≥20, 21%; IES intrusion ≥20, 16%; Khitab et al., 2013). Positive screenings for PTSD at nine months after ICU admission were based on a subset of the sample ($n = 37$) and resulted in similar rates (DTS, 38%; PTSS, 29%; IES avoidance, 22%; IES intrusion, 8%; Khitab et al., 2013). A recent prospective cohort study examined patients with non-neurological (i.e., traumatic brain or spinal cord) injuries who were admitted to a Level 1 trauma centre and were assessed for PTSD using the PCL-C (the selected cut-off score was not reported) (Bell, Vetor, & Zarzaur, 2018). The PCL-C was administered at five time points including initial hospitalization, one, two, four, and 12 months after injury, with 44.4% of participants screening positive for PTSD during at least one of the administrations (Bell et al., 2018).

Migrant Populations

Canadian immigrant, refugee, and asylum-seeking populations have emerged as a subpopulation within the PTSD epidemiological literature. An initial cross-sectional study examined rates of PTSD in Sri Lankan Tamil refugees ($n = 1,603$) from Toronto, Ontario. A prevalence rate of 12% was identified based on the International Classification of Diseases, tenth revision (ICD-10) and a prevalence rate of 5.8% was identified based on DSM-IV PTSD criteria (Beiser et al., 2011). A pilot investigation of alcohol use, substance use, and mental disorders among Iraqi, Afghani, and Iranian government-assisted refugees in Vancouver, British Columbia ($n = 68$) reported a "clinical concern" for PTSD (IES-R score > 19) in 22.1% of the sample (22.2% women; 21.8% men; Miremadi, Ganesan, & McKenna, 2011). A prospective cohort study in which researchers examined the post-birth health of women and infants ($n = 2,254$) from different migrant classes as compared to Canadian-born women-infant pairs. Based on scores from the Harvard Trauma Questionnaire (HTQ; Mollica et al., 1992) exceeding 2.5, asylum seekers had the highest prevalence of PTSD symptoms (48.2%), followed by refugees (33.8%), and immigrants (15%) (Gagnon et al., 2013). The rate of PTSD symptoms among Canadian-born participants was not provided; nevertheless, the comparison indicated a statistically significant ($p < .001$) association between PTSD and immigrant status (Gagnon et al., 2013). In a 2013 study using the HTQ, results indicated 37.7% of detained adult asylum seekers and 18.2% of non-detained adult asylum seekers exhibited symptoms of PTSD (Cleveland & Rousseau, 2013).

Homeless Populations

Researchers from three studies have examined rates of PTSD among homeless populations in Canada. The first study involved a cross-sectional sample of homeless people ($n = 51$) undergoing treatment for substance-use disorder (SUD) issues. A Modified PTSD Symptom Scale (MPSS-SR; Falsetti et al.,

164   *Daniel Marrello et al.*

1993) score great than 50 indicated 49% of the subjects screened positive for a potential PTSD diagnosis (Lalonde & Nadeau, 2012). Several factors were associated with having PTSD; specifically, having a parent with alcoholism ($p < .01$), experiencing early life PPTE ($p < .05$), and employing maladaptive coping strategies ($p < .01$) (Lalonde & Nadeau., 2012). The second study used the Mini International Neuropsychiatric Interview-Plus (Sheehan et al., 1997; Sheehan et al., 1998), and scholars assessed PTSD-Substance Use Disorder (SUD) comorbidity in homeless adults who had previously participated in the BC Health of the Homeless Study ($n = 489$) (Torchalla et al., 2014). Overall, 20.5% of the sample screened positive for PTSD based on DSM-IV criteria and 92% of the PTSD-positive group also met criteria for SUD (Torchalla et al., 2014). Rates of PTSD were higher among female homeless adults as compared to their male counterparts (28% vs. 15.5%, $p < .001$) as was PTSD-SUD comorbidity (24.9% vs. 14.9%, $p < .01$) (Torchalla et al., 2014). The third study was based on analyses of the full BC Health of the Homeless Study sample comparing young (19–24 years of age) and older (25+ years of age) homeless individuals ($n = 500$). Results indicated that 23.2% of youth and 19.4% of older participants ($p = .432$) met Mini International Neuropsychiatric Interview-Plus (Sheehan et al., 1997; Sheehan et al., 1998) diagnostic criteria for PTSD (Saddichha, Linden, & Krausz, 2014).

Indigenous Populations

In the Canadian literature, researchers have also begun exploring rates of PTSD among Canada's Indigenous populations. The first was a cross-sectional study assessing mental health and substance use in a First Nations population ($n = 554$) from Hamilton, Ontario (Firestone et al., 2015). As per the PC-PTSD screening criterion (respondent answers "yes" to any three items in the instrument), 34% of the sample met criteria for PTSD (Firestone et al., 2015). Benoit and colleagues (2016) examined chronic stress and mental health concerns among urban indigenous women ($n = 90$), indicating that 83.2% of participants reported substantive PTSD symptoms based on PCL-C scores exceeding 30 (Benoit et al., 2016).

Miscellaneous Research

Maternal PTSD

Exposures to PPTE and subsequent PTSD symptoms have been examined in a population of Canadian single mothers receiving social assistance ($n = 247$; Samuels-Dennis, Ford-Giboe, & Ray, 2010). The prevalence of PTSD in the sample of women based on the Davidson Trauma Scale criteria (DTS ≥40; Davidson et al., 1997) was 31% (Samuels-Dennis, Ford-Giboe, & Ray, 2010). Incidence and risk factors associated with PTSD in post-partum women ($n = 308$) have also been examined (Verreault et al., 2012).

The Structured Clinical Interview-I (First et al., 1996) and Modified PTSD Symptom Scale (MPSS-SR; Falsetti et al., 1993) were administered at 1) 25–40 weeks' gestation, 2) four to six weeks post-partum, 3) three months post-partum and 4) six months postpartum. Verreault and colleagues (2012) reported that 5.6% met criteria for full or partial PTSD (based on the SCID-I), and 26% (based on MPSS-SR cut score not provided) of participants screened positive for full or partial PTSD, at some point during the six-month study period. Significantly more women reported symptoms consistent with PTSD at one-month post-partum (4.3% [based on SCID-I], 24.2% [based on MPSS-SR) than at three months (2.1% [based on SCID-I], 11.4% (based on MPSS-SR) and six months post-partum (2.9% [based on SCID-I], 9.2% (based on MPSS-SR) ($p < .001$ [one month vs. three months], $p < .001$ [one month vs. six months])). There was no statistically significant difference in PTSD symptom prevalence between three and six months post-partum ($p = .549$) (Verreault et al., 2012).

Youth Samples

The mental health needs of incarcerated youth ($n = 205$) in British Columbia have also been explored (Gretton & Clift, 2011). Based on the Diagnostic Interview Schedule for Children (DISC-4), PTSD prevalence appeared statistically significantly greater among incarcerated young women than among their men counterparts (13% vs. 1.7%, OR [95% CI] = 8.79 [1.76–43.85]; Gretton & Clift, 2011, p < .01). Hébert and colleagues also conducted two studies of PTSD prevalence in adolescent and child victims of sexual abuse. In the first study ($n = 694$; Hébert, Lavoie, and Blais, 2014), the results indicated that 27.8% of adolescent men and 14.9% of adolescent women screened positive for PTSD based on having Abbreviated University of California at Los Angeles PTSD Reaction Index scores greater than 9 (Steinberg et al., 2004). In the second study ($n = 158$; Hébert, Langevin, & Daigneault, 2016), the results indicated that 53.6% of children reported clinical levels of PTSD based on the PTSD subscale of the Children's Impact of Traumatic Events Scale – II (CITES-II). An investigation of mental health and substance use among bisexual youth (age 16–24 years, $n = 99$) and non-youth (≥25 years, $n = 302$) in Ontario assessed for clinically significant PTSD symptoms using two previously published PCL-C cut-off scores (≥50 and ≥44; Weather et al., 2013). The higher cut-off score estimated PTSD prevalence at 10.8% (youth: 11.6%, non-youth: 10.8%), whereas the lower cut-off score estimated PTSD prevalence at 17.7% (youth: 26.1%, non-youth: 15.5%) (Ruggiero et al., 2003 cited in Ross et al., 2014).

Other Populations

PTSD in elderly Canadian patients has also been examined. In one cross-sectional study from primary health clinics in Quebec, elderly patients were

166 *Daniel Marrello et al.*

interviewed (≥65 years of age, $n = 1,765$) and diagnosed using DSM-IV PTSD criteria. The authors found that 1.76% and 1.81% qualified for full and partial PTSD respectively (Préville et al., 2014). The prevalence rates appear comparable to the general population (Préville et al., 2014).

Among a sample of Canadian adults who met criteria for pathological gambling ($n = 150$) 19% met SCID criteria (First et al., 1996) for lifetime PTSD (Ledgerwood & Milosevic, 2013). Participants with lifetime PTSD were statistically significantly more likely to use gambling as a coping mechanism for negative emotions ($F = 15.25$, $p < .001$) and experienced stronger negative emotions ($F = 8.61$, $p < .01$). PTSD symptoms are also prevalent amongst Canadian women with HIV ($n = 1,405$). An abbreviated version of the PTSD checklist (PCL-6) was administered to women in the Canadian HIV Women's Sexual Reproductive Health Cohort living in British Columbia, Ontario, and Quebec. Overall, 47.1% of the entire sample reported PTSD symptoms with the PCL-6 scores exceeding 13 (Lang & Stein, 2005), with rates highest in British Columbia (55.9%), followed by Quebec (54.1%), and Ontario (39.1%) (Wagner et al., 2018).

Future Directions

Over a decade has passed since PTSD prevalence estimates in the general Canadian population were first published. Existing estimates of PTSD prevalence in Canada have used older (pre-DSM-V) criteria to assess presence of lifetime PTSD. Further, due to the vast and diverse number of diagnostic scales of varying reliability and variability employed in the scientific literature, there is a glaring issue in terms of standardization of PTSD prevalence measurement. Given the substantial changes to PTSD criteria in the DSM-5 informed by more recent work in the field, coupled with the measurement issue associated by using a wide variety of PTSD diagnostic tools, the prevalence rates should be revaluated. Therefore, a standardized, "gold standard" assessment of prevalence rates using DSM-5 criteria for PTSD is necessary to accurately depict epidemiology of PTSD in Canada.

More recent reports of PTSD among Canadians are drawn from specific demographic, occupational, and social groups. Rates vary significantly between groups; consequently, such groups warrant consideration in future investigations of PTSD prevalence in the general Canadian population. Excepting the armed forces, most research analysing Canadian subpopulations is limited. There are some significant demographic groups that have yet to be investigated, most notably a number of the LGBTQ+ subpopulations, adult criminal/incarcerated populations, and anorexia nervosa and binge-eating disorder patients. Accurate measures of PTSD prevalence among different demographic groups would allow for the identification of at-risk subpopulations as well as establish novel risk factors for PTSD development.

Conclusion

Current PTSD prevalence in the general population ranges from 1% to 2.4%, compared to ranges of 2.8% to 17.8% in the armed forces. Rates of lifetime PTSD range from 4.8% to 6.6% in the armed forces; there have not been any large-scale general population estimates of PTSD prevalence in Canada since 2008, where a lifetime prevalence rate of 9.2% was reported (Van Ameringen et al., 2008). More Canadian epidemiological studies exploring the prevalence rate of PTSD are clearly warranted, particularly considering the potential impact of the change in diagnostic criteria to DSM-5 and the proposed ICD-11 criteria. Interestingly, the Canadian lifetime PTSD estimate of 9.2% is higher than similar estimates reported in the United States – 6.1% (DSM-5) (Goldstein et al., 2016) or 6.8% (DSM-IV) (Kessler et al., 2005). The higher rate in Canada is likely attributable to methodological issues, including gross variations in instrumentation, sampling methods and sizes, use of the respondents' personally selected "worst event" (Van Ameringen et al., 2008) versus a randomly selected event (Kessler et al., 2008), as well as potential differences in the classification of psychiatric disorders (i.e., DSM-IV to DSM-5). Nevertheless, the puzzling differences in prevalence rates support the necessity for further Canadian epidemiological studies to be conducted in larger samples using more rigorous sampling methods and for the PTSD research community to establish gold-standard measures of PTSD symptom severity and diagnosis. The elevated prevalence of PTSD within many of the Canadian subpopulations indicates that there may be a number of experiences that contribute to the development of PTSD that have not been fully explored. Further investigation of PTSD prevalence within Canadian subpopulations may identify novel risk-factors/experiences that contribute to the development of PTSD.

References

American Psychiatric Association (APA). (2000). *Diagnostic and statistical manual of mental disorders: DSM-IV-TR.* Arlington, VA: American Psychiatric Association.

American Psychiatric Association (APA). (2013). *Diagnostic and statistical manual of mental disorders: DSM-5.* Arlington, VA: American Psychiatric Association.

Beiser, M., Simich, L., Pandalangat, N., Nowakowski, M., & Tian, F. (2011). Stresses of passage, balms of resettlement, and posttraumatic stress disorder among Sri Lankan Tamils in Canada. *The Canadian Journal of Psychiatry, 56*(6), 333–340. https://doi.org/10.1177/070674371105600604

Bell, T. M., Vetor, A. N., & Zarzaur, B. L. (2018). Prevalence and treatment of depression and posttraumatic stress disorder among trauma patients with non-neurological injuries. *Journal of Trauma and Acute Care Surgery, 85*(5), 999–1006. https://doi.org/10.1097/ta.0000000000001992

Benoit, A. C., Cotnam, J., Raboud, J., Greene, S., Beaver, K., Zoccole, A., O'Brien-Teengs, D., Balfour, L., Wu, W., & Loutfy, M. (2016). Experiences of chronic stress and mental health concerns among urban Indigenous women.

Archives of Women's Mental Health, 19(5), 809–823. https://doi.org/10.1007/s00737-016-0622-8

Bond, S., Gourlay, C., Desjardins, A., Bodson-Clermont, P., & Boucher, M.-È. (2017). Anxiety, depression and PTSD-related symptoms in spouses and close relatives of burn survivors: When the supporter needs to be supported. Burns, 43(3), 592–601. https://doi.org/10.1016/j.burns.2016.09.025

Breslau, N. (2001). The epidemiology of posttraumatic stress disorder: What is the extent of the problem? Journal of Clinical Psychiatry, 62(17), 16–22. https://pubmed.ncbi.nlm.nih.gov/11495091/

Breslau, N., Davis, G., Andreski, P., & Peterson, E. (1991). Traumatic events and posttraumatic stress disorder in an urban population of young adults. Archives of General Psychiatry, 48(3), 216–222. https://doi.org/10.1001/archpsyc.1991.01810270028003

Breslau, N., Kessler, R. C., Chilcoat, H. D., Schultz, L. R., Davis, G. C., & Andreski, P. (1998). Trauma and posttraumatic stress disorder in the community. Archives of General Psychiatry, 55(7), 626–632. https://doi.org/10.1001/archpsyc.55.7.626

Bromet, E., Sonnega, A., & Kessler, R. C. (1998). Risk factors for DSM-III-R posttraumatic stress disorder: Findings from the National Comorbidity Survey. American Journal of Epidemiology, 147(4), 353–361. https://doi.org/10.1093/oxfordjournals.aje.a009457

Brunet, A., Monson, E., Liu, A., & Fikretoglu, D. (2015). Trauma exposure and posttraumatic stress disorder in the Canadian military. The Canadian Journal of Psychiatry, 60(11), 488–496. https://doi.org/10.1177/070674371506001104

Canadian Institute for Public Safety Research and Treatment (CIPSRT). (2019). Glossary of terms: A shared understanding of the common terms used to describe psychological trauma (version 2.0). Regina, SK: CIPSRT.

Carleton, R. N., Afifi, T. O., Turner, S., Taillieu, T., Duranceau, S., LeBouthillier, D. M., ... & Hozempa, K. (2018). Mental disorder symptoms among public safety personnel in Canada. The Canadian Journal of Psychiatry, 63(1), 54–64. https://doi.org/10.1177/0706743717723825

Cleveland, J., & Rousseau, C. (2013). Psychiatric symptoms associated with brief detention of adult asylum seekers in Canada. The Canadian Journal of Psychiatry, 58(7), 409–416. https://doi.org/10.1177/070674371305800706

Davidson, J. R. T., Book, S. W., Colket, J. T., Tupler, L. A., Roth, S., David, D., Hertzberg, M., Mellman, T., Beckham, J. C., Smith, R. D., Davison, R. M., Katz, R., & Feldman, M. E. (1997). Assessment of a new self-rating scale for post-traumatic stress disorder. Psychological Medicine, 27(1), 153–160. https://doi.org/10.1017/s0033291796004229

Davidson, J. R. T., Hughes, D., Blazer, D. G., & George, L. K. (1991). Post-traumatic stress disorder in the community: An epidemiological study. Psychological Medicine, 21(3), 713–721. https://doi.org/10.1017/s0033291700022352

Engdahl, R. M., Elhai, J. D., Richardson, J. D., & Frueh, B. C. (2011). Comparing posttraumatic stress disorder's symptom structure between deployed and nondeployed veterans. Psychological Assessment, 23(1), 1–6. https://doi.org/10.1037/a0020045

Falsetti, S. A., Resnick, H. S., Resick, P. A., & Kilpatrick, D. G. (1993). The Modified PTSD Symptom Scale: A brief self-report measure of posttraumatic stress disorder. The Behavior Therapist, 16, 161–162.

Fetzner, M. G., McMillan, K. A., & Asmundson, G. J. G. (2012). Similarities in specific physical health disorder prevalence among formerly deployed Canadian forces veterans with full and subsyndromal PTSD. *Depression and Anxiety*, *29*(11), 958–965. https://doi.org/10.1002/da.21976

Fikretoglu, D., & Liu, A. (2012). Prevalence, correlates, and clinical features of delayed-onset posttraumatic stress disorder in a nationally representative military sample. *Social Psychiatry and Psychiatric Epidemiology*, *47*(8), 1359–1366. https://doi.org/10.1007/s00127-011-0444-y

Firestone, M., Smylie, J., Maracle, S., McKnight, C., Spiller, M., & O'Campo, P. (2015). Mental health and substance use in an urban First Nations population in Hamilton, Ontario. *Canadian Journal of Public Health*, *106*(6), e375–e381. https://doi.org/10.17269/cjph.106.4923

First, M. B., Spitzer, R. L., Gibbon, M., & Williams, J. B. W. (1996). *Structured clinical interview for DSM-IV axis I disorders, clinician version (SCID-CV)*. Washington, DC: American Psychiatric Press.

Gagnon, A. J., Dougherty, G., Wahoush, O., Saucier, J.-F., Dennis, C.-L., Stanger, E., Palmer, B., Merry, L., & Stewart, D. E. (2013). International migration to Canada: The post-birth health of mothers and infants by immigration class. *Social Science & Medicine*, *76*, 197–207. https://doi.org/10.1016/j.socscimed.2012.11.001

Garber, B. G., Rusu, C., Zamorski, M. A., & Boulos, D. (2016). Occupational outcomes following mild traumatic brain injury in Canadian military personnel deployed in support of the mission in Afghanistan: A retrospective cohort study. *BMJ Open*, *6*(5), e010780. https://doi.org/10.1136/bmjopen-2015-010780

Gardner, P. J., Knittel-Keren, D., & Gomez, M. (2012). The Posttraumatic Stress Disorder Checklist as a screening measure for posttraumatic stress disorder in rehabilitation after burn injuries. *Archives of Physical Medicine and Rehabilitation*, *93*(4), 623–628. https://doi.org/10.1016/j.apmr.2011.11.015

Goldstein, R. B., Smith, S. M., Chou, S. P., Saha, T. D., Jung, J., Zhang, H., ... & Grant, B. F. (2016). The epidemiology of DSM-5 posttraumatic stress disorder in the United States: Results from the National Epidemiologic Survey on Alcohol and Related Conditions-III. *Social Psychiatry and Psychiatric Epidemiology*, *51*(8), 1137–1148.

Goodwin, R. D., Pagura, J., Cox, B., & Sareen, J. (2010). Asthma and mental disorders in Canada: Impact on functional impairment and mental health service use. *Journal of Psychosomatic Research*, *68*(2), 165–173. https://doi.org/10.1016/j.jpsychores.2009.06.005

Gretton, H. M., & Clift, R. J. W. (2011). The mental health needs of incarcerated youth in British Columbia, Canada. *International Journal of Law and Psychiatry*, *34*(2), 109–115. https://doi.org/10.1016/j.ijlp.2011.02.004

Hébert, M., Langevin, R., & Daigneault, I. (2016). The association between peer victimization, PTSD, and dissociation in child victims of sexual abuse. *Journal of Affective Disorders*, *193*, 227–232. https://doi.org/10.1016/j.jad.2015.12.080

Hébert, M., Lavoie, F., & Blais, M. (2014). Post traumatic stress disorder/PTSD in adolescent victims of sexual abuse: Resilience and social support as protection factors. *Ciência & Saúde Coletiva*, *19*(3), 685–694. https://doi.org/10.1590/1413-81232014193.15972013

Helzer, J. E., Robins, L. N., & McEvoy, L. (1987). Post-traumatic stress disorder in the general population. *New England Journal of Medicine*, *317*(26), 1630–1634. https://doi.org/10.1056/nejm198712243172604

Hilton, N. Z., Ham, E., & Dretzkat, A. (2017). Psychiatric hospital workers' exposure to disturbing patient behavior and its relation to post-traumatic stress

170 Daniel Marrello et al.

disorder symptoms. *Canadian Journal of Nursing Research*, *49*(3), 118–126. https://doi.org/10.1177/0844562117719202

Kessler, R. C., Berglund, P., Demler, O., Jin, R., Merikangas, K. R., & Walters, E. E. (2005). Lifetime prevalence and age-of-onset distributions of DSM-IV disorders in the National Comorbidity Survey Replication. *Archives of General Psychiatry*, *62*(6), 593–602. https://doi.org/10.1001/archpsyc.62.6.593

Kessler, R. C., Sonnega, A., Bromet, E., Hughes, M., & Nelson, C. B. (1995). Posttraumatic stress disorder in the National Comorbidity Survey. *Archives of General Psychiatry*, *52*(12), 1048. https://doi.org/10.1001/archpsyc. 1995.03950240066012

Khitab, A., Reid, J., Bennett, V., Adams, G. C., & Balbuena, L. (2013). Late onset and persistence of post-traumatic stress disorder symptoms in survivors of critical care. *Canadian Respiratory Journal*, *20*(6), 429–433. https://doi.org/10.1155/2013/861517

Lalonde, F., & Nadeau, L. (2012). Risk and protective factors for comorbid posttraumatic stress disorder among homeless individuals in treatment for substance-related problems. *Journal of Aggression, Maltreatment & Trauma*, *21*(6), 626–645. https://doi.org/10.1080/10926771.2012.694401

Lang, A. J., & Stein, M. B. (2005). An abbreviated PTSD checklist for use as a screening instrument in primary care. *Behaviour Research and Therapy*, *21*(5), 585–594. https://doi.org/10.1016/j.brat.2004.04.005

Ledgerwood, D. M., & Milosevic, A. (2013). Clinical and personality characteristics associated with post traumatic stress disorder in problem and pathological gamblers recruited from the community. *Journal of Gambling Studies*, *31*(2), 501–512. https://doi.org/10.1007/s10899-013-9426-1

Long, V., Guertin, M.-C., Dyrda, K., Benrimoh, D., & Brouillette, J. (2018). Descriptive study of anxiety and posttraumatic stress disorders in cardiovascular disease patients: From referral to cardiopsychiatric diagnoses. *Psychotherapy and Psychosomatics*, *87*(6), 370–371. https://doi.org/10.1159/000491581

Martin, M., Marchand, A., Boyer, R., & Martin, N. (2009). Predictors of the development of posttraumatic stress disorder among police officers. *Journal of Trauma & Dissociation*, *10*(4), 451–468. https://doi.org/10.1080/15299730903143626

Miremadi, S., Ganesan, S., & McKenna, M. (2011). Pilot study of the prevalence of alcohol, substance use and mental disorders in a cohort of Iraqi, Afghani, and Iranian refugees in Vancouver. *Asia-Pacific Psychiatry*, *3*(3), 137–144. https://doi.org/10.1111/j.1758-5872.2011.00136.x

Mollica, R. F., Caspi-Yavin, Y., Bollini, P., Truong, T., Tor, S., & Lavelle, J. (1992). The Harvard Trauma Questionnaire. Validating a cross-cultural instrument for measuring torture, trauma, and posttraumatic stress disorder in Indochinese refugees. *The Journal of Nervous and Mental Disease*, *180*(2), 111–116. PMID: 1737972

Norris, F. H. (1992). Epidemiology of trauma: Frequency and impact of different potentially traumatic events on different demographic groups. *Journal of Consulting and Clinical Psychology*, *60*(3), 409–418. https://doi.org/10.1037/0022-006x.60.3.409

Ohayon, M. M., & Shapiro, C. M. (2000). Sleep disturbances and psychiatric disorders associated with posttraumatic stress disorder in the general population. *Comprehensive Psychiatry*, *41*(6), 469–478. https://doi.org/10.1053/comp.2000.16568

The Epidemiology of PTSD in Canada 171

Préville, M., Lamoureux-Lamarche, C., Vasiliadis, H.-M., Grenier, S., Potvin, O., Quesnel, L., Gontijo-Guerra, S., Mechakra-Tahiri, S. D., & Berbiche, D. (2014). The 6-month prevalence of posttraumatic stress syndrome (PTSS) among older adults: Validity and reliability of the PTSS Scale. *The Canadian Journal of Psychiatry*, *59*(10), 548–555. https://doi.org/10.1177/070674371405901008

Raphael, B., Lundin, T., & McFarlane, C. (1989). A research method for the study of psychological and psychiatric aspects of disaster. *Acta Psychiatrica Scandinavica*, *80*(S353), 1–75. https://doi.org/10.1111/j.1600-0447.1989.tb03041.x

Regehr, C., LeBlanc, V. R., Barath, I., Balch, J., & Birze, A. (2013). Predictors of physiological stress and psychological distress in police communicators. *Police Practice and Research*, *14*(6), 451–463. https://doi.org/10.1080/15614263.2012.736718

Richardson, J. D., Long, M. E., Pedlar, D., & Elhai, J. D. (2010). Posttraumatic stress disorder and health-related quality of life in pension-seeking Canadian World War II and Korean War veterans. *The Journal of Clinical Psychiatry*, *71*(08), 1099–1101. https://doi.org/10.4088/jcp.09l05920blu

Roberge, M.-A., Dupuis, G., & Marchand, A. (2010). Post-traumatic stress disorder following myocardial infarction: Prevalence and risk factors. *Canadian Journal of Cardiology*, *26*(5), e170–e175. https://doi.org/10.1016/s0828-282x(10)70386-x

Ross, L. E., Bauer, G. R., MacLeod, M. A., Robinson, M., MacKay, J., & Dobinson, C. (2014). Mental health and substance use among bisexual youth and non-youth in Ontario, Canada. *PLoS One*, *9*(8), e101604. https://doi.org/10.1371/journal.pone.0101604

Roth, M. L., St. Cyr, K., Harle, I., & Katz, J. D. (2013). Relationship between pain and post-traumatic stress symptoms in palliative care. *Journal of Pain and Symptom Management*, *46*(2), 182–191. https://doi.org/10.1016/j.jpainsymman.2012.07.015

Saddichha, S., Linden, I., & Krausz, M. (2014). Physical and mental health issues among homeless youth in British Columbia, Canada: Are they different from older homeless adults? *Journal of the Canadian Academy of Child and Adolescent Psychiatry*, *23*(3), 200–206.

Samuels-Dennis, J. A., Ford-Gilboe, M., & Ray, S. (2010). Single mother's adverse and traumatic experiences and post-traumatic stress symptoms. *Journal of Family Violence*, *26*(1), 9–20. https://doi.org/10.1007/s10896-010-9337-1

Sareen, J., Cox, B. J., Stein, M. B., Afifi, T. O., Fleet, C., & Asmundson, G. J. G. (2007). Physical and mental comorbidity, disability, and suicidal behavior associated with posttraumatic stress disorder in a large community sample. *Psychosomatic Medicine*, *69*(3), 242–248. https://doi.org/10.1097/PSY.0b013e31803146d8

Sheehan, D., Lecrubier, Y., Sheehan, K., Amorim, P., Janavs, J., Weiller, E., Hergueta, T., Baker, R., & Dunbar, G. (1998). The Mini-International Neuropsychiatric Interview (M.I.N.I.): The development and validation of a structured diagnostic psychiatric interview for DSM-IV and ICD-10. *Journal of Clinical Psychiatry*, *59*, 22–33.

Sheehan, D., Lecrubier, Y., Sheehan, K., Janavs, J., Weiller, E., Keskiner, A., Schinka, J., Knapp, E., Sheehan, M., & Dunbar, G. (1997). The validity of the Mini International Neuropsychiatric Interview (MINI) according to the

SCID-P and its reliability. *European Psychiatry, 12*(5), 232–241. https://doi.org/10.1016/s0924-9338(97)83297-x

Stein, M. B., Walker, J. R., Hazan, A. L., & Forde, D. R. (1997). Full and partial posttraumatic stress disorder: Findings from a community survey. *American Journal of Psychiatry, 154*(8), 1114–1119. https://doi.org/10.1176/ajp.154.8.1114

Steinberg, A. M., Brymer, M. J., Decker, K. B., & Pynoos, R. S. (2004). The University of California at Los Angeles post-traumatic stress disorder reaction index. *Current Psychiatry Reports, 6*(2), 96–100. https://doi.org/10.1007/s11920-004-0048-2

Thompson, J. M., Maclean, M. B., Van Til, L., Sweet, J., Poirier, A., Pedlar, D., Adams, J., Horton, V., Sudom, K., & Campbell, C. (2011). *Survey on Transition to Civilian Life: Report on regular force veterans*. Ottawa, ON: Veterans Affairs Canada. Retrieved from http://publications.gc.ca/collections/collection_2011/acc-vac/V32-231-2011-eng.pdf.

Thompson, J. M., Van Til, L., Poirier, A., Sweet, J., McKinnon, K., Sudom, K., Dursun, S., & Pedlar, D. (2014, July 3). *Health and well-being of Canadian forces veterans: Findings from the 2013 life after service survey*. Research Directorate Technical Report. Charlottetown, PE: Research Directorate, Veterans Affairs Canada. Retrieved from www.veterans.gc.ca/eng/about-vac/research/research-directorate/publications/reports/2013-survey-caf-health.

Torchalla, I., Strehlau, V., Li, K., Aube Linden, I., Noel, F., & Krausz, M. (2014). Posttraumatic stress disorder and substance use disorder comorbidity in homeless adults: Prevalence, correlates, and sex differences. *Psychology of Addictive Behaviors, 28*(2), 443–452. https://doi.org/10.1037/a0033674

Van Ameringen, M., Mancini, C., Patterson, B., & Boyle, M. H. (2008). Posttraumatic stress disorder in Canada. *CNS Neuroscience & Therapeutics, 14*(3), 171–181. https://doi.org/10.1111/j.1755-5949.2008.00049.x

Verreault, N., Da Costa, D., Marchand, A., Ireland, K., Banack, H., Dritsa, M., & Khalifé, S. (2012). PTSD following childbirth: A prospective study of incidence and risk factors in Canadian women. *Journal of Psychosomatic Research, 73*(4), 257–263. https://doi.org/10.1016/j.jpsychores.2012.07.010

Wagner, A. C., Jaworsky, D., Logie, C. H., Conway, T., Pick, N., Wozniak, D., … & Ion, A. (2018). High rates of posttraumatic stress symptoms in women living with HIV in Canada. *PloS One, 13*(7), e0200526. https://doi.org/10.1371/journal.pone.0200526

Watkins, K., Lee, J. E. C., & Zamorski, M. A. (2017). Moderating effect of marital status on the association between combat exposure and post-deployment mental health in Canadian military personnel. *Military Psychology, 29*(3), 177–188. https://doi.org/10.1037/mil0000153

Weathers, F. W., Litz, B. T., Herman, D.S., Huska, J. A., & Keane, T. M. (1993). *The PTSD Checklist: Reliability, validity, & diagnostic utility*. Paper presented at the Meeting of the International Society for Traumatic Stress Studies, San Antonio, TX.

Weathers, F. W., Litz, B. T., Keane, T. M., Palmieri, P. A., Marx, B. P., & Schnurr, P. P. (2013). *The PTSD Checklist for DSM-5 (PCL-5)*. Scale available from the National Center for PTSD at www.ptsd.va.gov.

Weiss, D. S., & Marmar, C. R. (1996). The impact of event scale – Revised. In J. Wilson & T. M. Keane (eds), *Assessing psychological trauma and PTSD* (pp. 399–411). New York: Guilford Press.

Wilberforce, N., Wilberforce, K., & Aubrey-Bassler, F. K. (2010). Post-traumatic stress disorder in physicians from an underserviced area. *Family Practice*, *27*(3), 339–343. https://doi.org/10.1093/fampra/cmq002

Zamorski, M. A., Bennett, R. E., Rusu, C., Weeks, M., Boulos, D., & Garber, B. G. (2016). Prevalence of past-year mental disorders in the Canadian Armed Forces, 2002–2013. *The Canadian Journal of Psychiatry*, *61*(1_suppl), 26S–35S. https://doi.org/10.1177/0706743716628854

Part 2
Perspectives and Populations

6 Psychology of Men and Masculinities

Implications for Men's Experiences of Posttraumatic Stress Disorder

Donald R. McCreary

Introduction

Researchers have provided evidence that most individuals will experience at least one potentially psychologically traumatic event in the course of their lifetime (Benjet et al., 2016). Some individuals, especially those whose occupation puts them at a greater risk for exposure to potentially psychologically traumatic events (e.g., military, public safety personnel), may experience multiple exposures across their lifetime (Carleton et al., 2018). In such cases, additional exposures may further increase the risk of experiencing adverse psychological outcomes, such as Posttraumatic Stress Disorder (PTSD; Kilpatrick et al., 2013).

Self-identified men are often over-represented among those working in occupations at higher risk for exposure to potentially psychologically traumatic events (e.g., police, firefighting, military; McCreary, Fong, & Groll, 2017; Shafer, Sutter, & Gibbons, 2015); however, occupation is not the sole risk factor for men. If men are unfortunate enough to be exposed to something, or multiple somethings, potentially psychologically traumatic, and if they subsequently develop an adverse psychological outcome such as PTSD, depression, generalized anxiety, or substance abuse issues, their gender role socialization (i.e., their masculinities) will often serve as a barrier to three important treatment-related elements: (1) identifying that they have a problem; (2) seeking treatment for that problem; and (3) working with their mental health professionals in a manner that does not sabotage the treatment outcome (Seidler et al., 2016).

Despite a growing body of literature examining the intersection of masculinities and mental disorders (e.g., major depressive disorder), few researchers have explored the associations between masculinities and men's experiences with PTSD. In the current chapter, I will explore the current evidence regarding masculinities and men's experiences with PTSD in more detail. I argue that masculinities are a significant obstacle to the effective identification and treatment of PTSD, as well as to a range of other mental health disorders in self-identified men. To elucidate that expected relationship, I will initially provide a general overview of masculinities and how masculinities can adversely influence men's mental health. I structure the

DOI: 10.4324/9781351134637-7

178 *Donald R. McCreary*

chapter in three parts. First, I briefly review the main concepts underpinning the psychological approach to the scientific study of masculinities. Second, I describe how masculinities may be a barrier to men understanding that they are experiencing poor mental health, in general. Third, I shift my focus to the limited research examining the links between masculinities and men's experiences of PTSD.

In this chapter, I provide a cursory overview to encourage interested readers to seek out additional information about the importance of masculinities when studying men's experiences with PTSD and related mental health disorders, not an exhaustive review of the literature on masculinities and mental health. Psychological gender plays an undeniable role, as both a barrier and a facilitator, in people's positive mental health; however, much of the research I describe here has been conducted within the context of traditionally Western, Euro-centric cultures. The extent to which the results generalize to other cultures is unknown and needs further examination. The described associations may be the same, stronger, or weaker. Other variables may mediate or moderate the associations in some cultures, but not others. In any case, keep in mind these caveats while reading the chapter.

Masculinities

Understanding the role of masculinities is well-warranted when trying to understand the barriers that men face in both acknowledging the presence of a mental health concern (e.g., depression, anxiety, PTSD) and then seeking and engaging in treatment for that concern. Many people think of "masculinity" as a single, unidimensional concept (i.e., from not at all masculine to very masculine); however, such a simple conceptualization ignores important variance in the construct "masculinities", which refers to a wide-ranging, broad-based, and multidimensional individual difference characteristic. The activities, emotions, and related characteristics that define masculinities are socially constructed and can vary as a function of person, time, space, culture, and positioning. The actual display of masculine characteristics, as well as what constitutes such characteristics, varies according to what psychologists often refer to as a person-by-situation interaction (Addis & Mahalik, 2003). In other words, when individual differences and context-dependent elements of masculinities interact, some situations will be more or less likely to lead to a display of traditional or normative masculinities in some (but not all) self-identifying men (McCreary, 2016).

Masculinities are taught to both boys and girls as a part of the gender role socialization process, in which conforming to normative gender constructions is reinforced through social rewards, but failing to conform or transgressing, is socially punished (Halim & Ruble, 2010). The socializing agents are parents, peers, and societal members, as well as various forms of media. Researchers have provided evidence that boys and men are more frequently and more harshly punished for transgressing gender role norms than are girls and women (McCreary, 1994; Vandello & Bosson, 2013). Such realities lead to a more rigid degree of gender role conformity among males than among females. Developmental researchers have suggested that social pressures to conform to societal gender role norms are lessened for older men (Hyde & Phillis, 1979).

To better understand the complexity of masculinities, I briefly review the main psychological approaches to their conceptualization: male-valued personality traits; masculinity ideology; traditional male role norms; and the overlapping notions of stress, strain, conflict, precarious manhood, and masculinity contest cultures (Cochran, 2010). Several different ways of thinking about masculinities are summarized in Table 6.1 (also see McCreary, 2016).

Table 6.1 General overview of reviewed masculinity constructs

Authors	Construct focus	Aspects or dimensions of masculinity
Bem (1974)	Instrumentality	socially desirable personality traits stereotypically associated with men more than women
Spence & Helmreich (1975)	Agency	socially desirable personality traits stereotypically associated with men more than women
Spence et al. (1979)[a]	Unmitigated Agency	socially undesirable personality traits stereotypically associated with men more than women
Brannon (1976)	Traditional Male Role Norms	no sissy stuff the big wheel the sturdy oak give 'em hell
Pleck (1981, 1995)	Gender Role Strain	discrepancy strain trauma strain dysfunction strain
Thompson & Pleck (1986)	Traditional Male Role Norms	status toughness power anti-femininity
Levant et al. (2010)	Traditional Male Role Norms	avoidance of femininity negative attitudes towards sexual minorities extreme self-reliance dominance toughness importance of sex restrictive emotionality

(continued)

180   *Donald R. McCreary*

Table 6.1 Cont.

Authors	Construct focus	Aspects or dimensions of masculinity
Mahalik et al. (2003)	Conformity to Traditional Male Role Norms	winning emotional control risk-taking violence dominance playboy self-reliance primacy of work power over women disdain for homosexuals physical toughness pursuit of women
O'Neil et al. (1986)	Male Gender Role Conflict	success, power, & competition restrictive emotionality restrictive affectionate behaviour conflict between work & family relationships
Eisler & Skidmore (1987)	Masculine Gender Role Stress	physical inadequacy being subordinate to women emotional expression intellectual inferiority fear of performance failure
Vandello et al. (2008)[a]	Precarious Manhood	manhood is something that is achieved or earned manhood can be lost or taken away at any time manhood is something that is affirmed by others, not the individual himself
Berdahl et al., 2018	Masculinity Contest Culture	show no weakness strength and stamina put work first dog-eat-dog

Notes:
a The description of Precarious Manhood outlines its three tenets, not three measured dimensions of the construct. There is currently no self-report measure of the Precarious Manhood concept.

Masculine-typed Personality Traits

The modern study of masculinities is fairly recent, beginning in the early 1970s with the advent of Bem's notion of psychological androgyny (Bem, 1974). Androgyny theory was the first approach that disentangled biological

Psychology of Men and Masculinities 181

sex from psychological gender and sexual orientation. In other words, Bem (1974) posited that any individual could internalize and enact elements of both male and female gender roles. As such, men who internalized female-stereotypic gender role characteristics were not expected to be gay; conversely, it was equally expected that gay men could (and would) internalize and enact stereotypically masculine characteristics. Such positions had not always been the case with previous models of gender roles (e.g., Hathaway & McKinley, 1943).

To measure what were referred to at the time as masculine and feminine gender roles, Bem (1974) developed the Bem Sex Role Inventory, a measure of socially desirable personality traits that were stereotypic of either men or women. The male-typed traits (i.e., masculinities) were focused on the area of instrumentality, while the female-typed traits (i.e., femininities) were concentrated in the area of expressivity. Other measures of masculine and feminine personality traits soon followed, the most notable being the Personal Attributes Questionnaire (Spence, Helmreich, & Stapp, 1975; Spence & Helmreich, 1978) which measured socially desirable traits focused on agency (masculinities) and communion (femininities). Spence, Helmreich, and Holahan (1979) also created measures of socially undesirable masculine and feminine personality traits (unmitigated agency and unmitigated communion) to address concerns about social desirability that may confound the measurement of positive gender-related personality traits. The socially desirable and undesirable traits, especially unmitigated agency, have been used in several studies exploring adverse physical and psychological health outcomes for men (Helgeson, 1994). As a result of measurement concerns, many of the questionnaires used to examine the socially desirable masculine personality traits are no longer being used (Smiler & Epstein, 2010).

Masculinity Ideology

Masculinity ideology (Pleck, 1981, 1995) includes notions that, although boys are taught about masculinities, traditional male role norms, and society's gendered expectations for them, not all boys or men feel compelled to act in traditionally gender-typed ways at all times. Pleck argued that the central reason behind this lack of consistency in men's and boys' expression of traditional masculinities is due to differences in the way individuals perceive the need to conform to traditionally defined male role norms. Like most individual difference constructs, masculinity ideology is expected to follow a normal distribution: a small number of men (approximately 16%) at the front end will feel a great deal of self-induced pressure to conform to traditional male role norms in most instances; an equally small number of men (about 16%) at the back end will feel very little need to conform to traditional male role norms in their daily interactions; and the remainder (about 68%) will feel varying degrees of pressure to conform to traditional male role norms in the various social contexts within which

182 *Donald R. McCreary*

they interact. Between- and within-person variability regarding conformity helps to explain why we do not see all men acting at all times in ways that support our socially constructed expectations for men and masculinities. Masculinity ideology is part of the reason why, even though research shows that there are statistically significant correlations between men's need to conform to traditional male role norms and various mental health-related variables (e.g., negative attitudes towards mental health help-seeking behaviour; Vogel et al., 2011), those correlations tend to be only small to moderate in magnitude.

Traditional Male Role Norms

The concept of traditional male role norms evolved in parallel with the development of masculinity ideology, and is the most enduring way of thinking about and measuring masculinities within psychology. The concept represents the prescriptive, socially constructed expectations we teach boys and girls about how boys and men are expected to think, feel, and act. As the concept evolved, various authors identified, focused on, and defined different elements, or dimensions, of traditional male role norms. Below, I outline selected fundamental contributions.

Brannon (1976) was the first modern masculinities researcher to outline the dimensions of traditional male role norms, identifying four main components. The first, what he calls *No Sissy Stuff*, means that men should avoid doing things that society has constructed as feminine-typed; for example, men should not display things like openness or vulnerability, which can be seen as signs of weakness. The limitation has potential implications for several aspects of men's lives, including their relationships with others and their willingness to seek help when needed (e.g., for a mental health condition, such as PTSD, depression, anxiety, anger management, or substance abuse). Brannon's second aspect of male role norms, *The Big Wheel*, is focused on status, success, and the importance of being looked up to by others. Beyond income, there are several other ways to achieve success, including being successful at work (e.g., promotion, being a manager of others), in sports, or in various social activities. Focusing on success, however, often means the importance of family and friends can be minimized; resulting in a reduced degree of in-depth social connections that are key to recognizing and coping with mental health needs. The third element of Brannon's model, *The Sturdy Oak*, focuses on displaying toughness, confidence, and self-reliance. Displaying vulnerability in any form, including not being able to handle what life throws at you (e.g., physical and mental health concerns), is perceived as weakness, is not considered to be masculine, and thus must be avoided. The implications for those suffering from PTSD symptoms is that one must always appear strong, tough, and confident, even when they are re-experiencing the emotions from a psychologically traumatic event, are being hypervigilant, or are feeling emotionally numb. The final element Brannon discusses, *Give'Em Hell*, focuses on the value of violence, aggression, and daring. Traditional male role norms involve tackling personal and interpersonal threats with physical aggression and violence. *Give'Em Hell* also means that taking physical, psychological, interpersonal, social, and other kinds of risk is a way of displaying masculinities. Unsurprisingly, men experiencing depression are more likely to act out in aggressive and violent ways (Cavanagh et al., 2017). The implications for PTSD seem pretty clear.

Since Brannon's (1976) work, several others have developed their own taxonomies of male role norms. Essentially, newer taxonomic approaches are expansions of Brannon's original model. Authors of the updated approaches often take Brannon's four categories and identify important sub-elements that they feel need to be brought to the forefront. For example, when Thompson and Pleck (1986) attempted to create a self-report scale of traditional male role norms based on Brannon's model, they chose to focus on status, toughness, power over others, and anti-femininity. Levant et al. (2010) kept the toughness and anti-femininity aspects in their model but also highlighted five additional elements of traditional male role norms: negative attitudes towards sexual minorities, dominance over others, extreme self-reliance, the importance of sex, and restrictive emotionality. By giving these aspects their own focused domains, Levant and his colleagues highlight the fundamental importance for traditional masculinities of homophobia, preferences for managing one's own physical and mental health problems, and keeping one's emotions repressed or hidden, as well as being better than those around you and having an active sex life. Many of these aspects of male role norms can influence men's responses to their experience of poor mental health. For example, preferring to manage one's mental health problems is associated with less likelihood of seeking treatment, while the value of repressing or hiding emotions from others can prove to be a barrier to the successful treatment of conditions, such as PTSD (e.g., Addis & Mahalik, 2003; Seidler et al., 2016).

Mahalik and colleagues' (2003) Conformity to Masculine Norms Inventory (CMNI) presents a second popular taxonomy of male role norms. While continuing to focus on some of the more traditional elements of these norms, including risk-taking, status-seeking, and the importance of violence, Mahalik and colleagues (2003) suggested other additions. Specifically, they highlighted the significance for traditional masculinities of winning, the primacy of work, men's power over women, and men's sexual pursuit of women.

All of the expanded dimensions are now part of the canon of traditional male role norms and highlight key factors that can affect men's overall health and well-being, as well as the quality of their interactions with others. Traditional male role norms are typically measured using self-report questionnaires that give researchers an index of the degree to which men agree or disagree with these norms (Thompson & Bennett, 2015). Hundreds of research studies have been conducted since 1986 (e.g., Levant & Richmond, 2007; Wong et al., 2017) and, as alluded to throughout this section, many of the results indicate that the more strongly men agree with these traditional male role norms, the more harm they tend to do to themselves and to those around them, especially when PTSD and other mental health concerns are involved.

Masculine Gender Role Strain, Stress, Conflict, and Precarious Manhood

Pleck (1981, 1995) was the first to provide a theoretical underpinning for understanding the many adverse associations between traditional masculine beliefs and men's mental and physical health, as well as masculinities' potentially harmful impact on others (especially women and gender non-conforming individuals). Pleck's theoretical underpinning formed the basis of his notion of *Gender Role Strain*. The tenets of gender role strain are based on the potential, cumulative effects of ten inherent features of traditional male role norms. The features include that male role norms are inconsistent and often contradictory, that men often overconform to masculine norms in order to avoid being punished for transgressing them, that certain norms are psychologically dysfunctional, and that the norms will change over time which, as a result, will serve as compounding stressors because men will not know how to respond to various situations or in various contexts. Thus, while men are expected to conform to traditional male role norms, doing so can lead to stress and potential psychological and physical harm (i.e., strain) (Folkman & Moskowitz, 2004). In this vein, Pleck identified three different types of gender role strain: discrepancy strain (e.g., feeling that you are not as masculine as other men because you cannot or do not conform to role norms as often as you think you should); trauma strain (e.g., disengaging from your emotions to cope with stressful outcomes associated with the male gender role); and dysfunction strain (e.g., negative physical, psychological, and interpersonal impacts of masculinities).

Researchers have linked elements of gender role strain to numerous adverse outcomes for men (McCreary, 2016). Researchers evidence an example of trauma strain by showing that men who report higher levels of agreement with traditional male role norms also report higher levels of alexithymia, which is an inability to identify one's emotions (Levant & Richmond, 2007). Other researchers have provided multiple examples of dysfunction strain, showing that masculinities are associated with a wide array of other personal and interpersonal dysfunction, including substance abuse, depression, low self-esteem, poor relationship and life satisfaction, as well as more negative attitudes about women, more supportive views of sexual harassment, and a greater tendency to accept myths about rape (Levant & Richmond, 2007; Wong et al., 2017). More recent research has linked traditional male role norms about self-reliance to increased suicide ideation (Pirkis et al., 2017).

Masculinities are also thought to negatively impact men's health and well-being in other important ways. There are two popular theories that describe adverse relationships between masculinities and men's health and well-being; specifically, Eisler & Skidmore's notion of *Masculine Gender Role Stress* (1987) and O'Neil and colleagues' theory of men's *Gender Role Conflict* (O'Neil et al., 1986). Eisler (1995) felt that men would experience stress in two types of situation: (i) where men were forced to act in stereotypically feminine ways (even if the situation required that type of response); and (ii) where men felt they were not conforming strongly enough to traditionally masculine gender role expectations. Eisler identified five different causes of potential stress: feelings of physical inadequacy; being subordinate to women; emotional expression; intellectual inferiority; and fearing performance failure (Eisler & Skidmore, 1987). Eisler conceptualized Masculine Gender Role Stress as a form of internal stress; accordingly, ineffective coping strategies could lead to the development of psychological strain. There is substantial research evidence supporting the association between masculine gender role stress and a number of indicators of poor well-being and interpersonal conflict, including anger, hostility, lower social support, poor body image, homophobia, and physical and verbal abuse towards female partners (McCreary, 2016).

O'Neil and colleagues' model of Gender Role Conflict (O'Neil et al., 1986) has received a significant degree of support. According to this concept,

> [g]ender-role conflict is a psychological state where gender roles have negative consequences or impact on a person or others. The ultimate outcome of this conflict is the restriction of the person's ability to actualize their human potential or the restriction of some[one] else's potential.
>
> (O'Neil et al., 1986, p. 336)

O'Neil and his colleagues have identified four main dimensions of men's gender role conflict: a focus on success, power, and competition; a restriction on the types and degree of emotions that can be expressed; restrictions around the display of affectionate behaviour, especially towards other men; and conflict between the primacy of work and family. Researchers have demonstrated significant associations between gender role conflict (overall, or one or more of the sub-dimensions) and numerous mental health concerns and interpersonal problems. The concerns and problems include higher levels of depression, anxiety, and alcohol abuse, as well as lower self-esteem and greater likelihood of engaging in intimate partner violence (McCreary, 2016; O'Neil, 2008).

A new approach to understanding the adverse impact that masculinities can have on men is the notion of precarious manhood (Vandello & Bosson, 2013). The concept has three main tenets: (i) manhood is something that is achieved or earned, not inherent within the person; (ii) manhood can be taken away at any time, meaning that men are constantly under threat of losing their sense of masculinity and being seen as unmanly or not masculine; and (iii) manhood is something that is awarded by others, so men are always attempting to reaffirm their masculinity in a public manner. Researchers studying precarious manhood show that, when their sense of masculinity is threatened, men will avoid acting in feminine ways and enhance their expression of traditional masculinities (e.g., Cheryan et al., 2015). Examples include acting more aggressively (Bosson & Vandello, 2011), exaggerating reports of physical strength (Frederick et al., 2017), and taking more driving (Braly, Parent, & Delucia, 2018) and economic (Parent, Kalenkoski, & Cardella, 2018) risks. Threatening men's sense of masculinity can encourage behaviours that increase the likelihood they may harm themselves or those around them.

More recently, Berdahl et al. (2018) proposed a workplace-based extension of precarious manhood: Masculinity Contest Culture (MCC). Berdahl and colleagues argue that certain workplace cultures over-emphasize traditionally negative elements of masculinities, giving men in such cultures more latitude to behave in ways that will negatively impact the health and well-being of themselves and others. Engaging in workplace MCCs is perceived as a way of expressing dominance, status, and success; in contrast, failing to engage in MCC-type behaviours (or not winning at MCC activities) is perceived as a way of losing dominance, status, and success. Occupations and workplaces can incorporate MCCs to varying degrees from highly engaged in MCC, to not engaged at all, to only moderately engaged.

Berdahl et al. (2018) have identified four main components to MCCs: *Show No Weakness* (e.g., be confident, always be correct, avoid displaying feminine-typed behaviours and emotions); *Strength and Stamina* (e.g., work long, work hard, don't take breaks or vacations); *Put Work First* (e.g., work is more important than friends or family; taking family or sick leave is not acceptable); and *Dog-Eat-Dog* (e.g., work is a hypercompetitive environment where there are winners and losers; win at all costs). Thus, MCC is similar to precarious manhood in several ways: the dimensions of MCC reflect notions of traditional masculinities; winning in an MCC environment is equivalent to earning one's manhood; the status obtained or lost in MCCs is conferred by others; and, once earned, that status can be taken away by others at any time.

Given the types of activities incorporated in them, MCCs may create or reflect workplace environments that penalize men who wish to engage in health promotive behaviours, such as taking fewer risks (physical, psychological, financial), having a stronger work–life balance (e.g., by working fewer hours), prioritizing their non-work life (e.g., by taking paternity leave), seeking help for psychological health concerns, and taking a health-related leave of absence. The actual health impacts of workplace MCCs are still being explored, but initial results suggest people who work in organizations with greater degrees of MCCs report higher levels of workplace bullying and harassment, more job-related burnout, and poorer psychological well-being (Glick, Berdahl, & Alonso, 2018). Many of the

Psychology of Men and Masculinities 187

occupations that put men at greater risk for poor mental health (e.g., public safety personnel, including first responders, as well as military), including greater risk for PTSD, also tend to engage in MCCs to at least some degree (Rawski & Workman-Stark, 2018; Reid, O'Neill, & Blair-Loy, 2018).

Masculinities and Mental Health

Researchers have shown evidence of significant correlations between several aspects of masculinities and indices of poor mental health in men and boys (McCreary, 2016; Wong et al., 2017); however, I will not focus on such relationships here. One could argue that socially constructed role norms are too distal (i.e., too many steps away) from our measurement of mental health. Rather, we need to be measuring more proximal variables; variables that are influenced by masculinities, but which also influence behaviours that help or hinder recovery from a psychological ailment. Thus, I concentrate here on the ways the various facets of masculinities can serve as indirect barriers to the diagnosis and effective treatment of men experiencing poor mental health. Brannon's (1976) original emphasis on avoiding being vulnerable, needing to be looked up to, being seen as tough, confident, and reliable, and taking risks, can all be translated to the mental health sphere as edicts against admitting to a mental illness, not seeking (or delaying) treatment, and not disclosing mental health concerns to friends, loved ones, or even professionals. Similar notions emerged from Levant and Richmond's (2007) and Mahalik et al.'s (2003) models of traditional male role norms, especially with regard to the focus on extreme self-reliance and emotional control. As such, I now turn to explore some of the ways in which traditional masculinities are associated with two of those more proximal variables: mental health stigma and men's experiences with the mental health treatment process.

Men, Masculinities, and Mental Health Stigma

Men are much less likely than women to seek treatment for most health issues, including mental health problems (Addis & Mahalik, 2003). Not seeking treatment can either prevent men from achieving recovery or can significantly delay recovery, depending on the severity of the problem. Internalized self-stigma about mental health may be a factor in this delay. Self-stigma represents a set of negative attitudes and beliefs about mental health treatment (e.g., perceived need for psychotherapy, confidence in mental health practitioners, preference to cope on their own; Fischer & Turner, 1970; Picco et al., 2016) and is associated with reduced treatment-seeking behaviour (Clement et al., 2015). Numerous studies have evidenced that, when compared to women, men possess a higher degree of mental health self-stigma (Coppens et al., 2013; Elhai, Schweinle, & Anderson, 2008; Komiya, Good, & Sherrod, 2000; Vogel, Wade, & Haake, 2006; Vogel & Wester, 2003). Some researchers have even suggested that men

188 *Donald R. McCreary*

may possess twice the level of mental health self-stigma when compared to women (Jadego et al., 2009). Thus, men's higher levels of internalized self-stigma about mental health may be an important factor in better understanding their delays in treatment-seeking behaviour for mental disorders, including PTSD.

But to what extent is men's greater mental health self-stigma a function of traditional masculinities? The association between masculinities and mental health stigma has only been examined in a small handful of studies, but researchers have consistently shown that people with higher levels of restrictive emotionality (i.e., a dimension of the masculine gender role conflict construct proposed by O'Neil et al., 1986) tend to report higher levels of self-stigma (e.g., Heath et al., 2017; Vogel et al., 2014; Wahto & Swift, 2016). Researchers have also evidenced that men with higher levels of adherence to traditional male role norms, or who are experiencing gender role conflict, also report significantly more negative attitudes about mental health treatment-seeking and were significantly less likely to seek treatment (e.g., Good, Dell, & Mintz, 1989; Good & Wood, 1995). The average effect size for these associations tends to be moderate, suggesting a meaningful relationship (also see Seidler et al., 2016). Thus, one way to improve men's poorer mental health experiences may involve addressing the relationship between masculinities and self-stigma. How to do this effectively, especially across a wide range of men and social contexts, has not yet been examined.

Men, Masculinities, and Mental Health Treatment Experiences

Masculinities can also act as a barrier to men's mental health by adversely influencing the treatment process. To date, much of the limited scientific research addressing this issue has been focused on treatments for depression. Qualitative and quantitative research in the area was recently summarized by Seidler et al. (2016), whose results highlight the potential limiting role of masculinities in mental health treatment more broadly. In their overview of the quantitative research, Seidler and colleagues (2016) reported that men tend to perceive other men who seek mental health treatment as more feminine than masculine. Avoiding femininity is an important dimension of traditional male role norms and a feature of men's gender role stress, strain, and conflict; as such, avoiding femininity may be a significant barrier for men who need treatment for depression, PTSD, or any other mental health challenge. Seidler and colleagues (2016) also described research evidencing that men typically would not want to speak with male friends, or even a family doctor, about their experiences of depression; if men speak with anyone, it would likely be a close, ideally female, family member. Seidler and colleagues (2016) also reported that, when presented with a scenario of a typically depressed person, men rated their depression as less severe than did women; perhaps an indication of men's impaired ability to judge the severity of depression in both themselves and others.

The qualitative research summarized by Seidler and colleagues (2016) indicated several close links between men's perceptions of masculinities and treatment outcomes. Seidler and colleagues identified six aspects of the treatment process where masculinities appeared to have an important impact on men's experiences. First, because of limitations and restrictions around emotional expression, men often had difficulty telling their therapists how they felt. In fact, men typically avoided the term depression and used words like "stressed" or "overwhelmed" instead. Second, men experiencing depression often felt shame, weakness, and being out of control, as opposed to the masculine norms of strength, toughness, and being in control of their lives. Third, therapy is often seen as feminine and to be avoided until all other options have been exhausted. Furthermore, once they started therapy, men often under-reported their symptoms and problems to their therapist. Such practices may be thought to help maintain at least some semblance of a masculine identity, but also represent a significant barrier to successful treatment (and thus their healing potentiality). Fourth, men wanted to avoid talking therapies and instead take on more action-focused interventions. The choice of intervention strategy may be related to emotional control and appearing strong in the eyes of the therapist. Additionally, there was some evidence that men wanted to avoid medication because of a fear of losing control. Fifth, some men avoided seeking professional help and adopted a wide range of maladaptive coping strategies often linked to masculinities (e.g., risk-taking). Substance abuse was a common strategy and is often referred to as a form of self-medication. Finally, Seidler and colleagues' (2016) review suggests that the content of messages put forth in society about depression (e.g., using a battle analogy, such as "fighting it") can help men feel less marginalized.

Seidler et al.'s (2016) systematic review focused on men's experiences with depression, but may be relevant to a wider range of mental health challenges, including PTSD. Until the DSM-V placed PTSD in a Trauma and Stress-related Disorder category, it was classified as an anxiety disorder (Pietrzak et al., 2010). More importantly, however, PTSD sufferers have almost three times the risk of also experiencing co-morbid depression (Pietrzak et al., 2010). That is, more than one third of those with a full PTSD diagnosis also experience co-morbid depression, with that number climbing to more than two-thirds if those with a subthreshold diagnosis of PTSD are also included (Pietrzak et al., 2010). Future researchers need to determine how strongly the findings from Seidler and colleagues' review generalize to people experiencing PTSD and other forms of poor mental health.

Applications to PTSD

Masculinities are an obstacle to men overcoming mental health concerns; accordingly, what roles might masculinities play as a barrier to the effective identification and treatment of PTSD? As I have already noted, many research results related to masculinities and depression (both the self-stigma and treatment aspects) may also apply to PTSD. However, to date, the number of studies examining the associations between masculinities and men's experiences with PTSD is very small and there is very little overlap between the types of questions being asked in the research about depression and in the research on PTSD. Most of the empirical research on masculinities and PTSD has been conducted within military and veteran populations, especially those who attend outpatient treatment facilities for mental health concerns. Furthermore, much of the research has been quantitative in nature, using measures such as the Male Role Norms Scale (Thompson & Pleck, 1986), the Conformity to Masculine Norms Inventory (Mahalik et al., 2003), and the Masculine Gender Role Stress Scale (Eisler & Skidmore, 1987). The relative lack of qualitative research exploring self-perceptions of the relationships between masculinities and PTSD is a potential limitation because qualitative research can often inform new directions for quantitative study. Finally, many of the studies, whether qualitative or quantitative, were comprised of very small sample sizes, limiting the generalizability and replicability of results.

Despite the aforementioned limitations to the literature, there are some potentially interesting research results that may help inform us about how masculinities influence men's experiences with PTSD. First, among men with PTSD, self-perceptions of masculinities are heightened (Elder et al., 2017). That is, men with PTSD feel the need to appear strong, hoping to avoid seeming weak to themselves and others. As part of trying to appear strong, men may avoid expressing most emotions. The exception to avoiding emotions is anger, which is often seen as a form of masculine expression rather than an emotion. Mostly, however, men display a flattened affect (e.g., stoicism) that is thought to be a sign of masculine strength and independence. Stoicism as an aspect of masculinities has been linked to what Caddick, Smith, and Phoenix (2015) call *Military Masculinity* because, as they noted, military men are trained to emphasize characteristics such as internal strength and unimpacted perseverance in the face of hardship.

Second, not all aspects of masculinities appear to be directly correlated with PTSD symptoms or diagnosis. Jakupcak et al. (2013), in their study of military veterans in the United States, suggested that toughness is a significant predictor of higher levels of both PTSD and depression symptoms. In another study of American veterans, Garcia et al. (2011) suggested that an exaggerated sense of self-reliance and self-control were both significantly associated with greater levels of PTSD. McDermott et al.'s (2010) study of crack cocaine-addicted men in the United States showed that masculine gender role stress (Eisler, 1995) was a significant positive correlate of PTSD symptoms. In other words, research results support notions that the higher their self-reported traditional male role norms or gender role stress scores, the greater degree men will manifest PTSD symptoms.

Third, masculinity may be part of mediated or moderated associations between third party variables and PTSD. For example, Cox and

Loughlin's (2017) results suggested that the association between PTSD symptoms and relationship satisfaction in military veterans was partially mediated by elements of traditional male role norms (i.e., avoiding femininity, and emphasizing toughness, dominance, restrictive emotionality, and the importance of sex). Data from Jakupcak et al. (2006) suggested that masculinity may be indirectly associated with PTSD symptoms via high levels of alexithymia and poor social support. Unfortunately, the latter suggestions by Jakupcak and colleagues were *post hoc* and based on bivariate correlations, and no mediational analyses were used to test the suppositions. Regarding potential moderation, Morrison (2011) examined the relationship between conformity to traditional male role norms, PTSD, and cardiac health behaviours. Morrison found no evidence of a significant relationship between risky cardiac health behaviours (e.g., alcohol use, higher fat diet, tobacco use) and PTSD among men who did not feel a need to conform to traditional masculinities; in contrast, when their perceived need to conform to traditional masculinities was higher, the men in the higher PTSD symptom group reported poorer cardiac health behaviours. Evidence of an inverse relationship was replicated when masculine gender role stress replaced traditional male role norms as the moderating variable.

Conclusions

Overall, current social constructions of masculinities present several direct and indirect barriers to men's mental health. The same barriers appear to increase risk and add an extra hurdle to recovery for men experiencing a mental health condition, including those with PTSD. The increased risk and additional barriers are particularly troublesome for people working in male-dominated occupations (e.g., public safety personnel, including first responders, military) where there is a greater risk for exposure to single or multiple potentially psychologically traumatic events (e.g., Carleton et al., 2018). Many of these occupations often have a strong, masculine-influenced ethos or culture in which weakness is neither desired nor tolerated; as such, mental health challenges resulting from occupational exposures may be seen as a sign of being unfit to do the job well, leading men in such occupations to hide their symptoms from themselves and others.

The importance of masculinities in the way men experience poor mental health is also an important consideration for mental health practitioners. Being aware of the many ways in which masculinities can influence mental health and mental health treatment processes, may improve clinician effectiveness in treating men. There has been a significant increase in the availability of clinical resources stemming from research focused on the psychological study of men and masculinities since Bem's work in 1974. There are now more professional organizations, journals, conferences, and training materials available than in the past (Cochran, 2010). The available resources can aid in knowledge building, knowledge translation, and clinician capacity building. For example, members of the Society for the

192   *Donald R. McCreary*

Psychological Study of Men and Masculinity (Division 51 of the American Psychological Association) have a well-respected journal and conferences with several continuing education training sessions. Members of that organization also have developed numerous resources for clinicians seeking greater knowledge for the treatment of men, including recently released Guidelines for Psychological Practice with Boys and Men (American Psychological Association, Boys and Men Guidelines Group, 2018).

Applying a gendered lens, including sex and gender-based analysis, to the ways in which we approach the issues of men's mental health (in both practice and research) can lead to better proactive behaviours, treatments, and outcomes for all men, especially those working in highly masculinized workplace cultures. A gendered lens allows theories and models of gender to inform research, which then informs practice, which leads to more refined research questions, more effective practices, and so on, helping men achieve increasingly optimal health outcomes in the process.

References

Addis, M. E., & Mahalik, J. R. (2003). Men, masculinity, and the contexts of help seeking. *American Psychologist*, *58*, 5–14. https://doi.org/10.1037/0003-066X.58.1.5.

American Psychological Association, Boys and men guidelines group. (2018). *APA guidelines for psychological practice with boys and men.* Retrieved from www.apa.org/about/policy/boys-men-practice-guidelines.pdf.

Bem, S. L. (1974). The measurement of psychological androgyny. *Journal of Consulting and Clinical Psychology*, *42*, 155–162.

Benjet, C., Bromet, E., Karam, E. G., Kessler, R. C., McLaughlin, K. A., Ruscio, A. M., ... & Alonso, J. (2016). The epidemiology of traumatic event exposure worldwide: Results from the World Mental Health Survey Consortium. *Psychological Medicine*, *46*, 327–343. http://dx.doi.org/10.1017/S0033291715001981.

Berdahl, J. L., Cooper, M., Glick, P., Livingston, R. W., & Williams, J. C. (2018). Work as a masculinity contest. *Journal of Social Issues*, *72*, 422–448. https://doi.org/10.1111/josi.12289

Bosson, J. K., & Vandello, J. A. (2011). Precarious manhood and its links to action and aggression. *Current Directions in Psychological Science*, *20*, 82–86. https://doi.org/10.1177/0963721411402669.

Braly, A. M., Parent, M. C., & DeLucia, P. R. (2018). Do threats to masculinity result in more aggressive driving behavior? *Psychology of Men & Masculinity*, *19*, 540–546. http://dx.doi.org/10.1037/men0000135.

Brannon, R. (1976). The male sex role: Our culture's blueprint for masculinity and what it's done for us lately. In D. S. David & R. Brannon (eds), *The forty-nine percent majority: The male sex role* (pp. 1–45). Reading, MA: Addison-Wesley.

Caddick, N., Smith, B., & Phoenix, C. (2015). Male combat veterans' narratives of PTSD, masculinity, and health. *Sociology of Health and Illness*, *37*, 97–111. https://doi.org/10.1111/1467-9566.12183.

Carleton, R. N., Afifi, T. O., Turner, S., Taillieu, T., Duranceau, S., LeBouthillier, D. M., ... & Hozempa, K. (2018). Mental disorder symptoms among public safety personnel in Canada. *The Canadian Journal of Psychiatry*, *63*(1), 54–64. https://doi.org/10.1177/0706743717723825.

Cavanagh, A., Wilson, C. J., Kavanagh, D. J., & Caputi, P. (2017). Differences in the expression of symptoms in men versus women with depression: A systematic review and meta-analysis. *Harvard Review of Psychiatry, 25*, 29–38. https://doi.org/10.1097/HRP.0000000000000128.

Cheryan, S., Cameron, J. S., Katagiri, Z., & Monin, B. (2015). Manning up: Threatened men compensate by disavowing feminine preferences and embracing masculine attributes. *Social Psychology, 46*, 218–227. http://dx.doi.org/10.1027/1864-9335/a000239.

Clement, S., Schauman, O., Graham, T., Maggioni, F., Evans-Lacko, S., Bezborodovs, N., ... & Thornicroft, G. (2015). What is the impact of mental health-related stigma on help-seeking? A systematic review of quantitative and qualitative studies. *Psychological Medicine, 45*, 11–27. https://doi.org/10.1017/S0033291714000129.

Cochran, S. V. (2010). Emergence and development of the psychology of men and masculinity. In J. C. Chrisler & D. R. McCreary (eds), *Handbook of gender research in psychology, Volume 1: Gender research in general and experimental psychology* (pp. 43–58). New York: Springer. https://doi.org/10.1007/978-1-4419-1465-1_3.

Coppens, E., Van Audenhove, C., Scheerder, G., Arensman, E., Coffey, C., Costa, S., ... & Postuvan, V. (2013). Public attitudes toward depression and help-seeking in four European countries baseline survey prior to the OSPI-Europe intervention. *Journal of Affective Disorders, 150*(2), 320–329. http://dx.doi.org/10.1016/j.jad.2013.04.013.

Cox, D. W., & Loughlin, J. O. (2017). Posttraumatic stress mediates traditional masculinity ideology and romantic relationship satisfaction in veteran men. *Psychology of Men & Masculinity, 18*, 382–389. http://dx.doi.org/10.1037/men0000067.

Eisler, R. M. (1995). The relationship between masculine gender role stress and men's health risk: The validation of a construct. In R. F. Levant & W. S. Pollack (eds), *A new psychology of men* (pp. 207–225). New York: Basic Books.

Eisler, R., & Skidmore, J. (1987). Masculine gender role stress: Scale development and component factors in the appraisal of stressful situations. *Behavior Modification, 11*, 123–136.

Elder, W. B., Domino, J. L., Mata-Galán, E. L., & Kilmartin, C. (2017). Masculinity as an avoidance symptom of posttraumatic stress. *Psychology of Men & Masculinity, 18*, 198–207. http://dx.doi.org/10.1037/men0000123.

Elhai, J. D., Schweinle, W., & Anderson, S. M. (2008). Reliability and validity of the attitudes toward seeking professional psychological help scale-short form. *Psychiatry Research, 159*, 320–329. 10.1016/j.psychres.2007.04.020.

Fischer, E. H., & Turner, J. L. (1970). Orientations to seeking professional help: development and research utility of an attitude scale. *Journal of Consulting and Clinical Psychology, 35*, 79–90.

Folkman, S., & Moskowitz, J. T. (2004). Coping: Pitfalls and promise. *Annual Review of Psychology, 55*, 745–774. 10.1146/annurev.psych.55.090902.141456.

Frederick, D. A., Shapiro, L. M., Williams, T. R., Seoane, S.M., McIntosh, R. T., & Fischer, E. W. (2017). Precarious manhood and muscularity: Effects of threatening men's masculinity on reported strength and muscle dissatisfaction. *Body Image, 22*, 156–165. http://dx.doi.org/10.1016/j.bodyim.2017.07.002.

Garcia, H. A., Finley, E. P., Lorber, W., & Jakupcak, M. (2011). A preliminary study of the association between traditional masculine behavioral norms and PTSD symptoms in Iraq and Afghanistan veterans. *Psychology of Men & Masculinity*, *12*, 55–63. https://doi.org/10.1037/a0020577

Glick, P., Berdahl, J. L., & Alonso, N. M. (2018). Development and validation of the Masculinity Contest Culture Scale. *Journal of Social Issues*, *74*, 449–476. https://doi.org/10.1111/josi.12280.

Good, G. E., Dell, D. M., & Mintz, L. B. (1989). Male role and gender role conflict: Relations to help seeking in men. *Journal of Counseling Psychology*, *36*, 295–300. http://dx.doi.org/10.1037/0022-0167.36.3.295.

Good, G. E., & Wood, P. K. (1995). Male gender role conflict, depression, and help seeking: Do college men face double jeopardy? *Journal of Counseling and Development*, *74*, 70–75.

Halim, M. L., & Ruble, D. (2010). Gender identity and stereotyping in early and middle childhood. In J. C. Chrisler & D. R. McCreary (eds), *Handbook of gender research in psychology, Volume 1: Gender research in general and experimental psychology* (pp. 495–525). New York: Springer. https://doi.org/10.1007/978-1-4419-1465-1_24.

Hathaway, S. R., & McKinley, J. C. (1943). *The Minnesota Multiphasic Personality Inventory*. New York: Psychological Corporation.

Heath, P. J., Seidman, A. J., Vogel, D. L., Cornish, M. A., & Wade, N. G. (2017). Help-seeking stigma among men in the military: The interaction of restrictive emotionality and distress. *Psychology of Men and Masculinity*, *18*, 193–197. http://dx.doi.org/10.1037/men0000111.

Helgeson, V. S. (1994). Relation of agency and communion to well-being: Evidence and potential explanations. *Psychological Bulletin*, *116*, 412–428.

Hyde, J. S., & Phillis, D. E. (1979). Androgyny across the lifespan. *Developmental Psychology*, *15*, 334–336.

Jadego, A., Cox, B. J., Stein, B. S., & Sareen, J. (2009). Negative attitudes toward help seeking for mental illness in 2 population-based surveys from the United States and Canada. *Canadian Journal of Psychiatry*, *54*, 757–766. https://doi.org/10.1177/070674370905401106

Jakupcak, M., Blais, R. K., Grossbard, J., Garcia, H., & Okiishi, J. (2013). "Toughness" in association with mental health symptoms among Iraq and Afghanistan war veterans seeking Veterans Affairs health care. *Psychology of Men & Masculinity*, *15*, 100–104. https://doi.org/10.1037/a0031508.

Jakupcak, M., Osborne, T. L., Michael, S., Cook, J. W., & McFall, M. (2006). Implications of masculine gender role stress in male veterans with post-traumatic stress disorder. *Psychology of Men & Masculinity*, *7*, 203–211. https://doi.org/10.1037/1524-9220.7.4.203.

Kilpatrick, D. G., Resnick, H. S., Milanak, M. E., Miller, M. W., Keyes, K. M., & Friedman, M. J. (2013). National estimates of exposure to traumatic events and PTSD prevalence using DSM-IV and DSM-5 criteria. *Journal of Traumatic Stress*, *26*, 537–547. https://doi.org/10.1002/jts.21848.

Komiya, N., Good, G. E., & Sherrod, N. B. (2000). Emotional openness as a predictor of college students' attitudes toward seeking psychological help. *Journal of Counseling Psychology*, *37*, 138–143. http://dx.doi.org/10.1037/0022-0167.47.1.138.

Levant, R. F., Rankin, T. J., Williams, C., Hasan, N. T., & Smalley, K. B. (2010). Evaluation of the factor structure and construct validity of the Male Role Norms Inventory – Revised (MRNI-R). *Psychology of Men & Masculinity*, *11*, 25–37. https://doi.org/10.1037/a0017637.

Levant, R. F., & Richmond, K. (2007). A review of research on masculinity ideologies using the Male Role Norms Inventory. *Journal of Men's Studies*, *15*, 130–146. https://doi.org/10.3149/jms.1502.130.

Mahalik, J. R., Locke, B., Ludlow, L., Diemer, M., Scott, R. P. J., Gottfried, M., & Freitas, G. (2003). Development of the Conformity to Masculine Norms Inventory. *Psychology of Men & Masculinity*, *4*, 3–25. https://doi.org/10.1037/1524-9220.4.1.3.

McCreary, D. R. (1994). The male role and avoiding femininity. *Sex Roles*, *31*, 517–531.

McCreary, D. R. (2016). Masculinity. In V. Zeigler-Hill & T. K. Shackelford (eds), *Encyclopedia of personality and individual differences* (pp. 1–16). New York: Springer. https://doi.org/10.1007/978-3-319-28099-8_1087-1.

McCreary, D. R., Fong, I., & Groll, D. L. (2017). Measuring policing stress meaningfully: Establishing norms and cut-off values for the Operational and Organizational Police Stress Questionnaires. *Police Practice and Research*, *18*, 612–623. https://doi.org/10.1080/15614263.2017.1363965.

McDermott, M J., Tull, M. T., Soenke, M., Jakupcak, M., & Gratz, K. L. (2010). Masculine gender role stress and posttraumatic stress disorder symptom severity among inpatient male crack/cocaine users. *Psychology of Men & Masculinity*, *11*, 225–232. https://doi.org/10.1037/a0016671.

Morrison, J. A. (2011). Masculinity moderates the relationship between symptoms of PTSD and cardiac-related health behaviors in male veterans. *Psychology of Men & Masculinity*, *13*, 158–165. https://doi.org/10.1037/a0024186.

O'Neil, J. M. (2008). Summarizing 25 years of research on men's gender role conflict using the Gender Role Conflict Scale: New research paradigms and clinical implications. *The Counseling Psychologist*, *36*, 358–445. https://doi.org/10.1177/0011000008317057.

O'Neil, J. M., Helms, B. J., Gable, R. K., David, L., & Wrightsman, L. S. (1986). Gender-role conflict scale: College men's fear of femininity. *Sex Roles*, *14*, 335–350.

Parent, M. C., Kalenkoski, C. M., & Cardella, E. (2018). Risky business: Precarious manhood and investment portfolio decisions. *Psychology of Men & Masculinity*, *19*, 195–202. http://dx.doi.org/10.1037/men0000089.

Picco, L., Abdin, E., Chong, S. A., Pang, S., Shafie, S., Chua, B. Y., … & Subramaniam, M. (2016). Attitudes toward seeking professional psychological help: Factor structure and socio-demographic predictors. *Frontiers in Psychology*, *7*, 1–10. 10.3389/fpsyg.2016.00547.

Pietrzak, R. H., Goldstein, R. B., Southwick, S. M., & Grant, B. F. (2010). Prevalence and Axis I comorbidity of full and partial posttraumatic stress disorder in the United States: Results from Wave 2 of the National Epidemiologic Survey on Alcohol and Related Conditions. *Journal of Anxiety Disorders*, *25*, 456–465. DOI: 10.1016/j.janxdis.2010.11.010.

Pirkis, J., Spittal, M. J., Keogh, L., Mousaferiadis, T., & Currier, D. (2017). Masculinity and suicidal thinking. *Social Psychiatry and Psychiatric Epidemiology*, *52*, 319–327. 10.1007/s00127-016-1324-2.

Pleck, J. H. (1981). *The myth of masculinity*. Cambridge, MA: MIT Press.

Pleck, J. H. (1995). The gender role strain paradigm: An update. In R. F. Levant & W. S. Pollack (eds), *A new psychology of men* (pp. 11–32). New York: Basic Books.

Rawski, S. L., & Workman-Stark, A. L. (2018). Masculinity contest cultures in policing organizations and recommendations for training interventions. *Journal of Social Issues*, *74*, 607–627. https://doi.org/10.1111/josi.12286.

Reid, E. M., O'Neill, O. A., & Blair-Loy, M. (2018). Masculinity in male-dominated occupations: How teams, time, and tasks shape masculinity contests. *Journal of Social Issues*, *74*, 579–606. https://doi.org/10.1111/josi.12285.

Shafer, K., Sutter, R., & Gibbons, S. (2015). Characteristics of individuals and employment among first responders. Retrieved from https://pdfs.semanticscholar.org/ff85/3f4c94d62f3b5e12e7e753d2a372f780ba04.pdf?_ga=2.71015955.2073355937.1585489613-1207191193.1585489613.

Seidler, Z. E., Dawes, A. J., Rice, S. M., Oliffe, J. L., & Dhillon, H. M. (2016). The role of masculinity in men's help-seeking for depression: A systematic review. *Clinical Psychology Review*, *49*, 106–118. http://dx.doi.org/10.1016/j.cpr.2016.09.002.

Smiler, A. P., & Epstein, M. (2010). Measuring gender: Options and issues. In J. C. Chrisler & D. R. McCreary (eds), *Handbook of gender research in psychology, Volume 1: Gender research in general and experimental psychology* (pp. 133–157). New York: Springer. https://doi.org/10.1007/978-1-4419-1465-1_7.

Spence, J. T. & Helmreich, R. L. (1978). *Masculinity and femininity: Their psychological dimensions, correlates, and antecedents*. Austin, TX: University of Texas Press.

Spence, J. T. & Helmreich, R. L., & Holahan, C. K. (1979). Negative and positive components of psychological masculinity and femininity and their relationships to self-reports of neurotic and acting out behaviors. *Journal of Personality and Social Psychology*, *37*, 1673–1682.

Spence, J. T., Helmreich, R. L., & Stapp, J. (1975). Ratings of self and peers on sex role attitudes and their relation to self-esteem and conceptions of masculinity and femininity. *Journal of Personality and Social Psychology*, *32*, 29–39.

Thompson, E. H., Jr., & Bennett, K. M. (2015). Measurement of masculinity ideologies: A (critical) review. *Psychology of Men & Masculinity*, *16*, 115–133. http://dx.doi.org/10.1037/a0038609.

Thompson, E. H., Jr., & Pleck, J. H. (1986). The structure of male role norms. *American Behavioral Scientist*, *29*, 531–543.

Vandello, J. A., & Bosson, J. K. (2013). Hard won and easily lost: A review and synthesis of theory and research on precarious manhood. *Psychology of Men & Masculinity*, *14*, 101–113. https://doi.org/10.1037/a0029826.

Vandello, J. A., Bosson, J. K., Cohen, D., Burnaford, R. M., & Weaver, J. R. (2008). Precarious manhood. *Journal of Personality and Social Psychology*, *95*, 1325–1339. https://doi.org/10.1037/a0012453.

Vogel, D. L., Heimerdinger-Edwards, S. R., Hammer, J. H., & Hubbard, A. (2011). "Boys don't cry": Examination of the links between endorsement of masculine norms, self-stigma, and help-seeking attitudes for men from diverse backgrounds. *Journal of Counseling Psychology*, *58*, 368–382. https://doi.org/10.1037/a0023688.

Vogel, D. L., Wade, N. G., & Haake, S. (2006). Measuring the self-stigma associated with seeking psychological help. *Journal of Counseling Psychology*, *53*, 325–337. https://doi.org/10.1037/0022-0167.53.3.325.

Vogel, D. L., & Wester, S. R. (2003). To seek help or not to seek help: The risks of self-disclosure. *Journal of Counseling Psychology*, *50*, 351–361. https://doi.org/10.1037/0022-0167.50.3.351.

Vogel, D. K., Wester, S. R., Hammer, J. H., & Downing-Matibag, T. M. (2014). Referring men to seek help: The influence of gender role conflict and stigma. *Psychology of Men and Masculinity*, *15*, 60–67. https://doi.org/10.1037/a0031761.

Wahto, R., & Swift, J. K. (2016). Labels, gender-role conflict, stigma, and attitudes toward seeking psychological help in men. *American Journal of Men's Health*, *10*, 181–191. https://doi.org/10.1177/1557988314561491.

Wong, Y. J., Ho, M-H., R., Wang, S-Y., & Miller, I. S. K. (2017). Meta-analyses of the relationship between conformity to masculine norms and mental health-related outcomes. *Journal of Counseling Psychology*, *64*, 80–93. http://dx.doi.org/10.1037/cou0000176.

7 Implications of PTSD for Military Veteran Families

Heidi Cramm, Deborah Norris, Chloé Houlton, Molly Flindall-Hanna, and Linna Tam-Seto

Introduction

Posttraumatic stress disorder (PTSD) is a psychological response associated with exposure to potentially psychologically traumatic events (PPTE; Canadian Institute for Public Safety Research and Treatment [CIPSRT], 2019), particularly events that are life-threatening, and can affect people of any age, culture, sex, or gender (Veterans Affairs Canada, 2015). PTSD is characterized by persistent re-experiencing of the PPTE, effortful avoidance of PPTE-related stimuli, negative changes in cognition and moods, and alterations in arousal and reactivity levels. PTSD symptoms may present at different times in different individuals, and not all affected individuals experience all symptoms (American Psychiatric Association, 2013).

Rates of PTSD among militaries vary. In the United Kingdom, for example, PTSD rates among serving members returning from Iraq or Afghanistan range between 1.3% and 4.8%, comparable to the 3% rate found in the general civilian population (Rona et al., 2014). In Canada, posttraumatic stress disorder is the most common mental health diagnosis among Canadian Armed Forces (CAF) personnel involved in the recent missions in Afghanistan (Boulos & Zamorski, 2013). The current prevalence of PTSD has risen to 10% for all Canadian military members in active combat and 30% over their lifetime (Pare, 2011). In terms of prevalence, the rates are even higher for veterans in the United States, with at least 20% of Iraq and Afghanistan veterans reporting PTSD and/or depression (Tanielian & Jaycox, 2008). In addition to the methodological differences in estimating PTSD, the nature of the military service, motivation for joining the military, societal recognition of service-related injuries, and pre-service history of adverse childhood events are among factors thought to have an impact in the differences in the reported rates (Sundin et al., 2010).

PTSD can have significant impacts on the daily functioning of affected military veterans. PTSD is also associated with changes in family functioning, including the emergence of marital problems, parenting problems, and readjustment difficulties (Link & Palinkas, 2013). Despite the growth in research focusing on the impact of mental health disorders on military veterans, there is less attention to the impact PTSD has on family

DOI: 10.4324/9781351134637-8

members (Cramm et al., 2015). The gap in family research is a significant omission because veteran families experience the effects of PTSD and can also play an instrumental role in supporting the recovery of the military veteran. According to ongoing research in Veteran Affairs PTSD clinics in the United States, 80% of spouses are involved in the management of the military veteran's PTSD symptoms (Galovski & Lyons, 2004), leading to recommendations of their inclusion in treatment protocols available for military veterans diagnosed with PTSD (Reisman, 2016). As the research examining the impacts of PTSD on military and veteran families grows, and as the instrumental role that families play in supporting the military veteran living with PTSD is acknowledged, a review of the literature is imperative to examine knowledge gaps and to inform the development of evidence-based supports and programs. In the current chapter, we provide a literature review focused on PTSD and military veteran families, with recommendations for research, theory, and practice.

Methods

Scoping reviews are useful for synthesizing understanding of understudied phenomena, exposing the breadth and depth of related research, and identifying strategic directions for future research and program and policy development (Mays, Roberts, & Popay, 2001). Unlike a systematic review, scoping reviews synthesize key themes emerging from in-depth and strategic analysis of research aligned with a particular focus. Scoping reviews generally do not assess the quality of the studies reviewed as the studies are not assessed in light of methods, sampling strategies, or analysis procedures (Arksey & O'Malley, 2005). The process we employed in conducting the scoping review followed the protocol originally developed by Arksey and O'Malley (2005) and later refined by Levac, Colquhoun, and O'Brien (2010).

Identifying the Research Question

According to Arksey and O'Malley (2005), to be useful, the research question guiding a scoping review must strike a balance between capturing the breadth of relevant issues and the specificity required to define database search strategies. The research question guiding our scoping review is, "How does the research literature describe the impact of PTSD on military and veteran families?"

Identifying Relevant Studies

Studies fitting the parameters of the question(s) guiding a scoping review are identified through the planned selection of search terms, databases, time frames, and language (Arksey & O'Malley, 2005). Databases used for this review included Ovid MEDLINE, PsycINFO, Embase, CINAHL, and

200 *Heidi Cramm et al.*

Sociological Abstracts. Search terms relating to links between families and the intergenerational transmission of PTSD were combined. A complete list of the search terms used can be found in Table 7.1.

Inclusion criteria for the current review were: publication in a peer-reviewed journal; works published in English; and studies that discuss

Table 7.1 Complete list of search terms across databases—PTSD and Secondary Trauma

Ovid MEDLINE Search Strategy

#	Searches
1	stress disorders, post-traumatic/
2	stress disorders, traumatic/
3	Combat Disorders/
4	posttrauma*.mp.
5	post trauma*.mp.
6	1 or 2 or 3 or 4 or 5
7	((second* or vicarious) adj1 (trauma* or victim*)).mp.
8	secondary survivor*.mp.
9	compassion fatigue.mp.
10	intergeneration*.mp.
11	transgeneration*.mp.
12	exp Compassion Fatigue/
13	7 or 8 or 9 or 10 or 11 or 12
14	6 and 13

PsycINFO Search Strategy

#	Searches
1	exp posttraumatic stress disorder/
2	post-traumatic stress/
3	posttrauma*.mp.
4	trauma*.mp.
5	1 or 2 or 3 or 4
6	((second* or vicarious) adj1 (trauma* or victim*)).mp.
7	secondary survivor*.mp.
8	compassion fatigue.mp.
9	intergeneration*.mp.
10	transgeneration*.mp.
11	compassion fatigue/
12	exp Transgenerational Patterns/
13	6 or 7 or 8 or 9 or 10 or 11 or 12
14	5 and 13
15	limit 14 to ("0200 book" or "0240 authored book" or "0280 edited book")
16	14 not 15

Embase Search Strategy

#	Searches
1	posttraumatic stress disorder/
2	posttrauma*.mp.
3	trauma*.mp.

4	1 or 2 or 3
5	((second* or vicarious) adj1 (trauma* or victim*)).mp.
6	secondary survivor*.mp.
7	compassion fatigue.mp.
8	intergeneration*.mp.
9	transgeneration*.mp.
10	5 or 6 or 7 or 8 or 9
11	4 and 10

CINAHL Search Strategy

#	Query
S11	S4 AND S10
S10	S5 OR S6 OR S7 OR S8 OR S9
S9	transgeneration*
S8	intergeneration*
S7	compassion fatigue
S6	secondary survivor*
S5	((second* or vicarious) N1 (trauma* or victim*))
S4	S1 OR S2 OR S3
S3	trauma*
S2	posttrauma*
S1	(MH "Stress Disorders, Post-Traumatic")

Sociological Abstracts Search Strategy

Set	Search
S3	(SU.EXACT("Posttraumatic Stress Disorder") OR posttrauma* OR trauma*) AND (transgeneration* OR intergeneration* OR compassion fatigue OR secondary survivor* OR secondary trauma* OR second* victim* OR vicarious* trauma*)
S2	transgeneration* OR intergeneration* OR compassion fatigue OR secondary survivor* OR secondary trauma* OR second* victim* OR vicarious* trauma*
S1	SU.EXACT("Posttraumatic Stress Disorder") OR posttrauma* OR trauma*

PTSD in the military veteran family context. Databases were searched from 1990 until January 2017. During the searched time frame, the tempo of combat engagement escalated globally and new tactics such as the use of child soldiers began to emerge. We excluded studies where researchers: discussed children living in war/conflict situations/child soldiers; examined trauma involving families but not specifically PTSD; described PTSD and secondary trauma but did not involve family; or were describing grey literature including theses and conference abstracts.

A total of 6,085 articles were retrieved through the database search. After de-duplication, 4,408 articles underwent abstract reviews by two independent reviewers and 583 articles were deemed relevant to the current scoping review. An additional review was conducted using Covidence software (Veritas Health Innovation, 2017) to support the process of blinded

202   Heidi Cramm et al.

abstract reviews across multiple reviewers, yielding 155 abstracts. Screening was then undertaken using our inclusion criteria, identifying 70 sources for full text screening within Covidence by the two independent reviewers. Once exclusion criteria were applied, a total of 57 articles were retained and the full text of each of these articles was reviewed.

Charting the Data

All 57 articles were reviewed using an analytic data guide that included authors' names, article titles, keywords, year of publication, research location, purpose of the article, nature of the military service (e.g., deployment, context of combat, length of service, operational tempo), description of family (e.g., definition, family culture, family relationships), descriptions of trauma (e.g., nature of trauma, proximity to trauma, exposure type), type and nature of transmission (e.g., epigenetic, environmental), and other factors (e.g., resilience, adaptive coping mechanism, social support and family socio-economic status). The described process-oriented approach to data extraction is consistent with the data-charting approach recommended by Levac and colleagues (2010).

Collating, Summarizing, and Reporting Results

The results of scoping reviews are determined through the application of an analytic process of identifying and comparing key themes within the extracted data (Levac et al., 2010). A qualitative analysis software program called MAXQDA (VERBI Software Consult Sozialforschung GmbH, 1989-2017) was used to support thematic analysis. Results were organized and reported thematically using the review question as a guide.

Results

The traditional family, specifically a male military veteran with a female civilian spouse, is the predominant unit of analysis within the studies reviewed (Renshaw et al., 2011). Studies focusing on the female civilian spouse of a military veteran ($n = 33$) predominate, followed by the children of a military veteran ($n = 23$). Researchers have increasingly explored the experiences of dual military veteran families. Only one study addressed the issues faced by parents of military veterans. Determining the similarities and/or differences of who is considered an "active military member", a "combat veteran", or a "veteran," in the literature remains complicated because the terms are understood differently in different countries. For the current review, "military veteran" refers to a family member who has previously served, or is currently serving, in the armed forces, regardless of their combat or deployment experience. Also included were studies of the effects of being prisoners of war.

The current review process identified 57 articles from seven different countries, including the United States ($n = 16$), Iran ($n = 2$), Australia ($n = 3$), Israel

PTSD and Military Veteran Families 203

($n = 28$), Croatia ($n = 3$), United Kingdom ($n = 3$), and the Netherlands ($n = 2$). The military veterans covered by the studies reviewed served in a range of combat missions, including the Lebanese Civil War, the Yom Kippur War, the Vietnam War, World War II, and the first and second Gulf Wars.

In the military research literature, we found researchers study various family and spousal dynamics and arrangements. Most couples studied were married (Galovski & Lyons, 2004; Bjornestad, Schweinle, & Elhai, 2014; Campbell & Renshaw, 2012), but the literature also includes spousal cohabitation, separation (Bjornestad et al., 2014; Dekel et al., 2016), and divorce (Galovski & Lyons, 2004).

Children and civilian spouses are the subject of some of the family-oriented studies reviewed, focusing on how the military veteran's combat-related trauma and PTSD affects them. Here, we identified three themes: 1) PTSD disrupts family functioning and well-being; 2) trauma ripples through family systems; and 3) family adaptation to military veteran PTSD is complex.

Theme 1: PTSD Disrupts Family Functioning and Well-Being

The impact of PTSD on the functioning and well-being of all members of the family is evident throughout the literature reviewed. Outcomes that have garnered particular attention include changes in relationships, communication patterns within the family, shifting roles and responsibilities, and child development. The impact of PTSD on various dimensions of family well-being and functioning highlights the bidirectional patterns of symptom transmission, when the presence of PTSD symptoms in one family member contributes to the presentation of similar symptoms in another, suggested by the literature (Ahmadi et al., 2011; Arzhi, Solomon, & Dekel, 2000; Cohen, Zerach, & Solomon, 2011; Dinshtein, Dekel, & Polliack, 2011; Galovski & Lyons, 2004; Lambert, Holzer, & Hasbun, 2014; Levin, Bachem, & Solomon, 2016; Ray & Vanstone, 2009; Renshaw et al., 2011; Smith Osborne, Wilder, & Reep, 2013; Teague Caselli & Motta, 1995).

Changes in Relationships

One significant disruption in family functioning emerges from changes in family relationships. The literature reviewed provides evidence that PTSD typically leaves a significant mark on family relationships. Families come to the realization that the military veteran returning from combat is not the same individual who left, generating relationship changes that must be accommodated (Ahmadi et al., 2011; Campbell & Renshaw, 2012; Galovski & Lyons, 2004; Lambert et al., 2012; Leiner, 2009). Increased strain in family relationships can be attributed to avoidant attachment, increased aggression, and gender.

Based on attachment theory, avoidant attachment includes avoidance of support seeking and the suppression of negative emotions to maintain behavioural independence, emotional distance, and self-sufficiency, although this style of attachment can instead perpetuate distress (Ein-Dor et al., 2010; Silverman, 2011). Avoidant attachment is a risk factor for poor health that is associated with higher PTSD symptoms, namely withdrawal and avoidance, which are seen as some of the most significant symptoms interfering with the quality of relationships (Galovski & Lyons, 2004). Often, the spouse's desire for intimacy and closeness is set aside to avoid provoking or aggravating PTSD symptoms. Spouses report feelings of loneliness and emotional neglect; however, spouses tend to continue to attend to their military veteran partner and set aside such emotions (Levin, Greene, & Solomon, 2016). If the civilian spouse physically and emotionally avoids their military veteran partner as a response to the military veteran partner's withdrawal, this can perpetuate further withdrawal and avoidance (Ein-Dor et al., 2010; Zerach, Greene, & Solomon, 2015). Another significant strain on spousal relationships is increased aggression related to PTSD. Civilian spouses report incidences of increased verbal aggression (Arzhi et al., 2000; Dekel & Solomon, 2006) sometimes leading to intimate partner violence (Ahmadi et al., 2011; Figley, 2005; Nelson & Wright, 1996). Periods of intimate partner violence reportedly occur when the military veteran partner is experiencing flashbacks and nightmares that can increase anxiety (Nelson & Wright, 1996) and feelings of insecurity within the civilian spouse (Lambert et al., 2012). The cycle of aggression and violence within military veteran couples may be halted if there are sufficient feelings of guilt and shame (Solomon et al., 1992), leading to the acknowledgement of the military veteran's need for treatment, especially following acts of violence (Galovski & Lyons, 2004).

The impact of PTSD on heterosexual relationships varies by gender. PTSD symptoms in male trauma survivors exert a greater negative influence on the intimate partnership compared to relationships where the trauma is experienced by a female partner (Lambert et al., 2012). The differences may be attributed to "differences in emotional attunement to partners, differences in expression of symptoms, or other facets of gender roles" (Lambert et al., 2012, p. 734). Furthermore, the impact of military veterans' PTSD on spousal and intimate relationships is compounded when the PTSD symptoms, particularly anger, irritability, and hostility, affect communication patterns (Galovski & Lyons, 2004).

Communication Patterns

The degree to which spouses of military veterans living with PTSD engage in effective communication influences relational intimacy (Campbell & Renshaw, 2012). The frequency, style, and content communicated with partners has a significant impact on their overall satisfaction in their relationships (Campbell & Renshaw, 2012). Similar experiences emerge with respect to the children of military veteran parents with PTSD. Communication styles among and across family members can have knock-on effects in how individuals within family systems relate to one another. For example, a highly reactive communication pattern can lead to disengaged relational engagement. The communication pattern can produce a continuous feedback loop that shapes two distinct emergent communication behaviours in families with a military veteran living with PTSD: over-disclosure and avoidance of wartime experiences.

Prolonged avoidance of PPTE and war-related disclosure is said to impact the military veteran's mental and physical health, which may underscore the importance of discussing PPTE experiences (Dinshtein et al., 2011). Also, by avoiding combat-related conversations, family members are unaware of the extent to which military veterans have suffered throughout their time in combat (Dias et al., 2014). Alternatively, over-disclosure may also create an atmosphere of fear, cautiousness, and guilt within families dealing with a military veteran's PTSD (McCormack & Sly, 2013; Zerach & Aloni, 2015). Symptoms of withdrawal or emotional numbing can reduce effective communication (Davidson & Mellor, 2001), impairing relationship functioning and distancing the military veteran from everyday life (Galovski & Lyons, 2004). Such a dynamic forces the military veteran into deeper isolation and worsens distress levels and communication (Galovski & Lyons, 2004).

Avoidance tends to be more common than over-disclosure. As noted by Leiner (2009), society in general and families in particular tend to engage in conspiracies of silence justified by the belief that not discussing the PPTE experienced by the military veteran will lessen the impact. Lack of communication about the PPTE experience contributes not only to ongoing interpersonal tensions but also increases the risk for transmission of PTSD symptoms as "silence is a powerful means of transmission of trauma from one generation to the next" (Leiner, 2009, p. 3838).

Families may remain silent about war-related experiences and issues (Leiner, 2009), thereby reinforcing the belief that discussion is harmful and counter-productive. Paradoxically, children of military veterans living with PTSD may still exhibit signs of distress even when details and consequences of combat are not disclosed within the family. Implicitly or explicitly understanding that such matters are not to be discussed exacerbates distress and anxiety for children of military veterans living with PTSD. Overall, poor communication within the family unit leaves military veterans unsatisfied with their families' ability to face and resolve issues and demonstrate care and interest towards one another (Dias et al., 2014; Galovski & Lyons, 2004).

Roles and Responsibilities

PTSD symptoms may be manifested in shifts in family roles and responsibilities. Most of the research focusing on the familial disruptions incited by PTSD highlights changes in roles and responsibilities of civilian female spouses partnered with male soldiers in traditional, heteronormative families (Renshaw et al., 2011). Civilian female spouses assume maternal and caretaking roles, and, in so doing, reinforce traditional gender roles that assign women to the familial sphere (Franciskovic et al., 2007). Terms such as "over responsibility" (Nelson & Wright, 1996), "caregiver burnout" (Lambert et al., 2012), and "compassion trap" (Solomon et al., 1992) emerge within the literature focusing on the experiences of female civilian spouses who take on the role of caregiver. Unexpected changes in role behaviour and role expectations typically lead to feelings of sadness, hopelessness, worthlessness, anxiety, guilt, anger, and rejection (Solomon et al., 1992).

PTSD symptoms may also impact parenting. Withdrawal and avoidance, symptoms associated with PTSD, may affect the capacity of military veteran parents to assume parenting responsibilities, shifting the care of children to the civilian parent (Franciskovic et al., 2007; Leiner, 2009). By assuming additional parenting responsibilities, spouses may actually be inadvertently contributing to the ongoing withdrawal and disengagement of their military veteran partners (Franciskovic et al., 2007). Civilian spouses are expected to care for the physical, emotional, psychological, and spiritual needs of their children. In addition, the family's financial responsibilities may also shift to the civilian spouse (Nelson & Wright, 1996). The same shift may occur in responsibilities for care of other family members, such as aging parents (Lyons & Root, 2001).

Children of military veteran parents living with PTSD may also assume family responsibilities normally considered to be developmentally inappropriate. The avoidance and withdrawal displayed by the military veteran parent may precipitate changes in roles or responsibilities, inciting a compulsion in the children to rescue the injured parent (Leiner, 2009). Some children may be compensating for the injured parent by taking over the family roles previously assumed by the compromised military veteran parent (Leiner, 2009). Furthermore, behavioural changes in the military veteran parent, specifically the lack of patience and/or increased verbal and physical aggression may weigh heavily on children who then may choose to shoulder additional responsibilities in an effort to mitigate further upset (Franciskovic et al., 2007).

Upon returning home from protracted separations due to combat or deployment, military veterans may attempt to resume responsibility for previously held family roles. However, living with PTSD may limit their capacity to do so effectively (Dekel, 2017; Koic et al., 2002; Zerach & Aloni, 2015). Reactions to changes in roles and role expectations emerging in the military veteran's absence from the family may further compound PTSD symptoms, as the veterans may feel that their families have learned to live without them and that they are no longer contributing family members (Levin, Greene, et al., 2016). A further complication is present for military veteran parents exhibiting increased aggression, perhaps as a result of exposure to violence during service (Galovski & Lyons, 2004). Military veteran who are parents may also experience feelings of shame and loss of control contributing to increased withdrawal and unwillingness to assume familial roles and responsibilities (Galovski & Lyons, 2004).

Child Development

Researchers have also examined whether PTSD is affecting the daily functioning and development of veterans' children. For example, Davidson and Mellor (2001) posited that the younger ages of children would exhibit lower self-esteem, with the argument being that they may not have adequate coping skills or resiliency to face the adverse familial environment (Davidson & Mellor, 2001). Lower scores were found for children in measured self-esteem and family functioning but the differences were not significant. However, violence associated with the military veteran parent's PTSD appears to incite emotional distress (i.e., depression, anxiety, hyperactivity) as well as interpersonal relationship difficulties (i.e., socialization) in offspring (Galovski & Lyons, 2004).

Relationships between children and their military veteran parents can experience significant upheaval on multiple fronts. Children report feelings of physical and emotional detachment from their military veteran fathers living with PTSD, with some even considering them to be strangers (McCormack & Sly, 2013). A child's sense of safety and trust towards their military veteran parent may also be compromised (Leiner, 2009; McCormack & Sly, 2013). Perceptions of overprotectiveness, intrusiveness, and vigilance attributed to the military veteran parent with PTSD often cause strain in parent–child relationships (Davidson & Mellor, 2001). Changes within the family and in the relationship with the military veteran parent may invoke shame, anger, and guilt focused on the PTSD and its impacts (McCormack & Sly, 2013). Furthermore, the military veteran parents' difficulties in forming and maintaining interpersonal and intimate relationships, especially with their own families, are transmitted to their offspring who may also struggle with interpersonal relationships beyond the family (Dias et al., 2014). Long-term impacts on parent-child relationships also emerge for adult children of military veterans living with PTSD. Adult children offer recollections of parents' aggression, withdrawal, depression, and irritability during their formative years (Galovski & Lyons, 2004) and suggest that the PTSD symptoms impacted their capacity to develop and sustain intimate relationships later in life (Dinshtein et al., 2011). Relationships between children and the civilian parent can also be affected. Children of warm and caring mothers appear less emotionally distressed, less vulnerable, and less impacted by their fathers' symptoms than children with less warm and caring mothers (Dinshtein et al., 2011).

Theme 2: Trauma Ripples Through Family Systems

The appearance of PTSD-like symptoms in the spouses and children of military veterans living with combat-related PTSD suggests transmission

208 *Heidi Cramm et al.*

within the family system (Leiner, 2009). There is strong evidence in the literature suggesting that PTSD symptoms can be transferred to civilian spouses and children of military veterans even when these family members have not been exposed to trauma themselves. The family's emotional and psychological distress concerning the military veteran partner's war-related deployment increases the risk for secondary traumatization (Franciskovic et al., 2007).

Emotional demands (Koic et al., 2002), family environment and communication styles (Waysman et al., 1993), adaptive and maladaptive responses, and overlapping cognitive and behavioural difficulties (Zerach, 2015) further add to the complexity of the relationship between the military veteran's PTSD and family health and well-being, creating the potential for a downward spiral of isolation and worsening of symptoms (Fals Stewart & Kelley, 2005; Greene et al., 2014). The veteran and the family member can both contribute to the perpetuation of PTSD symptoms that, in turn, affect overall health and well-being for both. For example, there appears to be a relationship between secondary traumatization in civilian spouses resulting from the direct transmission of PPTE sequala from military veteran to spouse and lower marital satisfaction compared to civilian spouses of military veterans without PTSD. The secondary traumatization exacerbates the negative effects of PTSD on spousal mental health and well-being (Levin, Bachem, et al., 2016) and creates stress within a vital support system, the marriage, that otherwise could serve as a protective and buffering resource. Other social networks are also negatively affected, causing a vicious circle of impaired coping and psychological distress (Dekel, Solomon, & Rozenstreich, 2013; Nelson & Wright, 1996) of both partners, which can also contribute to relationship conflict.

Secondary Trauma in Spouses

Family members are typically the first people to witness the onset of PTSD symptoms in the veteran family member and thus have the potential to act as primary sources of support (Koic et al., 2002). Initial support is vital to the recovery process, which includes the reintegration into family and community life (Leiner, 2009). The family, primarily the spouse, are called upon to take on a significant role in providing the veteran family member with social support; however, family members may also need their own support network. The nature of PTSD may leave families isolated and removed from extended family members or friends, or they may lose support all together (Dirkzwager et al., 2005; Solomon et al., 1992). For example, a lack of social support appears to be a predictor of secondary traumatization in civilian spouses (Ein-Dor et al., 2010; Galovski & Lyons, 2004).

Pre-existing mental health problems or past PPTE exposures also appear to be factors that increase spousal vulnerability to the effects of the military veteran's PTSD (Dekel, Levinstein, Siegel, Fridkin, & Svetlitzky, 2016; Renshaw et al., 2011). The behaviours of the military veteran with

PTSD and Military Veteran Families 209

PTSD may trigger a civilian spouse's recollections of previous PPTE experiences unrelated to the military veteran's PTSD, producing symptoms (Dekel et al., 2016; Ein-Dor et al., 2010) and reducing the capacity of the spouse to support the military veteran.

Discussion of combat experiences with a spouse may be beneficial to the military veteran; however, sharing information may also lead to secondary traumatization (Campbell & Renshaw, 2012). Spouses may not benefit from hearing about the PPTE and have often reported feeling more distressed as a result (Campbell & Renshaw, 2012); as such, spousal relationships may be negatively impacted by excessive disclosure (Lev-Wiesel & Amir, 2001). The processes of disclosure, re-enactment, and identification have the potential to create a cycle of behaviours that can ultimately increase tension in family relationships and decrease quality of life (Campbell & Renshaw, 2012; Dekel & Solomon, 2006; Galovski & Lyons, 2004; Koic et al., 2002; McCormack & Sly, 2013; Thachil & Bhugra, 2006; Zerach et al., 2016).

The distress felt by spouses hearing about their partners' traumatic experiences is greater when the military veteran's symptoms of PTSD are severe (Campbell & Renshaw, 2012). The available evidence indicates greater levels of anxiety and depression, and higher frequencies of panic attacks and suicide attempts among civilian spouses of military veterans living with PTSD compared to civilian spouses living with military veterans without a diagnosis of PTSD (Beckham, Lytle, & Feldman, 1996; Calhoun, Beckham, & Bosworth, 2002; Campbell & Renshaw, 2012; Evans et al., 2003; Galovski & Lyons, 2004; Klaric et al., 2012; Lambert et al., 2012; Renshaw et al., 2011; Taft et al., 2011). Similar mental health symptoms have been reported by spouses of prisoners of war (POW) (Dekel & Solomon, 2006). Mental health symptoms contribute to decreased overall functioning and well-being including difficulties with sleep (Figley, 2005; Nelson & Wright, 1996; Waysman et al., 1993), decreased marital satisfaction (Arzhi et al., 2000; Campbell & Renshaw, 2012; Dinshtein et al., 2011; Galovski & Lyons, 2004; Renshaw et al., 2011), and decreased sociability (Ahmadi et al., 2011; Thachil & Bhugra, 2006).

Secondary Trauma in Children

Scholars have reported PTSD-like symptoms in the children of military veterans. Studies of the transmission of symptoms reveal behavioural changes in the children, including hyper-arousal, withdrawal, emotional numbing, and increased isolation (Dias et al., 2014; Dinshtein et al., 2011; Galovski & Lyons, 2004; Herzog, Everson, & Whitworth, 2011; Renshaw et al., 2011). In addition to symptoms associated with PTSD, some children experience co-occurring mental health disorders including anxiety, depression, eating disorders, attention deficit disorder, and learning disabilities (Galovski & Lyons, 2004; Renshaw et al., 2011). The combat-related stress experienced by ex-POWs has significant adverse effects on the psychological health of their children (Zerach & Aloni, 2015). There

210   *Heidi Cramm et al.*

is some disagreement about whether the ex-POW's captivity is associated with the adult children's symptoms of exposure to PPTE; comparisons of adult children of ex-POWs with PTSD with a control group reveal higher levels of secondary PPTE exposure symptoms including intrusion, avoidance, and hyperarousal, even decades after the parent's combat (Zerach, Kanat-Maymon, et al., 2016). For some children, military veteran parents can create emotional distance to separate themselves from the PPTE experiences of war; however, that emotional distance can impact the parent–child relationship, leading some children to press for details about the traumatic war and combat experiences despite the parent's silence on the issue. The children's inquiries may be an effort to regain emotional and physical closeness with their parent; nevertheless, the inquiries can lead to potentially graphic and distressing disclosure of war experiences that can inadvertently influence the child's perception of war and of the world more generally and contribute to children's fears about the surrounding environment (Leiner, 2009).

Research on adult children of military veterans living with PTSD brings into view the long-term and ongoing nature of PTSD transmission within families. Negative mental health outcomes in adult children, including depression and anxiety, are among a number of difficulties affecting social and intimate relationships for adult children of military veterans (Beckham et al., 1996; Ein-Dor et al., 2010; Galovski & Lyons, 2004; Leiner, 2009; Levin, Bachem, et al., 2016; McCormack & Sly, 2013).

Directionality of Transmission

Most of the literature highlights a uni-directional and linear translation of the military veteran's symptoms into negative outcomes for family members, but there are studies underscoring the complex contextual family ecological factors that impact the mental health of the military veteran. Military veteran PTSD has clear impacts on family health and well-being. Concurrently, changing family circumstances can also impact the course of PTSD. The severity and course of the veteran's PTSD symptoms are affected by shifting familial roles and responsibilities (Franciskovic et al., 2007; Galovski & Lyons, 2004; Koic et al., 2002; Leiner, 2009; Nelson & Wright, 1996; Renshaw et al., 2011), relational changes (Ahmadi et al., 2011; Campbell & Renshaw, 2012; Ein-Dor et al., 2010; Lambert et al., 2012; Leiner, 2009), child development (Davidson & Mellor, 2001; Dias et al., 2014; Dinshtein et al., 2011; Galovski & Lyons, 2004; Zerach et al., 2015) and communication patterns (Campbell & Renshaw, 2012; Davidson & Mellor, 2001; Dias et al., 2014; Dinshtein et al., 2011; Galovski & Lyons, 2004; Leiner, 2009).

Theme 3: Family Adaptation to Military Veteran PTSD

Distress in the family environment may ultimately prove adaptive, prompting the military veteran to acknowledge their experiences and communicate their thoughts and feelings with their family (Dekel & Solomon, 2006). Openness in communication can also contribute to strengthening the relationship (Nelson & Wright, 1996). Supporting spouses towards becoming more flexible and adaptive in the familial environment is significant in the development of coping strategies that can minimize relationship distress (Zerach et al., 2015). Spouses' acknowledgment and acceptance of their experiences facilitates adaptation and coping in their current environment as they become more settled in their own lives and well-being (McCormack & Sly, 2013). Similarly, positive parent–child communication such as open dialogue restores trust, enhances the family's understanding of the military veteran's experiences (Dekel & Solomon, 2006; Leiner, 2009), and reassures the children that they are not responsible for the PTSD symptoms experienced by their military veteran parent (Leiner, 2009).

Enhancing Resilience

Some familial environments can increase military veteran's symptoms of PTSD, but a supportive and empathic family can help the military veteran build resilience (Waysman et al., 1993). There are several possible definitions of resilience (CIPSRT, 2019), which can be defined as a dynamic process that includes positive adaptation within the context of significant adversity (Zerach & Solomon, 2016). Resilience supports outcomes that enable individuals to withstand or resist the negative impacts of stressors (Luthar, Cicchetti, & Becker, 2000; Masten, 2001). The mechanisms facilitating resilience are activated within networks of personal, environmental, and biological systems (Herrman et al., 2011). Spouses with greater resilience are able to adjust to their partners' emotional distress (Dekel & Solomon, 2006) and, in turn, to support the development of resilience in the partner. There is seemingly contradictory evidence from one study that repeated PPTE exposures may make some individuals more resilient (Dekel et al., 2013). There is also the suggestion that some individuals exposed to multiple PPTE develop coping mechanisms that both increase their resiliency and their preparedness for other PPTE (Dekel et al., 2013).

Treatment and Support Programs

Providing military veterans and families with the best possible mental healthcare is a responsibility of society (Herzog et al., 2011). Given the significant impact that PTSD has on all members of the family, there is consensus in the literature on the need for family-centred care provided by multidisciplinary teams using a biopsychosocial perspective (Campbell & Renshaw, 2012; Dinshtein et al., 2011; Leiner, 2009; Nelson & Wright, 1996).

Therapy should target emotion regulation, communication skills, gender role expectations, resilience (Nelson & Wright, 1996), establishing routines, family relationships and conflict (Leiner, 2009), problem solving (Galovski & Lyons, 2004), and adaptation (Zerach & Aloni, 2015). Other components

212 *Heidi Cramm et al.*

of treatment suggested by Galvoski & Lyons (2004) are improving social support and providing skills training, for example in coping techniques, for the military veteran and family members. Found to be helpful for this population is cognitive behavioural therapy (Herzog et al., 2011). In addition, family participation in psychoeducational groups, designed to enhance the understanding of PTSD, is useful for learning adaptive strategies. Couple therapy sessions that focus on communication and problem solving are equally important (Galovski & Lyons, 2004).

Mental health professionals can help military veterans and their family members develop adaptive coping strategies that may be crucial to the recovery journey (Leiner, 2009; Lester et al., 2013; Masten, 2013). Families connected with the Canadian Armed Forces have access to the Military Family Resource Centres located in base communities that offer an array of mental health and parenting supports (Edmonton Garrison Military Family Resource Centre, 2018). Military veteran parents can learn how to communicate appropriately with their children about lived experiences of war, and support children in gaining a developmentally appropriate understanding of the nature of their parents' emotions and their association with events outside of the parent–child relationship (Leiner, 2009). In one program, veteran fathers were provided with support and psychoeducation (information about PTSD and the transmission of trauma), which allowed them to be involved in treatment sessions with their children designed to help them gain emotional and social independence (Leiner, 2009). Another program, Families Overcoming Under Stress (FOCUS), has demonstrated the benefits of decreasing child and parental distress and of children's positive coping strategies (Lester et al., 2013; Saltzman et al., 2016).

Discussion

Our review of the literature has identified a growing body of research investigating the impact of PTSD on heterosexual spouses and on dependent children. Yet, despite the established body of research on the impact of PTSD on military veteran families, we identified gaps in the examined literature. The search revealed that little research exists on other family members such as parents of adult military veterans, siblings of military veterans, same-sex civilian parents, and adult children. In addition, family systems, as a whole, need to be studied in order to determine how best to support military and veteran families.

There is overwhelming evidence that the effects of PTSD go well beyond the military veteran family member; as such, more research is warranted focusing on the impacts of PTSD as well as on assessment and interventions for families (Galovski & Lyons, 2004; Nelson & Wright, 1996; Suozzi & Motta, 2004). Research on the impact of PTSD on the family system is relatively new; as such, there is a lack of evidence to inform how assessment should be conducted. Various interventions are being provided to support military families, but research is required to determine the efficacy and

PTSD and Military Veteran Families   213

effectiveness of the available programs and services (Galovski & Lyons, 2004; Norris et al., 2015).

Prospective longitudinal research on the prolonged consequences of PTSD on family members (Dekel et al., 2016; Fals Stewart & Kelley, 2005; Lambert et al., 2012; Zerach, 2015) is also warranted. Some longitudinal studies have been completed on secondary traumatization, attachment, and suicidal ideation among spouses of POWs (Lahav, Kanat-Maymon, & Solomon, 2016; Zerach, Levi-Belz, et al., 2016a, 2016b), as well as on intergenerational transmission of POW trauma (Zerach, Kanat-Maymon, et al., 2016); however, there is a paucity of research examining the long-term impacts of PTSD on family systems, functioning, well-being, and child development. Generalizing results to other populations (Ahmadi et al., 2011) with larger samples and diverse types of trauma (Lambert et al., 2012) and diverse severity is essential (Yahyavi et al., 2015). Research may also benefit from developing a wider range of tools (Bjornestad et al., 2014) and more general mental health measures (Davidson & Mellor, 2001) for assessing symptoms related to PTSD.

The current literature includes descriptions of intergenerational PTSD symptoms transmission (Babcock Fenerci, Chu, & DePrince, 2016; Dekel & Goldblatt, 2008); however, intergenerational transmission continues to be under-studied (Cramm et al., 2018; Dekel & Solomon, 2006; Leiner, 2009). In the context of recent and ongoing global conflicts and our current understanding of the familial impact of PTSD, there is an urgent need to undertake further exploration of intergenerational transmission given the potential impact of PTSD on future generations. Here, controlling for effect differences between pre-traumatic and posttraumatic experiences will be significant (Ein-Dor et al., 2010; Franciskovic et al., 2007).

Growing interest around the intergenerational mechanism and nature of PTSD transmission is intensifying the need for research focusing on affected children. More research is needed on the anatomical and neurological impacts of PTSD on the development of children. However, scholars should design studies focused on accounting for the impact of comorbid psychopathologies, genetic contribution (Smith Osborne et al., 2013), and environmental factors such as domestic violence (Galovski & Lyons, 2004). Lambert et al. (2012) emphasize how researchers need to understand the moderators of PTSD which would also help improve treatment strategies.

The most disabling factors experienced by military veteran families remain unclear (Bjornestad et al., 2014). Researchers examining marital intimacy problems (Campbell & Renshaw, 2012) gathering data from multiple sources (Fals Stewart & Kelley, 2005), and using objective measures may also help uncover the intersecting effects of PTSD on spouses (Zerach et al., 2015). Sources may extend to examining how family members with a mental disorder and chronic conditions can exacerbate stress in the family environment (Waysman et al., 1993).

In a study by Fals Stewart and Kelley (2005), the authors suggested that evaluations of peacekeeper couples without PTSD symptoms might help uncover the ways we can help protect those who are most vulnerable. The authors also highlighted that couples with female peacekeepers and military veterans need to be included, as gender may alter stress transmission. Similarly, couples in which both partners were military veterans should also be studied (Dekel et al., 2016). In future studies, researchers need to identify coping strategies and treatment approaches for living with a traumatized military veteran (Dekel & Solomon, 2006); such work may also inform future strategies for proactively supporting mental health (Klaric et al., 2012).

The literature included in the current scoping review has assumed a heteronormative and traditional family structure in which the male partner is the military veteran and the female partner is the civilian. Assessing whether or not the issues identified as pertinent to military families also pertain to other family systems remains unknown. We still know very little about the unique or specific needs of other types of families—including two gay male partners, two female lesbian partners, single parents, dual serving families, and so forth—supporting a veteran with PTSD. Moreover, the experiences of all family members, including siblings and parents, are not fully represented within the existing literature.

Application of an ecological, family-centred model of PTSD to assessment and intervention will be of benefit as research with this population proceeds. There is a promising proposed formative model emphasizing families as open systems, ideally with semi-permeable boundaries, operating within interdependent networks so as to develop and maintain equilibrium. Future program and policy development that recognizes the significant role of families in sustaining positive outcomes for veterans with PTSD in treatment and thereafter requires such a holistic lens.

Families warrant support to be effective in supporting the veteran. Learning about optimal communication practices, strategies for handling the veteran's disclosure of PPTE and experiences, and role transitions will enhance the family member's understanding of the veteran with PTSD and their capacity to support him/her. Moreover, challenges in recruitment and retention of serving members may intensify if family tension and strains detract from the ability to maintain employment in the military. The health needs of families outside of their role in maintaining operational readiness are receiving increasing attention from diverse groups. Family members require support in managing their own health issues that emanate from the experience of supporting the veteran with PTSD. For example, family members may be no longer connected to the veteran yet continue to experience their own mental health and well-being issues without eligibility for support through military veteran agencies. The impacts of PTSD on them are separate and distinct from the health issues ongoing with their veterans. The daily experience of "walking on eggshells", so often reported in the literature, elicits stresses for family members that are not yet well-understood. Failing to recognize and address the health needs of family members supporting veterans with PTSD carries costs for all involved.

The current scoping review results contrast conceptualizations of PTSD transmission as a linear process moving from the individual with the primary diagnosis to family members. Our results also suggest that research gaps can be addressed through integration of multiple research models and methods. Principal among these are prospective longitudinal studies following families from intake into the military system across the familial life course.

References

Ahmadi, K., Azampoor Afshar, S., Karami, G., & Mokhtari, A. (2011). PTSD research: The association of veterans' PTSD with secondary trauma stress among veterans' spouses. *Journal of Aggression, Maltreatment and Trauma, 20*(6), 636.

American Psychiatric Association. (2013). *Diagnostic and statistical manual of mental disorders: DSM-5.* Arlington, VA: American Psychiatric Association.

Arksey, H., & O'Malley, L. (2005). Scoping studies: Towards a methodological framework. *International Journal of Social Research Methodology, 8*(1), 19–32.

Arzhi, N. B., Solomon, Z., & Dekel, R. (2000). Secondary traumatization among wives of PTSD and post-concussion casualties: Distress, caregiver burden and psychological separation. *Brain Injury, 14*(8), 725.

Babcock Fenerci, R. L., Chu, A. T., & DePrince, A. P. (2016). Intergenerational transmission of trauma-related distress: Maternal betrayal trauma, parenting attitudes, and behaviors. *Journal of Aggression, Maltreatment and Trauma, 25*(4), 382–399. http://dx.doi.org/10.1080/10926771.2015.1129655.

Beckham, J. C., Lytle, B. L., & Feldman, M. E. (1996). Caregiver burden in partners of Vietnam War veterans with posttraumatic stress disorder. *Journal of Consulting and Clinical Psychology, 64*(5), 1068–1072.

Bjornestad, A. G., Schweinle, A., & Elhai, J. D. (2014). Measuring secondary traumatic stress symptoms in military spouses with the posttraumatic stress disorder checklist military version. *The Journal of Nervous and Mental Disease, 202*(12), 864–869.

Boulos, D., & Zamorski, M. A. (2013). Deployment-related mental disorders among Canadian Forces personnel deployed in support of the mission in Afghanistan, 2001–2008. *Canadian Medical Association Journal, 185*(11), E545–E553. https://doi.org/10.1503/cmaj.122120.

Calhoun, P. S., Beckham, J. C., & Bosworth, H. B. (2002). Caregiver burden and psychological distress in partners of veterans with chronic posttraumatic stress disorder. *Journal of Traumatic Stress, 15*(3), 205–222.

Campbell, S. B., & Renshaw, K. D. (2012). Distress in spouses of Vietnam veterans: Associations with communication about deployment experiences. *Journal of Family Psychology, 26*(1), 18.

Canadian Institute for Public Safety Research and Treatment (CIPSRT). (2019). *Glossary of terms: A shared understanding of the common terms used to describe psychological trauma (version 2.0).* Regina, SK: Author.

Cohen, E., Zerach, G., & Solomon, Z. (2011). The implications of combat-induced stress reaction, PTSD, and attachment in parenting among war veterans. *Journal of Family Psychology, 25*, 688–698.

Cramm, H., Murphy, S., Godfrey, C. M., Dekel, R., & McKeown, S. (2018). Experiences of children exposed to parental post-traumatic stress disorder while

216 *Heidi Cramm et al.*

growing up in military and veteran families: A systematic review protocol. *JBI Database of Systematic Reviews and Implementation Reports, 16*(4), 852–859.

Cramm, H., Norris, D., Tam-Seto, L., Eichler, M., & Smith-Evans, K. (2015). Making military families in Canada a research priority. *Journal of Military, Veteran and Family Health, 1*(2), 8–12. https://doi.org/10.3138/jmvfh.3287.

Davidson, A. C., & Mellor, D. J. (2001). The adjustment of children of Australian Vietnam veterans: Is there evidence for the transgenerational transmission of the effects of war-related trauma? *Australian and New Zealand Journal of Psychiatry, 35*(3), 345.

Dekel, R. (2017). My personal and professional trauma resilience truisms. *Traumatology, 23*(1), 10.

Dekel, R., & Goldblatt, H. (2008). Is there intergenerational transmission of trauma? The case of combat veterans' children. *American Journal of Orthopsychiatry, 78*(3), 281–289. https://doi.org/10.1037/a0013955.

Dekel, R., Levinstein, Y., Siegel, A., Fridkin, S., & Svetlitzky, V. (2016). Secondary traumatization of partners of war veterans: The role of boundary ambiguity. *Journal of Family Psychology, 30*(1), 63–71. http://dx.doi.org/10.1037/fam0000163.

Dekel, R., & Solomon, Z. (2006). Secondary traumatization among wives of Israeli POWs: The role of POWs' distress. *Social Psychiatry and Psychiatric Epidemiology, 41*(1), 27.

Dekel, S., Solomon, Z., & Rozenstreich, E. (2013). Secondary salutogenic effects in veterans whose parents were Holocaust survivors? *Journal of Psychiatric Research, 47*(2), 266.

Dias, A., Sales, L., Cardoso, R. M., & Kleber, R. (2014). Childhood maltreatment in adult offspring of Portuguese war veterans with and without PTSD. *European Journal of Psychotraumatology, 5*(1), 20198.

Dinshtein, Y., Dekel, R., & Polliack, M. (2011). Secondary traumatization among adult children of PTSD veterans: The role of mother-child relationships. *Journal of Family Social Work, 14*(2), 109. https://doi.org/10.1080/10522158.2011.544021.

Dirkzwager, A. J., Bramsen, I., Ader, H., & van der Ploeg, H. M. (2005). Secondary traumatization in partners and parents of Dutch peacekeeping soldiers. *Journal of Family Psychology, 19*(2), 217–226. https://doi.org/10.1037/0893-3200.19.2.217.

Edmonton Garrison Military Family Resource Centre. (2018). MFRC programs. Retrieved from www.cafconnection.ca/Edmonton/Contact-Us/Military-Family-Resource-Centre/MFRC-Programs.aspx.

Ein-Dor, T., Doron, G., Solomon, Z., Mikulincer, M., & Shaver, P. R. (2010). Together in pain: Attachment-related dyadic processes and posttraumatic stress disorder. *Journal of Counseling Psychology, 57*(3), 317.

Evans, L., McHugh, T., Hopwood, M., & Watt, C. (2003). Chronic posttraumatic stress disorder and family functioning of Vietnam veterans and their partners. *Australasian Psychiatry, 37*(6), 765–772.

Fals Stewart, W., & Kelley, M. (2005). When family members go to war – A systemic perspective on harm and healing: Comment on Dirkzwager, Bramsen, Ader, and van der Ploeg (2005). *Journal of Family Psychology, 19*(2), 233.

Figley, C. R. (2005). Strangers at home: Comment on Dirkzwager, Bramsen, Ader, and van der Ploeg (2005). *Journal of Family Psychology, 19*(2), 227–229. https://doi.org/10.1037/0893-3200.19.2.227

Franciskovic, T., Stevanovic, A., Jelusic, I., Roganovic, B., Klaric, M., & Grkovic, J. (2007). Secondary traumatization of wives of war veterans with posttraumatic stress disorder. *Croatian Medical Journal, 48*(2), 177.

PTSD and Military Veteran Families 217

Galovski, T., & Lyons, J. A. (2004). Psychological sequelae of combat violence: A review of the impact of PTSD on the veteran's family and possible interventions. *Aggression and Violent Behavior, 9*(5), 477–501. https://doi.org/10.1016/s1359-1789(03)00045-4.

Greene, T., Lahav, Y., Bronstein, I., & Solomon, Z. (2014). The role of ex-POWs' PTSD symptoms and trajectories in wives' secondary traumatization. *Journal of Family Psychology, 28*(5), 666.

Herrman, H., Stewart, D. E., Diaz-Granados, N., Berger, E. L., Jackson, B., & Yuen, T. (2011). What is resilience? *The Canadian Journal of Psychiatry, 56*(5), 258–265. https://doi.org/10.1177/070674371105600504

Herzog, J. R., Everson, R. B., & Whitworth, J. D. (2011). Do secondary trauma symptoms in spouses of combat-exposed national guard soldiers mediate impacts of soldiers' trauma exposure on their children? *Child & Adolescent Social Work Journal, 28*(6), 459.

Klaric, M., Franciskovic, T., Obrdalj, E. C., Petric, D., Britvic, D., & Zovko, N. (2012). Psychiatric and health impact of primary and secondary traumatization in wives of veterans with posttraumatic stress disorder. *Psychiatria Danubina, 24*(3), 280.

Koic, E., Franciskovic, T., Muzinic Masle, L., Dordevic, V., Vondracek, S., & Prpic, J. (2002). Chronic pain and secondary traumatization in wives of Croatian war veterans treated for post traumatic stress disorder. *Acta Clinica Croatica, 41*(4), 295.

Lahav, Y., Kanat-Maymon, Y., & Solomon, Z. (2016). Secondary traumatization and attachment among wives of former POWs: A longitudinal study. *Attachment & Human Development, 18*(2), 141–153. http://dx.doi.org/10.1080/14616734.2015.1121502.

Lambert, J. E., Engh, R., Hasbun, A., & Holzer, J. (2012). Impact of posttraumatic stress disorder on the relationship quality and psychological distress of intimate partners: A meta-analytic review. *Journal of Family Psychology, 26*(5), 729.

Lambert, J. E., Holzer, J., & Hasbun, A. (2014). Association between parents' PTSD severity and children's psychological distress: A meta-analysis. *Journal of Traumatic Stress, 27*(1), 9–17. https://doi.org/10.1002/jts.21891.

Leiner, B. (2009). The legacy of war: An intergenerational perspective. *Smith College Studies in Social Work, 79*(3), 375.

Lester, P., J.A., S., Saltzman, W., Woodward, K., MacDermid, S. W., Milburn, N., … Beardslee, W. (2013). Psychological health of military children: Longitudinal evaluation of a family-centered prevention program to enhance family resilience. *Military Medicine, 178*(8), 838–845. https://doi.org/10.7205/MILMED-D-12-00502.

Lev-Wiesel, R., & Amir, M. (2001). Secondary traumatic stress, psychological distress, sharing of traumatic reminisces, and marital quality among spouses of Holocaust child survivors. *Journal of Marital and Family Therapy, 27*, 433–444. https://doi.org/10.1111/j.1752- 0606.2001.tb00338.x.

Levac, D. E., Colquhoun, H., & O'Brien, K. K. (2010). Scoping studies: Advancing the methodology. *Implementation Science, 5*(69).

Levin, Y., Bachem, R., & Solomon, Z. (2016). Traumatization, marital adjustment, and parenting among veterans and their spouses: A longitudinal study of reciprocal relations. *Family Process, 56*(4), 926–942. http://dx.doi.org/10.1111/famp.12257.

Levin, Y., Greene, T., & Solomon, Z. (2016). PTSD symptoms and marital adjustment among ex-POWs' wives. *Journal of Family Psychology, 30*(1), 72–81. https://doi.org/https://dx.doi.org/10.1037/fam0000170.

218   *Heidi Cramm et al.*

Link, P. E., & Palinkas, L. A. (2013). Long-term trajectories and service needs for military families. *Clinical Child and Family Psychological Review, 16*(4), 376–393. https://doi.org/10.1007/s10567-013-0145-z.

Luthar, S. S., Cicchetti, D., & Becker, B. (2000). The construct of resilience: A critical evaluation and guidelines for future work. *Child Development, 71*(3), 543–562. https://doi.org/10.1111/1467-8624.00164.

Lyons, J. A., & Root, L. P. (2001). Family members of the PTSD veteran: Treatment needs and barriers. *National Center for Posttraumatic Stress Disorder Clinical Quarterly, 10*(3), 48–52.

Masten, A. S. (2001). Ordinary magic: Resilience processes in development. *American Psychologist, 56*(3), 227.

Masten, A. S. (2013). Competence, risk, and resilience in military families: Conceptual commentary. *Clinical Child and Family Psychology Review, 16*(3), 278–281. https://doi.org/10.1007/s10567-013-0150-2.

Mays, N., Roberts, E., & Popay, J. (2001). *Synthesising research evidence*. London: Routledge.

McCormack, L., & Sly, R. (2013). Distress and growth: The subjective "lived" experiences of being the child of a Vietnam veteran. *Traumatology, 19*(4), 303.

Nelson, B. S., & Wright, D. W. (1996). Understanding and treating post-traumatic stress disorder symptoms in female partners of veterans with PTSD. *Journal of Marital and Family Therapy, 22*(4), 455.

Norris, D., Cramm, H., Eichler, M., Tam-Seto, L., & Smith-Evans, K. (2015). *Operational stress injury: The impact on family mental health and well-being*. Military and Veteran Health Research.

Pare, J. R. (2011). *Post-traumatic stress disorder and the mental health of military personnel and veterans* [Background Paper]. Publication No. 2011-97-E. Library of Parliament. Retrieved from https://lop.parl.ca/staticfiles/PublicWebsite/Home/ResearchPublications/BackgroundPapers/PDF/2011-97-e.pdf.

Ray, S. L., & Vanstone, M. (2009). The impact of PTSD on veterans' family relationships: An interpretative phenomenological inquiry. *International Journal of Nursing Studies, 46*, 838–847. https://doi.org/10.1016/j.inurstu.2009.01.002.

Reisman, M. (2016). PTSD treatment for veterans: What's working, what's new, and what's next. *Pharmacy and Therapeutics, 41*(10), 623–634.

Renshaw, K. D., Allen, E. S., Rhoades, G. K., Blais, R. K., Markman, H. J., & Stanley, S. M. (2011). Distress in spouses of service members with symptoms of combat-related PTSD: Secondary traumatic stress or general psychological distress? *Journal of Family Psychology, 25*(4), 461.

Rona, R. J., Jones, M., Keeling, M., Hull, L., Wessely, S., & Fear, N. T. (2014). Mental health consequences of overstretch in the UK Armed Forces, 2007–09: A population cohort study. *The Lancet, 1*(7), 531–538. https://doi.org/10.1016/S2215-0366(14)00062-5.

Saltzman, W. R., Lester, P., Milburn, N., Woodward, K., & Stein, J. (2016). Pathways of risk and resilience: Impact of a family resilience program on active-duty military parents. *Family Process, 55*(4), 633–646. https://doi.org/10.1111/famp.12238.

Silverman, D. K. (2011). A clinical case of an avoidant attachment. *Psychoanalytic Psychology, 28*(2), 293–310. https://doi.org/10.1037/a0022342.

Smith Osborne, A., Wilder, A., & Reep, E. (2013). A review of reviews examining neurological processes relevant to impact of parental PTSD on military children: Implications for supporting resilience. *Journal of Aggression, Maltreatment and Trauma, 22*(5), 461.

PTSD and Military Veteran Families 219

Solomon, Z., Waysman, M., Levy, G., Fried, B., Mikulincer, M., Benbenishty, R., ... Bleich, A. (1992). From front line to home front: A study of secondary traumatization. *Family Process*, *31*(3), 289.

Sundin, J., Fear, N. T., Iversen, A., Rona, R. J., & Wessely, S. (2010). PTSD after deployment to Iraq: Conflicting rates, conflicting claims. *Psychological Medicine*, *40*(3), 367–382.

Suozzi, J. M., & Motta, R. W. (2004). The relationship between combat exposure and the transfer of trauma-like symptoms to offspring of veterans. *Traumatology*, *10*(1), 17–37.

Taft, C. T., Watkins, L. E., Stafford, J., Street, A. E., & Monson, C. M. (2011). Posttraumatic stress disorder and intimate relationship problems: A meta-analysis. *Journal of Consulting and Clinical Psychology*, *79*(1), 22–33. https://doi.org/10.1037/a0022196.

Tanielian, T., & Jaycox, L. H. (2008). *Invisible wounds of war: Psychological and cognitive injuries, their consequences, and services to assist recovery*. Santa Monica, CA: RAND Corporation.

Teague Caselli, L., & Motta, R. W. (1995). The effect of PTSD and combat level on Vietnam veterans' perceptions of child behavior and marital adjustment. *Journal of Clinical Psychology*, *51*(1), 4–13.

Thachil, A., & Bhugra, D. (2006). Literature update: A critical review. *Sexual and Relationship Therapy*, *21*(2), 229–235. https://doi.org/10.1080/14681990600637689.

VERBI Software Consult Sozialforschung GmbH. (1989–2017). MAXQDA software for qualitative data analysis. Berlin.

Veritas Health Innovation. (2017). Covidence systematic review software. Melbourne. Retrieved from www.covidence.org.

Veterans Affairs Canada. (2015). Mental Health. Retrieved from www.veterans. gc.ca/eng/services/health/mental-health.

Waysman, M., Mikulincer, M., Solomon, Z., & Weisenberg, M. (1993). Secondary traumatization among wives of posttraumatic combat veterans: A family typology. *Journal of Family Psychology*, *7*(1), 104–118.

Yahyavi, S. T., Zarghami, M., Naghshvar, F., & Danesh, A. (2015). Relationship of cortisol, norepinephrine, and epinephrine levels with war-induced posttraumatic stress disorder in fathers and their offspring. *Revista Brasileira de Psiquiatria*, *37*(2), 93–98. https://doi.org/10.1590/1516-4446-2014-1414.

Zerach, G. (2015). Secondary traumatization among ex-POWs' adult children: The mediating role of differentiation of the self. *Psychological Trauma: Theory, Research, Practice, and Policy*, *7*(2), 187.

Zerach, G., & Aloni, R. (2015). Secondary traumatization among former prisoners of wars' adult children: The mediating role of parental bonding. *Anxiety, Stress & Coping: An International Journal*, *28*(2), 162.

Zerach, G., Greene, T., & Solomon, Z. (2015). Secondary traumatization and self-rated health among wives of former prisoners of war: The moderating role of marital adjustment. *Journal of Health Psychology*, *20*(2), 222–235. https://doi.org/10.1177/1359105313502563.

Zerach, G., Kanat-Maymon, Y., Aloni, R., & Solomon, Z. (2016). The role of fathers' psychopathology in the intergenerational transmission of captivity trauma: A twenty three-year longitudinal study. *Journal of Affective Disorders*, *190*(84), 84–92. http://dx.doi.org/10.1016/j.jad.2015.09.072.

Zerach, G., Levi-Belz, Y., Michelson, M., & Solomon, Z. (2016a). Suicidal ideation among former prisoners of war's wives–A longitudinal dyadic study. *European Psychiatry*, *33*, S331–S332. https://doi.org/10.1016/j.eurpsy.2016.01.735

Zerach, G., Levi-Belz, Y., Michelson, M., & Solomon, Z. (2016b). Suicidal ideation among wives of former prisoners of war: A longitudinal dyadic study. *Psychiatry: Interpersonal and Biological Processes, 79*(2), 147–163. https://dx.doi.org/http://dx.doi.org/10.1080/00332747.2015.1124643.

Zerach, G., & Solomon, Z. (2016). A relational model for the intergenerational transmission of captivity trauma: A 23-year longitudinal study. *Psychiatry, 79*(3), 297–316. http://dx.doi.org/10.1080/00332747.2016.1142775.

8 Posttraumatic Stress Symptoms in Workers within the Homeless Serving Sector

The Impact of Organizational Factors

Jeannette Waegemakers Schiff and Annette M. Lane

Working within the homeless serving sector is recognized as very difficult work. The challenges lie in a multiplicity of factors including the complexity of stressors and challenges in the lives of persons who are homeless (Hopper, Bassuk, & Olivet, 2009), as well as the range of instrumental and supportive tasks required to address a complex array of physical, psychosocial, and legal issues with clients. Further, the limited individual preparation of staff for these roles (Waegemakers Schiff & Lane, 2019), the limited experience of many managers and supervisors, and organizational dynamics in chaotic environments (Hopper et al., 2009) all have impacts on the work lives of front-line workers in this sector.

Individuals who are homeless have often experienced potentially psychologically traumatic events (Canadian Institute for Public Safety Research and Treatment, 2019) prior to, or as a direct result of, their situation including abuse, violence and entanglements with the legal system (Bride, Radey, & Figley, 2007; Coates & McKenzie-Mohr, 2010; Mullen & Leginski, 2010), prolonged experiences in the child welfare system (Jankowski, Schifferdecker et al., 2018), and mental disorders and addictions (Bride, 2007; Howell, 2012; Kosny & Eakin, 2008; Mullen & Leginski, 2010; Taylor & Sharpe, 2008). Living on the streets often exacerbates the issues arising from prior experience through additional potentially psychologically traumatic events as well as a wide range of ongoing health challenges. The additional health challenges include cardio-pulmonary disabilities, chronic diseases such as diabetes and asthma (Waegemakers Schiff & Lane, 2016), foot problems, chronic obstructive pulmonary disorder (Hwang & Burns, 2014), mental disorders, addictions, and communicable diseases such as hepatitis, tuberculosis, and HIV/AIDS (Cheung & Hwang, 2004; Waegemakers Schiff & Lane, 2016). Health issues are often not effectively addressed, as persons who are homeless may not trust staff in some helping organizations such as shelters (Kryda & Compton, 2009). In the U.S., the homeless often have difficulty accessing health services. Even in Canada, following through with recommended care is complicated by lack of access to necessary medications and care for post-hospital recovery (Baggett

DOI: 10.4324/9781351134637-9

et al., 2010). The impact of inadequate care for physical conditions is often aggravated by lack of adequate mental health supports.

Working in homelessness services with clients who have numerous unmet needs is challenging for staff and often complicated by meagre organizational and staffing resources and insufficient funding (Olivet et al., 2010). Workers may experience difficulties maintaining boundaries with their clients (Juhila, 2007; Waegemakers Schiff, 2015). In addition, the interpersonal and systemic problems experienced by persons who are homeless frequently trigger in staff their own issues related to personal trauma or loss. As progress in clients' lifestyle, habits and coping mechanisms is often slow, sometimes imperceptible, and frequently beset with setbacks, workers may become emotionally drained by their work (Fahy, 2007; Kidd et al., 2007). The high early and mid-life death rates of individuals who are homeless as compared to the general population (Cheung & Hwang, 2004) mean that workers serving homeless populations may witness multiple deaths, and in turn, experience significant grief and loss (Lakeman, 2011). Frontline workers often have little academic or professional training and thus have significant knowledge gaps in relation to the health challenges, mental disorders, and addictions faced by their clients (Guirguis-Younger, McNeil, & Runnels, 2009; Waegemakers Schiff & Lane, 2019). Inadequate training comes from both the scarcity of specialized post-secondary programs and courses (Waegemakers Schiff, 2015) and the minimal qualifications most often required for accreditation in both Canada and the United States (Council on Accreditation, 2019).

Organizational factors that complicate the work of those in homelessness services include limited educational preparation and training of staff, high rates of staff stress leave and turn-over (Waegemakers Schiff & Lane, 2019), organizational dynamics and systemic elements. Some reports indicate that those working in this sector, especially those at entry-level and front-line positions, often have limited educational preparation for handling the complex challenges faced by the homeless (Waegemakers Schiff & Lane, 2019). Salaries are low, staff turnover high, and organizations have limited resources to provide ongoing and extensive staff training or direct supervision of front-line staff (Olivet et al., 2010). Supervisors are often promoted from the frontline with two years of direct practice experience or less because of high staff turnover; as such, the leaders often lack the knowledge and skills to provide effective input and support for their staff.

Homelessness involves both extreme poverty and high needs for relatively scarce social services; as such, front-line workers also face limited resources to which they can refer their homeless clients for essentials such as income, food, clothing, and stable affordable housing. Even where appropriate services exist, the systems governing access to them are frequently rife with bureaucratic requirements and hard to navigate (Rowe, Styron, & David, 2016). The numerous obstacles to the provision of care can result in staff demoralization and burnout (Baker, O'Brien, & Salahuddin, 2007).

The high incidence of Posttraumatic Stress Disorder (PTSD) in the lives of homeless people (Fazel et al., 2008) and the prevalence of trauma in their lives (Hopper et al., 2009) undoubtedly combine to give rise to the stress and feelings of helplessness among staff. However, the literature is devoid of any research that examines this association and thus of any exploration of organizational responses to this type of occupational hazard. Several studies (of which we cite some representative examples) report on potentially psychologically traumatic events-related stress in a wide range of frontline workers—mental health therapists (Baum, 2015), social work clinicians (Cunningham, 2003), critical care nurses (Burgess, Irvine, & Wallymahmed, 2010), mental health professionals (Finklestein et al., 2015) and domestic violence services providers (Kulkarni et al., 2013).

Workers serving homeless populations may also experience compassion fatigue, burnout, and secondary traumatic stress. Figley (2002) initially presented compassion fatigue as a separate construct; however, subsequent work by his protégé Stamm (2009) suggests compassion fatigue consists of a combination of burnout and secondary traumatic stress. Burnout is widely regarded as a work-related reaction characterized by three dimensions: emotional exhaustion, depersonalization, and diminished feelings of personal accomplishment (Baker et al., 2007; Maslach, Schaufeli, & Leiter, 2001; Stamm, 1995). Emotional exhaustion includes feelings of depletion of physical and emotional resources, being over-extended and no longer being able to give of themselves. Depersonalization refers to the development of excessively detached attitudes and feelings towards work and clients. The third component is diminished feelings of personal accomplishment and self-efficacy (Demerouti, Karina Mostert, & Bakker, 2010; Maslach et al., 2001). Burnout consists of multiple physical and psychological symptoms: physical exhaustion, fatigue and insomnia; feelings of helplessness and hopelessness; a negative attitude towards work, life, and other people; attempts at coping through alcohol and drug abuse; and the psychosocial complications of marital discord and family problems. In some instances, suicide has been reported (Maslach et al., 2001; Yaniv, 1995). Secondary traumatic stress, a phenomenon identified in various helping professions, consists of a constellation of physical and emotional reactions that occur as a result of exposure to the stories and emotions of trauma survivors (Figley, 1995). Secondary traumatic stress includes symptoms that are also characteristic of PTSD, such as dissociation and flashbacks, feelings of anger, caution, sadness, vigilance, irritability, intolerance, denial and sensitivity, as well as sleeplessness and nightmares resulting from a worker's engagement with clients' potentially psychologically traumatic events experiences (Crothers, 1995; Stamm, 2009; Van Hook & Rothenberg, 2009). Burnout is widely acknowledged as involving organizational and individual factors, but there is no evidence to indicate whether organizational components have an impact on either direct traumatization or secondary traumatic stress.

224 Waegemakers Schiff and Lane

Burnout, secondary traumatic stress, and compassion fatigue have been widely studied in various helping professions; however, there are no studies that examine this range of stress- related responses in persons who work in homelessness services. We conducted a study on burnout, compassion fatigue, and potentially psychologically traumatic events-related stress in homeless sector workers in two large urban centres in Western Canada and also explored some of the organizational factors that may exacerbate or alleviate these responses.

In the current chapter, we briefly review the methods and results for the study, including a brief discussion of the high reported rates of PTSD symptoms experienced by participating workers. We then provide an examination of the issues of managerial and supervisory supports and their impact on the high rate of PTSD symptoms. We conclude the chapter with a brief overview of the ways organizations determine whether workers are impacted by burnout or by potentially psychologically traumatic events-related stress and how they can provide support that is suited to the specific origins of the stress.

Our Research

Study Design and Methodology

We recruited frontline staff, those providing direct support and intervention services in organizations offering either crisis (less than seven days), short-term (less than 30 days), or transitional stay shelters (up to one year) for persons who are homeless in two major Canadian cities. All organizations providing shelter services were invited to participate and over 80% of these organizations and 85% of their staff agreed to participate. In total, the staff of 23 organizations, ten in one city and 13 in the other, participated. Surveys were distributed to 499 staff; 479 completed the survey for a 96% response rate. We attribute the rate to our having met with all staff at a regular staff meeting, distributed surveys with an unmarked return envelope and given staff time to go to a private location and complete the survey—or not—and then return for a debriefing. As there were some missing responses, the research team understood that participants did not feel obliged to participate, responding to an important ethical concern that staff were not pressured into participation. Our response rate also suggests that staff felt a strong desire to voice their concerns. Our response rate was an important factor in reliability and generalizability, in that the results could be attributed to the entire population (both organizations and staff). The current results are unlikely to be attributed to selection bias. These two considerations were frequent limitations in previous studies involving organizations that work with traumatized clients (Hales et al., 2018).

Anecdotal reports indicate high levels of burnout in homelessness services in two western Canadian cities, and previous research indicating that burnout, secondary traumatic stress, and compassion fatigue are concerns in the homelessness sector; accordingly, we expected participants would report substantial levels of burnout and secondary traumatic stress. We assessed burnout and secondary traumatic stress using the Professional Quality of Life (PROQoL) instrument (Stamm, 2010), described below. Persons who become homeless report frequent exposure to potentially psychologically traumatic events, directly and as secondary traumatic stress (Stamm, 2010). We included the PTSD Check List, Civilian version (PCL-C) to determine this possibility (Wilkins, Lang, & Norman, 2011). Only one previous study has examined primary and secondary traumatic stress symptoms simultaneously (Finklestein et al., 2015), the results of this comparison of direct and indirect traumatic stress we consider an important addition to our understanding of their inter-relationships. In addition to individual factors, organizational factors may also impact levels of burnout (Awa, Plaumann, & Walter, 2010); accordingly, we included a series of items about managerial and supervisory supports and training that we organized into a scale measuring these components.

Respondents were recruited through their workplaces. The foundations in each western Canadian city that coordinate services for homeless people identified the lead agencies that provide significant outreach and shelter services such as day programs, drop-in services, overnight and short-term shelters, and programs of case-management and family supports. The participating organizations all agreed to allow the researchers to present our study at a general staff meeting. At that time, research plans and protocols were explained, informed consent was outlined, and surveys were distributed. At shelters where staff work on a shift basis, several meetings were arranged to correspond with the availability of evening and night staff.

The PROQoL is one of the most widely used instruments to measure burnout and secondary traumatic stress (Stamm, 2010). The PROQoL has a multi-dimensional structure that captures both compassion satisfaction and compassion fatigue. The PROQoL scale is a 30-item instrument that has been used in numerous studies to assess the quality of professional life of individuals experiencing very stressful events (Stamm, 2010), and is often used to assess burnout. The PROQoL consists of three scales: compassion satisfaction, secondary traumatic stress, and burnout (Stamm, 2010). Each scale has a strong alpha (Cronbach's): compassion satisfaction = .87; compassion fatigue = .80; and burnout = .72 (Bride, Radley, & Figley, 2007; Stamm 2010). The PROQoL covers experiences over the previous 30 days and uses a 5-point Likert scale to measure frequency of experiences.

The PCL-C is a widely accepted measure of PTSD symptoms that provides a quick assessment of potentially psychologically traumatic events-related stress with minimal additional respondent burden. The PCL-C has a 6-item version which is 95% accurate for detection of symptoms indicative of a potential PTSD diagnosis (Lang et al., 2012). The PCL-C is one of the most frequently used measures and correlates strongly with other measures of PTSD (Wilkins, Lang, & Norman, 2011). The

226 *Waegemakers Schiff and Lane*

DSM-5 allows PTSD to be the result of "experiencing repeated or extreme exposure to aversive details of the traumatic events" (American Psychiatric Association, 2013, p. 271). Thus, the PCL-C screen can now be considered a suitable indicator of potentially psychologically traumatic events-related stress that may be associated with a PTSD diagnosis. We chose the PCL-C instrument based on brevity, well-documented validity, and accuracy in detecting potential PTSD. Throughout the chapter, however, we refer to potentially psychologically traumatic events-related symptoms and not to the diagnosis of PTSD because while the PCL-C may be an indicator, the measure is not a diagnostic instrument and we thus prefer a more cautious use of the terminology.

Results: Demographics

Levels of education, job preparation, and length of experience in the homeless sector were very low, arguably problematically so, for the high needs and high risk of the population that workers are assigned to help. As not all respondents completed all items in the demographic information, the totals and percentages reported in Table 8.1 are based on information received and do not always include all 479 respondents.

Table 8.1 provides the details of participant characteristics. Important characteristics include highlighting discrepancies between high needs, client loads, and work assignments on the one hand, and low levels of preparation and experience on the other. Over half of all respondents reported only two years of post-secondary education or less and only 25% had a two-year diploma. Social work, nursing, and rehabilitative studies are three healthcare-related professions that provide preparation in client/staff interactions and interviewing skills. Only just over one third of all respondents had a background that included human behaviour in the social environment, interpersonal communication, and interviewing training. Over a third of the respondents have a Bachelor of Arts (BA) or equivalent, but their areas of concentration were not in professional social services or health care but spanned the fields of liberal arts and social sciences, such as psychology, sociology, anthropology, fine arts, and theology. An undergraduate degree in psychology is an academic degree that does not provide specific education in counselling and intervention methods. Only 13% of participants had a graduate degree, and just over half of these (55%) were in social work or psychology. Most participants reported inadequate educational preparation for their jobs. Nonetheless, 78% report feeling "mostly or totally" adequately trained for their job and an almost identical number felt competent to do their job.

Our survey results indicate expertise in helping homeless people was further compromised by the fact that the homeless services workforce had relatively low levels of experience working in homelessness services and considerable turnover, often switching employers in homelessness services during the first few years of employment. A sizable group (43%) had worked

Table 8.1 Participant demographics

Role	Frequency	Valid Per Cent
Intake/outreach	28	6.1
Support/counsellor	129	28
Shelter/residential staff	91	19.7
Clinical/case manager	78	16.9
Reception/front desk	27	5.9
Supervisor/mgr.	34	7.4
Administration	22	4.8
Facilities	17	3.7
Other	35	7.6
Length of time employed in homeless sector		
Less than 1 year	120	25.1
1–2 years	87	18.2
2–5 years	147	30.7
5–10 years	72	15
Greater than 10 years	52	10.9
Length of time in current position		
Less than 1 year	185	38.9
1–2 years	110	23.1
2–5 years	125	26.3
5–10 years	39	8.2
Greater than 10 years	17	3.6
Total	476	100
Highest level of education		
Some High School	13	2.7
High School	25	5.5
Some University/College	86	18
College Diploma	119	24.9
B.A./B.S.	169	35.4
Graduate Degree	64	13.4
Total	476	100
Area of concentration		
Social Work	127	28.6
Psychology	69	15.5
Business	39	8.8
Social Sciences	55	12.4
Rehabilitation Studies	9	2
Other	88	19.8
Nursing	15	3.4
Education	20	4.5
Arts	21	4.7
Annual income		
Less than $20,000	43	9.4
$20,000 to $29,000	39	8.5
$30,000 to $39,000	79	17.2
$40,000 to $49,000	163	35.6
$50,000 to $59,000	89	19.4
$60,000 to $69,000	22	4.8
Greater than $70,000	23	5

228 *Waegemakers Schiff and Lane*

in homeless services for less than two years. Most (73%) had worked in the homeless sector for less than five years. Over 62% had worked in their current position for less than two years. As there has been little growth in homeless services jobs in the last five years these numbers strongly indicate that many staff are new, inexperienced, and inadequately trained. Lack of longevity in homeless services also supports perceptions that this sector has a very high rate of staff turnover, with new persons typically starting with little or no applicable prior experience. Furthermore, those in supervisory positions are most likely to have been promoted based on seniority rather than training. This further compromises the expertise of this workforce.

Educational background did not, for the most part, have any impact on the job roles held by most staff, as almost all positions were occupied by people from diverse backgrounds. In many instances (38%), respondents had multiple roles that included both administrative and direct service functions. Based on reports of low salaries leading many to work more than one job, we explored this possibility and found that most respondents (71%) earn less than $50,000 a year from all employment and that many of our respondents (31%) were working one or more part-time jobs in addition to their full-time duties. The relationship between part-time hours and income was supported. The length of time that a person had been employed in the homeless sector was modestly (but significantly) correlated ($r = .407, p < .01$) with income, and with highest achieved educational level ($r = .346, p < .01$), but only slightly ($r = .131, p < .05$) with the respondent's stated primary role. In other words, people were likely to earn more over time, which is understandable, and this was also dependent, but less so, on their educational achievement. How much they earned was not associated with their job role and those with more education were not any more likely to stay in their jobs than those with less preparation. It stands to reason that people who remain employed by the same organization will earn more over time, but the level of these earnings remained modest and forced many to seek additional work. When we examined the associations between job stability and emotional stress, we found no correlation between reported potentially psychologically traumatic events-related stress and length of employment in the sector, the type of position, or the length of employment in the present position. This lack of correlation between the incidence of trauma symptoms and many factors that would normally be associated with increased symptoms needs further investigation.

Rates of burnout and secondary traumatic stress were comparable to those in other health and human service professionals who work with traumatized individuals: we found that 24% of workers experienced burnout and secondary traumatic stress at sufficiently elevated levels that they should consider stepping back from direct care duties (see also Stamm, 2010). In addition, 20% had a seriously diminished sense of compassion satisfaction, that is, they no longer derived any inherent positive feelings from helping others and may, indeed, be more negative than is therapeutically helpful to those in need. But, as indicated above, the length of time in this field was not a significant driver in the development of the PTSD symptoms, which suggests that management and supervisory staff need to consider identifying and addressing potentially psychologically traumatic events responses in all staff regardless of length of service.

When we looked at symptoms of potentially psychologically traumatic events-related stress, we found that 33% of respondents reported PTSD symptoms that were at a score of 14 or higher. PCL-C scores of 14 or greater are consistent with a positive screen for PTSD (Lang et al., 2012). As under-reporting of stressful symptoms has been noted by others (De Leeuw, Schmidt, & Carlson, 2005), we examined slightly lower scores as well. Those who were on the cusp—that is, having a score of 13— raise the incidence of PTSD symptoms to 45%. The implications of this rate, substantially higher than that found among health and human service professionals in general, will be discussed below.

Because there were high and very significant correlations between PTSD and burnout (.580), between secondary traumatic stress and burnout (.594), and between secondary traumatic stress and PTSD symptoms (.611), with all p < .000, we explored these relationships with a regression analysis which is provided in Table 8.2. Not surprisingly, secondary traumatic stress has the highest predictive relationship to PTSD symptoms with a Beta coefficient of .624; when burnout is added to the equation, the Beta coefficient rises to .752 (p < .000). While peer and supervisory supports and the availability of free health benefits reduce the impact of potentially psychologically traumatic events-related stress (the relationships are negative), these contributions are very small (–.111 and –.094) and thus do not suggest that these organizational components mitigate potentially psychologically traumatic events-related stress symptoms to any significant extent.

Organizational Factors

We included several questions on workplace practices, including supervision, use of teams, and the availability of peer support in our survey because we wanted to understand how organizational factors may contribute to burnout, secondary traumatic stress, and PTSD symptoms. A principal components factor analysis (with Varimax rotation and Kaiser normalization) was used to extract the main factors from the relevant variables. The set of questions focused on worker and managerial job-related behaviours such as adequate, regular administrative and clinical supervision (administrative support), peer support by workers, debriefing of critical incidents, and the availability of mental health benefits, including time off (health support). This analysis produced three strong scales (scale alphas > .75) that were identified as peer support (n = 5, Cronbach's alpha .826), administrative support (n = 6, Cronbach's alpha .874) and health support (n = 6, Cronbach's alpha .784). Cumulatively, they represented 36% of the total variance and were statistically strong. They indicate that administrative support, peer support, and adequate benefits impact PTSD symptoms

230 Waegemakers Schiff and Lane

Table 8.2 Regression analysis of burnout, secondary traumatic stress, and trauma symptoms

ANOVA[a]

Model		Sum of Squares	df	Mean Square	F	Sig.
1	Regression	3,047.39	1	3,047.39	223.406	.000[b1]
	Residual	4,774.201	350	13.641		
	Total	7,821.591	351			
2	Regression	3,525.884	2	1,762.942	143.228	.000[c]
	Residual	4,295.707	349	12.309		
	Total	7,821.591	351			
3	Regression	3,701.419	3	1,233.806	104.21	.000[d]
	Residual	4,120.172	348	11.84		
	Total	7,821.591	351			
4	Regression	3,751.642	4	937.911	79.965	.000[e]
	Residual	4,069.948	347	11.729		
	Total	7,821.591	351			

a. Dependent Variable: PCL
b. Predictors: (Constant), STS
c. Predictors: (Constant), STS, burnout
d. Predictors: (Constant), STS, burnout, Support

Regression Coefficients[a]

Model		Unstandardized Coefficients		Standardized Coefficients		
		B	Std. Error	Beta	T	Sig.
1	(Constant)	−2.32	1.013		−2.29	.023
	STS	.294	.02	.624	14.947	.000
2	(Constant)	−5.451	1.086		−5.022	.000
	STS	.212	.023	.449	9.244	.000
	burnout	.144	.023	.303	6.235	.000
3	(Constant)	−2.151	1.367		−1.574	.116
	STS	.219	.023	.465	9.715	.000
	burnout	.123	.023	.258	5.26	.000
	Support	−.111	.029	−.155	−3.85	.000
4	(Constant)	−1.098	1.453		−.756	.45
	STS	.216	.022	.458	9.612	.000
	burnout	.118	.023	.249	5.089	.000
	Support	−.079	.032	−.111	−2.442	.015
	health support	−.096	.046	−.094	−2.069	.039

Note:
a Dependent Variable: PCL.

thus supporting the importance of professional relationships in the workplace. However, while these components of workplace life are important, the total variance explained by them is not large enough to account for the major portion of the potentially psychologically traumatic events-related

Workers within the Homeless Serving Sector   231

Table 8.3 Correlational analysis of organizational factors

Correlations

		PCL	STS	burnout	support	peer support	health support
PCL	Pearson Correlation	1	.611**	.58**	−.273**	−.165**	−.296**
	Sig. (2-tailed)		.000	.000	.000	.000	.000
	N	461	427	429	429	433	432
STS	Pearson Correlation	.611**	1	.594**	−.067	−.063	−.127**
	Sig. (2-tailed)	.000		.000	.174	.2	.01
	N	427	438	413	413	416	413
burnout	Pearson Correlation	.58**	.594**	1	−.272**	−.269**	−.283**
	Sig. (2-tailed)	.000	.000		.000	.000	.000
	N	429	413	440	413	417	414
support	Pearson Correlation	−.273**	−.067	−.272**	1	.639**	.532**
	Sig. (2-tailed)	.000	.174	.000		.000	.000
	N	429	413	413	439	425	413
peer_ support	Pearson Correlation	−.165**	−.063	−.269**	.639**	1	.384**
	Sig. (2-tailed)	.001	.2	.000	.000		.000
	N	433	416	417	425	444	424
health_ support	Pearson Correlation	−.296**	−.127**	−.283**	.532**	.384**	1
	Sig. (2-tailed)	.000	.01	.000	.000	.000	
	N	432	413	414	413	424	443

Note: ** Correlation is significant at the .01 level (2-tailed).

stress in staff. Further work is necessary to identify additional components that may influence and mitigate PTSD symptoms.

Most of the correlations between managerial support, peer support, health care support, burnout, secondary traumatic stress, and compassion satisfaction, presented in Table 8.3 were highly significant ($p < .000$) but modest. Managerial support in the form of supervision, time out for stressful events, and individual and team supervision, have a small but significant impact on reducing burnout (−.272) while increasing compassion satisfaction (.329). On the other hand, while there was no relationship between managerial support and secondary traumatic stress, there was a small negative correlation between managerial support and PCL-C scores. Staff saw managerial supports as related to lower experiences of burnout symptoms and potentially psychologically traumatic events-related stress symptoms but not of secondary traumatic stress, which raises the issue of the extent to which these constructs are different or if the results is a measurement artifact.

The relationships among variables for peer support were nearly identical to the relationships for managerial support. Workers with higher perceived peer support also report reduced experiences of PTSD symptoms. At the same time, participants reported a somewhat larger reduction in burnout but no impact on secondary traumatic stress. These results suggested there are conceptual differences in these three constructs. A closer inspection of some individual organizational practices clarifies some supports or lack thereof. While debriefing after critical incidents on the job is considered by researchers to be a central aspect of providing support for staff (Healy & Tyrrell, 2013), over 46% of our respondents reported that this practice was not routine for general incidents and 42% reported that debriefing was not routine for incidents involving clients. Debriefing was found to have a very modest impact on reducing PTSD responses ($r = -.164$, $p < .000$) and on reducing burnout ($r = -.268$). However, the effects were too small to suggest anything but a minimal impact on individuals.

Our current results suggest that concern is justified about the lack of administrative supports for staff who deal with troubling events. Of those who identified as having a managerial role, 45% had a BA or higher and only 24% had a graduate degree. Few managers had education in the helping professions, as only 41% had a degree in a relevant area (social work, psychology, nursing). This implies that most managers lack the education and training necessary to support workers in frontline positions. The fact that 63% of our respondents report that they regularly or always debrief with peers suggests that many turn to peers to provide the debriefing and support they are not getting from their managers. These supports, administrative and peer, are important in all organizational contexts, and certainly have an effect in environments with regular potentially psychologically traumatic events exposures. They also mitigate experiences of burnout. However, these peer supports are not sufficient to stem the effects of primary PTSD symptoms or to help prevent their exacerbation.

Despite the high rates of personal PTSD symptoms reported by participants, half of all respondents report that they feel pressured to keep working and 38% indicated that they did not feel free to take time off when needed. The pressure to keep working correlates directly with increased PCL-C scores (.333, p < .000), while the ability to take time off correlates negatively with PCL-C scores ($-.273$, p < .000). It is unclear if this lack of perceived freedom stems from individual personality characteristics (the drive to keep working) or from organizational demands. However, as this item was situated in the survey in the context of work-related practices, it is likely that the workplace does not support the need for employees to have some control over work-related activities, which is an aspect of self-care. Having enough mental health days was also associated with decreased burnout ($-.297$, $p < .000$) and with decreased potentially psychologically traumatic events-related stress ($-.305$, p < .000). Additional mental health time off was one of the most frequently mentioned needs of staff expressed in their write-in responses. Unlike other occupations that encounter potentially psychologically traumatic events on a regular basis, such as police and firefighters, there is no provision for "paid time off" after a stressful event in homeless services environments despite the fact that these workers are even more frequently exposed to trauma in their clientele (Hopper et al., 2009; Olivet et al., 2010; Tischler, Edwards, & Vostanis, 2009).

Fundamental to addressing potentially psychologically traumatic events experiences is the need to restore and assure a safe environment for those affected. Of considerable concern is the fact that, while about half of our respondents reported feeling mostly safe at work, only 23% felt safe "all of the time". The relationships between feeling safe and reduction in potentially psychologically traumatic events-related stress and burnout were both reported at (–.336, p < .000) but, interestingly, there was no significant correlation between safety and secondary traumatic stress. Our findings support the conclusion that the secondary traumatic stress scale may be measuring a different construct than the primary traumatic symptoms that the PCL-C does, despite the fact that both target potentially psychologically traumatic events experiences. This may be attributable to the construct of individual questions in the PROQoL scale which position all questions related to secondary traumatic stress in the context of "in your work with clients" whereas the PCL-C asks about the extent to which a person experiences certain feelings and behaviours without assigning any cause. A regression analysis indicated a small, but positively predictive, impact of lower PTSD symptoms with increased feelings of safety (Beta –.336, $p < .000$). The examination of the issue of safety supports the claims that homeless services are not inherently safe places to work (Hopper et al., 2009; Olivet et al., 2010) and that staff feel emotionally vulnerable much of the time. The issue of psychological safety is also the first and most important consideration for those who have been traumatized (Briere & Scott, 2015) and thus these findings support other studies and their underlying theoretical constructs. However, our study does not tell us anything about the extent to which staff are also reacting to previous potentially psychologically traumatic events that predate their employment in the homeless sector. There is a strong possibility that memories and feelings associated with potentially psychologically traumatic events or serious adverse childhood experiences may also be activating PTSD responses.

Qualitative Responses

In order to gain some understanding of the role organizational support plays in the stress levels of workers, we also invited respondents to provide additional information. Four questions addressed coping methods, how workers dealt with negative outcomes in the workplace, as well as what formal supports they might seek if experiencing difficulties.

One concern of our respondents is the number of administrative and bureaucratic requirements for access to job supports. When we asked if there were "requirements for staff in your program who want to access formal support" (e.g., referral by a health professional, scheduling, advanced notice, etc.), one third of all respondents provided additional information. Of the 151 responses, 42 indicated that they did not know or were not sure of any requirements. Many workers stated that in order to access professional support, they need to talk to their "supervisor", "manager", or "upper management". Those who were able to describe the supports available (beyond talking to management) raised concerns about the availability of support or the requirements for accessing help. For instance, several participants noted that they did not have access to ongoing mental health treatment, that counselling was only short term and was available for fulltime staff only or only for those who have completed their probationary period, that they have to book appointments two weeks in advance, or that staff cannot use sick days for mental health issues. One participant summed up the limits to available support as follows:

> The organization does not have readily available professionals to support staff experiencing any form of trauma; the program is only for crisis situations, no help is available for long term support and continuous care for workers.

Other reflections included that support "should be mandatory to see on a regular basis" suggesting that worker support should be an essential feature of the workplace. One participant stated that many workers are "wounded healers", implying that workers themselves have been wounded by their own potentially psychologically traumatic events exposures but still try to help others who are affected. This comment warrants further examination, as it appears to support our postulate that many workers have their own histories of potentially psychologically traumatic events and are "triggered" and thus potentially re-traumatized at work. Current prevalence studies place the rate of lifetime exposure to potentially psychologically traumatic events for the general public at between 80% and 90% (Frans et al., 2005; Kilpatrick et al., 2013), with many people reporting multiple events. Thus, it is safe to assume that most staff have also been personally exposed to potentially psychologically traumatic events and that work events may trigger previous emotional states. The lack of organizational acknowledgment that the workplace can catalyse additional mental health problems among homeless services staff is an important finding with implications for mental health in the workplace (Mental Health Commission of Canada, 2017). It also has implications for occupational health and safety coverage, as the high rates of potentially psychologically traumatic events-related stress in the homelessness sector means that workers' compensation boards need to extend the coverage they provide first responders to include homelessness staff. While this has recently been implemented in some provinces, it is not yet a universal practice across Canada.

How Do You Cope with the Stresses of Your Job?

Many participants (60%) reported high levels of stress at work, and this stress is highly correlated (.501, p < .000) with PCL-C scores. When we asked about coping with job stresses, we were told that a variety of responses were available, such as debriefing with co-workers and managers, talking with a mental health professional, social and physical activities, using substances (e.g., alcohol, marijuana, etc.), and talking with a significant other or with friends. Additional responses included religious or spiritual practices, including church attendance, prayer, reading scripture, meditation, sweat lodges, and accessing elders or Indigenous teachings. A few individuals mentioned that they engage in quiet activities such as reading, TV watching, writing, resting, or listening to music. These write-in responses reminded us that the response options offered in the survey's other questions were too limited. One additional observation is that while practices such as mindfulness, meditation and yoga have been shown to markedly reduce potentially psychologically traumatic events-related stress responses (Metcalf et al., 2016), few respondents said they utilized these resources. One reason may be that few staff have considered their stress reactions to have origins such as potentially psychologically traumatic events exposures since many had originally referred to feelings of burnout. Re-framing the conversation in terms of potentially psychologically traumatic events exposures could result in more staff thinking of these types of interventions.

While most of the participants referred to healthy coping methods that can be employed outside of work or perhaps during work (e.g., prayer, spirituality), a few individuals suggested coping methods that deliberately take them away from work or provide the possibility of leaving work in the homelessness serving sector. For instance, one individual stated that s/he "takes time off every 6 weeks or so" and another "use(s) flex time to get distance from work" but notes that there are "not enough MH days". One participant cited a strategy that provides both physical and mental distance from work, that is, "look(ing) for other jobs until my frustration is gone". Another coping mechanism that has been reported by some respondents is the use of specific end-of-the-work-day rituals or routines that help to create distance between the stress of the workplace and home. Some involve deliberately going for a walk before going home or alternatively, taking a shower immediately upon arrival at home to "wash off all of the negative debris".

What Do You Do When You Have a Negative Outcome?

In light of the complex past and current situations faced by many persons who are homeless, negative outcomes are an inevitability for people who work with this client population. This open-ended question elicited written responses from 82% of all participants, which is an extremely high rate for open-ended questions and strongly indicates the need felt by staff to express their reactions to adverse details of their jobs. As one participant noted, "10 staff and 360 clients makes for a lot of negative client outcomes". Although the overwhelming majority of those who responded (91%) reported seeing positive changes in clients, many also indicated that they experience clients as challenging, frequently changeable in mood and intent, and prone to reversals of prior decisions. This suggests that the path to a better life is often not a straight linear one and may be fraught with set-backs that, in turn, affect staff. We received 471 responses to this question about negative outcomes, some of them multiple responses from the same individual. Of these responses, 142 (30%) stated that they always debrief with colleagues, 63% with peers always or almost all of the time. In the survey, debriefing with colleagues and debriefing as a team were reported as related but separate constructs (.473, $p < .000$). Both were differentiated from Critical Incident Debriefing, which was a separate item. When asked about how often they debriefed as a team, 57% indicated they did so "regularly" but only 30% indicated that they always debriefed as a team. Thus, while the need to share with colleagues and supervisors is viewed as an important aspect of coping, it comes with the reality that many managers discount the importance of team discussion. Formal debriefing is infrequent, despite the fact that staff see this as an important coping strategy. As a substitute, many staff turn to one another for the support they need but do not get from supervisors.

Many participants provided answers that demonstrate positive self-care. Notably, many recognized the importance of being able to learn from negative situations and to recognize the boundaries between their responsibilities and the choices and decisions of their clients. This involved debriefing about a negative outcome (reflection) and purposefully engaging in forward thinking. For instance, one worker stated that s/he "debrief(s) and stay(s) future-oriented, troubleshooting what could bring success".

Although most responses revealed an understanding by staff of how to take care of themselves following a negative outcome and the ability to move forward, several responses were concerning. A few participants mentioned that they felt bad when there were negative outcomes and provided responses that were very negative, such as "I tend to think about it all the time and beat myself up", or "I feel personally affected and think I must have done something wrong; I internalize the issue", or "I feel that maybe I missed some information. Maybe I didn't ask the right questions". Several participants indicated that they "withdrew" or "isolated" themselves or that they self-medicated through substances or behaviours, such as "drink(ing) alcohol", "use substances", "I use marijuana, smoke and/ or drink, or [have] become more interested in extreme sex". One participant responded in a more cavalier manner, stating that s/he does "Nothing. Water off a duck's back. If we have high expectations in this field, then we will burn out. Low expectations mean a longer career." While decreased expectations may be a self-protective approach, it could become problematic in the future.

Workers within the Homeless Serving Sector 237

All of these self-care responses, whether positive or less than healthy coping mechanisms, are undoubtedly influenced by a lack of professional preparation for this type of work. While disciplines such as social work, nursing, and psychology include topics on self-awareness and the professional use of self[1] in their curricula, most workers in the homeless sector have not been exposed to this content. Thus, in addition to lacking the requisite skills for appropriate interventions with very vulnerable and high-risk individuals, they do not have the self-awareness and the skills needed to take care of themselves. Such a lack of preparation inevitably adds to the work-related stress they experience. Traumatic stress is also not mitigated in the workplace, as staff development activities tend to focus on client-related needs and interventions and not on worker supports.

What Supports Would You Like to Have Added or Increased in Your Workplace and Your Job?

Another open-ended question that received many responses asked staff about additional supports that they would like in the workplace. Over two-thirds (69%) of all respondents provided input beyond the list of options provided about work hours and benefits. Many comments repeated options that had been listed, which gave emphasis to their importance. The most prevalent response (37%) focused on mental health support (e.g., counselling or mental health days on which workers can stay home), followed by a substantial number (27%) who indicated that they would like better compensation (money) and supports (such as mental health supports/counselling, health care plan). These respondents presented the job supports as separate from benefits; a distinction for management to consider. Almost one in five participants (19%) stated that they would like more training to perform their work more effectively. The requests for training reflected varied needs and work-related demands and demonstrate the challenges of working with people who are homeless.

The training requested varied considerably and included: handling bed bugs, restraining clients, self-defence, critical incident response (including when to call police or emergency medical services), and responding to substance abuse. Participants also requested education in the areas of leadership, stress management, suicide intervention, bereavement response, disease control, first aid, working with individuals who are mentally ill, and working with Indigenous individuals. Some participants did not specify the focus of the training but wanted more workshops and seminars and more direct supervision by management. All education areas reflect the complexity, extensiveness, and severity of problems faced by homeless staff and those they serve.

Discussion

The rates of burnout we found were commensurate with other helping professions that are exposed to potentially psychologically traumatic events

(Stamm, 2010); however, the rates of clinically significant PTSD symptoms were substantially higher than those found among other health and human service professionals such as nurses (Gillespie et al.; Lee et al., 2015), emergency responders (Donnelly, 2012), and, depending upon their experiences, military personnel (United States Department of Veterans Affairs, 2018). The high rates of potentially psychologically traumatic events-related stress may be due to several factors. Some individuals who work in the homeless serving sector have suffered from potentially psychologically traumatic events exposures in childhood and may, in the past, have been homeless themselves. Potentially psychologically traumatic events exposures at work may be triggering old injuries, thereby potentiating the trauma response; this hypothesis is based on evidence that exposure to averse childhood events is a risk factor for PTSD in adulthood (Jacobowitz et al., 2015). We also have to consider whether workers in the homeless sector are actually understating the incidence of PTSD either because they are confusing PTSD with burnout or because they feel less stigmatized reporting difficulties with burnout than PTSD. Informal discussions with participants presented with the results of the current study support that this use of the burnout terminology has wide acceptance and may result in the misapplication of labels and under-reporting of PTSD symptoms.

Many respondents noted that they debriefed with their teammates and/ or supervisors following a negative outcome and some individuals reported employing healthy coping methods to deal with work stress; nevertheless, the rate of reported PTSD symptoms is high. Why are coping methods and debriefing not very effective? Several hypotheses are worth considering. Do opportunities to debrief not suffice for the number of recognized and unrecognized potentially psychologically traumatic events exposures? Is the amount of time spent debriefing not sufficient for the type of potentially psychologically traumatic events experienced? Not only are workers exposed to frequent potentially psychologically traumatic events, they also work in environments where they continuously expect potentially psychologically traumatic events or critical incidents.

Debriefing protocols that are most often employed are usually directed at major single incidents and use external consultants for this process (Pack, 2013). Many of the numerous individual potentially psychologically traumatic events that workers are exposed to, such as witnessing the sudden death of a client through an opioid overdose, are typically not seen as requiring a major organizational response, especially when these events occur on a weekly basis in some locations. Ancillary to this is the question of mandatory initial counselling for workers who are routinely exposed to potentially psychologically traumatic events? Such referrals could remove some of the stigma surrounding requirements to talk with managers about the need for counselling and could ensure that individuals receive some kind of psychological support. The issue of support is complicated for part-time or casual workers many of whom mentioned, in their write-in responses, that counselling is not available to them. Such a policy on referrals would imply that only full-time workers are exposed to the negative incidents that lead to PTSD symptoms, which is inaccurate. Given the large percentage of workers in the homelessness sector who work part-time or have not yet finished their probationary period, excluding them from eligibility for support services seems unwise.

Many respondents requested additional training in a multitude of areas. The diversity of requested training topics ranged from practical issues of living such as dealing with bed bugs and with imminent evictions, to behavioural challenges such as managing anger and aggression, and dealing with avoidant and hyper-vigilant individuals. The work of homeless services sector staff appears varied, complex, demanding and, at times, dangerous. The training provided is generally focused on documentation and legal requirements and often does not include counselling and support skills and is thus insufficient for the challenges of working with complex problems and vulnerable people. As one quarter of our respondents had worked with the homeless for less than one year and 43% had worked in this area for less than two years, they lack experience and work under supervisors with limited preparation for their jobs. Continual and ongoing education is crucial so that new staff receive the knowledge and skill sets they need. In addition, respondents requested more direct supervision from their team leads/supervisors. Direct supervision of workers' approaches to situations and actions with persons who are homeless can allow for interactions to be deconstructed in order to strategize how to conceptualize situations differently, and then respond differently.

Inadequate salaries are always a concern in human and social services where average wages are below those provided in industry and commerce. Over 71% of our respondents make less than $50,000 a year. The pay may reflect years of service, but does not reflect the stress that staff experience. Certainly, salary levels are not commensurate with the complexity of skills required for working with homeless and vulnerable people. Additional income would help staff to access better mental health support and allow some to seek additional education beyond what is provided through their place of employment.

Many workers answered the open-ended items with positive suggestions regarding work supports and the importance of their supervisors/managers in providing supports; however, some of their responses were alarmingly negative. A few respondents reported using substances to cope with work stress, or perseverating over work situations and personalizing blame when confronted by negative outcomes; nevertheless, reports may not accurately reflect usage. Actual substance use may be more substantial but the rates reported may reflect socially desirable responses, since those who counsel clients with substance abuse may be reluctant to acknowledge their own misuse. Questions about how staff cope with work stressors also elicited some important responses. Comments that workers are "wounded healers" and that mental health support "should be mandatory to see on a regular basis" exemplify the level of work stress.

Conclusion

Our preliminary inquiry examined the prevalence of potentially psychologically traumatic events-related stress, secondary traumatic stress, and burnout. We anticipated finding high rates of burnout and secondary traumatic stress, but we did not anticipate the large proportion of staff who reported primary PTSD symptoms. The PTSD symptoms raise important issues about development of trauma-informed care for staff in high-risk organizations. Since the publication of the treatment protocol on trauma-informed care by the National Institute of Mental Health (Substance Abuse and Mental Health Services Administration, 2014), there has been an upsurge of interest in providing trauma-informed care for clients and, to a lesser extent, for staff (Kusmaul et al., 2018). Little research has yet provided documentation of the impact and importance of trauma-informed care (Unick et al., 2019). However, some work has been done to demonstrate these connections in child welfare services in the U.S. (Purtle, 2018). Based on the emerging body of knowledge and the current work on staff stress in homeless organizations, we suggest that attention be given to the connection between trauma-informed organizational cultures and their impact on mitigating potentially psychologically traumatic events-related stress in staff who are continually exposed to stress and trauma.

Our data leave unresolved questions regarding the extent to which previous potentially psychologically traumatic events experiences may re-activate responses in staff and the extent to which organizations can anticipate this or have responsibility for work-activated stressors. The results also raise the delicate legal and ethical issues of the extent to which organizations can screen for this possibility and the degree to which they are then responsible for work-exacerbated PTSD symptoms. Thus, we are left with some puzzling issues to clarify. Workers appear to often seek peer and supervisory support, but then find organizational support lacking and not helpful in mitigating their PTSD reactions.

Staff do not routinely have opportunities to address critical incidents at team meetings and do not regularly receive the individual supports that these events necessitate. Formalized Critical Incident Stress Debriefing may give participants the opportunity to express emotional reactions, ventilate these feelings, learn that their reactions are common and shared by others involved in the event, and recognize that these reactions may recur. Some reports indicate that such debriefing is helpful (Hammond & Brooks, 2001). There is debate regarding the impact of Critical Incident Stress Debriefing (Pender & Prichard, 2009), which has been criticized for including all those involved in the incident while failing to recognize that many may resolve their emotional reactions without intervention and that recalling the event may actually traumatize some survivors. Some researchers also suggest that Critical Incident Stress Debriefing may have little impact in preventing PTSD in emergency workers (Harris, Baloğlu, & Stacks, 2002). In any case, Critical Incident Stress Debriefing is often used after potentially psychologically traumatic events exposure and does not usually refer to work-related complaints. More routine use of Critical Incident Stress Debriefing in the workplace where potentially psychologically traumatic events are a continuing occurrence should be explored to assess its impact in reducing staff stress in these situations.

Underlying all the responses we received is that most staff reported inadequate educational background that would help them acquire both intervention skills and personal awareness of the stresses of their work. Many have been working in the homelessness services field for only a short time and others may move into supervisory positions without specialized training in this job function. What is alarming is that many participants with two years or less of post-secondary education report feeling mostly or totally adequately trained for their job. Given the complex nature of the client population, this confidence may be both over-stated and indicative of a lack of awareness of the intricacies of client problems. At the same time, over two-thirds of all respondents indicated that they did not always feel safe on the job, and this lack of safety may very well exacerbate potentially psychologically traumatic events-related stress symptoms.

Previous research results indicate that supervisory and managerial supports may mitigate the impact of work stress and consequent burnout in stressful occupations (Galek et al., 2011). In our work, we found that burnout and secondary stress do not completely align with experiences of primary traumatic events-related stress in staff and that organizational responses may need to be modified to be effective for these experiences. Although supervisors well-versed in potentially psychologically traumatic events and related stress responses would be in a better position to support staff who are impacted by work-related potentially psychologically traumatic events, few supervisors in the current study had this professional preparation. Furthermore, supervisory support appears to have modest effects on secondary traumatic stress and primary PTSD symptoms, but greater impact on burnout (which is acknowledged to have both individual and organizational precipitants) (Galek et al., 2011). As supervision and peer support are not in and of themselves sufficient to mitigate the impact of working in environments with regular potentially psychologically traumatic events exposures, we face the challenge of identifying the individual and organizational dynamics that may mitigate the inevitable primary potentially psychologically traumatic events-related stress in homeless services work. Primary and secondary (vicarious) PTSD symptoms should also be examined because effective interventions may not be appreciably different.

The work presented here provides evidence for policy makers and funders of several essential needs within the homelessness sector. Pervasive lack of adequate educational preparation for work with people who have complex problems indicates a clear mandate to increase job preparation for the workforce. The strong evidence of how stressful this kind of work is should convince both agency administrators and policy makers to carefully

242 Waegemakers Schiff and Lane

consider the workplace risk and safety issues that employees confront. We hope that further examination of the issues raised by the current study results will help to address staff stress and retention in agencies helping persons who are homeless.

Note

1 The term "professional use of self" is frequently found in social work practice as indicative of the importance of the helping relationship and the social worker's engagement with clients in this professional helping relationship. See also Briggs & Corcoran (2001).

References

American Psychiatric Association. (2013). *Diagnostic and statistical manual of mental disorders* (5th edn). Arlington, VA: American Psychiatric Association.

Awa, W. L., Plaumann, M., & Walter, U. (2010). Burnout prevention: A review of intervention programs. *Patient Education and Counseling*, *78*(2), 184–190.

Baggett, T. P., O'Connell, J. J., Singer, D. E., & Rigotti, N. A. (2010). The unmet health care needs of homeless adults: A national study. *American Journal of Public Health*, *100*(7), 1326–1333.

Baker, L. M., O'Brien, K. M., & Salahuddin, N. M. (2007). Are shelter workers burned out? An examination of stress, social support, and coping. *Journal of Family Violence*, *22*(6), 465–474.

Baum, N. (2015). Secondary traumatization in mental health professionals: A systematic review of gender findings. *Trauma, Violence, & Abuse*, *17*(2), 221–235.

Bride, B. E. (2007). Prevalence of secondary traumatic stress among social workers. *Social Work*, *52*(1), 63–70.

Bride, B. E., Radey, M., & Figley, C. R. (2007). Measuring compassion fatigue. *Clinical Social Work Journal*, *35*(3), 155–163.

Briere, J., & Scott, C. (2015). *Principles of trauma therapy: A guide to symptoms, evaluation, and treatment* (2nd edn). Thousand Oaks, CA: SAGE Publications, Inc.

Briggs, H. & Corcoran, K. (2001). *Social work practice*. Chicago, IL: Lyceum Books, Inc.

Burgess, L., Irvine, F., & Wallymahmed, A. (2010). Personality, stress and coping in intensive care nurses: A descriptive exploratory study. *Nursing in Critical Care*, *15*(3), 129–140.

Canadian Institute for Public Safety Research and Treatment. (2019). Glossary of terms: A shared understanding of the common terms used to describe psychological trauma (version 2.0). Regina, SK: Author. Retrieved from http://hdl.handle.net/10294/9055.

Cheung, A. M., & Hwang, S. W. (2004). Risk of death among homeless women: A cohort study and review of the literature. *Canadian Medical Association Journal*, *170*(8), 1243–1247.

Coates, J., & McKenzie-Mohr, S. (2010). Out of the frying pan, into the fire: Trauma in the lives of homeless youth prior to and during homelessness. *Journal of Sociology & Social Welfare*, *37*, 65.

Council on Accreditation. (2019). What is accreditation? Retrieved from https://coanet.org/accreditation/.

Workers within the Homeless Serving Sector   243

Crothers, D. (1995). Vicarious traumatization in the work with survivors of childhood trauma. *Journal of Psychosocial Nursing and Mental Health Services*, *33*(4), 9–13.

Cunningham, M. (2003). Impact of trauma work on social work clinicians: Empirical findings. *Social Work*, *48*(4), 451–459.

De Leeuw, R., Schmidt, J. E., & Carlson, C. R. (2005). Traumatic stressors and post-traumatic stress disorder symptoms in headache patients. *Headache: The Journal of Head and Face Pain*, *45*(10), 9.

Demerouti, E., Karina Mostert, K., & Bakker, A. (2010). Burnout and work engagement: A thorough investigation of the independency of both constructs. *Journal of Occupational Health Psychology*, *15*(3), 209–222.

Donnelly, E. (2012). Work-related stress and posttraumatic stress in emergency medical services. *Prehospital Emergency Care*, *16*(1), 76–85.

Fahy, A. (2007). The unbearable fatigue of compassion: Notes from a substance abuse counselor who dreams of working at Starbucks. *Clinical Social Work Journal*, *35*(3), 199–205.

Fazel, S., Khosla, V., Doll, H., & Geddes, J. (2008). The prevalence of mental disorders among the homeless in western countries: Systematic review and meta-regression analysis. *PLoS Medicine*, *5*(12), e225.

Figley, C. R. (ed.). (1995). *Compassion fatigue: Coping with secondary traumatic stress disorder in those who treat the traumatized.* New York: Routledge.

Figley, C. R. (2002). Compassion fatigue: Psychotherapists' chronic lack of self care. *Journal of Clinical Psychology*, *58*(11), 1433–1441.

Finklestein, M., Stein, E., Greene, T., Bronstein, I., & Solomon, Z. (2015). Posttraumatic stress disorder and vicarious trauma in mental health professionals. *Health & Social Work*, *40*(2), E24–E31.

Frans, Ö., Rimmö, P. A., Åberg, L., & Fredrikson, M. (2005). Trauma exposure and post-traumatic stress disorder in the general population. *Acta Psychiatrica Scandinavica*, *111*(4), 291–290.

Galek, K., Flannelly, K. J., Greene, P. B., & Kudler, T. (2011). Burnout, secondary traumatic stress, and social support. *Pastoral Psychology*, *60*(5), 633–649.

Gillespie, G. L., Bresler, S., Gates, D. M., & Succop, P. (2013). Posttraumatic stress symptomatology among emergency department workers following workplace aggression. *Workplace Health & Safety*, *61*(6), 247–254.

Guirguis-Younger, M., McNeil, R., & Runnels, V. (2009). Learning and knowledge-integration strategies of nurses and client care workers serving homeless persons. *CJNR: Canadian Journal of Nursing Research*, *41*(2), 20–34.

Hales, T. W., Green, S. A., Bissonette, S., Warden, A., Diebold, J., Koury, S. P., & Nochajski, T. H. (2018). Trauma-informed care outcome study. *Research on Social Work Practice*, *29*(5), 529–539.

Hammond, J., & Brooks, J. (2001). The World Trade Center attack: Helping the helpers: The role of critical incident stress management. *Critical Care*, *5*(6), 315.

Harris, M. B., Baloğlu, M., & Stacks, J. R. (2002). Mental health of trauma-exposed firefighters and critical incident stress debriefing. *Journal of Loss & Trauma*, *7*(3), 223–238.

Healy, S., & Tyrell, M. (2013). Importance of debriefing following critical incidents. *Emergency Nurse*, *20*, 32–47.

Hopper, E. K., Bassuk, E. L., & Olivet, J. (2009). Shelter from the storm: Trauma-informed care in homelessness services settings. *The Open Health Services*

244 *Waegemakers Schiff and Lane*

and Policy Journal, *2*, 131–151. Retrieved from https://benthamopen.com/ ABSTRACT/TOHSPJ-3-80.

Howell, A. M. (2012). *Working in the trenches: Compassion fatigue and job satisfaction among workers who serve homeless clients.* MSW thesis, St. Catherine University, St. Paul, MN. Retrieved from http: //sophia.stkate.edu/msw. _papers/ 116 (116).

Hwang, S. W., & Burns, T. (2014). Health interventions for people who are homeless. *The Lancet*, *384*(9953), 1541–1547.

Jacobowitz, W., Moran, C., Best, C., & Mensah, L. (2015). Post-traumatic stress, trauma-informed care, and compassion fatigue in psychiatric hospital staff: A correlational study. *Issues in Mental Health Nursing*, *36*(11), 890–899.

Jankowski, M. K., Schifferdecker, K. E., Butcher, R. L., Foster-Johnson, L., & Barnett, E. R. (2018). Effectiveness of a trauma-informed care initiative in a state child welfare system: A randomized study. *Child Maltreatment*, *24*(1), 86–97.

Juhila, K. (2007). From care to fellowship and back: Interpretative repertoires used by the social welfare workers when describing their relationship with homeless women. *British Journal of Social Work*, *39*(1), 128–143.

Kidd, S. A., Miner, S., Walker, D., & Davidson, L. (2007). Stories of working with homeless youth: On being "mind-boggling". *Children and Youth Services Review*, *29*(1), 16–34.

Kilpatrick, D. G., Resnick, H. S., Milanak, M. E., Miller, M. W., Keyes, K. M., & Friedman, M. J. (2013). National estimates of exposure to traumatic events and PTSD prevalence using DSM-IV and DSM-5 criteria. *Journal of Traumatic Stress*, *26*(5), 537–547.

Kosny, A. A., & Eakin, J. M. (2008). The hazards of helping: Work, mission and risk in non-profit social service organizations. *Health, Risk & Society*, *10*(2), 149–166.

Kryda, A. D., & Compton, M., T. (2009). Mistrust of outreach workers and lack of confidence in available services among individuals who are chronically street homeless. *Community Mental Health Journal*, *45*(2), 144–150. https://doi. org/10.1007/s10597-008-9163-6.

Kulkarni, S., Bell, H., Hartman, J. L., & Herman-Smith, R. L. (2013). Exploring individual and organizational factors contributing to compassion satisfaction, secondary traumatic stress, and burnout in domestic violence service providers. *Journal of the Society for Social Work & Research*, *4*(2), 114–130.

Kusmaul, N., Wolf, M. R., Sahoo, S., Green, S. A., & Nochajski, T. H. (2018). Client experiences of trauma-informed care in Social Service Agencies. *Journal of Social Service Research*, *45*(4), 589–599.

Lakeman, R. (2011). How homeless sector workers deal with the death of service users: A grounded theory study. *Death Studies*, *35*(10), 925–948.

Lang, A. J., Wilkins, K., Roy-Byrne, P. P., Golinelli, D., Chavira, D., Sherbourne, C., ... Craske, M. G. (2012). Abbreviated PTSD Checklist (PCL) as a guide to clinical response. *General Hospital Psychiatry*, *34*(4), 332–338.

Lee, J., Daffern, M., Ogloff, J. R., & Martin, T. (2015). Towards a model for understanding the development of post-traumatic stress and general distress in mental health nurses. *International Journal of Mental Health Nursing*, *24*(1), 49–58.

Maslach, C., Schaufeli, W. B., & Leiter, M. P. (2001). Job burnout. *Annual Review of Psychology*, *52*, 379–422.

Workers within the Homeless Serving Sector   245

Mental Health Commission of Canada. (2017). Mental health in the workplace. Retrieved from www.mentalhealthcommission.ca/English/focus-areas/workplace.

Metcalf, O., Varker, T., Forbes, D., Phelps, A., Dell, L., DiBattista, A., … O'Donnell, M. (2016). Efficacy of fifteen emerging interventions for the treatment of Posttraumatic Stress Disorder: A systematic review. *Journal of Traumatic Stress*, *29*(1), 88–92. https://doi.org/10.1002/jts.22070.

Mullen, J., & Leginski, W. (2010). Building the capacity of the homeless service workforce. *Open Health Services and Policy Journal*, *3*, 101–110.

Olivet, J., McGraw, S., Grandin, M., & Bassuk, E. (2010). Staffing challenges and strategies for organizations serving individuals who have experienced chronic homelessness. *The Journal of Behavioral Health Services and Research*, *37*(2), 226–238.

Pack, M. J. (2013). Critical incident stress management: A review of the literature with implications for social work. *International Social Work*, *56*(5), 608–627.

Pender, D.A., & Prichard, K. (2009). ASGW Best Practice Guidelines as a research tool: A comprehensive examination of the critical incident stress debriefing. *The Journal of Specialists in Group Work*, *34*(2), 175–192.

Purtle, J. (2018). Systematic review of evaluations of trauma-informed organizational interventions that include staff trainings. *Trauma, Violence, & Abuse*, *21*(4), 1524838018791304.

Rowe, M., Styron, T., & David, D. H. (2016). Mental health outreach to persons who are homeless: Implications for practice from a statewide study. *Community Mental Health Journal*, *52*(1), 56–65.

Stamm, B. H. (1995). *The ProQOL manual: The professional quality of life scale: Compassion satisfaction, burnout & compassion fatigue/secondary trauma scales.* Baltimore, MD: Sidaren Press.

Stamm, B. H. (2009). *Professional quality of life: Compassion satisfaction and fatigue version 5 (ProQOL).* Pocatello, ID: ProQOL.org.

Stamm, B. H. (2010). *The ProQOL manual: The professional quality of life scale: Compassion satisfaction, burnout & compassion fatigue/secondary trauma scales* (2nd edn). Retrieved from https://proqol.org/uploads/ProQOLManual.pdf.

Substance Abuse and Mental Health Services Administration. (2014). *A treatment improvement protocol: Trauma-informed care in behavioural services: TIP 57.* Rockville, MD: US Department of Health and Human Services.

Taylor, K. M., & Sharpe, L. (2008). Trauma and post-traumatic stress disorder among homeless adults in Sydney. *Australian and New Zealand Journal of Psychiatry*, *42*(3), 206–213.

Tischler, V., Edwards, V., & Vostanis, P. (2009). Working therapeutically with mothers who experience the trauma of homelessness: An opportunity for growth. *Counselling and Psychotherapy Research*, *9*(1), 42–46.

Unick, G. J., Bassuk, E. L., Richard, M. K., & Paquette, K. (2019). Organizational trauma-informed care: Associations with individual and agency factors. *Psychological Services*, *16*(1), 134.

United States Department of Veterans Affairs. (2018). PTSD: National Center for PTSD – How common is PTSD in veterans? Retrieved from www.ptsd.va.gov/understand/common/common_veterans.asp

Van Hook, M. P., & Rothenberg, M. (2009). Quality of life and compassion satisfaction/fatigue and burnout in child welfare workers: A study of the child welfare workers in community based care organizations in central Florida. *Social Work and Christianity*, *36*(1), 36.

Waegemakers Schiff, J. (2015). *Working with homeless and vulnerable people.* Chicago, IL: Lyceum Books.

Waegemakers Schiff, J., & Lane, A. (2016). Understanding pandemic preparedness by homeless services in the context of an influenza outbreak: The Calgary response. In K. S. Bucierri and R. Schiff (eds), *Pandemic preparedness in the homeless sector* (pp. 99– 126). Toronto, ON: York University Homeless HUB Press.

Waegemakers Schiff, J., & Lane, A. (2019). PTSD symptoms, vicarious traumatization, and burnout in front line workers in the homeless sector. *Community Mental Health Journal*, *55*(3), 454–462, https://doi.org/10.1007/s10597-018-00364-7.

Wilkins, K. C., Lang, A. J., & Norman, S. B. (2011). Synthesis of the psychometric properties of the PTSD checklist (PCL) military, civilian, and specific versions. *Depression and Anxiety*, *28*(7), 596–606.

Yaniv, G. (1995). Burnout, absenteeism, and the overtime decision. *Journal of Economic Psychology*, *16*(2), 297–309.

9 Emotional Labour, Police, and the Investigation of Sex Crimes Perpetrated Against Children

Posttraumatic Stress and the Toll of Dirty Work

Dale Spencer, Alexa Dodge, Rosemary Ricciardelli, and Dale Ballucci

Introduction

Technological developments over the last 30 years significantly challenge traditional forms of policing, leading scholars to suggest that the digital world is increasingly the "new frontline" for police work (Blakemore, 2012, p. 16). Traditional crimes, as well as emergent criminal activities, characterize this new frontline of policing. The policing of online environments and digital communication technologies involves challenges that require particular types of expertise such as the navigation of the darknet. The challenges include acquiring an intimate familiarity with the ever-changing online landscape and associated manners of criminal activity. In relation to sex crimes perpetrated against children, sex crime unit investigators must respond to a dizzying array of online activities, many of which continue to morph in response to technological innovation and the resulting new opportunities for sexual exploitation (Yar, 2013). Sex crimes targeting children are not new, but digital innovations have increased the ways and extents to which children can be victimized.

Police officers – like other first responders, public safety personnel, doctors, nurses, and military personnel – experience high rates of posttraumatic stress disorder (PTSD) and other mental health impacts (Canadian Mental Health Association, 2014; Carleton et al., 2018a; Acquadro Maran et al., 2015; Ménard & Arter, 2013). Persons working in sex crime units are exposed to numerous potentially psychologically traumatic events (PPTE; Canadian Institute for Public Safety Research and Treatment, 2019) involving sexual violence through interviewing victims and offenders and, in the digital age, through viewing graphic images and videos. The emotional effects of working in Internet Child Exploitation (ICE) units, in which officers are regularly exposed to photographs and videos of child sexual abuse, place investigators at significantly higher risk of developing secondary traumatic stress (Dodge & Spencer, 2018; Bourke & Craun, 2014; Burns et al., 2008;

DOI: 10.4324/9781351134637-10

248 *Spencer, Dodge, Ricciardelli, and Ballucci*

Krause, 2009; Perez et al., 2010). The number of images to which officers are exposed in often overburdened ICE units means that "over time, this constant exposure to human suffering may lead to a breakdown in normal coping mechanisms, placing officers at higher risk of developing secondary traumatic stress" (Burns et al., 2008, p. 21). With the increasing ubiquity and accessibility of child pornography in the digital age (Rogers, 2013), coupled with new challenges in policing child exploitation online (Yar, 2013), makes understanding and addressing the emotional effects of investigating child sex crimes increasingly necessary.

In the current chapter we document how investigators working in sex crime units across Canada manage emotions associated with lurid aspects of investigating forms of ICE, including online luring and the production, distribution and possession of sexually explicit images and videos of children. We examine the "dirty work" associated with investigating sex crimes against children and the emotional effects of such work, emphasizing the potential for posttraumatic stress injury (PTSI), including PTSD, that can arise from exposure to the sounds, sights, and faces of child sexual victimization and exploitation online. In addition, we demonstrate how cynicism engendered by dirty work produces barriers to getting much-needed help for PTSIs.

We have structured the current chapter into three main sections. In the first section, we outline the concepts of emotional labour and dirty work. In the second, we outline the research project methods from which the current chapter results are based. The final section demonstrates how, for police, emotional labour figures in the performance of dirty work associated with investigations of sex crimes against children and how such work can affect the well-being of police.

Emotional Labour, Policing and Dirty Work

Hochschild (1983) coined the term "emotional labour" to describe the ways that employees, particularly in service jobs, are required to "induce or suppress feeling in order to sustain the outward countenance that produces the proper state of mind in others" (Hochschild, 1983, p. 7). Hochschild argues that, "if we can become alienated from goods in a goods-producing society, we can become alienated from service in a service-producing society", as "the worker can become estranged or alienated from an aspect of self [...] that is *used* to do the work" (Hochschild, 1983, p. 7). Hochschild describes two types of emotional labour. The first type of emotional labour is surface acting, which is a type of self-monitoring that refers to

> the display of an emotional expression that is not actually felt. Surface acting corresponds with response- focused regulation in which an individual manipulates their emotional expression in accordance with the requirements of the situation, rather than trying to modify the entire situation or the cognition.
>
> (Bhowmick & Mulla, 2016, p. 48)

Posttraumatic Stress and Dirty Work 249

The second type of emotional labour is deep acting, which refers to "attempts to actually experience or feel the emotions that one wishes to display" (Ashforth & Humphrey, 1993, p. 93) so that "modification of the feeling takes place before the emotion is expressed behaviorally [... and] one attempts to bring consonance between the felt and the expressed emotion" (Bhowmick & Mulla, 2016, p. 48). Accordingly, the first type of emotional labour suggests a superficial interactional context that could easily be tied to consumeristic ideologies like the "customer is always right" and that, in essence, alienates service providers from their own reactions. In contrast, the second type of emotional labour is the more ingrained reaction that service providers feel but that most disassociate to some degree from their reaction in order to perform their occupational responsibilities. Police officers working in the area of child exploitation are often exposed to images and sounds of violently exploited children that are hard to forget and create deep-seated reactions that require emotional labour including surface acting and deep acting.

Organizational emotional labour involves "displaying organizationally desired emotions by controlling one's private feelings" (Bhowmick & Mulla, 2016, p. 47). The amount of emotional labour required in a given organization is determined by the feeling rules and display rules for that organization. Feeling rules are norms about what emotions workers should experience, and display rules are norms about what should be publicly expressed (Martin, 1999). Many authors have begun analysing emotional labour as a concept relevant for various forms of police work; however, the research assessing emotional labour and PTSIs is surprisingly limited (Chapman, 2009; Schaible & Gecas, 2010). PTSIs and emotional labour are particularly salient among police on account of the fact that they have rather high rates of cynicism, burnout, job dissatisfaction, substance abuse, divorce, and suicide ideation and completion (Carleton et al., 2018a, 2018b; Ricciardelli et al., 2018; Ricciardelli et al., 2018; Schaible & Gecas, 2010; Bhowmick & Mulla, 2016).

Policing requires officers to complete a wide range of tasks that demand "highly inconsistent and incompatible expectations for conduct" that may conflict with their values and lead to the frequent use of emotional labour (Schaible & Gecas, 2010, p. 317). There has been an increasing specialization of policing due at least in part to growing needs for unique and specialized skills among officers who work victim-sensitive crimes such as domestic violence calls and who must deal with the complex nature of victim–offender relationships (Loftus, 2010; Sewell, 1985). The increasing specialization is particularly evident for sexual violence-related units within police organizations across Canada and the United States. Sexual violence-related units, namely ICE units, child abuse, and adult sex crime units, specialize in investigating and responding to specific types of crimes and thus victims; as such, sex crime units tend to deal with some of the most morally charged aspects of policing.

Since sex crime investigations involve forms of labour that are considered socially and morally tainted (Ashforth et al., 2007; Dick, 2005; Powell et al., 2014a; Waddington, 1999), such investigations can be viewed as a type of "dirty work". In essence, dirty work includes any types of labour that are associated with the bad or dirty elements of society (see Ashforth et al., 2007). Just as associations with dirt can be viewed as contaminating, individuals who engage in dirty work can come to be understood as "dirty workers". In the eyes of the public and fellow police officers, sex crime investigators may become contaminated by their work (see Powell et al., 2014a; Spencer et al., 2019).

Sex crimes, specifically against children, are generally seen as the most abject of crimes and solicit powerful reactions from society in terms of shame and disgust vis-a-vis the sex offender (Simon, 1998; Ricciardelli & Moir, 2013; Ricciardelli & Spencer, 2017). Accordingly, sex crime investigators must both investigate and respond to calls that involve any form of sex-related offence. This dirty work includes hearing and seeing any details of a sex crime case, including details that are lurid and potentially psychologically traumatic as the investigators sort out specifics and decide what actually occurred involving the perspectives of victim, perpetrator, and possibly witnesses. The investigations may include watching and listening to video evidence of sex crimes committed against children, youth and/or adults. Being exposed to such content means sex crime investigators are intimately involved in dirty work. The investigators experience the taint attached to the crimes, which can include perceptions that there is something psychologically "wrong" with the investigators (see Edelmann, 2010; Powell et al., 2014a, 2014b). Burns and colleagues' (2008) study of ICE unit workers ($n = 14$) found evidence that the negative perceptions of the work interfered with the workers' coping mechanisms; for example,

> many team members felt stigmatized by others because of the work they did. Several described feeling isolated and unable to talk about their work because of the reaction of others. Team members felt this reaction was held by society in general, others in the criminal justice system, and even within their own policing community.
>
> (Burns et al. 2008, p. 24)

The taint from working in sex crimes can leave such work relegated to the lower end of the policing hierarchy, potentiating vulnerabilities to emotional and mental health impacts. The exposure to abject characteristics of sex crimes fosters distinct forms of cynicism relative to forms among frontline officers who may go through their entire careers without ever being so intimately exposed to some shocking aspects of sex-related criminality. The distinct forms of cynicism may manifest in reluctance to get much-needed help, particularly when such exposures result in PTSIs.

PTSD is highly pertinent to policing. Exposure to PPTEs is part of the policing profession (Carleton et al., 2019; Tuckey & Scott, 2013), exposure can lead to significant mental health problems such as depression and in some cases PTSD (Ainsworth, 2002; Becker et al., 2009; Greenberg,

Brooks, & Dunn, 2015). Indeed, rates of PTSD among police officers are particularly high, with up to one-third of officers experiencing symptoms associated with PTSD (Carleton et al., 2018a; Kirschman, 2017). What makes addressing PTSD in policing particularly complicated are broader cultural issues within policing that act as a barrier to seeking help. As a result, police officers are more likely to conceal their trauma than other groups in society (Becker et al., 2009; Heffren & Hausdorf, 2016). The factors explaining this reluctance can include fear of appearing weak, concern about breaching confidentiality, and a fear that pursuing help will harm their careers (Ellrich & Baier, 2017; Greenberg et al., 2005; Skogstad et al., 2013; Ricciardelli et al., 2018). In the specific area of investigating sex crimes against children, there is a need to explore the traumatizing aspects of this form of labour and the organizational barriers that impede investigators from seeking help. In the next section of this chapter, we discuss the methodology of the project that we designed to study these issues.

Methods

Focusing on the Canadian context, our research is part of a broader qualitative research project that examines how police investigate and respond to sexual violence committed against children, youth, and adults in diverse communities and on the internet.[1] Case studies were conducted with ten police service organizations across Canada. The organizations were selected from Central, Eastern, and Western cities that reflect the different urban landscapes in Canada and the different challenges police encounter in their approaches to investigating sex crimes with adult, child, and youth victims.[2] Utilizing a purposive sampling strategy (see Creswell & Poth, 2016; Patton, 2001), we chose participating police service organizations if they satisfied two criteria: 1) that they have one or more specialized units, separate from front-line officers that respond to sex crimes; 2) that they are located in an urban, as opposed to a rural, setting where these dedicated units tend to be located. We chose from three small urban centres (cities under 200,000), three medium urban centres (cities with a population between 200,000 and 500,000), and four large urban centres (populations over 500,000). Access to the participating police organizations was brokered through email and follow-up phone conversations with key gatekeepers of the various organizations.[3]

In addition to a pilot case study conducted with one police service organization in March 2014, case studies were conducted with nine other police service organizations across Canada from November 2015 to June 2016. In this chapter, we treat each police service organization as a distinct case that may have one or more sex crime units within its organization. While the police organization in the pilot study had four sex crime-related units that pertain to the sexual victimization of children, youth, and adults, police organizations across Canada vary in the number of units they form to investigate and respond to sex crimes. The largest police service organization

252 *Spencer, Dodge, Ricciardelli, and Ballucci*

included in our study has eight different sex crime-related units and the smallest police service had only one. As the size of the police organizations increase, the mandates of the individual sex crime units become narrower and more specialized in terms of the type of victims to whom they respond.[4]

Data Collection

The collected data included semi-structured, in-depth interviews ($n = 70$) and two focus groups with members of sex crime-related units in police service organizations. The research team conducted the semi-structured, in-depth interviews with individual unit officers to support participants providing greater detail and depth about their experiences than structured interviews and to allow interviewees to bring up unanticipated concerns, concepts, and topics (Wengraf, 2001). Our interviews provided insights into how the officers and analysts understand sex crimes, in-depth knowledge of their professions, an understanding of the meanings they attach to "offenders", as well as a grasp of their experiences in working with children, youth, and adult complainants (see Flick, 2014; Marshall & Rossman, 2011). A subset of questions derived from the interview guide were used to conduct the focus groups with multiple members of sex crimes units in two large police service organizations.[5] The focus groups were used to understand the mandates of the individual sex crimes units and their experiences of investigating and responding to sex crimes committed against children, youth, and adults. Follow-up interviews were then conducted with individual members of the same sex crime units.[6]

The interview guide consisted of 42 open-ended questions. Interviews were intentionally wide-ranging and covered such topics as the participant's experiences of investigating and responding to sex crimes, uses of technology, and interpretations of types of sex crimes and victims. The interviews were not psychological in nature, but some interviewees did disclose their own mental health needs or concerns (including diagnoses) or those of persons in their units currently on leave for reasons tied to mental health. Examples of questions include: "How do you envision justice for victims of crime?" and "What are the challenges you face in your position?" Interviews were digitally recorded and averaged 50 minutes in duration, ranging from 30 to 150 minutes. The length of each interview depended on the talkativeness of the interviewee. Interviews were transcribed verbatim and identifiers have been assigned to replace the names of all participants.

Interviews and focus groups were conducted only with respondents working in police units whose mandate is to respond to sexual violence. In terms of the types of victims the police in this project investigate and respond to, 29 officers work in units that respond to both adult and child victims of sexual violence, 23 officers investigate only sex crimes against children, and 18 investigate and respond only to sexual assaults committed against adults. In the current chapter, we analyse responses from the 52

Posttraumatic Stress and Dirty Work 253

respondents who work in units that respond to child and youth victims of sexual violence.

Data Analysis

We used QSR Nvivo qualitative research software to assist with the compilation, organization, and coding of the interview and focus group transcripts. Interview and focus group data were initially coded according to theoretical, process, and attribute codes defined by the research team prior to data analysis. A significant number of additional themes emerged (Charmaz, 2006) in the initial stages of the coding of the interview data. The research team met to discuss the additional themes and used a process of codebook revision and recoding to reach consensus regarding meanings (Campbell et al., 2013; Kurasaki, 2000). Over 80 themes emerged from the interview and focus group data. In the current chapter we focus on the themes related to officer mental health and well-being, specifically the themes titled "emotions", "emotional labour", and "victim support".

Results

Pogrebin and Poole (1991, p. 396) explain that police, like other professionals, are expected to act respectful towards clients, but to remain "detached and dispassionate". For police, the social distance allows for demonstrable professionalism necessary for being calm and in control during emotionally charged situations (Pogrebin & Poole, 1991, p. 396). The police believe the public expects a portrayed calm, controlled, and fearless demeanour; as such, "the standards that police set for themselves for managing emotions are often severe and uncompromising" (Pogrebin & Poole, 1991, p. 397). The repression of emotion then becomes a normalized and expected part of police culture such that appearing overly emotional could signal to others an inability to handle the pressures of police work (Pogrebin & Poole, 1991; Chapman, 2009; Martin, 1999).

In the policing of sex crimes against children, officers are arguably dealing with some of the most emotionally charged elements of policing. Sex crime unit investigators are charged with responding to the victimization of some of the most vulnerable members of society, primarily women and children. ICE units are a subset of sex crime units involving a reconfiguration of the policing labour process that is complicated by the continuously evolving nature of online sex crimes. ICE investigators require knowledge of new applications and must explore the darknet, which is a largely unregulated, criminogenic online space. At the same time, ICE investigators labour process involves an emotionally draining element of processing online evidence. Consider the following interview responses:

LUCY: I think it's, the biggest part, is obviously dealing with those, those really young children that are being, being exploited. And, and what

254 Spencer, Dodge, Ricciardelli, and Ballucci

we do is like, you know, we have to review all the images that we, that we get from the searches. And, cuz we have to categorize them and say, "ok that is child pornography, or that's age difficult, or."

BRYAN: Personally I mean just viewing some of the, the images and videos of child pornography and then especially if, uh, to deal with that alone is one thing but then when you end up dealing—discovering or dealing, discovering who—who that victim is and then dealing with them on a personal level, that makes it more difficult as well.

Lucy's words describe the labour process of the ICE investigators and the "dirty" elements of doing such work. ICE investigations involve viewing and categorizing images and determining whether the subject viewed in the images meets the mandate of their unit. Bryan notes that viewing illicit images of children impacts him personally, making the labour process more difficult. Officers report that the continuous visual and aural exposure to exploited children is a traumatizing element of their work and is further complicated by additional elements of digital media investigations:

LEO: When I first came into the unit I had to learn very quickly. Like I was doing a categorization and I had a video and I had not cut the sound off. That's different. When you see stuff, you can go, ok, ok. But when you hear the little, little girl screaming and crying and all that stuff that can mess with you. So when I first came into the unit there'd be times when I'd be doing a search warrant where you have to watch what they're downloading. Unfortunately, it was movies. And you just look at it, just say, "Ok. Enough for now." Shut it down and go for a walk. Go out for coffee. Stuff like that…

BARRY: … it's videos to me are worse and there's different reasons why they're worse. One because they're videos so now you have people moving, people talking, um especially ones with little kids. To me they're worse because those kids usually have a smile on their face which means they've probably been through this abuse forever and they don't know any different… Videos are worse. Because there are moving parts—you see little girls and little boys that have happy smiles on their face and they're being abused. Because they just don't know any better. And those are the bad guys that are in there. And they're cowards. The bad guys that are in there with masks on and disguises on and—you know? This is what they do. So it's—when you categorize it like that, yeah.

As Leo indicates, this dirty work involves having to examine videos that are visually disturbing and that affect the investigator in other ways. Here the aural component figures as a potent element of examination that deeply affects the investigator as he or she must listen to exploitation, abuse, and suffering. Video is interpreted as more traumatizing than pictures for Leo because of, inter alia, the aural aspects of the investigation. For Barry, the

Posttraumatic Stress and Dirty Work 255

movement of figures on the screen is the most devastating, as the investigator has to view the normalization of paedophilia and the furtive nature of those committing such atrocities. The movement and text behind the video provide more context for the trauma and more information about the extent of the abuse the victim(s) experiences. The dirty work associated with these investigations involves more than viewing images and videos. The investigations involve the emotional labour of managing difficult situations:

MARIE: We have a lot of cases that are difficult to deal with emotionally, uh, in terms of difficult victims. One girl in particular, who was not cooperative at all, she was 14 and the 20-year-old guy that lured her online, and she sent nude photos to and ended up meeting and having sex with, she was in love with him and she thought he was in love with her and she was very difficult to uh, to deal with. Mom was really good, Mom actually had to physically pry the phone from her daughter's hands to give to us and … I remember … she was crawling under the table, trying to get Mom's purse and going through, Mom and her struggling and it was, it was ridiculous and then she ended up running outside in like minus 25-degree weather in her school uniform… I mean we couldn't do anything, we can't keep her there, we can't kidnap her …

Marie describes a seemingly chaotic scene where she worked to acquire the corroborating evidence from the mother and daughter, while coping emotionally with the chaos of the scene. Marie had to engage in surface acting, while remaining within the mandates of the profession and not engaging emotionally with the daughter. Such internet child investigations can also involve more than just dealing with parent–child tumult. Consider the following narrative of an undercover officer posing as a young girl:

DIANE: So we start chatting and I ended up chatting with him online for three months he's a convicted sex offender and… [has] umpteen previous charges, [he] started sending me pictures and teaching me all the things he'd like me to do [to] him and …step by step where I was to put my hand where he put his, what it would feel like, what we do, and to the point where I finally said… [I] "can't be on the computer because he was talking marriage. I'm 13 he believes I'm 13 I've never sent him a picture never sent him anything but apparently I'm a very good 13-year-old" and he said "have you ever thought about making this permanent?" … And this goes on and on online, [he] gave me his full name, mailing address for [where] he works so that I can send him my dirty panties and the pictures, address, everything. Homeland Security checked it out, [he's a] convicted sex offender, he's on the sex offender registry…. So I'm actually just finishing up a three months [of work] package [that I] sent to Homeland Security… I have to say,

256   *Spencer, Dodge, Ricciardelli, and Ballucci*

mental health wise, that was the worst thing I've ever done. Because I don't think you realize the reality of the problem until you see it to that extent.... It's horrific and I felt so gross because I ... was naïve. I didn't understand anything "oh what is that?" Like I played this role and he handed me everything and it made my skin crawl; "You dirty pervert, how dare you talk to this innocent little girl." Because that's essentially what I was [pretending to be]; "I'm an innocent little girl, I knew you were corrupting me, you are ruining me...". It's the reality, I mean the files... It was horrible. Files other than undercover online stuff, the ones that probably bother me most, if I start to cry, forgive me I probably will, are the ones that we meet the child and you see the pictures, videos and then you're face-to-face with them.

Diane's narrative of luring an offender on the sex offender registry reveals the form of online surface acting that is expected of investigators, and the emotional labour tied to the deep-rooted feelings that arise from such exposures. This form of emotional labour is embedded in deep-rooted feelings and even helplessness (e.g., knowing such incidents do happen and most victims fail to come forward or even recognize that they are victims until much later) and involves playing compromising roles that can take a mental health toll on the investigator (cf. Spencer & Patterson, 2016). Diane informed us that she was suffering from PTSD and reported feeling as though she was taking on the taint of the dirty work by luring sex offenders online. In pretending to be lured, pretending to be sexually naïve, she felt "gross"; accordingly, she engaged in dirty work that she felt was traumatizing and left her feeling "dirty".

ICE investigations have deep and diverse impacts on the officers working in sex crime units. The investigators report that exposures to the materials invade their everyday lives in unpredictable ways:

RYAN: Emotionally the triggers for me are obviously youth and even some-times animals but, I've had a few cases with animals and I don't like animals being victimized either... In this field in particular videos are tough, with audio that really temporally places you [in the context or scene of the exploitation], like it's very easy to empathize and intern-alize and associate to something. Like videos are very powerful, audio in particular, hearing the offences, hearing victims' reactions, those are tough. I don't, I try not to focus on any one of those because that's unhealthy and in terms of for posttraumatic stress... you don't want to dwell on individual, you want to look at everything as a whole. I've had several, I've been exposed to material in this industry that is very disturbing, that has lingered with me for periods of time after.

Ryan's words showcase how exposures to traumatic materials can have long-lasting effects. Ryan describes frequent struggles to cope by actively avoiding focusing on particular cases or on aspects of particular videos;

Posttraumatic Stress and Dirty Work   257

moreover, Ryan appears to recognize feeling that his well-being is compromised such that he feels vulnerable to a PTSI given his unavoidable and disturbing work context. Like many other sex crime investigators, Ryan recognizes that he will never know when a video or image will result in his needing formal psychological supports. A related problem involves ascertaining when an officer is in need of formal psychological support:

SAMANTHA: So it's sitting down with a therapist. I haven't done it yet, which is awful. I'm two years in—two and two months. My partner is in his fourth year and he hasn't done it yet either. Our new boss ... is putting it together and we're supposed to be going at the end of February. So, I think it's just to create a sort of benchmark to see where you were before, where you are along the way, and where you are and how you're coping with the time after.

Samantha, who after being asked if she has accessed formal mental health services, explains that she and her partner have not yet done so. Samantha has also recognized that her mental health and that of her partner may be compromised because of her work; nevertheless, her response points to an overarching problem among police service members: the perceived inaccessibility of mental health services for officers in sex crimes units who need help coping with their jobs.

Our interviewees overwhelmingly acknowledged that responding to sex crimes takes an emotional toll. Jennifer, an ICE investigator, explained that she did not "believe in PTSD" until she joined her unit and experienced how her ICE investigations actually affected her well-being. The emotional and psychological toll of ICE work appears further compounded by the stigma attached by police officers to acknowledging mental health challenges and seeking mental health support. Corrigan, Druss, and Perlick (2014) reported that stigma continued to prevent people in general from accessing mental health services. Speaking specifically about police service organizations, Karaffa and Koch (2016) acknowledge the stigma within the policing occupation and suggest that addressing the stigma may help officers engage in help-seeking for mental health. Our participants evidence the ongoing challenges as even those that use mental health services reported cynicism:

TREVOR: ... you hear through the grapevine and people talking and—I don't usually get too involved in it. I just sit back and listen, "that's all you got time to do? Like, come on. You got work here!" But, you know, the shoptalk, yeah people do talk about it and people always question evidence, is that the human nature of a police officer? Questioning? Or second thought or second-guess someone's legitimacy? .... I think the people who are saying "yeah, I have these [mental health] issues". [But mental health concerns] are getting now, "it's like 'oh come on, really'?" I think it's more of a negative thing. It went from like the

258   Spencer, Dodge, Ricciardelli, and Ballucci

positive to the negative. "Like are people overusing it now? Are they using it as a way to escape from work?"

Cynicism can be the product of officers' experiences of the failure of other police officers to meet their expectations of the occupation culture (see Bennett & Schmitt, 2002; Caplan, 2003). In terms of responses to emotional triggering stimuli, the occupational culture prescribes a stoic form of surface acting and a form of deep acting in which officers are expected to cope privately with the emotionally distressing elements of their profession. Officers who transgress the acting forms can face accusations of malingering. Trevor reported accepting the need for psychological services, but his cynical disposition led him to interpret psychological services as being overused by some and unused by others. Sex-crime investigators in our sample tended to report mental health services as necessary, but reported viewing officers who use such services as weak or as taking advantage of available services. As such, support services for mental health are simultaneously valued and perceived as problematic. The rates of PTSD and other mental disorders are significantly higher in police than among the general population (see Carlton et al., 2018a, 2018b); accordingly, the need to improve access to services by dismantling barriers to care seekers among police is essential, particularly for those working in sex crime related units. Stigmatizing mental health service use may create a double bind for police officers who may feel pressures to address the most abject aspects of their police work on their own. Most police officers in the current study reported not voluntarily seeking psychological services to cope with PPTE exposures, even when reporting feeling at risk for PTSIs. The double bind involves investigators being confronted with the irreconcilable demand of engaging in dirty work that is potentially mentally injurious work and not wanting to be stigmatized for receiving much needed care.

Conclusion

The chapter demonstrates how sex crime investigators' occupational work can be interpreted as a form of dirty work, that involves forms of surface and deep acting associated with emotional labour. The realities of investigating child sex crimes include hearing or seeing content, talking to victims, presenting as an innocent youth online ready to be lured, or other PPTE-related tasks impact officers to varying degrees over time. Our interview and focus group responses show how exposure to illicit images of children makes the labour process of investigators more difficult, often impacting officers personally and professionally. Officers report being particularly susceptible to PTSI because of vicarious traumatization. Officers report that seeing child victims appear "happy" while being abused (i.e., youth being so accustomed to abuse they no longer recognize they are being sexually violated) is extremely disturbing and painful. Such investigations involve surface acting and can harm the mental health

Posttraumatic Stress and Dirty Work 259

and well-being of the investigators. The occupational culture prescribes a stoic form of surface acting and a form of deep acting where the officer is implicitly instructed to cope privately with the repeated PPTE exposures. Accordingly, many officers reported their own experiences with PTSI, including PTSD, or reported their colleagues had been diagnosed and consequently left their occupational duties.

Our results underscore the need for further research on the emotional impact of investigating child sex crimes, the emotional needs of these investigators, and the barriers that prevent police officers from gaining access to support services when experiencing a PTSI. Exposure to PPTEs is part of the policing profession and when such exposures are frequent and morally deplorable, there may be a particularly high risk for PTSI including PTSD. There is also evidence that cynicism among police officers is contributing to stigma and serving as a deterrent to mental health help-seeking behaviours, despite repeated reports of distressing intrusions after PPTE exposures.

Notes

1 This project was supported by an Insight Development Grant from the Social Sciences and Humanities Research Council (SSHRC).
2 We sampled from police organizations in five provinces, including Alberta, Manitoba, Ontario, Newfoundland and Labrador, and Nova Scotia.
3 We contacted 12 organizations to participate in our study. Ten of these organizations responded to and agreed to our request to be included in our study.
4 In this chapter, we do not differentiate between units that investigate online and those that investigate only or mainly "offline" sexual assaults, as the interviewees confirmed that digital evidence is a factor in almost all cases of sexual assault. Instead, we distinguish in the analysis between units that specialize in investigating particular types of sex crimes and the degree to which their cases are online.
5 The first focus group was conducted with three members and the second focus group had eight members. The focus groups were heuristic in orientation and consisted of 32 questions and focused primarily on the mandate of the units, collaborations between police officers in the units, and their experiences with investigating and responding to different types of sex crimes. Follow-up interviews were conducted with two members of these focus groups. Focus groups were conducted in cases where there were availability constraints on unit members.
6 This project was approved by the Carleton University Research Ethics Board. All participants signed an informed consent form.

References

Acquadro Maran, D., Varetto, A., Zedda, M., & Ieraci, V. (2015). Occupational stress, anxiety and coping strategies in police officers. *Occupational Medicine*, *65*(6), 466–473.
Ainsworth, P. (2002). *Psychology and policing*. Cullompton: Willan.

Ashforth, B. E., & Humphrey, R. H. (1993). Emotional labor in service roles: The influence of identity. *The Academy of Management Review, 18*(1), 88–115. https://doi.org/10.2307/258824

Ashforth, B. E., Kreiner, G. E., Clark, M. A., & Fugate, M. (2007). Normalizing dirty work: Managerial tactics for countering occupational taint. *Academy of Management Journal, 50*(1), 149–174.

Becker, C., Meyer, G., Price, J., Graham, M., Arsena, A., Armstrong, D., & Ramon, E. (2009). Law enforcement preferences for PTSD treatment and crisis management alternatives. *Behaviour Research and Therapy, 47*(3), 245–253.

Bennett, R. R., & Schmitt, E. L. (2002). The effect of work environment on levels of police cynicism: A comparative study. *Police Quarterly, 5*(4), 493–522. https://doi.org/10.1177/109861102237692

Bhowmick, S., & Mulla, Z. (2016). Emotional labour of policing: Does authenticity play a role? *International Journal of Police Science & Management, 18*(1), 47–60. https://doi.org/10.1177/1461355716638113.

Blakemore, B. (2012). Cyberspace, cyber crime and cyber terrorism. In I. Awan & B. Blakemore (eds), *Policing cyber hate, cyber threats and cyber terrorism* (pp. 5–20). Farnham: Ashgate.

Bourke, M. L. & Craun, S. W. (2014). Secondary traumatic stress among internet crimes against children task force personnel: Impact, risk factors, and coping strategies. *Sexual Abuse, 26*(6), 586–609.

Burns, C., Morley, J., Bradshaw, R., & Domene, J. (2008). The emotional impact on and coping strategies employed by police teams investigating internet child exploitation. *Traumatology, 14*(2), 20–31.

Campbell, J. L., Quincy, C., Osserman, J., & Pedersen, O. K. (2013). Coding in-depth semistructured interviews: Problems of unitization and intercoder reliability and agreement. *Sociological Methods & Research, 42*(3), 294–320.

Canadian Institute for Public Safety Research and Treatment. (2019). Glossary of terms: A shared understanding of the common terms used to describe psychological trauma (version 2.0). Regina, SK.

Canadian Mental Health Association. (2014). Post-traumatic stress disorder. Retrieved from www.cmha.ca/mental_health/post-traumatic-stress-disorder.

Caplan, J. (2003). Police cynicism: Police survival tool? *The Police Journal, 76*(4), 304–313.

Carleton, R. N., Afifi, T. O., Tailieu, T., Turner, S., Duranceau, S., LeBouthillier, D. M., ... Asmundson, G. J. G. (2018a). Mental disorder symptoms among Canadian first responder and other public safety personnel. *Canadian Journal of Psychiatry, 63*(1), 54–64. doi:10.1177/0706743717723825

Carleton, R. N., Afifi, T. O., Turner, S., Tailieu, T., Duranceau, S., LeBouthillier, D. M., ... Asmundson, G. J. G. (2018b). Suicidal ideation, plans, and attempts among public safety personnel in Canada. *Canadian Psychology, 59*(3), 220. https://doi.org/10.1037/cap00001369

Carleton, R. N., Afifi, T. O., Taillieu, T., Turner, S., Krakauer, R., Anderson, G. S., ... McCreary, D. (2019). Exposures to potentially traumatic events among public safety personnel in Canada. *Canadian Journal of Behavioural Science, 51*, 37–52. https://doi.org/10.1037/cbs0000115

Chapman, D. (2009). Emotional labour in the context of policing in Victoria: A preliminary analysis. *International Journal of Police Science & Management, 11*(4), 476–492. https://doi.org/10.1350/ijps.2009.11.4.145

Posttraumatic Stress and Dirty Work   261

Charmaz, K. (2006). *Constructing grounded theory: A practical guide through qualitative analysis* (1st edn). Thousand Oaks, CA: SAGE Publications Ltd.

Corrigan, P. W., Druss, B. G., & Perlick, D. A. (2014). The impact of mental illness stigma on seeking and participating in mental health care. *Psychological Science in the Public Interest*, *15*(2), 37–70. https://doi.org/10.1177/1529100614531398

Creswell, J. W., & Poth, C. N. (2016). *Qualitative inquiry and research design: Choosing among five approaches*. Thousand Oaks, CA: SAGE Publications, Inc.

Dick, P. (2005). Dirty work designations: How police officers account for their use of coercive force. *Human Relations*, *58*(11), 1363–1390. https://doi.org/10.1177/0018726705060242

Dodge, A. & Spencer, D. (2018). Online sexual violence, child pornography, or something else entirely? Police responses to non-consensual consensual intimate image sharing amongst youth. *Social and Legal Studies*, *27*(5), 636–657.

Edelmann, R. J. (2010). Exposure to child abuse images as part of one's work: Possible psychological implications. *The Journal of Forensic Psychiatry & Psychology*, *21*(4), 481–489. https://doi.org/10.1080/14789940903540792

Ellrich, K., and Baier, D. (2017). Post-traumatic stress symptoms in police officers following violent assaults: A study on general and police-specific risk and protective factors. *Journal of Interpersonal Violence*, *32*(3), 331–356.

Flick, U. (2014). *An introduction to qualitative research* (5th edn). Los Angeles, CA: SAGE Publications Ltd.

Greenberg, N., Brooks, S., & Dunn, R. (2015). Latest developments in post-traumatic stress disorder: Diagnosis and treatment. *British Medical Bulletin*, *114*(1), 1–9.

Greenberg, N., Cawkill, P., March, C., & Sharpley, J. (2005). How to TRiM away at post traumatic stress reactions: Traumatic risk management – Now and in the future. *Journal of the Royal Naval Medical Service*, *91*(1), 26–31.

Heffren, C., & Hausdorf, P. (2016). Post-traumatic effects in policing: Perceptions, stigmas and help seeking behaviours. *Police Practice and Research*, 17(5), 420–433.

Hochschild, A. R. (1983). *The managed heart: Commercialization of human feeling*. Berkeley, CA: University of California Press.

Karaffa, K. M., & Koch, J. M. (2016). Stigma, pluralistic ignorance, and attitudes toward seeking mental health services among police officers. *Criminal Justice and Behavior*, *43*(6), 759–777. https://doi.org/10.1177/0093854815613103

Kirschman, E. (2017). Cops and PTSD. Retrieved from www.psychologytoday.com/blog/cop-doc/201706/cops-and-ptsd-0.

Krause, M. (2009). Identifying and managing stress in child pornography and child exploitation investigators. *Journal of Police and Criminal Psychology*, *24*(1), 22–29.

Kurasaki, K. S. (2000). Intercoder reliability for validating conclusions drawn from open-ended interview data. *Field Methods*, *12*(3), 179–194. https://doi.org/10.1177/1525822X0001200301

Loftus, B. (2010). Police occupational culture: Classic themes, altered times. *Policing and Society*, *20*(1), 1–20. https://doi.org/10.1080/10439460903281547

Marshall, C., & Rossman, G. B. (2011). *Designing qualitative research* (5th edn). Los Angeles, CA: SAGE Publications, Inc.

Martin, S. E. (1999). Police force or police service? Gender and emotional labor. *The ANNALS of the American Academy of Political and Social Science*, *561*(1), 111–126. https://doi.org/10.1177/000271629956100108

Ménard, K., & Arter, M. (2013). Police officer alcohol use and trauma symptoms: Associations with critical incidents, coping, and social stressors. *International Journal of Stress Management*, *20*(1), 37–56.

Patton, M. Q. (2001). *Qualitative research & evaluation methods* (3rd edn). Thousand Oaks, CA: SAGE Publications.

Perez, L. M., Jones, J., Englert, D. R., & Sachau, D. (2010). Secondary traumatic stress and burnout among law enforcement investigators exposed to disturbing media images. *Journal of Police and Criminal Psychology*, *25*(2), 113–124.

Pogrebin, M. R., & Poole, E. D. (1991). Police and tragic events: The management of emotions. *Journal of Criminal Justice*, *19*, 395–403.

Powell, M., Cassematis, P., Benson, M., Smallbone, S., & Wortley, R. (2014a). Police officers' perceptions of their reactions to viewing internet child exploitation material. *Journal of Police and Criminal Psychology*, *30*(2), 103–111.

Powell, M., Cassematis, P., Benson, M., Smallbone, S., & Wortley, R. (2014b). Police officers' strategies for coping with the stress of investigating internet child exploitation. *Traumatology*, *20*(1), 32–42.

Ricciardelli, R., & Spencer, D. (2017). *Violence, sex offenders and corrections*. New York and Abingdon: Routledge.

Ricciardelli, R., Carleton, R. N., Cramm, H., & Groll, D. (2018). Qualitatively unpacking Canadian public safety personnel trauma experiences and their wellbeing. *Canadian Journal of Criminology and Criminal Justice*, *60*(4), 566–577. https://doi.org/10.3138/cjccj.2017-0053.r2

Ricciardelli, R., Carleton, R. N., Mooney, T., & Cramm, H. (2018). "Playing the system": Structural factors potentiating mental health stigma, challenging awareness, and creating barriers to care for Canadian Public Safety Personnel. *Health*. https://doi.org/10.1177/1363459318800167

Ricciardelli, R., & Moir, M. (2013). Stigmatized among the stigmatized: Sex offenders in Canadian penitentiaries. *Canadian Journal of Criminology and Criminal Justice*, *5*(3), 353–386. https://doi.org/10.3138/cjccj.2012.E22

Rogers, A. (2013). From peer-to-peer networks to cloud computing: How technology is redefining child pornography laws. *St. John's Law Review*, *87*(4), 1013–1049.

Schaible, L. M., & Gecas, V. (2010). The impact of emotional labor and value dissonance on burnout among police officers. *Police Quarterly*, *13*(3), 316–341. https://doi.org/10.1177/1098611110373997

Sewell, J. (1985). *Police: Urban policing in Canada*. Toronto, ON: Lorimer.

Skogstad, M., Skorstad, A., Lie, H., Conradi, T., Heir, T., & Weisaeth, L. (2013) Work related post traumatic stress disorder. *Occupational Medicine*, *63*(3), 175–182.

Simon, J. (1998). Managing the monstrous: Sex offenders and the new penology. *Psychology, Public Policy, and Law*, *4*(1–2), 452–467. https://doi.org/10.1037/1076-8971.4.1-2.452

Spencer, D. C., & Patterson, J. (2016). Still worlds apart? Habitus, field, and masculinities in victim and police interactions. In D. C. Spencer & S. Walklate (eds), *Reconceptualizing critical victimology: Interventions and possibilities* (pp. 15–31). Lanham, MD: Lexington Books.

Spencer, D., Ricciardelli, R., Walby, K., & Ballucci, D. (2019). Cynicism, dirty work, and policing sex crimes. *Policing: An International Journal*, *43*(1), 151–165.

Tuckey, M., & Scott, J. (2013) Group critical incident stress debriefing with emergency services personnel: A randomized controlled trial. *Anxiety, Stress, and Coping*, *27*(1), 38–54.

Waddington, P. A. J. (1999). Police (canteen) sub-culture. An appreciation. *The British Journal of Criminology*, *39*(2), 287–309. https://doi.org/10.1093/bjc/39.2.287

Wengraf, T. (2001). *Qualitative research interviewing*. London: SAGE Publications, Ltd.

Yar, M. (2013). Internet sex offending: Patterns, problems, and policy. In J. Brayford, F. Cowe, & J. Deering (eds), *Sex offending: Punish, help, change or control* (pp. 188–204). Abingdon: Routledge.

10 Firefighters and Posttraumatic Stress Disorder

A Scoping Review

Heidi Cramm, Linna Tam-Seto, Alyson Mahar, Lucia Rühland, and R. Nicholas Carleton

Background

Firefighting is inherently dangerous and entails cumulative exposure to a wide range of potentially psychologically traumatic events (Canadian Institute for Public Safety Research and Treatment [CIPSRT], 2019) related to occupational activities. In addition to fire-specific emergencies, firefighters respond to medical emergencies, rescue and recovery, crime, motor vehicle accidents, high-angle rescue, marine disasters, ice rescue, natural disasters, hazardous material incidents, and trench rescue (International Association of Fire Fighters [IAFF], 2003). Occupational demands require that firefighters place themselves in close proximity to peril, deal with acute loss and grief at the scene—both their own and that of the people they are helping—and confront exposure to human remains. The number and range of emergencies an individual or a team of firefighters faces vary by shift and by jurisdiction, from recurrent small-scale events (e.g., single car motor vehicle accidents) up to and including large-scale catastrophes (e.g., the 2016 Alberta wildfires). Firefighter work is unpredictable and dynamic, lacking in daily structure, and featuring layers of shiftwork and disrupted sleep schedules (Beaton & Murphy, 1995; Beaton et al., 1998), all of which facilitates the accumulation of stress that may elevate risk of mental disorder (IAFF, 2000).

According to the American Psychiatric Association (APA), posttraumatic stress disorder (PTSD) can occur after exposure to one or more traumatic events and involves symptoms including intrusive thoughts, avoidance, negative changes in cognition and mood, and alterations in arousal and reactivity (APA, 2013). These symptoms can produce individual, social, and vocational impairments that compromise daily life

DOI: 10.4324/9781351134637-11

Firefighters and PTSD 265

(APA, 2013). Because of the impact of mental illness on productivity, there has been increased focus in workplace legislation over recent years (Fien, 2017; IAFF, 2016; Vogel, 2017), including the spread of presumptive legislation regarding occupational risk and PTSD for first responders (IAFF, 2003). There are calls for a national action plan to address PTSD among Canadian Public Safety Personnel (Oliphant, 2016); however, success with such a plan requires as much information as possible about the challenge. The current scoping review was designed to identify and describe what is available in the scholarly research literature about PTSD among firefighters.

Method

A scoping review was appropriate to synthesize the emerging field of PTSD scholarship concerning firefighters to inform potential actions in support of firefighters. A structured five-step process was used to guide the current review (Arksey & O'Malley, 2005).

Step 1: Identifying the Research Question

To balance scope and depth, while maintaining accessibility, the research question was narrowed to, "How does the research literature identify and describe PTSD among firefighters?"

Step 2: Identifying the Relevant Studies

The search and retrieval of relevant studies involved identification of pertinent databases, which were determined through consultation with a health sciences librarian. Relevant databases included PsycINFO, Cochrane, Medline, Embase, and CINAHL. See Box 10.1 for search terms used for each database accessed. Reference mining of relevant literature was used to identify additional studies. Database searches were conducted by combining search terms associated with firefighters and with PTSD. Boolean operators were used to combine search terms to generate multiple searches. Search criteria were limited to peer-reviewed articles published in the English language between 1990 and November 2017. Database searches were completed relating to the experience of living with PTSD and the occupation of firefighting (e.g., "firefighters" + "stress disorders, posttraumatic" OR "coping behaviour" OR "stress" OR "occupational exposure" OR "post traumatic stress" OR "mental health" OR "operational stress").

266   *Heidi Cramm et al.*

BOX 10.1 Search terms for each database

PsycINFO:
- fire fighters
- posttraumatic stress disorder

- coping behaviour
- stress
- occupational exposure
- post traumatic stress
- mental health
- operational stress

MEDLINE:
- firefighters
- stress disorders, posttraumatic
- adaptation, psychological
- occupational exposure
- post traumatic stress
- mental health
- operational stress

CINAHL:
- firefighters
- occupational exposure
- mental health
- operational stress
- stress disorders, posttraumatic
- post traumatic stress
- coping
- stress

EMBASE:
- fire fighter
- operational stress
- stress
- mental health
- occupational exposure
- coping behavior
- post traumatic stress
- posttraumatic stress disorder

Cochrane:
- fire fighter
- fire fighters
- fire service worker
- firefighter

The database search yielded 1,120 articles. After de-duplication, 731 remained. An additional 11 articles were identified through reference mining. Title and abstract screening left 155 for full text review.

Step 3: Study Selection

At least two authors reviewed each abstract for potential inclusion. Articles were included if they were English-language, peer-reviewed articles that specifically referenced PTSD within a firefighter sample. Conference abstracts and theses were excluded. Ultimately, the study included 121 studies that proceeded to full analytic extraction.

Step 4: Charting the Data

The literature on scoping reviews indicates research teams should develop a data-charting form to determine the variables that would be most helpful

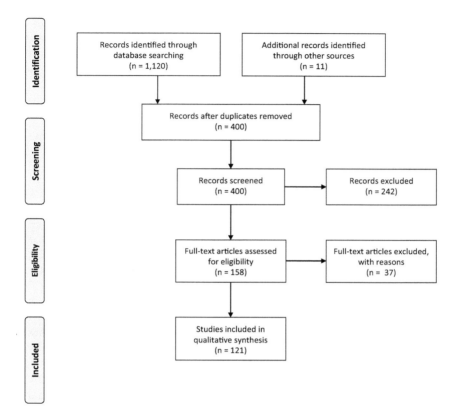

Figure 10.1 Prisma chart.

to answer the research question (Levac, Colquhoun, & O'Brien, 2010). The scoping review process should be iterative so that researchers are updating the form as required (Levac et al., 2010). The extracted data included the following from each article as available: key focus, stated objectives, description of population, type of source, sample size, details of sampling, symptoms of PTSD, types of trauma exposure, comparisons of firefighters to other groups, sociodemographic information, organizational culture variables, PTSD self-management strategies, PTSD interventions, post-trauma outcomes/implications, and models/theories/frameworks.

Step 5: Collating, Summarizing, and Reporting the Results

The final step of a scoping review involves analysing the data, reporting results, and applying meaning to the results (Levac et al., 2010). Our data analysis included both a descriptive numerical summary as well as a thematic analysis. The descriptive numerical summary included identifying characteristics of the studies including: the overall number of studies; study design type; year of publications; types of interventions; characteristics of

268 *Heidi Cramm et al.*

the study populations; and countries where studies were completed (Arksey & O'Malley, 2005). Directed content analysis was selected as the most suitable approach for data analysis to address the current research question. Directed content analysis is suitable for qualitative research designed to extend the understanding of a body of literature by providing predictions about variables or about relationships among variables (Hsieh & Shannon, 2005). We used the computer software MAXQDA 12.3.2 to support qualitative data analysis (VERBI Software Consult Sozialforschung GmbH, 1989–2017).

Results

The review included 121 articles from 16 different countries. The countries were primarily the United States ($n = 53$), Australia ($n = 24$), the Netherlands ($n = 7$), Canada ($n = 7$), the United Kingdom ($n = 6$), Japan ($n = 6$), and South Korea ($n = 3$). One or two studies came from each of Germany, Greece, Israel, Norway, Iran, Saudi Arabia, Sweden, Korea, Portugal, Ireland, and Kuwait. Most of the articles were published after the year 2000 ($n = 103$) and most were published between 2010 and 2017 ($n = 63$). The majority of the articles included in this review were research studies ($n = 88$); however, literature reviews, case study reviews, perspective/ position papers, and reports were also included. Most studies were cross-sectional and used survey methods to measure potentially psychologically traumatic event exposure and PTSD symptoms/status, though some included clinical interviews. Sample sizes ranged from a few participants in a neuroimaging study (e.g., Shin et al., 2004) to national surveys of thousands (e.g., Carleton et al., 2018); however, most involved convenience samples of several hundred. The firefighters included in the studies were typically in their late 30s to their early 40s and most were male.

The review identified three themes from the literature: 1) descriptions of the nature of the trauma exposure among firefighters; 2) efforts to understand PTSD among firefighters; and 3) approaches to dealing with PTSD among firefighters.

Theme 1: Descriptions of the Nature of Potentially Psychologically Traumatic Event Exposure among Firefighters

The literature describes a variety of "critical incidents" that involve significant and intense amounts of the potentially traumatic exposure. We define a critical incident as that which might overwhelm a firefighter's ability to deal with the situation, such as an exposure to threat of personal injury, dead bodies, or severely injured victims (Harris, Baloglu, & Stacks, 2002). Through their daily work, firefighters are exposed to unpredictable critical incidents of varying types, durations, and intensities that necessitate

Firefighters and PTSD 269

a state of constant readiness to react (e.g., Armstrong et al.; Benedek, Fullerton, & Ursano, 2007; Brown & Campbell, 1991; Bryant & Guthrie, 2007; Corneil et al., 1999; Huizink et al., 2006; Kehl et al., 2014; Monteiro et al., 2013; Shin et al., 2004; Witteveen et al., 2007). Most firefighters have been exposed to at least one critical incident over the course of their careers (Homish, Frazer, & Carey, 2012; Regehr, Hemsworth, & Hill, 2001) and can expect regular exposure to potentially psychologically traumatic events such as exposure to fires or explosions (Carleton et al., 2018). The critical incidents can include events that affect large numbers of individuals, such as the World Trade Center 9/11 terrorist attacks (Bacharach, Bamberger, & Doveh, 2008; Beaton & Murphy, 2002; Maslow et al., 2015), political violence (Brown & Campbell, 1991), earthquakes (Chang et al., 2003; Fushimi, 2012; Hagh-Shenas et al., 2005), gas explosions (De Soir et al., 2012), motor vehicle accidents (Eid, Helge Johnsen, & Weisæth, 2001; Hill & Brunsden, 2009), plane crashes (Homish et al., 2012; Huizink et al., 2006; Kaufmann et al., 2013), and natural disasters (Komarovskaya et al., 2014; McFarlane, 1990).

Volunteer and career firefighters can experience different potentially psychologically traumatic events in the course of their work, with different role demands. Researchers have tried to assess the types, frequencies, and characteristics of the potentially psychologically traumatic events encountered (Wagner, Heinrichs, & Ehlert, 1998). There is evidence that such exposures may be a function of the varying nature of firefighting duties of volunteers as compared to career firefighters (Baker & Williams, 2001). Volunteer firefighters are primarily exposed to building-related fire emergencies, while career firefighters are additionally responsible for, and exposed to, emergency medical calls, hazardous materials responses, woodland firefighting, and search and rescue (DeLorme, 2014; IAFF, 2003). Career firefighters respond to a wider array of potentially psychologically traumatic events. Given that two-thirds of the calls to fire stations involve requests for medical aid and that many everyday medical interventions, even by medically trained responders, can be considered as traumatic (Beaton et al., 1998), inadequate medical training can contribute to the experience of potentially psychologically traumatic events among firefighters (Jacobsson et al., 2015).

Firefighters who are regularly exposed to potentially psychologically traumatic events "see the devastation, smell the odour of lost life, and hear the cries of families and victims alike" (Eriksson, Foy, & Larson, 2004, p. 246). Nevertheless, the frequency of acute potentially psychologically traumatic events exposures does not sufficiently account for the onset and course of PTSD among firefighters (McFarlane, 1992; McFarlane & Papay, 1992; Meyer et al., 2012). Firefighters are also exposed to sub-acute trauma repeatedly over time and from multiple sources, including potentially psychologically traumatic events exposures outside of their work duties (Armstrong et al., 2014; Carleton et al., 2019).

270   *Heidi Cramm et al.*

Theme 2: Efforts to Understand PTSD among Firefighters

Prevalence

The available research literature generally indicates firefighters are at significant risk for developing clinical and subclinical symptoms of PTSD (e.g., Carleton et al., 2018; Chen et al., 2007; Kimbrel et al., 2011; Komarovskaya et al., 2014; Monteiro et al., 2013; Witteveen et al., 2006). Many available studies on PTSD symptoms among firefighters do not provide concrete data on the size of that risk; however, representative prevalence data used in cross-sectional survey methods has provided defensible estimates ranging from 14 to 57%, within and across countries including Australia (24%; Bryant & Harvey, 1995), Kuwait (18.5%; Al-Naser & Everly, 1999), Germany (18.2%; Wagner et al., 1998), Canada (13.5–17.3%; (Carleton et al., 2018; Corneil et al., 1999), and Japan (8.4–17.6%; Mitani, 2008). PTSD diagnostic status has been assessed using multiple, diverse self-screening tools and definitions, and sample sizes varied from a few individuals to hundreds or even thousands (Bryant & Harvey, 1995; Carleton et al., 2018). Accordingly, comparisons across studies are unreliable. Evaluating the quality of current prevalence study estimates is outside the scope of the current review; nevertheless, there appears to be sufficient evidence to state that PTSD prevalence among firefighters is a substantive and pervasive problem.

Comorbidity

Firefighters report high levels of mental disorders other than PTSD. Researchers argue that among firefighters, "the pure constellation of PTSD symptoms is the exception rather than the rule" (McFarlane & Papay, 1992, p. 502). The most commonly comorbid mental health disorder associated with PTSD among firefighters appears to be major depressive disorder (e.g., Arbona, Fan, & Noor, 2016; Wagner, McFee, & Martin, 2010). In one study, half of the firefighters with PTSD also met diagnostic criteria for major depressive disorder (McFarlane & Papay, 1992) or for moderate to severe depression symptoms (Harvey et al., 2016). A recent Canadian survey indicated that one in five firefighters screened positive for major depressive disorder, closely followed by anxiety disorder at 19.4% (Carleton et al., 2018). This is in addition to the 13.5% of surveyed Canadian firefighters who screened positive for PTSD (Carleton et al., 2018).

In the general firefighter population, there is increased risk for suicidal behaviours (i.e., ideation, planning, attempts) alongside other mental health challenges including PTSD symptoms (Boffa et al., 2017; Martin, Tran, & Buser, 2017; Martin, Vujanovic, et al., 2017), depression (Martin, Tran, et al., 2017; Martin, Vujanovic, et al., 2017), and alcohol dependence (Martin, Vujanovic, et al., 2017). For women firefighters, suicidal

Firefighters and PTSD 271

symptoms prior to the start of a career in firefighting may increase the risk of dying by suicide during their career (Stanley, Hom, & Joiner, 2016).

Panic and phobic disorders are reported as particularly associated with a chronic and persistent trajectory of PTSD (Benedek et al., 2007; McFarlane & Papay, 1992). More intense PTSD symptoms may be associated with disorders that impact affect or arousal regulation (Guthrie & Bryant, 2005; McFarlane, 1992; McFarlane & Papay, 1992). Avoidance may have no direct relationship with the onset of symptoms, serving instead as a defensive strategy to contain the distress generated by re-experiencing the event (McFarlane, 1992); however, individuals who experience elevated auditory and skin conductance responses to startle may be at greater risk for developing PTSD symptoms after potentially psychologically traumatic events exposure (Guthrie & Bryant, 2005).

PTSD and alcohol misuse comorbidity appears to increase with each additional potentially psychologically traumatic event exposure (Harvey et al., 2016). Increased use of alcohol is reported throughout the literature and may represent a style of coping with mental health symptoms (e.g., Arbona et al., 2016; Chiu, et al., 2011; North et al., 2002; Osofsky et al., 2011; Yip et al., 2016). Comorbid associations extend beyond mental health and addictions to include other medical issues.

Firefighters with PTSD report significantly higher levels of gastrointestinal, cardiorespiratory, and neurological symptoms than those without, and the presence of PTSD has been associated with intensified physical decline during ageing (Milligan-Saville et al., 2017). PTSD can also emerge after potentially psychologically traumatic events involving considerable physical injuries and attention to the relationship between PTSD and physical injuries is critical because of the reflexive relationship (Asmundson et al., 2002). Firefighters with posttraumatic stress symptoms also reported physical symptoms involving cardiovascular, respiratory, musculoskeletal, and neurological systems (McFarlane et al., 1994; Wagner et al., 1998). Firefighters with PTSD experienced sleep disturbances that influenced physical and mental aspects of their quality of life (Chen et al., 2007) and are more likely to present with overall sleep disturbances than other public safety personnel (Witteveen et al., 2007).

A Complex Interplay of Factors

Researchers underscored the need for more research to understand how different potentially psychologically traumatic events exposures interact with person-level and occupational factors to reduce the likelihood of firefighters developing PTSD and comorbid conditions (Bryant & Harvey, 1996). In addition to the type and dose of potentially psychologically traumatic events exposure, researchers typically identify a multitude of other variables as factors contributing to the development of PTSD by firefighters.

272   *Heidi Cramm et al.*

Person Level Factors

Potentially psychologically traumatic events exposure occurring either in childhood or in a firefighter's personal life may be a component cause of PTSD symptoms experienced during their career. Among firefighters, childhood physical abuse, neglect, or sexual abuse has been correlated with a higher presence of PTSD symptoms (Komarovskaya et al., 2014). Difficult situations with close friends or family members' terminal diseases, injuries, or deaths can be experienced as traumatic and can potentiate PTSD symptoms (Alghamdi, Hunt, & Thomas, 2015; Bracken-Scally et al., 2014; Haslam & Mallon, 2003). For example, in a study of 751 firefighters in Australia, one-quarter reported experiencing significant PTSD symptoms although many participants indicated that their stress was related to personal, rather than professional, events (Bryant & Harvey, 1996). Bryant and Harvey (1996) suggest that firefighters who have experienced previous personal potentially psychologically traumatic events had a lower threshold for managing stress or that increased PTSD symptoms creates additional challenges that are themselves stressful. A history of psychiatric illness may also create vulnerabilities that facilitate the onset of PTSD in firefighters (Corneil et al., 1999; McFarlane, 1988), but the evidence among firefighters is mixed, with some studies finding support (McFarlane, 1990, 1992) and other studies not (Guidotti, 1992).

Very few firefighters are women and most research on women firefighters involves very small sample sizes (e.g., $n = 9$, Corneil et al., 1999; $n = 2$, Monteiro et al., 2013); nevertheless, there is initial evidence from larger samples of firefighters that gender may be a person-level factor influencing the PTSD symptom onset (Carleton et al., 2018; Sattler, Boyd, & Kirsch, 2014).

Individual personality traits may also be associated with a greater propensity of developing PTSD after being exposed to a potentially psychologically traumatic event. McFarlane postulated that pre-exposure personality factors could increase the risk for developing PTSD in firefighters, specifically, "adversity before the event, neuroticism, a history of treated past mental disorder, and a tendency to avoid thinking about unwanted or negative experiences" (McFarlane, 1988, p. 35). In a prospective follow-up study with firefighters, Heinrichs has referred to the aforementioned as "pretrauma personality traits" (Heinrichs et al., 2005; Riolli & Savicki, 2012, p. 2282), such as high levels of hostility and low levels of efficacy, a result replicated in other studies (Regehr, Hill, & Glancy, 2000). Other factors that have been associated with the presence of PTSD symptoms include high levels of hostility (Heinrichs et al., 2005) or conflict (Saijo, Ueno, & Hashimoto, 2012), low levels of self-efficacy (Heinrichs et al., 2005; Regehr et al., 2000), and high levels of introversion or neuroticism (Guidotti, 1992; McFarlane, 1990; Wagner et al., 2010); however, the available data assessing the relationships between person-level factors such as personality traits and PTSD in firefighters have been primarily cross-sectional which limits our ability to distinguish between correlation and causation.

Firefighters and PTSD 273

A tendency towards avoidant coping strategies as individuals struggle to integrate intrusive memories (Spurrell & McFarlane, 1993) correlates with increased risk of PTSD (Chang et al., 2003; Holland, 2011; Sattler et al., 2014; Skeffington, Rees, & Mazzucchelli, 2017; Whealin, Ruzek, & Southwick, 2008). Doley and colleagues recently reported that, for volunteer firefighters continuing to experience PTSD symptoms several years after a bushfire disaster, those coping better did so when avoiding intrusive images rather than re-living them (Doley, Bell, & Watt, 2016). Difficulties managing intrusive and distressing memories may produce chains of PTSD symptom activations (McFarlane, 1992) that include fear generalization (e.g., fear caused by the loud noise of an explosion incites fear of other loud noises, such as fireworks; Levy-Gigi, Richter-Levin, & Kéri, 2014). The generalized fear can persist without meeting criteria for PTSD, which some have referred to as the "price of repeated traumatic exposure" (Levy-Gigi et al., 2014, p. 343). PTSD may also impair problem-solving skills as people struggle to manage post-exposure symptoms (Bryant, Sutherland, & Guthrie, 2007; Otis et al., 2012; Thomas et al., 2012). A more flexible capacity to shift between strategies may act as a buffer against developing PTSD (Levy-Gigi et al., 2016).

Occupational Factors

Several researchers have reported greater years of service, exposure related to years "on the job", and higher rank as significant risk factors for PTSD, acting as proxy measures for cumulative potentially psychologically traumatic event exposures (Carleton et al., 2018; Chamberlin & Green, 2010; Chang et al., 2003; Corneil et al., 1999; Monteiro et al., 2013; Pinto et al., 2015; Sattler et al., 2014; Wagner et al., 1998). Length of service has been associated with increased likelihood of distress (Chamberlin & Green, 2010), higher rates of alcohol consumption (Monteiro et al., 2013), and more frequent depression symptoms (Monteiro et al., 2013). By extension, higher rank within the fire service may also be associated with increased risk for PTSD (Corneil et al., 1999), as years of service and rank are logically related. In contrast, several researchers have also concluded there is no association between increased age and PTSD (Pinto et al., 2015) or even that there is an inverse relationship with age (Epstein, Fullerton, & Ursano, 1998) and with years of service (Bracken-Scally et al., 2014; Bryant & Harvey, 1995; Bryant & Harvey, 1996; Chamberlin & Green, 2010; Regehr et al., 2003; Saijo et al., 2012; Wagner et al., 2010).

Social support within an organization also appears to interact with PTSD. Perceived support from supervisors in the workplace (Saijo et al., 2012) interacts with bullying and co-worker conflict (Bracken-Scally et al., 2014) to increase stress. The perceived and actual availability of social support appears critically related to PTSD (Bernabé & Botia, 2016; Maslow et al., 2015; Meyer et al., 2012; Mitani et al., 2006; Smith et al., 2015; Regehr et al., 2000; Sripada et al., 2015).

Factors Related to Potentially Psychologically Traumatic Event Exposures

Cumulative Exposures

Most research literature supports a relationship between cumulative potentially psychologically traumatic event exposures and the risk of PTSD; however, there is no evidence of a consistent, clearly defined linear relationship. Firefighters who report more than six potentially psychologically traumatic event exposures also report significantly more symptoms of PTSD than those reporting fewer than four exposures (Lee et al., 2017). There is a positive linear relationship between total accumulated potentially psychologically traumatic event exposure and risk for PTSD, major depressive disorder symptoms, and heavy drinking for current and retired firefighters (Harvey et al., 2016). Firefighters may perceive each subsequent potentially psychologically traumatic event as more threatening than the last because of an enduring sense of helplessness and a reduced coping repertoire that depletes the personal resources required for adaptive responses (Bryant & Harvey, 1996; Lee et al., 2014; Riolli & Savicki, 2012) resulting from a "buildup of stress from 'close saves' and 'witnessing injured children'" (Coupland, 2009, p. E5). Previous potentially psychologically traumatic event exposures may increase the risk of developing PTSD upon subsequent exposure (Carleton et al., 2019; Chen et al., 2007; McFarlane, 1990; Osofsky et al., 2011), but does not always manifest more PTSD symptoms (Bryant & Guthrie, 2007; Jahnke et al., 2016). Cumulative potentially psychologically traumatic event exposures may explain why older firefighters report significantly higher emotional and mental demands than their younger peers (Plat, Frings-Dresen, & Sluiter, 2012). Those exposed to potentially psychologically traumatic events early in their careers may be at elevated risk for developing PTSD later in their careers (Komarovskaya et al., 2014), as are those who experienced helplessness during a potentially psychologically traumatic event (Bryant & Guthrie, 2005; Hill & Brunsden, 2009). There are also researchers who have evidenced that cumulative potentially psychologically traumatic event exposures do not necessarily lead to PTSD (Haddock et al., 2017; Harvey et al., 2016; Jahnke et al., 2016; Jeong, Kang, et al., 2015; Lee et al., 2014; Pinto et al., 2015) and some argue repeated potentially psychologically traumatic event exposures may facilitate resilience (Jeong, Jeon, et al., 2015; Lee et al., 2014). Cumulative potentially psychologically traumatic event exposures may also increase perceptions of personal safety as a function of increasing experience and skill, providing a buffer against developing PTSD symptoms (Pinto et al., 2015).

Critical Incident Characteristics

Occupational potentially psychologically traumatic event exposure characteristics can interact with individual roles, the scope and extent of

Firefighters and PTSD 275

property damage, the number of people involved, and the number of people killed or injured to influence subsequent responses. Experiencing large-scale critical incidents with widespread devastation and horror has been associated with the development of PTSD (Benedek et al., 2007; Bracken-Scally et al., 2014; Leon, 2004; Van der Velden et al., 2006; Whealin et al., 2008). Increase PTSD incidence rates have been reported in firefighters after responding to catastrophes such as earthquakes (Benedek et al., 2007; Chen et al., 2007) and airline disasters (Fullerton, Ursano, & Wang, 2004; Homish et al., 2012; Maslow et al., 2015; Van der Velden et al., 2006). The scale of the potentially psychologically traumatic event may interact with timing to influence vulnerability. Persons who are at a disaster sooner or work longer tend to report higher rates of PTSD (Berninger, Webber, Niles, et al., 2010; Soo et al., 2011). Specific firefighter activities (e.g., such as being a frontline fire suppression, driver, or senior officer) may be risk factors for subsequent mental health challenges (Baker & Williams, 2001) possibly linked to exposure proximity or perceptions of responsibility. Firefighters directly interacting with loss of life, including recovery of bodies at an incident, may also be at greater risk for PTSD than those who are more remotely involved (e.g., Marmar et al., 1996; Morren et al., 2005; Wagner et al., 2010).

The size or scale of the critical incident may be less important when a potentially psychologically traumatic event involves children, a small community, or individuals known to the fire team (Brazil, 2017). Incidents involving children and the death of coworkers are reported as particularly problematic for firefighters (e.g., Beaton et al., 1998; Bracken-Scally et al., 2014; De Soir et al., 2012; Katsavouni et al., 2016; Soo et al., 2011). Firefighters who are parents may be more affected by the death of children as a function of identifying with the victims (Baker & Williams, 2001; Monteiro et al., 2013).

Time since exposure may also be a factor (Benedek et al., 2007; Maslow et al., 2015; Skogstad et al., 2016). Specifically, events that happened more recently may be more likely to be associated with PTSD symptoms (Bracken-Scally et al., 2014; Bryant & Harvey, 1996), even though symptoms can persist for years (Bracken-Scally et al., 2014; Doley et al., 2016). Time since exposure has not been significantly associated with reducing the level of distress experienced (Regehr et al., 2001). For example, the longitudinal analyses of New York City firefighters who participated in rescue and recovery efforts for the World Trade Center 2001 attack showed that, at nine years post-9/11, PTSD remained a significant issue among the exposed firefighter population (Maslow et al., 2015; Soo et al., 2011). Regardless of the critical incident type, the experience of helplessness or futility of effort can be a powerful determinant of how a firefighter reacts to such events (Baker & Williams, 2001; Bracken-Scally et al., 2014; Bryant & Harvey, 1996; De Soir et al., 2012; Jacobsson et al., 2015; Vargas de Barros et al., 2013). The inherent intention of firefighting is to help others; as such, when firefighters' efforts are futile, their sense of self and identity can be undermined, exacerbating their risk for a mental health injury (Richardson & James, 2017).

276 *Heidi Cramm et al.*

Theme 3: Approaches to Dealing with PTSD among Firefighters

Many approaches have been described in the literature for addressing the development and management of PTSD in firefighters. Within firefighting organizations, suggestions have been made to address structural and cultural challenges that may facilitate environments that compromise member mental health. Various mitigation strategies have been explored in attempts to address individual risk factors, such as training to increase resiliency, but there are significant and substantial research gaps with respect to effectiveness.

Organizational Factors

The organizational features of a fire hall or fire association can negatively or positively impact the mental health of firefighters. Occupational stressors, including organizational (e.g., staff shortages, inconsistent leadership styles) and operational elements (e.g., shift work, public scrutiny), can negatively impact firefighter stress (Saijo et al., 2012; Sakuma et al., 2015). In contrast, perceived support and workplace connections have associated with lower rates of PTSD symptoms (Armstrong et al., 2014; Baker & Williams, 2001; Brown & Campbell, 1991). Structural barriers (e.g., cost and availability of resources) may also influence the development and management of PTSD. Stanley and colleagues reported significant differences in PTSD symptoms reported by volunteer firefighters relative to career firefighters, differences that may be linked to the availability of resources (Stanley et al., 2017); however, other researchers have not found significant differences between volunteer and career firefighters (Carleton et al., 2018).

Workplace stigma related to PTSD (Miller, 1995) and cultural influences that promote stoicism and minimize the importance of mental health issues can all reduce help-seeking behaviours (Barnes, 1997; Berninger, Webber, Cohen, et al., 2010; Corneil et al., 1999; Kehl et al., 2015; North et al., 2002). Firefighters may develop maladaptive self-appraisals and poor coping while managing potentially psychologically traumatic event exposures and PTSD symptoms using a "macho" identity (Admon et al., 2013; Bryant & Harvey, 1996; Fushimi, 2012; Hill & Brunsden, 2009; Holland, 2011; Richardson & James, 2017). Tension may emerge if new individuals enter a fire service who conflict with traditional hypermasculine role concepts by readily and broadly challenging mental health stigma (Richardson & James, 2017).

Early Identification and Critical Incidents

Firefighter experience ongoing exposure to critical incidents and other potentially psychologically traumatic events (Carleton et al., 2019). The frequent exposures require early symptom detection to mitigate the development of PTSD symptoms (Harvey et al., 2016; Jeong, Kang, et al., 2015;

Firefighters and PTSD 277

Pinto et al., 2015). PTSD with comorbid mental health issues is more likely to lead to chronicity (Asmundson et al., 2002), underscoring the need for early detection and intervention among firefighters. Raising awareness of PTSD symptoms in firefighters and creating a culture of early intervention may also be critical for reducing the exceedingly negative outcome of suicide (Martin, Tran, et al., 2017; Stanley et al., 2016; Stanley et al., 2017).

How organizations manage their responses during and after a critical incident may also affect the development of PTSD symptoms in firefighters. During large-scale critical incidents that affect communities, such as natural disasters, communication with firefighters regarding the whereabouts and safety of their loved ones may mitigate the impact of potentially psychologically traumatic event exposures for firefighters (Osofsky et al., 2011). Particularly important is the climate within a department after a critical incident (Bacharach et al., 2008), including use of rituals that provide meaning and dignity to what may otherwise be gruesome experiences that remain difficult to process and that can interfere with operational readiness (Barnes, 1997; Miller, 1995). Dark humour has been described as a way to create social cohesion and help process an event (e.g., Haslam & Mallon, 2003; Hill & Brunsden, 2009; Sliter, Kale, & Yuan, 2014).

Responses to critical incidents can include many varieties and formats of workforce-wide debriefing interventions (Gist & Woodall, 1995). Some researchers report positive impacts of debriefings (Guidotti, 1992; North et al., 2002; Sattler et al., 2014), but others disagree and recommend caution (Benedek et al., 2007; Harris et al., 2002; Tuckey & Scott, 2014). Bryant and Harvey assert that the use of such approaches fails to account for individual factors that may interact with potentially psychologically traumatic event exposures (Bryant & Harvey, 1996). Miller cautions that workplace-wide debriefings are most problematic when used indiscriminately or exclusively, and Paterson, Whittle, and Kemp (2015) caution that some aspects of critical incident debriefing may actually increase intrusive thoughts or lead to misinformation or reinterpretation of events. Paterson and colleagues recommend the creation of more effective post-potentially psychologically traumatic event interventions.

Role of Belonging and Social Supports

The positive role of social support in maintaining firefighter mental health has been strongly asserted by researchers (e.g., Alghamdi et al., 2015; Homish et al., 2012; Meyer et al., 2012; North et al., 2002; Regehr et al., 2003; Wagner et al., 2010). Organizations that create a sense of belonging and respect may facilitate help-seeking (Armstrong et al., 2016). Organizations that are prepared to train, anticipate, and respond to PTSD were more likely to see resiliency among firefighters as compared to organizations that provide less support (Armstrong et al., 2014; Osofsky et al., 2011). Armstrong and colleagues highlight the role of "organizational

278 *Heidi Cramm et al.*

belongingness" in facilitating an inclusive and supportive environment (Armstrong et al., 2016). Several studies indicate using social networks to provide instrumental (i.e., information gathering) and psycho-emotional support can be associated with decreased depressive and PTSD symptoms (Alghamdi et al., 2015; Farnsworth & Sewell, 2011; Hagh-Shenas et al., 2005; Maslow et al., 2015; Smith et al., 2011). Firefighters appear to prefer peers as a source of support (Carleton et al., 2020; Chamberlin & Green, 2010; Hill & Brunsden, 2009); however, some have suggested that the reliance on peer support may also contribute to a reluctance to seek out professional help (Hill & Brunsden, 2009). Informal supports outside of the fire hall may also provide a buffer against the development of PTSD in firefighters (Hagh-Shenas et al., 2005; Maslow et al., 2015). The strength of peer relationships may be inversely correlated with mental health challenges (Regehr et al., 2000; Saijo et al., 2012), but may also propagate "emotional contagion" (Homish et al., 2012) and make cultural changes more difficult to initiate. Supportive supervisory relationships are also likely to facilitate earlier referrals for effective assessment and treatment (Bacharach et al., 2008). Accordingly, reducing occupational stressors, co-worker conflicts, and stressors (Armstrong et al., 2014; Mitani et al., 2006), as well as fostering respectful and effective communications across ranks and divisions (Burke, 2006; Miller, 1995; Murphy et al., 1999; Regehr et al., 2001; Regehr et al., 2000; Saijo et al., 2012) and with the community served (Jacobsson et al., 2015), may all help to mitigate the impact of potentially psychologically traumatic event.

Bolstering Individual Resiliency and Supporting Mental Health

Resiliency is diversely defined (CIPSRT, 2019), but can be argued as being "a process to harness resources in order to sustain well-being" (Southwick et al., 2014, p. 4) that may help to mitigate PTSD symptoms (Jeong, Kang, et al., 2015; Lee et al., 2014; Leon, 2004). Ongoing training in resilience and coping for individuals over the course of their careers (Chamberlin & Green, 2010) has been referred to as "countermeasures" for PTSD symptom onset (Mitani et al., 2006). There are no best practices yet for resilience training, but such best practices are widely accepted as a critical next step (Skeffington et al., 2016).

Firefighters tend to have high levels of psychological health at the beginning of their careers (Bracken-Scally et al., 2014; Meyer et al., 2012). The regular physical training of firefighters may reduce their risk for PTSD (Sakuma et al., 2015), but does not appear to offset the impact of regular potentially psychologically traumatic event exposures. There is agreement that services and programs should be implemented to mitigate the elevated risk (Armstrong et al., 2014; Osofsky et al., 2011; Sakuma et al., 2015; Tuckey & Scott, 2014), but contemporary research

Firefighters and PTSD 279

has not clarified which services and programs are effective. The occupational health model, which views PTSD as the result of exposures to potentially psychologically traumatic event at work, may be effective for implementing mitigation strategies (Tuckey & Scott, 2014), including regular assessments of occupational stress and mental health (Chang et al., 2003; Corneil et al., 1999; Jeong, Kang, et al., 2015; Kimbrel et al., 2011; Murphy et al., 1999).

Primary prevention efforts may help to anticipate potentially psychologically traumatic event exposures and deploy adaptive cognitive strategies (Marmar et al., 1996; Bryant & Harvey, 1996). For example, maladaptive coping strategies such as reliance on alcohol should be a focus for engaging early intervention for PTSD (Skeffington et al., 2017). Practising problem solving and cognitive reframing with positive self-coaching statements may also be helpful for decreasing emotional arousal levels and maintaining self-efficacy and control (e.g., Baker & Williams, 2001; Dudek & Koniarek, 2000; Lambert et al., 2012).

Developing adaptive and problem-solving coping strategies can be part of a broader stress management approach (e.g., Armstrong et al., 2014; Burke, 2006; Chamberlin & Green, 2010; Chang et al., 2003; Holland, 2011; Wagner et al., 2010) that includes reduction of alcohol use (e.g., Homish et al., 2012; Skeffington et al., 2017; Vargas de Barros et al., 2013; Whealin et al., 2008) alongside the sustained exercise activities that are likely already supporting firefighter resiliency (e.g., Abdollahi et al., 2017; LeBouthillier & Asmundson, 2017; Powers, Asmundson, & Smits, 2015). Negative sequelae to potentially psychologically traumatic event may persist long after exposure; as such, services should continue to be offered for extended periods (Homish et al., 2012).

Some researchers suggest that peer counsellors can be trained to support stress management (Dowdall-Thomae et al., 2012; Homish et al., 2012; Kitchiner, 2004). Firefighters appear to prefer services provided by professionals who have no role in administrative decisions, such as fitness for duty (Osofsky et al., 2011). Under certain circumstances, employee assistance programs that explicitly look to enhance personal resources and resiliency skills can be helpful (Jeong, Kang, et al., 2015; Sattler et al., 2014). Van der Velden and colleagues reported that almost three-quarters of the firefighters in their study were offered access to a victim assistance program as mandated by the Working Conditions Act in the Netherlands in 1994 and most (85%) participated (Van der Velden et al., 2006).

The type, intensity, and duration of mental health supports offered to firefighters varies (e.g., Gist & Woodall, 1995; North et al., 2002; Osofsky et al., 2011), but mental health services can improve individual quality of life and should be made available. Volunteer firefighters may have fewer available resources than career firefighters, which suggests that enhanced access to services might offset access to psychological services (Stanley,

Boffa, et al., 2017). Family members of firefighters may also require access to psychological support (Stanley, Boffa, et al., 2017). Strategic onboarding for firefighters' partners may help them to recognize symptoms of stress and PTSD, learn how to provide social support related to potentially psychologically traumatic event exposures, and balance family with shiftwork; however, methods for family members to effectively support firefighters without vicarious traumatization remain debated (Richardson & James, 2017).

Discussion

The current scoping review was designed to synthesize the research literature on PTSD among firefighters. There were three overarching themes identified: 1) describing the nature of potentially psychologically traumatic event exposure among firefighters; 2) understanding PTSD among firefighters, and 3) developing approaches to dealing with PTSD among firefighters.

The current results support the dynamic and diverse ways firefighters are vulnerable to sequala of work-related potentially psychologically traumatic event exposures. Firefighters must have the capacity to pivot from run-of-the-mill calls with low risk to calls with high degrees of risk, volatility, and complexity. The volume and nature of calls can vary across departments and across stations within departments, creating different clusters of vulnerabilities for firefighters. For example, in some regions firefighters act in a dual role as paramedics (District of Columbia Fire and EMS, n.d.; Sagert, 2011) or serve in a volunteer capacity for small communities, responding to calls at the homes of friends and relatives.

Researchers have provided important insights into the diversity of stressors and sequala related to firefighting. Firefighters appear to report mental health challenges at much higher rates than the general population (Carleton et al., 2018). Previous potentially psychologically traumatic event exposures appear to increase risk for PTSD (Carleton et al., 2019) alongside other diverse occupational stressors (Carleton et al., 2020); nevertheless, human responses to similar potentially psychologically traumatic events can vary greatly and there is currently no definitive predictive algorithm for PTSD (Benedek et al., 2007; Liu, Tarigan, Bromet, & Kim, 2014; Mitani et al., 2006). The best course of action may be to develop and iteratively evaluate processes that support ongoing efforts at mitigation, early detection, and evidence-based interventions for PTSD and other mental health challenges. For firefighters, regular exercise may be serving as a particularly poignant mitigation factor against mental health challenges (Abdollahi et al., 2017; Asmundson et al., 2013; LeBouthillier & Asmundson, 2017; Powers et al., 2015).

There may be significant differences in such work-specific factors across different public safety personnel professions that help explain individual

Firefighters and PTSD 281

differences in mental health (Carleton et al., 2018). The available research indicates important influences of workplace variables on public safety personnel mental health broadly (Carleton et al., 2020), as well as more specifically among paramedics (Sterud et al., 2008), police officers (Shane, 2010), and correctional workers (Finney et al., 2013). In contrast, much of the research on firefighter health and well-being has focused on musculoskeletal injuries (e.g., McFalane et al., 1994) and occupational exposure, with less research on mental health than has been conducted for other public safety personnel (e.g., Asmundson et al., 2002).

Comorbidity may also be important for understanding and supporting individual differences in mental health among firefighters (Carleton et al., 2017), but the available data are currently limited. In the general population, there is substantial evidence of comorbidity between chronic pain and mental disorders (Alschuler & Otis, 2014; Baumeister, Knecht, & Hutter, 2012; Bernik, Sampaio, & Gandarela, 2013; Demyttenaere et al., 2007; McWilliams, Cox, & Enns, 2003), particularly PTSD and chronic pain (Asmundson, et al., 2002; Asmundson et al., 1998; Gibson, 2012; Koren, Hemel, & Klein, 2006). More than one-third of firefighters report difficulties with chronic pain and often report that the pain resulted from a work-related injury (Carleton et al., 2017). Psychological and biological vulnerabilities may interact with potentially psychologically traumatic event exposures to produce emotional responses characterized by hypervigilance, cognitive biases, and avoidance (Asmundson et al., 2002), and those symptoms may become mutually maintaining (Sharp & Harvey, 2001). Somatic complaints may translate into earlier presentation to the healthcare system (McFarlane, 2017) and offer important opportunities for early detection of mental health challenges among firefighters suffering from pain, headaches, and sleep disturbances (Sareen, 2014).

Help-seeking behaviour outside the fire service may be discouraged by the dominant firefighter culture that maintains traditional hypermasculine values and stoicism (Henderson et al., 2016). Traditional hypermasculinity in the face of frequent potentially psychologically traumatic event exposures may interact with perceptions of being abandoned by municipal, provincial, and federal governments to compromise coping skills, reduce help-seeking, and facilitate fatalistic attitudes that undermine mental health (Ricciardelli, Carleton, Groll, & Cramm, 2018). There is very little explicit research assessing the help-seeking behaviours of public safety personnel in general, and even less assessing among firefighters. A recent qualitative study underscored the pervasive and punitive impact of stigma on help-seeking (Ricciardelli Carleton, Mooney, & Cramm, 2018). The results describe a pernicious cycle of injuries leading to understaffing, resentment, cynicism, and guilt, all of which may serve as barriers to care seeking. Unfortunately, efforts at institutionalizing evidence-based training and support systems that reduce stigma and support care-seeking appear

282　*Heidi Cramm et al.*

underdeveloped for all public safety personnel, including firefighters (Beshai & Carleton, 2016).

Next Steps

As researchers continue to investigate the individual differences among firefighters' experience of PTSD, work can be completed to identify and develop evidence-based social and organizational supports for this population. An international Delphi study that included identifying the needs of ambulance staff and possible supports for them, can serve as a starting point for further discipline-specific research (Drury et al., 2013). One of the key implications of that study is that training and education programs need to be developed to support the specific psychosocial needs of these workers in order to help them develop their skills in addressing them. Participants requested help learning how to identify stress in themselves and their colleagues and to be better equipped to provide guidance for those who are stressed. Emphasis was also made on enhancing peer support programs and acquiring specialized training in listening skills and other psychosocial techniques for peer supporters (Drury et al., 2013).

A collaboration between the Department of National Defense and the Canadian Institute of Public Safety Research and Treatment has led to the translation of a mental health training program used widely within the Canadian Armed Forces to public safety sectors, including fire (Firefighter Behavioral Health Alliance, 2016; IAFF, 2018; Ontario Association of Fire Chiefs, 2018). Resilience-enhancing cultural interventions that create social support, belonging, and respect while reducing stigma related to both mental health and help seeking behavior may be promising. The literature has also explored resilience as a preventative factor that buffers against psychological distress and vicarious traumatic stress (Harker et al., 2016; Pietrzak et al., 2014). An organizational-level approach to supporting mental health difficulties has been shown to impact help-seeking behaviour within a military context (Fikretoglu et al., 2017). Resilience-oriented expertise may help communities respond to cumulative experiences or risk of social and physical stressors typically connected to natural disasters, violence, and economic downturns (Madrigano et al., 2017). Understood as being different from emergency preparedness, having a resilience-oriented workforce is defined:

> not as a single and unique set of professionals trained in resilience, but rather a goal state whereby all professions involved in protecting and promoting health of places and people possess the capacity (knowledge, attitudes, and skills) necessary to be integrated with each other (not just connected) and thus resilient in the face of a disaster or other widespread stress.
>
> (Madrigano et al., 2017, p. 1563)

Limitations

The ways PTSD prevalence rates were determined, along with the associated sample sizes, were variable. PTSD diagnostic criteria have evolved considerably over the timeframe covered by the review, which further complicates any comparison of prevalence rates. Firefighters who participated in the studies may have had variable potentially psychologically traumatic event exposures in the months leading up to the research and this may have influenced their reporting of symptoms. Studies tied to a specific large-scale incident, such as an earthquake, may capture the experience differently than studies of samples without an externally identifiable and specific potentially psychologically traumatic event. Many studies were cross-sectional, which limits the ability to identify causal factors associated with the development of PTSD, as well as protective factors.

Given the small proportion of women firefighters, data from women are often excluded from analyses (Arbona et al., 2016; Martin, Tran, et al., 2017; Paulus et al., 2017), further limiting our ability to understand any unique factors at play involving sex and gender. There is evidence that female firefighters are at greater risk of mental disorders than their male counterparts (Carleton et al., 2018), underscoring the need to focus more research on women firefighters.

The extent to which those serving as firefighters who served previously in the military or in other roles with elevated potentially psychologically traumatic event exposure risks remains unclear (e.g., 28.3% in Arbona et al., 2016), as is the interaction of potentially psychologically traumatic event exposures and organizational cultures across such experiences.

The current research literature relies primarily on cross-sectional survey data representing the experience of mostly urban, professional firefighters. Few studies with firefighters have used clinical or diagnostic interviews to identify PTSD; instead researchers tend to rely on self-reported cases of PTSD. Longitudinal studies that follow firefighters from before entry into the fire service throughout the course of their careers and beyond are needed to advance the field.

Conclusion

Firefighters are exposed to a diverse and unpredictable range of potentially psychologically traumatic event as a function of their employment. Such exposures can have negative effects on mental health and well-being such as PTSD. The research on prevalence relies predominantly on cross-sectional studies that use varied approaches to determining a PTSD diagnosis. Comorbidity with other mental health disorders appears common and extends to comorbidities with other medical issues. A myriad of person-level factors such as adverse childhood events, gender, and personality traits appear to interact with occupational factors such as years of service, age, and rank, as well as with elements specific to each potentially psychologically traumatic event exposure. Supportive organizations may be critical for destigmatizing mental health issues and enabling early identification of struggles; however, there is no consensus on the key elements for managing potentially psychologically traumatic event exposures. Firefighters who perceive social support from peers, leaders, families, and their communities seem to do better, as do firefighters with access to diverse mental health programming. Longitudinal and prospective studies are urgently required that can explore the myriad complexities of firefighter mental health and allow the field to develop appropriate and effective programming and policies that appreciate the unique culture of and demands within firefighting.

References

* Denotes references included in qualitative synthesis

*Abdollahi, A., LeBouthillier, D. M., Najafi, M., Asmundson, G. J. G., Hosseinian, S., Shahidi, S., … Jalili, M. (2017). Effect of exercise augmentation of cognitive behavioural therapy for the treatment of suicidal ideation and depression. *Journal of Affective Disorders*, 219, 58–63. https://doi.org/10.1016/j.jad.2017.05.012.

*Admon, R., Leykin, D., Lubin, G., Engert, V., Andrews, J., Pruessner, J., & Hendler, T. (2013). Stress-induced reduction in hippocampal volume and connectivity with the ventromedial prefrontal cortex are related to maladaptive responses to stressful military service. *Human Brain Mapping*, 34(11), 2808.

*Al-Naser, F., & Everly, J. G. (1999). Prevalence of posttraumatic stress disorder among Kuwaiti firefighters. *International Journal of Emergency Mental Health*, 1(2), 99–101.

*Alghamdi, M., Hunt, N., & Thomas, S. (2015). The effectiveness of narrative exposure therapy with traumatised firefighters in Saudi Arabia: A randomized controlled study. *Behaviour Research and Therapy*, 66, 64–71.

*Alschuler, K. N., & Otis, J. D. (2014). An examination of the impact of clinically significant levels of posttraumatic stress disorder symptomatology on the classification of pain as mild, moderate, or severe in a sample of veterans with chronic pain. *Psychological Services*, 11(3), 273.

American Psychiatric Association (APA). (2013). *Diagnostic and statistical manual of mental disorders (DSM-5®)*. American Psychiatric Association.

Arbona, C., Fan, W., & Noor, N. (2016). Factor structure and external correlates of posttraumatic stress disorder symptoms among African American firefighters. *Psychology Research and Behavior Management*, 9, 201–209.

Arksey, H., & O'Malley, L. (2005). Scoping studies: Towards a methodological framework. *International Journal of Social Research Methodology*, 8(1), 19–32.

Armstrong, D., Shakespeare Finch, J., & Shochet, I. (2014). Predicting post-traumatic growth and post-traumatic stress in firefighters. *Australian Journal of Psychology*, 66(1), 38.

*Armstrong, D., Shakespeare-Finch, J., & Shochet, I. (2016). Organizational belongingness mediates the relationship between sources of stress and posttrauma outcomes in firefighters. *Psychological Trauma: Theory, Research, Practice, and Policy*, 8(3), 343.

*Asmundson, G. J., Coons, M. J., Taylor, S., & Katz, J. (2002). PTSD and the experience of pain: Research and clinical implications of shared vulnerability and mutual maintenance models. *The Canadian Journal of Psychiatry, 47*(10), 930–937.

*Asmundson, G. J., Fetzner, M. G., Deboer, L. B., Powers, M. B., Otto, M. W., & Smits, J. A. (2013). Let's get physical: A contemporary review of the anxiolytic effects of exercise for anxiety and its disorders. *Depression & Anxiety, 30*, 362–373. https://doi.org/10.1002/da.22043

*Asmundson, G. J., Norton, G. R., Allerdings, M. D., Norton, P. J., & Larsen, D. K. (1998). Posttraumatic stress disorder and work-related injury. *Journal of Anxiety Disorders, 12*(1), 57–69.

*Bacharach, S. B., Bamberger, P. A., & Doveh, E. (2008). Firefighters, critical incidents, and drinking to cope: The adequacy of unit-level performance resources as a source of vulnerability and protection. *Journal of Applied Psychology, 93*(1), 155.

*Baker, S. R., & Williams, K. (2001). Relation between social problem-solving appraisals, work stress and psychological distress in male firefighters. *Stress and Health, 17*(4), 219–229.

*Barnes, P. (1997). A risk-based approach to occupational stress among urban firefighters. *Journal of Occupational Health and Safety, 13*(6), 549–555.

*Baumeister, H., Knecht, A., & Hutter, N. (2012). Direct and indirect costs in persons with chronic back pain and comorbid mental disorders – A systematic review. *Journal of Psychosomatic Research, 73*(2), 79–85.

*Beaton, R., & Murphy, S. (1995). *Secondary traumatic stress of crisis workers: Research implications*. New York: Brunner/Mazel.

*Beaton, R., & Murphy, S. (2002). Psychosocial responses to biological and chemical terrorist threats and events: Implications for the workplace. *AAOHN Journal, 50*(4), 182.

*Beaton, R., Murphy, S., Johnson, C., Pike, K., & Cornell, W. (1998). Exposure to duty-related incident stressors in urban firefighters and paramedics. *Journal of Traumatic Stress, 11*(4), 821–828.

*Benedek, D. M., Fullerton, C., & Ursano, R. J. (2007). First responders: Mental health consequences of natural and human-made disasters for public health and public safety workers. *Annual Review of Public Health, 28*, 55–68.

*Bernabé, M., & Botia, J. M. (2016). Resilience as a mediator in emotional social support's relationship with occupational psychology health in firefighters. *Journal of Health Psychology, 21*(8), 1778–1786.

*Bernik, M., Sampaio, T. P., & Gandarela, L. (2013). Fibromyalgia comorbid with anxiety disorders and depression: Combined medical and psychological treatment. *Current Pain and Headache Reports, 17*(9), 358.

*Berninger, A., Webber, M. P., Cohen, H. W., Gustave, J., Lee, R., Niles, J. K., ... Prezant, D. J. (2010). Trends of elevated PTSD risk in firefighters exposed to the World Trade Centre Disaster: 2001–2005. *Public Health Reports, 125*, 556–566.

*Berninger, A., Webber, M. P., Niles, J. K., Gustave, J., Lee, R., Cohen, H. W., ... Prezant, D. J. (2010). Longitudinal study of probable post-traumatic stress disorder in firefighters exposed to the World Trade Center disaster. *American Journal of Industrial Medicine, 53*(12), 1177–1185. https://doi.org/10.1002/ajim.20894

Beshai, S., & Carleton, R. N. (2016). *Peer support and crisis-focused psychological intervention programs in Canada first responders: Blue Paper*. University of Regina, SK. Retrieved from: www.justiceandsafety.ca/rsu_docs/blue_paper_full_web_final_production_aug_16_2016.pdf.

286   *Heidi Cramm et al.*

*Boffa, J. W., Stanley, I. H., Hom, M. A., Norr, A. M., Joiner, T. E., & Schmidt, N. B. (2017). PTSD symptoms and suicidal thoughts and behaviors among firefighters. *Journal of Psychiatric Research*, *84*, 277–283.

*Bracken-Scally, M., McGilloway, S., Gallagher, S., & Mitchell, J. T. (2014). Life after the emergency services: An exploratory study of well being and quality of life in emergency service retirees. *International Journal of Emergency Mental Health*, *16*(1), 223–231.

*Brazil, A. (2017). Exploring critical incidents and postexposure management in a volunteer fire service. *Journal of Aggression, Maltreatment & Trauma*, *26*(3), 244–257.

*Brown, J. M., & Campbell, E. A. (1991). Stress among emergency services personnel: Progress and problems. *Occupational Medicine*, *41*(4), 149–150.

*Bryant, R. A., & Guthrie, R. M. (2005). Maladaptive appraisals as a risk factor for posttraumatic stress: A study of trainee firefighters. *Psychological Science*, *16*(10), 749–752.

*Bryant, R. A., & Guthrie, R. M. (2007). Maladaptive self-appraisals before trauma exposure predict posttraumatic stress disorder. *Journal of Consulting & Clinical Psychology*, *75*(5), 812.

*Bryant, R. A., & Harvey, A. G. (1995). Avoidant coping style and post-traumatic stress following motor vehicle accidents. *Behaviour Research & Therapy*, *33*(6), 631.

*Bryant, R. A., & Harvey, A. G. (1996). Posttraumatic stress reactions in volunteer firefighters. *Journal of Traumatic Stress*, *9*(1), 51–62.

*Bryant, R. A., Sutherland, K., & Guthrie, R. M. (2007). Impaired specific autobiographical memory as a risk factor for posttraumatic stress after trauma. *Journal of Abnormal Psychology*, *116*(4), 837–841. https://doi.org/10.1037/0021-843X.116.4.837

*Burke, K. J. (2006). Well-being in protective services personnel: Organisational influences. *Australasian Journal of Disaster and Trauma Studies*.

Canadian Institute for Public Safety Research and Treatment (CIPSRT). (2019). *Glossary of terms: A shared understanding of the common terms used to describe psychological trauma (version 2.0)*. Regina, SK: Author.

Carleton, R. N., Afifi, T. O., Taillieu, T., Turner, S., Krakauer, R., Anderson, G. S., … & McCreary, D. R. (2019). Exposures to potentially traumatic events among public safety personnel in Canada. *Canadian Journal of Behavioural Science/Revue canadienne des sciences du comportement*, *51*(1), 37.

Carleton, R. N., Afifi, T. O., Taillieu, T., Turner, S., Mason, J. E., Ricciardelli, R., … Griffiths, C. T. (2020). Assessing the relative impact of diverse stressors among public safety personnel. *International Journal of Environmental Research and Public Health*, *17*. https://doi.org/10.3390/ijerph17041234.

Carleton, R. N., Afifi, T. O., Turner, S., Taillieu, T., Duranceau, S., LeBouthillier, D. M., … Asmundson, G. J. G. (2018). Mental disorder symptoms among public safety personnel in Canada. *Canadian Journal of Psychiatry*, *63*(1), 54–64. https://doi.org/10.1177/0706743717723825.

*Carleton, R. N., Afifi, T. O., Turner, S., Taillieu, T., El-Gabalawy, R., Sareen, J., & Asmundson, G. J. G. (2017). Chronic pain among public safety personnel in Canada. *Canadian Journal of Pain*, *1*(1), 237–246. https://doi.org/10.1080/24740527.2017.1410431.

*Chamberlin, M. J. A., & Green, H. J. (2010). Stress and coping strategies among firefighters and recruits. *Journal of Loss and Trauma*, *15*(6), 548–560.

*Chang, C., Lee, L., Connor, K. M., Davidson, J. R. T., Jeffries, K., & Lai, T. (2003). Posttraumatic distress and coping strategies among rescue workers after an earthquake. *Journal of Nervous & Mental Disease, 191*(6), 391.

*Chen, Y. R., Chen, M., Chou, F., Sun, F., Chen, P., Tsai, K., & Chao, S. (2007). The relationship between quality of life and posttraumatic stress disorder or major depression for firefighters in Kaohsiung, Taiwan. *Quality of Life Research, 16*(8), 1289–1297.

*Chiu, S., Webber, M. P., Zeig-Owens, R., Gustave, J., Lee, R., Kelly, K. J., ... North, C. S. (2011). Performance characteristics of the PTSD Checklist in retired firefighters exposed to the World Trade Center disaster. *Annals of Clinical Psychiatry, 23*(2), 95–104.

*Corneil, W., Beaton, R., Murphy, S., Johnson, C., & Pike, K. (1999). Exposure to traumatic incidents and prevalence of posttraumatic stress symptomatology in urban firefighters in two countries. *Journal of Occupational Health Psychology, 4*(2), 131.

*Coupland, N. J. (2009). Treatment of insomnia in post-traumatic stress disorder. *Journal Of Psychiatry & Neuroscience: JPN, 34*(5), E5–6.

*De Soir, E., Knarren, M., Zech, E., Mylle, J., Kleber, R., & van der Hart, O. (2012). A phenomenological analysis of disaster-related experiences in fire and emergency medical services personnel. *Prehospital & Disaster Medicine, 27*(2), 115–122.

*DeLorme, J. (2014). *The investigation of repeated trauma exposure and psychological adjustment in firefighters.* Doctoral dissertation, Alliant International University, California School of Professional Psychology, San Diego, CA.

*Demyttenaere, K., Bruffaerts, R., Lee, S., Posada-Villa, J., Kovess, V., Angermeyer, M. C., ... Mneimneh, Z. (2007). Mental disorders among persons with chronic back or neck pain: Results from the World Mental Health Surveys. *Pain, 129*(3), 332–342.

*District of Columbia Fire and EMS. (n.d.). Become a dual role firefighter and EMT or paramedic and firefighter. Retrieved from https://fems.dc.gov/page/become-dual-role-firefighter-and-emt-or-paramedic-and-firefighter.

*Doley, R. M., Bell, R., & Watt, B. D. (2016). An investigation into the relationship between long-term posttraumatic stress disorder symptoms and coping in Australian volunteer firefighters. *Journal of Nervous and Mental Disease, 204*(7), 530–536.

*Dowdall-Thomae, C., Gilkey, J., Larson, W., & Arend-Hicks, R. (2012). Elite firefighter/first responder mindsets and outcome coping efficacy. *International Journal of Emergency Mental Health, 14*(4), 269–281.

*Drury, J., Kemp, V., Newman, J., Novelli, D., Doyle, C., Walter, D., & Williams, R. (2013). Psychosocial care for persons affected by emergencies and major incidents: A Delphi study to determine the needs of professional first responders for education, training and support. *Emergency Medicine Journal, 30*(10), 831–836. https://doi.org/10.1136/emermed-2012-201632.

*Dudek, B., & Koniarek, J. (2000). Relationship between sense of coherence and post-traumatic stress disorder symptoms among firefighters. *International Journal of Occupational Medicine and Environmental Health, 13*(4), 299–305.

*Eid, J., Helge Johnsen, B., & Weisæth, L. (2001). The effect of group psychological debriefing on acute stress reactions following a traffic accident: A quasi-experimental approach. *International Journal of Emergency Mental Health, 3*(3), 145–154.

288   *Heidi Cramm et al.*

*Eriksson, C., Foy, D., & Larson, L. (2004). *When the helpers need help: Early intervention for emergency and relief services personnel.* London: Guilford Press.

*Epstein, R. S., Fullerton, C. S., & Ursano, R. S. (1998). Posttraumatic stress disorder following an air disaster: A prospective study. *The American Journal of Psychiatry, 155*(7), 934–938. https://doi.org/10.1176/ajp.155.7.934

*Farnsworth, J. K., & Sewell, K. W. (2011). Fear of emotion as a moderator between PTSD and firefighter social interactions. *Journal of Traumatic Stress, 24*(4), 444–450.

*Fien, N. (2017). Manitoba's changes to workers compensation legislation regarding post-traumatic stress disorder: Analysis and legislative process. *Manitoba Law Journal, 40*(2), 1–27.

*Fikretoglu, D., D'Agata, M. T., Sullivan-Kwantes, W., Richards, K., & Bailey, S. (2017). *Mental health and mental health service use attitudes among Canadian Armed Forces (CAF) recruits and officer cadets.* Ottawa, ON. Retrieved from http://cradpdf.drdc-rddc.gc.ca/PDFS/unc273/p805331_A1b.pdf.

*Finney, C., Stergiopoulos, E., Hensel, J., Bonato, S., & Dewa, C. S. (2013). Organizational stressors associated with job stress and burnout in correctional officers: A systematic review. *BMC Public Health, 13*(1), 82.

Firefighter Behavioral Health Alliance. (2016). Workshops designed by a firefighter for a firefighter. Saving those who save others. Retrieved from www.ffbha.org/.

*Fullerton, C. S., Ursano, R. J., & Wang, L. (2004). Acute stress disorder, posttraumatic stress disorder, and depression in disaster or rescue workers. *American Journal of Psychiatry, 161*(8), 1370–1376.

*Fushimi, M. (2012). Posttraumatic stress in professional firefighters in Japan: Rescue efforts after the Great East Japan Earthquake (Higashi Nihon Dai-Shinsai). *Prehospital & Disaster Medicine, 27*(5), 416–418.

*Gibson, C.-A. (2012). Review of posttraumatic stress disorder and chronic pain: The path to integrated care. *Journal of Rehabilitation Research and Development, 49*(5), 753.

*Gist, R., & Woodall, S. J. (1995). Occupational stress in contemporary fire service. *Occupational Medicine, 10*(4), 763–787.

*Guidotti, T. L. (1992). Human factors in firefighting: Ergonomic, cardiopulmonary, and psychogenic stress-related issues. *International Archives of Occupational and Environmental Health, 64*(1), 1–12.

*Guthrie, R. M., & Bryant, R. A. (2005). Auditory startle response in firefighters before and after trauma exposure. *American Journal of Psychiatry, 162*, 283–290.

*Haddock, C. K., Poston, W. S., Jahnke, S. A., & Jitnarin, N. (2017). Alcohol use and problem drinking among women firefighters. *Women's Health Issues, 27*(6), 632–638.

*Hagh-Shenas, H., Goodarzi, M. A., Dehbozorgi, G., & Farashbandi, H. (2005). Psychological consequences of the Bam earthquake on professional and non-professional helpers. *Journal of Traumatic Stress, 18*(5), 477–483.

*Harker, R., Pidgeon, A. M., Klaassen, F., & King, S. (2016). Exploring resilience and mindfulness as preventative factors for psychological distress burnout and secondary traumatic stress among human service professionals. *Work: Journal of Prevention, Assessment & Rehabilitation, 54*(3), 631–637. https://doi.org/http://dx.doi.org/10.3233/WOR-162311.

*Harris, M. B., Baloglu, M., & Stacks, J. R. (2002). Mental health of trauma-exposed firefighters and critical incident stress debriefing. *Journal of Loss & Trauma, 7*(3), 223–238. https://doi.org/10.1080/10811440290057639

*Harvey, S. B., Milligan-Saville, J. S., Paterson, H. M., Harkness, E. L., Marsh, A. M., Dobson, M., ... Bryant, R. A. (2016). The mental health of fire-fighters: An examination of the impact of repeated trauma exposure. *Australian & New Zealand Journal of Psychiatry, 50*(7), 649–658. https://doi.org/10.1177/0004867415615217.

*Haslam, C., & Mallon, K. (2003). A preliminary investigation of post-traumatic stress symptoms among firefighters. *Work & Stress, 17*(3), 277–285.

*Heinrichs, M., Wagner, D., Schoch, W., Soravia, L. M., Hellhammer, D. H., & Ehlert, U. (2005). Predicting posttraumatic stress symptoms from pretraumatic risk factors: A 2-year prospective follow-up study in firefighters. *The American Journal of Psychiatry, 162*(12), 2276–2286.

*Henderson, S. N., Van Hasselt, V. B., LeDuc, T. J., & Couwels, J. (2016). Firefighter suicide: Understanding cultural challenges for mental health professionals. *Professional Psychology: Research and Practice, 47*(3), 224–230.

*Hill, R., & Brunsden, V. (2009). "Heroes" as victims: Role reversal in the Fire and Rescue Service. *The Irish Journal of Psychology, 30*(1–2), 75–86.

*Holland, M. (2011). The dangers of detrimental coping in emergency medical services. *Prehospital Emergency Care, 15*(3), 331.

*Homish, G. G., Frazer, B. S., & Carey, M. G. (2012). The influence of indirect collective trauma on first responders' alcohol use. *International Journal of Emergency Mental Health, 14*(1), 21–28.

Hsieh, H.-F., & Shannon, S. E. (2005). Three approaches to qualitative content analysis. *Qualitative Health Research, 15*(9), 1277–1288. https://doi.org/10.1177/1049732305276687

*Huizink, A. C., Slottje, P., Witteveen, A. B., Bijlsma, J. A., Twisk, J. W., Smidt, N., ... Bouter, L. M. (2006). Long term health complaints following the Amsterdam Air Disaster in police officers and fire-fighters. *Occupational and Environmental Medicine, 63*(10), 657–662.

International Association of Fire Fighters (IAFF). (2000). *Death and injury survey.* Washington, D.C.

IAFF. (2003). Project HEROES: Homeland emergency response operational and equipment systems. Retrieved from www.cdc.gov/niosh/npptl/pdfs/ProjectHEROES-508.pdf.

IAFF. (2016). Ontario introduces legislation to recognize post-traumatic stress as occupational illness. Retrieved from www.iaff244.org/?zone=/unionactive/view_article.cfm&HomeID=551710.

IAFF. (2018). IAFF Behavioral health program. Retrieved from www.iaff.org/behavioral-health/.

*Jacobsson, A., Backteman-Erlanson, S., Brulin, C., & Hornsten, A. (2015). Experiences of critical incidents among female and male firefighters. *International Emergency Nursing, 23*(2), 100–104.

*Jahnke, S. A., Poston, W. S. C., Haddock, C. K., & Murphy, B. (2016). Firefighting and mental health: Experiences of repeated exposure to trauma. *Work, 53*(4), 737–744. https://doi.org/10.3233/WOR-162255.

*Jeong, H. S., Jeon, Y., Ma, J., Choi, Y., Ban, S., Lee, S., ... Lyoo, I. K. (2015). Validation of the Athens Insomnia Scale for screening insomnia in South Korean firefighters and rescue workers. *Quality of Life Research, 24*(10), 2391–2395.

*Jeong, H. S., Kang, I., Namgung, E., Im, J. J., Jeon, Y., Son, J., ... Kim, J. E. (2015). Validation of the Korean version of the Connor-Davidson Resilience Scale-2 in firefighters and rescue workers. *Comprehensive Psychiatry, 59*, 123–128.

290 *Heidi Cramm et al.*

*Katsavouni, F., Bebetsos, E., Malliou, P., & Beneka, A. (2016). The relationship between burnout, PTSD symptoms and injuries in firefighters. *Occupational Medicine* (Oxford), *66*(1), 32–37.

*Kaufmann, C. N., Rutkow, L., Spira, A. P., & Mojtabai, R. (2013). Mental health of protective services workers: Results from the national epidemiologic survey on alcohol and related conditions. *Disaster Medicine & Public Health Preparedness*, *7*(1), 36–45.

*Kehl, D., Knuth, D., Hulse, L., Holubova, M., & Schmidt, S. (2014). Relationships between firefighters' postevent distress and growth at different times after distressing incidents. *Acta Anaesthesiologica Belgica*, *20*(4), 253.

*Kehl, D., Knuth, D., Hulse, L., & Schmidt, S. (2015). Predictors of postevent distress and growth among firefighters after work-related emergencies – A cross-national study. *Psychological Trauma: Theory, Research, Practice, and Policy*, *7*(3), 203.

*Kimbrel, N. A., Steffen, L. E., Meyer, E. C., Kruse, M. I., Knight, J. A., Zimering, R. T., & Gulliver, S. B. (2011). A revised measure of occupational stress for firefighters: Psychometric properties and relationship to posttraumatic stress disorder, depression, and substance abuse. *Psychological Services*, *8*(4), 294.

*Kitchiner, N. J. (2004). Psychological treatment of three urban fire fighters with post-traumatic stress disorder using eye movement desensitisation reprocessing (EMDR) therapy. *Complementary Therapies in Nursing and Midwifery*, *10*(3), 186–193.

*Komarovskaya, I., Brown, A. D., Galatzer-Levy, I. R., Madan, A., Henn-Haase, C., Teater, J., … Chemtob, C. M. (2014). Early physical victimization is a risk factor for posttraumatic stress disorder symptoms among Mississippi police and firefighter first responders to Hurricane Katrina. *Psychological Trauma: Theory, Research, Practice, and Policy*, *6*(1), 92.

*Koren, D., Hemel, D., & Klein, E. (2006). Injury increases the risk for PTSD: An examination of potential neurobiological and psychological mediators. *CNS Spectrums*, *11*(8), 616–624.

*Lambert, J. E., Benight, C. C., Harrison, E., & Cieslak, R. (2012). The firefighter coping self-efficacy scale: Measure development and validation. *Anxiety, Stress, & Coping*, *25*(1), 79–91.

*LeBouthillier, D. M., & Asmundson, G. J. G. (2017). The efficacy of aerobic exercise and resistance training as transdiagnostic interventions for anxiety-related disorders and constructs: A randomized controlled trial. *Journal of Anxiety Disorders*, *52*, 43–52. https://doi.org/10.1016/j.janxdis.2017.09.005.

*Lee, J.-S., Ahn, Y.-S., Jeong, K.-S., Chae, J.-H., & Choi, K.-S. (2014). Resilience buffers the impact of traumatic events on the development of PTSD symptoms in firefighters. *Journal of Affective Disorders*, *162*, 128–133.

*Lee, J. H., Lee, D., Kim, J., Jeon, K., & Sim, M. (2017). Duty-related trauma exposure and posttraumatic stress symptoms in professional firefighters. *Journal of Traumatic Stress*, *30*(2), 133–141.

*Leon, G. R. (2004). Overview of the psychosocial impact of disasters. *Prehospital and Disaster Medicine*, *19*(1), 4-9.

Levac, D. E., Colquhoun, H., & O'Brien, K. K. (2010). Scoping studies: Advancing the methodology. *Implementation Science*, *5*(69).

*Levy-Gigi, E., Bonanno, G. A., Shapiro, A. R., Richter-Levin, G., Keri, S., & Sheppes, G. (2016). Emotion regulatory flexibility sheds light on the elusive

Firefighters and PTSD 291

relationship between repeated traumatic exposure and posttraumatic stress disorder symptoms. *Clinical Psychological Science, 4*(1), 28–39.

*Levy-Gigi, E., Richter-Levin, G., & Kéri, S. (2014). The hidden price of repeated traumatic exposure: Different cognitive deficits in different first-responders. *Frontiers in Behavioral Neuroscience, 8*, 281.

*Liu, B., Tarigan, L. H., Bromet, E. J., & Kim, H. (2014). World Trade Center disaster exposure-related probable posttraumatic stress disorder among responders and civilians: A meta-analysis. *PLoS One,* 9(7), e101491.

*Madrigano, J., Chandra, A., Costigan, T., & Acosta, J. D. (2017). Beyond disaster preparedness: building a resilience-oriented workforce for the future. *Int J Environ Res Public Health, 14*(12), 1563. https://doi.org/10.3390/ijerph14121563.

*Marmar, C. R., Weiss, D. S., Metzler, T. J., Ronfeldt, H. M., & Foreman, C. (1996). Stress responses of emergency services personnel to the Loma Prieta earthquake Interstate 880 freeway collapse and control traumatic incidents. *Journal of Traumatic Stress, 9*(1), 63–85.

*Martin, C. E., Tran, J. K., & Buser, S. J. (2017). Correlates of suicidality in firefighter/EMS personnel. *Journal of Affective Disorders, 208*, 177–183. https://doi.org/10.1016/j.jad.2016.08.078.

*Martin, C. E., Vujanovic, A. A., Paulus, D. J., Bartlett, B., Gallagher, M. W., & Tran, J. K. (2017). Alcohol use and suicidality in firefighters: Associations with depressive symptoms and posttraumatic stress. *Comprehensive Psychiatry, 74*, 44–52.

*Maslow, C. B., Caramanica, K., Welch, A. E., Stellman, S. D., Brackbill, R. M., & Farfel, M. R. (2015). Trajectories of scores on a screening instrument for PTSD among World Trade Center rescue, recovery, and clean-up workers. *Journal of Traumatic Stress, 28*(3), 198–205.

*McFarlane, A. C. (1988). The longitudinal course of posttraumatic morbidity: The range of outcomes and their predictors. *The Journal of Nervous and Mental Disease, 176*(1), 30–39.

*McFarlane, A. C. (1990). An Australian disaster: The 1983 bushfires. *International Journal of Mental Health, 19*(2), 36–47.

*McFarlane, A. C. (1992). Avoidance and intrusion in posttraumatic stress disorder. *The Journal of Nervous and Mental Disease, 180*(7), 439–445.

*McFarlane, A. C. (2017). Post-traumatic stress disorder is a systemic illness, not a mental disorder: Is Cartesian dualism dead? *The Medical Journal of Australia, 206*(6), 248–249.

*McFarlane, A. C., Atchison, M., Rafalowicz, E., & Papay, P. (1994). Physical symptoms in post-traumatic stress disorder. *Journal of Psychosomatic Research, 38*(7), 715–726.

*McFarlane, A. C., & Papay, P. (1992). Multiple diagnoses in posttraumatic stress disorder in the victims of a natural disaster. *The Journal of Nervous and Mental Disease, 180*(8), 498–504.

*McWilliams, L. A., Cox, B. J., & Enns, M. W. (2003). Mood and anxiety disorders associated with chronic pain: An examination in a nationally representative sample. *Pain, 106*(1), 127–133.

*Meyer, E. C., Zimering, R., Daly, E., Knight, J., Kamholz, B. W., & Gulliver, S. B. (2012). Predictors of posttraumatic stress disorder and other psychological symptoms in trauma-exposed firefighters. *Psychological Services, 9*(1), 1–15.

*Miller, L. (1995). Tough guys: Psychotherapeutic strategies with law enforcement and emergency services personnel. *Psychotherapy, 32*(4), 592–600.

292 *Heidi Cramm et al.*

*Milligan-Saville, J. S., Paterson, H. M., Harkness, L., Marsh, A. M., Dobson, M., Kemp, R. I., ... Harvey, S. B. (2017). The amplification of common somatic symptoms by posttraumatic stress disorder in firefighters. *Journal of Traumatic Stress, 30*(2), 142–148.

*Mitani, S. (2008). Comparative analysis of the Japanese version of the revised impact of event scale: A study of firefighters. *Prehospital and Disaster Medicine, 23*, 20–26.

*Monteiro, J. K., Abs, D., Labres, I. D., Maus, D., & Pioner, T. (2013). Firefighters: Psychopathology and working conditions. *Estudos de Psicologia* (Campinas), *30*(3), 437–444.

*Morren, M., Yzermans, C. J., van Nispen, R. M. A., & Wevers, J. M. (2005). The health of volunteer firefighters three years after a technological disaster. *Journal of Occupational Health, 47*, 523–532.

*Murphy, L. M., Koranyi, K., Crim, L., & Whited, S. (1999). Disclosure, stress, and psychological adjustment among mothers affected by HIV. *AIDS Patient Care & STDs, 13*(2), 111.

*North, C. S., Tivis, L., McMillen, J. C., Pfefferbaum, B., Cox, J., Spitznagel, E. L., ... Smith, E. M. (2002). Coping, functioning, and adjustment of rescue workers after the Oklahoma City bombing. *Journal of Traumatic Stress*, 15(3), 171.

Oliphant, R. (2016). *Healthy minds, safe communities: Supporting our public safety officers through a national strategy for operational injuries.* Report of the Standing Committee on Public Safety and National Security. House of Commons, Canada. Retrieved from: www.ourcommons.ca/Content/Committee/421/SECU/Reports/RP8457704/securp05/securp05-e.pdf.

Ontario Association of Fire Chiefs. (2018). R2MR course and booking information. Road to mental readiness. Retrieved from www.oafc.on.ca/twmfr-course-and-booking-information.

*Osofsky, H. J., Osofsky, J. D., Arey, J., Kronenberg, M. E., Hansel, T., & Many, M. (2011). Hurricane Katrina's first responders: The struggle to protect and serve in the aftermath of the disaster. *Disaster Medicine & Public Health Preparedness, 5*(2), S214–219.

*Otis, C., Marchand, A., & Courtois, F. (2012). Peritraumatic dissociation as a mediator of peritraumatic distress and PTSD: A retrospective, cross-sectional study. *Journal of Trauma & Dissociation, 13*(4), 469–477.

*Paterson, H. M., Whittle, K., & Kemp, R. I. (2015). Detrimental effects of post-incident debriefing on memory and psychological responses. *Journal of Police and Criminal Psychology, 30*(1), 27–37.

*Paulus, D. J., Vujanovic, A. A., Schuhmann, B. B., Smith, L. J., & Tran, J. (2017). Main and interactive effects of depression and posttraumatic stress in relation to alcohol dependence among urban male firefighters. *Psychiatry Research, 251*, 69–75.

*Pietrzak, R. H., Feder, A., Singh, R., Schechter, C. B., Bromet, E. J., Katz, C. L., ... Southwick, S. M. (2014). Trajectories of PTSD risk and resilience in World Trade Center responders: An 8-year prospective cohort study. *Psychological Medicine, 44*(1), 205–219. https://doi.org/10.1017/S0033291713000597.

*Pinto, R. J., Henriques, S. P., Jongenelen, I., Carvalho, C., & Maia, A. C. (2015). The strongest correlates of ptsd for firefighters: Number, recency, frequency, or perceived threat of traumatic events? *Journal of Traumatic Stress, 28*(5), 434–440.

*Plat, M. J., Frings-Dresen, M. H., & Sluiter, J. K. (2012). Which subgroups of fire fighters are more prone to work-related diminished health requirements? *International Archives of Occupational and Environmental Health, 85*(7), 775–782. https://doi.org/10.1007/s00420-011-0720-x.

*Powers, M. B., Asmundson, G. J., & Smits, J. A. (2015). Exercise for mood and anxiety disorders: The state-of-the science. *Cogntive Behavioral Therapy, 44*, 237–239. https://doi.org/10.1080/16506073.2015.1047286.

*Regehr, C., Hemsworth, D., & Hill, J. (2001). Individual predictors of post-traumatic distress: A structural equation model. *The Canadian Journal of Psychiatry, 46*(2), 156–161.

*Regehr, C., Hill, J., & Glancy, G. D. (2000). Individual predictors of traumatic reactions in firefighters. *The Journal of Nervous and Mental Disease, 188*(6), 333–339.

*Regehr, C., Hill, J., Knott, T., & Sault, B. (2003). Social support, self-efficacy and trauma in new recruits and experienced firefighters. *Stress and Health, 19*(4), 189–193.

Ricciardelli, R., Carleton, R. N., Groll, D., & Cramm, H. (2018). Qualitatively unpacking Canadian public safety personnel experiences of trauma and their well-being. *Canadian Journal of Criminology and Criminal Justice, 60*(4), 566–577.

Ricciardelli, R., Carleton, R. N., Mooney, T., & Cramm, H. (2018). "Playing the system": Structural factors potentiating mental health stigma, challenging awareness, and creating barriers to care for Canadian Public Safety Personnel. *Health*. https://doi.org/10.1177/1363459318800167.

*Richardson, B. K., & James, E. P. (2017). The role of occupational identity in negotiating traumatic experiences: the case of a rural fire department. *Journal of Applied Communication Research, 45*(3), 313–332.

*Riolli, L., & Savicki, V. (2012). Firefighters' psychological and physical outcomes after exposure to traumatic stress: The moderating roles of hope and personality. *Traumatology, 18*(3), 7–15.

Sagert, L. (2011, April 4). Dual Duty: April 2011. FIREFighting in Canada. Retrieved from www.firefightingincanada.com/fire-ems/dual-duty-8305.

*Saijo, Y., Ueno, T., & Hashimoto, Y. (2012). Post-traumatic stress disorder and job stress among firefighters of urban Japan. *Prehospital and Disaster Medicine, 27*(1), 59–63.

*Sakuma, A., Takahashi, Y., Ueda, I., Sato, H., Katsura, M., Abe, M., ... Matsumoto, K. (2015). Post-traumatic stress disorder and depression prevalence and associated risk factors among local disaster relief and reconstruction workers fourteen months after the Great East Japan Earthquake: A cross-sectional study. *BMC Psychiatry, 15*(1), 58.

Sareen, J. (2014). Posttraumatic stress disorder in adults: Impact, comorbidity, risk factors, and treatment. *The Canadian Journal of Psychiatry, 59*(9), 460–467.

*Sattler, D. N., Boyd, B., & Kirsch, J. (2014). Trauma-exposed firefighters: Relationships among posttraumatic growth, posttraumatic stress, resource availability, coping and critical incident stress debriefing experience. *Stress and Health: Journal of the International Society for the Investigation of Stress, 30*(5), 356.

*Shane, J. M. (2010). Organizational stressors and police performance. *Journal of Criminal Justice, 38*(4), 807–818.

294   *Heidi Cramm et al.*

*Sharp, T. J., & Harvey, A. G. (2001). Chronic pain and posttraumatic stress disorder: Mutual maintenance? *Clinical Psychology Review*, *21*(6), 857–877.

*Shin, L. M., Shin, P. S., Heckers, S., Krangel, T. S., Macklin, M. L., Orr, S. P., ... Richert, K. (2004). Hippocampal function in posttraumatic stress disorder. *Hippocampus*, *14*(3), 292–300.

*Skeffington, P. M., Rees, C. S., & Mazzucchelli, T. (2017). Trauma exposure and post-traumatic stress disorder within fire and emergency services in Western Australia. *Australian Journal of Psychology*, *69*(1), 20–28.

*Skeffington, P. M., Rees, C. S., Mazzucchelli, T. G., & Kane, R. T. (2016). The primary prevention of PTSD in firefighters: Preliminary results of an RCT with 12-month follow-up. *PLoS One*, *11*(7). https://doi.org/10.1371/journal.pone.0155873

*Skogstad, L., Heir, T., Hauff, E., & Ekeberg, Ø. (2016). Post-traumatic stress among rescue workers after terror attacks in Norway. *Occupational Medicine*, *66*(7), 528–535.

*Sliter, M., Kale, A., & Yuan, Z. (2014). Is humor the best medicine? The buffering effect of coping humor on traumatic stressors in firefighters. *Journal of Organizational Behavior*, *35*(2), 257–272.

*Smith, A. J., Donlon, K., Anderson, S. R., Hughes, M., & Jones, R. T. (2015). When seeking influences believing and promotes posttraumatic adaptation. *Anxiety, Stress, & Coping*, *28*(3), 340.

*Smith, B. W., Ortiz, J. A., Steffen, L. E., Tooley, E. M., Wiggins, K. T., Yeater, E. A., ... Bernard, M. L. (2011). Mindfulness is associated with fewer PTSD symptoms, depressive symptoms, physical symptoms, and alcohol problems in urban firefighters. *Journal of Consulting & Clinical Psychology*, *79*(5), 613–617.

*Soo, J., Webber, M. P., Gustave, J., Lee, R., Hall, C. B., Cohen, H. W., ... Prezant, D. J. (2011). Trends in probable PTSD in firefighters exposed to the World Trade Center disaster, 2001–2010. *Disaster Medicine and Public Health Preparedness*, *5*(S2), S197–S203.

*Southwick, S. M., Bonanno, G. A., Masten, A. S., PanterBrick, C., & Yehuda, R. (2014). Resilience definitions, theory, and challenges: Interdisciplinary perspectives. *European Journal of Psychotraumatology*, *5*(1), 25338.

*Spurrell, M. T., & McFarlane, A. C. (1993). Post-traumatic stress disorder and coping after a natural disaster. *Social Psychiatry & Psychiatric Epidemiology*, *28*(4), 194.

*Sripada, R. K., Pfeiffer, P. N., Rauch, S. A. M., & Bohnert, K. M. (2015). Social support and mental health treatment among persons with PTSD: Results of a nationally representative survey. *Psychiatric Services*, *66*, 65–71. https://doi.org/10.1176/appi.ps.201400029 PMID: 2526988.

*Stanley, I. H., Boffa, J. W., Hom, M. A., Kimbrel, N. A., & Joiner, T. E. (2017). Differences in psychiatric symptoms and barriers to mental health care between volunteer and career firefighters. *Psychiatry Research*, *247*, 236–242.

*Stanley, I. H., Hom, M. A., & Joiner, T. E. (2016). A systematic review of suicidal thoughts and behaviors among police officers, firefighters, EMTs, and paramedics. *Clinical Psychology Review*, *44*, 25–44.

*Stanley, I. H., Hom, M. A., Spencer-Thomas, S., & Joiner, T. E. (2017). Examining anxiety sensitivity as a mediator of the association between PTSD symptoms and suicide risk among women firefighters. *Journal of Anxiety Disorders, 50*, 94–102.

*Sterud, T., Hem, E., Ekeberg, Ø., & Lau, B. (2008). Occupational stressors and its organizational and individual correlates: A nationwide study of Norwegian ambulance personnel. *BMC Emergency Medicine, 8*(1), 1–11.

*Thomas, É., Saumier, D., & Brunet, A. (2012). Peritraumatic distress and the course of posttraumatic stress disorder symptoms: A meta-analysis. *The Canadian Journal of Psychiatry, 57*(2), 122–129.

*Tuckey, M. R., & Scott, J. E. (2014). Group critical incident stress debriefing with emergency services personnel: A randomized controlled trial. *Anxiety, Stress, & Coping, 27*(1), 38–54.

*Van der Velden, P. G., Christiaanse, B., Kleber, R. J., Marcelissen, F. G. H., Dorresteijn, S. A. M., Drogendijk, A. N., … Olff, M. (2006). The effects of disaster exposure and post-disaster critical incidents on intrusions, avoidance reactions and health problems among firefighters: A comparative study. *Stress, Trauma, and Crisis, 9*(2), 73–93.

*Vargas de Barros, V., Martins, L. F., Saitz, R., Bastos, R. R., & Ronzani, T. M. (2013). Mental health conditions, individual and job characteristics and sleep disturbances among firefighters. *Journal of Health Psychology, 18*(3), 350–358.

VERBI Software Consult Sozialforschung GmbH. (1989–2017). *MAXQDA software for qualitative data analysis (Version 12.3.2.)*. Berlin, Germany.

*Vogel, L. (2017). Health on the hill: Six health bills to watch. *CMAJ, 189*(44), E1373–E1374. https://doi.org/10.1503/cmaj.109-5514.

*Wagner, D., Heinrichs, M., & Ehlert, U. (1998). Prevalence of symptoms of posttraumatic stress disorder in German professional firefighters. *American Journal of Psychiatry, 155*(12), 1727–1732.

*Wagner, S. L., McFee, J. A., & Martin, C. A. (2010). Mental health implications of fire service membership. *Traumatology, 16*(2), 26.

*Whealin, J. M., Ruzek, J. I., & Southwick, S. (2008). Cognitive–behavioral theory and preparation for professionals at risk for trauma exposure. *Trauma, Violence, & Abuse, 9*(2), 100–113.

*Witteveen, A. B., Bramsen, I., Twisk, J. W. R., Huizink, A. C., Slottje, P., Smid, T., & Van Der Ploeg, H. M. (2007). Psychological distress of rescue workers eight and one-half years after professional involvement in the Amsterdam air disaster. *The Journal of Nervous and Mental Disease, 195*(1), 31–40.

*Witteveen, A. B., Van der Ploeg, E., Bramsen, I., Huizink, A. C., Slottje, P., Smid, T., & Van der Ploeg, H. M. (2006). Dimensionality of the posttraumatic stress response among police officers and fire fighters: An evaluation of two self-report scales. *Psychiatry Research, 141*(2), 213–228.

*Yip, J., Zeig-Owens, R., Hall, C. B., Webber, M. P., Olivieri, B., Schwartz, T., … Prezant, D. J. (2016). Health conditions as mediators of the association between World Trade Center exposure and health-related quality of life in firefighters and EMS workers. *Journal of Occupational & Environmental Medicine, 58*(2), 200–206.

11 Correctional Officers

Experiences of Potentially Psychologically Traumatic Events and Mental Health Injuries

Rosemary Ricciardelli, Nicole Gerarda Power, and Daniella Simas Medeiros

Introduction

There is a large body of evidence demonstrating the negative impacts on the physical and mental health of workers of workplace violence (Baines & Cunningham, 2011); bullying and harassment (Mayhew & Chappell, 2007); occupational stressors (Bourbonnais et al., 2007; Mayhew & Chappell, 2007); and non-standard (e.g., shift work) and precarious employment relations (Quinlan, Mayhew, & Mohle, 2001). In addition to the impact of occupational stressors (e.g., staff shortages, inconsistent leadership styles, shift work, public scrutiny) on individual workers' well-being (Carleton et al., 2020), researchers have demonstrated the impacts on workers' families and communities, livelihoods, and the productivity of organizations. Regarding economic impact, Shain (2009) estimates that the implementation of organization-wide and managerial interventions aimed at reducing harm to the mental health of employees could save the Canadian economy between 3 and 11 billion dollars a year, while contributing to increases in productivity, social capital, and efficiency. Perhaps motivated by the recognition of the costs associated with occupational stressors, scholars and the public have been paying more attention to occupation-related mental health over the last decade (Carleton et al., 2018; Duxbury & Higgins, 2001; Ricciardelli et al., 2018).

In Canada, federal and provincial jurisdictions are mandating employers to create psychologically safer workplaces that can include assessments of mental health hazards and risks, as well as implementation of proactive measures to at least partially safeguard employee health (Shain, 2009). Public concerns about Posttraumatic Stress Disorder (PTSD; American Psychiatric Association [APA], 2013) in particular appear to be influencing legislative changes (see House of Commons Public Safety Committee Report, Parliament of Canada, 2016). Much of this legislation centres on compensation for PTSD or other mental health injury via presumption of an occupation-related cause, such as exposure to one or more traumatic events; however, the specifics of the legislation vary across provinces (see

DOI: 10.4324/9781351134637-12

Keefe, Bornstein, & Neis, 2018). At the time of writing, the governments of British Columbia, New Brunswick, Saskatchewan, Ontario, Manitoba, Alberta, Prince Edward Island, Nova Scotia, Newfoundland and Labrador, and the Yukon have rebuttable presumptive legislation, though the type of psychological injury covered and qualifying occupations vary. In their review of provincial and territorial legislation in Canada, Keefe, Bornstein and Neis (2018) found that most presumptive legislation is limited to first-responders, front-line workers or emergency response workers. Some provinces (e.g. Saskatchewan, Prince Edward Island) extend presumptive legislation to all occupations. Across jurisdictions, legislation requires a professional diagnosis using the Diagnostic and Statistical Manual of Mental Disorders. Some jurisdictions limit presumption to PTSD, while others include a broader range of psychological injury (e.g., British Columbia, Saskatchewan, Prince Edward Island). Finally, jurisdictions tend to define the kinds of workplace events to which the legislation applies. While most jurisdictions cover exposure to a single traumatic event and cumulative exposures, legislation applies to exposures that are considered extraordinary, horrific, shocking or violent (Keefe, Bornstein, & Neis, 2018, p. 14). In other words, legislation does not account for the potentially psychologically injurious impacts of everyday or "normal" work experiences.

The variability among regulatory approaches to compensable occupational stressors highlights two main tensions: first, how to designate compensable occupational groups; and second, how to define occupational stressors. There have been progressive changes in legislation acknowledging PTSD among first responders and some other public safety personnel (e.g., border services, communications officials, firefighters, paramedics, police; CIPSRT, 2019) that have brought positive outcomes to some workers who have experienced, or continue to experience, PTSD (see Hall et al., 2019). Nevertheless, other workers in high-risk environments or those who have experienced potentially psychologically traumatic events, defined as "a stressful event that may cause psychological trauma" (CIPSRT, 2019), or other occupational stressors that do not meet the legislative criteria have been largely excluded from compensation.

In the current chapter, we consider the case of correctional workers—who are sometimes not included as a qualifying occupational category in presumptive legislation—and examine how correctional officers' accounts of occupation-related potentially psychologically traumatic events and subsequent stress challenge the limited scope of legislation regarding compensation for mental health injury and PTSD. Correctional officers in Canada and elsewhere work in environments characterized by overcrowding of prisons (Public Services Foundation of Canada, 2015), understaffing (Martin et al., 2012), and insufficient programming for prisoners. Correctional workplace conditions have been linked to increased reports of stress; perceived or actual instances of violence; and victimization, burnout, and mental health illnesses (e.g., Boudoukha et al., 2013; Gordon, Proulx, & Grant, 2013). We argue that legislative approaches to compensation for occupational stressors should reflect how potentially psychologically traumatic events are actually experienced in real life on the job. Correctional officers are frequently exposed to diverse potentially psychologically traumatic events as a function of their daily occupational duties (Carleton et al., 2019; Ricciardelli & Power, 2020; Ricciardelli, 2019); as such, correctional officers should be included in presumptive legislation to support their mental health. Drawing on interviews with provincial correctional officers, we offer a complex interpretation of the relationship among exposure to potentially psychologically traumatic events, work processes, and health that conceptualizes trauma as embedded in the labour process. Rather than understanding PTSD and other mental health injuries as responses to a specific anomalous workplace event or events, our understanding of correctional officers' experiences suggests that mental health injuries can result from the common, everyday conditions, and organizational elements (see Baines, 2006; Baines & Cunningham, 2011; Ricciardelli, 2018, for similar arguments in different work environments). In doing so, we enter into the ongoing and controversial debate about the nature of potentially psychologically traumatic events and PTSD. We argue for recognizing the injurious nature of diverse traumatic events and other occupational stressors within a framework that recognizes cumulative experience.

We divide our chapter into three sections. First, we present an overview of the Canadian correctional system and the specific carceral space in which the men and women in our sample have worked. Second, we briefly review our methods and then move to a description of our results. Third, we offer some thoughts about how best to think about and address PTSD and occupational stressors in the context of correctional work.

Contextualizing Correctional Services

Canadian correctional services function as one arm of the three-pronged Canadian criminal justice system—the other two being courts and policing. Different levels of government, federal versus provincial or territorial and often different ministries or departments, administer youth and adult correctional services (Correctional Service Canada [CSC], 2014). Correctional services in turn are broken down into 14 separate but connected systems—the federal system that houses individuals sentenced to two or more years in prison and the provincial and territorial systems that house those remanded into custody, or sentenced to, a maximum of two years less a day. Nonetheless, some provincial and territorial prisons house federally sentenced prisoners under specific circumstances (see Ricciardelli, 2014). In the current chapter, we limit our discussion to adult correctional services at the provincial level, which is the responsibility of provincial departments of justice or public safety rather than of Correctional Service Canada (CSC, 2014; Ricciardelli, 2019).

Correctional officers, often referred to as prison officers in the international literature, are responsible for the care, confinement, and supervision of the people in their custody (CSC, 2019); accordingly, correctional officers perform a wide variety of job tasks deemed essential to the operation of prisons, including maintaining the safety of prisoners, co-workers, visitors and themselves. One of the distinguishing characteristics of correctional officers' work is they are responsible for people who are held, often against their preference (Ricciardelli, 2019; Ricciardelli, Power, & Simas Medeiros, 2018).

There is a discrepancy between Canada's crime rate and its incarceration rates. Canada's crime rate has been stable or has steadily decreased for the past 50 years, yet the number of incarcerated persons had continued to rise (Brosnahan, 2013) until quite recently. The number of employed correctional officers has also increased, but not proportionately; consequently, many penal institutions (before Covid-19) operate well above prisoner capacity and are understaffed. Overcrowded facilities intensify correctional officers' work and take a toll on their occupational health and safety (Ricciardelli, 2019; Ricciardelli, Power, & Simas Medeiros, 2018; Weinrath, 2009). Martin and colleagues (2012) demonstrate that correctional officers in crowded facilities report high levels of stress related to issues of safety, increased violence, and impaired job performance, and correctional officers attribute chronic health issues (e.g., headaches, obesity, heart attacks, diabetes, weak immune systems, alcoholism) to their stressful work environment. Correctional officers also work in environmental conditions that have negative impacts on their health and well-being. For example, a review of the prison system in Newfoundland and Labrador described the environmental conditions in which correctional officers work as deplorable (e.g., built-up dirt and grime, paint peeling off the walls, holes in the walls; poor air quality; poor mattress conditions) and harmful to the health and the sense of well-being of both prisoners and staff (Poirier, Brown, & Carlson, 2008). A United States study by Bierie (2012) connected the harsh environmental conditions of the prison (e.g., noise, dilapidation, clutter, lack of privacy) to physical and mental health issues for prison staff. Staff who perceived harsh working conditions were likely to report negative impacts on their psychological health (e.g., depression, concentration problems) and their physical health (e.g., increased headaches, back pain, and stomach aches).

The prison workspace is also shaped by an omnipresent potential for violence, which has implications for the health and well-being of employees (see Ricciardelli, 2014; Ricciardelli & Sit, 2016; Ricciardelli, Power, & Simas Medeiros, 2018; Wolff et al., 2007). Correctional officers, like prisoners, are often victims of physical or verbal assaults as well as of threats of violence at work (Ricciardelli & Gazso, 2013; Ricciardelli, Power, & Simas Medeiros, 2018; Ricciardelli, 2019). Investigating the relationship between working conditions and health and safety in federal corrections, Samak's research (2003) documents "alarmingly" high levels of harassment and

300 *Ricciardelli, Power, and Simas Medeiros*

finds that occupational stressors "spilled over" into the private lives of officers. Similarly, a 2014 study published by Correctional Service Canada (CSC) documents the excessive violence experienced by federal correctional officers in Canada. Among the 122 correctional officers included in the study, 15% reported being physically assaulted more than three times. Other types of potentially psychologically traumatic events reported by correctional officers include witnessing physical assault and murder, and responding to attempted death by suicide and riots (CSC, 2014). The authors reported that 17% of the correctional officers in their sample had been clinically diagnosed with PTSD (CSC, 2014). The Canadian Institute of Public Safety Research and Treatment (CIPSRT) administered a prevalence study from September 2016 to January 2017 to measure, among other mental health injuries, the rates of PTSD symptoms among correctional workers (Carleton et al., 2018; Ricciardelli, Carleton, Groll, & Cramm, 2018). The researchers report that 54.6% of correctional workers screened positive for one or more mental illnesses; a rate of self-reported positive screens much higher than the 10.1% rate of all diagnosed mental health disorders in the general population (Statistics Canada, 2018). Approximately 29.1% of correctional worker participants screened positive for PTSD, 31.1% for major depressive disorder, and 23.6% for generalized anxiety disorder (Carleton et al., 2018).

The available Canadian prevalence results align with results from international research on the impact of prison violence on health. In France, researchers examining the relationships among interpersonal violence (e.g., a prisoner assault on a correctional officer), burnout, and posttraumatic stress report that, in a random sample of 240 correctional officers, 233 had been assaulted by a prisoner, either verbally, physically or with a weapon, and 224 officers had experienced other potentially psychologically traumatic events, such as witnessing violent assaults or completed or attempted suicides by prisoners (Boudoukha et al., 2013). In fact, Boudoukha et al. (2013) concluded that correctional officers who experienced high levels of emotional exhaustion, depersonalization, stress, intrusion, avoidance, and hyper-reactivity were at risk of developing PTSD. Similarly, researchers in the United States suggest that correctional officers are more likely than other government employees or public safety personnel to use sick leave to deal with a physical injury or to take a "mental health day" (Lambert, Hogan, & Altheimer, 2010).

In Canada, the Trudeau Liberal government elected in 2015 spoke about rescinding the "tough on crime" legislative changes introduced by the previous government (e.g., the Safe Streets and Communities Act formerly known as Bill C-10). The rescinding of legislative changes was expected to improve prison conditions by, among other things, reducing overcrowding (see Heck, 2016; Killpatrick, 2015; Prutischi, 2015); however, correctional officers continued to work in harsh environments, characterized by overcrowding, understaffing and high rates of employee stress, burnout, and absenteeism (see Ricciardelli, 2019). In Canada, full-time officers are generally unionized, but there is increasing reliance on casual and part-time staff who are not. Correctional officers tend to do shift work (12-hour rotating shifts) and overtime; in some cases, correctional officers are mandated to work on weekends and holidays (Nova Scotia Government & General Employees Union, 2006–2009). Part-time employees are not guaranteed minimum or maximum hours of work (Nova Scotia Government & General Employees Union, 2006–2009). Nevertheless, few researchers have explicitly investigated the health and well-being of provincial and territorial correctional officers. Drawing on semi-structured interviews with provincial officers, we explore the nature and extent of potentially psychologically traumatic events and other occupational stressors. Correctional officers' understandings and experiences of potentially psychologically traumatic events and other occupational stressors appear more complex than is currently reflected by compensation legislation. In addition, the factors that affect their health and well-being stem from elements common to the institutional prison environment that *should be* largely preventable with proper resources and enforcement of existing health and safety regulations. Notably, very few of our participants reported having mental health problems before starting work in corrections, and most participants reported that the carceral work environment had negatively impacted their mental health and emotional well-being.

Methods

To examine the extent to which prison conditions affect correctional officers' health and well-being, we draw on semi-structured interviews conducted over a three-year period (2012–2015) with over 130 correctional officers working in provincial or territorial prisons. Interview questions focused on, among other things, the occupational role and responsibilities of correctional officers, relations between management and correctional officers, and how work in the prison impacted correctional officers' health and safety as well as their personal lives. Participation was voluntary and participants included both self-identifying men and women employed full-time, part-time, and casually. In the current chapter, we limit our analysis to the transcripts of correctional officers working with adult prisoner populations housed in facilities for men or women. The semi-structured nature of the interviews provided the interviewer with the flexibility necessary to follow emergent conversational paths and to create a safe space for correctional officers to discuss their experiences openly. Transcripts were coded thematically (see Strauss and Corbin, 1990) in line with a constructed grounded approach, focusing on self-reported health impacts (Charmaz, 2006). We do not intend to provide diagnoses; instead, we are documenting correctional officers' self-reported health impacts to demonstrate the effects of working under stressful conditions based on how correctional officers say they experience their workplaces and associated impacts on their health and well-being.

Results

Consistent themes emerged across our interviews including that correctional work is stressful, that the correctional environment is stressful, that there are insufficient supports in place to recognize and address the stressors, and that the stressors have a negative impact on the psychological well-being of officers. In other words, correctional officers understand their work and their workplace to be damaging. Prison work includes attending to a range of critical, and sometimes violent, incidents as well as managing the everyday tensions among prisoners and the harassment, and sometimes the violence, directed at correctional officers by prisoners. In the remainder of the current chapter, we unpack the realities of correctional work as experienced by the research participants and we discuss the results that emerged from our interviews. First, the interviews document how mental health injuries can result from a single traumatic event exposure or from cumulative potentially psychologically traumatic event exposures associated with the generalized context of workplace violence. Second, the interviews document difficulties in accessing care for some potentially psychologically traumatic events and other occupational stressors. Third, we explore how the organization and conditions of prison work exacerbate, and in some cases produce, occupational stressors and the associated psychological effects. Fourth, we show how, without appropriate workplace supports, correctional officers feel they must cope with occupational stressors individually using informal means outside of work, and how their reality impacts their personal well-being as well as their familial and social relationships. Finally, we argue that correctional officers should be included in presumptive legislation and we consider some of the consequences of failing to do so.

Potentially Psychologically Traumatic Events, Critical Incidents, and Mental Health

As part of their work, correctional officers are subjected to diverse potentially psychologically traumatic events, some of which may be categorized as critical incidents (i.e., a designation used to distinguish potentially psychologically traumatic events (PPTE) thought more likely to cause a mental health injury; CIPSRT, 2019), including suicides, murders, riots, assaults, and hostage takings. A correctional officer may experience potentially psychologically traumatic events directly or indirectly, and in either case the exposure may cause a mental health injury. In addition, there is evidence that any PPTE may be associated with one or more mental health injuries, including PTSD (Carleton et al., 2019), which raises important questions and caveats regarding any classification system for critical incidents that is not defined by the individual person experiencing the PPTE. One correctional officer explains:

Correctional Officers 303

> So, let's say you and I are best friends and somebody dies in your unit, and I'm called to the, what's called the, "medical alert", which means you're calling for the nurses to come down and all available correctional officers come assist you with this medical issue you're having. And I get there and see you either with your finger in the neck with someone trying to cut themselves open and trying to stop bleeding and I can't get to help you because there's four or five other people trying to help you. I'm helpless watching you go through this and I have to watch you do CPR on somebody that's dead. There's blood coming out of them, they're bleeding all over, there's water coming out of them and you're doing. I'm still, it may not be me doing it, but me watching you go through it is just as bad or worse for me.

As evidenced in the words of this officer, such events can have a significant impact on bystanders. Critical incidents and other potentially psychologically traumatic events can also impact employees who must continue the routine work required in the prison. For example, another officer describes being left alone on the unit while their partner dealt with a riot:

> I was a casual actually... it was very stressful for me because I just started... I was left in my unit by myself. Everybody was secured but I was in my bubble wondering what was going on down in the unit. And I was left there for 12 hours.... I was left by myself for pretty much for the rest of the shift because my partner was gone dealing with the riot. So that was stressful for the fact for not knowing what was going on.

In cases like the one described above, a traumatic event diverts correctional officers away from their routine work, leaving their co-workers to, at least temporarily, manage the relatively increased workload. Depending on their level of experience, officers may feel more or less prepared to take on the increased workload, which may include working alone. In the aforementioned case, the correctional officer had recently been hired as a casual employee and was, thus, new to the job. Staffing issues, like being understaffed or out of communication with a partner, as well as other workplace conditions, can all mediate the impact of critical incidents. For example, some correctional officers reported experiencing psychological distress when required by management to stay on shift after a critical incident and to complete paperwork, instead of being able to take needed time away. In other words, irrespective of whether a potentially psychologically traumatic event is a critical incident, the normal work practices and the conditions of prison work may exacerbate the impacts of such events.

Officers expressed two main responses to their experiences of potentially psychologically traumatic events classified as critical incidents: some reported feeling "anxious", "scared", or "afraid" in their work environment

304 *Ricciardelli, Power, and Simas Medeiros*

after such incidents, while others reported little emotional impact or feeling emotionally detached. Various factors (e.g., years of experience; the target of the violence) can explain the different reactions of correctional officers (see Ricciardelli & Power, 2020). In some cases, correctional officers reported difficulty performing operational duties following a critical incident: "I couldn't write a report for a couple of days…" Especially in cases where correctional officers had been assaulted by a prisoner, they reported a decreased sense of safety on duty: "I didn't feel that [fear] before, but now I feel it, so to live with that every day is, you know, it's hard." Another correctional officer reported: "And I mean if you were to ask me prior to that, I would have been [like] 'yeah, I feel safe' but after that happened, I don't trust anybody anymore." Similarly, some admitted becoming "nervous" around prisoners after having been assaulted:

> I can't go into the male units yet, I can't. I can't even you know because we have two male units. They're so similar to each other in say design or whatever so I decided to go with the one that it didn't happen in and I couldn't make, I couldn't make it down to the hallway, my legs just got numb, I just wanted to puke and I turned around and I just said it ain't worth it, it ain't worth the stress today.
>
> But even now, when I'm in the day rooms and they're coming around me, it's just, I'm the first one to say you need to back up because you're too close to me which normally I'd be right there and wouldn't care and other officers, I seen one sitting down the other day sitting down to the table, doing paperwork or whatever and the inmates were just all gathered around her and my anxiety just went through the roof, cause I'm like oh my God, they could smash you, bang your head and you wouldn't even know it.

Both of the excerpts above document how experiencing a critical incident that involves bodily harm directed against correctional officers produced a sense of concern and anxiety about safety that persists well after the violent event. The participants reported that anxiety can manifest physically (as when the correctional officer's legs feel numb and she feels physically sick) and impact their view of, and interactions with, prisoners (e.g., insisting that prisoners keep their distance). Correctional officers were more likely to report emotional distress when they or a co-worker, as opposed to prisoners, were the targets of a critical incident (see Ricciardelli & Power, 2020). In contrast, most correctional officers reported feeling detached, somewhat numb, or desensitized to prisoner-on-prisoner violence. Emotional detachment may be a coping strategy to deal with the pervasiveness of violence in the prison context, but can impact how correctional officers perceive prisoners and do their jobs (Crawley & Crawley, 2008)—a point to which we will return in the next section.

In addition to self-reports of feeling "traumatized", depressed, and anxious, a significant subset of our sample spontaneously reported a personal

Correctional Officers 305

diagnosis of PTSD or knowing someone diagnosed with PTSD. Other correctional officers described experiencing many "symptoms" consistent with PTSD diagnostic criteria. Correctional officers described potentially psychologically traumatic events that involved exposure to bodily fluids, including salvia, urine or faeces as particularly problematic (Ricciardelli, 2019; Ricciardelli, Power, & Simas-Mederios, 2018):

> You know, you kind of have to watch your back and a year ago I got shit-bombed in the dayroom as kind of a warning and I was alone in the dayroom by myself and I was doing the round and an inmate had a whole cup full of feces and he throw it right in my face, right? So, that's why I get emotional about it... And I was still had to see male offenders in the East in the garage because they would bring the Sheriff's truck in, offload the females and go to the male side, and there were a couple times, you know, they'd be like, hey [nick name removed], how did it feel to eat shit and then all the female inmates knew and... It was just really badly dealt with and I don't think management knew how to deal with it because it hadn't really happened to a female or a guard before.

The correctional officer above is describing being significantly affected by a traumatic event, underscoring the potential impact of being targeted for a faecal bombing, and describing the subsequent harassment she endured because of inappropriate workplace accommodation following the incident. Correctional officers also reported that the follow-up procedures for potentially psychologically traumatic events involving exposure to body fluids (e.g., health screenings and testing for infections, such as HIV/AIDS, Hepatitis B or C, could be required for up to a year) produced substantial fear and anxiety. For example, screening is required after being spat on, which is such a common event that the potential psychological impact is often discounted; however, the cumulative effects of routine exposure to any traumatic event that requires testing can be psychologically injurious (Carleton et al., 2019), as can be the testing process and the associated uncertainty (Carleton, 2016). Many correctional officers indicated that they would rather be stabbed than spat on for this very reason. After exposure to bodily fluids, a correctional officer explained: "I went to a hospital that night and they basically said the guy [prisoner] had Hep C and HIV... I had a year of blood tests and everything..." Another officer explained his reported good fortune:

> They [medical staff] had said luckily I was wearing, I think two shirts, so the second shirt seemed to cushion his teeth marks more because had their not been he probably would have basically torn off flesh. [*Did you still have to go through testing then?*]. Oh yeah.

Correctional officers described waiting for tests results as distressing, in part because of the uncertainty of the results and the long wait period

306 *Ricciardelli, Power, and Simas Medeiros*

required for some results. Given that such testing is required for many PPTE, not only PPTE designated as critical incidents, correctional officers likely experience pervasive physical and psychological effects from repeated exposures to bodily fluids and subsequent testing.

Everyday Violence in Prison

In addition to the more egregious types of potentially psychologically traumatic events (e.g., faecal bombing, responding to death by suicide), correctional officers, particularly those working in remand centres or higher security institutions, described their everyday work environments as characterized by a general and pervasive threat of violence. Violence was described as an omnipresent "part of the job". A large part of the correctional officer's job involves managing tensions and negotiating how best to enforce the rules without inciting violence from and among prisoners. For correctional officers, proactively managing violence was described as especially difficult because of deteriorating conditions of confinement and inadequate staffing and material resources (see Boyd, 2011; Ricciardelli, Power, & Simas Medeiros, 2018).

Correctional officers described circumstances that triggered violence among prisoners; for example, when prisoners are placed on a unit with others with whom they are not compatible (e.g., persons who have a history of conflict, members of opposing gangs). Officers must pay special attention to the complex, and often changing, social relationships in prison to diffuse or prevent violence (Crawley & Crawley, 2008; Martin et al., 2012; Ricciardelli, Power, & Simas Medeiros, 2018; Ricciardelli, 2019; Weinrath, 2016). Correctional officers reported arguments, fistfights among prisoners, and their use of everyday objects (e.g., toothbrushes) to handcraft weapons ("shanks") as normal risks of the job. As one correctional officer explained:

> This last stabbing I was involved with, one of the young staff grabbed the offender before he fell to the floor and was, so many puncture holes in him; it was holding a strainer up and watching the water come down through. And, we just get so accustomed to stuff like that in this building.

Correctional officers suggested that percolating just beneath the surface of the mundane prison environment was the potential for violence, injury, and death among prisoners, with implications for the safety and well-being of officers. Correctional officers also reported being the targets of verbal harassment, threats, assault, and badgering from prisoners. For some, being targeted was an everyday experience. During interviews, the impact of verbal abuse on some correctional officers became evident when the participant broke down in tears or expressed anxiety while telling their story.

Correctional Officers 307

Correctional officers explained how verbal abuse can escalate into physical assaults on officers and, more often, how correctional officers became targets of verbal abuse from prisoners for "just doing their job". Correctional officers reported that prisoners most often target colleagues who adhered strictly to formal procedures and policies. As one correctional officer explained:

> The only reason she [the correctional officer] was attacked... is because she locked down a range and they didn't like it... Just doing her job. And the other guard [who was also attacked] was a regular officer and maybe she wrote more levels than she should of. But, she stuck to policy and procedure, and there's nothing wrong with that. She did her job. She did her job, and she got targeted.

As suggested above, the constant threat of conflict is built into the occupational role of controlling prisoners. For example, the nearly everyday task of moving prisoners often resulted in violence:

> I went into a day room and we had a female offender in there... my Captain asked me to remove her from one day room [and move her] to the other because she was acting [up]. So we ran [to] her cell, packin' up her stuff and she gave me a hard time, just arguing with me and so, she was packin' up her and she was, so instead of that, I said "You know what forget it, you just move, we'll just go". I said "I'll pack up your stuff". And with that, I went to grab for her bag and she hauled off and she punched me in the face three times and knocked me out, I was unconscious.
>
> Well, the, the, we were moving someone from the, for instance from the West unit to seg and half way there he just wanted to fight. [*Just angry?*] Yeah. So, we basically had to use force on him and then we got him there and then he started wrestling with us, we were just holding him down trying to take off his cuffs and, and then I can re-call me goin', my eyes are lit up and I was like, the fuckin' guy is bitin' me. Just had me here with his teeth and then I could feel blood and then I was like, but then, same as now, you don't wanna hit him because...

As demonstrated by the examples above, the movement and placement of prisoners can be difficult because of tense social relationships among prisoners, all of which is exacerbated by prison overcrowding (see Ricciardelli, Power, & Simas Medeiros, 2018; Weinrath, 2009). As a correctional officer explained, prisoner overcrowding means "double-bunking" (i.e., two persons per cell) and sometimes "triple-bunking" (i.e., three persons per cell) is required and understandably resisted by prisoners. Correctional officers are then left with the impossible task of trying to find

308   Ricciardelli, Power, and Simas Medeiros

a bunk for a new prisoner and, at the same time, managing tensions that arise from double-bunking:

> I have to find somewhere for him [the prisoner] to go. I come in the dayroom, I bring him in. So, I bring him in and I have to lock him in a cell. And they're all double bunked and they're saying there's no room. I'm saying well, we're gonna have to make room right. There's no double bunking. Well, listen, you know you might think there's no double bunking… he has to be double bunked somewhere. So, they're saying you know I have a medical note, I have this, I have that. So, I say well how about this, he has to be locked in somewhere so I'll lock him in. You say you have a medical note, I'll follow up on that and if he does I'll find somewhere else for him to go. And if not this is where he's gonna stay… So, I said if you do have a no double bunking healthcare I'll come back and we'll move him into another cell. One of the inmates stood up and said this is fucking bullshit, I don't give a fuck, as soon as they open his door I'm gonna throw him off the top tier. Really, if you're gonna try and throw him off the top tier, that's your own problem. He's locked in there for 24 hours I don't know why you're yelling at me. And then he spit at me. So, I said alright, time for you to lock up. You know, you don't spit at me. And then he just attacked me, charged at me and attacked me. So, I didn't even have time to call a code, I tried to call a code but I had to stop because I would have got punched in the face.

Practices of double- and triple-bunking that have become "routine" and can provoke resistance among prisoners as a direct result of the larger institutional problem of overcrowding. Correctional officers have little to no control over the broader management of correctional services, but must deal with the consequences of organizational policies in their everyday work. Correctional officers are expected to carry out routine duties and to manage the uncertain responses of prisoners, including violent responses that ensue. Given the pervasiveness of violence in prisons and the lack of control that correctional officers can exercise to change their conditions of work, correctional officers reported simply accepting violence as part of the job. Correctional officers, like prisoners, reported a need to appear unfazed by the regular exposures to violence and other potentially psychologically traumatic events as part of coping with the occupational context. In practice, appearing unfazed means correctional officers carefully manage the presentation of their emotions for fear of being "eaten alive". Correctional officers reported also feeling that they must at least appear emotionally detached. For example, one officer states that "you will definitely fall apart if you let them know if they got to you. I wouldn't give them the satisfaction of knowing." This kind of emotional labour (Hochschild, 1983) must be understood in part as a coping response to the conditions of work in prison, a response that has consequences for correctional

Correctional Officers 309

officers' well-being and that often deters help-seeking behaviour. Similarly, researchers have shown that service professionals must manage their presentation of self, retaining control of their emotions by repressing feelings and appearing even-keeled despite diverse stressors. Studies by Baines (2006) and Baines and Cunningham (2011) found that social service workers frequently tolerated being injured by their clients to protect the professional–client care relationship as well as their jobs in an organizational context of spending cuts and job insecurity. The organizational norms for social service workers resulted in under-reporting of violence to management and downplaying injuries sustained and the stress resulting from interactions with clients (Baines, 2006; Baines & Cunninham, 2011). Correctional workers also operate under an organizational norm that requires tolerating harsh working conditions (see Ricciardelli & Power, 2020 for discussion of the relationship between the emotional labour of correctional officers and mental health injury).

Coping and Impacts on Personal and Social Life

Correctional officers reported engaging in few help-seeking strategies despite their repeated exposure to traumatic events that can impact the safety and well-being of prisoners, co-workers and themselves. A minority of correctional officers reported seeking some kind of counselling or were under the care of a physician for assistance in dealing with psychological injury and occupational stress: "I suffered from posttraumatic stress ... I still suffer from posttraumatic stress and still go to therapists." However, many correctional officers reported coping with psychological distress informally and unofficially—or not at all. Beyond the minority of correctional officers who received formal counselling or medical care, the respondents who did describe how they coped with psychological distress disclosed taking antidepressants or anti-anxiety medications or turning to other substances (e.g., alcohol). Correctional officers who reported taking antidepressants or anti-anxiety medications did not always report having had a formal diagnosis, and many of those who reported taking prescribed medications had not formally disclosed the information to their employer. Others opted to cope by using other drugs and alcohol:

> I'm very anxious. Okay, anxiety is—if you talk to anybody who has any type of, like the type work we do, we are all anxious. Like, we all have anxiety and most of us are medicated. And this week I got home and I'm like, oh my god! I've never—do you know they say some people pass their stress like reaching for the bottle, or reaching for this and I was actually thinking, "Ok, I'm—like I—this, like, physical feeling needs to go", like, what could I do and I was actually, "Geez we have alcohol". I—I—I never—never reached for it, but it crossed my mind and I'm like, "Woah. Something is wrong here."

310 Ricciardelli, Power, and Simas Medeiros

Correctional officers tend to substitute informal strategies for help-seeking behaviours and to avoid disclosure in the workplace, at least partially reflecting inadequate organizational and managerial support and, in some cases, an outright hostility on the part of management towards requests for accommodation. Some correctional officers reported their concerns and complaints were downplayed, unrecognized, or ignored by management and by the prison organization more broadly. In particular, participants reported being discouraged by management and co-workers alike from expressing emotions at work that could be perceived as weakness (see Ricciardelli & Power, 2020). To illustrate, a correctional officer explained that, after responding to a suicide, a correctional officer must "go back to your unit and finish your rounds ... Oh, it's traumatizing." In response to the interviewer asking if a correctional officer can get relieved from their shift after a traumatic event, the correctional officer replied, "Oh God, no. Unless you tell them that you're sick, 'I'm goin' home, I'm sick' and then you get looked at as being weak." In this interview, the correctional officer points to an inappropriate managerial response to a potentially psychologically traumatic events (e.g., insisting that correctional officers complete their shifts) and an informal but normative expectation that correctional officers must not complain and should instead simply get on with the job. As an officer explained: "Nobody wants to really admit that we're sensitive and have feelings and are affected by things, right? That's what I find."

Given the severity of many potentially psychologically traumatic events, the everyday experience of workplace violence, and a lack of organizational support, correctional officers explain that occupational stressors spills over into their familial and social relationships outside the workplace. One participant described the "spillover" in his account of an incident in which he is reminded of a prisoner suicide while doing laundry at home:

> [Name], he went and hung himself and we're doing the laundry and I went to empty the dryer [Name of town where person was from] kid who hung himself and I went to, I opened up the dryer door and when I opened up the dryer door, I guess I had the dryer overloaded, and I went, to take and reach, they were washin' their bed linen, and I pulled the sheet and the sheet was all twisted. It was all twisted, and I sort of froze, it was just the only one time it had ever happened to me and I sort of froze and my wife had come in behind me about 10 seconds, and she said "what's wrong?" And I was sort of lost in a gaze almost and that was the only time it had happened to me, and when I, 'cause I pulled it out and I was lookin' at the sheet and it was just like... and I probably hadn't even thought by that time, it had been three or four months before the thought had even, by the time we started talkin' about this, it hadn't really entered my mind.

The officer's story above demonstrates the impact of work experiences on his ability to do normal day-to-day tasks at home (e.g., knotted bed linens

Correctional Officers   311

when doing laundry triggered a memory of a critical incident at work, which in turn caused him to freeze). Another officer from the same institution, points to how management's failure to address the impacts of a traumatic event on his health and well-being has consequences for his family:

> You [management] don't care. My family has to deal with that not you, you know what I mean? But they were only concerned about the offender in regards to that. They didn't and I just, basically at one point I had to shut up because I was so internally mad and so frustrated. I was so mad and so emotional about it that I couldn't say anything because anything that I said, wasn't going to be respectful.

The officer above expresses frustration at the lack of support he received from management following a critical incident and how this lack of support translated into a downloading of the consequences onto his family. The officer reported approaching management, but more often than not officers reported keeping their mental health issues to themselves. The organizational norm to not appear weak in front of prisoners, co-workers, and management alike serves, intentionally or not, to discourage or limit help-seeking behaviour among correctional officers and perpetuates silence among colleagues and managers rather than conversation after a correctional officer has experienced a potentially psychologically traumatic event:

> That segregation unit, as far as I'm concerned, everybody's an individual. I had a terrible experience for 14 months. It was coming to the point where I was considering resignation, I was gonna quit, if they didn't move me, I was gonna quit... It was [horrible at the time], that was the straw because by that time I'd been shit bombed, I had urine thrown on me, I had been assaulted. The mental torture, right? And nobody ever spoke to me about it. My, my boss at the time [name], he was pretty good, but I never even spoke to him. Just my wife. I remember comin' home that, actually that morning [after] I was in a fist fight with a guy, and that was bad enough, [but it was] Christmas eve, right? That was bad enough, fist fightin' on Christmas Eve. Anyway, that was bad enough, and then by the time I came home that, I came home, you got your wife, your wife comin' home, "how's your day at work?" And I was like "where's the bottle of vodka?"

Again, the participant above, like many others, experienced an event that he found particularly salient alongside a host of other PPTE exposures, all of which can have serious negative consequences for his physical and mental well-being, as well as for his familial and interpersonal relationships. With no formal support from management and a lack of informal support from colleagues (e.g., talking about the incidents), he must find other ways to cope (e.g., engaging in fist fights, drinking alcohol) with consequences for his health and his wife's well-being. An additional source of stress is the possibility of being formally investigated for their actions related to incidents at work. For example, some correctional officers reported problems with work procedures and arrangements following critical incidents, including how such incidents are investigated:

> They don't charge me but [they] charged my partner for excessive use of force. So we did that, I had to go through court and all that. My partner was off for six weeks, he's still off for posttraumatic stress. I was out for six months and they suspended me 'cause they had to investigate me. The [unit] had to investigate me and they thought I was. They said "did you hit the inmate?" "No, I did everything I had to do".

Based on the above results, the impact of potentially psychologically traumatic events may be better mitigated by changes to the organizational norms, conditions of work, and labour processes that better recognize and address the needs of correctional officers before the burden of their occupational work becomes too much to bear for the officers and their families.

Discussion

Our current research results suggest that correctional officers should be included in presumptive legislation. The evidence suggests the work of correctional officers is just as potentially psychologically injurious as that of other public safety personnel and other categories of workers currently included in most presumptive legislation. In addition, our results point to normal, everyday work as potentially psychologically injurious. The organization and conditions of prison work exacerbate, and in some cases produce, occupational stressors and associated psychological effects. Correctional work in Canada and elsewhere is characterized by diverse potentially psychologically traumatic events, including generalized violence, and occupational stressors, all of which impact the mental health of correctional officers (Boudoukha et al., 2013; Carleton et al., 2019; Carleton et al., 2020). Officers in the current study described experiencing single particularly salient traumatic events that may be directly linked to a formal diagnosis of PTSD, but also underscored the cumulative impact of exposures to diverse potentially psychologically traumatic events and other occupational stressors (e.g., daily harassment; the uncertain potential for violence during routine duties). The contemporary PTSD diagnostic criteria allow for a single traumatic event or cumulative exposures to traumatic events to meet the first criterion and therein facilitate provision of a diagnosis (APA, 2013); however, our interviews with correctional officers suggest that presumptive legislation should reflect the complex realities of potentially psychologically traumatic events for correctional officers that include the everyday, "normal" parts of the job that may be injurious.

Our current research results emphasize that potentially psychologically traumatic events are embedded in the labour process of correctional work, and the impact of potentially psychologically traumatic events exposures can be intensified by how correctional officers' experiences are understood and recognized by their employer. In other words, PTSD and mental health challenges are a response to workplace anomalies as well as a response to many daily occupational elements (Carleton et al., 2020). Inadequate workplace supports and employers' refusal to provide accommodations can cause or exacerbate negative psychological outcomes for officers working in prisons. Some aspects of correctional officers' work may be difficult to change; however, potentially psychologically traumatic events including generalized workplace violence might be mitigated by changes to the organizational norms, conditions of work, and labour processes. Such changes might include additional resources, increased staffing, and improved conditions of confinement for prisoners, as well as mandatory accommodations when individual correctional officers experience potentially psychologically traumatic events as particularly impactful. Making reasonable and mandatory accommodations policy (e.g., time off work, movement to a different unit) can remove or reduce stigma and moral accusations of weakness that officers who seek help may experience after a potentially psychologically traumatic event. Mandatory accommodations shift responsibility to the employer and may mitigate negative judgements of co-workers and management by removing the onus from the individual worker to request assistance (see Ricciardelli & Power, 2020).

Our current results inform new questions regarding the cumulative impacts of daily emotional labour required to carry out correctional duties and the status of cumulative exposures to potentially psychologically traumatic events and other occupational stressors within policy and compensable legislation. The need to constantly suppress emotional responses to traumatic events may exacerbate the cumulative impact of repeated exposures; if correct, stakeholders involved with supporting correctional officer well-being will need to innovate solutions that fit the work environment and protect mental health. Accordingly, we encourage researchers to examine the relationship between exposure to cumulative potentially psychologically traumatic events and the emotional labour required to manage the potential of experiencing daily violence in the workplace.

In the absence of changes to their conditions of work (e.g., overcrowding of prisons, understaffing), correctional officers will have to continue to bear the costs of cumulative occupational stressors. Correctional officers must manage their emotions to protect themselves against becoming targets of harassment and violence from prisoners. Suppressing emotions and maintaining a detached façade are coping strategies to deal with the pervasiveness of violence in the prison context. Our interviews with correctional officers suggest that emotional detachment also affects how correctional officers perceive prisoners and how they do their job (e.g., desensitization to violence among prisoners may mean that correctional officers are less attentive to the needs of prisoners), with long-term consequences on health and well-being, such as those documented elsewhere (e.g., Boudoukha

314 *Ricciardelli, Power, and Simas Medeiros*

et al., 2013; Ricciardelli & Power, 2020). Correctional officers who seek treatment also have to manage accusations from co-workers and managers of being weak and not having what it takes to do their job. Legislation that fails to effectively recognize and proactively mitigate the effects of cumulative occupational stressors, including but not limited to potentially psychologically traumatic events, perpetuates the downloading of the effects of a damaging work environment onto individual officers and their families. We can better support the mental health of correctional officers first by ensuring compensation legislation effectively recognizes the impact of individual and cumulative potentially psychologically traumatic events, and other occupational stressors resulting from an unhealthy work environment; and, second, by ensuring appropriate measures are put in place to lessen the damaging conditions of the prison work environment.

References

American Psychiatric Association (APA). (2013). *Diagnostic and statistical manual of mental disorders* (5th edn). Washington, DC: Author.

Baines, D. (2006). Staying with people who slap us around. Gender, juggling responsibilities and violence in paid (and unpaid) care work. *Gender, Work and Organization, 13*(2), 129–151.

Baines, D., & Cunningham, I. (2011). "White knuckle care work": Violence, gender and new public management in the voluntary sector. *Work, Employment and Society, 25*(4).

Bierie, D. (2012). The impact of prison conditions on staff well-being. *International Journal of Offender Therapy and Comparative Criminology, 56*(1), 81–95.

Boudoukha, A. H., Altinas, E., Rusinek, S., Fautini-Hauwel, C., & Hautekeete, M. (2013). Inmates-to-staff assaults, PTSD and burnout: Profiles of risk and vulnerability. *Journal of Interpersonal Violence, 28*(100), 2332–2350.

Bourbonnais, R., Jauvin, N., Dussault, J., & Vezina, M. (2007). Psychosocial work environment, interpersonal violence at work and mental health among correctional officers. *International Journal of Law and Psychiatry, 30*, 355–368.

Boyd, N. (2011). *Correctional officers in British Columbia: Abnormal working conditions.* Retrieved from www.sfu.ca/content/dam/sfu/pamr/pdfs/final%20 boyd-report-2011.pdf.

Brosnahan, M. (2013, November 25). Canada's prison population at all-time high: Number of visible minority inmates increased by 75% in past decade. *CBC.* Retrieved from www.cbc.ca/news/canada-s-prison-population-at-all-time-high-1.2440039.

Canadian Institute for Public Safety Research and Treatment (CIPSRT). (2019). Glossary of terms: A shared understanding of the common terms used to describe psychological trauma (version 2.0). Regina, SK: Author. Retrieved from http://hdl.handle.net/10294/9055.

Carleton, R. N. (2016). Into the unknown: A review and synthesis of contemporary models involving uncertainty. *Journal of Anxiety Disorders, 39*, 30–43. https://doi.org/10.1016/j.janxdis.2016.02.007.

Carleton, N., Afifi, T., Turner, S., Taillieu, T., Duranceau, S., LeBouthillier, D., ... & Asmundson, G. (2018). Mental disorder symptoms among public safety personnel in Canada. *The Canadian Journal of Psychiatry, 63*(1), 54–64.

Correctional Officers 315

Carleton, R. N., Afifi, T. O., Taillieu, T., Turner, S., Krakauer, R., Anderson, G. S., ... McCreary, D. (2019). Exposures to potentially traumatic events among public safety personnel in Canada. *Canadian Journal of Behavioural Science, 51,* 37–52. https://doi.org/10.1037/cbs0000115.

Carleton, R. N., Afifi, T. O., Taillieu, T., Turner, S., Mason, J. E., Ricciardelli, R., ... Griffiths, C. T. (2020). Assessing the relative impact of diverse stressors among public safety personnel. *International Journal of Environmental Research and Public Health, 17.* https://doi.org/10.3390/ijerph17041234.

Charmaz, K. (2006). *Constructing grounded theory: A practical guide through qualitative analysis.* London: Sage Publication.

Correctional Service Canada (CSC). (2014). FORUM on corrections research. Exposure to critical incidents: What are the effects on Canadian correctional officers? Retrieved from www.csc-scc.gc.ca/research/forum/e041/e041m-eng.shtml#archived.

Correctional Service Canada (CSC). (2019). Care, custody and supervision. Retrieved from www.csc-scc.gc.ca/publications/005007-3003-en.shtml.

Correctional Service Canada. (1992). Corrections and Conditional Release Act. Canada: Correctional Services Canada Retrieved from http://laws-lois.justice.gc.ca/eng/acts/C-44.6/page-1.html.

Crawley, E., & Crawley, P. (2008). Understanding prison officers: Culture, cohesion and conflict. In J. Bennett, B. Crewe, & A. Wahidin (eds), *Understanding prison staff* (pp. 134–152). London: Taylor & Francis.

Duxbury, L. & Higgins, C. (2001) *Work-life balance in the new millennium: Where are we? Where do we need to go?* CPRM Discussion Paper No. W|12, Canadian Policy Research Network, Ottawa, ON. Retrieved from https://files.eric.ed.gov/fulltext/ED465060.pdf.

Gordon, J, A., Proulx, B., & Grant, P.H. (2013). Trepidation among the "keepers": Gendered perceptions of fear and risk of victimization among corrections officers. *American Journal of Criminal Justice, 38,* 245–265.

Hall, A., Ricciardelli, R., Sitter, K., Simas-Medeiros, D., deBoer, C., & Small, S. (2019). Occupational stress injuries in two Atlantic provinces: A policy analysis. *Canadian Public Policy, 44*(4), 384–399. https://doi.org/10.3138/cpp.2017-071

Heck, A. (2016, January 22). Undoing the Tories: A complete guide to all Harperisms that the Liberals might or have killed. *National Post.* Retrieved from http://nationalpost.com/news/politics/undoing-the-tories-a-guide-to-harperisms-that-the-liberals-have-or-might-kill.

Hochschild, A. (1983). *The managed heart: Commercialization of human feeling.* Berkeley, CA: University of California Press.

Keefe, A., Bornstein, S., & Neis, B. (2018). *An environmental scan of presumptive coverage for work-related psychological injury (including post-traumatic stress disorder) in Canada and selected international jurisdictions.* Prepared for Workplace NL by the SafetyNet Centre for Occupational Health and Safety Research at Memorial University.

Killpatrick, S. (2015, October 20). After a decade-long Conservative reign, what's Trudeau's justice agenda? *The Globe and Mail.* Retrieved from www.theglobeandmail.com/news/politics/after-a-decade-long-conservative-reign-whats-on-trudeaus-justice-agenda/article26885833/.

Lambert, E. G., Hogan, N. L., & Altheimer, I. (2010). An exploratory examination of the consequences of burnout in terms of life satisfaction, turnover intent, and absenteeism among private correctional staff. *The Prison Journal, 90*(1), 94–114.

316 *Ricciardelli, Power, and Simas Medeiros*

Nova Scotia Government & General Employees Union. (2006–2009). Agreement between her Majesty the Queen in the right of the province of Nova Scotia represented by the Minister of Justice. Retrieved from http://novascotia.ca/psc/pdf/employeeCentre/collectiveAgreements/Correctional_Services_Local_480-November_1_2006-October_31_2009.pdf.

Martin, J. L., Lichtenstein, B., Jenkot, R. B., & Forde, D. R. (2012). They can take us over at any time they want: Correctional officers' responses to prison crowding. *The Prison Journal, 91*(1), 88–105.

Mayhew, C., & Chappell, D. (2007). Workplace violence: An overview of patterns of risk and the emotional/stress consequences on targets. *International Journal of Law and Psychiatry, 30*(4–5), 327–339.

Parliament of Canada. (2016). *Operational stress injuries and post traumatic stress disorder in public safety officers and first responders.* House of Commons. Retrieved from www.parl.gc.ca/Committees/en/SECU/StudyActivity?studyActivityId=8818269.

Poirier, S., Brown, G. R., & Carlson, T. M. (2008). *Decades of darkness moving towards the light: A review of the prison system in Newfoundland and Labrador.* St. John's, NL. Retrieved from www.gov.nl.ca/jps/files/publications-ac-report.pdf.

Prutischi, E. (2015, December 10). Law in the age of Justin Trudeau. *Slaw.* Retrieved from www.slaw.ca/2015/12/10/law-in-the-age-of-justin-trudeau/.

Public Services Foundation of Canada. (2015). Crisis in correctional services: Overcrowding and inmates with mental health problems in provincial correctional facilities. Retrieved from http://former.bcgeu.ca/sites/default/files/page/attachments/Crisis%20in%20Correctional%20Services%20April%202015%5B2%5D.pdf.

Quinlan, M., Mayhew, C., & Bohle, P. (2001). The global expansion of precarious employment, work disorganization, and consequences for occupational health: A review of recent research. *International Journal of Health Services, 31*(2), 335–414.

Ricciardelli, R. (2014). *Surviving incarceration: Inside Canadian prisons.* Waterloo, ON: Wilfred Laurier University Press.

Ricciardelli, R. (2018). "Risk it out, risk it out": Occupational and organizational stresses in rural policing. *Police Quarterly, 21*(4), 415–439.

Ricciardelli, R. (2019). *Also serving time: Canadian provincial and territorial correctional officers.* Toronto, ON: University of Toronto Press.

Ricciardelli, R., Carleton, R. N., Groll, D., & Cramm, H. (2018). Qualitatively unpacking Canadian public safety personnel experiences of trauma and their well-being. *Canadian Journal of Criminology and Criminal Justice, 60*(4), 566–577.

Ricciardelli, R., Carleton, R. N., Mooney, T., & Cramm, H. (2018). "Playing the system": Structural factors potentiating mental health stigma, challenging awareness, and creating barriers to care for Canadian Public Safety Personnel. *Health: An Interdisciplinary Journal for the Social Study of Health, Illness and Medicine, 24*(3), 259–278. doi.org/10.1177/1363459318800167

Ricciardelli, R., & Gazso, A. (2013). Investigating threat perceptions among correctional officers in the Canadian provincial correctional system. *Qualitative Sociology Review, 9*(3), 97–120.

Ricciardelli, R., & Power, N.. (2020). How "conditions of confinement" impact "conditions of employment": The work-related wellbeing of provincial correctional officers in Atlantic Canada. *Victims and Violence, 35*(1), 88–107.

Ricciardelli, R., Power, N., & Simas Medeiros, D. (2018). Correctional officers in Canada: Interpreting workplace violence. *Criminal Justice Review*, 43(4), 458–476.

Ricciardelli, R., & Sit, V. (2016). The effects of administrative controls on prisoner-on-prisoner violence. *The Prison Journal*, 96(2), 210–231.

Samak, Q. (2003). Correctional officers of CSC and their working conditions: A questionnaire based study. Retrieved from http://ucco-sacc-csn.ca/wp-content/uploads/2015/05/Correctional-Officers-and-their-working-conditions1.pdf.

Shain, M., Mental Health Commission of Canada, & Canadian Electronic Library. (2009). *Stress at work, mental injury and the law in Canada: A discussion paper for the mental health commission of Canada.* (Final Report). Calgary, AB: Mental Health Commission of Canada.

Statistics Canada. (2018). 2015 Canadian Community Health Survey. Ottawa, ON.

Strauss, A. L., & Corbin, J. (1990). *Basics of qualitative research: Techniques and procedures for developing grounded theory*. Newbury Park, CA: Sage Publishing Ltd.

Weinrath, M. (2009). Inmate perspectives on the remand crisis in Canada. *Canadian Journal of Criminology and Criminal Justice*, 51(3), 355–379.

Weinrath, M. (2016). *Behind the walls: Inmates and correctional officers on the state of Canadian prisons*. Vancouver, BC: UBC Press.

Wolff, N., Blitz, C., Shi, J., Siegel, J., & Bachman, R. (2007). Physical violence inside prison: Rates of victimization. *Criminal Justice and Behavior*, 34(5), 588–599.

12 Posttraumatic Growth among Prisoners

Findings, Controversies, and Implications

Esther F. J. C. van Ginneken and Siebrecht Vanhooren

Life, Interrupted

The adaptive resources of an individual are significantly challenged leading up to and during imprisonment (Tedeschi & Calhoun, 2004, p. 1)[1] and cumulative stress on adaptive resources can leave an individual susceptible to symptoms of posttraumatic stress disorder (PTSD; American Psychiatric Association, 2013). Not all imprisoned individuals will experience symptoms of PTSD because not all individuals adapt to imprisonment the same way. Imprisonment will cause some people to suffer debilitating mental health problems, after which some will eventually return to their pre-trauma levels of well-being, while others will report positive changes after coming to terms with the event. The substantial negative consequences of imprisonment are well-documented (e.g., Cohen & Taylor, 1972; Crewe, 2012; Crewe, Hulley, & Wright, 2017; Hannah-Moffat, 2001; Liebling & Ludlow, 2016; Sykes, 1958); however, much less attention has been paid to the accounts and mechanisms of positive transformation, or to posttraumatic growth. Posttraumatic growth may be a helpful framework for understanding accounts of positive transformation, particularly if the transformation is reported to be an improvement over pre-imprisonment well-being. Posttraumatic growth entails the experience of persistent positive change (e.g., a sense of purpose, increased self-worth, improved relationships) following the struggle to overcome an emotionally or physically threatening event (Tedeschi & Calhoun, 1996, 2004). Imprisonment is rarely an isolated incident or a happenstance occurrence; therefore, the effects of imprisonment must be interpreted within a broader context of cumulative experience, individual vulnerability, and relative disadvantage. The experience of imprisonment can be a potentially psychologically traumatic event (Canadian Institute for Public Safety Research and Treatment, 2019); however, notions of posttraumatic growth allow for the possibility that some individuals may overcome suffering and experience positive transformation.

DOI: 10.4324/9781351134637-13

Prisons expose an already vulnerable population to further deprivation (Liebling & Ludlow, 2016); accordingly, the harmful effects of imprisonment are extensively documented. Levels of distress, serious mental illness, and risk of suicide are significantly elevated among prisoners in comparison to the general population (Butler et al., 2006; Fazel & Danesh, 2002; Fazel et al., 2011; Sirdifield et al., 2009). The first period of imprisonment, including pre-trial detention, can be especially stressful (Liebling et al., 2005; Fazel et al., 2008; Sapsford, 1983; Van Ginneken et al., 2018; Vanhooren, Leijssen, & Dezutter, 2017c). The sudden separation from loved ones, uncertainty about the future, and exposure to a new and potentially hostile environment can be major challenges for men and women entering prison; accordingly, the challenges of imprisonment can further exacerbate a life narrative that already included disadvantage and injury. Prisoners may be exposed to three types of traumatic events: 1) the prison experience itself, including entry into prison; 2) the offence that led to imprisonment, particularly if the crime was violent, defensive, or impulsive; and 3) instances of victimization prior to imprisonment. Women in prison can experience added stress from comparatively longer distances between the carceral facility and their home, as well as being more likely to be primary caregivers of children (Gelsthorpe & Sharpe, 2007). Women often have even more pronounced histories of victimization and marginalization that relate to their offending in complex ways (Bosworth, 1990; Carlen & Worrall, 2004; Comack, 1996; Hannah-Moffat, 2001; Worrall, 1990).

There has been relatively limited research focused on prisoners who report posttraumatic growth after imprisonment. Any positive sequelae following imprisonment should be considered in light of the thoroughly disadvantaged circumstances (e.g., homelessness, unemployment, low educational attainment, financial problems, substance abuse, victimization, mental health problems) that often precede a person's incarceration (Durcan, 2008; Social Exclusion Unit, 2002). Despite the multiple pains of imprisonment, distress and mental health problems abate as prisoners acclimate to the new environment, underscoring the relatively robust adaptability of humans (Dirkzwager & Nieuwbeerta, 2018; Hassan et al., 2011; Plugge, Douglas, & Fitzpatrick, 2011). Some prisoners report positive effects such as mental health benefits, a greater appreciation of life, increased self-worth, a better understanding of people, and newfound purpose (Crewe et al., 2017; Depner et al., 2017; Douglas, Plugge, & Fitzpatrick, 2009; Elisha, Idisis & Ronel, 2013; Frois, 2017; Guse & Hudson, 2014; Kazemian, 2020; Maphan & Hefferon, 2012; Maruna, Wilson, & Curran, 2006; Novek, 2005; Van Ginneken, 2016; Vanhooren, 2018; Vanhooren et al., 2017a, 2017b).

In the current chapter, we present information about posttraumatic growth among prisoners, including manifestations and potential explanations. We begin by providing a methodological justification and a brief general background on posttraumatic growth. We then critically

320   *van Ginneken and Vanhooren*

assess whether posttraumatic growth can exist in prison and endure beyond release, highlighting the debate surrounding whether real growth is possible in the prison context or if positive stories are a product of coping efforts. We conclude by discussing the implications of actual or illusory posttraumatic growth among prisoners.

Methodological Note

In the current chapter, we draw on existing literature on the experience and effects of imprisonment, as well as on results from two empirical studies conducted independently by the two authors. Much of the chapter focuses on a study conducted by the first author (see Van Ginneken, 2015, 2016 for details); specifically, research conducted in prisons in England and Wales, which consisted of 30 in-depth interviews among men and women who were near the end of their sentences. The prisoners were asked about the experience of imprisonment, psychological adjustment, and preparation for release. The author did not intend to explore posttraumatic growth when originally designing the study; instead, positive interpretations of the prison experience emerged spontaneously and appeared to warrant analyses. We did not conduct new data analyses for the purpose of the current chapter; however, we used interview material from the study for the purpose of illustration. Quotations from the interviews are accompanied by the interviewee's pseudonym and, where applicable, the first author's (the interviewer) initials ("EvG"). All quotations are from Van Ginneken's study, unless indicated otherwise.

In the current chapter, we also provide a synthesis of studies conducted by the second author in prisons and forensic psychiatry hospitals in Belgium. The studies were designed to explore the experience of loss of meaning invoked by crime and imprisonment, meaning-making processes, and posttraumatic growth among prisoners (except for Gunst & Vanhooren, 2018). The studies include a quantitative cross-sectional study in three prisons ($n = 365$; Vanhooren, 2018; Vanhooren, et al., 2016, 2017c, 2018a), a mixed-methods study with former prisoners in a forensic hospital ($n = 30$; Vanhooren et al., 2017b), a qualitative study in a prison ($n = 10$; Vanhooren et al., 2017a), and ongoing case studies (Gunst & Vanhooren, 2018; Vanhooren et al., 2018b).

Posttraumatic Growth

The reported benefits of incarceration can be understood from research on the effects of potentially psychologically traumatic event exposures, which can include clinically significant distress and impairment next to posttraumatic growth. Posttraumatic growth is an enduring positive change following an adverse event. "Posttraumatic growth is not simply a return to baseline—it is an experience of improvement that for some persons is deeply profound" (Tedeschi & Calhoun, 2004, p. 4). Growth may be experienced in terms of positive interpretations and cognitions about the traumatic event, improved perceptions of the self and life, and increased psychological well-being. Growth and distress are not mutually exclusive. The struggle to overcome traumatic event exposures can precipitate growth (Tedeschi & Calhoun, 2004), which implicates the experience of distress in the experience posttraumatic growth. Potentially psychologically traumatic events can challenge people's assumptions about the world and their self-narratives, and posttraumatic growth can result from a "re-scripting" of the traumatic event and of one's life story.

Imprisonment and other traumatic events can pose a challenge to a person's assumptive world (i.e., a collection of beliefs about the world and the self; Janoff-Bulman, 1989; Janoff-Bulman, 1992). Assumptive worlds include assumptions about how other people will behave, how events should unfold, and to what extent a person believes they can influence events. Janoff-Bulman distinguished three categories of fundamental assumptions: 1) benevolence of the world refers to the extent to which a person believes the world is a good place and people are basically good; 2) meaningfulness of the world refers to a person's beliefs about the distribution of good and bad outcomes—including beliefs about justice, controllability, and chance; and 3) self-worth refers to a person's beliefs about being good, worthy, and moral. Imprisonment can substantively impact our fundamental assumptions. For example, individuals who perceive their sentence as unjust or unexpected may have their assumptions about the meaningfulness of the world threatened. Imprisonment and the associated stigma may also severely damage a person's sense of self-worth. Posttraumatic growth may result from attempts to restore fundamental assumptions by allowing an individual to turn bad outcomes into meaningful experiences. However, research on the relationship between assumptions and posttraumatic growth is scant and does not indicate a straightforward relationship between specific beliefs and distress or growth (Nygaard & Heir, 2012).

Traumatic events and other difficult life events can also threaten a person's identity or constructed life story. A person's constructed life story integrates a person's reconstructed past, perceived present, and anticipated future, providing a sense of coherence, meaning, and purpose (McAdams, 1996). Efforts to assign meaning to a traumatic event and integrate the traumatic event into one's life story may facilitate posttraumatic growth by framing the traumatic event as leading to an ultimately positive result. Potentially positive outcomes of traumatic event have been made apparent by individuals who draw from their own past problems with crime or substance abuse to support others in the desistance from crime or through the recovery process (Heidemann et al., 2016; LeBel, Richie, & Maruna, 2015).

In their pioneering work on posttraumatic growth, Tedeschi and Calhoun (1996) identified five domains of growth: 1) appreciation of life; 2) relationships with others; 3) personal strength; 4) new possibilities in life; and 5) spiritual change. Positive changes in the five domains of growth have been reported as responses to a wide range of traumatic events, including life-threatening illness, bereavement, war, natural disasters, and violent victimization (Kunst, 2011; Powell et al., 2003; Stanton, Bower, & Low, 2006; Znoj, 2006; Zhou, Wu, & Chen, 2015). Posttraumatic growth has also been reported among ex-prisoners of war and former political prisoners (Dekel, Ein-Dor, & Solomon, 2012; Erbes et al., 2005; Salo, Qouta, & Punamäki, 2005). Posttraumatic growth as indicated by the five domains is commonly measured using Tedeschi and Calhoun's (1996) Posttraumatic Growth Inventory. Protracted traumatic events (e.g., war captivity) can have long-lasting positive and negative outcomes, including increased appreciation of life and confidence in personal strength (Dekel et al., 2012); however, not all aspects of posttraumatic growth are positive.

Focusing on positive changes such as posttraumatic growth may facilitate avoiding acknowledging the harm associated with the traumatic events (Sledge & Boydstun, 1980). Perhaps from here stems the debate about whether posttraumatic growth leads to real identity change or is only a mechanism of cognitive avoidance to maintain aspects of identity (including self-esteem, coherence, and a sense of control). The suggestion that posttraumatic growth is simply a form of avoidance implies that posttraumatic growth is illusory (Sumalla, Ochoa, & Banco, 2009; Zoellner & Maercker, 2006). Illusory growth may have counter-productive effects, including posttraumatic stress symptoms at a later time (Blix et al., 2016; Engelhard, Lommen, & Sijbrandij, 2015).

Manifestation of Posttraumatic Growth among Prisoners

Similar to posttraumatic growth resulting from other potentially psychologically traumatic events, posttraumatic growth among prisoners may result from efforts to integrate the traumatic event of incarceration into their constructed life story. Many prisoners integrate traumatic events experienced prior to imprisonment into their life story (Ferrito, Needs, & Adshead, 2017; Kazemian, 2020), complicating efforts to delineate the diverse impacts of their cumulative experiences. Past events intertwine with new events during imprisonment, and the experiences readily and repeatedly resurface. Imprisonment can also cause a person to hit "rock bottom", which can lead to existential questioning (Maruna et al., 2006). Imprisonment may then provide time and space for self-reflection, as well as access to previously unavailable supports and resources (including assured shelter and subsistence), all of which can support the creation of meaning and a coherent self-narrative that facilitates positive growth.

Need for Survival

Individuals who are incarcerated prior to conviction and sentencing (i.e., pre-trial detention) face a great deal of uncertainty about their future, which can be inherently problematic for mental health. The novel environment,

Posttraumatic Growth among Prisoners 323

separation from loved ones, and concerns about life outside prison can be emotionally challenging, exacerbating experiences of uncertainty and distress. The timeframe of the initial high-stress period varies and can depend on the length of a person's sentence, their incarceration history, and the crime for which they are imprisoned. For prisoners with a long sentence, adjustment may take years (Crewe et al., 2017), whereas prisoners with shorter sentences may adjust in a matter of months (Van Ginneken, 2016). Longitudinal studies indicate that, on average, mental health disorder symptom intensity decreases linearly within a few months of imprisonment, but remains at an elevated level compared to the general population (Dirkzwager & Nieuwbeerta, 2018; Hassan et al., 2011; Gonçalves et al., 2016; Lennox et al., 2013).

Adaptation to imprisonment is necessary for survival because the alternative to coping would be "psychological disintegration" (Crewe et al., 2017, p. 524):

> You've got two choices when you're faced with a sentence like this: sink or swim, really, and there's a multitude of ways to sink and only one way to swim.
>
> (Neil, 30s, 18-yr tariff [minimum sentence to serve], served 12, as cited in Crewe et al., 2017, p. 525)

Sinking is experienced by many prisoners at the beginning of their sentence and can manifest as mental health disorders such as depression, anxiety, suicidal ideation, or attempted suicide (Liebling et al., 2005). Even though average levels of mental health disorder symptoms appear to decline over the course of imprisonment, some prisoners fail to cope. Failure to adapt can lead to a number of outcomes from hospital admission to, in the most extreme cases, death by suicide. Misconduct as a manifestation of failure to adapt can result in consequences, such as punishment and withholding of privileges that can have complex interactions with mental health and adaptation. Consider, for example, this female prisoner's description of the first six months of her prison sentence:

EVG: How were those six months?
RACHEL: They weren't good at all, I was always, like, I rebelled against being in jail, I kept getting into trouble and stuff, but obviously, if you get into trouble, then you don't get anywhere in the prison system. So I just knocked it down and started to be good, 'cause I wanna go home.

Rachel's words demonstrate how imprisonment regulates the body and mind to the point that there appears to be no alternative to *appearing to cope well*. Posttraumatic growth may be a way of coping with the pains of imprisonment. Research on the relationship between posttraumatic growth and distress has been inconsistent (Vanhooren, 2018; Vanhooren, et al., 2017b; Zoellner & Maercker, 2006), but in Vanhooren's studies the relationship was inverse, significant and strong.[2]

324   *van Ginneken and Vanhooren*

Not all examples of personal transformation and adaptation are positive. Posttraumatic growth requires a change that goes beyond mere coping or a return to baseline well-being. Posttraumatic growth requires finding new meaning and purpose and the perception of change relative to pre-imprisonment as being positive. True posttraumatic growth involves the persistence of a positive transformation after release (for additional discussion see "Posttraumatic Growth or Positive Illusion?").

Need for Meaning

A key element of positive personal transformation among prisoners is the positive re-interpretation of the prison experience to imbue meaning and purpose that contributes to a coherent life narrative. Frequently, positive re-interpretation involves (a) coming to terms with one's past and (b) using time for self-improvement. Imprisonment may serve as a catalyst for rewriting a self-narrative because of the radically new experience with respect to one's sense of self, assumptions about the world, and sense of meaning.

Entry into prison can disrupt an individual's self-identity through displacement, degradation rituals, the loss of personal possessions, and the forced adoption of an "inmate" identity (Goffman, 1961). In order to cope with pains of imprisonment, prisoners may adopt certain roles in prison, allowing them to better adapt (Sykes, 1958). Prison roles may help prisoners manage levels of distress (Zamble & Porporino, 1988), but still leave prisoners anxious about the impact of imprisonment on their identity (Cohen & Taylor, 1972). Imprisonment is an interruption of the life story that has the potential to impact self-identity through irreparable damage to relationships, job prospects, and accommodation, and perhaps only prisoners with dire life circumstances prior to incarceration will see the changes as improvements. Prisoners' psychological suffering has been strongly related to an overall sense of having lost meaning in life (Vanhooren et al., 2017c). Lower levels of meaning in life have been associated with mental and physical health problems (Friedman & Kern, 2014; Steger, 2012). Frankl (1959/2006) and other existentialist scholars (Yalom, 1980) suggest human beings have a primary need for meaning in life. Prisoners who embark on a search for meaning during their imprisonment—and who succeed in finding new meaning—show higher levels of posttraumatic growth and well-being than those who give up searching (Vanhooren, 2018; Vanhooren et al., 2016). For prisoners who experience a loss of meaning, acknowledge and face the loss, and search for new meaning, imprisonment can be a fundamental turning point in life (Ferrito et al., 2017; Guse & Hudson, 2014; Kazemian, 2020; Schinkel, 2014; Van Ginneken, 2016; Vanhooren et al., 2017a).

The meaning given to imprisonment needs to be contextualized within the individual's pre-imprisonment experiences. Unfortunately, imprisonment can be an important intervention for preventing further harm by

Posttraumatic Growth among Prisoners 325

enabling access to hard-to-reach groups with complex needs (Prison Health Policy Unit and Prison Health Task Force, 2002, p. 1). Pre-prison life is often characterized by disadvantage, including low income, unemployment, and homelessness (Social Exclusion Unit, 2002). Other issues may include substance abuse, victimization (e.g., abusive relationships), and other traumatic events (e.g., abortion, bereavement). Imprisonment can also provide relative safety and relief from one's chaotic life outside of prison, such as offering a refuge from an abusive relationship, subsistence to the criminalized homeless, and detoxification (Codd, 2008). "The absence of adequate support mechanisms in the community renders imprisonment the only 'alternative' option - the only way to interrupt cycles of abuse, addiction and/or financial pressure that leads [sic] to lifestyles focused on survival" (Segrave & Carlton, 2010, pp. 295–296). Katie, whose story merits quoting at length, described the following chaotic lifestyle prior to incarceration:

EvG: Can you describe to me what your life was like before you came to prison this time?

KATIE: It was pretty hectic, pretty hectic. I was on the road a lot, didn't really get to see much of my kids. Mom had my kids before I come in. I was travelling from one end of the country to the other, drug habit, beer habit, business to run. (…) It was very, very hectic.

EvG: How has prison changed that now?

KATIE: Because you just have no choice but to have a clear head. There's no way you can get [drugs]. Obviously you get the times where there's a lot of things, but that's very, very rare. People say there's more drugs inside than outside, that's a lie. You probably have a week where there's a good bit going around, but after that week, it can be seven to eight, nine, ten weeks before anything else will come in. (…) I find it less stressful, less depressing in prison than I actually do outside.

EvG: Why do you think that is?

KATIE: Because I don't have as many things going on in prison, so I can't really let it get all to me. Whereas outside, something's always going on. Too much at one time, I don't like that.

As evidenced in Katie's words, prison can provide a space for clarity in mind. Prison may also be the first time that people receive support in dealing with past trauma or mental health issues, which can help increase individuals' sense of self-worth and can lead to the perception of imprisonment as a catalyst for positive transformation (Van Ginneken, 2016; Vanhooren et al., 2017a, 2018a). For Nicole, imprisonment symbolized a fresh start, as prison offered her an escape from an abusive relationship.

NICOLE: I think now, 'cause I'm due to be released tomorrow, that if, had I walked out of court that day, that I'd probably gone back to a life of what I had, when [prison] has given me a new life, basically. I've gone from one extreme to another; I've had two years of being controlled by some bully, not being allowed to wear the clothes that I want to wear, my hair the way I want to wear, can't see my kids, can't eat what I want, have to do what he wants. And tomorrow, I'm going to a new address, in a different city and being-, I can do whatever. (...) And it's the prison, that's basically enabled me to start a different [life] tomorrow, really.

An essential ingredient for a prisoner to feel supported in dealing with current and older issues is feeling perceived as human by people providing help (Vanhooren et al., 2017a). Unfortunately, prisoners often have the experience of being stripped of their humanity and seen only as a "criminal" by prison personnel, former friends, society in general, and sometimes even family members. Feeling as though another person can see beyond the committed crime and find something valuable in the prisoner can encourage the prisoner's search for new meaning (Maruna, 2001; Vanhooren et al., 2017a). Feeling understood and seen by others has predicted posttraumatic growth in prisoners (Vanhooren et al., 2018a) and helped prisoners to face older traumatic events that are often connected to the committed crime (Gunst & Vanhooren, 2018; Vanhooren, 2018; Vanhooren et al., 2017a, 2018b).

Adverse childhood events may work against prisoners experiencing posttraumatic growth (Vanhooren, 2018; Vanhooren et al., 2016). For example, participants who experienced sexual abuse and physical violence during childhood were less likely to search for meaning and to experience posttraumatic growth (Vanhooren, 2018; Vanhooren et al., 2016). Unaddressed traumatic events may result in prisoners lacking enough understanding about their current situation to recover, which may support perceptions that life is meaningless (Vanhooren et al., 2016). The right support from someone who affirms the prisoner's worthiness can help them find meaning, not only about the committed crime and imprisonment, but also about life as a whole. Giving meaning to imprisonment is also a way to reconstitute a person's assumptive worlds, including the assumptions that the world is essentially a good and just place and that the person in question is worthy. Reconstitution of assumptive worlds is especially relevant considering that prisoners may be dealing with feelings of guilt and shame in relation to their crime and incarceration.

Religion and Redemption

Spiritual change is considered one of the domains of posttraumatic growth (Tedeschi & Calhoun, 1996). Conversion narratives, in which prisoners report turning to religion, are not uncommon. Maruna, Wilson, and Curran (2006) interviewed 75 prisoners in the UK who self-identified as having converted to Christianity. Participants reported that imprisonment

Posttraumatic Growth among Prisoners 327

was first experienced as devastating, describing a profound sense of loss and a questioning of their self-identity. The crime they committed would contradict prisoners' assumptions about themselves. One interviewee is quoted saying:

> In the past, I think I was quite sort of satisfied that I knew who I was and, you know when somebody would say, "Oh I think you're really good at that" or "We appreciate you for this." Then all this happens. The big crash, everything lying in smithereens, and all of a sudden I'm thinking, "Hang on a minute, the person who's responsible for this cannot have been the person who all those people were saying nice things about, because he wouldn't have done that." So that takes some resolving.
>
> (Interviewee 66 in Maruna et al., 2006, pp. 171–172)

Religious conversion can create a new social identity, which can help to resolve the identity crisis and give purpose and meaning to imprisonment. Religious conversion may also provide a framework for self-forgiveness and hope for the future (Clear & Sumter, 2002; Maruna et al., 2006; Spalek & El-Hassan, 2007). In the typical conversion narrative, imprisonment becomes part of "God's plan" and past involvement with crime and addiction can inform one's missionary work. The forgiveness element in Christianity was particularly important for interviewees who had committed serious crimes, including murder (Maruna et al., 2006). Forgiveness facilitated posttraumatic growth by allowing prisoners to regain a sense of self-worth and move on from crippling guilt. Other research also supports the idea that religious coping is associated with posttraumatic growth (Vanhooren, Leijssen, & Dezutter, 2018a). Likely influencing the potential for religious or spiritual growth is country and context (O'Connell, Abbott, & White, 2017). Conversions to Islam may also be quite common in the UK and US (Spalek & El-Hassan, 2007; Ammar, Weaver, & Saxon, 2004).

Religious conversion can be seen as a sub-type of a redemption script. Redemption scripts are self-narratives that frame a person's past as an unfortunate and inevitable precursor to a worthy life in which they can fully realize their true self (Maruna, 2001). In the Liverpool Desistance Study, 65 men and women, who had successfully stopped committing crime, reported similar redemption scripts in which they felt their past led them to where they were at the time of the interview (Maruna, 2001). The participants also reported another important element of a redemption script: the desire to give back to society (Maruna, 2001).

Commitment to helping others, also referred to as generativity, is defined as a concern for the next generation and making a contribution that has a lasting, positive impact (Erikson, 1968; McAdams & de St. Aubin, 1998). The theme of "giving something back" has also been identified in other studies among prisoners, including ex-prisoners (Crewe et al., 2017; Depner et al., 2017; Ferrito et al., 2017; Guse & Hudson, 2014; Halsey

328   *van Ginneken and Vanhooren*

& Harris, 2011; Maruna, 2001). Various prisoners report taking up volunteering opportunities, which provided them with a sense of self-worth, purpose, and, occasionally, a direction for the future.

EvG: Why did you decide to become a Listener [peer supporter in prison]?
AUDREY: Ehm… because… I've took a lot of help and support of other people, and I just wanted to give something back. You know, I've been in the jail a long time and I thought, well, I'd got to a point where I felt I was ready to be able to support other people. I'd had all the support all the way along, but now it was a time where I was ready to give that support, you know, and just listen to people. As a Listener you don't give an opinion and you don't give advice, that's not what you're there for. You are there just to listen, and to talk about the way that person feels. And if out of twenty people I help one person, then that makes being in jail worthwhile, you know, for all the help and support it's given me in my own life, if I can help one person, then my time here ain't been wasted. You know, I've used the beginning of my sentence to get off the drugs and do all the courses and, you know, help myself and now… it's just giving something back, I suppose.

Audrey found imprisonment meaningful by helping other prisoners as peer supporter; in doing so, Audrey also experienced personal growth. Researchers have evidenced personal transformation through participation in peer support roles that leads to a positive self-image, the establishment of new purpose and meaning, and the ability to relate to others in new ways (Einat, 2017; Perrin & Blagden, 2014). Peer supporters have also reported experiencing a sense of trust and responsibility within their role, which validated their positive transformation (Perrin & Blagden, 2014).

Self-Improvement and Strengthening Relationships

Time in prison can be used to come to terms with the past and for future-oriented efforts at self-improvement. For example, prisoners can seek to improve existing skills or learn new ones through educational and vocational courses, as well as participate in work assignments and volunteer opportunities. The opportunities for skill development are much more restricted in prison, but the threshold to begin and complete these opportunities may appear much lower to prisoners once incarcerated. For example, Rachel reported experiencing personal growth in terms of skills and confidence resulting from courses she took during her prison sentence.

EvG: When you look back on the past year, is there anything on your mind that would describe your experience?
RACHEL: I just think that you have to make the most of a bad situation. I've done quite a bit since I've been in here, like, cookery, like, got qualifications, like, I could open up my own catering business if

Posttraumatic Growth among Prisoners 329

I wanted to, 'cause I've done all the courses that you could do. I've done health and safety, I've done-, I've got better grades in, like, maths and English than when I went to college, stuff like that. It's been a good experience for me I think. I know it's a bad place to be, but I've just made the most of it.

Posttraumatic growth also has a relational dimension (Tedeschi & Calhoun, 1996). Researchers have mostly studied the negative impact of imprisonment on relationships as the pain of separation and deprivation of intimacy is glaring (Richards, 1978; Sykes, 1958). Nevertheless, imprisonment can occasionally help to repair damaged relationships, increase the value prisoners place on interpersonal relationships, and give rise to new ways of relating to others (Guse & Hudson, 2014; Kazemian, 2020; Vanhooren et al., 2017a). Multiple examples of perceived improvement in the quality of family relationships during imprisonment were found in Van Ginneken's study (2015, 2016).

ADENA: Since I've come to prison I've matured a lot. Definitely a lot. When I was on road, ehm... I was very immature, and I used to, like, party and drink and do drugs, and just do a lot of silly things like that. But since I've come in here, I've learned like a lot of things really. And I've just grown up so much, and become more respectful as well of people and that. Cause I never used to care about anyone else, really. So in one way I'm glad I've come to prison and I also met my mom when I come into prison as well. So, I'm kind of glad really. (...) I've only just met my mom since I've come to prison. She found out I was in prison. I haven't seen her since I'm like five and I'm 20 now, so it's like a big 15-year gap, so she comes to visit me every so often and it's just-, it's awkward, but I'm just trying to build up a relationship with her again, really.

Adena's words describe experiencing personal growth and a strengthening of her relationships, which gave her confidence for the future. There may also be variation in the extent to which narratives of personal transformation are oriented towards the future. Prisoners with shorter sentences or who are closer to their release may be more concerned with their post-release future. Prisoners with lengthy sentences may focus more on building a purposeful life *in prison*. Arguably, building a purposeful life in prison has consequences for the extent to which the personal transformation has a positive effect that endures beyond imprisonment.

Posttraumatic Growth or Positive Illusion?

There is still disagreement in the literature as to whether posttraumatic growth is real or illusory (Frazier et al., 2009; McFarland & Alvaro, 2000; Tedeschi, Park, & Calhoun, 1998). Posttraumatic growth is usually measured through retrospective self-report rather than measuring changes between pre- and posttrauma functioning. The reliance on self-report measures of growth has led to some critics suggesting that posttraumatic growth is simply an illusion (Frazier et al., 2009; Smith & Cook, 2004). Arguably, a positive mindset may also result in actual growth (Calhoun & Tedeschi, 2006). Ascribing positive meaning to imprisonment may provide a sense of cognitive relief and enable prisoners to cope with the difficulties in their lives and the pains of imprisonment (Halsey, 2007); however, distinguishing genuine personality change or growth from successful coping with traumatic events is difficult (Jayawickreme & Blackie, 2014; Tennen & Affleck, 2002). The relationship between imprisonment and posttraumatic growth can also be impacted by: 1) the explicit and implicit expectations about prisoners' behaviour and cognitions; and 2) the endurance and effects of personality transformations post-release.

The difficulty with in-prison activities and deriving conclusions about growth from prisoners' participation in such activities is that participation is often seen as good and desirable behaviour within the prison system and may even be mandated as part of a sentence plan. Thus, self-reported transformation may be partly shaped by the external demands and expectations associated with power relations in prison. Prisoners may appear to have a choice in terms of participation in activities and programs, but there can be negative consequences for deviations from the norms regarding good behaviour. The negative consequences can effectively create an illusory sense of autonomy (Crewe, 2012; Hannah-Moffat, 2001). Thus, administrative criteria for "rehabilitation" such as program participation do not necessarily equate to signs of positive transformation that are conducive to desistance; instead, true generativity may occur outside the parameters of prison programmes (Halsey & Harris, 2011).

Growth reported in prison may dissipate rapidly without opportunities for a stable and supported life after prison. Many prisoners lack social, cultural, economic, and symbolic capital to turn aspirations into actual change (Hart, 2017); therefore, transformation narratives are easier to maintain in prison, when the obstacles of outside life are not interfering (Schinkel, 2014; Soyer, 2014). For example, narratives of desistance were omnipresent among a sample of juvenile prisoners, but the perceived desistance did not result in actual desistance once released (Soyer, 2014). Participants were deterred by the thought of reimprisonment, but were not prepared for the difficulties they faced after release. Soyer (2014) argues that

> incarceration generates a structural environment conducive to framing imprisonment as a turning point while simultaneously failing to provide tools that could sustain the narrative of desistance on the outside. (…) The responses are shaped by the immediate experience of having lost one's freedom and the rather intensive attention teenagers

Posttraumatic Growth among Prisoners 331

receive from staff, probation officers and judges. One may argue that the emotions felt and plans made during this particular moment may be insignificant for a life that still needs to be lived.

(Soyer, 2014, pp. 93–94)

Currently, any causal links between posttraumatic growth and desistance are speculative. Hypothetically, posttraumatic growth may contribute to the formation of a non-offender identity and strengthens one's motivation to live a crime-free life. Posttraumatic growth can initiate a transformation that can sustain desistance even in the face of substantial impediments (Kazemian, 2020). Personal transformation is considered an important causal factor in desistance (Giordano, Cernkovich, & Rudolph, 2002; LeBel et al., 2008; Paternoster & Bushway, 2009). Redemption narratives are common among people who have successfully desisted from crime (Maruna, 2001), but causal attributions for such narratives are problematically based on retrospective research. Redemption narratives are also not necessarily equitable with posttraumatic growth. Evidence of posttraumatic growth was found among individuals who had participated in a rehabilitation program ("Silence to Violence") two to five years prior to being interviewed (Mapham & Hefferon, 2012). Participants were still incarcerated or had just recently been released when participating in the "Silence to Violence" program and had not been reincarcerated since completion of the program. The 14 respondents described growth in their relationships, emotional intelligence, identity, and sense of agency as a result of their participation in "Silence to Violence".

A final concern is that personality transformation in prison may be maladaptive upon release. These problems, also known as post-incarceration syndrome are reminiscent of, and can co-exist with, posttraumatic stress disorder. The symptoms of post-incarceration syndrome present in three clusters: institutionalized personality traits, social-sensory deprivation syndrome, and social/temporal alienation (Liem & Kunst, 2013). The manifestation of post-incarceration syndrome could be explained by the contrast between coping mechanisms that are adaptive inside prison and those that are adaptive outside prison. "Mastering the psychological rigors of prison does little to facilitate successful reintegration into the free world. ... The ability to successfully adapt to certain prison contexts may be inversely related to subsequent adjustment in the community" (Haney, 2006, p. 170). Such profound problems reintegrating into the community, which may suggest personality change, have also been found among wrongfully convicted and political ex-prisoners (Grounds, 2005; Jamieson & Grounds, 2005). Due to these serious post-release problems, it is important to consider alternatives to imprisonment, to create prison conditions that stimulate autonomy and personal development, and to support prisoners with re-entry.

Concluding Comments

In the current chapter, we have critically discussed the occurrence of post-traumatic growth among prisoners. We have taken an inclusive approach to what may be considered posttraumatic growth by including changes in life narratives (based on qualitative interviews) and self-reported growth in the domains identified by Tedeschi and Calhoun (1996; based on survey research using the posttraumatic growth inventory). Imprisonment is generally associated with a loss of meaning and an interruption, disruption, or even destruction of life; nevertheless, some prisoners have the ability to positively reinterpret the experience. The process of reinterpretation can be explained by the human needs for survival and meaning, in combination with the use of support and resources that prisoners previously did not perceive as accessible. The current chapter was primarily focused on the cognitive and existential disruptions and transformations following imprisonment; however, the emotional dimension remains important. There are clear indications that the experience and recall of strong emotions, emotional coping, affective personality style, openness to one's bodily felt senses, and emotional support are related to posttraumatic growth (Fredrickson et al., 2003; Kunst, 2011, 2012; O'Connell et al., 2017; Vanhooren et al., 2018a; Zwiercan & Joseph, 2018). Further investigation in the prison context may help shine a light on the complex relationship between distress and growth and may provide some answers in regards to the ongoing debate (Helgeson, Reynolds, & Tomich, 2006; Zoellner & Maercker, 2006).

We have also discussed various areas in life where prisoners found new meaning and experienced personal transformation. A hopeful outlook on the future was an important factor in their transformations. Nevertheless, it remains an unsettled debate whether posttraumatic growth in the prison context can be regarded as a precursor to lasting change beyond imprisonment (including desistance) or as a mode of adjustment to highly distressing circumstances. The association between desistance and posttraumatic growth needs to be studied more in depth, and posttraumatic growth seems to have the potential to buffer risk factors that can lead to re-offending (e.g., hopelessness, existential alienation, meaninglessness; Ronel & Segev, 2014; Wolff, Morgan, & Shi, 2013). As prisoners often carry potentially psychologically traumatic event experiences of the past and may also experience or witness trauma in prison, psychotherapeutic help might be needed to process previous traumatic event to make sense of current life experiences. In order to facilitate posttraumatic growth through therapy, a wider perspective than a risk-management approach towards offenders and prisoners is necessary. Instead, therapists and prisoners need to engage in a process of facing the existential questions that are linked with former traumas, the committed crime, and the experienced loss of meaning during imprisonment (Vanhooren, 2018; Vanhooren et al., 2018b). Without dealing with emotional wounds prior to release, prisoners

Posttraumatic Growth among Prisoners   333

will find it very challenging return to the community (Kazemian, 2020). Posttraumatic growth among prisoners means understanding one's past in a different way, taking responsibility and coping with the outcomes of the committed crime, and making sense of one's life by finding new purpose for the future.

Notes

1 This is a broader interpretation of trauma than its DSM-V definition in the context of a clinical diagnosis of posttraumatic stress disorder (PTSD), in which case an event should involve actual or threatened death or serious injury (American Psychiatric Association, 2013).
2 In our cross-sectional study, the posttraumatic growth inventory had a Cronbach's alpha of .91 (Vanhooren et al., 2018a) which is comparable to its internal consistency of .9 in other populations (Tedeschi & Calhoun, 1996). Pearson's correlation between posttraumatic growth and distress measured by the General Health Questionnaire (Goldberg & Williams, 1988) was significant ($r = -.405$; $p < .001$) and showed a large effect size (Cohen's $d = -.886$).

References

American Psychiatric Association. (2013). *Diagnostic and statistical manual of mental disorders* (5th edn). Washington, DC: American Psychiatric Association.

Ammar, N. H., Weaver, R. R., & Saxon, S. (2004). Muslims in prison: A case study from Ohio state prisons. *International Journal of Offender Therapy and Comparative Criminology*, 48(4), 414–428.

Blix, I., Birkeland, M. S., Hansen, M. B., & Heir, T. (2016). Posttraumatic growth— An antecedent and outcome of posttraumatic stress: Cross-lagged associations among individuals exposed to terrorism. *Clinical Psychological Science*, 4(4), 620–628.

Bosworth, M. (1990). *Engendering resistance: Agency and power in women's prisons.* Aldershot: Ashgate.

Butler, T., Andrews, G., Allnutt, S., Sakashita, C., Smith, N. E., & Basson, J. (2006). Mental disorders in Australian prisoners: A comparison with a community sample. *Australian and New Zealand Journal of Psychiatry*, 40(3), 272–276.

Calhoun, L., & Tedeschi, R. (2006). The foundations of posttraumatic growth: An expanded framework. In L. Calhoun & R. Tedeschi (eds), *Handbook of post-traumatic growth: Research and practice* (pp. 1–23). New York: Routledge

Canadian Institute for Public Safety Research and Treatment. (2019). *Glossary of terms: A shared understanding of the common terms used to describe psycho-logical trauma (version 2.0).* Regina, SK: Author.

Carlen, P., & Worrall, A. (2004). *Analysing women's imprisonment.* Cullompton: Willan Publishing.

Clear, T. R., & Sumter, M. T. (2002). Prisoners, prison, and religion: Religion and adjustment to prison. *Journal of Offender Rehabilitation*, 35(3–4), 125–156.

Codd, H. (2008). *In the shadow of prison: Families, imprisonment, and criminal justice.* Cullompton: Willan Publishing.

Cohen, S., & Taylor, L. (1972). *Psychological survival: The experience of long-term imprisonment.* Harmondsworth: Penguin Books.

334   van Ginneken and Vanhooren

Comack, E. (1996). *Women in trouble: Connecting women's law violations to their histories of abuse*. Halifax, NS: Fernwood Publishing.

Crewe, B. (2012). *The prisoner society: Power, adaptation and social life in an English prison*. Oxford: Oxford University Press.

Crewe, B., Hulley, S., & Wright, S. (2017). Swimming with the tide: Adapting to long-term imprisonment. *Justice Quarterly*, *34*(3), 517–541.

Dekel, S., Ein-Dor, T., & Solomon, Z. (2012). Posttraumatic growth and post-traumatic distress: A longitudinal study. *Psychological Trauma: Theory, Research, Practice, and Policy*, *4*(1), 94.

Depner, R. M., Grant, P. C., Byrwa, D. J., Breier, J. M., Lodi-Smith, J., Kerr, C. W., & Luczkiewicz, D. L. (2017). A consensual qualitative research analysis of the experience of inmate hospice caregivers: Posttraumatic growth while incarcerated. *Death Studies*, *41*(4), 199–210.

Dirkzwager, A. J. E., & Nieuwbeerta, P. (2018). Mental health symptoms during imprisonment: A longitudinal study. *Acta Psychiatrica Scandinavica*, *138*(4), 300–311.

Douglas, N., Plugge, E., & Fitzpatrick, R. (2009). The impact of imprisonment on health–What do women prisoners say? *Journal of Epidemiology & Community Health*, *63*(9), 749–754.

Durcan, G. (2008). *From the inside: Experiences of prison mental health care*. London: Sainsbury Centre for Mental Health.

Einat, T. (2017). The wounded healer: Self-rehabilitation of prisoners through providing care and support to physically and mentally challenged inmates. *Journal of Crime and Justice*, *40*(2), 204–221.

Elisha, E., Idisis, Y., & Ronel, N. (2013). Positive criminology and imprisoned sex offenders: Demonstration of a way out from a criminal spin through acceptance relationships. *Journal of Sexual Aggression*, *19*(1), 66–80.

Engelhard, I. M., Lommen, M. J .J., & Sijbrandij, M. (2015). Changing for better or worse? Posttraumatic growth reported by soldiers deployed to Iraq. *Clinical Psychological Science*, *3*(5), 789–796.

Erbes, C., Eberly, R., Dikel, T., Johnsen, E., Harris, I., & Engdahl, B. (2005). Posttraumatic growth among American former prisoners of war. *Traumatology*, *11*(4), 285–295.

Erikson, E. (1968). *Identity: Youth and crisis*. New York: Norton.

Fazel, S., Cartwright, J., Norman-Nott, A., & Hawton, K. (2008). Suicide in prisoners: A systematic review of risk factors. *The Journal of Clinical Psychiatry*, *69*(11), 1721–1731.

Fazel, S., & Danesh, J. (2002). Serious mental disorder in 23,000 prisoners: A systematic review of 62 surveys. *The Lancet*, *359*(9306), 545–550.

Fazel, S., Grann, M., Kling, B., & Hawton, K. (2011). Prison suicide in 12 countries: An ecological study of 861 suicides during 2003–2007. *Social Psychiatry and Psychiatric Epidemiology*, *46*(3), 191–195.

Ferrito, M., Needs, A., & Adshead, G. (2017). Unveiling the shadows of meaning: Meaning-making for perpetrators of homicide. *Aggression and Violent Behavior*, *34*, 263–272.

Frankl, V. (1959/2006). *Man's search for meaning*. Boston, MA: Beacon Press.

Frazier, P., Tennen, H., Gavian, M., Park, C., Tomich, P., & Tashiro, T. (2009). Does self-reported posttraumatic growth reflect genuine positive change? *Psychological Science*, *20*(7), 912–919.

Fredrickson, B. L., Tugade, M. M., Waugh, C. E., & Larkin, G. R. (2003). What good are positive emotions in crisis? A prospective study of resilience and emotions following the terrorist attacks on the United States on September 11th, 2001. *Journal of Personality and Social Psychology*, *84*(2), 365–376.

Friedman, H. S., & Kern, M. L. (2014). Personality, well-being, and health. *Annual Review of Psychology*, *65*, 719–742.

Frois, C. (2017). *Female imprisonment: An ethnography of everyday life in confinement*. London: Palgrave.

Gelsthorpe, L., & Sharpe, G. (2007). Women and resettlement. In A. Hucklesby & L. Hagley-Dickinson (eds), *Prisoner resettlement: Policy and practice* (pp. 199–223). Cullompton: Willan Publishing.

Giordano, P. C., Cernkovich, S. A., & Rudolph, J. L. (2002). Gender, crime, and desistance: Toward a theory of cognitive transformation. *American Journal of Sociology*, *107*(4), 990–1064.

Goffman, E. (1961). *Asylums: Essays on the social situation of mental patients and other inmates*. Garden City, NY: Anchor Books.

Goldberg, D., & Williams, P. (1988). A users guide to the General Health Questionnaire. GL Assessment. Windsor, ON: NFER-Nelson.

Gonçalves, L. C., Endrass, J., Rossegger, A., & Dirkzwager, A. J. (2016). A longitudinal study of mental health symptoms in young prisoners: Exploring the influence of personal factors and the correctional climate. *BMC Psychiatry*, *16*(1), 91.

Grounds, A.T. (2005). Understanding the effects of wrongful imprisonment. *Crime and Justice: A Review of Research*, *32*, 1–58.

Gunst, E., & Vanhooren, S. (2018). The destructive pattern: An experiential and existential theory-building case study. *Person-centered & Experiential Psychotherapies*, *17*, 1–18.

Guse, T., & Hudson, D. (2014). Psychological strengths and posttraumatic growth in the successful reintegration of South African ex-offenders. *International Journal of Offender Therapy and Comparative Criminology*, *58*(12), 1449–1465.

Halsey, M. (2007). Assembling recidivism: The promise and contingencies of post-release life. *Journal of Criminal Law and Criminology*, *97*(4), 1209–1260.

Halsey, M., & Harris, V. (2011). Prisoner futures: Sensing the signs of generativity. *Australian & New Zealand Journal of Criminology*, *44*(1), 74–93.

Haney, C. (2006). *Reforming punishment: Psychological limits to the pains of imprisonment*. Washington, DC: American Psychological Association.

Hannah-Moffat, K. (2001). *Punishment in disguise: Penal governance and federal imprisonment of women in Canada*. Toronto, ON: University of Toronto Press.

Hart, E. L. (2017). Women prisoners and the drive for desistance: Capital and responsibilization as a barrier to change. *Women & Criminal Justice*, *27*(3), 151–169.

Hassan, L., Birmingham, L., Harty, M. A., Jarrett, M., Jones, P., King, C., ... & Thornicroft, G. (2011). Prospective cohort study of mental health during imprisonment. *The British Journal of Psychiatry*, *198*(1), 37–42.

Heidemann, G., Cederbaum, J. A., Martinez, S., & LeBel, T. P. (2016). Wounded healers: How formerly incarcerated women help themselves by helping others. *Punishment & Society*, *18*(1), 3–26.

Helgeson, V. S., Reynolds, K. A., & Tomich, P. L. (2006). A meta-analytic review of benefit finding and growth. *Journal of Consulting and Clinical Psychology*, *74*(5), 797–816.

336 van Ginneken and Vanhooren

Jamieson, R., & Grounds, A. (2005). Release and adjustment: Perspectives from studies of wrongly convicted and politically motivated prisoners. In A. Liebling & S. Maruna (eds), *The effects of imprisonment* (pp. 33–65). Cullompton: Willan Publishing.

Janoff-Bulman, R. (1989). Assumptive worlds and the stress of traumatic events: Applications of the schema construct. *Social Cognition, 7*(2), 113–136.

Janoff-Bulman, R. (1992). *Shattered assumptions: Towards a new psychology of trauma.* New York: Free Press.

Jayawickreme, E., & Blackie, L. E. (2014). Post-traumatic growth as positive personality change: Evidence, controversies and future directions. *European Journal of Personality, 28*(4), 312–331.

Kazemian, L. (2020). *Positive growth and redemption in prison: Finding light behind bars and beyond.* Abingdon: Routledge.

Kunst, M. J. J. (2011). Affective personality type, post-traumatic stress disorder symptom severity and post-traumatic growth in victims of violence. *Stress and Health, 27*(1), 42–51.

Kunst, M. J. J. (2012). Recalled peritraumatic distress in survivors of violent crime: Exploring its impact on the relationship between posttraumatic stress disorder symptoms and posttraumatic growth. *The Journal of Nervous and Mental Disease, 200*(11), 962–966.

LeBel, T. P., Burnett, R., Maruna, S., & Bushway, S. (2008). The "chicken and egg" of subjective and social factors in desistance from crime. *European Journal of Criminology, 5*(2), 131–159.

LeBel, T. P., Richie, M., & Maruna, S. (2015). Helping others as a response to reconcile a criminal past: The role of the wounded healer in prisoner reentry programs. *Criminal Justice and Behavior, 42*(1), 108–120.

Lennox, C., Bell, V., O'Malley, K., Shaw, J., & Dolan, M. (2013). A prospective cohort study of the changing mental health needs of adolescents in custody. *BMJ Open, 3*(3), e002358.

Liebling, A., & Ludlow, A. (2016). Suicide, distress and the quality of prison life. In Y. Jewkes, B. Crewe, & J. Bennett (eds), *Handbook on prisons* (pp. 224–245). Abingdon: Routledge.

Liebling, A., Tait, S., Durie, L., Stiles, A., & Harvey, J. (2005). *An evaluation of the Safer Locals Programme: Final report.* Cambridge: Cambridge Institute of Criminology.

Liem, M., & Kunst, M. (2013). Is there a recognizable post-incarceration syndrome among released "lifers"? *International Journal of Law and Psychiatry, 36*(3–4), 333–337.

Mapham, A., & Hefferon, K. (2012). "I used to be an offender—Now I'm a defender": Positive psychology approaches in the facilitation of posttraumatic growth in offenders. *Journal of Offender Rehabilitation, 51*(6), 389–413.

Maruna, S. (2001). *Making good: How ex-convicts reform and rebuild their lives.* Washington, DC: American Psychological Association.

Maruna, S., Wilson, L., & Curran, K. (2006). Why God is often found behind bars: Prison conversions and the crisis of self-narrative. *Research in Human Development, 3*(2–3), 161–184.

McAdams, D. (1996). Personality, modernity, and the storied self: A contemporary framework for studying persons. *Psychological Inquiry, 7*(4), 295–321.

McAdams, D. P., & de St. Aubin, E. (1998). Introduction. In D. P. McAdams & E. de St. Aubin (eds), *Generativity and adult development: How and why we care for*

Posttraumatic Growth among Prisoners 337

the next generation (pp. xix–xxiv). Washington, DC: American Psychological Association.

McFarland, C., & Alvaro, C. (2000). The impact of motivation on temporal comparisons: Coping with traumatic events by perceiving personal growth. *Journal of Personality and Social Psychology*, *79*(3), 327–343.

Novek, E. M. (2005). "Heaven, hell, and here": Understanding the impact of incarceration through a prison newspaper. *Critical Studies in Media Communication*, *22*(4), 281–301.

Nygaard, E., & Heir, T. (2012). World assumptions, posttraumatic stress and quality of life after a natural disaster: A longitudinal study. *Health and Quality of Life Outcomes*, *10*(1), 76.

O'Connell, E., Abbott, R. P., & White, R. S. (2017). Emotions and beliefs after a disaster: A comparative analysis of Haiti and Indonesia. *Disasters*, *41*(4), 803–827.

Paternoster, R., & Bushway, S. (2009). Desistance and the "feared self": Toward an identity theory of criminal desistance. *The Journal of Criminal Law and Criminology*, *99*(4), 1103–1156.

Perrin, C., & Blagden, N. (2014). Accumulating meaning, purpose and opportunities to change "drip by drip": The impact of being a listener in prison. *Psychology, Crime & Law*, *20*(9), 902–920.

Plugge, E., Douglas, N. & Fitzpatrick, R. (2011). Changes in health-related quality of life following imprisonment in 92 women in England: A three month follow-up study. *International Journal for Equity in Health*, *10*(1), 21–27.

Powell, S., Rosner, R., Butollo, W., Tedeschi, R. G., & Calhoun, L. G. (2003). Posttraumatic growth after war: A study with former refugees and displaced people in Sarajevo. *Journal of Clinical Psychology*, *59*(1), 71–83.

Prison Health Policy Unit and Prison Health Task Force (2002). *Health promoting prisons: A shared approach*. London: HMSO/DH.

Richards, B. (1978). The experience of long-term imprisonment – An exploratory investigation. *British Journal of Criminology*, *18*(2), 162–169.

Ronel, N., & Segev, D. (2014). How the positive can influence criminal behavior: Growing out of criminal spin by positive criminology approaches. In D. Pollizi, M. Braswell, & M. Draper (eds), *Transforming corrections: Humanistic approaches to corrections and offender treatment* (pp. 229–243). Durham, NC: Carolina Academic Press.

Salo, J. A., Qouta, S., & Punamäki, R. L. (2005). Adult attachment, posttraumatic growth and negative emotions among former political prisoners. *Anxiety, Stress, and Coping*, *18*(4), 361–378.

Sapsford, R. (1983). *Life sentence prisoners: Reaction, response and change*. Milton Keynes: Open University Press.

Schinkel, M. (2014). *Being imprisoned: Punishment, adaptation and desistance*. Basingstoke: Palgrave Macmillan.

Segrave, M., & Carlton, B. (2010). Women, trauma, criminalisation and imprisonment. *Current Issues in Criminal Justice*, *22*(2), 287–305.

Sledge, W. H., & Boydstun, J. A. (1980). Self-concept changes related to war captivity. *Archives of General Psychiatry*, *37*(4), 430–443.

Sirdifield, C., Gojkovic, D., Brooker, C., & Ferriter, M. (2009). A systematic review of research on the epidemiology of mental health disorders in prison populations: A summary of findings. *The Journal of Forensic Psychiatry & Psychology*, *20*(S1), S78–S101.

338 *van Ginneken and Vanhooren*

Smith, S. G., & Cook, S. L. (2004). Are reports of posttraumatic growth positively biased? *Journal of Traumatic Stress*, *17*(4), 353–358.

Social Exclusion Unit. (2002). *Reducing re-offending by ex-prisoners*. London: SEU.

Soyer, M. (2014). The imagination of desistance: A juxtaposition of the construction of incarceration as a turning point and the reality of recidivism. *British Journal of Criminology*, *54*(1), 91–108.

Spalek, B., & El-Hassan, S. (2007). Muslim converts in prison. *The Howard Journal of Crime and Justice*, *46*(2), 99–114.

Stanton, A. L., Bower, J. E., & Low, C. A. (2006). Posttraumatic growth after cancer. In L. G. Calhoun & R. G. Tedeschi (eds), *Handbook of posttraumatic growth: Research and practice* (pp. 138–175). Mahwah, NJ: Lawrence Erlbaum.

Steger, M.F. (2012). Making meaning in life. *Psychological Inquiry*, *23*(4), 381–385.

Sumalla, E. C., Ochoa, C., & Blanco, I. (2009). Posttraumatic growth in cancer: Reality or illusion? *Clinical Psychology Review*, *29*(1), 24–33.

Sykes, G.M. (1958). *The society of captives*. Princeton, NJ: Princeton University Press.

Tedeschi, R. G., & Calhoun, L. G. (1996). The Posttraumatic Growth Inventory: Measuring the positive legacy of trauma. *Journal of Traumatic Stress*, *9*(3), 455–471.

Tedeschi, R. G., & Calhoun, L. G. (2004). Posttraumatic growth: Conceptual foundations and empirical evidence. *Psychological Inquiry*, *15*(1), 1–18.

Tedeschi, R., Park, C., & Calhoun, L. (1998). Posttraumatic growth: Conceptual issues. In R. Tedeschi, C. Park, & L. Calhoun (eds), *Posttraumatic growth: Positive changes in the aftermath of crisis* (pp. 1–23). Mahwah, NJ: Erlbaum.

Tennen, H., & Affleck, G. (2002). Benefit-finding and benefit-reminding. In C. R. Snyder & S. J. Lopez (eds), *Handbook of positive psychology* (pp. 584–597). New York: Oxford University Press.

Van Ginneken, E. F. J. C. (2015). Doing well or just doing time? A qualitative study of patterns of psychological adjustment in prison. *The Howard Journal of Criminal Justice*, *54*(4), 352–370.

Van Ginneken, E. F. J. C. (2016). Making sense of imprisonment: Narratives of posttraumatic growth among female prisoners. *International Journal of Offender Therapy and Comparative Criminology*, *60*(2), 208–227.

Van Ginneken, E. F. J. C., Palmen, H., Bosma, A. Q., Nieuwbeerta, P., & Berghuis, M. L. (2018). The Life in Custody Study: The quality of prison life in Dutch prison regimes. *Journal of Criminological Research, Policy and Practice*, *4*(4), 253–268.

Vanhooren, S. (2018). Een existentieel keerpunt? Gedetineerden, betekenisverlies en posttraumatische groei [An existential turning point? Prisoners, loss of meaning, and posttraumatic growth]. *Tijdschrift Persoonsgerichte Experiëntiële Psychotherapie*, *56*, 63–73.

Vanhooren, S., Leijssen, M., & Dezutter, J. (2016). Profiles of meaning and search for meaning among prisoners. *The Journal of Positive Psychology*, *11*(6), 622–633.

Vanhooren, S., Leijssen, M., & Dezutter, J. (2017a). Ten prisoners on a search for meaning: A qualitative study of loss and growth during incarceration. *The Humanistic Psychologist*, *45*, 162–178.

Vanhooren, S., Leijssen, M., & Dezutter, J. (2017b). Posttraumatic growth in sex offenders: A pilot study with a mixed-method design. *International Journal of Offender Therapy and Comparative Criminology*, *61*, 171–190.

Vanhooren, S., Leijssen, M., & Dezutter, J. (2017c). Loss of meaning as a predictor of distress in prison. *International Journal of Offender Therapy and Comparative Criminology, 61*, 1411–1432.

Vanhooren, S., Leijssen, M., & Dezutter, J. (2018a). Coping strategies and posttraumatic growth in prison. *The Prison Journal, 98*, 123–142.

Vanhooren, S., Leijssen, M., & Dezutter, J. (2018b). Posttraumatic growth during incarceration: A case study from an experiential-existential perspective. *Journal of Humanistic Psychology, 58*, 144–167.

Wolff, N., Morgan, R. D., & Shi, J. (2013). Comparative analysis of attitudes and emotions among inmates: Does mental illness matter? *Criminal Justice and Behavior, 40*, 1092–1108.

Worrall, A. (1990). *Offending women: Female lawbreakers and the criminal justice system*. London: Routledge.

Zamble, E., & Porporino, F. J. (1988). *Coping, behavior and adaptation in prison inmates*. New York: Springer-Verlag.

Zhou, X., Wu, X., & Chen, J. (2015). Longitudinal linkages between posttraumatic stress disorder and posttraumatic growth in adolescent survivors following the Wenchuan earthquake in China: A three-wave, cross-lagged study. *Psychiatry Research, 228*(1), 107–111.

Znoj, H. (2006). Bereavement and posttraumatic growth. In L. G. Calhoun & R. G. Tedeschi (eds), *Handbook of posttraumatic growth: Research and practice* (pp. 176–196). Mahwah, NJ: Lawrence Erlbaum.

Zoellner, T., & Maercker, A. (2006). Posttraumatic growth in clinical psychology – A critical review and introduction of a two component model. *Clinical Psychology Review, 26*(5), 626–653.

Zwiercan, A., & Joseph, S. (2018). Focusing manner and posttraumatic growth. *Person-centered & Experiential Psychotherapies, 17*, 191–200

Yalom, I. (1980). *Existential psychotherapy*. New York: Basic Books.

Part 3

Biology, Understanding, and Treatment

13 The Use, Validity, and Translational Utility of Animal Models of Posttraumatic Stress Disorder

Eric D. Eisenmann, Chelsea E. Cadle, and Phillip R. Zoladz

Posttraumatic stress disorder (PTSD) is a debilitating mental disorder reflecting enduring abnormalities in cognitive, emotional, and physiological processes following exposure to a traumatic event (American Psychiatric Association, 2013). The APA first acknowledged PTSD as an independent mental disorder in the 1980s with the release of the Diagnostic and Statistical Manual of Mental Disorders, third edition (DSM-III; American Psychiatric Association, 1987). Since the inception of PTSD, the literature has rested on the core assumption that traumatic events involving actual or threatened death or serious injury (i.e., Criterion A, DSM-V) are causally linked to a distinct set of reactions (i.e., Criteria B to E, DSM-V), making PTSD unique among mental disorders recognized in the DSM (Davidson & Foa, 1991). The underlying assumption that traumatic events provide the most potent (Meehl, 1977) a etiologic agent to account for PTSD development has endured, despite changes to the definition of Criterion A in subsequent DSM editions (APA, 2013; Rosen & Lilienfeld, 2008). The logic of this position is that different types of stressors (i.e., combat, rape, motor vehicle accidents) have different magnitudes, which significantly influence an individual's response.

If the magnitude of a traumatic event was adequate for predicting PTSD development and/or severity post-exposure, one would expect Criterion A to be necessary for the syndrome to develop and to contribute the greatest variance to PTSD symptom expression (Rosen & Lilienfeld, 2008), which includes intrusion symptoms (Criterion B), persistent avoidance of stimuli associated with the trauma (Criterion C), negative alterations in cognitions and mood that are associated with the traumatic event (Criterion D), and alterations in arousal and reactivity that are associated with the traumatic event (Criterion E) (APA, 2013). To date, epidemiological PTSD studies have failed to provide consistent support linking the severity of a distinct traumatic event to a specific set of symptom responses; accordingly, there are concerns about the validity underlying Criterion A-driven assumptions (Breslau & Davis, 1987). Among the greatest challenges are results indicating that (1) non-criterion A events (e.g., marital infidelity) can elicit many of the symptoms associated with PTSD (Burstein, 1984; Dattilio,

DOI: 10.4324/9781351134637-14

2004; Dreman, 1991; Helzer, Robins, & McEvoy, 1987) and (2) there is little support for a simple dose–response relationship between stressor intensity and resulting symptomatology (Brewin, Andrews, & Valentine, 2000; Ehlers, Mayou, & Bryant, 1998). Consistent with these results are epidemiological studies for the prevalence of lifetime trauma exposure that demonstrate that most adults are exposed to at least one Criterion A event, but only a minority of those exposed develop symptoms consistent with PTSD (Breslau, Davis, Andreski, & Peterson, 1991; Breslau & Kessler, 2001; Breslau et al., 1998; Landgraf & Wigger, 2002). For example, the National Comorbidity Survey (NCS) Report estimated the lifetime prevalence of PTSD among American adults was 7.8%, despite the fact that 60.7% of men and 51.2% of women respondents reported exposure to at least one traumatic event (Van Ameringen et al., 2008). Moreover, women (10.4%) were twice as likely as men (5%) to meet the criteria for PTSD (Van Ameringen et al., 2008). Canadians were estimated to have a 9.2% lifetime prevalence of PTSD (Van Ameringen et al., 2008), even though 76.1% of Canadian respondents reported exposure to at least one traumatic event. Taken together, the available results suggest that Criterion A events are not always necessary or sufficient for the development of PTSD (McFarlane & De Girolamo, 1996; Shalev et al., 1996; Yehuda, McFarlane, & Shalev, 1998). The lack of evidence to support a relationship between exposure to a traumatic event (Criterion A) and the development of PTSD has led to increased research into individual difference factors that could help account for the variability in response to trauma exposure. Research efforts have focused attention on potential risk factors (before, during, and after traumatic events) that predispose some individuals to develop and maintain PTSD (Bowman, 2013; Yehuda & McFarlane, 1995).

The Role of Animal Models in PTSD Research

Clinical studies are able to answer questions related to PTSD prevalence in comparative groups but have a limited ability to indicate why certain factors increase the risk for PTSD development. Epidemiological data provide crucial information, but researchers have not yet identified a distinct pathophysiology or other validating marker of the PTSD construct. Preclinical research using valid animal models can complement clinical investigations, allowing researchers to test theories of PTSD aetiology and pathophysiology, as well as offering opportunities to develop and test novel treatments. Animal models enable explorations that are difficult to conduct in clinical studies and provide several unique advantages when studying PTSD. First, animal models make it possible to directly test for different PTSD comorbidities and risk factors that might explain causation and influence treatment responses in humans. Second, a stressor that is comparable to a traumatic event experienced by humans can be carefully controlled, allowing for the direct study of events that result in PTSD-like phenotypes and, thus, helping refine our definition of Criterion A. Third,

Animal Models of PTSD 345

valid animal models induce certain translational PTSD-like symptoms in non-human animals and allow investigators to link such symptoms to physiological mechanisms. Lastly, animal models can circumvent ethical limitations observed in clinical research, enabling the assessment of treatment outcomes for novel pharmacological agents with direct measurement of the molecular changes. However, despite the advantages, animal models cannot perfectly replicate human pathophysiology in uniquely human conditions, such as PTSD, because the cognitive and linguistic processes underlying the stress response in humans are largely absent in other mammals (Shalev & Rogel-Fuchs, 1993; Stam, 2007b).

Preclinical research often attempts to reproduce features of human psychiatric disorders in laboratory animals by correlating observed physiological and behavioural changes with specific emotional states (face validity), the aetiology of pathology (construct validity), and responses to pharmacological treatments (predictive validity). A defendable animal model of PTSD is one that produces variability in responses that are predicted by factors other than the severity of the stressor. Determining the degree to which an animal model is representative of a human syndrome requires an evaluation of whether the model captures critical aspects of the entire condition (i.e., underlying a etiological mechanisms, symptom expression, and treatment response). Many researchers have provided such evaluations for the face validity of animal models (Goswami et al., 2013; Schöner et al., 2017); however, construct and predictive validity have been less extensively explored. We designed the present chapter to describe contemporary animal models of PTSD, determine their construct and predictive validity, and offer experimental evidence highlighting their translational utility. We have organized our coverage of these animal models around the type of stressor utilized by investigators to induce PTSD-like physiological and behavioural sequelae.

Early Life Stressors

Stress that occurs early in life increases one's susceptibility to PTSD. In humans, prenatal stress has been associated with long-lasting behavioural, emotional, and cognitive changes. Such changes are suggestive of neurodevelopmental changes, which could result in increased susceptibility to develop PTSD after exposure to trauma later in life (Van den Bergh et al., 2005). Furthermore, exposure to childhood trauma (e.g., physical abuse, emotional neglect) increases the risk of developing PTSD as an adult (Bremner et al., 1993; Delahanty & Nugent, 2006; Epstein, Saunders, & Kilpatrick, 1997; Heim & Nemeroff, 2001; Sanchez, Ladd, & Plotsky, 2001). Childhood trauma may result in maladaptive developmental changes that lead to decreased hippocampal volume, abnormal baseline cortisol levels, and enhanced negative feedback of the hypothalamus-pituitary-adrenal (HPA) axis (Bremner, 2002; De Bellis, 2001; De Bellis et al., 1999). The hippocampus is a medial temporal lobe structure that is important for learning and memory. A smaller hippocampus has been observed in multiple studies involving PTSD patients, and some evidence suggests that a smaller, or less functional, hippocampus is a pre-existing risk factor for developing PTSD following trauma exposure, possibly due to impairing one's ability to process trauma-related contextual cues (Gilbertson et al., 2002, 2007). The HPA axis is the physiological system that controls the synthesis and release of cortisol, a steroid hormone that is important for the body's response to stress. Following its release, cortisol exerts negative feedback on receptors throughout the body to regulate its own production. A properly controlled cortisol response and feedback system is important for the stress response to fulfill its adaptive purpose. In other words, having abnormal baseline cortisol levels or enhanced negative feedback of the HPA axis can result in a maladaptive stress response that predisposes one to psychiatric conditions, such as PTSD. Because cortisol exerts significant negative feedback on receptors in the hippocampus, it is unsurprising that extensive work has shown that chronically occurring abnormal cortisol levels can result in the shortening of hippocampal neurons and impaired hippocampal function (McEwen, Nasca, & Gray, 2016), thereby predisposing one to the development of PTSD. Unfortunately, studies of childhood trauma are often confounded by environmental issues, such as parental response to traumatic events, which is important to note because parental PTSD symptoms increase the likelihood that a child will develop PTSD (Nugent et al., 2007; Pelcovitz et al., 1998).

Researchers have attempted to identify the underlying pathology that is associated with an increased risk of developing PTSD by using animal models. Juvenile rats exposed to severe psychological stress or high levels of glucocorticoids early in life react more severely to subsequent stressors (Bazak et al., 2009; Cohen et al., 2006). Prenatal (Glover, O'Connor, & O'Donnell, 2010) and postnatal (Claessens et al., 2011) stressors have been used with rodents to study the effect of early life stressors on future stress responses. Prenatal rodent studies have exposed pregnant mothers to social stressors, such as overcrowding (Dahlöf, Hård, & Larsson, 1978), or physical stressors, such as electric tail shocks (Takahashi, Haglin, & Kalin, 1992), noise and flashing lights (Freide & Weinstock, 1984), restraint (Alonso et al., 1991), or cold water immersion (Velazquez-Moctezuma, Salazar, & Rueda, 1993). In general, these studies have found that prenatal stress produces sustained changes in physiology and behaviour, including learning deficits, heightened anxiety, reduced attention, altered immune system function, and altered cardiovascular reactivity (Glover et al., 2010). An advantage of animal models examining prenatal stress is the ability to control confounds such as the postnatal environment, potential genetic differences, and the timing and intensity of the stressor (Weinstock, 2001).

Postnatal stress studies commonly use a model involving maternal separation from neonatal pups and have demonstrated similar results. Pups are separated from their mother for prolonged periods, ranging from one to 24 hours. Results from maternal separation studies show HPA axis

Animal Models of PTSD 347

hyper-responsiveness (Plotsky & Meaney, 1993) and impaired cognitive performance (Levine, 2005). Differential glucocorticoid responsiveness is believed to underlie the changes in the HPA axis and cognition (Levine, 2005); however, postnatal stress studies are not necessarily the most defendable models for studying trauma-like events. The responses to stress in these studies are not solely accounted for by the acute stressor; a lack of maternal care may account for more of the variance seen in responses to the stressor (Stam, 2007a). Another possible confounding variable is the developmental stage of rodents when they are born. Rodents are born at a much less developed stage than humans, which further limits the translational utility of postnatal stress studies. There are also significant differences between rodents and humans in the regulation of maternal-placental-foetal neuroendocrine processes (Weinstock, 2001).

Physical Stressors

Animal models of PTSD have been developed which directly stress subjects through administration of controlled aversive stimuli. Broadly referred to as physical stressors, aversive stimuli can be controlled for in terms of quality, intensity, and duration. Numerous animal models with diverse paradigms have been developed that use one or more physical stressors as a means to replicate Criterion A requirements. Representative physical stressors include electric shock, underwater/forced swim models, restraint stress, and the single prolonged stress model. Models have also been developed using multiple physical stressors over a period of time (i.e., chronic stress). Preclinical research using physical stressors in rodent subjects typically produces enduring physiological and behavioural signs of anxiety and/or fear, such as an exaggerated startle response, cognitive impairments, enhanced fear conditioning, resistance to fear extinction, and reduced social interaction.

Electric Shock

Electric foot-shock is a physical stressor with emotional consequences that has been used to study PTSD (Bali & Jaggi, 2015b). Electric foot-shock has been used in animal research to study the response of an animal to a disruption in homeostasis (i.e., stress) since 1908 (Yerkes & Dodson, 1908). Since that time, foot-shock has been incorporated as a stimulus in various animal models of human disease, including anxiety (Geller & Seifter, 1960; Louvart et al., 2006; Van Dijken et al., 1992b), depression (Seligman, 1972; Vollmayr & Henn, 2001), and PTSD (Bali & Jaggi, 2015b; Pynoos et al., 1996; Yu et al., 2014).

Numerous foot-shock models have been used to induce PTSD-like symptoms in animals by invoking long-term sensitization of the stress response. The models involve rats or mice that are exposed to a single or limited number of electric foot-shock sessions. Each session uses one long

348   Eisenmann, Cadle, and Zoladz

(10 seconds to 3 minutes) or a small number of shorter inescapable, unpredictable shocks (between 1 and 6 seconds, repeated 1–10 times) at relatively high intensities ranging from 1 to 2.5 mA that are delivered to the feet through floor grids (Louvart et al., 2006; Pawlyk et al., 2005; Philbert et al., 2011; Pynoos et al., 1996; Siegmund & Wotjak, 2007). Some studies combine the foot-shock model with a situational reminder of the stressful experience which serves as contextually conditioned Pavlovian cue (e.g., re-exposure to the box where the shocks were administered) (Pynoos et al., 1996). Exposure to repeated situational reminders induces a progressive increase in the startle response in rats, similar to behavioural changes observed in PTSD patients (Pynoos et al., 1996). Foot-shock offers significant experimental control over intensity and duration, allowing researchers to see the relationship between intensity and behavioural sensitization. Higher current intensity results in stronger behavioural sensitization than lower current intensity (Anderson et al., 1976; Pijlman, Wolterink, & van Ree, 2002).

In general, foot-shock models meet the criteria for face validity as models of PTSD. Rodents exposed to foot-shock models of PTSD exhibit high levels of persistent freezing (fear development), exaggerated responsiveness to external stimuli (hyperarousal), persistent sleep disturbances, and hypocortisolism (Li et al., 2005; Louvart et al., 2005; Pawlyk et al., 2005; Philbert et al., 2011; Pynoos et al., 1996; Shimizu et al., 2004). Furthermore, selective serotonin reuptake inhibitor (SSRI) treatment decreases sensitized fear, hyperarousal, and avoidance-like behaviour in rodents exposed to foot-shock models (Shimizu et al., 2004; Siegmund & Wotjak, 2007). SSRIs (e.g., sertraline), which increase serotonin levels in the synapse, are the first line of treatment for PTSD. Accordingly, models of PTSD using foot-shock appear to have face and predictive validity. The major advantage of foot-shock relative to other physical stressors is that rodents do not readily habituate to foot-shock (Bali & Jaggi, 2015a, 2015b; Hajos-Korcsok et al., 2003; Van den Berg et al., 1998). By way of contrast, immobilization, restraint, and water immersion result in habituation after repeated exposure (Agrawal, Jaggi, & Singh, 2011; Chauhan et al., 2015).

Animal models that use electric foot-shock to model PTSD are different from those used to model depression. Paradigms modelling depression also involve inescapable foot-shocks; however, these models generally involve delivery of lower intensity shocks (~.7mA) for a longer period of time (40–60 min) (Sherman et al.; Sherman, Sacquitne, & Petty, 1982; Vollmayr & Henn, 2001; Wang et al., 2007). Inescapable foot-shocks lead to a state of "learned helplessness", where animals will later allow themselves to be shocked at a low intensity (.4 mA) even when they have the opportunity to escape. The learned helplessness model was first described in dogs (Overmier & Seligman, 1967; Seligman & Maier, 1967), but has since been validated in fish, pigeons, mice, and rats (McKinney Jr, 2012).

Differentiating between foot-shock models of depression and PTSD, rats exposed to the depression, or learned helplessness, model typically do not respond to antipsychotic or anxiolytic treatment and exhibit a decreased sensitivity and responsiveness to reward (sucrose) (Sanchis-Segura et al., 2005). Rodents in PTSD models typically show an aversion to a sucrose reward on the first day of testing; however, the aversion seems to be due to neophobia (i.e., fear of novelty) rather than anhedonia (i.e., a lack of pleasure or desire for pleasure) (Pijlman et al., 2003; Pijlman, Wolterink, & Van Ree, 2003; Stam, 2007a; Van Dijken et al., 1992a).

The translational utility of foot-shock in neuroscience has been well-documented (Bali & Jaggi, 2015b). For example, foot-shock allows comparisons between novel treatment strategies (e.g., nisoldipine) and previously effective therapies (e.g., sertraline) (Verma et al., 2016). One particularly interesting study incorporated foot-shock as an early life stressor in transgenic mice (i.e., mice that had their DNA altered) (Joseph et al., 2013). Transgenic manipulations are often used in preclinical work to examine the involvement of specific genes in the aetiology of a disorder. Such methodology affords investigators the ability to identify genes that might predispose humans to develop PTSD following trauma exposure. In the study, at postnatal day 25 (i.e., adolescence), cholecystokinin receptor-2 (CCK-2) transgenic mice were subjected to high-intensity foot-shocks (1.0mA, 2 s) five times during a one-minute trial. Because of the CCK-2 genetic alteration, these mice exhibited greater expression of CCK activity. At postnatal day 60 (i.e., adulthood), the mice were subjected to an additional stress trial consisting of a .8 mA shock for two seconds. The results revealed that the transgenic mice exhibited impaired glucocorticoid negative feedback inhibition and impaired spatial learning; however, if the CCK-2 gene was suppressed during adolescent stress, the impairments to the negative feedback system in adult rats were diminished. Transgenic mice treated with the SSRI fluoxetine evidenced diminished impairment of glucocorticoid negative feedback, but they still exhibited learning deficits (Joseph et al., 2013). The researchers effectively used foot-shock to investigate the role of the CCK-2 gene in the development of PTSD-like symptoms (i.e., avoidance, cognitive impairment) in rodents. By presenting the foot-shock in adolescence and adulthood, the researchers were better able to determine the impact of transgenic modification on the development of a PTSD-like phenotype (Joseph et al., 2013).

PTSD is typified by dysfunctional fear modulation and decreased extinction of fear (Pitman et al., 2012). The modification of classical fear conditioning techniques using foot-shock has been able to replicate core PTSD-like symptoms in rodents; however, foot-shock is not an ecologically valid stressor in rodents because the stimulus does not naturally occur in the rat habitat (Bali & Jaggi, 2015b). Further, the overlap of depression-like and PTSD-like symptoms also raises limitations for the use of foot-shock to solely model PTSD (Goswami et al., 2013).

350 Eisenmann, Cadle, and Zoladz

Restraint Stress and Single Prolonged Stress (SPS)

Restraint stress has been used to model aspects of PTSD. Animals are restrained to a wooden board or in a plastic restraint device for 15 minutes to 2 hours (Vallès, Martí, & Armario, 2006). Restrained rats have increased behavioural anxiety and nociception, as measured via behavioural responses (e.g., head flinching, rubbing the painful region) (Gameiro et al., 2006). The increased anxiety and pain can be blocked by stimulation of alpha-2a adrenoreceptors with guanfacine (Hains, Yabe, & Arnsten, 2015). Restraint stress generates PTSD-like anxiety, but when used alone does not produce the entire array of symptoms observed with better validated animal models of PTSD (Borghans & Homberg, 2015). The single prolonged stress (SPS) model expands on the restraint stress model by using several different stressors in a single session to elicit PTSD-like symptoms in rats (Liberzon, Krstov, & Young, 1997). In the SPS model, rats are immobilized for two hours, then forced to swim for 20 minutes, and then exposed to diethyl ether until they become unconscious (Liberzon et al., 1997; Liberzon et al., 1999). After 30 minutes of unconsciousness, the rats may be exposed to a single electric foot-shock of 1 mA intensity for 4 seconds (Wang et al., 2008). The single foot-shock allows for the testing of a conditioned fear response by re-exposure to the shock context.

SPS has face and predictive validity as a model of PTSD in rodents. One week after SPS, rats exhibit significantly increased startle responses compared against both a control group and their own pre-exposure responses (Khan & Liberzon, 2004). SPS also leads to diminished fear extinction (Knox et al., 2012), anxiety-like behaviour, and increased nociception (Zhang, Gandhi, & Standifer, 2012), all of which have been reversed by administering an SSRI (Lin, Tung, & Liu, 2016; Takahashi et al., 2006). Furthermore, rats exposed to the SPS model evidence increased negative feedback of the HPA axis (Liberzon et al., 1997; Liberzon et al., 1999). PTSD patients display similar physiologic abnormalities, including low baseline cortisol levels and increased negative feedback of cortisol (Yehuda, 2001; Yehuda et al., 1993); accordingly, SPS is supported as a model for PTSD in humans.

A recent translational utilization of the SPS model studied the model's impact on sleep (Vanderheyden et al., 2015). Rodents were exposed to the SPS model after being implanted with electrodes capable of recording electrical activity in the brain (i.e., electroencephalogram [EEG]) and peripheral muscle activity (i.e., electromyography [EMG]). The rodents were monitored with EEG and EMG for seven days after exposure to the SPS. Altered EEG waveforms and altered sleep, including increased REM sleep and transitions to REM sleep, were seen. The researchers effectively used SPS to study changes from baseline sleep patterns, including changes that occurred over the course of the development of a PTSD-like phenotype (Liberzon et al., 1997; Liberzon et al., 1999; Yamamoto et al.,

Animal Models of PTSD   351

2009). Ultimately, the results may have supported the identified waveform abnormalities as potential biomarkers for increased PTSD susceptibility (Vanderheyden et al., 2015).

Underwater Trauma

Underwater trauma has been used to model PTSD in rodents as well (Richter-Levin, 1998). In the underwater model, rats are forced to swim for one minute in a large tub of water and are then submerged underwater for 30 seconds. The submergence is thought to be the traumatic stressor and is more ecologically valid than electric foot-shocks, as drowning is a real-life possibility for rats in the wild. The rats are then removed from the water and returned to their home cages. Spatial learning is impaired for up to three weeks after submergence (Richter-Levin, 1998). Simply immersing a rat in water will cause anxiety-like behaviour and a physiological stress response; however, the underwater trauma model produces significant decreases in basal corticosterone one week after trauma (Moore, Gauchan, & Genovese, 2012). Contrasted against water immersion, the underwater trauma model has been uniquely characterized as a traumatic stressor in rats (Moore et al., 2012). Accordingly, underwater trauma has been used to investigate the role of the hippocampus in the development of traumatic memories using biochemical assays (Sood et al., 2014) and electrophysiology (Ardi et al., 2014; Wang, Akirav, & Richter-Levin, 2000). The available results indicate reduced ability to develop long-term potentiation in the dentate gyrus after exposure to the traumatic stressor (Ardi et al., 2014; Wang et al., 2000). Results associated with underwater trauma studies in rats could improve our understanding of the relationship between stress, cognition, and learning.

Chronic Stress Models

Chronic stress models (e.g., chronic mild stress model; Willner et al., 1987) are primarily used to study depression (Schöner et al., 2017); however, models of chronic variable stress (CVS) have been developed to study PTSD (McGuire et al., 2010). The CVS model is potentially critical for understanding the influence of repeated exposure to traumatic events, such as incidents that can be experienced by public safety personnel (PSP; APA, 2013; Carleton et al., 2018). PSP includes, but is not limited to, border services officers, correctional workers, firefighters, paramedics, public safety communications officials, police, and search and rescue personnel. In the CVS model, rats are exposed twice daily to alternating stressors for one week. Stressors include swimming, hypoxia, shaking, cold, or restraint. Testing is performed either 16 hours or seven days after CVS. Rats exposed to CVS experience sensitization of the HPA axis and hyperarousal to fearful contexts (McGuire et al., 2010). Rats have also demonstrated anxiety-like behaviour and anhedonia (Zurita et al., 2000). Despite the correlates with

352　*Eisenmann, Cadle, and Zoladz*

PTSD, the CVS model also has important limitations. The co-morbidity between major depressive disorder and PTSD is high (Kessler et al., 1995), in part because of significant symptom overlap (i.e., the negative thoughts or feelings symptom cluster of PTSD); however, researchers have suggested that PTSD induction should use a brief and very intense stressor (Yehuda & Antelman, 1993), which is inconsistent with the CVS model.

Psychosocial Stressors

Several models of PTSD have been developed that rely on psychosocial stressors (e.g., social defeat stress, predator exposure) rather than physical stressors.

Social Defeat Stress

Social defeat has been used as a social stressor in rodents for over 40 years (Miczek, 1979). Social defeat stress has typically been used as a model of depression (Krishnan, Berton, & Nestler, 2008); as such, there are challenges in using social defeat for differentiating depression and PTSD. Recent modifications to social defeat stress models (Hammamieh et al., 2012) have demonstrated efficacy for producing anxiety and PTSD-like phenotypes (Daskalakis & Yehuda, 2014; Huhman, 2006). Contemporary social defeat stress now appears to be well-validated to model aspects of PTSD (Bhatnagar et al., 2006; Golden et al., 2011; Hammamieh et al., 2012; Koolhaas et al., 2013; Miczek, 1979; Vasconcelos, Stein, & de Almeida, 2015).

Social defeat stress generally involves placing a test male rodent ("intruder") into the home cage of a more aggressive rodent ("resident"). The resulting defeat of the intruder rodent results in social stress. Social defeat stress models may expose C57BL/6J mice to CD-1 (Golden et al., 2011; Koolhaas et al., 2013) or SJL albino mice (Warren et al., 2013). Generally, C57BL/6J mice are more docile than CD-1 or SJL albino mice (Golden et al., 2011; Koolhaas et al., 2013). Several variations of social defeat stress have been used as a social stressor in rodents. A classic experiment using the resident-intruder model places the resident in direct contact with the intruder for 5–10 minutes for 5–10 consecutive days. Following direct exposure, for an hour or for the rest of the day, the resident is placed in sensory contact with the intruder. That is, a barrier physically separates the two animals, but the intruder rodent experiences social stress via visual, olfactory, and auditory cues (Pulliam et al., 2010).

Variants of classical social defeat have been developed. For example, one animal may witness another animal undergo physical defeat by an aggressor and then the witness spends the rest of the day in sensory contact with the intruder (Patki, Solanki, & Salim, 2014; Warren et al., 2013). Ten days of witnessing social defeat produces a PTSD-like phenotype

Animal Models of PTSD 353

in a percentage of rodents similar to those directly exposed to the social defeat. Another PTSD-focused variation of social defeat stress is the cage-within-cage resident-intruder model (Hammamieh et al., 2012). For one month prior to the experiment, SJL albino male mice are placed in isolation to induce aggressiveness. These aggressor mice are then trained to assault intruders by occasional pairing with olfactory bulbectomized (OBx) male C57BL/6J mice. Adult male C57BL/6J mice are then placed in sensory contact with the trained aggressors for six hours daily for 5–10 days. During experimental aggressor exposures, the C57BL/6J mice are physically exposed to the aggressor for one minute. These physical exposures occur one to three times per session, mirroring the unpredictability of trauma in the human population (Hammamieh et al., 2012). Behavioural abnormalities found using social defeat stress include anhedonia-like symptoms, anxiety-like symptoms, persistent enhancement of the acoustic startle response, and an increased susceptibility to addictive behaviours (Berton et al., 2006; Covington & Miczek, 2005; Nikulina et al., 2004). Social defeat stress also leads to physical abnormalities, including elevated corticosteroids, increased oxidative stress, and inflammation in submissive animals (Huhman et al., 1992; Patki et al., 2013). Rodents exposed to the cage-within-cage resident-intruder variant display characteristic PTSD-like behaviour, including prolonged grooming, freezing, and retarded locomotion (Hammamieh et al., 2012). The symptoms produced by social defeat stress can last for more than a month after the initial event (Huhman, 2006). Evidencing a dose–response relationship, multiple social defeats elicit a more severe stress response than single exposures (Meerlo et al., 1996); however, even one social defeat episode causes defeated animals to engage in submissive behaviours (Jasnow & Huhman, 2001).

Studies using social defeat stress models indicate variability in anxiety-like response between animals; that is, not all animals exposed to social defeat display significant PTSD-like symptoms. For example, only 60–70% of C57BL/6J exposed to chronic social defeat stress display most of the aforementioned behavioural and physical symptoms. The remaining 30–40% of mice are classified as "resilient" (Golden et al., 2011). Identification of differential susceptibility allows researchers to study the mechanisms by which other mice develop resistance. Similar differential susceptibility in rodents exposed to predator odour stress led to formally dividing rats based on severity of symptoms (Cohen, Matar, & Joseph, 2013; Cohen et al., 2006).

A sophisticated use of social defeat looking at neurochemistry evidences both the predictive and translational validity of social defeat stress in modelling aspects of PTSD. Mice exposed to social defeat stress who were given chronic treatment with either fluoxetine or imipramine evidenced normal social contact, aligning with successful treatment of PTSD using antidepressants with humans (Burstein, 1984; Davidson, Roth, & Newman, 1991); however, the symptom and treatment overlap between major

354 *Eisenmann, Cadle, and Zoladz*

depressive disorder and PTSD complicate support for social defeat stress models as specific PTSD analogues (Tsankova et al., 2006). Researchers replicated the efficacy of chronic antidepressant administration for treating PTSD with viral-mediated, mesolimbic dopamine pathway-specific knock-down of brain-derived neurotrophic factor (BDNF) (Tsankova et al., 2006). The results indicated an essential role for BDNF in response to aversive social experiences (Berton et al., 2006). Future studies using social defeat stress to study PTSD should emphasize characteristics specific to PTSD; for example, making the traumatic event unpredictable (Hammamieh et al., 2012) and dividing rats based on the severity of their stress response (Cohen et al., 2006).

Predator Stress

Commonly used animal models of PTSD utilize predator exposure to produce PTSD-like symptoms (Clinchy, Sheriff, & Zanette, 2013). The use of an ecologically valid, trauma-like event which presents the threat or perceived threat of death or serious injury makes predator stress an effective stressor to elicit PTSD-like symptoms (Daskalakis, Yehuda, & Diamond, 2013). Predator stress models have been independently referred to as "psychological models" of PTSD because they do not typically involve physical harm (Goswami et al., 2013). Controlled biomedical studies have consistently evidenced a sustained psychological stress response after predator exposure (Apfelbach et al., 2005; Stam, 2007a)

Researchers have demonstrated that rats exhibit an innate fear of cats (Blanchard et al., 1990). Adamec and colleagues (1993) were the first group to formally develop a model of PTSD using cat exposure. Unprotected, but supervised, rodents exposed to a cat for 10 minutes led to anxiety-like behaviour and arousal, avoidance of trauma-related cues, and social withdrawal (Adamec & Shallow, 1993; Daskalakis & Yehuda, 2014). Predator exposure in rodents has demonstrated PTSD-like effects on learning and memory, the HPA axis, and brain chemistry after exposure (Diamond et al., 1999; Masini et al., 2006; Park et al., 2008; Woodson et al., 2003). PTSD models have been designed using different predators, such as a snake (Khonicheva et al., 2008; Mendes-Gomes et al., 2014), but researchers have generally found cat exposure to be the most stressful for rodents (Travis & Genovese, 2016). Notable animal models of PTSD expanding on the work of Adamec and colleagues include using predator odour or a social stress component (i.e., the psychosocial predator stress model).

Predator Odour

Evidencing outcomes similar to those resulting from direct predator exposure, investigators have used predator scents to model PTSD. For example, Cohen and colleagues (2013) formally developed a model of PTSD which stresses rodents by exposing them to urine-soiled cat litter for 5–10 minutes in a closed environment, where both "fight" and "flight" options are ineffective. Rodents exposed to cat litter displayed similar behavioural responses to those directly exposed to a cat; however, subgroups of rats displayed differential behavioural responses.

Cohen and colleagues (2013) further examined such individual variability in stress reactivity, which is an important consideration for identifying putative mechanisms and susceptibility for PTSD. After verifying an overall effect between stressed and unstressed rats, stressed rats were further subdivided into "extreme behavioural response" (EBR), "partial behavioural response" (PBR), and "minimal behavioural response" (MBR) groups based on tests assessing anxiety (EPM) and arousal (acoustic startle response [ASR]). An extreme behavioural response on both tests was used to classify a rat as EBR. Roughly 20% of rats exposed to the model were classified as exhibiting EBR (Cohen et al., 2013), which closely mirrors the prevalence of PTSD in traumatized humans (15% to 35%; Breslau et al., 1991; Breslau et al., 1998). The results add predictive validity to the predator odour model. The predator odour model has been the most commonly used model for studying individual variance in PTSD susceptibility, but other models have been used to identify PTSD biomarkers or predisposing factors as well (Krishnan et al., 2007; Siegmund et al., 2009).

A recent translational application of the Cohen model was used to assess the impact of sleep deprivation on PTSD symptoms. Cohen and colleagues (2012) reported a significant decrease in PTSD-like symptoms when rats were sleep deprived by gentle handling for six hours following a traumatic experience. The suggested mechanism is that sleep deprivation leads to impairment of the formation and consolidation of hippocampus-dependent traumatic memories (Cohen et al., 2012b). Cohen's team replicated their results using modafinil, a wakefulness-promoting agent prescribed for narcolepsy. The researchers suggested modafinil therapeutically promoted an adaptive stress response by stimulating a hypothalamic circuit linking neuropeptide Y, the orexin system, and the HPA axis (Cohen et al., 2016).

Animal research using the predator odour model of PTSD has the ability to identify potential prophylactic treatments that could be given after a traumatic exposure, which would decrease susceptibility to PTSD development. The sleep deprivation study is a particularly effective example of the potential offered by the predator odour model; specifically, the predator odour model can assess interventions designed to reduce symptoms, while allowing for inherent differences in susceptibility.

Predator-Based Psychosocial Stress

Instead of predator odour, the predator-based psychosocial stress model combines live predator exposure with chronic social stress to induce symptoms of PTSD. Rats are exposed to a combination of predator and social stress throughout a 31-day time frame. On the first day of the paradigm, rats are immobilized and exposed to a cat for one hour. The cat exposure is repeated 10 days later to mimic the intrusive, re-experiencing symptoms that people with PTSD endure (Zoladz et al., 2008). A second exposure to a cat is used because it is nearly impossible to induce an intrusive, flashback memory of a "traumatic" event in a rat. The second cat exposure occurs 10 days following the first exposure because research has evidenced amygdala hypertrophy (i.e., increased growth) 10 days following a single stress experience (Fuchs, Flugge, & Czeh, 2006; Mitra et al., 2005). Amygdala hypertrophy may prime the rodent to react more severely to a second predator exposure. The amygdala is a medial temporal lobe structure that identifies threats in the environment and is highly involved in emotions, particularly fear. If the amygdala exhibits increased neural growth 10 days following a single stress experience, one might expect it to have increased function and respond more strongly to a stressor at that time point.

To add an element of chronic mild stress, rats in the cat-exposed stress group are also exposed to chronic social instability; the housing partner of stressed rats is changed daily throughout the entire 31-day paradigm. Housing instability is a social stressor known to cause long-lasting anxiety-like behaviour in rodents (Park, Campbell, & Diamond, 2001; Saavedra-Rodríguez & Feig, 2013). By including housing instability in the model, researchers are able to mirror a lack of social support, which appears to increase the likelihood of developing PTSD in humans (Hyman, Gold, & Cott, 2003; King et al., 1998). Following the 31-day paradigm, rats exposed to the predator-based psychosocial stress model of PTSD exhibit reduced growth rate, reduced thymus weight, increased adrenal gland weight, increased anxiety, an exaggerated startle response, cognitive impairments, increased negative feedback of HPA axis, lower baseline corticosterone levels, a robust fear-conditioned memory of the cat exposures (likened to traumatic memory in people), and greater cardiovascular reactivity to an acute stressor (Zoladz et al., 2008; Zoladz, Fleshner, & Diamond, 2012). Furthermore, rats exposed to the model have exhibited such PTSD-like responses up to four months following the initial cat exposure (Zoladz et al., 2015). Taken together, the results show a high amount of face validity for the predator-based psychosocial stress model.

There is also evidence of predictive validity for predator-based psychosocial stress as a model of PTSD in rodents. Rats exposed to the model exhibit abnormally low baseline levels of serotonin and significant elevations of baseline levels of norepinephrine (Wilson et al., 2014; Wilson et al., 2013), similar to neurotransmitter profiles observed in human PTSD patients. Medications that have demonstrated efficacy in human PTSD patients have also demonstrated efficacy at decreasing PTSD-like symptoms in stressed rats. Tianeptine (a novel antidepressant that normalizes glutamatergic transmission under stress conditions) and clonidine (an alpha-2 receptor agonist that decreases noradrenergic activity) decreased PTSD-like sequelae in stressed rats when administered throughout most of the 31-day period of stress (Zoladz, Fleshner, & Diamond, 2013). Valproic acid, which was administered after the conclusion of the 31-day stress paradigm, led to a decrease in anxiety-like behaviour and a decrease in reactive oxygen species (Wilson, McLaughlin, Ebenezer, Nair, & Francis, 2014). Sertraline, which was also administered after the conclusion of the 31-day stress paradigm, attenuated inflammatory markers and normalized serotonin levels in stressed rodents (Wilson, Ebenezer, et al., 2014). However, sertraline also led to increased norepinephrine levels, which could partially explain contradictory results of sertraline's efficacy (Brady et al., 2000; Friedman et al., 2007; Rothbaum, Ninan, & Thomas, 1996), despite US–FDA approval for this indication (Hoskins et al., 2015).

An example of a particularly effective translational utility of the predator-based psychosocial stress model is recent work directed at the pathology underlying worse cardiac outcomes (e.g., greater mortality following myocardial infarction) observed in PTSD patients (Dimsdale, 2008; Edmondson & Cohen, 2013; Edmondson et al., 2013; Eisenmann, Rorabaugh, & Zoladz, 2016). To determine whether the predator-based psychosocial stress model would impact the amount of damage to the heart following a myocardial infarction, rats were exposed to the 31-day stress paradigm and then had their hearts removed. Using a Langendorff isolated heart system, the rat hearts were kept alive and then oxygen supply to the hearts was stopped to mimic a myocardial infarction. Rodents exposed to the predator-based psychosocial stress model exhibited more dead heart tissue following the induced myocardial infarction than controls (Rorabaugh et al., 2015). The predator-based psychosocial stress model is particularly effective for studies measuring damage to the heart using the Langendorff isolated heart system (Eisenmann et al., 2016). The predator-based psychosocial stress model decreases the amount of rodents necessary by precipitating PTSD-like symptoms in all exposed rodents. Because all stressed rodents display a similar phenotype, researchers can more directly study the effect of severe stress on the heart by comparing stressed versus non-stressed hearts. Differential susceptibility could confound evidence of a decrease in heart damage or overall stress response across groups. Future work examining the underlying molecular mechanisms or directed at decreasing tissue damage will translate to a better understanding of the pathology and patient outcomes associated with PTSD (Eisenmann et al., 2016).

Future Models

The animal models reviewed so far provide a robust overview of the current processes for studying PTSD with animal analogue research designs. Animal researchers continue to refine animal models using advanced techniques to study PTSD; for example, researchers can explore optogenetic modelling, genetic modification, and viral gene transfer to further investigate putative biochemical pathways, biomarkers, predisposing factors, drug targets, and neuronal circuitry.

358 Eisenmann, Cadle, and Zoladz

Genetic Models of PTSD-Like Symptoms

Genetics play an important role in the development of PTSD (Yehuda et al., 2011). For example, the concordance rate for PTSD symptoms following trauma exposure is greater in monozygotic twins than in dizygotic twins (True et al., 1993). Most of the genetic work in humans has focused on genetic differences predisposing individuals to resilience or susceptibility for PTSD (Paris, 2000). Children of individuals with PTSD appear to have lower baseline cortisol and a higher likelihood to develop PTSD (Yehuda, Halligan, & Bierer, 2002); however, the mechanism of these changes is not defined and a non-genomic intergeneration transmission may be mediated by parental behaviour (Yehuda et al., 2000). Studies have examined the entire genome or specific gene variations to identify potentially putative genes that result in an increased likelihood of PTSD development (Yehuda et al., 2011). Gene variations of interest include those impacting the stress response (i.e., genes affecting the HPA axis or cortisol function; Bachmann et al., 2005; Nugent, Amstadter, & Koenen, 2008; Yehuda, 2009) or other putative neurotransmitters (Drury et al., 2009; Gelernter et al., 1999; Grabe et al., 2009).

Genetic studies have provided some insight into the genetic differences leading to increased susceptibility for PTSD, but the results are inconsistent. There is a need for clinical research to focus on genome–environmental interactions or the entire genome (as opposed to only testing specific genes) (Broekman, Olff, & Boer, 2007; Koenen et al., 2013). Complicating clinical genetic studies, environmental exposure to stress leads to epigenetic changes resulting in increased susceptibility to stress (Vialou et al., 2013). Clinical studies examining gene–environment interactions in PTSD development are scarce. One such study conducted by Yehuda et al. (2009) demonstrated down-regulated gene expressions affecting glucocorticoid receptor activity (i.e., FKBP5, STAT5B) in persons who developed PTSD after the 9/11 attack on New York City. Without baseline genetic data, PTSD development cannot be attributed to the genetic code or epigenetic changes in response to trauma. The utility of genetics for future study of PTSD has been reviewed extensively elsewhere, in which the author argues that inherited genetic variation might influence environmentally mediated epigenetic changes and should thus be considered in genetic studies addressing PTSD susceptibility (Yehuda et al., 2011).

The role of genetics in susceptibility to stress has been investigated with animal models. Genetic differences in monkeys have been found to result in altered anxiety-like responses (Fox et al., 2008; Kalin, 2002). Strains of rats and mice have been developed which exhibit high trait anxiety and marked fear extinction deficits (Holmes & Singewald, 2013; Landgraf & Wigger, 2002). Studies examining the amygdala, hippocampus, medial prefrontal cortex, nucleus accumbens, and ventral tegmental area have identified genome-wide changes in gene expression associated with susceptibility to social defeat stress (Russo et al., 2012). Animal models examining

Animal Models of PTSD 359

individual genes have used the aforementioned stressors (e.g., soiled cat litter, social defeat; Cohen et al., 2012a, Briand et al., 2015, respectively) to induce a PTSD-like phenotype. The results implicate individual genes as producing resilience to PTSD-like behaviours; accordingly, direct manipulation using optogenetic modelling is a promising translational avenue for genetics research with PTSD.

Optogenetics

Optogenetic modelling involves the genetic modification of neurons to express light-sensitive ion channels; specifically, researchers can use light to control the relationship between specific neurons or groups of neurons. Optogenetic techniques have not yet been used to study PTSD, but have been used to study depressive behaviour. Optogenetic activation of the medial prefrontal cortex led to a rapid, sustained alleviation of social avoidance and anhedonia in susceptible mice exposed to chronic social defeat stress (Covington et al., 2010). Similarly, researchers have demonstrated that optogenetic activation of the mesolimbic dopamine neurons induces a state of susceptibility to social defeat stress; optogenetic inhibition of these same neurons appears to reverse the susceptibility phenotype (Chaudhury et al., 2013). Optogenetics and similarly advanced neuronal-manipulation techniques will allow for future high-impact research investigating the underlying pathology of PTSD.

Future research examining genetics and genetically modified animals in PTSD studies will help identify predisposing factors, biomarkers, and important pharmacogenomic variations (Amstadter, Nugent, & Koenen, 2009; Koenen, 2007; Yehuda, 2006; Yehuda & Bierer, 2009; Yehuda et al., 2011). The development of new molecular techniques and sampling strategies will continue to explore the contributions of genetic and environmental factors to PTSD development (Yehuda et al., 2011).

Conclusion

PTSD is a multi-faceted psychological disorder uniquely complicated by differential individual susceptibility to a wide array of traumatic events; furthermore, several PTSD symptoms can manifest at different degrees of intensity within the same diagnostic category. By definition, no animal model of PTSD can perfectly mimic the human disorder; however, as reviewed in the current chapter, animal models can reproduce key features of PTSD, including individual susceptibility, abnormal fear responses, hyperarousal, and changes in hormone balance and neurochemistry. All contemporary animal models of PTSD have limitations with translatability to human models. For example, the predator-based psychosocial stress model is not robust for studying differential individual behavioural responses. Animal models with differential susceptibility, as in models using the predator odour and social defeat stress, are especially effective

360 *Eisenmann, Cadle, and Zoladz*

for identifying strategies to improve resilience or factors which underlie increased susceptibility. Alternatively, the predator-based psychosocial stress model, which uses social stress to precipitate a PTSD-like phenotype in exposed rodents, is effective for studying the pathology of overall PTSD-induced dysfunction (e.g., increased cardiac susceptibility to myocardial injury). Leveraging unique strengths of several animal models of PTSD increases translatability of results and supports efforts into improving human patient outcomes. Future models will likely incorporate advanced techniques more specifically targeting brain areas (i.e., optogenetics) and will study polymorphisms and epigenetic changes, which result in increased predisposition to the development of PTSD. As a result, sophisticated translation of bench research to clinical research will continue to result in an enhanced understanding of PTSD and improved patient outcomes.

References

Adamec, R. E., & Shallow, T. (1993). Lasting effects on rodent anxiety of a single exposure to a cat. *Physiology & Behavior, 54*(1), 101–109.

Agrawal, A., Jaggi, A. S., & Singh, N. (2011). Pharmacological investigations on adaptation in rats subjected to cold water immersion stress. *Physiology & Behavior, 103*(3), 321–329.

Alonso, S., Arevalo, R., Afonso, D., & Rodriguez, M. (1991). Effects of maternal stress during pregnancy on forced swimming test behavior of the offspring. *Physiology & Behavior, 50*(3), 511–517.

American Psychiatric Association. (1987). *Diagnostic and statistical manual of mental disorders* (3rd edn, rev.). Washington, DC : American Psychiatric Association.

American Psychiatric Association. (2013). *Diagnostic and statistical manual of mental disorders* (5th edn). Washington, DC : American Psychiatric Association.

Amstadter, A. B., Nugent, N. R., & Koenen, K. C. (2009). Genetics of PTSD: Fear conditioning as a model for future research. *Psychiatric Annals, 39*(6), 358.

Anderson, D., Crowell, C., Koehn, D., & Lupo, J. (1976). Different intensities of unsignalled inescapable shock treatments as determinants of non-shock-motivated open field behavior: A resolution of disparate results. *Physiology & Behavior, 17*(3), 391–394.

Apfelbach, R., Blanchard, C. D., Blanchard, R. J., Hayes, R. A., & McGregor, I. S. (2005). The effects of predator odors in mammalian prey species: A review of field and laboratory studies. *Neuroscience and Biobehavioral Reviews, 29*, 1123–1144.

Ardi, Z., Ritov, G., Lucas, M., & Richter-Levin, G. (2014). The effects of a reminder of underwater trauma on behaviour and memory-related mechanisms in the rat dentate gyrus. *International Journal of Neuropsychopharmacology, 17*(4), 571–580.

Bachmann, A. W., Sedgley, T. L., Jackson, R. V., Gibson, J. N., Young, R. M., & Torpy, D. J. (2005). Glucocorticoid receptor polymorphisms and post-traumatic stress disorder. *Psychoneuroendocrinology, 30*(3), 297–306.

Bali, A., & Jaggi, A. S. (2015a). Electric foot shock stress adaptation: Does it exist or not? *Life Sciences, 130*, 97–102.

Bali, A., & Jaggi, A. S. (2015b). Electric foot shock stress: A useful tool in neuro-psychiatric studies. *Reviews in the Neurosciences, 26*(6), 655–677.

Animal Models of PTSD 361

Bazak, N., Kozlovsky, N., Kaplan, Z., Matar, M., Golan, H., Zohar, J., ... Cohen, H. (2009). Pre-pubertal stress exposure affects adult behavioral response in association with changes in circulating corticosterone and brain-derived neurotrophic factor. *Psychoneuroendocrinology*, *34*(6), 844–858.

Berton, O., McClung, C. A., DiLeone, R. J., Krishnan, V., Renthal, W., Russo, S. J., ... Rios, M. (2006). Essential role of BDNF in the mesolimbic dopamine pathway in social defeat stress. *Science*, *311*(5762), 864–868.

Bhatnagar, S., Vining, C., Iyer, V., & Kinni, V. (2006). Changes in hypothalamic-pituitary-adrenal function, body temperature, body weight and food intake with repeated social stress exposure in rats. *Journal of Neuroendocrinology*, *18*(1), 13–24.

Blanchard, D. C., Blanchard, R. J., Tom, P., & Rodgers, R. J. (1990). Diazepam changes risk assessment in an anxiety/defense test battery. *Psychopharmacology*, *101*(4), 511–518.

Borghans, B., & Homberg, J. R. (2015). Animal models for posttraumatic stress disorder: An overview of what is used in research. *World Journal of Psychiatry*, *5*(4), 387.

Bowman, M. L. (2013). *Individual differences in posttraumatic response: Problems with the adversity-distress connection*. Abingdon: Routledge.

Brady, K., Pearlstein, T., Asnis, G. M., Baker, D., Rothbaum, B., Sikes, C. R., & Farfel, G. M. (2000). Efficacy and safety of sertraline treatment of posttraumatic stress disorder: A randomized controlled trial. *Journal of the American Medical Association*, *283*(14), 1837–1844.

Bremner, J. D. (2002). *Does stress damage the brain? Understanding trauma-related disorders from a mind-body perspective*. New York: WW Norton & Company.

Bremner, J. D., Southwick, S. M., Johnson, D. R., Yehuda, R., & Charney, D. S. (1993). Childhood physical abuse and combat-related posttraumatic stress disorder in Vietnam veterans. *The American Journal of Psychiatry*, *150*(2), 235–239.

Breslau, N., & Davis, G. C. (1987). Posttraumatic stress disorder: The stressor criterion. *The Journal of Nervous and Mental Disease*, *175*(5), 255–264.

Breslau, N., Davis, G. C., Andreski, P., & Peterson, E. (1991). Traumatic events and posttraumatic stress disorder in an urban population of young adults. *Archives of General Psychiatry*, *48*(3), 216–222.

Breslau, N., & Kessler, R. C. (2001). The stressor criterion in DSM-IV posttraumatic stress disorder: An empirical investigation. *Biological Psychiatry*, *50*(9), 699–704.

Breslau, N., Kessler, R. C., Chilcoat, H. D., Schultz, L. R., Davis, G. C., & Andreski, P. (1998). Trauma and posttraumatic stress disorder in the community: The 1996 Detroit Area Survey of Trauma. *Archives of General Psychiatry*, *55*(7), 626–632.

Brewin, C. R., Andrews, B., & Valentine, J. D. (2000). Meta-analysis of risk factors for posttraumatic stress disorder in trauma-exposed adults. *Journal of Consulting and Clinical Psychology*, *68*(5), 748. https://doi.org/10.1037/0022-006X.68.5.748

Briand, L. A., Hilario, M., Dow, H. C., Brodkin, E. S., Blendy, J. A., & Berton, O. (2015). Mouse model of OPRM1 (A118G) polymorphism increases sociability and dominance and confers resilience to social defeat. *The Journal of Neuroscience*, *35*(8), 3582–3590.

Broekman, B. F., Olff, M., & Boer, F. (2007). The genetic background to PTSD. *Neuroscience & Biobehavioral Reviews*, *31*(3), 348–362.

Burstein, A. (1984). Treatment of post-traumatic stress disorder with imipramine. *Psychosomatics*, *25*(9), 681–687.

362 *Eisenmann, Cadle, and Zoladz*

Carleton, R. N., Afifi, T. O., Turner, S., Taillieu, T., Duranceau, S., LeBouthillier, D. M.,... Asmundson, G. J. G. (2018). Mental disorder symptoms among public safety personnel in Canada. *Canadian Journal of Psychiatry, 63*, 54–64.

Chaudhury, D., Walsh, J. J., Friedman, A. K., Juarez, B., Ku, S. M., Koo, J. W., ... Christoffel, D. J. (2013). Rapid regulation of depression-related behaviours by control of midbrain dopamine neurons. *Nature, 493*(7433), 532–536.

Chauhan, E., Bali, A., Singh, N., & Jaggi, A. S. (2015). Pharmacological investigations on cross adaptation in mice subjected to stress immobilization. *Life Sciences, 127*, 98–105.

Claessens, S. E., Daskalakis, N. P., van der Veen, R., Oitzl, M. S., de Kloet, E. R., & Champagne, D. L. (2011). Development of individual differences in stress responsiveness: An overview of factors mediating the outcome of early life experiences. *Psychopharmacology, 214*(1), 141–154.

Clinchy, M., Sheriff, M. J., & Zanette, L. Y. (2013). Predator-induced stress and the ecology of fear. *Functional Ecology, 27*(1), 56–65. https://doi.org/10.1111/1365-2435.12007.

Cohen, H., Liu, T., Kozlovsky, N., Kaplan, Z., Zohar, J., & Mathé, A. A. (2012). The neuropeptide Y (NPY)-ergic system is associated with behavioral resilience to stress exposure in an animal model of post-traumatic stress disorder. *Neuropsychopharmacology, 37*(2), 350–363.

Cohen, H., Matar, M. A., & Joseph, Z. (2013). Animal models of post-traumatic stress disorder. *Current Protocols in Neuroscience, 64*(1), 9–45.

Cohen, H., Matar, M. A., Richter-Levin, G., & Zohar, J. (2006). The contribution of an animal model toward uncovering biological risk factors for PTSD. *Annals of the New York Academy of Sciences, 1071*(1), 335–350.

Cohen, S., Ifergane, G., Vainer, E., Matar, M. A., Kaplan, Z., Zohar, J., ... Cohen, H. (2016). The wake-promoting drug modafinil stimulates specific hypothalamic circuits to promote adaptive stress responses in an animal model of PTSD. *Translational Psychiatry, 6*(10), e917.

Cohen, S., Kozlovsky, N., Matar, M. A., Kaplan, Z., Zohar, J., & Cohen, H. (2012). Post-exposure sleep deprivation facilitates correctly timed interactions between glucocorticoid and adrenergic systems, which attenuate traumatic stress responses. *Neuropsychopharmacology, 37*(11), 2388–2404.

Covington, H. E., Lobo, M. K., Maze, I., Vialou, V., Hyman, J. M., Zaman, S., ... Tamminga, C. A. (2010). Antidepressant effect of optogenetic stimulation of the medial prefrontal cortex. *The Journal of Neuroscience, 30*(48), 16082–16090.

Covington, H. E., & Miczek, K. A. (2005). Intense cocaine self-administration after episodic social defeat stress, but not after aggressive behavior: Dissociation from corticosterone activation. *Psychopharmacology, 183*(3), 331–340.

Dahlöf, L.-G., Hård, E., & Larsson, K. (1978). Influence of maternal stress on the development of the fetal genital system. *Physiology & Behavior, 20*(2), 193–195.

Daskalakis, N. P., & Yehuda, R. (2014). Principles for developing animal models of military PTSD. *European Journal of Psychotraumatology, 5*(1), 23825.

Daskalakis, N. P., Yehuda, R., & Diamond, D. M. (2013). Animal models in translational studies of PTSD. *Psychoneuroendocrinology, 38*(9), 1895–1911.

Dattilio, F. M. (2004). Extramarital affairs: The much-overlooked PTSD. *The Behavior Therapist, 27*, 76–78.

Davidson, J., & Foa, E. (1991). Diagnostic issues in posttraumatic stress disorder: Considerations for the DSM-IV. *Journal of Abnormal Psychology, 100*(3), 346–355.

Animal Models of PTSD   363

Davidson, J., Roth, S., & Newman, E. (1991). Fluoxetine in post-traumatic stress disorder. *Journal of Traumatic Stress, 4*(3), 419–423.

De Bellis, M. D. (2001). Developmental traumatology: The psychobiological development of maltreated children and its implications for research, treatment, and policy. *Development and Psychopathology, 13*(3), 539–564.

De Bellis, M. D., Baum, A. S., Birmaher, B., Keshavan, M. S., Eccard, C. H., Boring, A. M., ... Ryan, N. D. (1999). Developmental traumatology part I: Biological stress systems. *Biological Psychiatry, 45*(10), 1259–1270.

Delahanty, D. L., & Nugent, N. R. (2006). Predicting PTSD prospectively based on prior trauma history and immediate biological responses. *Annals of the New York Academy of Sciences, 1071*(1), 27–40.

Diamond, D. M., Park, C. R., Heman, K. L., & Rose, G. M. (1999). Exposing rats to a predator impairs spatial working memory in the radial arm water maze. *Hippocampus, 9*(5), 542–552.

Dimsdale, J. E. (2008). Psychological stress and cardiovascular disease. *Journal of the American College of Cardiology, 51*(13), 1237–1246.

Dreman, S. (1991). Coping with the trauma of divorce. *Journal of Traumatic Stress, 4*(1), 113–121.

Drury, S. S., Theall, K. P., Keats, B. J., & Scheeringa, M. (2009). The role of the dopamine transporter (DAT) in the development of PTSD in preschool children. *Journal of Traumatic Stress, 22*(6), 534–539.

Edmondson, D., & Cohen, B. E. (2013). Posttraumatic stress disorder and cardiovascular disease. *Progress in Cardiovascular Disease, 55*(6), 548–556.

Edmondson, D., Kronish, I. M., Shaffer, J. A., Falzon, L., & Burg, M. M. (2013). Posttraumatic stress disorder and risk for coronary heart disease: A meta-analytic review. *American Heart Journal, 166*(5), 806–814.

Ehlers, A., Mayou, R. A., & Bryant, B. (1998). Psychological predictors of chronic posttraumatic stress disorder after motor vehicle accidents. *Journal of Abnormal Psychology, 107*(3), 508–519.

Eisenmann, E. D., Rorabaugh, B. R., & Zoladz, P. R. (2016). Acute stress decreases but chronic stress increases myocardial sensitivity to ischemic injury in rodents. *Frontiers in Psychiatry, 7*, 71.

Epstein, J. N., Saunders, B. E., & Kilpatrick, D. G. (1997). Predicting PTSD in women with a history of childhood rape. *Journal of Traumatic Stress, 10*(4), 573–588.

Fox, A. S., Shelton, S. E., Oakes, T. R., Davidson, R. J., & Kalin, N. H. (2008). Trait-like brain activity during adolescence predicts anxious temperament in primates. *PLoS One, 3*(7), e2570.

Freide, E., & Weinstock, M. (1984). The effects of prenatal exposure to predictable or unpredictable stress on early development in the rat. *Developmental Psychobiology, 17*(6), 651–660.

Friedman, M. J., Marmar, C. R., Baker, D. G., Sikes, C. R., & Farfel, G. M. (2007). Randomized, double-blind comparison of sertraline and placebo for posttraumatic stress disorder in a Department of Veterans Affairs setting. *Journal of Clinical Psychiatry, 68*, 711–720.

Fuchs, E., Flugge, G., & Czeh, B. (2006). Remodeling of neuronal networks by stress. *Frontiers in Bioscience, 11*, 2746–2758.

Gameiro, G. H., Gameiro, P. H., da Silva Andrade, A., Pereira, L. F., Arthuri, M. T., Marcondes, F. K., & de Arruda Veiga, M. C. F. (2006). Nociception-and anxiety-like behavior in rats submitted to different periods of restraint stress. *Physiology & Behavior, 87*(4), 643–649.

Gelernter, J., Southwick, S., Goodson, S., Morgan, A., Nagy, L., & Charney, D. S. (1999). No association between D 2 dopamine receptor (DRD2) "A" system alleles, or DRD2 haplotypes, and posttraumatic stress disorder. *Biological Psychiatry*, *45*(5), 620–625.

Geller, I., & Seifter, J. (1960). The effects of meprobamate, barbiturates, d-amphetamine and promazine on experimentally induced conflict in the rat. *Psychopharmacology*, *1*(6), 482–492.

Gilbertson, M. W., Shenton, M. E., Ciszewski, A., Kasai, K., Lasko, N. B., Orr, S. P., & Pitman, R. K. (2002). Smaller hippocampal volume predicts pathologic vulnerability to psychological trauma. *Nature Neuroscience*, *5*(11), 1242–1247.

Gilbertson, M. W., Williston, S. K., Paulus, L. A., Lasko, N. B., Gurvits, T. V., Shenton, M. E., ... Orr, S. P. (2007). Configural cue performance in identical twins discordant for posttraumatic stress disorder: Theoretical implications for the role of hippocampal function. *Biological Psychiatry*, *62*(5), 513–520.

Glover, V., O'Connor, T., & O'Donnell, K. (2010). Prenatal stress and the programming of the HPA axis. *Neuroscience & Biobehavioral Reviews*, *35*(1), 17–22.

Golden, S. A., Covington III, H. E., Berton, O., & Russo, S. J. (2011). A standardized protocol for repeated social defeat stress in mice. *Nature Protocols*, *6*(8), 1183–1191.

Goswami, S., Rodríguez-Sierra, O., Cascardi, M., & Paré, D. (2013). Animal models of post-traumatic stress disorder: Face validity. *Frontiers in Neuroscience*, *7*, 89.

Grabe, H. J., Spitzer, C., Schwahn, C., Marcinek, A., Frahnow, A., Barnow, S., ... Wallaschofski, H. (2009). Serotonin transporter gene (SLC6A4) promoter polymorphisms and the susceptibility to posttraumatic stress disorder in the general population. *American Journal of Psychiatry*, *166*(8), 926–933.

Hains, A. B., Yabe, Y., & Arnsten, A. F. (2015). Chronic stimulation of alpha-2A-adrenoceptors with guanfacine protects rodent prefrontal cortex dendritic spines and cognition from the effects of chronic stress. *Neurobiology of Stress*, *2*, 1–9.

Hajos-Korcsok, E., Robinson, D., Yu, J., Fitch, C., Walker, E., & Merchant, K. (2003). Rapid habituation of hippocampal serotonin and norepinephrine release and anxiety-related behaviors, but not plasma corticosterone levels, to repeated footshock stress in rats. *Pharmacology, Biochemistry and Behavior*, *74*(3), 609–616.

Hammamieh, R., Chakraborty, N., De Lima, T. C., Meyerhoff, J., Gautam, A., Muhie, S., ... Jett, M. (2012). Murine model of repeated exposures to conspecific trained aggressors simulates features of post-traumatic stress disorder. *Behavioural Brain Research*, *235*(1), 55–66.

Heim, C., & Nemeroff, C. B. (2001). The role of childhood trauma in the neurobiology of mood and anxiety disorders: Preclinical and clinical studies. *Biological Psychiatry*, *49*(12), 1023–1039.

Helzer, J. E., Robins, L. N., & McEvoy, L. (1987). Post-traumatic stress disorder in the general population. *New England Journal of Medicine*, *317*(26), 1630–1634.

Holmes, A., & Singewald, N. (2013). Individual differences in recovery from traumatic fear. *Trends in Neurosciences*, *36*(1), 23–31.

Hoskins, M., Pearce, J., Bethell, A., Dankova, L., Barbui, C., Tol, W. A., ... Chen, H. (2015). Pharmacotherapy for post-traumatic stress disorder: Systematic review and meta-analysis. *The British Journal of Psychiatry*, *206*(2), 93–100.

Huhman, K. L. (2006). Social conflict models: Can they inform us about human psychopathology? *Hormones and Behavior*, *50*(4), 640–646.

Animal Models of PTSD 365

Huhman, K. L., Moore, T. O., Mougey, E. H., & Meyerhoff, J. L. (1992). Hormonal responses to fighting in hamsters: Separation of physical and psychological causes. *Physiology & Behavior, 51*(5), 1083–1086.

Hyman, S. M., Gold, S. N., & Cott, M. A. (2003). Forms of social support that moderate PTSD in childhood sexual abuse survivors. *Journal of Family Violence, 18*(5), 295–300.

Jasnow, A. M., & Huhman, K. L. (2001). Activation of GABA(A) receptors in the amygdala blocks the acquisition and expression of conditioned defeat in Syrian hamsters. *Brain Research, 920*(1–2), 142–150.

Joseph, A., Tang, M., Mamiya, T., Chen, Q., Yang, L.-L., Jiao, J., ... Tang, Y.-P. (2013). Temporal association of elevated cholecystokininergic tone and adolescent trauma is critical for posttraumatic stress disorder-like behavior in adult mice. *Proceedings of the National Academy of Sciences, 110*(16), 6589–6594.

Kalin, N. H. (2002). Nonhuman primate studies of fear, anxiety, and temperament and the role of benzodiazepine receptors and GABA systems. *The Journal of Clinical Psychiatry, 64*, 41–44.

Kessler, R. C., Sonnega, A., Bromet, E., Hughes, M., & Nelson, C. B. (1995). Posttraumatic stress disorder in the National Comorbidity Survey. *Archives of General Psychiatry, 52*(12), 1048–1060.

Khan, S., & Liberzon, I. (2004). Topiramate attenuates exaggerated acoustic startle in an animal model of PTSD. *Psychopharmacology, 172*(2), 225–229.

Khonicheva, N., Livanova, L., Tsykunov, S., Osipova, T., Loriya, M., Élbakidze, A., ... Airapetyants, M. (2008). Blood testosterone in rats: Correlation of the level of individual anxiety and its impairment after "death threat". *Neuroscience and Behavioral Physiology, 38*(9), 985–989.

King, L. A., King, D. W., Fairbank, J. A., Keane, T. M., & Adams, G. A. (1998). Resilience–recovery factors in post-traumatic stress disorder among female and male Vietnam veterans: Hardiness, postwar social support, and additional stressful life events. *Journal of Personality and Social Psychology, 74*(2), 420–434.

Knox, D., George, S. A., Fitzpatrick, C. J., Rabinak, C. A., Maren, S., & Liberzon, I. (2012). Single prolonged stress disrupts retention of extinguished fear in rats. *Learning & Memory, 19*(2), 43–49.

Koenen, K. C. (2007). Genetics of posttraumatic stress disorder: Review and recommendations for future studies. *Journal of Traumatic Stress, 20*(5), 737–750.

Koenen, K. C., Duncan, L. E., Liberzon, I., & Ressler, K. J. (2013). From candidate genes to genome-wide association: The challenges and promise of post-traumatic stress disorder genetic studies. *Biological Psychiatry, 74*(9), 634–636.

Koolhaas, J. M., Coppens, C. M., de Boer, S. F., Buwalda, B., Meerlo, P., & Timmermans, P. J. (2013). The resident-intruder paradigm: A standardized test for aggression, violence and social stress. *JoVE (Journal of Visualized Experiments), 77*, e4367–e4367.

Krishnan, V., Berton, O., & Nestler, E. (2008). The use of animal models in psychiatric research and treatment. *American Journal of Psychiatry, 165*(9), 1109.

Krishnan, V., Han, M.-H., Graham, D. L., Berton, O., Renthal, W., Russo, S. J., ... Lagace, D. C. (2007). Molecular adaptations underlying susceptibility and resistance to social defeat in brain reward regions. *Cell, 131*(2), 391–404.

Landgraf, R., & Wigger, A. (2002). High vs low anxiety-related behavior rats: An animal model of extremes in trait anxiety. *Behavior Genetics, 32*(5), 301–314.

Levine, S. (2005). Developmental determinants of sensitivity and resistance to stress. *Psychoneuroendocrinology, 30*(10), 939–946.

366 Eisenmann, Cadle, and Zoladz

Li, Z., Zhou, Q., Li, L., Mao, R., Wang, M., Peng, W., ... Cao, J. (2005). Effects of unconditioned and conditioned aversive stimuli in an intense fear conditioning paradigm on synaptic plasticity in the hippocampal CA1 area in vivo. *Hippocampus*, *15*(6), 815–824.

Liberzon, I., Krstov, M., & Young, E. A. (1997). Stress-restress: Effects on ACTH and fast feedback. *Psychoneuroendocrinology*, *22*(6), 443–453.

Liberzon, I., Lopez, J. F., Flagel, S. B., Vazquez, D. M., & Young, E. A. (1999). Differential regulation of hippocampal glucocorticoid receptors mRNA and fast feedback: Relevance to post-traumatic stress disorder. *Journal of Neuroendocrinology*, *11*, 11–17.

Lin, C.-C., Tung, C.-S., & Liu, Y.-P. (2016). Escitalopram reversed the traumatic stress-induced depressed and anxiety-like symptoms but not the deficits of fear memory. *Psychopharmacology*, *233*(7), 1135–1146.

Louvart, H., Maccari, S., Ducrocq, F., Thomas, P., & Darnaudéry, M. (2005). Long-term behavioural alterations in female rats after a single intense footshock followed by situational reminders. *Psychoneuroendocrinology*, *30*(4), 316–324.

Louvart, H., Maccari, S., Lesage, J., Léonhardt, M., Dickes-Coopman, A., & Darnaudéry, M. (2006). Effects of a single footshock followed by situational reminders on HPA axis and behaviour in the aversive context in male and female rats. *Psychoneuroendocrinology*, *31*(1), 92–99.

Masini, C., Sauer, S., White, J., Day, H., & Campeau, S. (2006). Non-associative defensive responses of rats to ferret odor. *Physiology & Behavior*, *87*(1), 72–81.

McEwen, B. S., Nasca, C., & Gray, J. D. (2016). Stress effects on neuronal structure: Hippocampus, amygdala, and prefrontal cortex. *Neuropsychopharmacology*, *41*(1), 3–23.

McFarlane, A. C., & De Girolamo, G. (1996). The nature of traumatic stressors and the epidemiology of posttraumatic reactions. In B. A. van der Kolk, A. C. McFarlane, & L. Weisaeth (eds), *Traumatic stress: The effects of overwhelming experience on mind, body, and society* (pp. 129–154). New York: Guilford Press.

McGuire, J., Herman, J. P., Horn, P. S., Sallee, F. R., & Sah, R. (2010). Enhanced fear recall and emotional arousal in rats recovering from chronic variable stress. *Physiology & Behavior*, *101*(4), 474–482.

McKinney Jr, W. T. (2012). *Models of mental disorders: A new comparative psychiatry*. Berlin: Springer Science & Business Media.

Meehl, P. E. (1977). Specific etiology and other forms of strong influence: Some quantitative meanings. *Journal of Medicine and Philosophy*, *2*(1), 33–53.

Meerlo, P., Overkamp, G., Daan, S., Van Den Hoofdakker, R., & Koolhaas, J. (1996). Changes in behaviour and body weight following a single or double social defeat in rats. *Stress*, *1*(1), 21–32.

Mendes-Gomes, J., Paschoalin-Maurin, T., Freitas, R., Donaldson, L., Lumb, B., & Coimbra, N. (2014). Unconditioned fear induces antinociception in sham rats threatened by wild snakes but not in those with neurophatic pain. *European Neuropsychopharmacology*, *24*(2), S587.

Miczek, K. A. (1979). A new test for aggression in rats without aversive stimulation: Differential effects of d-amphetamine and cocaine. *Psychopharmacology*, *60*(3), 253–259.

Mitra, R., Jadhav, S., McEwen, B. S., Vyas, A., & Chattarji, S. (2005). Stress duration modulates the spatiotemporal patterns of spine formation in the basolateral amygdala. *Proceedings of the National Academy of Sciences of the United States of America*, *102*(26), 9371–9376.

Animal Models of PTSD 367

Moore, N. L., Gauchan, S., & Genovese, R. F. (2012). Differential severity of anxiogenic effects resulting from a brief swim or underwater trauma in adolescent male rats. *Pharmacology, Biochemistry and Behavior*, *102*(2), 264–268.

Nikulina, E. M., Covington, H. E., 3rd, Ganschow, L., Hammer, R. P., Jr., & Miczek, K. A. (2004). Long-term behavioral and neuronal cross-sensitization to amphetamine induced by repeated brief social defeat stress: Fos in the ventral tegmental area and amygdala. *Neuroscience*, *123*(4), 857–865.

Nugent, N. R., Amstadter, A. B., & Koenen, K. C. (2008, May). Genetics of posttraumatic stress disorder: Informing clinical conceptualizations and promoting future research. In *American Journal of Medical Genetics Part C: Seminars in Medical Genetics*, *148*(2), 127–132.

Nugent, N. R., Ostrowski, S., Christopher, N. C., & Delahanty, D. L. (2007). Parental posttraumatic stress symptoms as a moderator of child's acute biological response and subsequent posttraumatic stress symptoms in pediatric injury patients. *Journal of Pediatric Psychology*, *32*(3), 309–318.

Overmier, J. B., & Seligman, M. E. (1967). Effects of inescapable shock upon subsequent escape and avoidance responding. *Journal of Comparative and Physiological Psychology*, *63*(1), 28.

Paris, J. (2000). Predispositions, personality traits, and posttraumatic stress disorder. *Harvard Review of Psychiatry*, *8*(4), 175–183.

Park, C. R., Campbell, A. M., & Diamond, D. M. (2001). Chronic psychosocial stress impairs learning and memory and increases sensitivity to yohimbine in adult rats. *Biological Psychiatry*, *50*(12), 994–1004.

Park, C. R., Zoladz, P. R., Conrad, C. D., Fleshner, M., & Diamond, D. M. (2008). Acute predator stress impairs the consolidation and retrieval of hippocampus-dependent memory in male and female rats. *Learning & Memory*, *15*(4), 271–280.

Patki, G., Solanki, N., Atrooz, F., Allam, F., & Salim, S. (2013). Depression, anxiety-like behavior and memory impairment are associated with increased oxidative stress and inflammation in a rat model of social stress. *Brain Research*, *1539*, 73–86.

Patki, G., Solanki, N., & Salim, S. (2014). Witnessing traumatic events causes severe behavioral impairments in rats. *International Journal of Neuropsychopharmacology*, *17*(12), 2017–2029.

Pawlyk, A. C., Jha, S. K., Brennan, F. X., Morrison, A. R., & Ross, R. J. (2005). A rodent model of sleep disturbances in posttraumatic stress disorder: The role of context after fear conditioning. *Biological Psychiatry*, *57*(3), 268–277.

Pelcovitz, D., Libov, B. G., Mandel, F., Kaplan, S., Weinblatt, M., & Septimus, A. (1998). Posttraumatic stress disorder and family functioning in adolescent cancer. *Journal of Traumatic Stress*, *11*(2), 205–221.

Philbert, J., Pichat, P., Beeske, S., Decobert, M., Belzung, C., & Griebel, G. (2011). Acute inescapable stress exposure induces long-term sleep disturbances and avoidance behavior: A mouse model of post-traumatic stress disorder (PTSD). *Behavioural Brain Research*, *221*(1), 149–154.

Pijlman, F. T., Herremans, A. H., van de Kieft, J., Kruse, C. G., & van Ree, J. M. (2003). Behavioural changes after different stress paradigms: Prepulse inhibition increased after physical, but not emotional stress. *European Neuropsychopharmacology*, *13*(5), 369–380.

Pijlman, F. T., Wolterink, G., & van Ree, J. M. (2002). Cueing unavoidable physical but not emotional stress increases long-term behavioural effects in rats. *Behavioural Brain Research*, *134*(1), 393–401.

368 Eisenmann, Cadle, and Zoladz

Pijlman, F. T., Wolterink, G., & Van Ree, J. M. (2003). Physical and emotional stress have differential effects on preference for saccharine and open field behaviour in rats. *Behavioural Brain Research*, *139*(1), 131–138.

Pitman, R. K., Rasmusson, A. M., Koenen, K. C., Shin, L. M., Orr, S. P., Gilbertson, M. W., ... Liberzon, I. (2012). Biological studies of post-traumatic stress disorder. *Nature Reviews Neuroscience*, *13*(11), 769–787.

Plotsky, P. M., & Meaney, M. J. (1993). Early, postnatal experience alters hypothalamic corticotropin-releasing factor (CRF) mRNA, median eminence CRF content and stress-induced release in adult rats. *Molecular Brain Research*, *18*(3), 195–200.

Pulliam, J. V., Dawaghreh, A. M., Alema-Mensah, E., & Plotsky, P. M. (2010). Social defeat stress produces prolonged alterations in acoustic startle and body weight gain in male Long Evans rats. *Journal of Psychiatric Research*, *44*(2), 106–111.

Pynoos, R. S., Ritzmann, R. F., Steinberg, A. M., Goenjian, A., & Prisecaru, I. (1996). A behavioral animal model of posttraumatic stress disorder featuring repeated exposure to situational reminders. *Biological Psychiatry*, *39*(2), 129–134.

Richter-Levin, G. (1998). Acute and long-term behavioral correlates of underwater trauma—potential relevance to stress and post-stress syndromes. *Psychiatry Research*, *79*(1), 73–83.

Rorabaugh, B. R., Krivenko, A., Eisenmann, E. D., Bui, A. D., Seeley, S., Fry, M. E., ... Zoladz, P. R. (2015). Sex-dependent effects of chronic psychosocial stress on myocardial sensitivity to ischemic injury. *Stress*, *18*(6), 645–653.

Rosen, G. M., & Lilienfeld, S. O. (2008). Posttraumatic stress disorder: An empirical evaluation of core assumptions. *Clinical Psychology Review*, *28*(5), 837–868.

Rothbaum, B. O., Ninan, P. T., & Thomas, L. (1996). Sertraline in the treatment of rape victims with posttraumatic stress disorder. *Journal of Traumatic Stress*, *9*(4), 865–871.

Russo, S. J., Murrough, J. W., Han, M.-H., Charney, D. S., & Nestler, E. J. (2012). Neurobiology of resilience. *Nature Neuroscience*, *15*(11), 1475–1484.

Saavedra-Rodríguez, L., & Feig, L. A. (2013). Chronic social instability induces anxiety and defective social interactions across generations. *Biological Psychiatry*, *73*(1), 44–53.

Sanchez, M. M., Ladd, C. O., & Plotsky, P. M. (2001). Early adverse experience as a developmental risk factor for later psychopathology: Evidence from rodent and primate models. *Development and Psychopathology*, *13*(3), 419–449.

Sanchis-Segura, C., Spanagel, R., Henn, F., & Vollmayr, B. (2005). Reduced sensitivity to sucrose in rats bred for helplessness: A study using the matching law. *Behavioural Pharmacology*, *16*(4), 267–270.

Schöner, J., Heinz, A., Endres, M., Gertz, K., & Kronenberg, G. (2017). Posttraumatic stress disorder and beyond: An overview of rodent stress models. *Journal of Cellular and Molecular Medicine*, *21*(10), 2248–2256.

Seligman, M. E. (1972). Learned helplessness. *Annual Review of Medicine*, *23*(1), 407–412.

Seligman, M. E., & Maier, S. F. (1967). Failure to escape traumatic shock. *Journal of Experimental Psychology*, *74*(1), 1–9.

Shalev, A. Y., Peri, T., Canetti, L., & Schreiber, S. (1996). Predictors of PTSD in injured trauma survivors: A prospective study. *The American Journal of Psychiatry*, *153*(2), 219–225.

Shalev, A. Y., & Rogel-Fuchs, Y. (1993). Psychophysiology of the posttraumatic stress disorder: From sulfur fumes to behavioral genetics. *Psychosomatic Medicine, 55*(5), 413–423.

Sherman, A. D., Allers, G., Petty, F., & Henn, F. (1979). A neuropharmacologically-relevant animal model of depression. *Neuropharmacology, 18*(11), 891–893.

Sherman, A. D., Sacquitne, J., & Petty, F. (1982). Specificity of the learned helplessness model of depression. *Pharmacology, Biochemistry and Behavior, 16*(3), 449–454.

Shimizu, K., Sawamura, T., Nibuya, M., Nakai, K., Takahashi, Y., & Nomura, S. (2004). An animal model of posttraumatic stress disorder and its validity: Effect of paroxetine on a PTSD model in rats. *Nihon Shinkei Seishin Yakurigaku Zasshi, 24*(5), 283–290.

Siegmund, A., Kaltwasser, S. F., Holsboer, F., Czisch, M., & Wotjak, C. T. (2009). Hippocampal N-acetylaspartate levels before trauma predict the development of long-lasting posttraumatic stress disorder-like symptoms in mice. *Biological Psychiatry, 65*(3), 258–262.

Siegmund, A., & Wotjak, C. T. (2007). A mouse model of posttraumatic stress disorder that distinguishes between conditioned and sensitised fear. *Journal of Psychiatric Research, 41*(10), 848–860.

Sood, R., Ritov, G., Boltyansky, B., Spector-Chotiner, A., Richter-Levin, G., & Barki-Harrington, L. (2014). Underwater trauma causes a long-term specific increase in the expression of cyclooxygenase-2 in the ventral CA 1 of the hippocampus. *Psychoneuroendocrinology, 49*, 62–68.

Stam, R. (2007a). PTSD and stress sensitisation: A tale of brain and body Part 2: Animal models. *Neuroscience & Biobehavioral Reviews, 31*(4), 558–584.

Stam, R. (2007b). PTSD and stress sensitisation: A tale of brain and body: Part 1: Human studies. *Neuroscience & Biobehavioral Reviews, 31*(4), 530–557.

Takahashi, L. K., Haglin, C., & Kalin, N. H. (1992). Prenatal stress potentiates stress-induced behavior and reduces the propensity to play in juvenile rats. *Physiology & Behavior, 51*(2), 319–323.

Takahashi, T., Morinobu, S., Iwamoto, Y., & Yamawaki, S. (2006). Effect of paroxetine on enhanced contextual fear induced by single prolonged stress in rats. *Psychopharmacology, 189*(2), 165–173.

Travis, C. M. G., & Genovese, R. F. (2016). Cat-exposure results in significantly more elicited alarm calls (22kHz ultrasonic vocalizations, USVs) compared to snake-, ferret-, or sham-exposure during a rodent model of traumatic stress. *The FASEB Journal, 30*(1 Supplement), 938.9.

True, W. R., Rice, J., Eisen, S. A., Heath, A. C., Goldberg, J., Lyons, M. J., & Nowak, J. (1993). A twin study of genetic and environmental contributions to liability for posttraumatic stress symptoms. *Archives of General Psychiatry, 50*(4), 257–264.

Tsankova, N. M., Berton, O., Renthal, W., Kumar, A., Neve, R. L., & Nestler, E. J. (2006). Sustained hippocampal chromatin regulation in a mouse model of depression and antidepressant action. *Nature Neuroscience, 9*(4), 519–525.

Vallès, A., Martí, O., & Armario, A. (2006). Long-term effects of a single exposure to immobilization: A c-fos mRNA study of the response to the homotypic stressor in the rat brain. *Journal of Neurobiology, 66*(6), 591–602.

Van Ameringen, M., Mancini, C., Patterson, B., & Boyle, M. H. (2008). Posttraumatic stress disorder in Canada. *CNS Neuroscience & Therapeutics, 14*(3), 171–181.

370 *Eisenmann, Cadle, and Zoladz*

Van den Berg, C. L., Lamberts, R. R., Wolterink, G., Wiegant, V. M., & Van Ree, J. M. (1998). Emotional and footshock stimuli induce differential long-lasting behavioural effects in rats; Involvement of opioids. *Brain Research, 799*(1), 6–15.

Van den Bergh, B. R., Mulder, E. J., Mennes, M., & Glover, V. (2005). Antenatal maternal anxiety and stress and the neurobehavioural development of the fetus and child: Links and possible mechanisms. A review. *Neuroscience & Biobehavioral Reviews, 29*(2), 237–258.

Van Dijken, H. H., Mos, J., van der Heyden, J. A., & Tilders, F. J. (1992a). Characterization of stress-induced long-term behavioural changes in rats: Evidence in favor of anxiety. *Physiology & Behavior, 52*(5), 945–951.

Van Dijken, H. H., van der Heyden, J. A., Mos, J., & Tilders, F. J. (1992b). Inescapable footshocks induce progressive and long-lasting behavioural changes in male rats. *Physiology & Behavior, 51*(4), 787–794.

Vanderheyden, W. M., George, S. A., Urpa, L., Kehoe, M., Liberzon, I., & Poe, G. R. (2015). Sleep alterations following exposure to stress predict fear-associated memory impairments in a rodent model of PTSD. *Experimental Brain Research, 233*(8), 2335–2346.

Vasconcelos, M., Stein, D. J., & de Almeida, R. M. (2015). Social defeat protocol and relevant biomarkers, implications for stress response physiology, drug abuse, mood disorders and individual stress vulnerability: A systematic review of the last decade. *Trends in Psychiatry and Psychotherapy, 37*(2), 51–66.

Velazquez-Moctezuma, J., Salazar, E. D., & Rueda, M. L. C. (1993). The effect of prenatal stress on adult sexual behavior in rats depends on the nature of the stressor. *Physiology & Behavior, 53*(3), 443–448.

Verma, M., Bali, A., Singh, N., & Jaggi, A. S. (2016). Investigating the role of nisoldipine in foot-shock-induced post-traumatic stress disorder in mice. *Fundamental & Clinical Pharmacology, 30*, 128–136.

Vialou, V., Feng, J., Robison, A. J., & Nestler, E. J. (2013). Epigenetic mechanisms of depression and antidepressant action. *Annual Review of Pharmacology and Toxicology, 53*, 59–87.

Vollmayr, B., & Henn, F. A. (2001). Learned helplessness in the rat: Improvements in validity and reliability. *Brain Research Protocols, 8*(1), 1–7.

Wang, J., Akirav, I., & Richter-Levin, G. (2000). Short-term behavioral and electrophysiological consequences of underwater trauma. *Physiology & Behavior, 70*(3), 327–332.

Wang, W., Lei, Y., Tseng, T., Hsu, W., Wang, C., Hsu, C., & Ho, Y. (2007). Effects of apomorphine on the expression of learned helplessness behavior. *Chinese Journal of Physiology, 50*(2), 63–68.

Wang, W., Liu, Y., Zheng, H., Wang, H. N., Jin, X., Chen, Y. C., ... Tan, Q. R. (2008). A modified single-prolonged stress model for post-traumatic stress disorder. *Neuroscience Letters, 441*(2), 237–241.

Warren, B. L., Vialou, V. F., Iñiguez, S. D., Alcantara, L. F., Wright, K. N., Feng, J., ... Nestler, E. J. (2013). Neurobiological sequelae of witnessing stressful events in adult mice. *Biological Psychiatry, 73*(1), 7–14.

Weinstock, M. (2001). Alterations induced by gestational stress in brain morphology and behaviour of the offspring. *Progress in Neurobiology, 65*(5), 427–451.

Willner, P., Towell, A., Sampson, D., Sophokleous, S., & Muscat, R. (1987). Reduction of sucrose preference by chronic unpredictable mild stress, and its restoration by a tricyclic antidepressant. *Psychopharmacology, 93*(3), 358–364.

Animal Models of PTSD 371

Wilson, C. B., Ebenezer, P. J., McLaughlin, L. D., & Francis, J. (2014). Predator exposure/psychosocial stress animal model of post-traumatic stress disorder modulates neurotransmitters in the rat hippocampus and prefrontal cortex. *PLoS One*, *9*(2), e89104.

Wilson, C. B., McLaughlin, L. D., Ebenezer, P. J., Nair, A. R., & Francis, J. (2014). Valproic acid effects in the hippocampus and prefrontal cortex in an animal model of post-traumatic stress disorder. *Behavioural Brain Research*, *268*, 72–80.

Wilson, C. B., McLaughlin, L. D., Nair, A., Ebenezer, P. J., Dange, R., & Francis, J. (2013). Inflammation and oxidative stress are elevated in the brain, blood, and adrenal glands during the progression of post-traumatic stress disorder in a predator exposure animal model. *PLoS One*, *8*(10), e76146.

Woodson, J. C., Macintosh, D., Fleshner, M., & Diamond, D. M. (2003). Emotion-induced amnesia in rats: Working memory-specific impairment, corticosterone-memory correlation, and fear versus arousal effects on memory. *Learning & Memory*, *10*(5), 326–336.

Yamamoto, S., Morinobu, S., Takei, S., Fuchikami, M., Matsuki, A., Yamawaki, S., & Liberzon, I. (2009). Single prolonged stress: Toward an animal model of posttraumatic stress disorder. *Depression and Anxiety*, *26*(12), 1110–1117.

Yehuda, R. (2001). Biology of posttraumatic stress disorder. *Journal of Clinical Psychiatry*, *62*, 41–46.

Yehuda, R. (2006). Advances in understanding neuroendocrine alterations in PTSD and their therapeutic implications. *Annals of the New York Academy of Sciences*, *1071*(1), 137–166.

Yehuda, R. (2009). Status of glucocorticoid alterations in post-traumatic stress disorder. *Annals of the New York Academy of Sciences*, *1179*(1), 56–69.

Yehuda, R., & Antelman, S. M. (1993). Criteria for rationally evaluating animal models of postraumatic stress disorder. *Biological Psychiatry*, *33*(7), 479–486.

Yehuda, R., & Bierer, L. M. (2009). The relevance of epigenetics to PTSD: Implications for the DSM-V. *Journal of Traumatic Stress*, *22*(5), 427–434.

Yehuda, R., Bierer, L. M., Schmeidler, J., Aferiat, D. H., Breslau, I., & Dolan, S. (2000). Low cortisol and risk for PTSD in adult offspring of holocaust survivors. *American Journal of Psychiatry*, *157*(8), 1252–1259.

Yehuda, R., Cai, G., Golier, J.A., Sarapas, C., Galea, S., Ising, M., ... Buxbaum, J.D. (2009). Gene expression patterns associated with posttraumatic stress disorder following exposure to the World Trade Center attacks. *Biological Psychiatry*, *66*, 708–711.

Yehuda, R., Halligan, S. L., & Bierer, L. M. (2002). Cortisol levels in adult offspring of Holocaust survivors: Relation to PTSD symptom severity in the parent and child. *Psychoneuroendocrinology*, *27*(1), 171–180.

Yehuda, R., Koenen, K. C., Galea, S., & Flory, J. D. (2011). The role of genes in defining a molecular biology of PTSD. *Disease Markers*, *30*(2–3), 67–76.

Yehuda, R., McFarlane, A., & Shalev, A. (1998). Predicting the development of posttraumatic stress disorder from the acute response to a traumatic event. *Biological Psychiatry*, *44*(12), 1305–1313.

Yehuda, R., & McFarlane, A. C. (1995). Conflict between current knowledge about posttraumatic stress disorder and its original conceptual basis. *American Journal of Psychiatry*, *152*(12), 1705–1713.

Yehuda, R., Southwick, S. M., Krystal, J. H., Bremner, D., Charney, D. S., & Mason, J. W. (1993). Enhanced suppression of cortisol following dexamethasone

372 *Eisenmann, Cadle, and Zoladz*

administration in posttraumatic stress disorder. *American Journal of Psychiatry*, *150*, 83–83.

Yerkes, R. M., & Dodson, J. D. (1908). The relation of strength of stimulus to rapidity of habit-formation. *Journal of Comparative Neurology and Psychology*, *18*(5), 459–482.

Yu, B., Zhang, X., Cui, X., Cui, S., & Zhang, Y. (2014). Establishment and evaluation of physical and psychological stress-induced PTSD animal model (1144.7). *The FASEB Journal*, *28*(1 Supplement), 1144.7.

Zhang, Y., Gandhi, P. R., & Standifer, K. M. (2012). Increased nociceptive sensitivity and nociceptin/orphanin FQ levels in a rat model of PTSD. *Molecular Pain*, *8*(1), 76.

Zoladz, P. R., Conrad, C. D., Fleshner, M., & Diamond, D. M. (2008). Acute episodes of predator exposure in conjunction with chronic social instability as an animal model of post-traumatic stress disorder. *Stress*, *11*(4), 259–281.

Zoladz, P. R., Fleshner, M., & Diamond, D. M. (2012). Psychosocial animal model of PTSD produces a long-lasting traumatic memory, an increase in general anxiety and PTSD-like glucocorticoid abnormalities. *Psychoneuroendocrinology*, *37*(9), 1531–1545.

Zoladz, P. R., Fleshner, M., & Diamond, D. M. (2013). Differential effectiveness of tianeptine, clonidine and amitriptyline in blocking traumatic memory expression, anxiety and hypertension in an animal model of PTSD. *Progress in Neuropsychopharmacology & Biological Psychiatry*, *44*, 1–16.

Zoladz, P. R., Park, C. R., Fleshner, M., & Diamond, D. M. (2015). Psychosocial predator-based animal model of PTSD produces physiological and behavioral sequelae and a traumatic memory four months following stress onset. *Physiology & Behavior*, *147*, 183–192.

Zurita, A., Martijena, I., Cuadra, G., Brandão, M. L., & Molina, V. c. (2000). Early exposure to chronic variable stress facilitates the occurrence of anhedonia and enhanced emotional reactions to novel stressors: Reversal by naltrexone pretreatment. *Behavioural Brain Research*, *117*(1), 163–171.

14 Developing a Reliable Animal Model of PTSD in Order to Test Potential Pharmacological Treatments

Predator Stress and the Mechanistic Target of Rapamycin

Phillip MacCallum, Jesse Whiteman, Therese Kenny, Katelyn Fallon, Sriya Bhattacharya, James Drover, and Jacqueline Blundell

Posttraumatic Stress Disorder (PTSD)

Several current models in psychology and neuroscience describe post-traumatic stress disorder (PTSD) as a condition of disturbed emotional learning and memory processes in which the *consolidation* of **traumatic fear memories** is enhanced, fear *cues* are generalized, and the *extinction* of fear memories is impaired (Murray et al., 2014; Mahan & Ressler, 2012). Bailey and Balsam (2013) describe PTSD as a syndrome where "old memories evoke responses ill-suited to current circumstances" (p. 245). Bailey and Balsam's description of PTSD reflects the plight of a traumatized combat veteran induced to panic, terror, or rage by the gunshot-like sounds of holiday firecrackers or an otherwise innocuous car backfire. Such vividness ensures that understanding trauma is not just another research goal in behavioural science, but that the quality of life and well-being of these individuals drives our interest in understanding the mechanisms that contribute to the development and maintenance of PTSD. The considerable suffering experienced by people with PTSD and the relatively high prevalence of PTSD (i.e., lifetime prevalence is estimated to be 6.1% and 9.2% among the general population in the United States and Canada, respectively; Goldstein et al., 2016; Kessler & Wang, 2008; Van Ameringen et al., 2008) contribute to the urgency for research on the brain mechanisms underlying the disorder. Clarification of brain mechanisms will help clinicians and other scientists understand the aetiology of PTSD, which may ultimately help identify candidate drug treatments (Steckler & Risbrough, 2012; Hauger et al., 2012; Reul & Nutt, 2008).

DOI: 10.4324/9781351134637-15

374 *Phillip MacCallum et al.*

The Dynamic Nature of Memory

Research linking basic neuroscience to behavioural models of learning and memory has primarily focused on "simple system" learning models using invertebrates and rodents (for comprehensive reviews, see Kandel, Dudai, & Mayford, 2014; Mayford, Siegelbaum, & Kandel, 2012; Sweatt, 2010; Squire & Kandel, 2008). The simple system approach distinguishes between **associative** and **non-associative** learning. Associative learning is typified by **Pavlovian fear conditioning**, a laboratory paradigm in which the pairing of a neutral stimulus (the *Conditioned Stimulus*) with an aversive stimulus (the *Unconditioned Stimulus*) allows the animal to learn to respond to the previously neutral stimulus with fear on subsequent encounters. In the Pavlovian model, **fear** is usually defined as the visible performance of species-typical defence behaviours, such as freezing or fleeing, which have evolved to allow evasion of environmental dangers like predators (Bolles, 1975; Ledoux, 1995, Panksepp, 1998). Associative processes allow an animal to learn about relations between environmental events and how to respond appropriately to such events (Rescorla, 1988; Timberlake, 1994; Gallistel, 2003). For example, the prey animal that learns to freeze in the presence of a predator is more likely to survive and transmit its genes to the next generation. Non-associative learning includes the contrasting phenomena of **habituation** and **sensitization**. Habituation and sensitization typically occur with reflexive behaviours (e.g., when you jump in response to a loud noise), the intensity of which can be attenuated (habituation) or increased (sensitization) by repeated exposure to the triggering stimulus. Habituation is a decreased response to a stimulus, whereas sensitization is an increased response to a stimulus. While much of our knowledge of the physiology of non-associative learning comes from studies of invertebrates (e.g. Aplysia (a sea slug); Byrne, 2012; Kandel, 2001; Carew & Kandel, 1973; Lau et al., 2013); habituation and sensitization are conserved across phyla and studied in rodents and humans as well (Lissek & van Meurs, 2015; Davis et al., 2008; Orr, Metzger, & Pitman (2002); Piltz & Schnitzler, 1996; Leaton & Supple, 1986; Davis, 1970, 1972).

Distinguishing associative and non-associative learning is useful in the context of PTSD because symptoms can be split into those shaped by associative learning (i.e., re-experiencing and avoidance symptoms) and those shaped by non-associative learning (i.e., hyperarousal symptoms and negative alterations in cognitions and mood). Thus, clarification of the respective neural substrates for associative and non-associative learning processes is crucial to understanding how these symptoms emerge and are maintained in PTSD. Any animal model designed to study the neural mechanisms of PTSD should produce as many symptom clusters analogues of the human disorder as possible by eliciting species-specific responses to species-relevant threats in the animal of choice (Goswami et al., 2013; Adamec, 1997; Skolnick & Paul, 1983). Associative and non-associative fear memories both follow the standard stages of processing for any memory trace;

Predator Stress and Rapamycin   375

specifically, fear memories are subject to acquisition and consolidation, and can be altered by intrinsic updating processes like reconsolidation and extinction. Consolidation is the critical inflection point in the survival of new fear memories and the molecular biological processes underlying consolidation is mostly well understood; as such, consolidation is the aspect of a potentially psychologically traumatic event (PPTE) memory perhaps most amenable to development of therapeutic drugs.

Consolidation

Neuroscientists define *learning* two ways: either as a relatively permanent change in behaviour as a result of experience (Pearce & Bouton, 2001; Bouton, 2007; Smock, 1999) or as the acquisition of information as a result of experience (Squire, 1987; Tulving, 2000). Accordingly, a *memory* is an experience-dependent internal representation (Dudai, 2004) formed by the capacity of the brain to retain learned information (Alberini, 2009). Researchers describing one particular memory are typically referring to a neural pattern carrying information about an aspect of the experienced world; however, such a memory is not a static entity within the brain. Five decades of research on the pharmacological manipulation of learning and memory in animals have led to the broadly accepted proposal that there are two stages of memory formation: **acquisition** and **consolidation** (Nader & Hardt, 2009; Alberini & LeDoux, 2013; McGaugh & Izquierdo, 2000; Squire, 1987). The learning experience is the crux of memory acquisition. In simplest terms, acquisition can be considered as the *generation of a memory trace*. Once information is learned and a memory is acquired (i.e., a *memory trace* is generated in the brain), the memory trace remains in a labile state where its strength (and perhaps existence) is acutely sensitive to pharmacological manipulations. The lability of memory is evidenced by several drug interventions, but most comprehensively with protein synthesis inhibitors (e.g., *Anisomycin*; McGaugh, 1966; McGaugh & Herz, 1972; Davis & Squire, 1984; McGaugh, 2000; Klann & Sweatt, 2008).

Protein synthesis inhibitors given after memory acquisition have been shown to block the formation of certain types of memories, but not others. For example, a "long-term memory" (i.e., memories evident when tested hours to years following training) can be blocked with protein synthesis inhibitors; however, a "short-term memory" (i.e., memories evident minutes to hours following training) cannot be blocked with protein synthesis inhibitors.[1] The difference indicates a time-limited neural process where the initial memory trace must be "laid down" in the brain in order to be transferred to a long-term/permanent storage format. The process of "laying down" the memory is referred to as **consolidation** (Müller & Pilzecker, 1900; Dudai, 1996; 2004; McGaugh, 2000; Squire & Bayley, 2007; Kandel et al., 2014) and occurs on a timescale of minutes to hours.

Consolidation requires new protein synthesis that provides a physical basis for changes in synaptic efficacy. These physical changes are thought

376   *Phillip MacCallum et al.*

to represent the instantiation of the new memory or the engram (Nader, 2003 Dudai, 2004; Kandel, 2001). Synaptic changes embed the memory within patterns of neuronal connections over broad timescales, which allows consolidation to be formally defined as a "time-dependent stabilization process leading eventually to permanent storage of a new memory" (Nader & Hardt, 2009, p. 224). In other words, consolidation is the process that transfers the new trace from a nebulous entity in short-term memory to a stable component of long-term memory.

From Molecule to Memory

Much of what we presently know about how brains create, maintain, and modify memory traces comes from invertebrate models of non-associative learning and rodent models of associative learning (particularly Pavlovian fear conditioning). Beginning with the insights of McGill's Donald O. Hebb (1949), behavioural neuroscientists have searched for a physiological process in neural connections that parallels the nature of the behavioural associative learning process (i.e., a process where a **synapse** linking two neurons is strengthened when both of these neurons are active at the same time; Bliss & Collingridge, 1993). Bliss and Lømo (1973) discovered such a process, which they termed *long-term potentiation*. Briefly, long-term potentiation refers to the enhancement of neural transmission at a given synapse (i.e., a communicative juncture between brain cells or neurons) by repeated, high-frequency stimulation of presynaptic neural inputs.

For example, when both a weak and a strong input arrive at a synapse *at the same time* and are intended for the *same postsynaptic cell*, the weak input becomes *potentiated* through association, and the weak pathway consequently responds to the tetanic electrical stimulation with greater depolarization than would have previously occurred (Nicoll & Roche, 2013; Dudek & Bear, 1992). The phenomena of long-term potentiation was anticipated in 1949 by Hebb's ground-breaking theorem, which is commonly paraphrased as "neurons that fire together, wire together". Hebb's rule can be illustrated in a population of neurons (typically CA1 neurons) with stimulating electrodes, recording electrodes, and an oscilloscope. In this setup, a weak pulse of electrical stimulation will only produce a weak electrophysiological response (weak depolarization). But if a weak pulse is followed up in short succession with a pulse of strong stimulation, then subsequent responses to weak stimulation on the oscilloscope are shown to be enhanced or potentiated, demonstrating the "fire together, wire together" logic across a neural population (Rudy, 2014; Sweatt, 2010).

Researchers have resolved in detail the molecular mechanisms underlying long-term potentiation (see Frankland & Josslyn, 2016; Malenka & Bear, 2004). Consistent with the hypothesis of long-term potentiation as a mechanism for memory consolidation, long-lasting long-term potentiation—like behavioural consolidation—requires protein synthesis. At the synaptic level, researchers have shown the N-methyl-D-aspartate

Predator Stress and Rapamycin 377

(NMDA) glutamate receptor to have the properties needed to underlie a synaptic potentiation process. Despite many of the identified synaptic elements (e.g., NMDA receptors) that participate in long-term potentiation (Panja & Branham, 2014; Mayford et al., 2012), how action at the synapse contributes to protein synthesis, and ultimately memory consolidation, remains relatively unresolved. Thus, researchers have recently focused on the cellular signalling cascades (second-messenger pathways) that mediate synaptic changes by driving protein synthesis in neurons. Brain-Derived Neurotrophic Factor (BDNF) has emerged as a key molecule in synaptic plasticity and long-term potentiation as related to learning and memory (Panja & Branham, 2014). The BDNF molecule provides a mechanistic link between learning and consolidation of a fear memory (Monfils, Cowansage, & Ledoux, 2007). Research suggests the sub-cortical **amygdala** is a key neural hub for plasticity in fear learning-related processes (Rogan, Stäubli, & Ledoux, 1997; Blair et al., 2001); therefore, researchers have focused on the role of amygdalar BDNF activity in fear memory consolidation. Many such studies report BDNF transcription (synthesis of RNA from DNA) during fear memory consolidation (Rudy, 2014). Based on these and other results, there is now a large and growing body of literature on the role of the *mechanistic (formerly mammalian) Target of Rapamycin (mTOR) kinase* pathway in memory processes. The literature specifically addresses how upstream signals from the synapse (e.g., the BDNF receptor tyrosine receptor kinase B (TrkB)) activate mTOR, and how mTOR, in turn, drives translation (synthesis of protein from RNA) of molecular products needed for the ongoing plasticity underlying fear memory acquisition and consolidation. The molecular and pharmacological aspects of mTOR can further inform Pavlovian and predator stress models of fear learning.

mTOR and Rapamycin

mTOR is a kinase (i.e., enzyme) at the centre of a signalling pathway that is strongly conserved from bacteria to humans (Li, Kim, & Blenis, 2014; Hay & Sonenberg, 2004). In the brain, mTOR contributes to synaptic plasticity by controlling a subset of protein synthesis (translation) through downstream target effector proteins (e.g., p70s6k and 4E-BP1). The mTOR kinase also responds to signals initiated by receptors (e.g., NMDA, TrkB) that are crucial to synaptic plasticity required in long-term potentiation (Graber, McCamphill, & Sossin, 2013; Hoeffer & Klann, 2010). The mTOR molecule is found in cells as a component of two distinct molecular complexes, complex 1 (mTORC1) and complex 2 (mTORC2; Hay & Sonenberg, 2004; Hoeffer & Klann, 2010). The mTORC1 structure and function is well characterized with much of what we understand about the biochemistry of mTORC1 coming from research using the bacterium-derived mTORC1 allosteric inhibitor drug **rapamycin**. The drug specifically inhibits the complex by first binding with FK506-binding protein 12 (FKBP12), which

378 *Phillip MacCallum et al.*

then binds to the FKB12 rapamycin-binding (FRB) domain of mTORC1 forming a ternary complex preventing mTORC1 from carrying out its kinase activities to its substrates (Yang et al., 2013). mTORC2 is considered rapamycin-insensitive and is only mildly response to rapamycin treatment following chronic administration (Hay & Sonenberg, 2004; Sarbassov et al., 2006). Lacking any specific inhibitor, much less is known about the characteristics of mTORC2 biochemically, with even less know about its function in the biology of behaviour (Bockaert & Martin, 2015; Hoeffer & Klann, 2010; Huang et al., 2013). In the current chapter, we focus exclusively on mTORC1, referred to as mTOR hereafter.

Animal Models of PTSD: From Pavlov to Predation

Human psychobiology research on PTSD is large and includes neuroendocrine, psychophysiological, and neuroimaging approaches (e.g., Acheson, Geyer, & Risbrough, 2014; Pole, 2007; Etkin & Wager, 2007; Bryant et al., 2005; Yehuda, 2009; Rasmusson, Vythilingam, & Morgan, 2003). The approaches are largely non-invasive for practical and ethical reasons, limiting the bases of most results to correlational data. Direct manipulation of the brain to identify causal mechanisms requires the use of animal models. Substantial research efforts have gone into modelling PTSD symptoms in rodents to investigate underlying cellular and molecular mechanisms of PTSD (especially the mechanisms that underlie consolidation, extinction, and reconsolidation of traumatic memories). An understanding of these mechanisms offers opportunities to identify potential pharmacological treatment targets. However, no particular animal model of PTSD ideally recapitulates all symptoms of the disorder; with Pavlovian fear conditioning paradigms and predator stress paradigms being the major approaches used by researchers to date. Pavlovian fear conditioning effectively models the re-experiencing and cue-related symptoms of PTSD. Predator stress models capture re-experiencing and cue-related symptoms as well, but also produce hyperarousal and anxiety-like behaviour, making predator stress models arguably more comprehensive animal models of PTSD (Deslauriers et al., 2017).

Pavlovian Fear Conditioning

The fear memories produced by Pavlovian paradigms involve an organism learning that a previously innocuous or neutral cue (the conditioned stimulus; e.g., a light or buzzer) predicts the onset of a naturally fear-producing stimulus (the unconditional stimulus; e.g., a mildly painful foot shock). The unconditioned stimulus is a stimulus to which the animal has an innate and reflexive behavioural fear response (i.e., the unconditioned response). Unconditioned responses usually manifest as freezing or *tonic immobility* in both rodents and humans (Maren, 2001; Ledoux, 2003). Little experience is required for animals to associate the conditioned and unconditioned stimuli in memory, and the conditioned stimulus quickly comes to elicit the fear response. When the conditioned stimulus elicits the fear response without the presence of the unconditioned stimulus, the fear response is then referred to as the conditioned response (Pearce & Bouton, 2001). Pavlovian conditioning involves the animal learning relations between events in the world and fear has been powerfully shaped as a threat-avoidance mechanism over evolutionary time (Ledoux, 2012; Öhman & Mineka, 2001, Cosmides & Tooby, 2000). For example, a rat that freezes or hides in response to a hawk's cry is demonstrating an adaptive behaviour. Little experience is needed for objects and contexts predictive of danger or pain to prime the animal to respond with fear when these cues are encountered again. Pavlovian paradigms have been successful in modelling one set of PTSD symptoms, namely associative fear memories. The fear learning mechanisms activated in these protocols appear dramatically recalibrated in people with PTSD, where fear memories seem "over-consolidated". The process of extinction learning that allows an animal to update predictive relationships also appears compromised in PTSD (Mahan & Ressler, 2012; Morgan, Romanski, & LeDoux, 1993; Wessa & Flor, 2007), so cues and contexts reminiscent of the original PPTE exposure continue to generate powerful fear responses long after the predictive value has disappeared (Bailey & Balsam, 2013).

mTOR and Pavlovian Fear Conditioning

The role of mTOR in the formation and maintenance of associative fear memories as tested in Pavlovian fear conditioning models is well-established. As described above consolidation and other aspects of memory can be disrupted via global protein synthesis inhibitors. Unlike other inhibitors that arrest all cellular machinery related to protein synthesis, rapamycin only selectively inhibits mTOR, which allows for the precise investigation of the mTOR pathway contribution to memory consolidation. There is a discrete period of increased activation of p70S6K (a downstream target of mTOR) in two brain areas underlying fear memory after fear memory acquisition; specifically, the hippocampus (Bekinschtein et al., 2007; Gafford, Parsons, & Helmstetter, 2011) and the amygdala (Parsons, Gafford, & Helmstetter, 2006). The increase in p70S6K activation is thought to drive consolidation of the fear memory. Concordantly, inhibition of mTOR in the hippocampus by rapamycin blocks both consolidation of a shock-induced Pavlovian fear memory and the associated increase in p70S6K activation (Bekinschtein et al., 2007). Similar inhibitory effects follow direct rapamycin administration into the amygdala (Parsons et al., 2006), with systemic rapamycin following Pavlovian training inhibiting consolidation of associative fear memories (Mac Callum et al., 2014; Bekinschtein et al., 2007; Blundell, Kouser, & Powell, 2008; Tishmeyer et al., 2003). Together, the available results suggest that consolidation of a Pavlovian fear memory depends on mTOR, which highlights a role for mTOR in the development

380   *Phillip MacCallum et al.*

of persistent fear memories in PTSD. The data point to the importance of mTOR in context or stimulus-specific fear memories, but do not address hyperarousal or generalized anxiety symptoms.

Limitations of Pavlovian Fear Conditioning as a PTSD Model

Fear conditioning defensibly captures the associative aspects of PTSD symptoms by generating strong fear memories for contexts and cues. Notable disadvantages of Pavlovian fear conditioning include not exposing the organism to a truly life-threatening event and the inability to robustly mimic other PTSD symptoms (e.g., persistent hyperarousal; increased anxiety-like behaviour; Pitman, 1997; Pitman, Orr, & Shalev, 1993). Experiments in our lab have shown that while animals display normal freezing behaviour to the training context following contextual fear conditioning, other behaviours germane to PTSD remain relatively unbridled. Conditioned animals showed no difference from their untrained counterparts in arousal state or in levels of anxiety (as measured in the elevated plus maze and dark/light box). Fear conditioning has allowed us to learn a great deal about the neural basis of associative fear and stress, from critical structures (i.e., hippocampus, amygdala) to molecular components (i.e., mTOR, BDNF); but to truly model and understand the neurobiology of PTSD, an animal model is needed that recapitulates a more comprehensive set of symptoms of the disorder. A prominent candidate for such a model is the predator stress paradigm.

Predator Stress

Cat Exposure as a Paradigmatic Predator Stress Model

Predator stress typically involves acute exposure of a prey species (e.g., mouse, rat) to a predator (e.g., cat, rat, ferret). The classic predator stress paradigm developed by Adamec and Shallow (1993) involves a single, unprotected exposure of a rodent to an adult male domestic cat. Cat exposures last for 10 minutes and are videotaped to capture the activities of both the rodent and the cat. When the 10-minute test is completed, the rodent is gently removed from the cat exposure room and returned to its home cage. Video recordings can later be examined to determine locomotor activity of the rodent and cat, approaches to and flights from the cat by the rodent, the number of cat/rodent interactions, and the number of vocal calls made by the cat. Control groups for studies using the predator stress model are handled by experimenters rather than exposed to a predator (hereafter referred to as "handled control"). Cat exposures consistently generate high levels of associative fear, non-associative fear, and anxiety-like behaviour (Adamec & Shallow, 1993; Adamec, Shallow, & Budgell, 1997; Adamec, 1998; Adamec et al., 1999; Adamec, 2001; Adamec, Bartoszyk, & Burton, 2004; Adamec, Walling, & Burton, 2004; Adamec, Blundell, & Burton,

Predator Stress and Rapamycin   381

2005; Blundell, Adamec, & Burton, 2005; Adamec et al., 2008; Fifield et al., 2013; Fifield et al., 2015; Lau, Whiteman, & Blundell, 2015; therefore, unprotected domestic cat exposure may be an ecologically valid and comprehensive rodent model of PTSD. The ethological vividness of the feline predator stress model is attractive, but the effects can be highly variable (Adamec, Walling, & Burton, 2004; Fifield et al., 2013; 2015).

Predator Stress, Consolidation, and Protein Synthesis

Ample evidence demonstrates that protein synthesis is necessary for consolidation of predator stress-induced non-associative fear memories, such as hyperarousal and anxiety-like behaviour, paralleling associative fear memories from the fear conditioning literature (Adamec et al., 2006; Cohen et al., 2006; Blundell et al., 2005; Kozlovsky et al., 2008). Systemic injection of anisomycin (i.e., a global protein synthesis inhibitor) following predator exposure can block the increase in anxiety-like behaviour and exaggerated response to acoustic startle (a measure of hyperarousal) when measured one week later (Adamec et al., 2006). Similarly, infusion of anisomycin either before or after predator scent stress (i.e., exposure to predator odour stimulus, such as urine or fur) reduced anxiety and startle responses (Cohen et al., 2006). Collectively this work from the Adamec and Cohen labs has supported the hypothesis that the synthesis of novel proteins is necessary for consolidation of non-associative fear memories in predator stress paradigms as evidenced through the effects of protein synthesis inhibitors on non-associative memories. It follows that these memories likely require translation regulation in order to be consolidated.

Anisomycin is a global protein synthesis inhibitor as it inhibits ribosomal activity, which reduces protein synthesis by as much as 60–80%. In contrast, rapamycin selectively inhibits only mTOR activity and reduces protein synthesis by a mere 10% (Parsons et al., 2006). The selectivity of rapamycin makes it ideal for investigating the role of mTOR in predator stress. Work from the Blundell lab has demonstrated that the mTOR pathway plays a role in predator stress-induced associative and non-associative fear memories. Rats exposed to a cat and then injected with systemic rapamycin showed decreased freezing when re-exposed to the cat room context, suggesting reduced associative fear memories. Moreover, predator stressed rats given rapamycin showed lower anxiety-like behaviour in the elevated plus maze and decreased hyperarousal in the acoustic startle test compared with controls injected with a physiologically inert vehicle solution, suggesting reduced non-associative fear memories. In all cases, animals exposed to predator stress and treated with rapamycin exhibited similar behaviour to that of handled control animals (Fifield et al., 2013), suggesting that rapamycin blocks consolidation of the predator stress-induced associative *and* non-associative fear memories. As the results indicate a potential role for mTOR in both types of fear memory induced by

382 Phillip MacCallum et al.

predator stress, we were interested in examining the distribution of mTOR activity in the brain during consolidation of such memories.

Experimental Approaches to Predator Stress Models: Molecules, Drugs, and Behaviour

Experiment 1: What is the Neuroanatomical Distribution of mTOR Activation Underlying Predator Stress-Induced Fear Memories?

Data from the Blundell lab suggested that like shock-induced Pavlovian fear memories, predator stress-induced fear memories are regulated by mTOR activity. Unlike shock-induced fear memory, the localization of mTOR activation in the brain following predator stress is unknown. Thus, we intended to identify brain areas that could mediate consolidation of mTOR-dependent predator stress-induced fear memories. Rats were randomly assigned to predator stress or handled control conditions and were euthanized one hour or one week following cat exposure or control handling. Brains were extracted from rats of both groups and frozen for tissue analysis by immunohistochemistry. Immunohistochemistry was done using an antibody designed to detect "phospho-mTOR" (noted as p-mTOR) as a proxy of mTOR activity. p-mTOR expression was analysed using densitometry with respect to two brain areas commonly implicated in memory, stress, and anxiety: the hippocampus and the midbrain periaqueductal grey.

Decades of research results implicate the hippocampal complex as a critical brain structure in the formation of fear memories (Foster & Burman, 2010; Kim & Fansewlow, 1992; Phillips & LeDoux, 1992; Saxe et al., 2006). The role of the hippocampus as a critical structure in the formation of many types of memories in general is supported by a very diverse body of evidence (Andersen et al., 2006).

The hippocampus has a highly complex internal structure containing the CA1 and CA3 regions, hilus, and associated dentate gyrus amongst other subregions (Amaral & Lavenex, 2006). The CA1 pyramidal cell layer of the dorsal hippocampus is of particular relevance to the consolidation of fear memory. Recent studies have demonstrated that selective inhibition of excitatory CA1 neurons during fear conditioning sufficiently abolishes the acquisition and recall of contextual fear memory (Goshen et al., 2011). Studies using immunohistochemistry identified increased neuronal activation (e.g., c-Fos staining) in the CA1 region of the hippocampus in chronically stressed and fear conditioned rats (Hoffman et al.). In addition to the CA1 pyramidal cell layer, the dentate gyrus is a subregion of the dorsal hippocampus that has been implicated in the encoding of contextual fear memories (Hernandez-Rabaza et al., 2008; Khierbek et al., 2013). An analysis by Kheirbek et al. (2013) demonstrated that inhibition of the dorsal dentate gyrus during fear conditioning significantly reduced freezing behaviour to the learning context. Experimental lesions of the dentate

Predator Stress and Rapamycin 383

gyrus also appear to impair fear conditioning in rats when compared to "sham-lesion" animals (Hernandez-Rabaza et al., 2008).

The periaqueductal grey, a prominent feature of the midbrain, is an evolutionarily older structure than the hippocampus. Anatomists have divided the periaqueductal grey into three longitudinal columns that are termed dorsal, lateral, and ventral subregions (Bandler, Carrive, & Depaulis, 1991). The periaqueductal grey has been strongly implicated in cardiovascular functioning, nociception (pain), and vocalization (Jürgens, 1991; Kim et al., 2013). Evidence also indicates that the periaqueductal grey modulates fear memories and defensive behaviours through its connections with the structures of the limbic system (the emotional brain; e.g., hippocampus, amygdala; Adamec, Blundell, & Collins, 2001). Experimental evidence demonstrates increased activity in the periaqueductal grey in response to several different types of stress (Canteras & Goto, 1999; Adamec et al., 2012; Blundell & Adamec, 2006). For example, Adamec and colleagues (2012) showed that c-Fos (a ubiquitous marker of neuron activity) was elevated in the *dorsolateral* periaqueductal grey after predator stress and the *ventrolateral* periaqueductal grey after water submersion stress. Phosphorylated cAMP response element binding protein (pCREB), the activated form of a transcription factor (DNA binding protein that controls the rate of transcription) involved in memory formation, was also elevated in the lateral periaqueductal grey after predator stress (Blundell & Adamec, 2006). Further, electrical stimulation of the periaqueductal grey elicits fear in rodents (Kim et al., 2013; Di Scala et al., 1987). Specifically, in fear conditioning experiments, stimulation of the periaqueductal grey acts as an aversive stimulus, which elicits a fear state that is paired with a conditioned stimulus resulting in robust conditioned emotional responding to the conditioned stimulus in the absence of periaqueductal grey stimulation (Di Scala et al., 1987; Fanselow, 1991). Periaqueductal grey stimulation also provokes defensive behaviours, including bursts of activity, vocalizations, and robust freezing (Kim et al., 2013). The freezing behaviour is blocked by ventral periaqueductal grey lesions, which also attenuate the learned fear conditioned response (Amorapanth, Nader, & LeDoux, 1999).

Little is known about the long-term effects of mTOR activation. Therefore, we were interested in mTOR activation differences between the two brain areas at different time points. Our research has shown that anxiety-like behaviours in rodents can last up to seven days following exposure to a predator (Adamec & Shallow, 1993; Blundell & Ademec, 2006; Adamec et al., 2006). Accordingly, we wanted to determine whether changes in mTOR activation also persist at this approximate time point. If such changes persist, they could be a candidate for the expression of sustained associative and non-associative fear memories. We compared levels of p-mTOR expression in rats sacrificed one-hour following predator stress to those sacrificed one-week following predator stress. To our knowledge, the current study is the first study to examine mTOR activation patterns in

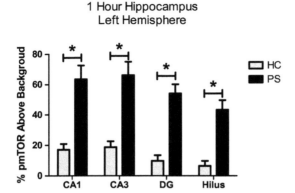

Figure 14.1 mTOR activation in control and stressed groups across subregions of the hippocampus in each hemisphere. C. mTOR activation by subregion of the periaqueductal grey.

the brain following predator stress. Based on behavioural-pharmacological data (Fifield et al., 2013) and previous molecular work using Pavlovian models (Parsons et al., 2006; Gafford et al., 2011), we hypothesized that p-mTOR levels would be elevated one hour following predator stress relative to handled control animals in both the hippocampus and periaqueductal grey. The current study was also designed to investigate whether altered levels of mTOR expression remained one week following predator stress.

As predicted, p-mTOR expression was significantly higher in the hippocampus of predator stress rats in comparison to handled control rats one-hour post-predator stress. This was the case bilaterally (i.e., in both right and left hemispheres) and across the major anatomical subregions of the hippocampus. p-mTOR expression was higher in predator stress rats in the CA1, CA3, dentate gyrus, and Hilus subregions in both left and right hemispheres (Figures 14.1 and 14.2). These results are consistent with previous Pavlovian research showing that the mTOR pathway is activated in the dorsal hippocampus in response to contextual fear conditioning (e.g., Gafford et al., 2011). The results also support the hypothesis that mTOR activation in the dorsal hippocampus is essential for the consolidation of predator stress-induced fear memories as well. Upon separating the periaqueductal grey into the three columnar regions (i.e., dorsal, ventral, and lateral periaqueductal grey), differences were identified across regions. Specifically, p-mTOR expression was significantly higher in the dorsal periaqueductal grey in predator stress rats compared to handled controls, with a *trend* towards an increase in p-mTOR expression in the lateral periaqueductal grey of predator stress animals (Figure 14.3).

There were no significant differences in p-mTOR expression between predator stress and handled control groups in the ventral periaqueductal

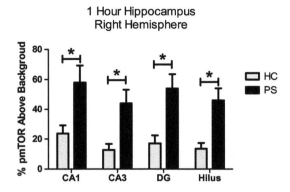

Figure 14.2 mTOR activation in control and stressed groups across subregions of the hippocampus in each hemisphere. C. mTOR activation by subregion of the periaqueductal grey.

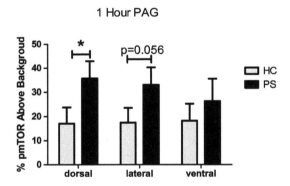

Figure 14.3 mTOR activation by subregion of the periaqueductal grey.

grey (Figure 14.3). The increase of p-mTOR expression in the dorsal and lateral regions of the periaqueductal grey is consistent with our hypothesis and previous literature implicating the periaqueductal grey in stress and fear processes. Following predator stress, pCREB expression increases in both the dorsal and lateral periaqueductal grey columns (Adamec et al., 2011), suggesting that increases in activity in these regions are important in the formation of fear memories. The results dovetail with our observed increases in mTOR activation. The parallel increase of p-mTOR and pCREB indicated activation of dorsal and lateral regions of the periaqueductal grey following predator stress provide compelling evidence for (and a clean picture of) dorsolateral periaqueductal grey activity during fear memory consolidation. The current results are also consistent with evidence demonstrating that the stimulation of the dorsal periaqueductal

386 *Phillip MacCallum et al.*

grey elicits anxiety-like and natural defensive behaviours in rodents (i.e., panic-like behaviour), implying that activity in the dorsal periaqueductal grey is a crucial substrate for expression of fear and anxiety (Panksepp, 1998; Pinto de Almeida et al., 2006; Borelli et al., 2013). No significant differences were found between predator stress and handled control groups in p-mTOR levels in either the hippocampus or periaqueductal grey at one week following exposure.

Research has shown that activity in the ventral region of the periaqueductal grey is increased in response to stress, as c-Fos was shown to be elevated in the ventrolateral periaqueductal grey following submersion stress (Adamec et al., 2012) and in all areas of the periaqueductal grey following predator stress (Cantera & Gota, 1999). Therefore, we expected alterations in mTOR activation in the ventral periaqueductal grey following predator stress. In reference to our negative results, there may have been insufficient statistical power to detect changes in mTOR activity in the periaqueductal grey region. Alternatively, changes in mTOR activation may occur on a different timescale in the ventral periaqueductal grey in comparison with other regions and molecular cascades with changes not detectable at the one-hour time point. Another consideration is that the ventral periaqueductal grey may not be involved in the processes of fear learning and memory *per se*, but may instead be an output nucleus responsible for mediating defensive behaviours and conditioned emotional fear responses since lesions to this area inhibit these behaviours typically evoked by electrical stimulation of the dorsal periaqueductal grey (Amorapanth et al., 1999). If this is the case, it would explain why increases in p-mTOR expression were not seen in the ventral region following predator stress. Perhaps the ventral area is involved in the production of a conditioned response but would not be activated simply upon the *formation* or consolidation of a fearful memory. Our experiment described here only examines the molecular basis of the consolidation of a putative fear memory; the roles of mTOR in behavioural expression of a predator stress-induced fear memory remain indirectly shown by rapamycin injection studies (Fifield et al., 2013).

We did not observe any differences between predator stress and handled control groups in p-mTOR levels in either the hippocampus or periaqueductal grey at one week following exposure. Accordingly, mTOR activation may be limited to the initial consolidation phase of memory formation and other changes (perhaps downstream of mTOR) may maintain the memory over the long term. In any event, the results suggest mTOR activation in the dorsal hippocampus and dorsal and lateral periaqueductal grey are important in mediating consolidation of predator stress-induced fear memories. We also demonstrated that changes in mTOR activation do not persist at one-week post-exposure, suggesting transient mTOR activation underlies changes in synaptic efficacy via protein synthesis in order to lay down the nascent memory.

Experiment 2A: The Rat-Exposure Test and Fear Memory

Despite research success, the feline predator stress model is associated with high economic costs (i.e., maintaining experimental felines), reliability issues (i.e., variability across studies) and threats to its validity (i.e. occasional docile cat behaviour). These important caveats coupled with benefits of mouse-rat models (i.e., lower cost, clear external validity, increased reliability) led us to examine another mammalian exposure model; The Rat-Exposure Test (Yang et al., 2004). The Blanchard group, based at the University of Hawaii, first developed the rat-exposure test to evaluate mouse defensive behaviours. Defensive behaviours are innate, unconditioned responses that are elicited in response to a perceived threatening situation (Blanchard & Blanchard, 1988). Defensive behaviours are the outputs of brain systems evolved to increase chances of escape and survival when an animal is exposed to a predator. Examples of defensive behaviours include freezing, defensive burying, and avoidance (Yang et al, 2004). The defensive behaviours are indicators that the animal perceives a situation as potentially life-threatening and therefore contributes to the construct validity of a predator stress model. For the initial study, Yang et al. (2004) used amphetamine-injected Long-Evans rats (to ensure mobility across trials) for predators and BALB/C or C57BL/6 strain mice as prey. On the exposure day, a mouse was placed in the exposure cage and either a live rat or a stuffed toy rat control (instead of the handled control condition) was immediately introduced behind the wire mesh screen. The mouse could investigate the rat in the exposure cage or return to its home cage through a tunnel connecting the two boxes. In response to a live rat, mice subsequently demonstrated high levels of defensive behaviours, including freezing and avoidance. The results from Yang et al. (2004) have been successfully replicated (Amaral, Santos-Gomes, & Nunes-de-Souza, 2010; Campos et al., 2013; Furuya-da-Cunha, Souza, & Canto-de-Souza, 2016), supporting the rat-exposure test as an effective way to induce predator stress in mice.

We modified the rat-exposure test to a simplified exposure model with the mouse on one side of a perforated Plexiglas wall-divided cage and the rat (or stuffed control rat) on the other side. Instead of amphetamine, the live rats were calorie-restricted to increase activity and motivation during exposures, but importantly were never able to physically interact with mice during interactions.

During initial exposure, C57BL/6 mice exposed to a live rat froze significantly more than mice exposed to a stuffed control (Figure 14.4), suggesting that mice in the predator stress condition did indeed perceive the stimulus of the live rat to be stressful.

Upon re-exposure to the predator stress context, mice previously exposed to a live rat also froze significantly more than those who had been exposed to a stuffed control rat (Figure 14.5), suggesting that a five-minute

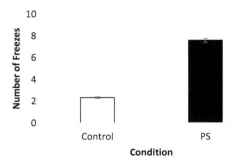

Figure 14.4 Exposure freezing for control and stressed animals during the rat-exposure test.

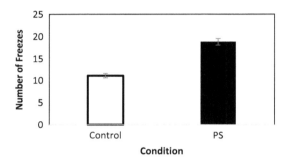

Figure 14.5 Re-exposure freezing for control and stressed animals following the rat-exposure test.

protected exposure of a mouse to a rat is sufficient to produce associative (contextual) fear memories upon re-exposure to the stressful context.

Non-associative memory testing was conducted over successive days with a different test carried out each day. Both groups of mice were first run through a battery of tests for anxiety-like behaviours using the elevated plus maze (EPM) on the first day, open field on the second day, and light–dark box on the third day, with acoustic startle testing on the final day to examine for hyperarousal (for a full description of these tests see Appendix 14: Methods). The results indicated control mice spent proportionately more time in the open arms of the EPM than did predator stress mice (Figure 14.6). Predator stress mice made fewer entries into the light side of the light–dark box (Figures 14.7). No differences were observed between groups in the time spent in the centre of the open field or acoustic startle response (data not shown).

Excluding the last results, the overall data suggest that a five-minute protected exposure of a mouse to a rat produces both associative and

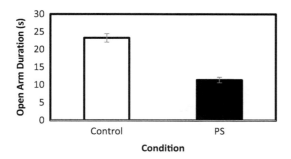

Figure 14.6 Time spent on open arms of elevated plus maze for control and stressed animals following the rat-exposure test.

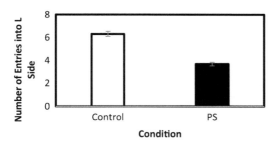

Figure 14.7 Number of entries into light side of light–dark box for control and stressed animals following the rat-exposure test.

non-associative fear memories in the mouse. Subsequent experiments in the Blundell lab have demonstrated increased startle behaviour following mouse exposure to a live rat. The overall results align with research indicating predator stress models produce both associative and non-associative fear memories in a prey animal following an acute non-lethal exposure to a predator (Adamec et al., 1998; Fifield et al., 2013).

Experiment 2B: Etho-Pharmacological Exploration of a Candidate PTSD Therapeutic—Rat-Exposure Test and Rapamycin

Initial results supporting the rat-exposure test as a reasonably robust model of PTSD-like fear memories led us to question whether the associative and non-associative fear memories elicited by the rat-exposure test were mTOR dependent. Mice were randomly assigned to predator or stuffed rat control groups and injected with either rapamycin (40 mg/kg) or an inert vehicle (VEH) immediately following exposure to the live or stuffed rat. The results were somewhat consistent with the previous experiment,

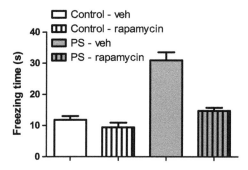

Figure 14.8 Freezing for the four Experiment 2B groups during re-exposure to the rat-exposure test context.

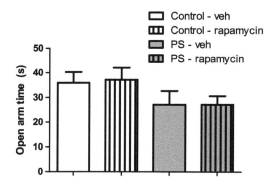

Figure 14.9 Ratio time (time in open arms/time in all arms) in the elevated plus maze for the four groups in Experiment 2B.

with no differences in the open field or startle across the drug and stress conditions (data not shown).

A strong context effect was demonstrated, and memory consolidation was shown to be at least partially mTOR dependent. Predator stress+VEH mice froze more on re-exposure compared to controls (Stuffed Control+VEH, Stuffed Control + rapamycin), while freezing in predator stress+rapamycin mice was comparable to control group levels (Figure 14.8). In the EPM, a similar pattern was seen for ratio time, with rapamycin increasing the proportion of time predator stress animals spent on the open arms as compared to VEH-treated mice. Unlike freezing, predator stress+rapamycin mice ratio times in the EPM were not as closely aligned with control levels (Figure 14.9). The "core" of a predator stress animal model of PTSD is sometimes reduced to contextual/cued fear, anxiety-like behaviour, and hyperarousal, as measured in predator context re-exposure, EPM, and startle, respectively (e.g., Cohen et al., 2006). Our results captured the first two components of the predator stress model, but without evidence of a startle effect as the curves over the course of the 30 trials did not differ (data not shown).

The results suggest that further research is needed to examine the involvement of mTOR in hyperarousal memory. Hyperarousal induced by the rat-exposure test may be impervious to rapamycin or might simply be more variable than the context or EPM effects. Given that consolidation of hyperarousal memory appears to be under mTOR control in the cat exposure test (Fifield et al., 2013), and that effects in other non-associative tests (light–dark box, open field) are somewhat variable, the latter is more likely the case. The contributions of mTOR to consolidation of hyperarousal may also be more nuanced than currently understood. Research using cat exposure indicated time-dependent effects of rapamycin on hyperarousal (Fifield et al., 2015). The ubiquity of mTOR in neurons (and all other cells) introduces complexity. Research on ingestive behaviour has come to the consensus that the effects of the mTOR pathway on eating and body weight are highly dependent on several factors (i.e., signalling stimulus, cell population, behavioural context; Haissaguerre, Saucisse, & Cota, 2014). Therefore, the effects of mTOR on learning and memory may be similarly complex. For example, amygdalar and hippocampal mTOR pathway activity promotes fear memory acquisition and consolidation, while prefrontal mTOR pathway activity promotes extinction or other forms of modulation to such memories (Bekinschtein et al., 2007; Gafford et al., 2011; Glover, Ressler, & Davis, 2010; Jobim et al., 2012; Levin et al., 2017; Mac Callum et al., 2014). Such a scenario would explain the variable nature of results following systemic rapamycin reported here and, in some experiments reported in Fifield et al. (2013, 2015). It will be critical for future research using the rat-exposure test to cannulate rapamycin into specific brain regions (e.g., hippocampus, periaqueductal grey) to measure its effects on contextual and non-associative fear memories. Doing so will allow the dissociation of effects of the mTOR pathway in different regions in parallel to work showing site-specific effects of mTOR in fear conditioning (Helmstetter, Parsons, & Gafford, 2008).

The slightly more modest results from experiment 2B suggest that the rat-exposure test generates contextual fear and speak to a role for mTOR in consolidation of fear memory. In contrast, the EPM results suggest that the non-associative fear memory/anxiety-like behaviour is also at least partially mTOR-dependent. The current results align with results using cat exposure (Fifield et al., 2013), but unlike cat exposure results, the rat-exposure test from Experiments 2A and B did not produce a startle effect or show that startle effect was subject to modification by mTOR blockade with rapamycin. Given that the unprotected cat exposure induces unwanted variability and can be complicated to execute, the rat-exposure test provides a more controlled alternative producing similar associative and non-associative fear behaviours. Thus, despite limitations and opportunities for refinement, the rat-exposure test represents a novel predator

392 Phillip MacCallum et al.

stress paradigm that holds much promise for elucidating the mechanisms underlying fear memories. As a final point, the still varying nature of the effects seen in these models reflect two important facts about real PPTE: (1) not every PPTE will produce the same constellation of behavioural and brain changes; and (2) the nature of symptoms appearing in humans with PTSD is itself highly variable, suggesting that models capturing such variability may be more accurate than appears intuitively.

Summary

The experimental results discussed above provide information relevant to PTSD. First, immunohistochemistry work using traditional cat exposure models provided the first evidence of region-specific mTOR activation underlying predator stress-induced memory formation, advancing our understanding of fear memory and potential treatments. Second, the rat-exposure test is a useful model for studying the modulation of predator stress-induced fear memories and a helpful tool in translational research aimed at modelling and developing treatments for PTSD symptoms. Indeed, the results of experiment 2B add to evidence that the blockade of mTOR with rapamycin may be a useful pharmacological treatment, given rapamycin lead to an attenuation of contextual fear memory and some anxiety-like behaviour. Finally, inconsistent results with respect to hyperarousal symptoms mean that future research will help to fully tease apart the complex contribution of mTOR to fear memory formation and modulation and clarify the best uses of rapamycin as a PTSD treatment.

Note

1 Note these neuroscientific definitions of long- and short-term memory differ from how the terms are used in cognitive psychology; cf. Atkinson & Schiffrin, 1968.

References

Acheson, D. T., Geyer, M. A., & Risbrough, V. B. (2014). Psychophysiology in the study of psychological trauma: Where are we and where do we need to be? In V. Kumari, P. Bob, & N. N. Boutros (eds), *Electrophysiology and Psychophysiology in Psychiatry and Psychopharmacology* (pp. 157–183). Berlin: Springer.

Adamec, R. E. (1997). Transmitter systems involved in neural plasticity underlying increased anxiety and defense – Implications for understanding anxiety following traumatic stress. *Neuroscience & Biobehavioral Reviews*, *21*(6), 755–765.

Adamec, R. E. (1998). Evidence that N-methyl-D-aspartate-dependent limbic neural plasticity in the right hemisphere mediates pharmacological stressor (FG-7142)-induced lasting increases in anxiety-like behavior: Study 3 – The effects on amygdala efferent physiology of block of N-methyl-D-aspartate receptors prior to injection of FG-7142 and its relationship to behavioral change. *Journal of Psychopharmacology*, *12*(3), 227–238.

Predator Stress and Rapamycin   393

Adamec, R. E. (2001). Does long term potentiation in periacqueductal gray (PAG) mediate lasting changes in rodent anxiety-like behavior (ALB) produced by predator stress? – Effects of low frequency stimulation (LFS) of PAG on place preference and changes in ALB produced by predator stress. *Behavioural Brain Research*, *120*(2), 111–135.

Adamec, R., Bartoszyk, G. D., & Burton, P. (2004). Effects of systemic injections of vilazodone, a selective serotonin reuptake inhibitor and serotonin 1A receptor agonist, on anxiety induced by predator stress in rats. *European Journal of Pharmacology*, *504*(1), 65–77.

Adamec, R. E., Blundell, J., & Burton, P. (2005). Neural circuit changes mediating lasting brain and behavioral response to predator stress. *Neuroscience & Biobehavioral Reviews*, *29*(8), 1225–1241.

Adamec, R. E., Blundell, J., & Collins, A. (2001). Neural plasticity and stress induced changes in defense in the rat. *Neuroscience and Biobehavioral Reviews*, *25*(7–8), 721–744.

Adamec, R., Hebert, M., & Blundell, J. (2011). Long lasting effects of predator stress on pCREB expression in brain regions involved in fearful and anxious behavior. Behavioral Brain Research, *221*(1), 118–133.

Adamec, R. E., Burton, P., Shallow, T., & Budgell, J. (1999). N-methyl-D-aspartate receptors mediate lasting increases in anxiety-like behavior produced by the stress of predator exposure – Implications for anxiety associated with posttraumatic stress disorder. *Physiology & Behavior*, *65*(4), 723–737.

Adamec, R., Head, D., Soreq, H., & Blundell, J. (2008). The role of the read-through variant of acetylcholinesterase in anxiogenic effects of predator stress in mice. *Behavioural Brain Research*, *189*(1), 180–190.

Adamec, R., Kent, P., Anisman, H., Shallow, T., & Merali, Z. (1998). Neural plasticity, neuropeptides, and anxiety in animals – Implications for understanding and treating affective disorder following traumatic stress in humans. *Neuroscience & Biobehavioral Reviews*, *23*(2), 301–318.

Adamec, R. E., & Shallow, T. (1993). Lasting effects on rodent anxiety of a single exposure to a cat. *Physiology & Behavior*, *54*(1), 101–109.

Adamec, R. E., Shallow, T., & Budgell, J. (1997). Blockade of CCK-B but not CCK-A receptors before and after the stress of predator exposure prevents lasting increases in anxiety-like behavior: Implications for anxiety associated with posttraumatic stress disorder. *Behavioral Neuroscience*, *111*(2), 435–449.

Adamec, R., Strasser, K., Blundell, J., Burton, P., & McKay, D. W. (2006). Protein synthesis and the mechanisms of lasting change in anxiety induced by severe stress. *Behavioural Brain Research*, *167*(2), 270–286.

Adamec, R., Toth, M., Haller, J., Halasz, J., & Blundell, J. (2012). A comparison of activation patterns of cells in selected prefrontal cortical and amygdala areas of rats which are more or less anxious in response to predator exposure or submersion stress. *Physiology & Behavior*, *105*(3), 628–638.

Adamec, R., Walling, S., & Burton, P. (2004). Long-lasting, selective, anxiogenic effects of feline predator stress in mice. *Physiology & Behavior*, *83*(3), 401–410.

Alberini, C. M. (2009). Transcription factors in long-term memory and synaptic plasticity. *Physiological Reviews*, *89*(1), 121–145.

Alberini, C. M., & LeDoux, J. E. (2013). Memory reconsolidation. *Current Biology*, *23*(17), R746–R750.

Amaral, V. C. S., Santos-Gomes, K., & Nunes-de-Souza, R. L. (2010). Increased corticosterone levels in mice subjected to the rat exposure test. *Hormones and Behavior*, *57*(2), 128–133.

Amorapanth, P., Nader, K., & LeDoux, J. E. (1999). Lesions of periaqueductal gray dissociate-conditioned freezing from conditioned suppression behavior in rats. *Learning & Memory*, *6*(5), 491–499.

Andersen, P., Morris, R., Amaral, D. G., Bliss, T., & O'Keefe, J. (eds). (2006). *The hippocampus book*. Oxford: Oxford University Press.

Amaral, D., & Lavenex, P. (2006). Hippocampal neuroanatomy. In P. Andersen, R. Morris, D. Amaral, T. Bliss, & J. O'Keefe (eds), *The hippocampus book* (pp. 37–115). Oxford University Press.

Atkinson, R. C., & Shiffrin, R. M. (1968). Human memory: A proposed system and its control processes. *Psychology of Learning and Motivation*, *2*, 89–195.

Bailey, M. R., & Balsam, P. D. (2013). Memory reconsolidation: Time to change your mind. *Current Biology*, *23*(6), R243–R245.

Bandler, R., Carrive, P., & Depaulis, A. (1991). Emerging principles of organization of the midbrain periaqueductal gray matter. In A. Depaulis, & R. Bandler (eds), *The midbrain periaqueductal gray matter: Functional, anatomical, and neurochemical organization* (pp. 1–8). Boston, MA: Springer.

Bekinschtein, P., Katche, C., Slipczuk, L. N., Igaz, L. M., Cammarota, M., Izquierdo, I., & Medina, J. H. (2007). mTOR signaling in the hippocampus is necessary for memory formation. *Neurobiology of Learning and Memory*, *87*(2), 303–307.

Blair, H. T., Schafe, G. E., Bauer, E. P., Rodrigues, S. M., & LeDoux, J. E. (2001). Synaptic plasticity in the lateral amygdala: A cellular hypothesis of fear conditioning. *Learning & Memory*, *8*(5), 229–242.

Blanchard, D. C., & Blanchard, R. J. (1988). Ethoexperimental approaches to the biology of emotion. *Annual Review of Psychology*, *39*(1), 43–68.

Bliss, T. V., & Lømo, T. (1973). Long-lasting potentiation of synaptic transmission in the dentate area of the anaesthetized rabbit following stimulation of the perforant path. *The Journal of Physiology*, *232*(2), 331–356.

Bliss, T. V., & Collingridge, G. L. (1993). A synaptic model of memory: Long-term potentiation in the hippocampus. *Nature*, *361*(6407), 31.

Blundell, J., & Adamec, R. (2006). Elevated pCREB in the PAG after exposure to the elevated plus maze in rats previously exposed to a cat. *Behavioural Brain Research*, *175*(2), 285–295.

Blundell, J., Adamec, R., & Burton, P. (2005). Role of NMDA receptors in the syndrome of behavioral changes produced by predator stress. *Physiology & Behavior*, *86*(1–2), 233–243.

Blundell, J., Kouser, M., & Powell, C. M. (2008). Systemic inhibition of mammalian target of rapamycin inhibits fear memory reconsolidation. *Neurobiology of Learning and Memory*, *90*(1), 28–35.

Bockaert, J., & Marin, P. (2015). mTOR in brain physiology and pathologies. *Physiological Reviews*, *95*(4), 1157–1187.

Bolles, R. C. (1975). *Theory of motivation* (2nd edn). New York: HarperCollins Publishers.

Borelli, K. G., Albrechet-Souza, L., Fedoce, A. G., Fabri, D. S., Resstel, L. B., & Brandao, M. L. (2013). Conditioned fear is modulated by CRF mechanisms in the periaqueductal gray columns. *Hormones and Behavior*, *63*(5), 791–799.

Bouton, M. E. (2007). *Learning and behavior: A contemporary synthesis*. Sunderland: Sinauer Associates.

Bryant, R. A., Felmingham, K. L., Kemp, A. H., Barton, M., Peduto, A. S., Rennie, C., ... & Williams, L. M. (2005). Neural networks of information processing in posttraumatic stress disorder: A functional magnetic resonance imaging study. *Biological Psychiatry*, *58*(2), 111–118.

Byrne, J.H. (2012). Learning and memory: Basic mechanisms. In L. R. Squire, D. Berg, F. E. Bloom, S. du Lac, A. Ghosh, & N. C. Spitzer (eds), *Fundamental neuroscience* (4th edn) (pp. 1009–1028). Amsterdam: Academic Press.

Campos, K. F. C., Amaral, V. C. S., Rico, J. L., Miguel, T. T., & Nunes-de-Souza, R. L. (2013). Ethopharmacological evaluation of the rat exposure test: A prey–predator interaction test. *Behavioural Brain Research*, *240*, 160–170.

Canteras, N. S., & Goto, M. (1999). Fos-like immunoreactivity in the periaqueductal gray of rats exposed to a natural predator. *Neuroreport*, *10*(2), 413–418.

Carew, T. J. & Kandel, E. R. (1973). Acquisition and retention of long-term habituation in *Aplysia*: Correlation of behavioral and cellular processes. *Science*, *182*(4117), 1158–1160.

Cohen, H., Matar, M. A., Richter-Levin, G. A. L., & Zohar, J. (2006). The contribution of an animal model toward uncovering biological risk factors for PTSD. *Annals of the New York Academy of Sciences*, *1071*(1), 335–350.

Cosmides, L. & Tooby, J. (2000). Evolutionary psychology and the emotions. In M. Lewis & J. M. Haviland-Jones (eds), *Handbook of emotions* (2nd edn) (pp. 91–115). New York: Guilford Press.

Davis, M. (1970). Effects of interstimulus interval length and variability on startle-response habituation in the rat. *Journal of Comparative and Physiological Psychology*, *72*(2), 177.

Davis, M. (1972). Differential retention of sensitization and habituation of the startle response in the rat. *Journal of Comparative and Physiological Psychology*, *78*(2), 260–267.

Davis, M., Antoniadis, E. A., Amaral, D. G., & Winslow, J. T. (2008). Acoustic startle reflex in rhesus monkeys: A review. *Reviews in the Neurosciences*, *19*, 171–185.

Davis, H. P., & Squire, L. R. (1984). Protein synthesis and memory: A review. *Psychological Bulletin*, *96*(3), 518.

de Almeida, L. P., Ramos, P. L., Pandossio, J. E., Landeira-Fernandez, J., Zangrossi, H., & Nogueira, R. L. (2006). Prior electrical stimulation of dorsal periaqueductal grey matter or deep layers of the superior colliculus sensitizes rats to anxiety-like behaviors in the elevated T-maze test. *Behavioural Brain Research*, *170*(2), 175–181.

Deslauriers, J., Toth, M., Der-Avakian, A., and Risbrough, V. B. (2017). Current status of animal models of PTSD: Behavioral and biological phenotypes, and future challenges in improving translation. *Biological Psychiatry*, *83*(10), 895.

Di Scala, G., Mana, M. J., Jacobs, W. J., & Phillips, A. G. (1987). Evidence of Pavlovian conditioned fear following electrical stimulation of the periaqueductal grey in the rat. *Physiology & Behavior*, *40*(1), 55–63.

Dudai, Y. (1996). Consolidation: Fragility on the road to the engram. *Neuron*, *17*(3), 367–370.

Dudai, Y. (2004). The neurobiology of consolidations, or, how stable is the engram? *Annual Review of Psychology*, *55*, 51–86.

Dudek, S. M., & Bear, M. F. (1992). Homosynaptic long-term depression in area CA1 of hippocampus and effects of N-methyl-D-aspartate receptor blockade. *Proceedings of the National Academy of Sciences*, *89*(10), 4363–4367.

Etkin, A., & Wager, T. D. (2007). Functional neuroimaging of anxiety: A meta-analysis of emotional processing in PTSD, social anxiety disorder, and specific phobia. *American Journal of Psychiatry*, *164*(10), 1476–1488.

Fanselow, M. S. (1991). The midbrain periaqueductal gray as a coordinator of action in response to fear and anxiety. In A. Depaulis & R. Bandler (eds), *The midbrain periaqueductal gray matter: Functional, anatomical, and neurochemical organization* (pp. 151–173). Boston, MA: Springer.

Fifield, K., Hebert, M., Angel, R., Adamec, R., & Blundell, J. (2013). Inhibition of mTOR kinase via rapamycin blocks persistent predator stress-induced hyperarousal. *Behavioural Brain Research*, 256, 457–463.

Fifield, K., Hebert, M., Williams, K., Linehan, V., Whiteman, J. D., Mac Callum, P., & Blundell, J. (2015). Time-dependent effects of rapamycin on consolidation of predator stress-induced hyperarousal. *Behavioural Brain Research*, 286, 104–111.

Foster, J. A., & Burman, M. A. (2010). Evidence for hippocampus-dependent contextual learning at postnatal day 17 in the rat. *Learning & Memory*, *17*(5), 259–266.

Frankland, P. W., & Josselyn, S. A. (2016). Neuroscience: In search of the memory molecule. *Nature*, *535*(7610), 41.

Furuya-da-Cunha, E. M., Souza, R. R., & Canto-de-Souza, A. (2016). Rat exposure in mice with neuropathic pain induces fear and antinociception that is not reversed by 5-HT2C receptor activation in the dorsal periaqueductal gray. *Behavioural Brain Research*, 307, 250–257.

Gafford, G. M., Parsons, R. G., & Helmstetter, F. J. (2011). Consolidation and reconsolidation of contextual fear memory requires mammalian target of rapamycin-dependent translation in the dorsal hippocampus. *Neuroscience*, *182*, 98–104.

Gallistel, C. R. (2003). Conditioning from an information processing perspective. *Behavioural Processes*, *62*(1), 89–101.

Glover, E. M., Ressler, K. J., & Davis, M. (2010). Differing effects of systemically administered rapamycin on consolidation and reconsolidation of context vs. cued fear memories. *Learning & Memory*, 17(11), 577–581.

Goldstein, R. B., Smith, S. M., Chou, S. P., Saha, T. D., Jung, J., Zhang, H., ... & Grant, B. F. (2016). The epidemiology of DSM-5 posttraumatic stress disorder in the United States: Results from the National Epidemiologic Survey on Alcohol and Related Conditions-III. *Social Psychiatry and Psychiatric Epidemiology*, *51*(8), 1137–1148.

Goshen, I., Brodsky, M., Prakash, R., Wallace, J., Gradinaru, V., Ramakrishnan, C., & Deisseroth, K. (2011). Dynamics of retrieval strategies for remote memories. *Cell*, *147*(3), 678–689.

Goswami, S., Rodríguez-Sierra, O., Cascardi, M., & Paré, D. (2013). Animal models of post-traumatic stress disorder: Face validity. *Frontiers in Neuroscience*, 7, 89.

Graber, T. E., McCamphill, P. K., & Sossin, W. S. (2013). A recollection of mTOR signaling in learning and memory. *Learning & Memory*, *20*(10), 518–530.

Haissaguerre, M., Saucisse, N., & Cota, D. (2014). Influence of mTOR in energy and metabolic homeostasis. *Molecular and Cellular Endocrinology*, *397*(1), 67–77.

Hauger, R. L., Olivares-Reyes, J. A., Dautzenberg, F. M., Lohr, J. B., Braun, S., & Oakley, R. H. (2012). Molecular and cell signaling targets for PTSD pathophysiology and pharmacotherapy. *Neuropharmacology*, *62*(2), 705–714.

Hay, N., & Sonenberg, N. (2004). Upstream and downstream of mTOR. *Genes & Development*, *18*(16), 1926–1945.

Hebb, D. O. (1949/1965). *The organization of behavior: A neuropsychological theory*. New York: Wiley.

Helmstetter, F. J., Parsons, R. G., & Gafford, G. M. (2008). Macromolecular synthesis, distributed synaptic plasticity, and fear conditioning. *Neurobiology of Learning and Memory*, *89*(3), 324–337.

Hernandez-Rabaza, V., Hontecillas-Prieto, L., Velázquez-Sánchez, C., Ferragud, A., Perez-Villaba, A., Arcusa, A., ... & Canales, J. J. (2008). The hippocampal dentate gyrus is essential for generating contextual memories of fear and drug-induced reward. *Neurobiology of Learning and Memory*, *90*(3), 553–559.

Hoeffer, C. A., & Klann, E. (2010). mTOR signaling: At the crossroads of plasticity, memory and disease. *Trends in Neurosciences*, *33*(2), 67–75.

Hoffman, A. N., Lorson, N. G., Sanabria, F., Olive, M. F., & Conrad, C. D. (2014). Chronic stress disrupts fear extinction and enhances amygdala and hippocampal Fos expression in an animal model of post-traumatic stress disorder. *Neurobiology of Learning and Memory*, *112*, 139–147.

Huang, W., Zhu, P. J., Zhang, S., Zhou, H., Stoica, L., Galiano, M., Krnjević, K., Roman, G., & Costa-Mattioli, M. (2013). mTORC2 controls actin polymerization required for consolidation of long-term memory. *Nature Neuroscience*, *16*(4), 441–448.

Jobim, P. F., Pedroso, T. R., Christoff, R. R., Werenicz, A., Maurmann, N., Reolon, G. K., & Roesler, R. (2012). Inhibition of mTOR by rapamycin in the amygdala or hippocampus impairs formation and reconsolidation of inhibitory avoidance memory. *Neurobiology of Learning and Memory*, *97*(1), 105–112.

Jürgens, U. (1991). Neurochemical study of PAG control of vocal behavior. In A. Depaulis & R. Bandler (eds), *The midbrain periaqueductal gray matter: Functional, anatomical, and neurochemical organization* (pp. 11–21). Boston, MA: Springer.

Kandel, E. R., Dudai, Y., & Mayford, M. R. (2014). The molecular and systems biology of memory. *Cell*, *157*(1), 163–186.

Kandel, E. R. (2001). The molecular biology of memory storage: A dialogue between genes and synapses. *Science*, *294*(5544), 1030–1038.

Kessler, R. C., & Wang, P. S. (2008). The descriptive epidemiology of commonly occurring mental disorders in the United States. *Annual Review of Public Health*, *29*, 115–129.

Kheirbek, M. A., Drew, L. J., Burghardt, N. S., Costantini, D. O., Tannenholz, L., Ahmari, S. E., ... & Hen, R. (2013). Differential control of learning and anxiety along the dorsoventral axis of the dentate gyrus. *Neuron*, *77*(5), 955–968.

Kim, J. J., & Fanselow, M. S. (1992). Modality-specific retrograde amnesia of fear. *Science*, *256*(5057), 675.

Kim, E. J., Horovitz, O., Pellman, B. A., Tan, L. M., Li, Q., Richter-Levin, G., & Kim, J. J. (2013). Dorsal periaqueductal gray-amygdala pathway conveys both innate and learned fear responses in rats. *Proceedings of the National Academy of Sciences*, *110*(36), 14795–14800.

Klann, E., & Sweatt, J. D. (2008). Altered protein synthesis is a trigger for long-term memory formation. *Neurobiology of Learning and Memory*, *89*(3), 247–259.

Kozlovsky, N., Kaplan, Z., Zohar, J., Matar, M. A., Shimon, H., & Cohen, H. (2008). Protein synthesis inhibition before or after stress exposure results in divergent endocrine and BDNF responses disassociated from behavioral responses. *Depression and Anxiety*, *25*(5), 24–34.

398 *Phillip MacCallum et al.*

Lau, H. L., Timbers, T. A., Mahmoud, R., & Rankin, C. H. (2013). Genetic dissection of memory for associative and non-associative learning in Caenorhabditis elegans. *Genes, Brain and Behavior, 12*(2), 210–223.

Lau, C., Whiteman, J. D., & Blundell, J. J. (2015). Endogenous glucocorticoids in traumatic memory extinction: Implications for PTSD. In C. R. Martin, V. R. Preedy, & V. B. Patel (eds), *The comprehensive guide to PTSD* (pp. 943–960). Cham: Springer International.

Leaton, R. N., & Supple, W. F. (1986). Cerebellar vermis: Essential for long-term habituation of the acoustic startle response. *Science, 232*(4749), 513–515.

LeDoux, J. E. (1995). Emotion: Clues from the brain. *Annual Review of Psychology, 46*(1), 209–235.

LeDoux, J. (2003). The emotional brain, fear, and the amygdala. *Cellular and Molecular Neurobiology, 23*(4–5), 727–738.

LeDoux, J. (2012). Rethinking the emotional brain. *Neuron, 73*(4), 653–676.

Li, J., Kim, S. G., & Blenis, J. (2014). Rapamycin: One drug, many effects. *Cell Metabolism, 19*(3), 373–379.

Lissek, S., & van Meurs, B. (2015). Learning models of PTSD: Theoretical accounts and psychobiological evidence. *International Journal of Psychophysiology, 98*(3), 594–605.

Levin, N., Kritman, M., Maroun, M., & Akirav, I. (2017). Differential roles of the infralimbic and prelimbic areas of the prefrontal cortex in reconsolidation of a traumatic memory. *European Neuropsychopharmacology: The Journal of the European College of Neuropsychopharmacology, 27*(9), 900–912.

Mac Callum, P. E., Hebert, M., Adamec, R. E., & Blundell, J. (2014). Systemic inhibition of mTOR kinase via rapamycin disrupts consolidation and reconsolidation of auditory fear memory. *Neurobiology of Learning and Memory, 112*, 176–185.

Mahan, A. L., & Ressler, K. J. (2012). Fear conditioning, synaptic plasticity and the amygdala: implications for posttraumatic stress disorder. *Trends in Neurosciences, 35*(1), 24–35.

Malenka, R. C., & Bear, M. F. (2004). LTP and LTD: An embarrassment of riches. *Neuron, 44*(1), 5–21.

Maren, S. (2001). Neurobiology of Pavlovian fear conditioning. *Annual Review of Neuroscience, 24*(1), 897–931.

Mayford, M., Siegelbaum, S. A., & Kandel, E. R. (2012). Synapses and memory storage. *Cold Spring Harbor Perspectives in Biology, 4*(6), a005751.

McGaugh, J. L. (1966). Time-dependent processes in memory storage. *Science, 153*(3742), 1351–1358.

McGaugh, J. L. (2000). Memory – A century of consolidation. *Science, 287*(5451), 248–251.

McGaugh, J. L., & Herz, M.J. (1972). *Memory consolidation.* San Francisco, CA: Albion.

McGaugh, J. L., & Izquierdo, I. (2000). The contribution of pharmacology to research on the mechanisms of memory formation. *Trends in Pharmacological Sciences, 21*(6), 208–210.

Monfils, M. H., Cowansage, K. K., & LeDoux, J. E. (2007). Brain-derived neurotrophic factor: Linking fear learning to memory consolidation. *Molecular Pharmacology, 72*(2), 235–237.

Müller G. E. & Pilzecker, A. (1900). Experimentelle Beiträge zur Lehre vom Gedächtnis. *Zeitschrift für Psychologie. Ergänzungsband, 1*, 1–300.

Predator Stress and Rapamycin 399

Morgan, M. A., Romanski, L. M., & LeDoux, J. E. (1993). Extinction of emotional learning: Contribution of medial prefrontal cortex. *Neuroscience Letters*, *163*(1), 109–113.

Murray, K. E., Keifer, O. P., Ressler, K. J., Norrholm, S. D., & Jovanovic, T. (2014). Neurobiology and treatment of PTSD. In D. S. Charney, P. Sklar, J. D. Buxbaum, & E. J. Nestler (eds), *Neurobiology of mental illness* (4th edn) (pp. 662–672). New York: Oxford University Press.

Nader, K. (2003) Memory traces unbound. *Trends in Neurosciences*, *26*, 65–72.

Nader, K., & Hardt, O. (2009). A single standard for memory: The case for reconsolidation. *Nature Reviews Neuroscience*, *10*(3), 224–234.

Nicoll, R. A., & Roche, K. W. (2013). Long-term potentiation: Peeling the onion. *Neuropharmacology*, *74*, 18–22.

Öhman, A., & Mineka, S. (2001). Fears, phobias, and preparedness: Toward an evolved module of fear and fear learning. *Psychological Review*, *108*(3), 483.

Orr, S. P., Metzger, L. J., & Pitman, R. K. (2002). Psychophysiology of posttraumatic stress disorder. *The Psychiatric Clinics of North America*, *25*(2), 271–293.

Panja, D., & Bramham, C. R. (2014). BDNF mechanisms in late LTP formation: A synthesis and breakdown. *Neuropharmacology*, *76*, 664–676.

Panksepp, J. (1998). *Affective neuroscience*. Oxford: Oxford University Press.

Parsons, R. G., Gafford, G. M., & Helmstetter, F. J. (2006). Translational control via the mammalian target of rapamycin pathway is critical for the formation and stability of long-term fear memory in amygdala neurons. *Journal of Neuroscience*, *26*, 12977–12983.

Pearce, J. M., & Bouton, M. E. (2001). Theories of associative learning in animals. *Annual Review of Psychology*, *52*(1), 111–139.

Phillips, R. G., & LeDoux, J. E. (1992). Differential contribution of amygdala and hippocampus to cued and contextual fear conditioning. *Behavioral Neuroscience*, *106*(2), 274.

Pilz, P. K., & Schnitzler, H. U. (1996). Habituation and sensitization of the acoustic startle response in rats: Amplitude, threshold, and latency measures. *Neurobiology of Learning and Memory*, *66*(1), 67–79.

Pitman, R. K. (1997). Overview of biological themes in PTSD. *Annals of the New York Academy of Sciences*, *821*, 1–9.

Pitman, R. K., Orr, S. P., & Shalev, A. Y. (1993). Once bitten, twice shy: Beyond the conditioning model of PTSD. *Biological Psychiatry*, *33*(3), 145–146.

Pole, N. (2007). The psychophysiology of posttraumatic stress disorder: A meta-analysis. *Psychological Bulletin*, *133*(5), 725.

Rasmusson, A. M., Vythilingam, M., & Morgan, C. A. (2003). The neuroendocrinology of posttraumatic stress disorder: New directions. *CNS Spectrums*, *8*(9), 651–667.

Reul, J. M. H. M., & Nutt, D. J. (2008). Glutamate and cortisol – A critical confluence in PTSD? *Journal of Psychopharmacology*, *22*(5), 469–472.

Rescorla, R.A. (1988). Pavlovian conditioning: It's not what you think it is. *American Psychologist*, *43*(3), 151–160.

Rogan, M. T., Stäubli, U. V., & LeDoux, J. E. (1997). Fear conditioning induces associative long-term potentiation in the amygdala. *Nature*, *390*(6660), 604–607.

Rudy, J.W. (2014). *Neurobiology of learning and memory* (2nd edn). Sunderland: Sinauer Associates.

400 *Phillip MacCallum et al.*

Sarbassov, D. D., Ali, S. M., Sengupta, S., Sheen, J. H., Hsu, P. P., Bagley, A. F., Markhard, A. L., & Sabatini, D. M. (2006). Prolonged rapamycin treatment inhibits mTORC2 assembly and Akt/PKB. *Molecular Cell, 22*(2), 159–168.

Saxe, M. D., Battaglia, F., Wang, J. W., Malleret, G., David, D. J., Monckton, J. E., … & Hen, R. (2006). Ablation of hippocampal neurogenesis impairs contextual fear conditioning and synaptic plasticity in the dentate gyrus. *Proceedings of the National Academy of Sciences, 103*(46), 17501–17506.

Skolnick, P. & Paul, S.M. (1983). New concepts in the neurobiology of anxiety. *Journal of Clinical Psychiatry, 44*, 12–19.

Smock, T.K. (1999). *Physiological psychology: A neuroscience approach.* Upper Saddle River, NJ: Prentice Hall.

Squire, L.R. (1987). *Memory and brain.* Oxford: Oxford University Press.

Squire, L. R., & Bayley, P. J. (2007). The neuroscience of remote memory. *Current Opinion in Neurobiology, 17*(2), 185–196.

Squire, L.R. & Kandel, E.R. (2008). *Memory: From mind to molecules* (2nd edn). London: Macmillan.

Steckler, T., & Risbrough, V. (2012). Pharmacological treatment of PTSD–established and new approaches. *Neuropharmacology, 62*(2), 617–627.

Sweatt, D.J. (2010). *Mechanisms of memory* (2nd edn). Amsterdam: Academic Press.

Timberlake, W. (1994). Behaviour systems, associationism, and Pavlovian conditioning. *Psychonomic Bulletin & Review, 1*(4), 405–420.

Tishmeyer, W., Schicknick, H., Kraus, M., Seidenbecher, C. I., Staak, S., Scheich, H., & Gundelfinger, E. D. (2003). Rapamycin-sensitive signaling in long-term consolidation of auditory cortex-dependent memory. *European Journal of Neuroscience, 18*, 942–950.

Tulving, E. (2000). Memory: Introduction. In M. S. Gazzaniga (ed.), *The new cognitive neurosciences* (pp. 727–732). Cambridge, MA: MIT Press.

Van Ameringen, M., Mancini, C., Patterson, B., & Boyle, M. H. (2008). Post-traumatic stress disorder in Canada. *CNS Neuroscience & Therapeutics, 14*(3), 171–181.

Wessa, M., & Flor, H. (2007). Failure of extinction of fear responses in post-traumatic stress disorder: Evidence from second-order conditioning. *The American Journal of Psychiatry, 164*(11), 1684–1692.

Yang, H., Rudge, D. G., Koos, J. D., Vaidialingam, B., Yang, H. J., & Pavletich, N. P. (2013). mTOR kinase structure, mechanism and regulation by the rapamycin-binding domain. *Nature, 497*(7448), 217–223.

Yang, M., Augustsson, H., Markham, C. M., Hubbard, D. T., Webster, D., Wall, P. M., … & Blanchard, D. C. (2004). The rat exposure test: A model of mouse defensive behaviors. *Physiology & Behavior, 81*(3), 465–473.

Yehuda, R. (2009). Status of glucocorticoid alterations in post-traumatic stress disorder. *Annals of the New York Academy of Sciences, 1179*(1), 56–69.

Appendix 14

Methods

Drug Administration

For experiment 2B, mice received an intraperitoneal (*i.p.*) injection of rapamycin (40 mg/kg dose, injection volumes of 10 ml/kg, volume dependent on mouse weight) or vehicle (5% ethanol, 4% PEG400, and 4% Tween 80 in sterile water, volume dependent on mouse weight).

Behavioural Testing

Elevated Plus MazeThe elevated plus maze consisted of four arms arranged in the shape of a plus sign, with two opposite arms uncovered and two covered. For the rat-sized apparatus, each arm was 10 cm wide, 50 cm long and elevated 50 cm above the ground. The four arms were joined at the centre by a 10-cm square platform. Two of the arms opposite each other had no sides while the other two arms had walls 40 cm high and were open at the top. For the mouse-sized elevated plus maze, each arm was 5.1 cm wide, 29.2 cm long and the maze was elevated 45.7 cm above the ground. The four arms were joined at the centre by a 6.4-cm square platform. The animal was placed in the centre of the elevated plus maze and behaviour was recorded for five minutes. Rodents were then returned to their home cages. Behavioural measures included time spent in the open arms, time spent in the closed arms, frequency in the open, frequency in the closed arms, and *ratio* measurements of these variables. Ratio time is defined as time in open arms/(time in open)+(time in closed). Ratio frequency follows the same formula.

Open Field

The open field is a square Plexiglas box (rat-sized apparatus:60 cm long x 60 cm wide x 35 cm high; mouse-sized apparatus: 48 cm x 48 cm x 48 cm) painted with grey enamel. Rodents were placed in the centre of the floor at the beginning of each trial. The rodents were then videotaped for five-minute trials. Behaviours measured included time in the centre of the box and number of rears. Rears were defined as any instance where the mouse or rat raised itself up on its hind legs, with its forepaws leaving the ground (with the exception of obvious grooming behaviour). Rodents were considered in the centre when the full body was within the centre area defined by white masking tape, and near the wall when all four feet were between the masking tape and the wall.

402   Phillip MacCallum et al.

Light/Dark Box

The light/dark box was a single alley apparatus constructed of Plexiglas, divided into two chambers of equal size. For the rat light–dark box, each chamber was 31.75 cm long, 10.48 cm wide and 14.6 cm high. Both chambers were covered by a transparent Plexiglas top, hinged so it could not be opened. Both tops had centre pieces cut out to provide ventilation. One chamber had a solid wooden floor and was painted white. The other chamber had a metal mesh floor and its walls were painted black. The chamber painted black had its Plexiglas top rendered opaque with a black plastic covering. In addition, a 100-Watt LED light was positioned 66 cm above the white chamber. Testing took place in a darkened room illuminated only by the lamp over the white chamber. This produced a light intensity at the centre of the floor of the white chamber of 55 foot candles (fc), and an intensity of two fc at the centre of the floor of the dark chamber.

The mouse light dark box was a 50 cm long, 15 cm high structure with two square-shaped boxes (20 x 20 cm) connected by a short (10cm) tunnel. The dark side was covered by a removable lid, while the light side had a hinged Plexiglas lid with air holes to provide proper ventilation. Illumination and light intensity were the same as for the rat apparatus. Behaviour in the testing apparatus was videotaped for later analysis with a video camera mounted directly over the apparatus. Rodents were placed in the light chamber at the start of the test and their activity was videotaped for five minutes. Rodents were then returned to their home cages. Behavioural measures included time spent in each chamber, number of entries into each chamber (defined as having all four paws in the chamber) and number of faecal boli in each chamber.

Acoustic Startle Testing

Startle testing took place in a San Diego Instruments standard startle chamber. During testing, rodents were placed in the chamber in a cylindrical small animal enclosure. The animal enclosure sat atop a piezo-electric transducer that produced an electrical signal sampled by a computer, providing a measure of rodent movement. Startle testing was done in a dark chamber. This involved acclimating rodents to the startle apparatus with a background of 60dB white noise for 5 minutes. Then the rodents were exposed to 30 pulses of 50 msec bursts of white noise of 120dB amplitude rising out of a background of 60dB of white noise with a 30 second inter-trial interval. Startle response was measured over a 250 msec recording window.

15 Severing the Trauma—PTSD Connection with Public Safety Personnel

The Role of Personal Social Support Networks

Grace B. Ewles, Peter A. Hausdorf,
Terry A. Beehr, and
M. Gloria González-Morales[1]

Public safety personnel, including but not limited to border services officers, correctional workers, firefighters, paramedics, police officers, public safety communication officials (i.e., dispatchers, 911 operators), and search and rescue personnel (Canadian Institute for Public Safety Research and Treatment [CIPSRT], 2019), experience a variety of potentially psychologically traumatic events at work that can have a debilitating effect on individual functioning and mental health (Alexander & Klein, 2009; Benedek, Fullerton, & Ursano, 2007). Over time, exposure to traumatic events can impact physical and psychological well-being, including various traumatic event-related disorders (e.g., posttraumatic stress disorder [PTSD]; McFarlane & Bryant, 2007). Worldwide, PTSD can develop in roughly 10% of public safety personnel following exposure to a traumatic event (Berger et al., 2012). In a recent survey of over 5,000 Canadian public safety personnel, 44.5% of the sample ($n = 1,998$) screened positively for one or more mental health disorders, including major depressive disorder, panic disorder, and alcohol use disorder (Carleton et al., 2018). Additionally, 23.2% ($n = 1,304$) of the sample screened positively for PTSD (Carleton et al., 2018). Compared to the lifetime estimate of PTSD from the general population in Canada (9.2%; see Wilson, Guliani, & Boichev, 2016 for a review), the prevalence rates of mental disorders in public safety personnel suggest their increased risk for developing mental disorders. The increased risk is likely due to single or cumulative exposure to occupational stressors (e.g., traumatic events).

Historically, a diagnosis of PTSD required a single, identifiable exposure to a traumatic event (American Psychiatric Association [APA], 2000). However, the most recent version of the Diagnostic and Statistical Manual of Mental Disorders (i.e., DSM-5) has eliminated the single event requirement and includes multiple exposures to traumatic events as meeting the diagnostic criterion (APA, 2013). The change benefits people

DOI: 10.4324/9781351134637-16

404 *Ewles, Hausdorf, Beehr, and González-Morales*

who experience an accumulation of traumatic events exposure, such as public safety personnel, as well as people who experience routine occupational stress (e.g., Kaufmann & Beehr, 1989; Liberman et al., 2002). Researchers link multiple exposures to traumatic events with negative long-term outcomes for individuals, including increased morbidity and functional impairments (Karam et al., 2014). Results from the World Health Organization's *World Mental Health Survey*, which surveyed 51,295 adults from the general population across 20 countries,[2] indicated that, of the participants who met the criteria for PTSD within the previous 12 months (1.1% of total sample), those exposed to multiple traumatic events experienced greater functional impairments at home and at work. In addition, they experienced symptoms for a longer duration and had higher rates of comorbidity with other psychological disorders, including anxiety and mood disorders (Karam et al., 2014).

The accumulation of traumatic events is particularly salient in public safety personnel occupations, where exposure occurs on a regular basis. In particular, due to the specific nature of their work, firefighters, paramedics, and police officers experience increased risk for traumatic events exposure compared to many other occupations (e.g., forensic personnel, therapists, and flight attendants; Skogstad et al., 2013). Despite the similarity of the type of traumatic events experienced by public safety personnel, there is wide variability with respect to the psychological impact of these events on individuals. For example, in a recent survey of Ontario police officers ($n = 256$) exposed to traumatic events, participants reported moderate levels of psychological impairment on average and a wide range of functional impairments (Ewles & Hausdorf, 2016). The wide range of impairments found are consistent with previous results wherein many individuals experience negative symptoms following exposure to a traumatic events, but most do not meet the diagnostic criteria for PTSD (Benedek et al., 2007; Creamer, Burgess, & McFarlane, 2001; Liberman et al., 2002). In the absence of clinically diagnosed PTSD, researchers have suggested that many public safety personnel experience a range of sub-clinical functional impairments and symptoms of PTSD, stemming from job- and traumatic event-related stress (e.g., Carleton et al., 2019; Donnelly, 2012; Gershon et al., 2009; Sommer et al., 2020).

The variability in reactions and responses to traumatic events exposure appears related to aspects of the traumatic event (e.g., Carleton et al., 2019; Ricciardelli, Carleton, Cramm, & Groll, 2018; Ricciardelli et al., 2020), individual characteristics (e.g., personality, resiliency; Skogstad et al., 2013), and individual responses (e.g., emotional reactions, dissociation; Ozer et al., 2003). As exposure to potentially psychologically traumatic events is a vocational requirement for public safety personnel, researchers and organizations need to focus on aspects of the events, the individual responses, and the individuals characteristics that can be influenced. In the current chapter, we contribute to the growing body of research on PTSD by exploring the role of social support after exposure to traumatic events at work as a potential risk-reduction strategy for public safety personnel, families, and organizations. The specific nature of support-seeking behaviours appears to vary across cultures (e.g., Kim, Sherman, & Taylor, 2008; Taylor et al., 2004), but the benefits of social support for long-term physical and psychological well-being may be universal (Kim et al., 2008).

Accordingly, in the current chapter we explore the role and impact of social support in reducing the negative impact of work-related traumatic event exposures for public safety personnel over time. We begin the chapter by reviewing current literature on the role of social support following exposure to a traumatic event. Using data from two recent studies, we explore the challenges and/or barriers faced by individuals seeking support and those providing support. We argue that better understanding of the complex and nuanced nature of social support will leave researchers and organizations better equipped to design targeted interventions and implement evidence-based best practices to support the long-term health and well-being of public safety personnel. We conclude with recommendations for individuals and organizations to strengthen available social support networks.

Role of Social Support Following Traumatic Event Exposure

Lack of social support after exposure to a traumatic event appears associated with an exacerbation of PTSD symptoms (Marmar et al., 2006; Wagner, Monson, & Hart, 2016) and the development of psychopathology (overall estimate based on 11 studies: weighted $r = .4$, $n = 3,276$; Brewin, Andrews, & Valentine, 2000). Meta-analyses have demonstrated the direct and indirect effects of social support on work-related stress (Viswesvaran, Sanchez, & Fisher, 1999). Social support was found to significantly mitigate the impact of work-related stressors (estimated underlying relationship: $r = -.12$) and strain (estimated underlying relationship: $r = -.21$), in addition to moderating the stressor–strain relationship (overall estimate based on 68 studies: frequency weighted $R^2 = .03$; Viswesvaran et al., 1999). Accordingly, individuals lacking social support may be more likely to experience a negative response following exposure to a traumatic event, which may increase their risk for mental illness. Social support (or a lack thereof) likely interacts with the type or severity of the traumatic event exposure in producing PTSD.

Critics of the social support literature point to the oversimplification of the social support construct, including the use of aggregate measures that fail to explore the underlying support process (Thoits, 2011; Walen & Lachmen, 2000). Aggregate measures often ignore the contextual nature of supportive interactions; for example, the source of social support (e.g., work versus non-work), types of support (e.g., instrumental, informational, emotional, self-esteem), forms of support (e.g., received, perceived, enacted), and the conditions under which support is provided. The different components of social support interact and shape subsequent outcomes

(Jackson, 1992; Nurullah, 2012; Veiel, 1985), suggesting that different support experiences for different traumatic events can result in a range of responses or reactions that can be either beneficial, neutral, or detrimental for individuals.

Additional theoretical and empirical work would facilitate understanding of the wide range of possible outcomes from social support following work-related traumatic events for public safety personnel. Increased understanding of social support may enhance the quality of mental health programs and promote long-term individual health and well-being across occupations and countries. The following sections explore current research on the role of support source (e.g., formal organizational supports, personal support networks) and support type (e.g., emotional, informational) in the social support process within the context of public safety personnel occupations.

Role of Formal Organizational Supports

The need to support employee mental health and well-being in response to a wide range of work-related stressors has inspired public safety personnel organizations to implement many internal programs. For example, the Toronto Police Service in Ontario, Canada offers access to Psychological Services, an internal branch providing psychological supports for its members (i.e., psychological evaluation of new constables, supervisor consultations for work-related psychological issues, access to Employee and Family Assistance Program [EFAP]; Toronto Police Service, n.d.). Many of the programs implemented by public safety organizations focus on managing the aftermath of work-related exposure to a traumatic event. Access to programs that provide psychological care, debriefing, and crisis intervention, is either voluntary or mandatory, and the organization (or representatives of the organization) often serve as the main provider of support.

Despite the good intentions of formal debriefing and crisis intervention programs, concerns have been raised about program efficacy and challenges with research assessing these programs (Anderson et al., 2020). Some research suggests that stress symptoms can worsen following participation (see Regehr, 2001 for a review). Single-session debriefings following exposure to a traumatic event have been associated with negative (Rose et al., 2002) or no impact on individual mental health outcomes (Rose et al., 2002).

Research on group debriefing outcomes have historically demonstrated mixed findings, likely also due, in part, to the lack of methodological rigor in the majority of the available research (Anderson, et al., 2020; Tuckey, 2007). More recently, researchers have used RCTs to demonstrate some potential benefits of group debriefing. For example, in a sample of Australian volunteer firefighters ($n = 67$), group debriefing following exposure to a shared traumatic event was associated with lower levels of self-reported alcohol consumption and higher levels of self-reported quality of life compared to a control condition (Tuckey & Scott, 2014). The authors suggest that group debriefings may offer individuals a critical aspect of social support that aids in adjustment after traumatic events (Tuckey & Scott, 2014).

Organizational social support (e.g., from supervisors) may also be beneficial for individual adjustment to traumatic events (e.g., Regehr, Hill, & Glancy, 2000; Stephens & Long, 2000); however, accessing social support from their organization can be problematic for public safety personnel (Ricciardelli et al., 2020). They must first recognize their own impairment and then actively seek out support, which is not common for public safety personnel. Canadian police officers (n = 421) in a large municipal organization in Ontario reported that many do not seek help from their organization following traumatic events (Heffren & Hausdorf, 2016). Specifically, few respondents indicated that they had sought help from a direct supervisor (10.8%), professional help at work (5%), or help from someone else at work (2%; Heffren & Hausdorf, 2016). Reasons for low levels of formal help-seeking behaviours among public safety personnel may include fear of negative repercussions, low levels of perceived organizational support, or perceived stigma (Corrigan, 2004; Fox et al., 2012; Ricciardelli, Carleton, et al., 2020). In particular, mental health disorders have historically carried social stigma, which can deter individuals from seeking or maintaining treatment (Corrigan, 2004; Heffren & Hausdorf, 2016). Stigma is still of significant concern for public safety personnel, with concerns regarding a lack of confidentiality, negative career impact, and perceived stigma being among the most commonly cited barriers for participants in the U.S. accessing formal mental health services through their organization (Fox et al., 2012; Ricciardelli, Carleton, et al., 2020).

The barrier of stigma is particularly noteworthy in male-dominated occupational contexts, as socialized gender roles (i.e., masculine ideologies that emphasize strength and assertiveness; see Ricciardelli, Clow, & White, 2010) make men particularly resistant to seeking help for mental health issues (Addis & Mahalik, 2003; Berger et al., 2013). Individuals within public safety personnel occupations may attempt to suppress emotional reactions to occupational stressors in line with social norms and expectations (Amaranto, Steinberg, Castellano, & Mitchell, 2003; Farnsworth & Sewell, 2011; Koch, 2010). Normative pressures may also limit help-seeking behaviour for all public safety personnel regardless of their gender identity (Anshel, 2000). Such findings are similar to the concept of "rugged individualism", an individual coping strategy reflecting the desire to manage or control a situation that is commonly seen in policing occupations (Beehr, Johnson, & Nieva, 1995).

To normalize support-seeking and promote well-being, many organizations have begun implementing peer support programs to supplement formal psychological services. Peer support programs emphasize the value of shared work experiences in the provision of mental health-informed social support (Hohner, 2017). These programs are designed to minimize

408   Ewles, Hausdorf, Beehr, and González-Morales

stigma and increase help-seeking by enhancing confidential internal support networks (Dowling, Genet, & Moynihan, 2005). For example, the Ottawa Police Association in Ontario, Canada, is currently developing a Resiliency and Performance Group, which is a peer support program directed towards member mental health (Yogaretnam, 2015). The Resiliency and Performance Group attempts to address concerns stemming from the Ontario Ombudsman's (2012) report on operational stress injuries (e.g., work stress, PTSD; CIPSRT, 2019), as well as members' Resiliency and Performance Group concerns about the adequacy and confidentiality of other internal service providers (e.g., internal health practitioners; Yogaretnam, 2015).

The concerns raised by public safety personnel highlight the need for alternative approaches to supplement current organizational mental health initiatives (e.g., formal crisis debriefing, psychological supports) to promote help-seeking behaviour. However, research supporting the efficacy of these alternative initiatives over time remains limited. Due to the lack of empirical support for specific programs, many organizations have adopted their own unique approach to peer support and crisis intervention, resulting in little consistency across current practices (Beshai et al., 2016). Further research is needed to standardize peer support and crisis intervention programs and to implement best practices across public safety organizations (Beshai et al., 2016).

Role of Personal Support Networks

Rather than seeking help from organizations or professionals, police officers in Ontario seem to be more likely to deal with the issues themselves (44.1%), or to seek help from friends (42.1% at work; 37.2% outside of work), or family members (56.9%; Heffren & Hausdorf, 2016). This suggests a preference for seeking support from personal support networks. Those who seek support from others are likely to fare better than those who attempt to deal with stressors themselves (Jackson, 1992; Walen & Lachmen, 2000). Such results are consistent with recent evidence that public safety personnel reach out to their spouses (74%), friends (62%), and colleagues who are not their leadership (45%) as their first choices for mental health supports (Carleton et al., 2020).

Over the past four decades, significant evidence demonstrating the positive effects of social support on adjustment to both work and life stressors has come to light (see Thoits, 2011 and Turner & Brown, 2010 for a review). In particular, personal support networks (e.g., support from friends, family, spouses/partners) are considered to be most effective in reducing emotional distress (Thoits, 2011). In a cross-sectional study of 267 married and employed parents from the U.S., spousal support and friend support demonstrated an inverse relationship with depression ($r = -.39$ and $r = -.31$, respectively; Jackson, 1992). The study results are consistent with the effect of perceived social support on mental health (e.g., lower levels of

PTSD and Public Safety Personnel 409

depression; Turner & Brown, 2010). Social support is argued to be a key feature of intimate relationships (Collins et al., 2010); accordingly, spousal support significantly predicts individual health and well-being outcomes compared to friend and family support (Feeney & Collins, 2003), which has weaker or indirect effects (Jackson, 1992; Walen & Lachmen, 2000).

Spousal support may also be important for public safety personnel. Canadian public safety personnel (n = 5,813) who report being single (OR 1.37 [95% CI 1.13 to 1.66]) or separated/divorced (OR 1.74 [95% CI 1.43 to 2.11]) were significantly more likely to report symptoms associated with a mental disorder than those who were married or in common-law relationships (Carleton et al., 2018). Although it may be possible that individuals with mental health disorders are more likely to become separated or divorced over time (e.g., Wade & Pevalin, 2004), spouses or romantic partners may serve as a buffer against the negative impact of work-related stressors for public safety personnel (Carleton et al., 2018).

Individuals are generally motivated to support and meet the needs of their romantic partners to maintain a healthy and secure relationship (Bowlby, 2005). Individuals may actively seek support from their romantic partners or spouses. Alternatively, a romantic partner or spouse may be required to observe or recognize signals that their partner is in need (Collins et al., 2010). During times of stress, emotional support (e.g., reassurance, comforting) from a romantic partner may be most important for individual well-being and adjustment (Collins et al., 2010). Further, the quality of that support is more important than the frequency (Collins et al., 2010). For support efforts to be effective, the spouse/romantic partner must: be sensitive to their partner's unique needs (Collins et al., 2010), provide support that is targeted at the specific nature of the stressor (Nurullah, 2012), and present the support in a way that allows the individual to feel cared for and validated (Collins et al., 2010). Support may be instrumental (e.g., booking an appointment), informational (e.g., giving advice), emotional (e.g., validating feelings), or self-esteem based (e.g., affirming abilities; Haber, Cohen, Lucas, & Baltes, 2007). High quality social support targeting the specific nature of the stressor experienced is most effective (Nurullah, 2012). Emotional support, especially from a romantic partner, may also be important in mitigating the symptoms of PTSD (Ozer et al., 2003) and in supporting individual coping following a personal crisis (e.g., severe illness; Revenson, Kayser, & Bodenmann, 2005). Thus, emotional support may be particularly important for public safety personnel following exposure to a traumatic event.

Emotional support from significant others includes actions that reflect love, care, and empathy for a partner, such as expressing concern, having a sympathetic ear, or simply being present (Thoits, 2011). Partners in intimate relationships can provide "safe haven support" during times of adversity or strain by responding to a partner's need for help, closeness, or reassurance (Feeney & Collins, 2003). Positive support provided by partners must be tailored to the unique stressor, but may include encouraging a partner to share thoughts or feelings, showing interest, validating concerns, communicating confidence in their abilities, reaffirming worth, love, or value, providing tangible resources, and/or reassuring availability for continued support (Collins et al., 2010). Emotional support sends a signal to the receiver that their romantic partner understands the significance of the stressor they experienced (Thoits, 2011). In contrast to providing tangible support (e.g., advice), emotional support allows public safety personnel to communicate their feelings and concerns about a work stressor to someone perceived as understanding their emotional response and the associated significance (Thoits, 2011). A romantic partner may have minimal experience with the occupational demands experienced by their public safety personnel partner; nevertheless, there is still an opportunity to provide effective social support, which is promising for public safety personnel families where spouses have different occupational backgrounds.

There is currently limited understanding of the role of social support from romantic partners within the specific context of public safety personnel; however, empirical evidence for the value of non-work support in adjusting to traumatic events exposure is growing. Results from a survey of Ontario police officers ($n = 266$, of whom 76 had experienced a traumatic event within the previous 12 months) indicated that the spouse/romantic partner was the most commonly sought source of support following traumatic events (73.7%; $n = 56$; Hausdorf, Heffren, & Klauninger, 2014), which is consistent with more recent results for all public safety personnel (Carleton et al., 2020). Officers were also asked which type(s) of support (i.e., self-esteem, emotional, informational, instrumental) were sought from each source. Most individuals who sought support (57.1%; $n = 32$) reported seeking emotional support from their spouse/romantic partner, reflecting the need to express feelings without any comments, just care and empathy (Hausdorf et al., 2014). Accordingly, there may be an opportunity for researchers and organizations to enhance family supports for public safety personnel (Carleton et al., 2018; Carleton et al., 2020), especially given that public safety personnel in male-dominated organizations are less likely to seek support from formal organizational networks. Despite the potential benefits, the research focus on public safety personnel families in this process remains nascent.

New Research Exploring the Social Support Process

We conducted two research studies to better understand the social support process from multiple perspectives, including both support seekers and support providers. The first study was designed to explore the experiences of support seekers, including their perception of support helpfulness following a work-related traumatic event. Respondents ($n = 158$ Ontario police officers) provided information on the type of support sought from seven potential sources after the experience of a traumatic event, as well as the perceived efficacy of the support received using several open-ended questions (Ewles et al., 2019). Participants were asked: 1) if they dealt with the situation on their own, what did they do, 2) who was the most helpful source of support and what that person did that helped, 3) who was the least helpful source of support and why did they feel the support was not helpful, and 4) whether or not the support received was what they felt they needed. Qualitative responses were analysed using content analysis.

In the second study we interviewed 38 spouses of Canadian public safety personnel (police $n = 13$; fire $n = 3$; paramedic $n = 22$) about their experiences providing support to their partners so we could explore the experiences of support providers (Ewles et al., 2020). Participants were asked about the unique pressures associated with being in a relationship with a public safety personnel, the signs or signals that indicated when their partner needed support, which support strategies they felt were successful, and what, if any, challenges or barriers did they face when providing support. Preliminary findings from both studies, including sample qualitative responses, will be used in subsequent sections to provide insight into the experiences of support seekers and support providers. We highlight the barriers that impact help-seeking and support provision initially, as well as the challenges associated when others attempt to provide effective social support. Together with empirical evidence from the work of other researchers, we will provide a more comprehensive understanding of social support, including recommendations for both public safety personnel and their families.

Helpful Support Following Traumatic Event Exposures

Consistent with Heffren and Hausdorf (2016), our quantitative survey data indicated that the most common source of support sought by police service members following exposure to a traumatic event was their spouse or romantic partner ($n = 139$). Participants reported seeking emotional support ($n = 59$), informational support ($n = 28$), instrumental support ($n = 30$), and support for self-esteem ($n = 22$). In terms of the qualitative data, the most commonly reported source of helpful support was a spouse or romantic partner and responses highlighted the importance of emotionally supportive actions (e.g., listening, validating feelings). Sample qualitative responses included:

> *"My spouse, just listened."*
> *"Spouse, listened and was empathetic."*
> *"My wife, she listened and put in a different perspective."*
> *"My spouse has been my sounding board and has been offering advice and support."*

Our results are consistent with the general social support literature (e.g., Collins et al., 2010) and underscore the importance of emotional support from partners or spouses when individuals deal with work-related traumatic

412 *Ewles, Hausdorf, Beehr, and González-Morales*

events. Based on this, future researchers can examine ways to strengthen the provision of support at home in order to promote help-seeking behaviours outside traditional organizational boundaries.

Perceived Barriers to Seeking and Providing Support

Public safety personnel who are dealing with stressors must be willing to seek or receive support from the sources available in their network in order to benefit from social supports; unfortunately, a large proportion of public safety personnel in previous research appear more interested in managing stress alone (e.g., 44.1%; Heffren & Hausdorf, 2016). The gendered and individualistic culture of policing that emphasizes the importance of inhibiting emotional reactions to work-related events may influence public safety personnel willingness to access help (Beehr et al., 1995; Koch, 2010; Moad, 2011; Pogrebin & Poole, 1991). The focus on self-reliance can become an ingrained approach to managing work demands that limits help-seeking behaviours for fear of appearing weak or inadequate (Kirschman, 2007; Pogrebin & Poole, 1991). Accordingly, many public safety personnel attempt to manage traumatic events alone, often using suppression or dissociation as coping strategies (Koch, 2010). We asked our policing participants to expand on the actions they took when attempting to manage traumatic events on their own (Ewles et al., 2019). Sample responses included:

> *"Just ignore and hope it goes away."*
> *"Held it in, although realizing it wasn't the best idea."*
> *"You have to detach yourself from the situation. Rationalize it."*
> *"I really haven't spoken much to someone about this. I have told the story but not the emotional impact it really has had on me."*
> *"[I relied on] myself. Dug deep and got it done."*
> *"Just dealt with it. Just accepted it."*

Our participant responses suggest that public safety personnel use a range of behaviours when attempting to manage the after-effects of traumatic events alone. Some participants reported behaviours consistent with positive coping strategies, including acceptance or allowing themselves to feel their emotions. However, the most commonly reported actions involved attempts to dissociate, distract, or separate oneself from emotion.

The focus on solving the problem on one's own (i.e., avoiding seeking help from others) can also be influenced by organizational culture (e.g., Kirschman, 2007; Pogrebin & Poole, 1991). Specifically, fear of stigmatization or concerns about job security (Fox et al., 2012) constrain the option of seeking support at work. The same barriers to help-seeking were echoed by spouses in our qualitative interviews, reflecting potential problems when attempting to provide social support (Ewles et al., 2020):

> *"There's still such a big stigma about [mental health] in police officers [because] they're supposed to be strong and they're there to protect us, and any sign of weakness, it's like smelling blood in the water."*
>
> *"I could only help to a certain point, I couldn't reach out to anyone [at work] and ask them, 'Is anything going on with him? Can you help him? Can you talk to him?' without fear of creating more issues for him at work."*
>
> *"Because there was a stigma, [when I would say] 'Go [seek help at work], maybe you could talk to someone there, they could relate to you'. [He would say], 'No one can relate to what's going on, I just have to power through this. I'm not going there. If I go there, they're going to take my gun, I'm going to lose my job.'"*

Our participants' spouses were aware that organizations were attempting to reduce the stigma associated with mental health, but many spouses felt stigma was still present within their partners' organizations. The ever-present stigma, concerns about confidentiality, and potential repercussions for their spouse/romantic partner constrained them from accessing organizational support. Our participant responses suggest that stigma not only limited help-seeking behaviour from the public safety personnel but also interfered with spouses' resource mobilization.

Beyond the perceived risks associated with help-seeking at work, spouses reported that public safety personnel also do not want to share their experiences outside of the workplace due to concerns about confidentiality, fear of traumatizing others, or appearing weak (Ewles et al., 2020). For example:

> *"There are unique stressors. [For example, they're] dealing with [a] file that's very confidential or of a covert nature. Some of the files [they] deal with, they even say, 'Don't let your spouse know about this' or 'You need to keep it close to the chest', and I don't think you [find] that in other employment."*
>
> *"When he would just shut down, he didn't want to talk to anyone; not friends, not family, not me, not anyone. So, that is difficult [because] even when you're reaching out and trying to help, saying, 'I'm here', he didn't want to talk to his family. So, whether that was [because] he didn't want to expose anyone to whatever he was going through or he didn't feel open enough to talk, I don't know."*
>
> *"In the last year there's been a huge difference [in how my partner seeks support]. Prior to that, him talking about things... you just buck up and deal with it, you don't cry, you just take it like a man, act like a man... Over time we started to talk about, not specific situations, but specific emotions with calls, and so, I've been able to get him now to talk about things that really, really bother him."*

414 *Ewles, Hausdorf, Beehr, and González-Morales*

There appears to be a range of barriers present at individual (e.g., willingness to share), organizational (e.g., fear of breaching confidentiality), and societal levels (e.g., social stigma) that negatively impact help-seeking behaviours from public safety personnel and their spouses/romantic partners after the experience of a work-related stressor. Policing participants often described the need to separate work and family life, rationalizing the experience of stress as part of their role (Ewles et al., 2019). For example:

> *"Deal with it, stress is part of the job."*
> *"I seem to be able to separate work related events and my personal life. I am not sure if this is a learned behaviour or if I have just accepted the things I will encounter in my job."*
> *"Nothing, accepted [stress] as part of the job."*

Public safety personnel appear to consider traumatic event exposures as part of their career and that career suitability involves being able to manage the aftermath on their own, which is consistent with previous research (Ricciardelli, Czarnuch, et al., 2020). Participants reported they managed occupational stressors by attempting to isolate work experiences from their families and compartmentalizing their emotional reactions. Despite these attempts, spouses reported wanting to know what their partner was experiencing (Ewles et al., 2020). For example:

> *"As a spouse, you want to be able to help them, you want to know what's going on."*
> *"You want to provide what they need but you don't necessarily know. And then, in the case of my partner, he's not very good at telling me what he needs."*
> *"If I had to request one change in our relationship it would be that I really wish there was someone, whether it's me or a family member or a friend, that I knew he was opening up to. That's what worries me… they do this 'tough man' exterior and they're dying inside. And everyone would have loved to have helped if they could have recognized it. And my fear is that something's happening that I don't see, that I haven't recognized, [or] that I don't realize is as serious as it might be. And that it'll end up being too late."*
> *"I don't really know exactly how best to help him and he's good at hiding it—well, maybe he isn't hiding it, maybe he just genuinely isn't too affected by things. But, I don't see how that's possible. I think they've got to carry a lot of weight on their shoulders. So, I would love tips on how to better help them. But, I mean, I ask, and he just says, 'Oh no, I'm fine, I'm fine'. So, I don't really know what else I can do."*

The excerpts above suggest that spouses are often highly motivated to support their partners but may not know exactly how to help. Spouses

PTSD and Public Safety Personnel   415

often described situations in which they experienced distress because of feelings of uncertainty and concern for the public safety personnel partner's emotional and physical well-being. This highlighted that public safety personnel efforts to compartmentalize work stress and not share it with their spouses/romantic partners may still produce the distress in the home that they were trying to avoid.

Researchers have demonstrated the crossover effects of traumatic events on partners, despite efforts to separate work and family. PTSD symptoms, such as emotional numbing, may limit individual abilities to express feelings and relate to others, which can negatively impact attachment relationships (Dekel & Monson, 2010). United States meta-analytic results of PTSD and intimate relationship research with military (i.e., active duty soldiers, veterans) and civilian (i.e., women who survived traumatic events) participants found a small negative effect size between PTSD symptoms and relationship quality ($r = -.24$ [95% CI $-.29$ to $-.19$], $k = 22$, $n = 3,421$), as well as a moderate effect size between PTSD symptoms and partner psychological distress (i.e., general distress, vicarious traumatization, caregiver burden; $r = .3$ [95% CI .23 to .36], $k = 25$, $n = 3,417$; Lambert et al., 2012).

Vicarious traumatization has been a central focus in research conducted with partners and families of those exposed to traumatic events (e.g., veterans with combat-related PTSD; Renshaw & Campbell, 2011). Hirschfeld (2005) examined symptoms of vicarious traumatization in spouses of newly recruited police officers ($n = 33$ couples) in the United States over a period of 12 months. There were discrepancies between officer-reported exposure to traumatic events and self PTSD symptoms as compared to spousal perceptions of traumatic event exposures and their partner's PTSD symptoms (the maximum agreement was 9% between partners). Officers reported a higher frequency of traumatic events and more PTSD symptoms than were being perceived by their spouses. Officer-reported traumatic event exposures and PTSD symptoms were not related to spousal distress unless the spouse perceived partner distress. Spouses who perceived distress in their partner had higher levels of distress, including vicarious traumatization ($r = .33$), general psychiatric distress ($r = .41$), depression ($r = .36$), and alcohol consumption ($r = .36$). That is, higher levels of perceived traumatic event exposures and partner distress were associated with negative implications for spouses. The discrepancy between partners may reflect officers' attempts to protect family members from vicarious traumatization, limited communication between partners, or the internalization and denial of emotional reactions to traumatic events (Hirschfeld, 2005).

A related study of spouses of urban police recruits ($n = 71$) had similar results (Meffert et al., 2014). Spouses' perceptions of their partner's symptoms of PTSD (i.e., without the public safety personnel partner sharing their symptoms) predicted vicarious traumatization (i.e., symptoms of PTSD expressed in close family or friends of those who have experienced a traumatic events) in the spouse after 12 months on the job ($\beta = .45$,

416   *Ewles, Hausdorf, Beehr, and González-Morales*

$p < .001$, 95% CI [.22, .67]). Cross-sectional data from U.S. police officers and their spouses has also evidenced that spouses of officers experiencing higher levels of job stress report higher levels of distress themselves and lower levels of relationship satisfaction compared to spouses of officers who experienced lower levels of job stress, possibly reflecting an empathetic response to partner distress (Pavett, 1986). In any case, there appears to be substantive evidence that public safety personnel spouses experience vicarious traumatization that may warrant additional attention by researchers and stakeholders, especially in the absence of public safety personnel partner communication.

There is little research exploring the reasons for these crossover experiences within public safety personnel families, but research on spouses caring for partners with critical illnesses (e.g., breast cancer) provides insight into the difficulty associated with feelings of powerlessness, while attempting to provide comfort and support for a loved one during times of suffering (Petrie, Logan, & DeGrasse, 2001). Public safety personnel spouses or romantic partners may experience similar feelings of powerlessness when witnessing their loved one attempt to manage the effects of exposure to traumatic events alone. Attempting to provide support during times of crisis is often difficult and can be further complicated if public safety personnel are not fully communicating their needs or struggles. Spouses are then left to infer or draw conclusions about their partner's needs in addition to managing their own distress, which limits their ability to provide effective support.

Challenges Providing Effective Support

Even when support is provided, it may not always benefit the recipient and, therefore, ineffective support can influence individual help-seeking behaviours and perceptions of caregiving efficacy over time (Heaney & Israel, 2008). For example, a recent theoretical review of PTSD found associations between negative reactions (e.g., minimizing a person's feelings, victim blaming) and higher levels of PTSD symptoms (Monson, Taft, & Fredman, 2009). The reviewed literature primarily focused on victims of sexual assault, but the authors described the importance of home environments for individual recovery, suggesting that hostile intimate relationships are associated with exacerbated PTSD symptoms (Monson et al., 2009).

Support providers who are unresponsive, react negatively, or provide ineffective support stemming from a lack of knowledge, skill, resources, or motivation, can unintentionally exacerbate symptoms and limit subsequent help-seeking behaviour (Collins et al., 2010). Several responses from police service members in our survey highlighted the potential for a negative support experience (Ewles et al., 2019). Officers perceived that spouses who reacted negatively or were unavailable as the least helpful source of support

PTSD and Public Safety Personnel 417

following traumatic events (Ewles et al., 2019). When spouses or romantic partners were identified as unsupportive, participants highlighted the disconnection between the support they needed and the support they received. Reported challenges included partners who were uninterested in discussing the issue, too busy, or lacked experience or understanding. For example:

> *"My spouse was not helpful. She said it sounded terrible and didn't want to hear about it."*
> *"My wife gave me pity but she really doesn't understand."*
> *"Partner [was] supportive but [was] dealing with other stressful issues at the same time."*

The reported challenges could be explained by a prototypical support interaction model (Collins & Ford, 2010). Within this model, support provided by a partner impacts various outcomes for the receiver, including their well-being and stress levels (Collins & Ford, 2010). The positive impact of the support provided depends on the ability of the support provider to meet the needs of the receiver (Collins et al., 2010). The support employed by the provider is moderated by their skills or abilities, available resources, and individual motives or goals, all of which can influence the outcomes of the support interaction (Collins & Ford, 2010). Thus, if an individual lacks the understanding, time, or motivation to support their partner, any efforts provided may be perceived as ineffective by the recipient (Collins & Ford, 2010).

Spouses who work in jobs unrelated to public safety may feel they lack the ability or understanding required to provide effective support, possibly due to their limited understanding of their partner's occupational demands (Ewles et al., 2020). For example:

> *"I try to offer as much help as I can, but I recognize that… I don't know her work environment, so I don't deal with the things that she deals [with]. So, … I feel bad that I cannot do more than listen and offer practical advice to seek support from the people [at work]."*
> *"I think the odd time that he does go through an incredibly stressful event at work, I don't necessarily know how to help him. I mean, I can listen, I can do the best that I can that way, but there's not much I can really provide in terms of support because I wasn't there in the situation…"*
> *"[My challenge is] just understanding and not letting my worry overtake that moment. So, when he is able to open up, it's hard for me not to get emotional, because I worry about what he's seen and how that's affected him… So, my barrier is [that I need] to be the strength that he needs in that moment because I'm not used to seeing what he's seeing…"*
> *"I think a challenge is [that] I never know if I'm doing enough. And there's the fine line between, 'Am I asking too much?' and 'Am I not*

helping enough?' So, I always have that in the back of my head… I guess it's always on my mind. Like, 'Is he okay?' and 'Am I doing enough?'"
"It's a build-up of these traumatic incidences, and you can only help with what they're willing to tell you about. And then, I don't even know if it's helpful."

The participating public safety personnel spouses who were not themselves public safety personnel reported a high level of motivation to help their romantic partners, but also highlighted difficulties in understanding how best to support them. Spouses who identified themselves as public safety personnel reported being able to provide support to their spouses, partly due to their shared understanding of the occupational demands (Ewles et al., 2020). For example:

"Because we do the same job—if he's got any issues, he's able to come home and talk to me about it [because] I understand the job and things that happen, where not many people can understand our job."
"I find it easier to be with someone in the same occupation, especially this one, because… we relate and we understand each other. It is a little more difficult though… as far as not wanting to talk about certain things, because there's that thing of weakness and exposure if you were to talk about certain issues, certain calls, things like that."
"[When dealing with a stressful event] you run down the event, let's go through the events that brought on these feelings and then… 'In my educated opinion, did you do anything that was outside of standard directive or standard protocol?' and then once that was cleared off, if there was anything of question, you go through it. We worked through the process of how the event went down, and then how we could better make peace with it in our mind."

Regardless of the spouses' occupational background, the support provided was often described as primarily instrumental (e.g., focused on providing immediate help). Instrumental support may be problematic given the relative importance of emotional support (e.g., showing interest, reaffirming worth, validating concerns) during times of adversity or strain (Collins et al., 2010; Thoits, 2011). Training programs to increase emotional support between public safety personnel and their spouse/romantic partner, both in terms of how individuals communicate their support needs and what support is provided after a traumatic event, may be particularly beneficial.

Our results suggest that effective social support begins with public safety personnel being willing to share their emotional experiences with their partner, followed by spouses providing emotional support. From here, effective support interactions can develop based on the situation, the needs of both partners, and openly honest communication. Future researchers should focus on interventions that support constructive interactions and

PTSD and Public Safety Personnel   419

effective communication between public safety personnel and their support networks (Monson et al., 2009).

Improving Social Support

There are several areas where training could improve the benefits of support; for example, aligning the type, timing, and quality of the support to the receiver's needs. public safety personnel may benefit most from seeking and accepting support early and often, particularly if the correct type of support (e.g., emotional) can be delivered in the correct way for a given situation, which may help to mitigate the impact of traumatic events. Researchers need to confirm that these will increase the benefits of social support.

Table 15.1 summarizes three dimensions of social support and associated example interventions that focus on education, communication, and skills-based training to support public safety personnel after exposure to traumatic events. Educating romantic partners on the different aspects of social support will help individuals effectively recognize their own support needs

Table 15.1 Social support dimensions summary

Dimension	Description	
	Less Effective	*More Effective*
Alignment	The social support provided does not align with the needs of the support seeker. For example, providing informational support (e.g., advice) when emotional support is needed (e.g., validating someone's feelings).	The social support provided (e.g., emotional, informational, instrumental, self-esteem) matches the needs of the support seeker.
Quality	Support providers are unable to meet the needs of the support seeker based on a lack of knowledge, skills, resources, or motivation, and may have negative reactions to partner distress, such as minimizing the person's feelings or blaming.	Support providers have the necessary knowledge, skills, resources (e.g., time), and motivation to meet the needs of the support seeker.
Availability	No social support is provided to the support seeker. Support providers may be unaware of partner's distress levels.	Support providers have the capacity and resources to provide support. Social support is readily available and provided in a timely manner to the support seeker.

and evaluate the support provided or received. By building communication skills, both individuals will be more likely to describe their needs effectively and to discuss how their mutual needs can be met. They can also identify and confront any challenges or barriers that are present in the relationship. Lastly, skills-based training can enhance individual skills and abilities for providing support. Interactions between spouses or romantic partners are unique and will be shaped by individual (e.g., personality), couple (e.g., relationship dynamics, previous experiences), and cultural influences (e.g., masculinity; Hofstede, Hofstede, & Minkov, 2010). Educating couples can help build the foundation to support the ongoing alignment, quality, and availability of social support in intimate relationships.

Researchers exploring interventions with couples in the military suggest that efforts to strengthen supportive relationships can reduce symptoms of PTSD (e.g., Monson et al., 2004). Integrative Behavioural Couple Therapy is a therapy designed to promote social support and decrease avoidance behaviours (e.g., distraction, withdrawal) and interpersonal conflict between U.S. military veterans and their partners (Erbes et al., 2008; originally developed by Jacobson & Christensen, 1996). Integrative Behavioural Couple Therapy is designed to enhance communication between partners through education (e.g., regarding PTSD symptoms and avoidance behaviours) and talk therapy.

By discussing recurring themes within the relationship related to distress, conflict, and PTSD symptoms (e.g., how symptoms impact the relationship), Integrative Behavioural Couple Therapy is designed to validate the experiences of both partners and examine the cyclical interaction between PTSD symptoms, withdrawal, and relationship distress. Exploring the links between symptoms of PTSD and relationship distress helps promote acceptance and understanding between partners and reduce avoidance behaviours, thereby increasing intimacy and emotional support (Erbes et al., 2008). Preliminary results suggest that participation in an Integrative Behavioural Couple Therapy program is associated with improvements in relationship satisfaction, qualitative reports of decreased conflict, and increases in positive interactions (Erbes et al., 2008). Couple-based therapy appears to be a promising avenue for future research to evaluate the effects of targeted support for public safety personnel couples following traumatic events.

Success from interventions like Integrative Behavioural Couple Therapy reflects the contextualized nature of stressors and the importance of tailoring specific learning and skill development to participant needs. Understanding that stressors are unique to each relationship is important to provide effective skills-based training and education (Erbes et al., 2008). The approach can be applied to public safety personnel populations by determining the unique nature of relationship stressors for couples that fall within the sub-clinical range of malfunctioning following traumatic events. Training programs like Integrative Behavioural Couple Therapy can improve the alignment, quality, and availability of social support between spouses and promote effective help-seeking behaviour.

What Can Individuals and Families Do?

Based on available research, there are several recommendations for improving social support interactions between public safety personnel and their personal support networks.

Support Seekers

Reflecting on and understanding one's own personal support needs is essential to effectively communicate with others. Some support providers may be more effective at providing specific types of support than others (e.g., work-related advice from a co-worker versus a family member). Multiple types of support (i.e., emotional, instrumental, informational, self-esteem) can be sought from each source, but it is unlikely for a single person to fulfil all social support needs. Thus, individuals must note which sources are most effective at providing each type of support and seek help from multiple sources in their network (i.e., co-workers, supervisors, partners, spouses, trained professionals).

Support Providers

Understanding spousal needs and personal limitations is necessary for providing effective support. Contrary to popular belief, not all support is helpful; providing ineffective support can be detrimental to the receiver and limit subsequent help-seeking behaviour (e.g., Kaufman & Beehr, 1989; Viswesvaran et al., 1999). Additionally, the support provider must be aware of their own personal support needs. Although the research reviewed in the current chapter emphasizes public safety personnel as receivers of support, social support is bidirectional. The ability to provide support also depends on an individual's personal resources and whether their support needs are also being met. Support providers must reflect on their own support needs and seek help from others when necessary.

There are organizations currently available that specifically target the stress experienced by spouses and partners of public safety personnel. For example, the First Responders Support Network based in the U.S. (www.frsn.org/) provides resources, training, and therapeutic retreats to support families of public safety personnel who have been managing traumatic events. Compared to other supports that specifically focus on public safety personnel, the First Responders Support Network offers programs that actively engage families following a family member's exposure to traumatic events. Such programs recognize the impact of traumatic events exposure on families, as well as the spouse's role in the

422 Ewles, Hausdorf, Beehr, and González-Morales

recovery process. Within Canada, there are several organizations available to support public safety personnel and their families, including Badge of Life Canada (https://badgeoflifecanada.org/), Wounded Warriors Canada (https://woundedwarriors.ca/how-we-help-first-responders/), and Boots on the Ground (www.bootsontheground.ca/). Community organizations like these provide promise for building an integrated support network involving public safety personnel, families, organizations, and the community.

Future Directions for Organizational and Community Supports

The prevalence of PTSD and the increased awareness surrounding mental health within public safety personnel groups has pushed various countries to recognize the impact of traumatic events on individual health and well-being. For example, in Canada, most provinces have passed legislation that classifies PTSD as a work-related illness and establishes the presumption of work-relatedness in all diagnosed cases of PTSD in public safety personnel (e.g., Government of Manitoba, 2015; Ontario Ministry of Labour, 2016). Presumption clauses in legislation are continuing across Canada because such clauses provide earlier access to care and compensation and reflect the recent concerns within public safety personnel communities regarding the ability of individuals to cope with work-related traumatic events. More work is needed to include more occupational groups in these laws, but the changes reflect a step in the right direction towards reducing the stigma associated with mental health and help-seeking in public safety personnel.

Social support provides a promising way to help mitigate the relationship between traumatic events and symptoms of PTSD for public safety personnel. To help promote social support outside of traditional boundaries, public safety personnel organizations should consider partnering with community organizations or third-party support groups to provide families with additional evidence-based resources, education, and programs. Organizations can take a more holistic approach by extending the conversation about well-being and mental health outside of formal structures. Informal approaches allow individuals to seek a variety of supports to help manage their diverse and specific experiences. Moreover, as a community, facilitating conversations that underscore the importance of mental health and the interactions with social support can help reduce stigma and create a more inclusive environment to promote health and well-being for public safety personnel and their families.

Notes

1 The views expressed in this paper are those of the authors and not of the organizations from which data were obtained.

2 Surveyed countries include Belgium, Brazil, Bulgaria, Colombia, France, Germany, Ireland, Italy, Israel, Japan, Lebanon, Mexico, the Netherlands, New Zealand, the People's Republic of China, Romania, South Africa, Spain, Ukraine, and the United States of America (Karam et al., 2014).

References

Addis, M. E., & Mahalik, J. R. (2003). Men, masculinity, and the contexts of help seeking. *American Psychologist*, *58*(1), 5–14.

Alexander, D. A., & Klein, S. (2009). First responders after disasters: A review of stress reactions, at-risk, vulnerability, and resilience factors. *Prehospital and Disaster Medicine*, *24*(2), 87–94.

Amaranto, E., Steinberg, J., Castellano, C., & Mitchell, R. (2003). Police stress interventions. *Brief Treatment and Crisis Intervention*, *3*(1), 47–54.

American Psychiatric Association (APA). (2000). *Diagnostic and statistical manual of mental disorders* (4th edn, text rev.). Washington, DC: American Psychiatric Association.

APA. (2013). *Diagnostic and statistical manual of mental disorders (DSM-5®)*. Washington, DC: American Psychiatric Association.

Anderson, G. S., Di Nota, P. M., Groll, D., & Carleton, R. N. (2020). Peer support and crisis-focused psychological interventions designed to mitigate post-traumatic stress injuries among public safety and frontline healthcare personnel: A systematic review. *International Journal of Environmental Research and Public Health*, *17*, 7645. https://doi.org/10.3390/ijerph17207645

Anshel, M. H. (2000). A conceptual model and implications for coping with stressful events in police work. *Criminal Justice and Behavior*, *27*(3), 375–400.

Beehr, T. A., Johnson, L. B., & Nieva, R. (1995). Occupational stress: Coping of police and their spouses. *Journal of Organizational Behavior*, *16*(1), 3–25.

Benedek, D. M., Fullerton, C., & Ursano, R. J. (2007). First responders: Mental health consequences of natural and human-made disasters for public health and public safety workers. *Annual Review of Public Health*, *28*, 55–68.

Berger, J. L., Addis, M. E., Green, J. D., Mackowiak, C., & Goldberg, V. (2013). Men's reactions to mental health labels, forms of help-seeking, and sources of help-seeking advice. *Psychology of Men & Masculinity*, *14*(4), 433–443.

Berger, W., Coutinho, E. S. F., Figueira, I., Marques-Portella, C., Luz, M. P., Neylan, T. C., ... Mendlowicz, M. V. (2012). Rescuers at risk: A systematic review and meta-regression analysis of the worldwide current prevalence and correlates of PTSD in rescue workers. *Social Psychiatry and Psychiatric Epidemiology*, *47*(6), 1001–1011.

Beshai, S., Carleton, R. N., Dirkse, D A., Duranceau, S., Hampton, A. J. D., Ivens, S. E., LeBouthillier, D. M., ... Zamorski, M. A. (2016). *Peer support and crisis-focused psychological intervention programs in Canadian first responders: Blue paper*. Regina, SK: Collaborative Centre for Justice and Safety, University of Regina.

Bowlby, J. (2005). *A secure base: Clinical applications of attachment theory*. New York: Routledge.

Brewin, C. R., Andrews, B., & Valentine, J. D. (2000). Meta-analysis of risk factors for posttraumatic stress disorder in trauma-exposed adults. *Journal of Consulting and Clinical Psychology*, *68*(5), 748–766.

Canadian Institute for Public Safety Research and Treatment (CIPSRT). (2019). Glossary of terms: A shared understanding of the common terms used to describe psychological trauma (version 2.0). http://hdl.handle.net/10294/9055.

Carleton, R. N., Afifi, T. O., Turner, S., Taillieu, T., Duranceau, S., LeBouthillier, D. M., ... Asmundson, G. J. G. (2018). Mental disorder symptoms among public safety personnel in Canada. *The Canadian Journal of Psychiatry/La revue canadienne de psychiatrie*, *63*(1), 54–64.

Carleton, R. N., Afifi, T. O., Taillieu, T., Turner, S., Krakauer, R., Anderson, G. S., ... McCreary, D. (2019). Exposures to potentially traumatic events among Public Safety Personnel in Canada. *Canadian Journal of Behavioural Science*, *51*, 37–52. https://doi.org/10.1037/cbs0000115

Carleton, R. N., Afifi, T. O., Turner, S., Taillieu, T., Vaughan, A. D., Anderson, G. S., ... Camp, R. D. II. . (2020). Mental health training, attitudes towards support, and screening positive for mental disorders. *Cognitive Behaviour Therapy*, *49*, 55–73. https://doi.org/10.1080/16506073.2019.1575900

Collins, N. L., & Ford, M. B. (2010). Responding to the needs of others: The caregiving behavioral system in intimate relationships. *Journal of Social and Personal Relationships*, *27*(2), 235–244.

Collins, N. L., Ford, M. B., Guichard, A. C., Kane, H. S., & Feeney, B. C. (2010). Responding to need in intimate relationships: Social support and caregiving processes in couples. In M. Mikulincer & P. R. Shaver (eds), *Prosocial motives, emotions, and behavior: The better angels of our nature* (pp. 367–389). Washington, DC: American Psychological Association.

Corrigan, P. (2004). How stigma interferes with mental health care. *American Psychologist*, *59*(7), 614–625.

Creamer, M., Burgess, P., & McFarlane, A. C. (2001). Post-traumatic stress disorder: Findings from the Australian National Survey of Health and Well-Being. *Psychological Medicine*, *31*(7), 1237–1247.

Dekel, R., & Monson, C. M. (2010). Military-related posttraumatic stress disorder and family relations: Current knowledge and future directions. *Aggression and Violent Behavior*, *15*(4), 303–309.

Donnelly, E. (2012). Work-related stress and posttraumatic stress in emergency medical services. *Prehospital Emergency Care*, *16*(1), 76–85.

Dowling, F. G., Genet, B., & Moynihan, G. (2005). A confidential peer-based assistance program for police officers. *Psychiatric Services*, *56*(7), 870–871.

Erbes, C. R., Polusny, M. A., MacDermid, S., & Compton, J. S. (2008). Couple therapy with combat veterans and their partners. *Journal of Clinical Psychology*, *64*(8), 972–983.

Ewles, G. B., & Hausdorf, P. A. (2016, August). *Investigating the role of social support in policing*. Paper presented at the PTSD Multidisciplinary Conference, St. John's, NL, Canada.

Ewles, G. B., Hausdorf, P. A., González-Morales, M. G., & Beehr, T. A. (2019). *Examining the role of enacted social support for police service members following a traumatic work-related event: A cross-sectional analysis*. Unpublished manuscript, Department of Psychology, University of Guelph, ON, Canada.

Ewles, G. B., Hausdorf, P. A., González-Morales, M. G., & Beehr, T. A. (2020). *When trauma comes home: Exploring the social support process within emergency first responder romantic relationships*. Manuscript in preparation.

Farnsworth, J. K., & Sewell, K. W. (2011). Fear of emotion as a moderator between PTSD and firefighter social interactions. *Journal of Traumatic Stress*, *24*(4), 444–450.

Feeney, B. C., & Collins, N. L. (2003). Motivations for caregiving in adult intimate relationships: Influences on caregiving behavior and relationship functioning. *Personality and Social Psychology Bulletin*, *29*(8), 950–968.

Fox, J., Desai, M. M., Britten, K., Lucas, G., Luneau, R., & Rosenthal, M. S. (2012). Mental-health conditions, barriers to care, and productivity loss among officers in an urban police department. *Connecticut Medicine*, *76*(9), 525–531.

PTSD and Public Safety Personnel 425

Gershon, R. R. M., Barocas, B., Canton, A. N., Li, X., & Vlahov, D. (2009). Mental, physical, and behavioral outcomes associated with perceived work stress in police officers. *Criminal Justice and Behavior*, *36*(3), 275–289.

Government of Manitoba (2015, June 8). Province introduces ground-breaking first-in-Canada presumptive posttraumatic stress disorder legislation. Retrieved from http://news.gov.mb.ca/news/index.html?item=35114.

Haber, M. G., Cohen, J. L., Lucas, T., & Baltes, B. B. (2007). The relationship between self-reported received and perceived social support: A meta-analytic review. *American Journal of Community Psychology*, *39*(1–2), 133–144.

Hausdorf, P. A., Heffren, C. D. J., Klauninger, L. (2014). *Coping and social support before and after traumatic events: Implications for adjustment and states of mind*. Unpublished manuscript, Department of Psychology, University of Guelph, ON, Canada.

Heaney, C. A., & Israel, B. A. (2008). Social networks and social support. In K. Glanz, B. K. Rimer, & K. Viswanath (eds), *Health behavior and health education: Theory, research, and practice* (4th edn) (pp. 189–210). San Francisco, CA: Jossey-Bass.

Heffren, C. D. J., & Hausdorf, P. A. (2016). Post-traumatic effects in policing: Perceptions, stigmas, and help seeking behaviours. *Police Practice and Research: An International Journal*, *17*(5), 1–14.

Hirschfeld, A. (2005). *Secondary effects of traumatization among spouses and partners of newly recruited police officers*. Unpublished doctoral dissertation, Alliant International University, San Francisco, CA.

Hofstede, G., Hofstede, G. J., & Minkov, M. (2010). *Culture and organizations: Software of the mind* (3rd edn). New York: McGraw-Hill.

Hohner, C. (2017). *"The environment says it's okay": The tension between peer support and police culture*. Unpublished master's thesis, Western University, London, ON.

Jackson, P. B. (1992). Specifying the buffering hypothesis: Support, strain, and depression. *Social Psychology Quarterly*, *55*(4), 363–378.

Jacobson, N. S., & Christensen, A. (1996). *Integrative couple therapy: Promoting acceptance and change*. New York: WW Norton & Co.

Karam, E. G., Friedman, M. J., Hill, E. D., Kessler, R. C., McLaughlin, K. A., Petukhova, M., ... Koenen, K. C. (2014). Cumulative traumas and risk thresholds: 12-month PTSD in the World Mental Health (WMH) surveys. *Depression and Anxiety*, *31*(2), 130–142.

Kaufmann, G. M., & Beehr, T. A. (1989). Occupational stressors, individual strains, and social supports among police officers. *Human Relations*, *42*(2), 185–197.

Kim, H. S., Sherman, D. K., & Taylor, S. E. (2008). Culture and social support. *American Psychologist*, *63*(6), 518–526.

Kirschman, E. (2007). *I love a cop: What police families need to know* (rev. edn). New York: The Guilford Press.

Koch, B. J. (2010). The psychological impact on police officers of being first responders to completed suicides. *Journal of Police and Criminal Psychology*, *25*(2), 90–98.

Lambert, J. E., Engh, R., Hasbun, A., & Holzer, J. (2012). Impact of posttraumatic stress disorder on the relationship quality and psychological distress of intimate partners: A meta-analytic review. *Journal of Family Psychology*, *26*(5), 729–737.

Liberman, A. M., Best, S. R., Metzler, T. J., Fagan, J. A., Weiss, D. S., & Marmar, C. R. (2002). Routine occupational stress and psychological distress in police.

426 *Ewles, Hausdorf, Beehr, and González-Morales*

Policing: An International Journal of Police Strategies and Management, 25(2), 421–439.

Marmar, C. R., McCaslin, S. E., Metzler, T. J., Best, S., Weiss, D. S., Fagan, J., Liberman, A., ... Neylan, T. (2006). Predictors of posttraumatic stress in police and other first responders. *Annals of the New York Academy of Sciences, 1071*(1), 1–18.

McFarlane, A. C., & Bryant R. A. (2007). Post-traumatic stress disorder in occupational settings: Anticipating and managing the risk. *Occupational Medicine, 57*(6), 404–410.

Meffert, S. M., Henn-Haase, C., Metzler, T. J., Qian, M., Best, S., Hirschfeld, A., ... Marmar, C. R. (2014). Prospective study of police officer spouse/partners: A new pathway to secondary trauma and relationship violence? *PLoS One, 9*(7), 1–8.

Moad, C. (2011). *Critical incidents: Responding to police officer trauma.* Criminal Justice Institute, University of Arkansas System, Little Rock, AR. Retrieved from www.cji.edu/wp-content/uploads/2019/04/chrismoad.pdf

Monson, C. M., Schnurr, P. P., Stevens, S. P., & Guthrie, K. A. (2004). Cognitive-behavioral couple's treatment for posttraumatic stress disorder: Initial findings. *Journal of Traumatic Stress, 17*(4), 341–344.

Monson, C. M., Taft, C. T., & Fredman, S. J. (2009). Military-related PTSD and intimate relationships: From description to theory-driven research and intervention development. *Clinical Psychology Review, 29*(8), 707–714.

Nurullah, A. S. (2012). Received and provided social support: A review of current evidence and future directions. *American Journal of Health Studies, 27*(3), 173–188.

Ontario Ministry of Labour (2016, April 5). Ontario passes legislation to support first responders with PTSD. Retrieved from https://news.ontario.ca/mol/en/2016/04/ontario-passes-legislation-to-support-first-responders-with-ptsd.html.

Ontario Ombudsman. (2012). In the line of duty. Retrieved from www.ombudsman.on.ca/Files/sitemedia/Documents/Investigations/SORT%20Investigations/OPP-final-EN.pdf.

Ozer, E. J., Best, S. R., Lipsey, T. L., & Weiss, D. S. (2003). Predictors of post-traumatic stress disorder and symptoms in adults: A meta-analysis. *Psychological Bulletin, 129*(1), 52–73.

Pavett, C. M. (1986). High stress professions: Satisfaction, stress, and well-being of spouses of professionals. *Human Relations, 39*(12), 1141–1154.

Petrie, W., Logan, J., & DeGrasse, C. (2001). Research review of the supportive care needs of spouses of women with breast cancer. *Oncology Nursing Forum, 28*(10), 1601–1607.

Pogrebin, M. R., & Poole, E. D. (1991). Police and tragic events: The management of emotions. *Journal of Criminal Justice, 19*(4), 395–403.

Regehr, C. (2001). Crisis debriefing groups for emergency responders: Reviewing the evidence. *Brief Treatment and Crisis Intervention, 1*(2), 87–100.

Regehr, C., Hill, J., Glancy, G. D. (2000). Individual predictors of traumatic reactions in firefighters. *The Journal of Nervous and Mental Disease, 188*(6), 333–339.

Renshaw, K. D., & Campbell, S. B. (2011). Combat veterans' symptoms of PTSD and partners' distress: The role of partners' perceptions of veterans' deployment experiences. *Journal of Family Psychology, 25*(6), 953–962.

Revenson, T. A., Kayser, K., & Bodenmann, G. (eds). (2005). *Couples coping with stress: Emerging perspectives on dyadic coping.* Washington, DC: American Psychological Association.

Ricciardelli, R., Carleton, R. N., Cramm, H., & Groll, D. (2018). Qualitatively unpacking Canadian public safety personnel experiences of trauma and their wellbeing: Physical manifestations, psychological implications, and fatalistic attitudes. *Canadian Journal of Criminology and Criminal Justice, 60,* 566–577. https://doi.org/10.3138/cjccj.2017-0053.r2

Ricciardelli, R., Carleton, R. N., Mooney, T., & Cramm, H. (2020). "Playing the system": Structural factors potentiating mental health stigma, challenging awareness, and creating barriers to care for Canadian public safety personnel. *Health, 24,* 259–278. https://doi.org/10.1177/1363459318800167.

Ricciardelli, R., Clow, K. A., & White, P. (2010). Investigating hegemonic masculinity: Portrayals of masculinity in men's lifestyle magazines. *Sex Roles, 63*(1/ 2), 64–78.

Ricciardelli, R., Czarnuch, S., Afifi, T. O., Taillieu, T., & Carleton, R. N. (2020). Public Safety Personnel's interpretations of potentially traumatic events. *Occupational Medicine, 70,* 155–161. https://doi.org/10.1093/occmed/kqaa007.

Rose, S. C., Bisson, J., Churchill, R., & Wessely, S. (2002). Psychological debriefing for preventing post-traumatic stress disorder (PTSD). *Cochrane Database of Systematic Reviews, 2002*(2), 1–49.

Skogstad, M., Skorstad, M., Lie, A., Conradi, H. S., Heir, T., & Weisaeth, L. (2013). Work-related posttraumatic stress disorder. *Occupational Medicine, 63*(3), 175–182.

Sommer, J. L., El-Gabalawy, R., Taillieu, T., Afifi, T. O., & Carleton, R. N. (2020). Associations between trauma exposure and physical health conditions among Public Safety Personnel. *Canadian Journal of Psychiatry, 65*(8), 548–558. https://doi.org/10.1177/0706743720919278.

Stephens, C., & Long, N. (2000). Communication with police supervisors and peers as a buffer of work-related traumatic stress. *Journal of Organizational Behavior, 21*(4), 407–424.

Taylor, S. E., Sherman, D. K., Kim, H. S., Jarcho, J., Takagi, K., & Dunagan, M. S. (2004). Culture and social support: Who seeks it and why? *Journal of Personality and Social Psychology, 87*(3), 354–362.

Thoits, P. A. (2011). Mechanisms linking social ties and support to physical and mental health. *Journal of Health and Social Behavior, 52*(2), 145–161.

Toronto Police Service (n.d.) Psychological services. Retrieved from www. torontopolice.on.ca/psychologicalservices/.

Tuckey, M. R. (2007). Issues in the debriefing debate for the emergency services: Moving research outcomes forward. *Clinical Psychology: Science and Practice, 14*(2), 106–116.

Tuckey, M. R., & Scott, J. E. (2014). Group critical incident stress debriefing with emergency services personnel: A randomized controlled trial. *Anxiety, Stress, & Coping, 27*(1), 38–54.

Turner, R. J., & Brown, R. L. (2010). Social support and mental health. In T. L. Scheid & T. N. Brown (eds), *A handbook for the study of mental health: Social contexts, theories, and systems* (2nd edn) (pp. 200–212). New York: Cambridge University Press.

Veiel, H. O. F. (1985). Dimensions of social support: A conceptual framework for research. *Social Psychiatry, 20*(4), 156–162.

Viswesvaran, C., Sanchez, J. I., & Fisher, J. (1999). The role of social support in the process of work stress: A meta-analysis. *Journal of Vocational Behavior, 54*(2), 314–334.

Wade, T. J., & Pevalin, D. J. (2004). Marital transitions and mental health. *Journal of Health and Social Behavior, 45*(2), 155–170.

Wagner, A. C., Monson, C. M., & Hart, T. L. (2016). Understanding social factors in the context of trauma: Implications for measurement and intervention. *Journal of Aggression, Maltreatment & Trauma, 25*(8), 831–853.

Walen, H. R., & Lachman, M. E. (2000). Social support and strain from partner, family, and friends: Costs and benefits for men and women in adulthood. *Journal of Social and Personal Relationships, 17*(1), 5–30.

Wilson, S., Guliani, H., & Boichev, G. (2016). On the economics of posttraumatic stress disorder among first responders in Canada. *Journal of Community Safety & Well-Being, 1*(2), 26–31.

Yogaretnam, S. (2015, July 14). Ottawa police approve mental health plan for officers. *Ottawa Citizen.* Retrieved from https://ottawacitizen.com/news/local-news/ottawa-police-approve-mental-health-plan-for-officers.

16 Group Cognitive Processing Therapy for PTSD

Preliminary Outcomes, Group Cohesion, Therapeutic Alliance, and Participant Satisfaction in Current and Former Members of the Canadian Military and Federal Police Force

Sarah J. Chaulk and David J. Podnar

There has been much research focused on the risk factors, etiology, and treatment of posttraumatic stress disorder (PTSD), since its original conceptualization as "shell shock". The current chapter and the presented study focuses on reviewing the background literature on PTSD treatments and examining the effectiveness of a group-based Cognitive Processing Therapy for PTSD in a Canadian military and police population. Cognitive behavioural therapy approaches to treatment have recently gained the most support in the literature for alleviating symptoms of PTSD. Most of the research on PTSD treatments for military and police populations has traditionally been done with individual-based therapies; however, the cost-effectiveness and greater service capacity of group-based interventions have encouraged efforts to experiment with combining the benefits of cognitive behavioural therapy with those of group psychotherapy. In the current chapter, we seek to assist in bridging the gap between research and practice by investigating the effectiveness of group-based Cognitive Processing Therapy for PTSD in the context of routine mental health care. We begin by discussing psychological trauma to contextualize the presented study and psychotherapy under examination. Next we summarize the literature on PTSD in the context of the military and police service, which leads us to the results of the presented study. We provide reflections and recommendations that link our results with the previous literature. We tie together the overall literature on treatment for PTSD and our presented study before putting forth the implications of our results in the context of the greater body of research on Cognitive Processing Therapy and PTSD treatment more generally. We conclude with suggested implications for administration of group-based Cognitive Processing Therapy in routine practice, cost-effectiveness of group psychotherapy for PTSD, and health care policy.

DOI: 10.4324/9781351134637-17

Psychological Trauma

A note on terminology used to describe psychological trauma. There are several terms used interchangeably throughout this chapter—these include trauma, potentially psychologically traumatic events, and psychological trauma. When thinking about events objectively, for example natural disaster, it is not an inherently traumatic event but rather a potentially psychologically traumatic event. However, if the individual is deemed to be experiencing posttraumatic stress in relation to that event it is then a traumatic event for that individual. It is also important to note that sometimes physical trauma and psychological trauma overlap such as a head injury during a serious car accident or combat.

Potentially psychologically traumatic events (Canadian Institute for Public Safety Research and Treatment [CIPSRT], 2019), can precipitate lasting psychological distress in individuals who experience them directly, witness them, or even learn about them. These extremely stressful and potentially traumatic events can affect individuals' cognitions, physiology, and social and emotional functioning (Wilson & Keane, 2004). The effects of trauma can include disruptions in terms of how an individual thinks and their beliefs about themselves and others (e.g., "I can never trust anyone again", "I am permanently damaged because of what happened to me"). It can also include biological changes whereby the nervous system and the fight-or-flight response become overactive. Individuals exposed to traumatic events may feel emotionally numb and distant or isolate themselves from others. While epidemiological data support that most people do experience one or more traumatic events over the course of their lifetime (Kessler et al., 1995; Breslau, 2009), the good news is that most posttraumatic stress is considered a normal reaction to extremely stressful life events and most people recovery naturally over time. Only a small proportion of individuals develop PTSD (APA, 2013).

What Leads to PTSD?

PTSD is one of the only psychological diagnoses whose origin can be directly linked to an external event. Since not all individuals develop PTSD from potentially psychologically traumatic events, much research has been conducted in an attempt to explain why some people develop PTSD and others recover naturally (e.g., over time and through natural social supports). Researchers have focused on different event types, individual demographics, psychosocial history, and peritraumatic factors. While there has not been a clear consensus, it is generally accepted that interpersonal traumas, as compared to natural disasters or accidents, are more likely to result in lasting psychological distress. In a systematic review, Santiago and colleagues (2013) found evidence that potentially psychologically traumatic events which involved intentional harm (e.g., assault/terrorism) demonstrate different trajectories. People exposed to intentional or interpersonal

Group Cognitive Processing Therapy for PTSD 431

traumatic events were more likely to report a severe and chronic course of PTSD. There is also evidence that some events are associated with more distress (e.g., combat trauma, sudden loss of a loved one, sexual assault, and sudden violent deaths; Carleton et al., 2019; Kessler et al., 2005). The number of exposures to potentially traumatic events has also been examined, with a relationship between the number of events and the probability and severity of PTSD increasing with chronic or repeated exposures (e.g., child maltreatment; Scott, 2007). Certain risk factors (i.e., younger age at the time of exposure, history of childhood adversity, pre-existing psychological conditions) have also been identified (Perkonigg et al., 2000). In addition, there has been a growing interest in studying the resiliency of individuals who have experienced potentially psychologically traumatic events and what factors may protect against or mitigate the psychological consequences of trauma. Social support (e.g., how the person is supported) during and following the event appears to be protective of individuals' mental health following trauma (James et al., 2013).

Prevalence of PTSD

Most people exposed to potentially psychologically traumatic events recover on their own; however, there are still many people who develop PTSD and could benefit from trauma-focused psychological treatment. PTSD prevalence rates vary from country to country, but the global estimates range from 9.2% to 13.6% (Atwoli et al., 2015). Canadian epidemiological estimates suggest a lifetime prevalence rate of 9.2% and a current rate of 2.4% (i.e., defined as symptoms reported in the past month; Van Ameringen et al., 2008). Accordingly, the current PTSD rate in the Canadian population of 36.7 million would be approximately 881,000 people (Statistics Canada, 2018).

Certain subsections of the Canadian population have increased exposure to traumatic events, such as those in military and policing (e.g., members of the Canadian Armed Forces [CAF] and the Royal Canadian Mounted Police [RCMP]). Additionally, Public safety personnel, including police, paramedics, firefighters, appear at much higher risk for exposure to potentially traumatic events than the general population (Carleton et al., 2019). Military service can involve increased risk for exposure to adverse and stressful events not experienced by civilians (i.e., combat-related peacekeeping, and emergency response deployments; Thompson et al., 2016, VanTil et al., 2017). Numerous researchers have suggested that exposure to trauma for public safety personnel and general combat exposure significantly increases the risk of developing posttraumatic stress and other stress-related disorders (Hoge et al., 2004; Hoge, Auchterlonie, & Milliken, 2006; Hotopf et al., 2006; Bertenthal et al., 2007; Carleton et al., 2018). In a recent study of Canadian public safety personnel, 19.5% of municipal/provincial police and 30% of active Royal Canadian Mounted Police members screened positive for symptoms of PTSD (Carleton et al., 2018). The Canadian Forces

Mental Health Survey, which indicates lifetime PTSD prevalence rates of 11.1% and 12-month prevalence rates of 5.3% for Canadian Armed Forces members (Pearson, Zamorski & Janz, 2014), supports the increased risk for the development of PTSD in military members. Further, 12-month prevalence rates for PTSD were twice as much for Canadian Armed Forces members who were deployed to Afghanistan compared to those who were not (Pearson et al., 2014). Risk factors specific to military members, police officers, and veterans (i.e., length of military service, higher number of deployments, longer cumulative length of deployments, combat specialization) predict a greater chance for developing PTSD (Brewin et al., 2000; Hidalgo & Davidson, 2000; Xue et al., 2015).

Combat exposure can increase the risk of developing PTSD, but in the military and the general population sexual trauma is a consistent predictor of PTSD. Within the military, sexual assault is quite prevalent and contributes to the development PTSD and other issues (Kang et al., 2005). In one survey of United States military reservists, higher proportions of self-identified female reservists reported sexual harassment (60% versus 27.2% for males) and sexual assault (13.1% versus 1.6% for males; Street et al., 2008). Participants who reported sexual harassment and assault, regardless of identifying as female or male, were significantly more likely to report issues with symptoms of major depressive disorder, somatic symptoms, and medical conditions; however, only female members who experienced sexual harassment and assault showed greater risks for developing current and lifetime PTSD. Regarding regular service members, in a study of United States female veterans receiving outpatient care, 55% of female veterans reported sexual harassment and 23% reported at least once incident of sexual assault over their military service (Skinner et al., 2000). Women who experienced sexual harassment or assault were significantly more likely to report social isolation and disconnection, as well as a variety of readjustment problems (e.g., anxiety, depression, alcohol or drug use problems).

PTSD is often complicated by high comorbidity with a number of other mental health conditions (Keane & Wolfe, 1990; Kessler et al., 1995; Carleton et al., 2018). Among the general population, PTSD most frequently co-occurs with disorders involving alcohol or substance use, mood and anxiety disorders, and personality disorders (especially antisocial and borderline personality disorder; Keane & Kaloupek, 1997). Similarly, comorbidity has been found in military and veteran populations. In a random sample of 50 outpatient veterans diagnosed with PTSD, high co-occurring rates of alcoholism (84%), substance abuse (42%), major depressive disorder (68%), dysthymia (34%), and antisocial personality disorder (26%) were reported (Keane & Wolfe, 1990). Other researchers argue that PTSD is a dominant disorder following exposure to potentially psychologically traumatic events and, if left untreated, could lead to the secondary development of mood, anxiety, and substance use disorders (Ginzburg, Ein-Dorb & Solomona, 2010).

Effectiveness of Psychological Interventions for PTSD

There has been significant research into various psychotherapies and pharmacotherapies to address PTSD (Haagen et al., 2015). There is a large literature on the efficacy of psychotherapies for PTSD; evidence on the use of psychopharmacological treatments indicates individuals are more likely to relapse after discontinuing medication treatment, but this is not true after discontinuing psychotherapy (Lancaster et al., 2016). Several effective evidence-based psychological treatments exist for PTSD, including Prolonged Exposure Therapy (Foa et al., 2019), Eye Movement and Desensitization and Reprocessing Therapy (Shapiro & Forrest,1997; Chen et al., 2014), and Cognitive Processing Therapy (Resick et al., 2002; Resick, Monson, & Chard, 2017). There are also non trauma-focused therapies, such as Transcendental Meditation (Nidich et al., 2018), Present-Centred Therapy (Ford et al., 2018), and Interpersonal Psychotherapy (Markowitz et al., 2015) that are gaining empirical support. Cognitive-based therapies for PTSD, such as Cognitive Processing Therapy, are designed to identify and change problematic negative beliefs and/or avoidant behaviours that contribute to the maintenance of PTSD symptoms. Cognitive Processing Therapy (Resick, Monson, & Chard, 2017) is one of the dominant cognitive therapies for PTSD and is our focus in the current chapter and the effectiveness study herein. Cognitive Processing Therapy is an effective treatment for PTSD for several clinical populations (Chard & La Greca, 2005; Resick et al., 2015).

What Is Cognitive Processing Therapy?

Cognitive Processing Therapy conceptualizes PTSD as a problem in recovery, wherein a traumatic event(s) has (have) fundamentally disrupted how individuals think about themselves, others, and the world (Resick, Monson, & Chard, 2017). Disrupted cognitions can have pervasive impacts on people and can cause distress and impairments related to problematic emotions, avoidance behaviours, and physiological changes. Since negative changes in cognition are viewed as the mechanism that elicits painful emotions (e.g., guilt, shame, fear) and behavioural avoidance in PTSD, cognitions are the focus of change in Cognitive Processing Therapy. A secondary focus in Cognitive Processing Therapy is on processing or feeling emotions associated with the traumatic event and to reduce avoidance of emotions as well. Changes to cognition are addressed in five areas of core psychological needs: safety, trust, intimacy, esteem, and power/control (McCann & Pearlman, 1990). As clients identify their trauma-related cognitions (e.g., "The world is completely dangerous"), Cognitive Processing Therapy therapists teach clients cognitive strategies to restructure the negative beliefs underlying their PTSD and encourage them to feel the associated emotions. Doing so helps to reduce avoidance and process the emotions associated with trauma (e.g., sadness, powerlessness).

These therapeutic strategies collectively facilitate recovery from PTSD. The benefits of Cognitive Processing Therapy include reduced symptoms of posttraumatic stress such as, reduced intrusive thoughts/images, less behavioural avoidance, reduced negative affect (e.g., fear, anger, and sadness), and a more balanced view of the self, others, and the world.

Cognitive Processing Therapy is composed of several components including psychoeducation on PTSD, the fight/flight/freeze response, universal emotions, cognitive biases, and recovery from posttraumatic stress. Another component is focused on increasing awareness of connections between thoughts, feelings, and behaviours. Ending with assisting the individual to develop skills for cognitive restructuring of problematic trauma-related cognitions. The original protocol for Cognitive Processing Therapy includes an exposure component where patients revisit their traumatic experience by writing out a narrative description and reading the narrative to their therapist during sessions and to themselves between sessions. This aspect of therapy is now optional and can be incorporated into the protocol. All psychotherapies, including Cognitive Processing Therapy, are carried out on the foundation of a therapeutic alliance. The therapeutic alliance also referred to as the working alliance, refers to the quality of the relationship between the therapist and client, and is characterized by collaboration and agreement on task, goals, and approach to treatment (Norcross, 2011). A strong and positive therapeutic alliance between patients and their treating clinicians is positively correlated with treatment outcomes (Horvath & Luborsky, 1993).

Cognitive Processing Therapy can be delivered in various formats, including, individual, couple (i.e., Cognitive Behavioural Conjoint Therapy), and group formats. Group psychotherapy has many benefits. The curative factors of group psychotherapy are universality, imparting information, altruism, interpersonal learning, imitative behaviours, and group cohesiveness (Yalom & Leszez, 2005). Individuals who struggle with PTSD often have difficulties in relationships. Interpersonal difficulties in combination with avoidance behaviours that are characteristic of PTSD and can lead to social isolation. One of the apparent differences between individual and group Cognitive Processing Therapy is the presence of others during therapy sessions and the cohesion among them. Group cohesion is often considered a central therapeutic factor that contributes to beneficial effects of group therapy (Bernard et al., 2008). There is a relationship between group cohesion and positive outcomes in psychotherapy, as well as a relationship with group processes facilitating self-disclosure and a supportive, reflective environment for producing change (Tschuschke & Dies, 1994).

The theory behind Cognitive Processing Therapy is that avoidance behaviours and maladaptive beliefs act to precipitate and maintain the symptoms of PTSD and prevent natural recovery from the trauma (Resick, Monson, & Chard, 2017). Moreover, this trauma-focused psychotherapy encourages approaching the memory of a traumatic event, experiencing the associated emotions, learning cognitive restructuring skills to assist

Group Cognitive Processing Therapy for PTSD 435

patients in thinking about their traumatic experience in a balanced and flexible way. The goal is to accommodate the traumatic memory; this means that the traumatic memory is integrated in a balanced way with the person's previously held beliefs. Over-accommodated beliefs are common in individuals experiencing posttraumatic stress where the person rejecting all previously held beliefs and adopting new extreme and often generalized opinions about themselves, others, and the world (e.g., "No men can be trusted" or "the world is not safe"). In people who have experienced significant childhood adversity, this more recent traumatic event, may serve to confirm previously held over-accommodated beliefs. Another cognitive process common in PTSD occurs when the individual attempts change or to undo the event in some way to have it fit with previously held beliefs (e.g., just world belief). This often presents as a pre-occupation with ideas about how the negative outcome could have been prevented or changed. These assimilated thoughts can revolve around blaming themselves or others for the event (e.g., "If I had have been able to see the explosive device I would be able to prevent my friend from dying", "If I hadn't have gone to the party I would not have been assaulted"). Individuals with PTSD typically experience both assimilated and over-accommodated thoughts and both are related to symptoms of PTSD.

The Cognitive Processing Therapy model aligns with what we know about the neurobiology of PTSD; imaging studies show over-activation in the amygdala, which is one of the brain regions associated with emotion, and a suppression of the pre-frontal cortex (i.e., the area of the brain responsible to logical thought, planning, and other executive functions; Shin et al., 2004 & Henigsberg et al., 2019). This functional connectivity as well as changes in other brain regions has been shown consistently in neuroimaging studies on individuals effected by PTSD (Henigsberg et al., 2019). The Cognitive Processing Therapy model postulates that the cognitive restructuring skills taught in the treatment activates the pre-frontal cortex, which in turn can down regulate the amygdala, resulting in decreased emotional distress, even when the memory of the traumatic events is activated (Shin et al., 2004; Resick, Monson, & Chard, 2017).

Cognitive Processing Therapy delivered individually is effective for treating those who have experienced multiple potentially psychologically traumatic events and who have co-occurring conditions (Forbes et al., 2012; Kaysen et al., 2014; Roberts et al., 2015). Randomized clinical trials have demonstrated that Cognitive Processing Therapy it is effective in treating PTSD in individuals who have experienced different types of trauma such as interpersonal violence, child sexual abuse, and military and combat-related trauma (e.g., Chard & La Greca, 2005; Monson et al., 2006; Resick et al., 2008; Resick et al., 2002).

The therapeutic benefits of Cognitive Processing Therapy and other trauma-focused psychological interventions delivered to individuals appear to be sustained over time. For example, in a study involving 171 female civilian sexual assault survivors, of the 126 they were able to locate for long-term follow-up five and ten years posttreatment, more than 80% no longer met full-criteria for PTSD post-treatment with Cognitive Processing Therapy or Prolonged Exposure (Resick et al., 2012). A Randomized Controlled Trial of civilians with a history of childhood sexual abuse evidenced that 93% no longer met the criteria for PTSD post-treatment (Chard & La Greca, 2005). Another Randomized Controlled Trail of Cognitive Processing Therapy evidenced that 80.5% of female civilians who experienced sexual assault did not meet criteria for PTSD post-treatment (Resick et al., 2002). The results of Cognitive Processing Therapy trials in military populations suggest that combat-related PTSD may be more treatment-resistant. For example, results from one trial indicate only 40% of veterans with military-related PTSD no longer met criteria for PTSD after Cognitive Processing Therapy (Monson et al., 2006); accordingly, some researchers theorize military veterans report less symptom improvement due to greater severity of symptomatology, isolation from support and help when returning from a deployment, reduced ability to recognize improvement, and possible inaccuracies in symptom reports for purposes of secondary gain (e.g., disability benefits; Iribarren et al., 2005).

Cognitive Processing Therapy can be delivered to individually and in group formats (Resick. Wachen, et al., 2017); however, most research on Cognitive Processing Therapy effectiveness has focused on individual treatments. Several recent research studies have focused on Cognitive Processing Therapy delivered in group formats and the results have been mixed. In 2014, Morland and colleagues compared individual Cognitive Processing Therapy to group Cognitive Processing Therapy delivered to male veterans in rural settings over videoconferencing and found that both were equivalent and led to significant reductions in PTSD symptoms that were maintained at three- and six-month follow-up (Morland et al., 2014). Resick and colleagues (2015) also found evidence supporting group Cognitive Processing Therapy. They compared group Cognitive Processing Therapy to group Present-Centred Therapy (PCT) in active military personnel (Resick, 2015). Both interventions led to significant reductions in PTSD with group Cognitive Processing Therapy showing greater rates of improvement and added reductions in depressive symptoms as compared to Present-Centred Therapy.

One recent Randomized Clinical Trial revealed divergent findings favouring individual Cognitive Processing Therapy at reducing PTSD symptoms among 268 active military members diagnosed with PTSD (Resick, Wachen, et al., 2017). Cognitive Processing Therapy delivered to individuals and groups both produced to significant reductions in PTSD symptoms, but patients treated with individual Cognitive Processing Therapy improved more (i.e., large effect sizes for individual Cognitive Processing Therapy versus medium effect sizes for group). Patients receiving individual Cognitive Processing Therapy also improved more rapidly with change between pre-versus post-treatment being almost twice as large for individual versus group Cognitive Processing Therapy. Group and individual Cognitive Processing Therapy did not differ with respect to loss-of-diagnosis pre- versus post-treatment. The authors of this study speculated that group Cognitive Processing Therapy did not perform as well as individual formats because group members received less individual attention, less accountability for completing practice assignments, and no opportunity to make up for any sessions missed (Resick, Wachen, et al., 2017).

The Current Study

The current study was designed to expand upon group-based Cognitive Processing Therapy research literature for Canadian service populations (e.g., military and police) by examining the effectiveness of group-based Cognitive Processing Therapy with help-seeking members and veterans of the Canadian Armed Forces and Royal Canadian Mounted Police. The current study was also designed to examine the relationship between traditional symptom reduction outcomes in addition to process variables related to outcomes (e.g., group cohesion) for group-based Cognitive Processing Therapy. Consistent with previous researchers, we hypothesized that the group-based Cognitive Processing Therapy treatment would lead to reductions in symptoms of PTSD. We also hypothesized that significant reductions in depressive symptoms, generalized anxiety, and general distress would be observed. In addition to clinical outcomes, we were also interested in process outcomes of group Cognitive Processing Therapy. It was hypothesized that strong therapeutic alliances with group Cognitive Processing Therapy facilitators, group cohesion among Cognitive Processing Therapy group members, and participant self-reported satisfaction with the program, would be associated with decreases in reported psychological symptoms.

Participants were 36 serving and retired members of the Canadian Armed Forces and Royal Canadian Mounted Police who were seeking treatment at a Canadian Operational Stress Injury Clinic. An operational stress injury is a non-clinical term developed by the Canadian Military which refers to

> An operational stress injury (OSI) is any persistent psychological difficulty resulting from operational duties performed while serving in the Canadian Forces (CF) or as a member of the Royal Canadian Mounted Police (RCMP). It is used to describe a broad range of problems which include diagnosed medical conditions such as anxiety disorders, depression, and post-traumatic stress disorder (PTSD) as well as other conditions that may be less severe, but still interfere with daily functioning.
>
> (Minister of Veterans Affairs Canada, 2006)

Furthermore the cause of these injuries is thought to be related to psychological trauma, prolonged periods of high stress, or fatigue while serving

438 *Sarah J. Chaulk and David J. Podnar*

as a member of the military or federal police force. More recently this term has been adopted by other public safety personnel, such as front-line emergency first responders including police, firefighters, paramedics, correctional officers, and emergency dispatchers. When defining Operational Stress Injuries more broadly they are "any mental disorder or other mental health condition resulting from operational stressors experienced while serving in a professional capacity, especially in military or other public safety professions" (CIPSRT, 2019).

The Operational Stress Injury Clinics are a network of outpatient clinics in various locations across Canada that provide specialized mental health care to Canadians who have sustained psychological injury related to serving in the Canadian Armed Forces or Royal Canadian Mounted Police. Most Operational Stress Injury Clinics have inter-professional teams who offer a wide array of programs and services to clients. Each participant in the current study was receiving services from an Operational Stress Injury Clinic and had been diagnosed with PTSD or subclinical PTSD (i.e., other trauma-and-stressor related disorder) by a licensed psychologist or psychiatrist. To be diagnosed, participants had to report experiencing one or more potentially psychologically traumatic events, as defined by the Diagnostic and Statistical Manual of Mental Disorders (DSM-5; i.e., Criterion A; American Psychiatric Association [APA], 2013), as well as reporting symptoms consistent with diagnostic criteria for each of the four symptoms clusters of PTSD: intrusion, avoidance, arousal, and negative cognition and mood. Symptoms must have caused distress and impairment socially and/or occupationally. Each participant was proficient in reading and writing in English. Participants were mostly male (~80%), with a mean age of 45 years (range: 25–65; see Table 16.1). Ethnicity was fairly homogeneous (i.e., 75.7% Caucasian, 11% Indigenous, and 3% Black, and 8% Other). In terms of professional background, 75% were current or former members of the Canadian Armed Forces and 25% were current members or veterans of the Royal Canadian Mounted Police. Additional participant demographics (e.g., education, rank, length of service, etc.) are reported in Table 16.1. Exclusionary criteria included imminent risk of suicide or homicide, active psychosis or mania, cognitive impairment, or severe personality pathology at the time of the pretreatment meeting; however, no participants were excluded for these reasons. Some potential participants were excluded based on scheduling conflicts or their preference not to participate in group-based therapy. Co-occurring conditions such as Major Depressive Disorder, Substance Use Disorders, or anxiety-related disorders were not reasons for exclusion.

Several self-report symptom measures were utilized to monitor symptom change throughout treatment and at three-month follow-up (Table 16.2). The Posttraumatic Stress Disorder Checklist for DSM-5 (PCL-5) is a 20-item measure of symptoms of PTSD with four subscales which reflect the four symptom clusters in DSM-5 (i.e., intrusion, negative cognition and mood, avoidance, and arousal; Weathers et al., 2013). The PTSD Checklist for DSM-5 has shown high levels of reliability and validity (Bovin et al.,

Group Cognitive Processing Therapy for PTSD 439

Table 16.1 Demographic variables

Characteristics		n	%
Age M (SD)	45.4 years (10.46)	36	100
Range	25–65 years		
Sample		n	%
Military (Canadian Armed Forces)		27	72.9%
Royal Canadian Mounted Police		9	24.3%
Gender			%
Male		29	78.3%
Female		7	18.9%
Education		n	%
High school		20	54%
Apprenticeship or Trade		2	5.4%
College / CEGEP / Non-university		6	16.2%
University Diploma / Degree		6	16.2%
None		2	5.4%
Married/Common-law (%)		25	69.4%
Ethnicity		n	%
Caucasian		28	75.7
Aboriginal		4	10.8%
Black		1	2.7%
Other		3	8.1%
Years of Service		n	%
<5		1	2.7%
5–9		5	13.5%
10–14		7	18.9%
15–19		8	21.6%
20–24		4	10.8%
25–29		5	13.5%
30+		6	16.2%
Rank – Military		n	%
Private/Ordinary		0	0%
Jr. Non-Commission		13	35.1%
Sr. Non-Commission		11	2.9%
Jr. Officer		0	0%
Sr. Officer		3	8.1%
Rank – RCMP		n	%
Civilian		1	2.7%
Constable/Corporal		7	18.9%
Sr. Non-Commission		1	2.7%
Inspector/Superintendent		0	0%
Commissioner		0	0%
Other		0	0%
Status – Military		n	%
Active		14	51.9%
Retired		13	48.1%
Status – RCMP		n	%
Active		5	55.6%
Retired		4	44.4%

Note: DND = Department of National Defense; RCMP = Royal Canadian Mounted Police.

440 *Sarah J. Chaulk and David J. Podnar*

Table 16.2 Data collection schedule

	Pre-treatment	Mid-treatment	Post-treatment	Three-month follow-up
Questionnaires administered	PCL-5 PHQ-9 GAD-7 OQ-45 GCQ-S ASC SRS	PCL-5 PHQ-9 GAD-7 OQ-45 GCQ-S ASC SRS	PCL-5 PHQ-9 GAD-7 OQ-45 GCQ-S ASC SRS	PCL-5 PHQ-9 GAD-7 OQ-45

2016). The mean score at group intake was 51.28 (SD = 12.23). A score of 33 or above reflects clinically significant symptoms and distress related to posttraumatic stress. The more frequent and severe the symptoms reported by the participant, the higher the score on the scale up to a maximum value of 80 (Weathers et al., 2013). The Patient Health Questionnaire is a nine-item measure of depressive disorders (PHQ-9; Spitzer, Kroenke, & Williams, 1999) with good psychometric properties (Kroenke, Spitzer, & Williams, 2001). A score of 10 or higher on the PHQ-9 reflects clinically significant symptoms of depressive disorders (Manea, Gilbody, & McMillan, 2012), with a range of scores from 0 to 27. The Generalized Anxiety Disorder-7 scale is a 7-item measure of anxiety symptoms (Spitzer et al., 2006) with good reliability and validity (Rutter & Brown, 2017). A score of seven or above reflects significant symptoms of anxiety (Plummer et al., 2016), with a range of scores from 0 to 21. The Outcome Questionnaire-45 is a 45-item psychometrically sound questionnaire that measures distress on three subscales: symptom distress, social role, and interpersonal relations (OQ-45; Lambert et al., 1996). A cut-score of 63 on the Outcome Questionnaire-45 indicates symptoms of clinical significance. The possible range of scores on the Outcome Questionnaire-45 is 0 to 180.

The PTSD Checklist for DSM-5 was administered at the outset of each session. While this tool was not used for purposes of diagnosis or screening in the current study, it was used to monitor progress in therapy in individuals previously diagnosed with PTSD or subclinical PTSD. Participants were asked to fill out the PTSD Checklist for DSM-5 on the stressful event that is currently causing them the most distress and related to their PTSD symptoms. All other measures were administered at four time points: pre-, mid-, post-treatment and at three-month follow-up (see Table 16.2). At the time the data was analysed, only half of the participants had reached the three-month follow-up. Therefore, results presented here are based on the three-month follow-up data available for 20 of the participants. We received responses from 14 of the 20 potential participants, yielding a response rate of 70%.

Self-report questionnaires were also used to measure the process variables. The Assessment for Signal Client (ASC; Lambert et al., 1996) and

Group Climate Questionnaire (GCQ-S; MacKenzie & Tschuschke, 1993) were administered at pre-, mid-, and post-treatment to measure therapeutic alliance and group cohesion, respectively. Participants also completed the Session Rating Scale (SRS; Campbell & Hemsley, 2009) each session to measure working alliance and satisfaction, which has good reliability and validity (Duncan et al., 2003; see Table 16.2 for a detailed data collection schedule). The participants completed the pre- and mid-measures in the group setting at the outset of the first and seventh session, respectively. The post measures were completed at the end of the 12th session. All participants were encouraged to attend the 13th session (i.e., three-month follow-up) and complete the follow-up measures at the final session in the group setting; however, if participants were unable to attend the final session the measures were either completed online or returned by mail. For those participants not in attendance, the measures were completed either the same-day or up to two weeks after the 13th session.

The Cognitive Processing Therapy Group consisted of 12 weekly two-hour sessions and a 13th "booster" session. The first 12 sessions occurred weekly with a 13th session scheduled three months after the 12th session. The number of participants per group ranged from eight to a maximum of ten. Of the 36 participants, only one participant discontinued the treatment after attending five sessions. The participant's data was included in the overall data analysis, and there did not appear to be any significant differences between analyses with or without the inclusion of their data. Participants attended on average 10.42 (SD = 1.65) sessions with a range of attendance from five to 12 sessions, and the modal number of sessions attended was 12.

Each therapy session was facilitated by two doctoral-level registered psychologists. Each psychologist has been trained in the delivery of Cognitive Processing Therapy. Each group therapist adhered to the manualized treatment protocol for Cognitive Processing Therapy: Veteran/Military Version, Therapist's Group Manual (Chard et al., 2009). This version included two sessions focused on the completion of a written Trauma Account. Several aspects in the administration of group-based Cognitive Processing Therapy. In this study appear unique when compared to previous studies. They include: routine offerings of individual intake sessions to screen for group which allow the participant the choice to participate in group or individual therapy, we offer make-up sessions to participants who missed sessions (primarily by phone, but also individual in-person sessions). We also provided weekly written individualized feedback on all homework assignments submitted by the participants.

Is Group-based Cognitive Processing Therapy Effective in Routine Clinical Practice?

Participants receiving the group intervention rated their symptoms as less severe over the course of the therapy. Table 16.3 contains the means and

442 *Sarah J. Chaulk and David J. Podnar*

Table 16.3 Means and standard deviations for the primary symptom variables (PCL-5, PHQ-9, GAD-7, and OQ-45) at pre-, post-, and three-month follow-up

	Pre-treatment [a]		Post-treatment [a]		Three-month Follow-up [b]	
	M	SD	M	SD	M	SD
PCL-5	51.28	13.28	40.98	15.38	35.57	8.56
PHQ-9	15.92	5.55	12.85	5.77	11.36	4.31
GAD-7	13.68	4.97	10.99	4.89	9.36	3.1
OQ-45	97.28	22.42	88.86	22.15	81.82	17.12

Notes:
a $n = 36$.
b $n = 14$.

standard deviations for each psychopathology outcome measure from pre- to post-treatment and at three-month follow-up. The greatest reductions in symptoms were noted for participant responses to questionnaires regarding PTSD at post-treatment and three-month follow-up. While symptoms of PTSD showed the largest change, statistically significant decreases were reported in symptoms across all symptom measures at post-treatment and three-month follow-up, with effect sizes exceeding Cohen's (1988) conventions. Participants reported a ten-point reduction on the Posttraumatic Disorder Checklist for DSM-5, $t(36) = 4.51$, $p < .001$, $d = .72$, which is a clinically significant reduction with a medium effect size (Weathers et al., 2013). Participant responses on the General Anxiety Disorder-7 also showed a mean reduction of three points from pre-treatment to post-treatment, $t(36) = 4.01$, $p < .001$, $d = .54$, with a medium effect size, although a change in three points does not reflect a clinically significant change (Touissaint et al., 2020). Mean participant responses on the Patient Health Questionnaire-9 decreased by three points from pre-treatment to post-treatment, $t(36) = 4.01$, $p < .001$, $d = .54$; this is statistically significant and shows a medium effect size. Participant responses on the Outcome Questionnare-45 also reflected a reliable reduction from pre-treatment to post-treatment, $t(36) = 3.27$, $p < .01$, $d = .38$; there is a statistically significant difference with a small effect size. Accordingly, compared to pre-treatment, Cognitive Processing Therapy group members experienced fewer PTSD, depressive, generalized anxiety, and general distress symptoms post-treatment.

At three-month follow-up the effect sizes increased in magnitude. All symptom measures showed further reductions at three-month follow-up. Most notably, on average participants reported a 16-point reduction on the PTSD checklist for DSM-5. Large effect sizes were found for self-reported PTSD symptoms ($g_{av} = 1.44$), depression symptoms ($g_{av} = .90$) and generalized anxiety symptoms ($g_{av} = 1.08$). Finally, at three-month follow-up a medium effect size was found for self-reported reductions in general distress ($g_{av} = .78$). As a reminder these follow-up data are based on few participants and should be interpreted with caution.

Group Cognitive Processing Therapy for PTSD 443

Were Reductions in Psychological Symptoms of Distress Related to Group Cohesion and Therapeutic Alliance?

Correlations were calculated between primary symptom measures (i.e., PTSD Checklist for DSM-5, Patient Health Questionnaire-9, Generalized Anxiety Disorder-7 and Outcome Questionnaire-45) and three process-related variables: (1) group cohesion as measured by the engaged subscale of the Group Climate Questionnaire (see Figure 16.1); (2) therapeutic alliance, as measured by the therapeutic alliance subscale of the Alert Signal Client Questionnaire (see Figure 16.2), and (3) participant satisfaction as measures by the Session Rating Scale. Participants ratings on the Engaged subscale of the Group Climate Questionnaire increased by mid-treatment as compared to pre-treatment and continued to increase at post-treatment. In contrast participants ratings on the Avoiding and Conflict subscales decreased from pre- to post-treatment. This reflects a decreasing level of negativity towards other group members over the course of the therapy and an increasing level of responsibility for group work among group members. Participant ratings of therapeutic alliance also increased from pre- to mid-treatment and from mid- to post-treatment. Participant satisfaction also increased steadily over the course of the intervention (see Figure 16.3) correlations were calculated for post-treatment data there were no statistically significant relationships between satisfaction and symptom reduction outcomes. Furthermore, analyses yielded no significant correlations, indicating that while strong cohesive relationships within

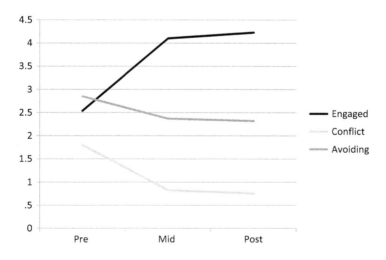

Figure 16.1 Participant mean ratings on the group climate questionnaire on the subscales of engaged, conflict, and avoiding at pre-, mid-, and post-treatment.

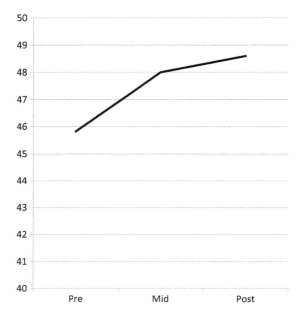

Figure 16.2 Participant mean scores on Therapeutic Alliance subscale of the Alert Signal Client questionnaire at pre-, mid-, and post-treatment.

the group and alliances with therapists were formed, these relationships were not associated with symptom scores at the end of treatment.

Discussion of Preliminary Results, Lessons Learned, and Plans for Future Research

Given the available body of literature supporting Cognitive Processing Therapy as an effective intervention for PTSD, we hypothesized that group-based Cognitive Processing Therapy would lead to reductions in symptoms of PTSD, symptoms of depression and generalized anxiety, and general distress. Our primary hypothesis was supported. Group-based Cognitive Processing Therapy appeared effective for reducing symptoms of PTSD, depression, generalized anxiety, and general distress. Small to medium effect sizes were noted across symptom domains between pre- and post-treatment. The greatest symptom reductions were noted for PTSD, which was expected given the specific intervention targets. In sum, the results suggest that participants reported experiencing less severe symptoms of PTSD, depression, generalized anxiety, and general distress at the termination of the intervention relative to the outset. The results are consistent with previous research results, further supporting that psychotherapeutic interventions are typically as effective in routine clinical practice as in

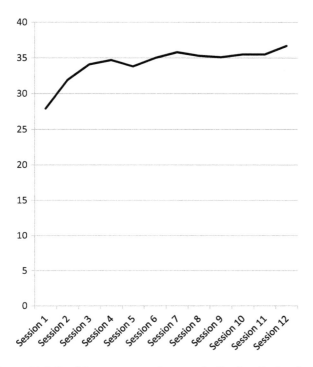

Figure 16.3 Participant mean ratings on the Session Rating Scale by session.

clinical trials (Minami & Wampold, 2008; Wales, Palmer, & Fairburn, 2009). Conversely, the magnitude of the therapeutic gains were not as significant as those seen with higher internal consistency (Resick et al., 2002). At post-treatment, our effect sizes were medium in contrast to large effect sizes noted in randomized controlled trials.

The observed reductions in symptoms of depression are consistent with the previous literature (e.g., Forbes et al., 2012) where Cognitive Processing Therapy is shown to reduce both symptoms of PTSD and depression. Participants also reported less general distress and generalized anxiety at the end of therapy, which is promising. Group Cognitive Processing Therapy appears to be effective in reducing not only symptoms of PTSD, but may more holistically reduce psychological distress in general. The overall decrease in general distress is noteworthy given that individuals with PTSD often have co-occurring conditions and/or psychological difficulties.

Results from the three-month follow-up are only available for a limited number of participants and should be interpreted with caution. Consistent with previous research (Abbass, Kisely, & Kroenke, 2006; Resick et al., 2012), the preliminary results show that positive treatment effects were sustained at three-month follow-up across all measures of psychopathology. Symptoms of PTSD showed a further reduction from post-treatment to three-month follow-up. Most longitudinal studies have found that treatment gains, such as symptom reduction, are sustained at follow-up (Resick et al., 2012).

In the current study measures of group cohesion reflected strong cohesion within groups, which has been an important agent of change in group psychotherapy (Yalom & Leszcz, 2005). We found that from mid-treatment onwards, group members shared positive regard for one another, valued participation in the group, and revealed personal information with other group members. Furthermore, participants reported low levels of negativity towards other group members throughout the intervention and participants indicated only minimal avoidance of the personal responsibility of group work; avoidance decreased over time, indicating that participants did not exclusively depend on group leaders for direction and they did not avoid important interpersonal issues. In contrast to our hypothesis, participants who reported higher levels of group cohesion did not report lower levels of psychological symptoms compared to those who reported more modest levels of group cohesion. That is, group cohesion did not appear to be related to treatment outcomes.

Participants reported positive therapeutic alliance at mid- and post-treatment, with the score increasing in a linear fashion from pre- to post-treatment. Despite the high reported levels of therapeutic alliance, there was no statistically significant correlation between therapeutic alliance and symptom reduction measured at the end of treatment. Our results contrast previous evidence regarding therapeutic alliance and effectiveness of psychotherapy (e.g., Lambert & Barley, 2001; Norcross, 2011), which has indicated most change can be attributed to a good working alliance between patients and therapists.

Participants' ratings of overall levels of satisfaction with sessions increased over the course of the treatment, suggesting that participants were very satisfied with the treatment they were receiving on the basis of the bond with therapists and the tasks and goals of the therapy, as reflected on the Session Rating Scale. There was no statistically significant correlation between participants' self-reported levels of satisfaction with sessions and post-treatment psychological symptoms. Our results are in contrast with research showing that explicitly asking clients for feedback can help make therapy more effective (Lambert & Shimokawa, 2011; Miller et al., 2006).

We expected that high ratings of therapeutic alliance, group cohesion, and participant satisfaction would be associated with decreases in reported psychological symptoms. Participants did report high ratings of therapeutic alliance, group cohesion, and satisfaction, but there were no significant correlations between therapeutic alliance, group cohesion, or satisfaction and symptom reduction. Therefore, the secondary hypotheses in this study were not supported, for which there are several possible explanations. First, the current study examined preliminary results with a small sample of 36 participants. The small sample size may preclude any observable effects of high rates of group cohesion on symptom reduction. The observed treatment effects may become more robust as more data is collected. Second, participants reported reductions in symptoms of PTSD and, while this is clinically and statistically significant, the pre-treatment mean score was only moderately elevated and may have resulted in insufficient variance in scores to be sensitive to correlational testing. Third, it is possible that individual differences may be responsible for symptom improvements. Cognitive Processing Therapy groups differ from some other psychotherapy groups because of the high levels of structure with progress relying heavily on individual members completing practice assignments between sessions and/or integrating skills into their everyday life. Individual effort and engagement with exercises that change thinking patterns may be more responsible for symptom change than group processes. Fourth, by examining Cognitive Processing Therapy effectiveness within a routine clinical practice, several confounding variables and extra-therapeutic factors could not be controlled for. For example, we did not control for individuals with varied treatment histories (e.g., previous participation in PTSD treatment) and/or participants receiving concurrent interventions (e.g., psychological, marital, psychopharmacological). External life events such as medical problems, family stress, or new relationships could have occurred throughout the duration of the treatment and affected the results. The confounding variables complicate efforts to discern what has accounted for the change in symptoms, particularly given that group process variables were not statistically significantly related to symptom reductions. Despite this, best efforts are made in clinical practice to appropriately time psychological and psychopharmacological interventions in the best interest of the participants; often limitations of the programs and resources and/or other extra-therapeutic life events preclude the level of control and internal validity attained in some experimental studies.

The current study was designed to examine the effectiveness, that is real-world application not the efficacy or application under ideal circumstances, of Group Cognitive Processing Therapy. We were interested in evaluating outcomes in the context of the above noted extraneous variables, with little exclusion of potential participants. In that case Group Cognitive Processing Therapy appears to be effective as delivered in a routine clinical setting. As noted above, doing so prevents us from drawing conclusions regarding what accounted for the observed changes. The inability to draw conclusions regarding observed outcomes is a limitation, but that limitation also reflects the reality in most outpatient treatment settings, arguably increasing ecological validity. We were able to examine the effectiveness of the treatment with a great deal of external validity, to see that despite the variability in treatment history and concurrent treatment, on average, participants report clinically significant reductions in symptoms after participating in Group Cognitive Processing Therapy. Our results reflect the overall quality of Cognitive Processing Therapy in a group format, as it was delivered in a realistic clinical setting.

Individual versus Group Cognitive Processing Therapy

Some studies comparing group and individual Cognitive Processing Therapy have found that Cognitive Processing Therapy delivered to individuals produces equivalent effects as compared to the therapy delivered in group format (Morland et al., 2014) and one study has found that individual therapy produced larger effects (Resick, Wachen, et al., 2017). It has been postulated that the larger effects in previous studies may be due to lack of screening potential participants for suitability for group delivered treatments, absence of make-up sessions, and less individually tailored treatment (Resick, Wachen, et al., 2017). The current study did not directly compare group and individual Cognitive Processing Therapy delivery modes; nevertheless, we completed individual intakes for the group treatment that also had the aim of increasing motivation for treatment (including client preference of group or individual cognitive processing therapy). To further elaborate on the intake process, all potential group members participated in a one-hour individual intake session assessing for inclusionary criteria, symptom levels, identification of a suitable traumatic event(s) to be targeted in therapy, and apparent motivation and readiness for group therapy. We employed motivational interviewing strategies by reminding participants that participation in the group is completely optional, we emphasized several potential costs and benefits associated with the group participation (e.g., intensive assignment work, ability to learn from others with lived experience of posttraumatic stress) as well as eliciting their perceived benefits of participation. Therefore participants all begin the group with clear expectations and understanding of the program. Lastly, we asked participants to explicitly identify reasons for working on their symptoms of posttraumatic stress (e.g., "How important is it for you to make these changes and why?"). Accordingly, our participants may have been more motivated and engaged than previous group participants reported in the literature. The intake process was designed to prepare participants and ensure favourable group composition based on intrinsic motivation. We also routinely offered individual make-up sessions for missed group sessions and provided individualized feedback to each participant on all submitted out-of-session assignments. The differences in administration of the therapy may explain why we observed clinically significant decreases in symptoms post-treatment with small to medium magnitudes. Our groups also demonstrated a lower drop-out rate and high attendance to sessions, whereby one participant dropped out and most participants attended all sessions. This is possibly attributable to the above-mentioned differences in administration of the group-based Cognitive Processing Therapy. This is particularly important to highlight given that rates of dropout from trauma-focused psychotherapies is higher than in other psychological treatment and there have been wide range of estimates in the literature of mean dropout rates from 16 to 36% (Szafranski et al., 2017; Lewis et al., 2020).

Limitations

There are limitations that also provide directions for future study. Despite the low drop-out rate and high attendance, there was substantial variability in engagement within the treatment sessions as well as for time invested in completing practice assignments between sessions. Therefore, it would be useful to examine whether treatment engagement (i.e., attendance, participation, homework completion, motivation) is related to therapeutic improvements as well. We also focused most outcome measurements on symptom reduction, which is important given that reduction in psychopathology is a central focus of intervention; however, quality of life and impairments in functioning for important domains may be useful as treatment outcomes. Some individuals may continue to experience clinically significant symptoms while noticing improvement in other areas (e.g., occupational functioning).

Currently, we cannot comment on the diagnostic status of participants' pre/post treatment because semi-structured interviews were not used routinely during the assessment process. Semi-structured interviews, such as the Clinician-Administered PTSD Scale for Diagnostic Statistical Manual-5 (CAPS-5; Weathers et al., 2013), would allow us to comment on what proportion of individuals would no longer meet diagnostic threshold for PTSD following the therapy. Such information is more valid and reliable than self-report data alone, would provide more information regarding the magnitude of improvements, and would allow for more direct comparisons to the previous research.

The sample included individuals who have a diagnosis of full threshold PTSD and those diagnosed with subthreshold PTSD; there was also quite a lot of variability in self-report measures of PTSD symptom severity at the outset of the Cognitive Processing Therapy intervention. While Cognitive Processing Therapy appears effective for treating subthreshold PTSD (Dickstein et al., 2013), perhaps treatment effects would have been more robust if the sample only included those meeting full threshold for diagnosis of PTSD. The subset of individuals experiencing significant distress and/or functional impartment due to subthreshold PTSD is large and our results add further support for the effectiveness of Cognitive Processing Therapy for subthreshold presentations.

Finally, our study did not include a control group or compare treatment delivery modes directly. Therefore, we are unable to comment on the potential superiority of Cognitive Processing Therapy relative to other psychotherapies or trauma-focused treatments. Again, the study was designed to bridge the gap between science and clinical practice. Our results support group-based Cognitive Processing Therapy is effective at reducing symptoms of PTSD and other associated psychopathologies. There are other trauma-focused psychotherapies (e.g., prolonged exposure, eye movement desensitization and reprocessing therapy) that have a good base of evidence to support their efficacy and there is mounting evidence for non-trauma-focused psychotherapies (e.g., mindfulness-based strategies; Hopwood & Schutte, 2017). Examining the effectiveness of various therapies with an active control condition in routine practice would also provide important information for using Group Cognitive Processing Therapy in practice.

Conclusion

Considering the prevalence of PTSD worldwide, and especially in military members and police officers (and other public safety personnel; i.e., correctional workers, firefighters, paramedics), empirically validating several treatment options that are able to be tailored to the particular needs of participants is warranted and necessary. The common factors, such as therapeutic alliance of psychotherapy, can account for many observed treatment gains relative to specific therapy ingredients (Norcross, 2002). In general, trauma-focused psychotherapy has a large amount of evidence supporting its effectiveness and appears superior to non-trauma-focused psychotherapies for treating PTSD. Having multiple options for effective trauma-focused or non-trauma-focused treatments provides therapists and participants with additional flexibility to choose a treatment that is best suited to the participants' current strengths, needs, abilities, and preferences in a variety of formats (i.e., individual, group, couple).

Group-based interventions are generally more cost-effective than those delivered individually or in dyads. The support for Group Cognitive Processing Therapy has implications in cost-effectiveness in our healthcare systems. Group psychotherapy is beneficial in health care based on cost-effectiveness and reduced wait-times for services. It also provided a good option for a stepped care model of service delivery that allows for increased intensity of intervention as required to assist individuals in their recovery from Operational Stress Injuries. Having effective treatments available to service members has the potential to reduce time off work due to Operational Stress Injuries and potentially reduce the attrition from military and police forces after experiencing potentially psychologically traumatic events and psychological injury (Hoge et al., 2006). Moreover, the external validity of our results allows for further generalizability to outpatient clinics and treatment centres that are using Group Cognitive Processing Therapy in routine clinical care.

When Group Cognitive Processing Therapy is being delivered in group format, we have several recommendations: (1) screening penitential participants for suitability based on group composition; (2) providing participants the choice of individual or group therapy if possible; (3) offering make-up sessions for missed materials; and (4) providing individualized feedback on out-of-session assignments. These modifications may help improve outcomes and reduce dropout rates. Despite numerous potential confounding factors, which are often present in clinical settings, the current study supports that group Cognitive Processing Therapy delivered

Group Cognitive Processing Therapy for PTSD   451

in routine clinical practice may be effective in helping people who are impacted by PTSD.

In conclusion, Group Cognitive Processing Therapy appears effective in treating symptoms of PTSD and associated symptoms in the context of routine practice. The effects of Group Cognitive Processing Therapy were sustained after the termination of treatment. We hypothesized that the effects of Cognitive Processing Therapy in a group format would be enhanced through social and peer support; however our results did not support Cognitive Processing Therapy as providing enhanced benefits. Replication of results with larger samples is necessary.

References

Abbass, A., Kisely, S., & Kroenke, K. (2006). Short-term psychodynamic psycho-therapy for somatic disorders: Systematic review and meta-analysis of clinical trials. *Psychotherapy and Psychosomatics, 78*, 265–274.

American Psychiatric Association (APA). (2013). *Diagnostic and statistical manual of mental disorders* (5th edn). Washington, DC: American Psychiatric Association.

Atwoli, L., Stein, D. J., Koenen, K. C., & McLaughlin, K. A. (2015). Epidemiology of posttraumatic stress disorder: Prevalence, correlates and consequences. *Current Opinion in Psychiatry, 28*(4), 307.

Bernard, H., Burlingame, G., Flores, P., Greene, L., Joyce, A., Kobos, J., ... Feirman, D. (2008). Clinical practice guidelines for group psychotherapy. *International Journal of Group Psychotherapy, 58*(4), 455–542.

Bertenthal, D., Miner, C., Sen, S., & Marmar, C. (2007). Bringing the war back home: Mental health disorders among 103,788 United States veterans returning from Iraq and Afghanistan seen at Department of Veterans Affairs facilities. *Archives of Internal Medicine, 167*(5), 476–482.

Bovin, M. J., Marx, B. P., Weathers, F. W., Gallagher, M. W., Rodriguez, P., Schnurr, P. P., & Keane, T. M. (2016). Psychometric properties of the PTSD checklist for Diagnostic and Statistical Manual of Mental Disorders – 5th edition (PCL-5) in veterans. *Psychological Assessment, 28*(11), 1379–1391.

Breslau, N. (2009). The epidemiology of trauma, PTSD, and other posttrauma disorders. *Trauma, Violence, & Abuse, 10*(3), 198–210. https://doi.org/10.1177/15248380 09334448

Brewin, C., Andrews, B., Valentine, J., & Kendall, P. C. (2000). Meta-analysis of risk factors for posttraumatic stress disorder in trauma-exposed adults. *Journal of Consulting and Clinical Psychology, 68*(5), 748–766.

Canadian Institute for Public Safety Research and Treatment (CIPSRT). (2019). *Glossary of terms: A shared understanding of the common terms used to describe psychological trauma (version 2.0)*. Regina, SK: Author.

Campbell, A., & Hemsley, S. (2009). Outcome rating scale and session rating scale in psychological practice: Clinical utility of ultra-brief measures. *Clinical Psychologist, 13*(1), 1–9.

Carleton, R. N., Afifi, T. O., Taillieu, T., Turner, S., Krakauer, R., Anderson, G. S., MacPhee, R. S., Ricciardelli, R., Cramm, H. A., Groll, D., & McCreary, D. (2019). Exposures to potentially traumatic events among public safety per-sonnel in Canada. *Canadian Journal of Behavioural Science, 51*, 37–52. https://doi.org/10.1037/cbs0000115.

452 *Sarah J. Chaulk and David J. Podnar*

Carleton, R. N., Afifi, T. O., Turner, S., Taillieu, T., Duranceau, S., LeBouthillier, D. M., ... & Hozempa, K. (2018). Mental disorder symptoms among public safety personnel in Canada. *The Canadian Journal of Psychiatry, 63*(1), 54–64.

Chard, K., & La Greca, A. M. (2005). An evaluation of for the treatment of post-traumatic stress disorder related to childhood sexual abuse. *Journal of Consulting and Clinical Psychology, 73*(5), 965–971.

Chard, K. M., Resick, P. A., Monson, C. M., & Kattar, K. (2009). *Cognitive processing therapy therapist group manual: Veteran/military version.* Washington, DC: Department of Veterans Affairs.

Chen, Y.-R., Hung, K.-W., Tsai, J.-C., Chu, H., Chung, M.-H., Chen, S.-R., Liao, Y.-M., Ou, K.-L., Chang, Y.-C., & Chou, K.-R. (2014). Efficacy of Eye-Movement Desensitization and Reprocessing for patients with posttraumatic-stress disorder: A meta-analysis of randomized controlled trials. *PLoS One, 9*(8), e103676. https://doi.org/10.1371/journal.pone.0103676

Cohen, J. (1988). *Statistical power analysis for the behavioral sciences* (2nd edn). Hillsdale, NJ: Erlbaum Associates.

Duncan, B. L., Miller, S. D., Sparks, J. A., Claud, D. A., Reynolds, L. R., Brown, J., Johnson, L. D. (2003). The Session Rating Scale: Preliminary psychometric properties of a "working" alliance measure. *Journal of Brief Therapy, 3*(1), 3–12.

Dickstein, B. D., Walter, K. H., Schumm, J. A., & Chard, K. M. (2013). Comparing response to cognitive processing therapy in military veterans with subthreshold and threshold posttraumatic stress disorder. *Journal of Traumatic Stress, 26*(6), 703–709. https://doi.org/10.1002/jts.21869

Foa, E. B. (2019). *Prolonged exposure therapy for PTSD: Emotional processing of traumatic experiences. Therapist guide* (2nd edn). New York: Oxford University Press.

Forbes, D., Lloyd, D., Nixon, R. D.V., Elliott, P., Varker, T., Perry, D., ... Creamer, M. (2012). A multisite randomized controlled effectiveness trial of cognitive processing therapy for military-related posttraumatic stress disorder. *Journal of Anxiety Disorders, 26*(3), 442–452.

Ford, J. D., Grasso, D. J., Greene, C. A., Slivinsky, M., & Deviva, J. C. (2018). Randomized clinical trial pilot study of prolonged exposure versus present centred affect regulation therapy for PTSD and anger problems with male military combat veterans. *Clinical Psychology & Psychotherapy, 25*(5), 641–649. https://doi.org/10.1002/cpp.2194

Ginzburg, K., Ein-Dorb, T., & Solomona, Z. (2010). Comorbidity of posttraumatic stress disorder, anxiety and depression: A 20-year longitudinal study of war veterans. *Journal of Affective Disorders, 123*(1–3), 249–257.

Haagen, J. F. G., Smid, G. E., Knipscheer, J. W., & Kleber, R. J. (2015). The efficacy of recommended treatments for veterans with PTSD: A metaregression analysis. *Clinical Psychology Review, 40*, 184–194.

Henigsberg, N., Kalember, P., Petrović, Z. K., & Šečić, A. (2019). Neuroimaging research in posttraumatic stress disorder – Focus on amygdala, hippocampus and prefrontal cortex. *Progress in Neuro-Psychopharmacology and Biological Psychiatry, 90*, 37–42. https://doi.org/10.1016/j.pnpbp.2018.11.003

Hidalgo, R., & Davidson, J. (2000). Posttraumatic stress disorder: Epidemiology and health-related considerations. *The Journal of Clinical Psychiatry, 61*, 5–13.

Hoge, C. W., Auchterlonie, J. L., & Milliken, C. S. (2006). Mental health problems, use of mental health services, and attrition from military service after returning from deployment to Iraq or Afghanistan. *JAMA, 295*(9), 1023–1032.

Group Cognitive Processing Therapy for PTSD 453

Hoge, C. W., Castro, C. A., Messer, S. C., McGurk, D., Cotting, D. I., & Koffman, R. L. (2004). Combat duty in Iraq and Afghanistan, mental health problems, and barriers to care. *The New England Journal of Medicine, 351*(1), 13–22.

Hopwood, T. L., & Schutte, N. S. (2017). A meta-analytic investigation of the impact of mindfulness-based interventions on post-traumatic stress. *Clinical Psychology Review, 57,* 12–20.

Horvath, A. O., & Luborsky, L. (1993). The role of the therapeutic alliance in psychotherapy. *Journal of Consulting and Clinical Psychology, 61*(4), 561–573.

Hotopf, M., Hull, L., Fear, N. T., Browne, T., Horn, O., Iversen, A., ... Wessely, S. (2006). The health of UK military personnel who deployed to the 2003 Iraq war: A cohort study. *The Lancet, 367*(9524), 1731–1741.

Iribarren, J., Prolo, P., Neagos, N., & Chiappelli, F. (2005). Post-traumatic stress disorder: evidence-based research for the third millennium. *Evidence-Based Complementary and Alternative Medicine, 2*(4), 503–512. https://doi.org/10.1093/ecam/neh127

James, L. M., Van Kampen, E., Miller, R. D., & Engdahl, B. E. (2013). Risk and protective factors associated with symptoms of post-traumatic stress, depression, and alcohol misuse in OEF/OIF veterans. *Military Medicine, 178*(2), 159–165.

Kang, H., Dalager, N., Mahan, C., & Ishii, E. (2005). The role of sexual assault on the risk of PTSD among gulf war veterans. *Annals of Epidemiology, 15*(3), 191–195.

Kaysen, D., Schumm, J., Pedersen, E. R., Seim, R. W., Bedard-Gilligan, M., & Chard, K. (2014). Cognitive processing therapy for veterans with comorbid PTSD and alcohol use disorders. *Addictive Behaviors, 39*(2), 420–427.

Keane, T. M., & Kaloupek, D. G. (1997). Comorbid psychiatric disorders in PTSD. *Annals of the New York Academy of Sciences, 821*(1), 24–34.

Keane, T. M., & Wolfe, J. (1990). Comorbidity in post-traumatic stress disorder an analysis of community and clinical studies 1. *Journal of Applied Social Psychology, 20*(21), 1776–1788.

Kessler, R. C., Berglund, P. A., Demler, O., Jin, R., Merikangas, K. R., & Walters, E. E. (2005). Lifetime prevalence and age-of-onset distributions of DSM-IV disorders in the National Comorbidity Survey Replication. *Archives of General Psychiatry, 62*(6), 593–602.

Kessler, R., Sonnega, A., Bromet, E., Hughes, M., & Nelson, C. (1995). Post-traumatic stress disorder in the national comorbidity survey. *Archives of General Psychiatry, 52*(12), 1048. https://doi.org/10.1001/archpsyc.1995.03950240066012

Kroenke, K., Spitzer, R. L., & Williams, J. B. (2001). The PHQ-9: Validity of a brief depression severity measure. *Journal of General Internal Medicine, 16,* 606–613.

Lambert, M. J., & Barley, D. E. (2001). Research summary on the therapeutic relationship and psychotherapy outcome. *Psychotherapy: Theory, Research, Practice, Training, 38*(4), 357–361. https://doi.org/10.1037/0033-3204.38.4.357

Lambert, M. J., Burlingame, G. M., Umphress, V., Hansen, N. B., Vermeersch, D. A., Clouse, G. C., & Yanchar, S. C. (1996). The reliability and validity of the outcome questionnaire. *Clinical Psychology & Psychotherapy, 3*(4), 249–258.

Lambert, M. J., & Shimokawa, K. (2011). Collecting client feedback. *Psychotherapy, 48,* 72–79.

Lancaster, C. L., Teeters, J. B., Gros, D. F., Back, S. E., Lambkin, F. K., & Barrett, E. (2016). Posttraumatic stress disorder: Overview of evidence-based assessment and treatment. *Journal of Clinical Medicine, 5*(11), 105.

Lewis, C., Roberts, N. P., Gibson, S., & Bisson, J. I. (2020). Dropout from psychological therapies for post-traumatic stress disorder (PTSD) in adults: Systematic review and meta-analysis. *European Journal of Psychotraumatology*, *11*(1), 1709709. https://doi.org/10.1080/20008198.2019.1709709

Mackenzie, K. R., & Tschuschke, V. (1993). The group relationship questionnaire. Unpublished manuscript.

Manea, L., Gilbody, S., & McMillan, D. (2012). Optimal cut-off score for diagnosing depression with the Patient Health Questionnaire (PHQ-9): A meta-analysis. *Canadian Medical Association. Journal*, *184*(3), E191–196.

Markowitz, J. C., Petkova, E., Neria, Y., Van Meter, P. E., Zhao, Y., Hembree, E., ... Marshall, R. D. (2015). Is exposure necessary? A randomized clinical trial of interpersonal psychotherapy for PTSD. *American Journal of Psychiatry*, *172*(5), 430–440. https://doi.org/10.1176/appi.ajp.2014.14070908

McCann, I., & Pearlman, L. (1990). Vicarious traumatization: A framework for understanding the psychological effects of working with victims. *Journal of Traumatic Stress*, *3*(1), 131–149.

Miller, S. D., Duncan, B. L., Brown, J., Sorrell, R., & Chalk, M. B. (2006). Using formal client feedback to improve retention and outcome: Making ongoing, real time assessment feasible. *Journal of Brief Therapy*, *5*, 5–22.

Minami, T., & Wampold, B. E. (2008). Adult psychotherapy in the real world. In W. B. Walsh (ed.), *Biennial review of counseling psychology: Volume 1* (pp. 27–45). New York: Routledge.

Monson, C., Schnurr, P., Resick, P., Friedman, M., Young-Xu, Y., Stevens, S., & La Greca, A. M. (2006). Cognitive processing therapy for veterans with military-related posttraumatic stress disorder. *Journal of Consulting and Clinical Psychology*, *74*(5), 898–907.

Morland, L., Mackintosh, M., Greene, C., Rosen, C., Chard, K., Resick, P., & Frueh, B. (2014). Cognitive processing therapy for posttraumatic stress disorder delivered to rural veterans via telemental health: A randomized noninferiority clinical trial. *The Journal of Clinical Psychiatry*, *75*(5), 470–476.

Nidich, S., Mills, P. J., Rainforth, M., Heppner, P., Schneider, R. H., Rosenthal, N. E., ... Rutledge, T. (2018). Non-trauma-focused meditation versus exposure therapy in veterans with post-traumatic stress disorder: A randomised controlled trial. *The Lancet Psychiatry*, *5*(12), 975–986. https://doi.org/10.1016/S2215-0366(18)30384-5

Norcross, J. C. (2002). *Psychotherapy relationships that work : Therapist contributions and responsiveness to patients.* Oxford and New York: Oxford University Press.

Norcross, J. C. (ed.). (2011). *Psychotherapy relationships that work: Evidence-based responsiveness* (2nd edn). New York: Oxford University Press.

Pearson, C., Zamorski, M. & Janz, T. (2014). *Mental health of the Canadian Armed Forces: Health at a glance.* Statistics Canada Catalogue No. 82-624-X. Retrieved from www.statcan.gc.ca/pub/82-624-x/2014001/article/14121-eng.htm

Perkonigg, A., Kessler, R. C., Storz, S., & Wittchen, H. U. (2000). Traumatic events and post-traumatic stress disorder in the community: Prevalence, risk factors and comorbidity. *Acta psychiatrica scandinavica*, *101*(1), 46–59.

Plummer, F., Manea, L., Trepel, D., & McMillan, D. (2016). Screening for anxiety disorders with the GAD-7 and GAD-2: A systematic review and diagnostic meta-analysis. *General Hospital Psychiatry*, *39*, 24–31.

Resick, P. A., Galovski, T., Uhlmansiek, M., Scher, C., Clum, G., Young-Xu, Y., & La Greca, A. M. (2008). A randomized clinical trial to dismantle components of cognitive processing therapy for posttraumatic stress disorder in female victims of interpersonal violence. *Journal of Consulting and Clinical Psychology, 76*(2), 243–258.

Resick, P. A., Monson, C. M., & Chard, K. M. (2017). *Cognitive processing therapy for PTSD: A comprehensive manual.* New York: Guilford Publications Inc.

Resick, P. A., Nishith, P., Weaver, T. L., Astin, M. C., Feuer, C. A., & Kendall, P. C. (2002). A comparison of cognitive-processing therapy with prolonged exposure and a waiting condition for the treatment of chronic posttraumatic stress disorder in female rape victims. *Journal of Consulting and Clinical Psychology, 70*(4), 867–879.

Resick, P. A., Wachen, J. S., Dondanville, K. A., Pruiksma, K. E., Yarvis, J. S., Peterson, A. L., Mintz, J., & the STRONG STAR Consortium (2017). Effect of group vs individual cognitive processing therapy in active-duty military seeking treatment for posttraumatic stress disorder: A randomized clinical trial. *JAMA Psychiatry, 74*(1), 28–36.

Resick, P. A., Wachen, J. S., Mintz, J., Young-Mccaughan, S., Roache, J. D., Borah, A. M., ... Peterson, A. L. (2015). A randomized clinical trial of group cognitive processing therapy compared with group present-centered therapy for PTSD among active duty military personnel. *Journal of Consulting and Clinical Psychology, 83*(6), 1058–1068.

Resick, P. A., Williams, L. F., Suvak, M. K., Monson, C. M., & Gradus, J. L. (2012). Long-term outcomes of cognitive-behavioral treatments for posttraumatic stress disorder among female rape survivors. *Journal of Consulting and Clinical Psychology, 80*(2), 201–210.

Roberts, N. P., Roberts, P. A., Jones, N., & Bisson, J. I. (2015). Psychological interventions for post-traumatic stress disorder and comorbid substance use disorder: A systematic review and meta-analysis. *Clinical Psychology Review, 38*, 25–38.

Rutter, L., & Brown, T. A. (2017). Psychometric properties of the generalized anxiety disorder scale-7 (GAD-7) in outpatients with anxiety and mood disorders. *Journal of Psychopathology and Behavioral Assessment, 39*(1), 140–146.

Santiago, P. N., Ursano, R. J., Gray, C. L., Pynoos, R. S., Spiegel, D., Lewis-Fernandez, R., ... & Fullerton, C. S. (2013). A systematic review of PTSD prevalence and trajectories in DSM-5 defined trauma exposed populations: intentional and non-intentional traumatic events. *PLoS One,* 8(4), e59236.

Scott, S. (2007). Multiple traumatic experiences and the development of posttraumatic stress disorder. *Journal of Interpersonal Violence, 22*(7), 932–938.

Shapiro, F., & Forrest, M. S. (1997). *EMDR: The breakthrough therapy for overcoming anxiety, stress, and trauma.* New York: Basic Books.

Shin, L. M., Orr, S. P., Carson, M. A., Rauch, S. L., Macklin, M. L., Lasko, N. B., ... Pitman, R. K. (2004). Regional cerebral blood flow in the amygdala and medial prefrontal cortex during traumatic imagery in male and female Vietnam veterans with PTSD. *Archives of General Psychiatry, 61*(2), 168–176. https://doi.org/10.1001/archpsyc.61.2.168

Skinner, K., Kressin, N., Frayne, S., & Tripp, T. (2000). The prevalence of military sexual assault among female veterans' administration outpatients. *Journal of Interpersonal Violence, 15*(3), 291–310.

Spitzer, R. L., Kroenke, K., & Williams, J. B. W. (1999). Validation and utility of a self-report version of PRIME-MD: The PHQ primary care study. *JAMA, 282*(18), 1737–1744.

Spitzer, R. L., Kroenke, K., Williams, J. B. W., & Löwe, B. (2006). A brief measure for assessing generalized anxiety disorder: The GAD-7. *Archives of Internal Medicine, 166*(10), 1092–1097.

Statistics Canada. (2018). Canada at a glance 2018: Population estimates. Retrieved from www150.statcan.gc.ca/n1/pub/12-581-x/2018000/pop-eng.htm

Street, A. E., Stafford, J., Mahan, C. M., & Hendricks, A. (2008). Sexual harassment and assault experienced by reservists during military service: Prevalence and health correlates. *Journal of Rehabilitation Research and Development, 45*(3), 409–419.

Szafranski, D.D., Smith, B.N., Gros, D. F., Resick, P. A. (2017). High rates of PTSD treatment dropout: A possible red herring? *Journal of Anxiety Disorders, 47*, 91–98.

Thompson, J. M., VanTil, L. D., Zamorski, M. A., Garber, B., Dursun, S., Fikretoglu, D., ... & Pedlar, D. J. (2016). Mental health of Canadian Armed Forces Veterans: Review of population studies. *Journal of Military, Veteran and Family Health, 2*(1), 70–86.

Toussaint, A., Huesing, P., Gumz, A., Wingenfeld, K., Haerter, M., Schramm, E., & Loewe, B. (2020). Sensitivity to change and minimal clinically important difference of the 7-item Generalized Anxiety Disorder Questionnaire (GAD-7). *Journal of Affective Disorders, 265*, 395–401.

Tschuschke, V., & Dies, R. R. (1994). Intensive analysis of therapeutic factors and outcome in long-term inpatient groups. *International Journal of Group Psychotherapy, 44*(2), 185–208.

Van Ameringen, M., Mancini, C., Patterson, B., & Boyle, M. (2008). Post-traumatic stress disorder in Canada. *CNS Neuroscience & Therapeutics, 14*(3), 171–181.

VanTil, L. D., Sweet, J., Poirier, A., McKinnon, K., Sudom, K., Dursun, S., & Pedlar, D. (2017). *Well-being of Canadian regular force veterans. Findings from LASS 2016 Survey.* Technical Report. Charlottetown, PE: Veterans Affairs Canada Research Directorate.

Wales, J. A., Palmer, R. L., & Fairburn, C. G. (2009). Can treatment trial samples be representative? *Behaviour Research and Therapy, 47*(10), 893–896.

Weathers, F. W., Litz, B. T., Keane, T. M., Palmieri, P. A., Marx, B. P., & Schnurr, P. P. (2013). The PTSD checklist for DSM-5 (PCL-5). Scale available from the National Center for PTSD. Retrieved from www.ptsd.va.gov/professional/assessment/adult-sr/ptsd-checklist.asp

Wilson, J. P., & Keane, T. M. (eds). (2004). *Assessing psychological trauma and PTSD* (2nd edn). Portland, OR: Ringgold Inc.

Yalom, I. D., & Leszcz, M. (2005). *The theory and practice of group psychotherapy* (5th edn). New York: Basic Books.

Xue, C., Ge, Y., Tang, B., Liu, Y., Kang, P., Wang, M., & Zhang, L. (2015). A meta-analysis of risk factors for combat-related PTSD among military personnel and veterans. *PLoS One, 10*(3), E0120270.

17 Eye Movement Desensitization and Reprocessing in PTSD
Neurobiology and its Applications in Other Mental Disorders

Cristina Trentini, Sara Carletto, and Marco Pagani

Introduction

Eye Movement Desensitization and Reprocessing (EMDR) has been recommended by several guidelines (American Psychological Association, 2017; International Society for Traumatic Stress Studies, 2018; National Institute for Health and Clinical Excellence, 2018; World Health Organization, 2013), along with trauma-focused Cognitive Behavioural Therapy, as a frontline treatment for posttraumatic stress disorder (PTSD). In the current chapter, we review the EMDR literature and provide an overview of the clinical value of EMDR. We focused on studies stressing the role of versatile psychotherapy in treating pathological conditions with a history of exposure to potentially psychologically traumatic events (Canadian Institute for Public Safety Research and Treatment, 2019).

EMDR has been increasingly used in clinical practice as effectiveness evidence has increased (Chen et al., 2014; Cusack et al., 2016; Moreno-Alcázar et al., 2017; Valiente-Gómez et al., 2017) and the speed in which positive outcomes result in comparison to other forms of psychotherapy (Ironson et al., 2002; Nijdam et al., 2012). Several investigations demonstrate the impact of EMDR on cortical and sub-cortical brain regions involved in PTSD. For example, there appears to be a clear association between the disappearance of symptoms and the normalization of cortical function as evidenced through monitoring of cortical activity, both statically (i.e., before and after therapy) and dynamically (i.e., during EMDR sessions). Proposed hypotheses for mechanisms of action in EMDR may help explain details regarding treatment effectiveness (Pagani et al., 2017; Hase et al., 2017; Baek et al., 2019). EMDR is also now applied beyond PTSD, with scholars evidencing EMDR effectiveness for treating other major public health problems (i.e., depression and addiction; Valiente-Gómez et al., 2017; Malandrone et al., 2019; Tapia, 2019).

DOI: 10.4324/9781351134637-18

An Overview on Eye Movement Desensitization and Reprocessing (EMDR)

EMDR is an integrative psychotherapeutic approach that was first described by Francine Shapiro in 1989 and further developed in the 1990s. EMDR was initially used for treating the sequelae of potentially psychologically traumatic events exposures and is now used to address a wide range of distress and mental health disorders (e.g., depression, Malandrone et al., 2019; bipolar disorder, Valiente-Gomez et al., 2019; psychosis, de Bont, de Jongh, & van den Berg, 2019; substance use disorder, Tapia, 2019). The procedures for EMDR are guided by the theoretical model of Adaptive Information Processing (Shapiro, 1989, 1995, 2001, 2002). Adaptive information processing theory posits the existence of an information processing system that assimilates new experiences into already existing memory networks that contain related thoughts, images, emotions, and sensations. Such adaptive associations result in "relief of emotional distress, and the availability of the material for future use", which guide the person's reactions and behaviours (Shapiro & Maxfield, 2002, p. 935). When working appropriately, the innate information processing system is thought to "metabolize" or "digest" new experiences (Shapiro, 2001).

The adaptive information processing hypothesizes that the intensely disturbing effect that occurs at the time of a potentially psychologically traumatic event may interrupt the brain's information processing system (Shapiro, 1995, 2001). The interruption may cause failure in proper processing and information storage of images, thoughts, emotions, and sensations associated with the potentially psychologically traumatic event. As Shapiro and Maxfield (2002) have underscored, "If the information related to a distressing or traumatic experience is not processed fully, the initial perceptions will be stored essentially as they were inputted, along with any distorted thoughts or perceptions experienced at the time of the event" (p. 935). Improperly processed information may be more easily triggered by reminders of the potentially psychologically traumatic event and could lead to symptoms of PTSD (i.e., negative affective, cognitive, somatic responses). In summary, the adaptive information processing model posits that activation of improperly processed and stored memories leads to symptoms of PTSD (Solomon & Shapiro, 2008). Reprocessing of inadequately stored traumatic memories is hypothesized to return the person to healthy functioning. EMDR is designed to access improperly stored experiences and facilitate integration by stimulating the natural neural processes of memory consolidation (Shapiro, 2012).

EMDR is applied by means of a standardized eight-phased protocol requiring the clients to focus on their traumatic memories (*target*), while simultaneously being exposed to bilateral stimulation (i.e., alternating left and right eye movements, tactile taps, or auditory tones; see Table 17.1).

Since Shapiro's first study in 1989, more than 30 randomized controlled trials have evaluated EMDR as a treatment for symptoms related

Eye Movement Desensitization and Reprocessing 459

Table 17.1 Overview of EMDR treatment

EMDR Phases	Description
Phase 1: *Client History*	A thorough history is taken, designed to identify the experiences that appear to be causing personal distress or psychopathology; client history also includes an overall treatment plan that is discussed with the client.
Phase 2: *Preparation*	The client is prepared for treatment by stabilizing and increasing access to positive affect. To do so, the client is asked to identify a "safe place" (i.e., an image or memory that elicits comfortable feelings and a positive sense of self). Such safe places can be used later to bring closure to an incomplete session or to help the client to deal with a particularly upsetting session.
Phase 3: *Assessment*	The client is asked to access the perceptual, cognitive, affective, and somatic components of the most disturbing moment of the targeted event. The level of emotional disturbance is rated using the Subjective Units of Disturbance scale, where 0 is no disturbance and 10 is worst possible disturbance. Then, the client is asked to identify a preferred self–referential positive cognition and rates how valid it feels using the Validity of Cognition scale, where 1 is not true and 7 is completely true (Shapiro, 2001).
Phase 4: *Desensitization*	The client is instructed to focus on the image, negative belief, and body sensations related to a distressing memory for about 30 seconds, while simultaneously engaging in therapist-directed bilateral stimulation, with lengthier sets during expression of emotional tension. After each set, the client is asked to report any other elicited material, so the material can be processed during bilateral stimulation, until the subjective units of disturbance scale score substantially decreases to zero.
Phase 5: *Installation*	The clinician asks the client to focus on his/her preferred self-referential positive cognition while thinking of the targeted memory and engaging in new sets of bilateral stimulation, until the validity of cognition scale score is 7. After several sets, clients generally report increased confidence in their positive cognition.
Phase 6: *Body Scan*	Any residual physical disturbances associated with the memories are processed. Possible negative sensations are processed as above, until the client reports that the body is clear and free of any disturbance. Positive sensations are further enhanced.
Phase 7: *Closure*	The therapist asks the client to keep a weekly log to document any other related material that may arise. Then, the client is reminded of the self-reassuring activities that were mastered during phase 2.
Phase 8: *Reevaluation*	Reevaluation occurs at the beginning of subsequent sessions to check whether achieved results are maintained or need further reprocessing. In addition to previous exposures to potentially psychologically traumatic events, current triggers and related future anxieties are targeted.

Source: Partially taken from Trentini et al. (2015).

460 *Trentini, Carletto, and Pagani*

to potentially psychologically traumatic events (for comprehensive reviews, see de Jongh et al., 2019; Shapiro, 2014). EMDR has been evidenced as more successful than psychopharmacological therapy (van der Kolk et al., 2007) and resulted in faster symptom reductions compared to brief eclectic psychotherapy (Nijdam et al., 2012). EMDR also appears to effectively reduce PTSD symptoms in a comparable fashion to cognitive behavioural therapy (CBT; Arabia, Manca, & Solomon, 2011; Capezzani et al., 2013; de Roos et al., 2011; Ironson et al., 2002; Jaberghaderi et al., 2004; Karatzias et al., 2007; Lee et al., 2002; Power et al., 2002; Rogers et al., 1999; Vaughan et al., 1994). There are also two meta-analyses that provide evidence that EMDR may be more effective than cognitive behavioural therapy among adults (Chen et al., 2015; Khan et al., 2018), as well as for children and adolescents (Rodenburg et al., 2009). Several scholars have also reported that, compared to cognitive behaviour therapy, EMDR therapy may work more rapidly for the psychological sequelae of natural and man-made disasters (Carr et al., 1997; Chemtob, Nakashima, & Carlson, 2002; Fernandez, 2007; Goenjian et al., 1995; Maslovaric et al., 2017; Morgan et al., 2003; Perkonigg et al., 2005; Trentini et al., 2018). The cited studies evidence that, although EMDR and cognitive behavioural therapy may be equally able to induce a long-term improvement of children's disaster-related mental disorder symptoms, treatment gains of EMDR are reached in fewer sessions (de Roos et al., 2011). Accordingly, EMDR has been recommended as a potential first-line treatment for potentially psychologically traumatic event sequalae by several organizations (e.g., American Psychiatric Association, 2004; the United States' Department of Defense and Department of Veterans Affairs, 2017).

There is consensus that EMDR can be effective for treating individuals who have experienced a single potentially psychologically traumatic event, but much less is known about the role of EMDR in alleviating the symptoms following chronic interpersonal potentially psychologically traumatic events (e.g., psychological maltreatment, physical and sexual abuse, neglect, separation from caregivers, traumatic loss, witnessing of domestic violence). Emerging research is providing the first preliminary evidence of the clinical effectiveness of EMDR in treating symptoms associated with the exposure to complex childhood potentially psychologically traumatic events, in both children and adults (Moreno-Alcázar et al., 2017; Trentini et al., 2015).

Proposed Mechanisms of Action of EMDR

There are still debates about the mechanisms of EMDR functioning. The adaptive information processing model views eye movements and other forms of bilateral stimulation (e.g., tapping) as one of the elements that facilitates information processing (Solomon & Shapiro, 2008). The specific mechanism by which information processing occurs is unclear and there has been disagreement as to whether eye movements or alternate bilateral

Eye Movement Desensitization and Reprocessing 461

stimulations add anything to the effectiveness of EMDR. A meta-analysis of treatment studies attempted to address the disagreement by investigating the effect size differences between EMDR with and without eye movements (Davidson & Parker, 2001). No statistically significant incremental effects of eye movements were reported (Davidson & Parker, 2001). More recently, another meta-analysis, with fewer methodological limits, investigated the additive effects of eye movements (Lee & Cuijpers, 2013). A moderate and statistically significant effect size for the additive effect of eye movements in EMDR was reported (Lee & Cuijpers, 2013).

Different hypotheses have been proposed regarding the mechanism of action related to EMDR eye movements or alternate bilateral stimulations (for reviews see Landin-Romero et al., 2018; Leeds, 2016; Maxfield, 2008; Pagani et al., 2017). Such hypotheses include the orienting response hypothesis (Barrowcliff et al., 2004), the working memory account (Gunter & Bodner, 2008; van den Hout & Engelhard, 2012), the thalamocortical binding model (Bergmann, 2008; Lanius & Bergmann, 2014), the rapid eye movement theory (Stickgold, 2002, 2008), and the slow wave sleep hypothesis (Carletto, Borsato, & Pagani, 2017; Pagani et al., 2017). There is no definitive evidence supporting any one hypothesis. A recent experiment on mice has shed light on the neural circuit that could underlie the effect of EMDR (Baek et al., 2019). A neuronal pathway, driven by the superior colliculus, was described and appears to mediate the persistent attenuation of fear (Baek et al., 2019). Further research combining these theoretical perspectives, molecular biology, neurophysiology, brain imaging, and clinical evidence in patient cohorts are needed to reach a comprehensive model of the mechanisms underlying EMDR.

Neurobiological Correlates of Trauma and EMDR

In recent years, non-invasive techniques have been used to investigate brain activity and shed light on the functional and anatomical changes associated with PTSD. These studies have substantially contributed to uncovering the role of each specific cerebral area in the complex mechanisms that mediate the processing of emotions and psychological trauma (for an extensive review, see Bremner, 2007).

Functional imaging studies (i.e., single photon emission computed tomography, positron emission tomography, and functional magnetic resonance imaging) have extensively measured regional cerebral blood flow. Studies conducted in adults with PTSD (for a review see Francati, Vermetten, & Bremner, 2007) and victims of childhood abuse (for a review see Hart & Rubia, 2012), have compared the regional cerebral blood flow of these individuals with that of healthy control groups (e.g., adults without PTSD, non-victims). Converging results from these investigations have identified a hyper–reactivity of the amygdala with acquisition of fear responses and an impairment of the medial prefrontal cortex in properly regulating fear extinction. Such abnormal cerebral activity could account for an increase in PTSD symptoms (e.g., intrusive thoughts, hyperarousal, flashbacks, nightmares and sleep disturbances, changes in memory and concentration, and startle reactions) in response to triggering stimuli (Bremner, 2007; Looi et al., 2010). It has been suggested that the abnormal cerebral activity may be due to an excess of prefrontal cortical catecholamine concentration (i.e., norepinephrine, dopamine) in response to potentially psychologically traumatic event exposures (Vanitallie, 2002). Extreme levels of dopamine, in particular, may impair frontal inhibition of the limbic system, which can lead to exaggerated attention and vigilance towards cues that are experienced as potentially psychologically traumatic (De Bellis, Spratt, & Hooper, 2011).

Several investigations using structural magnetic resonance imaging have also documented consistent changes in hippocampal and prefrontal cortex volumes among PTSD patients (Bromis et al., 2018). Changes in the hippocampal and prefrontal cortex volumes are associated with impairments in the encoding, consolidation, and retrieval of declarative memories. Reduced volume in ACC is associated with deficits in emotional awareness and affect regulation (Bremner, 2007; Looi et al., 2010; Pagani et al., 2012; Pagani et al., 2011; Nardo et al., 2010, 2013; van Strien, Cappaert, & Witter, 2009).

Research focused on the neurobiological correlates of EMDR has increased dramatically and neuroimaging represents a powerful tool to investigate the possible impact of EMDR on the cortical and sub-cortical brain regions involved in symptoms of PTSD (Pagani & Cavallo, 2014; Pagani, Högberg, Fernandez, & Siracusano, 2013). Single photon emission computed tomography studies have documented significant changes in regional cerebral blood flow patterns after EMDR (Lansing et al., 2005; Pagani et al., 2007). Post-treatment, the changes in regional cerebral blood flow reflect the recovered inhibitory role of the prefrontal cortex in reducing the hyperactivation of the limbic system (including the amygdala and the related nuclei and circuitry) in response to potentially psychologically traumatic event stimuli. Studies using functional magnetic resonance imaging data have indicated that EMDR may be associated with changes in limbic and paralimbic grey matter density, coinciding with the improvement of PTSD symptoms (Bossini, 2012; Nardo et al., 2010).

Bilateral stimulation and its effects on brain activation and deactivation has been extensively researched. Using an electroencephalogram, researchers have suggested that bilateral stimulation might be associated with: a reduced attention to novel stimuli and decreased levels of arousal after therapy (Lamprecht et al., 2004); a depotentiation of fear memory synapses in the amygdala (Harper, Rasolkhani-Kalhorn, & Drozd, 2009); and a decrease in the inter-hemispheric electroencephalogram coherence (i.e., the functional interaction or connectivity between the regions of the two hemispheres) which may reduce intrusions from potentially psychologically traumatic event memories (Propper & Christman, 2008). The

Eye Movement Desensitization and Reprocessing 463

available research studies were all conducted before and after treatment; therefore, the results do not show the relative neurobiological modifications occurring during EMDR. The possibility of conducting an electroencephalogram during EMDR has only recently been proposed (Pagani et al., 2011; 2012)

Pagani and colleagues (2011; 2012) monitored participants during their first EMDR session and during the session performed after processing the index potentially psychologically traumatic event. During the first session, participants showed an exaggerated limbic and orbitofrontal cortex hyperactivation as compared to normal individuals undergoing the same experimental protocol. Participants also showed hyperactivation relative to activation levels after having processed the potentially psychologically traumatic event. The comparison between electroencephalograms from the first and last session showed significant deactivation of the orbitofrontal and subcortical limbic structures, leading to higher emotional valence. There was also a greater activation in the fusiform gyrus and visual cortex, leading to higher cognitive and associative valence. The changes may suggest a better cognitive and sensorial (visual) processing of the potentially psychologically traumatic event during autobiographical reliving. As an effect of successful trauma elaboration, the visual images of the event are processed and stored in the primary and associative visual cortex and are likely decoupled from the emotional memory of faces and bodies linked to the event, which is typically recalled through the fusiform gyrus (Pagani et al., 2011; 2012).

Recent EMDR Research Results: Applications Beyond PTSD

Potentially psychologically traumatic event exposures have also been associated with the occurrence and development of psychiatric disorders other than PTSD (e.g., Kim & Lee, 2016; Nemeroff, 2016). A recent systematic review suggested EMDR may be helpful for reducing psychotic or affective symptoms (Valiente-Gómez et al., 2017). There was also evidence that EMDR might be effective as an add-on treatment in chronic pain conditions (Valiente-Gómez et al., 2017). A complete review of the existing literature about EMDR and potential clinical applications is beyond the scope of the current chapter; as such, the following are relevant examples of studies conducted by our team that focus on psychiatric conditions in participants with a history of potentially psychologically traumatic event exposures.

Contribution of EMDR in Restoring Emotional Problems in Child Survivors of Earthquakes

There is evidence demonstrating the psychopathological sequelae of natural disasters among children and adolescent survivors. Some individuals may show resilience after potentially psychologically traumatic event exposures by manifesting only temporary, sub-clinical stress responses (Bonanno, 2004); in contrast, some individuals may experience a wide range of psychopathological outcomes (for a systematic review, see Wang, Chan, & Ho, 2013). For example, severe psychopathological outcomes (e.g., anxiety, depression, PTSD, emotional distress; Oyama et al., 2012; Toyabe et al., 2006), difficulties in regulating anger (Becker-Blease, Turner, & Finkelhor, 2010; Kar & Bastia, 2006), and poorer quality of life (Tsai et al., 2007) are commonly observed in individuals who are exposed to natural disasters (Liu et al., 2011; Zhang et al., 2011). The prompt availability of psychological interventions in the aftermath of a natural disaster has become essential to reducing the risk of onset and worsening of psychopathological symptoms in exposed individuals (National Institute of Mental Health, 2002; Te Brake et al., 2009). Intervention is especially important in children, who are more vulnerable to the dramatic effects of critical events than adults (Norris, Foster, & Weishaar, 2002). Children's psychopathological responses may be enduring (Ularntinon et al., 2008), persisting until adulthood (Green et al., 1994), and potentiating significant impairments of function throughout the lifespan.

Our group recently investigated the effects of EMDR on a large sample of child survivors of both earthquakes that struck Umbria (a region of central Italy) on August 24 and on October 26 in 2016 (Trentini et al., 2018). An adjusted EMDR protocol (i.e., the EMDR Integrative Group Treatment Protocol) was used one day following the first earthquake to quickly restore psychological functioning in the child survivors. The EMDR-Integrative Group Treatment Protocol uses the standard EMDR protocol, along with a group therapy model, an art therapy format, and the Butterfly Hug (BH; i.e., a form of self-administered bilateral stimulation; Artigas et al., 2000; Artigas & Jarero, 2010; Jarero & Artigas, 2012).

Participants were children ($n = 332$), aged between five and 13, from the town of Norcia and nearby disrupted villages. Participants received EMDR-Integrative Group Treatment Protocol once a week for three weeks (i.e., three cycles) and scales (i.e., The Emotion Thermometers, Mitchell et al., 2010; Italian translation by Acquati; and the Children's Revised Impact of Event Scale; Perrin, Meiser-Stedman, & Smith, 2005) were administered before the protocol was started and about one week after the conclusion of the third treatment cycle.

Preliminary results show that EMDR-Integrative Group Treatment Protocol contributed significantly to the reduction of emotional disturbances and PTSD symptoms in exposed children, primarily in older children and in those who had received a timelier treatment. The use of EMDR-Integrative Group Treatment Protocol provided an opportunity to deliver psychological interventions to a great number of exposed children, increasing our ability to rapidly deal with the outcomes of an emergency situation.

Use of Electroencephalogram to Explore the Effects of EMDR on Brain Neurobiology in Maltreated Children

Early interpersonal potentially psychologically traumatic event exposures can jeopardize children's abilities to recognize, express, and regulate emotional states (van der Kolk & d'Andrea, 2010). Children exposed to early and prolonged potentially psychologically traumatic events often experience intense negative affect (e.g., rage, betrayal, fear, resignation, defeat, shame), as well as persistent sensitivity to others' negative emotions, which is used to detect early potential signs of threat (van der Kolk, 2007). Such enhanced sensitivity causes a long-term emotional dysregulation, characterized by over- or under-reactivity to minor emotional stimuli (i.e., stimuli that would have no significant impact on non-maltreated children; van der Kolk, 2007). Researchers have also evidenced that maltreated children have poor discriminatory abilities for different facial emotions and misinterpret many emotional faces (including neutral and happy ones) as being threatening or as a mask for more malevolent emotions (Leist & Dadds, 2009; Pollak et al., 2000; van Harmelen et al., 2013).

We used high-density electroencephalogram to explore the impact of EMDR on a sample of school-aged children with histories of early and prolonged maltreatment. We were interested in examining neural responses to adults' facial emotions, as well as the levels of distress related to potentially psychologically traumatic event and emotional-adaptive functioning. Children were examined before and within one month after the conclusion of EMDR treatment. High-density electroencephalogram were recorded while children passively viewed angry, afraid, happy, and neutral faces (Lundqvist, Flykt, & Öhman, 1998). The Trauma Symptom Checklist for Children (TSCC–A; Briere, 1996; Italian validation by Di Blasio, Piccolo, & Traficante, 2011) and the Child Behaviour Checklist/4–18 (CBCL/4–18; Achenbach, 1991; Italian validation by Frigerio et al., 2004) were administered. Correlation analyses were performed to look for associations between active brain regions and children's potentially psychologically traumatic event-related symptoms and emotional–adaptive problem scores.

Before EMDR, high-density electroencephalogram showed significantly higher activity on the right medial prefrontal and fronto–temporal limbic regions. After the intervention, activity shifted towards the left medial and superior temporal regions. The changes were associated with a decrease in symptoms of depression and PTSD, and the improvement of emotional–adaptive functioning over time.

Consistent with the results of previous research on adults with PTSD symptoms (Pagani et al., 2012), our results indicated that after EMDR children used higher-order cognitive resources when processing expressions of emotion. Our results are also consistent with the adaptive information processing model (Shapiro, 2001), which posits that once the memory retention of the potentially psychologically traumatic event can move from an implicit subcortical status to an explicit cortical one, the memories of

466   *Trentini, Carletto, and Pagani*

a potentially psychologically traumatic event and the related emotions may be processes at a higher cognitive level. Our results may have relevant implications in clinical practice, suggesting that interventions focused on the cognitive processing of emotions may be particularly beneficial for children.

EMDR as Adjunctive Treatment for Recurrent Depressive Disorder

Major depressive disorder has been associated with adverse childhood experiences (e.g., physical and sexual abuse, emotional neglect; Hughes et al., 2017; Infurna et al., 2016; Kendler & Gardner, 2016; Nemeroff, 2016). Several studies have highlighted a dose–response relationship between the number of adverse childhood experiences and the probability of major depressive episodes (Anda et al., 2006; Chapman et al., 2004). Adverse childhood experiences are also associated with a poorer clinical course of major depressive disorder, including earlier age of onset, greater symptom severity, and greater co-morbidity (Paterniti et al., 2017; Scott et al., 2012; Tunnard et al., 2014; Wiersma et al., 2009).

The first randomized controlled trial comparing the effectiveness of EMDR to cognitive behavioural therapy in participants affected by recurrent depression and treated with antidepressants was conducted by European Depression EMDR Network (Ostacoli et al., 2018), to which some of the authors of the current chapter belong. EMDR was hypothesized as addressing memories of adverse childhood experiences and other potentially psychologically traumatic events that could be clinically significant contributors to the onset and maintenance of major depressive episodes.

Participants ($n = 82$) were recruited between 2014 and 2016 in two centres in Italy and Spain. Participants were assessed at baseline, after treatment, and at a six-month follow-up with self-report questionnaires for several clinical measures (i.e., severity of depressive and anxiety symptoms, quality of life and general psychological functioning). Most participants reported previous adverse childhood experiences and other potentially psychologically traumatic event (e.g., sexual and physical abuse, traumatic mourning, abandonment), supporting the hypothesis that stressful life events can play a significant role in both the onset and the risk of recurrence of major depressive episodes. Participants received between 12 and 18 individual adjunctive EMDR or cognitive behavioural therapy sessions while continuing to receive antidepressant therapy. The EMDR treatment followed the DeprEnd protocol (i.e., the manual for EMDR in the treatment of depressive patients; Hofmann et al., 2016). A total of 66 participants (31 EMDR and 35 cognitive behaviour therapy) completed the protocol. The proportion of participants experiencing depressive symptoms, as measured by the Beck Depression Inventory-II (Beck & Steer, 1993), was similar across both the EMDR and cognitive behavioural therapy treatment groups at completion of treatment and at six months follow-up. The proportion of participants considered in remission at completion of treatment was statistically significantly higher in the EMDR treatment group than in the cognitive behavioural therapy group (χ^2 = 4.735, p = .046); however, no significant difference between the two groups was found at the six-month follow-up. Participants in the EMDR group did remain under the clinical threshold for depression symptoms in the long term.

As a secondary outcome of the study, the impact of EMDR or cognitive behavioural therapy on anxiety (as measured by Beck Anxiety Inventory, Beck & Steer, 2013), posttraumatic stress symptoms (as measured by Impact of Event Scale-Revised, Weiss & Marmar, 1997) and quality of life (as measured by WHO-Quality of Life, Murphy et al., 2000) were evaluated. Both EMDR and cognitive behavioural therapy resulted in a reduction of anxiety and posttraumatic symptoms and an improvement in quality of life, with the benefits still apparent after six months.

To our knowledge, this was the first randomized controlled trial that highlighted the effectiveness of EMDR compared to cognitive behavioural therapy in reducing symptoms of major depressive disorder as measured by Beck Depression Inventory-II, and anxiety symptoms and increasing quality of life in participants suffering from recurrent major depressive disorder who were already treated with antidepressant medications. After this study, other clinical trials aimed at broadening the investigation of EMDR effectiveness in depressive disorders in both adult and adolescent populations (for their results see Hase et al., 2018; Minelli et al., 2019; Paauw et al., 2019; Wood, Ricketts, & Parry, 2018).

EMDR as Add-On Treatment for Psychiatric and Traumatic Symptoms in Patients with Substance Use Disorder

We have also investigated the effectiveness of EMDR as an add-on treatment in patients with substance use disorder (Carletto et al., 2018). Substance abuse is frequently associated with adverse childhood events and other potentially psychologically traumatic event, as well as a high prevalence of PTSD symptoms (Dube et al., 2003; Green et al., 2010; Felitti et al., 1998). Therefore, using a trauma-informed approach could lead to better treatment outcomes for substance use disorder (e.g., greater symptom reduction, increased retention in treatment; LeTendre & Reed, 2017; Markus & Hornsveld, 2017). EMDR has been applied to substance use disorder using two main approaches: trauma-focused EMDR and addiction-focused EMDR. Trauma-focused-EMDR uses standard EMDR focused on the potentially psychologically traumatic event exposure and PTSD symptoms; addiction-focused-EMDR uses standard EMDR to target traumatic memories related to the history of addiction (Markus & Hornsveld, 2017).

Our quasi-experimental study was designed to assess the efficacy of a combined trauma-focused- and addiction-focused-EMDR protocol in treating PTSD and stress-related symptoms in patients with substance use

468   Trentini, Carletto, and Pagani

disorder (Carletto et al., 2018). Our study was conducted in two Italian centres for drug addiction treatment where participants (n = 40) with different substance use disorder s were enrolled. Half of the participants (n = 20) underwent treatment as usual, while the other half (n = 20) underwent treatment as usual plus 24 weekly sessions of a combined trauma-focused- and addiction-focused-EMDR protocol. This combined protocol was developed according to the Palette of EMDR Interventions in Addiction (Markus and Hornsveld, 2017; see Carletto et al., 2018 for more details). All participants were assessed with psychological self-report questionnaires to evaluate anxiety, depression and PTSD symptoms, as measured by State-Trait Anxiety Inventory (Spielberger et al., 1983), Beck Depression Inventory-II and Impact of Event Scale-Revised respectively, before and after the intervention. Moreover, dissociative symptoms and severity of psychopathology levels were assessed using the Dissociative Experiences Scale (Frischholz, Braun, Sachs, & Hopkins, 1990) and the Global Severity Index of the Symptom Checklist 90 Items revised version (Derogatis, 1994), respectively. Both groups reported statistically significant reductions in PTSD symptoms [treatment as usual: Mean Difference (MD) = -11.6 [95% CI: -20.912; -2.288], p = .016; TAU+EMDR: MD = -33.6 [95% CI: -42.912; -24.288], p < .001]. Also, the treatment as usual plus EMDR group showed a statistically significant improvement of dissociative symptoms (MD = -8.973 [95% CI: -13.071; -4.874], p < .001), and a statistically significant reduction in anxiety (MD = -3.05 [95% CI: -5.289; $-.811$], p = .009) and severity of psychopathology levels (MD = -10.65 [95% CI: -14.935; -6.365], p < .001). The results support the use of a combined trauma-focused- and addiction-focused-EMDR protocol in patients with substance use disorder with a wide range of psychological symptoms.

Clinical and Neurobiological Effects of EMDR for PTSD in Patients with Breast Cancer

Cancer diagnosis and subsequent treatment can be highly stressful experiences, with possible devastating effects on patients' psychological functioning and quality of life that may result in PTSD (Parikh et al., 2015). Trauma-focused interventions appear effective for reducing PTSD symptoms in patients with cancer (Dimitrov, Moschopoulou, & Korszun, 2019).

There is currently one published study investigating neurobiological correlates of EMDR treatment in patients with PTSD related to cancer (Carletto et al., 2019). The study was designed to (1) evaluate the effectiveness of EMDR as compared to treatment as usual in participants with PTSD related to breast cancer; (2) identify the neurophysiological changes underlying treatment effects via electroencephalogram; and (3) investigate associations between neurophysiological changes and clinical symptoms. Participants with breast cancer and PTSD diagnosis assessed by the

Clinician-Administered PTSD Scale (Weathers et al., 2018) ($n = 30$) were recruited and administered questionnaires, before and after EMDR or treatment as usual treatments, to assess symptoms of PTSD, anxiety, and depression with self-report questionnaires (by using Impact of Event Scale-Revised, State-Trait Anxiety Inventory, and Beck Depression Inventory-II, respectively). Post-treatment, participants in the EMDR group no longer met criteria for PTSD and had a statistically significant decrease in depressive symptoms (MD = -13.429 [95% CI: -17.334; -9.524], $p < .001$); anxiety levels were unchanged (MD = 4.643 [95% CI: $-.286$; 9.571], $p = .064$). Participants in the treatment as usual group did not demonstrate statistically significant differences in symptoms from pre- to post-treatment for PTSD (MD = -4.667 [95% CI: -12.961; 3.628], $p = .258$), depression (MD = .133 [95% CI: -3.639; 3.906], $p = .943$), and anxiety (MD = $-.4$ [95% CI: -5.161; 4.361], $p = .864$). Electroencephalograms were performed before and after EMDR treatment as usual to identify the neurophysiological changes underlying the two treatments. Pearson correlation analyses between electroencephalograms before and after treatment and the levels of clinical symptoms were calculated. Electroencephalogram results showed a greater neuronal synchronization in the areas of the left angular gyrus and right fusiform gyrus after EMDR therapy ($p < .05$, for further details see Figure 1 in Carletto et al., 2019).

Both the left angular gyrus and the right fusiform gyrus have previously been associated with statistically significant symptom improvements following EMDR therapy (p values: pairwise interaction with Impact of Event Scale-Revised: .016; with Beck Depression Inventory-II: .023; with Positive Symptom Distress Index: .03) in participants with PTSD (Pagani et al., 2012). During EMDR, re-elaboration of the potentially psychologically traumatic event memories may be associated with the recovery of connections between different areas of the brain that are involved in the elaboration at both associative and visual levels, favouring a better contextualization and integration of the traumatic memories in associative semantic networks. The previous results, along with our current results, support the use of EMDR to treat cancer-related PTSD, possibly from a clinical and a neurobiological perspective.

Summary

In the current chapter, the relevant literature about EMDR neurobiology and suggested mechanisms of action for patients with PTSD was reviewed. Some examples of the use of EMDR in psychiatric disorders other than PTSD were also reviewed. The current investigations provide support that EMDR: a) contributes to restoring psychological functioning in child survivors of earthquakes; b) appears comparable to cognitive behavioural therapy in reducing depressive symptoms, even at six months follow-up; c) appear more effective than treatment as usual at reducing symptoms in patients with substance use disorder; and d) appears effective at reducing

470 *Trentini, Carletto, and Pagani*

symptoms of PTSD and depression in women with breast cancer. The use of electroencephalogram to explore the effects of EMDR on brain neurobiology in adults and maltreated children was also discussed. It allowed to examine the experimental subjects in an ecological environment avoiding the possible bias on brain activity due to the physical and psychological confinement in a camera gantry, as in the case of functional magnetic resonance imaging, single photon emission computed tomography and positron emission tomography.

References

Achenbach, T. M. (1991). *Manual for the Child Behavior Checklist/4–18 and 1991 Profiles*. Burlington, VT: University of Vermont Department of Psychiatry.

American Psychiatric Association. (2004). *Practice guideline for the treatment of patients with acute stress disorder and posttraumatic stress disorder*. Arlington, VA: American Psychiatric Association Practice Guidelines.

American Psychological Association. (2017). Clinical practice guideline for the treatment of posttraumatic stress disorder (PTSD) in adults. Retrieved from www.apa.org/ptsd-guideline/ptsd.pdf

Anda, R. F., Felitti, V. J., Bremner, J. D., Walker, J. D., Whitfield, C., Perry, B. D., … Giles, W. H. (2006). The enduring effects of abuse and related adverse experiences in childhood: A convergence of evidence from neurobiology and epidemiology. *European Archives of Psychiatry and Clinical Neuroscience, 256*(3), 174–186.

Arabia, E., Manca, M. L., & Solomon, R. M. (2011). EMDR for survivors of life-threatening cardiac events: Results of a pilot study. *Journal of EMDR Practice and Research, 5*(1), 2–13. http://dx.doi.org/10.1891/1933-3196.5.1.2.

Artigas, L., & Jarero, I. (2010). The butterfly hug. In M. Luber (ed.), *Eye movement desensitization and reprocessing (EMDR) scripted protocols: Special populations.* (pp. 5–7). New York: Springer Publishing.

Artigas, L. A., Jarero, I., Mauer, M., López Cano, T., & Alcalá, N. (2000, September). EMDR and traumatic stress after natural disasters: Integrative treatment protocol and the butterfly hug. Poster presented at the 5th EMDR International Association Conference, Toronto, ON.

Baek, J., Lee, S., Cho, T., Kim, S. W., Kim, M., Yoon, Y., … & Shin, H. S. (2019). Neural circuits underlying a psychotherapeutic regimen for fear disorders. *Nature, 566*(7744), 339. https://doi.org/10.1038/s41586-019-0931-y

Barrowcliff, A. L., Gray, N. S., Freeman, T. C., & MacCulloch, M. J. (2004). Eye-movements reduce the vividness, emotional valence and electrodermal arousal associated with negative autobiographical memories. *Journal of Forensic Psychiatry & Psychology, 15*(2), 325–345. https://doi.org/10.1080/14789940410001673042

Beck, A., and Steer, R. (1993). *Manual for the Beck Depression Inventory*. San Antonio, TX: Psychological Corporation.

Beck, A., and Steer, R. (2013). *Manual for the Beck Anxiety Inventory*. San Antonio, TX: Psychological Corporation.

Becker-Blease, K. A., Turner, H. A., & Finkelhor, D. (2010). Disasters, victimization, and children's mental health. *Child Development, 81*(4), 1040–1052. https://doi.org/10.1111/j.1467-8624.2010.01453.x

Eye Movement Desensitization and Reprocessing 471

Bergmann, U. (2008). The Neurobiology of EMDR: Exploring the thalamus and neural integration. *Journal of EMDR Practice and Research, 2*(4), 300–314. https://doi.org/10.1891/1933-3196.2.4.300

Bonanno, G. A. (2004). Loss, trauma, and human resilience: Have we underestimated the human capacity to thrive after extremely aversive events? *The American Psychologist, 59*(1), 20–28. https://doi.org/10.1037/0003-066X.59.1.20

Bossini, L. (2012). Cortical and subcortical volumetric changes after EMDR treatment in PTSD. *Journal of Psychosomatic Research, 72*(6), 472–473. https://doi.org/10.1016/j.jpsychores.2012.03.004

Bremner, J. D. (2007). Neuroimaging in posttraumatic stress disorder and other stress-related disorders. *Neuroimaging Clinics of North America, 17*(4), 523–538, ix. https://doi.org/10.1016/j.nic.2007.07.003

Briere, J. (1996). *Trauma Symptom Checklist for Children: Professional manual.* Odessa, TX: Psychological Assessment Resources, Inc.

Bromis, K., Calem, M., Reinders, A. A., Williams, S. C., & Kempton, M. J. (2018). Meta-analysis of 89 structural MRI studies in posttraumatic stress disorder and comparison with major depressive disorder. *American Journal of Psychiatry, 175*(10), 989–998. https://doi.org/10.1176/appi.ajp.2018.17111199

Canadian Institute for Public Safety Research and Treatment (CIPSRT). (2019). *Glossary of terms: A shared understanding of the common terms used to describe psychological trauma* (version 2.0). Regina, SK: Author.

Capezzani, L., Ostacoli, L., Cavallo, M., Carletto, S., Fernandez, I., Solomon, R., ... Cantelmi, T. (2013). EMDR and CBT for cancer patients: Comparative study of effects on PTSD, anxiety, and depression. *Journal of EMDR Practice and Research, 7,* 134–143. https://doi.org/10.1891/1933-3196.7.3.134

Carletto, S., Borsato, T., & Pagani, M. (2017). The role of slow wave sleep in memory pathophysiology: Focus on post-traumatic stress disorder and eye movement desensitization and reprocessing. *Frontiers in Psychology, 8,* 2050. https://doi.org/10.3389/fpsyg.2017.02050

Carletto, S., Oliva, F., Barnato, M., Antonelli, T., Cardia, A., Mazzaferro, P., ... & Pagani, M. (2018). EMDR as add-on treatment for psychiatric and traumatic symptoms in patients with substance use disorder. *Frontiers in Psychology, 8,* 2333. https://doi.org/10.3389/fpsyg.2017.02333

Carletto, S., Porcaro, C., Settanta, C., Vizzari, V., Stanizzo, M. R., Oliva, F., ... & Ostacoli, L. (2019). Neurobiological features and response to eye movement desensitization and reprocessing treatment of posttraumatic stress disorder in patients with breast cancer. *European Journal of Psychotraumatology, 10*(1), 1600832. https://doi.org/10.1080/20008198.2019.1600832

Carr, V. J., Lewin, T. J., Webster, R. A., Kenardy, J. A., Hazell, P. L., & Carter, G. L. (1997). Psychosocial sequelae of the 1989 Newcastle earthquake: II. Exposure and morbidity profiles during the first 2 years post-disaster. *Psychological Medicine, 27*(1), 167–178. https://doi.org/10.1017/S0033291796004278

Chapman, D. P., Whitfield, C. L., Felitti, V. J., Dube, S. R., Edwards, V. J., & Anda, R. F. (2004). Adverse childhood experiences and the risk of depressive disorders in adulthood. *Journal of Affective Disorders, 82*(2), 217–225. https://doi.org/10.1016/j.jad.2003.12.013

Chemtob, C. M., Nakashima, J., & Carlson, J. G. (2002). Brief treatment for elementary school children with disaster-related posttraumatic stress disorder: A field study. *Journal of Clinical Psychology, 58*(1), 99–112. https://doi.org/10.1002/jclp.1131

472 Trentini, Carletto, and Pagani

Chen, L., Zhang, G., Hu, M., & Liang, X. (2015). Eye movement desensitization and reprocessing versus cognitive-behavioral therapy for adult posttraumatic stress disorder: Systematic review and meta-analysis. *The Journal of Nervous and Mental Disease, 203*, 443–451. https://doi.org/10.1097/NMD.0000000000000306

Chen, Y. R., Hung, K. W., Tsai, J. C., Chu, H., Chung, M. H., Chen, S. R., ... & Chou, K. R. (2014). Efficacy of eye-movement desensitization and reprocessing for patients with posttraumatic-stress disorder: A meta-analysis of randomized controlled trials. *PLoS One, 9*(8), e103676. https://doi.org/10.1371/journal.pone.0103676

Cusack, K., Jonas, D. E., Forneris, C. A., Wines, C., Sonis, J., Middleton, J. C., ... & Weil, A. (2016). Psychological treatments for adults with posttraumatic stress disorder: A systematic review and meta-analysis. *Clinical Psychology Review, 43*, 128–141. https://doi.org/10.1016/j.cpr.2015.10.003

Davidson, P. R., & Parker, K. C. H. (2001). Eye movement desensitization and reprocessing (EMDR): A meta-analysis. *Journal of Consulting and Clinical Psychology, 69*, 305–316. https://doi.org/10.1037//0022-006x.69.2.305

De Bellis, M. D., Spratt, E. G., & Hooper, S. R. (2011). Neurodevelopmental biology associated with childhood sexual abuse. *Journal of Child Sexual Abuse, 20*(5), 548–587. https://doi.org/10.1080/10538712.2011.607753

de Bont, P., de Jongh, A., & van den Berg, D. (2019). Psychosis: An emerging field for EMDR research and therapy. *Journal of EMDR Practice and Research, 13*(4), 313–324.

de Jongh, A., Amann, B. L., Hofmann, A., Farrell, D., & Lee, C. W. (2019). The status of EMDR therapy in the treatment of posttraumatic stress disorder 30 years after its introduction. *Journal of EMDR Practice and Research, 13*(4), 261–269. https://doi.org/10.1891/1933-3196.13.4.261

de Roos, C., Greenwald, R., den Hollander-Gijsman, M., Noorthoorn, E., van Buuren, S., & de Jongh, A. (2011). A randomised comparison of cognitive behavioural therapy (CBT) and eye movement desensitisation and reprocessing (EMDR) in disaster-exposed children. *European Journal of Psychotraumatology, 2*(1), 5694. https://doi.org/10.3402/ejpt.v2i0.5694

Derogatis, L. R. (1994). *SCL-90-R: Symptom Checklist-90-R: Administration, Scoring & Procedures Manual.* Minneapolis, MN: National Computer Systems, Inc.

Di Blasio, P., Piccolo, M., & Traficante, D. (2011). *TSCC – Trauma Symptom Checklist for Children. Valutazione delle conseguenze psicologiche di esperienze traumatiche.* Trento: Erikson.

Dimitrov, L., Moschopoulou, E., & Korszun, A. (2019). Interventions for the treatment of cancer-related traumatic stress symptoms: A systematic review of the literature. *Psycho-Oncology, 28*(5), 970–979. https://doi.org/10.1002/pon.5055

Dube, S. R., Felitti, V. J., Dong, M., Chapman, D. P., Giles, W. H., & Anda, R. F. (2003). Childhood abuse, neglect, and household dysfunction and the risk of illicit drug use: The adverse childhood experiences study. *Pediatrics, 111*(3), 564–572.

Felitti, V. J., Anda, R. F., Nordenberg, D., Williamson, D. F., Spitz, A. M., Edwards, V., & Marks, J. S. (1998). Relationship of childhood abuse and household dysfunction to many of the leading causes of death in adults: The Adverse Childhood Experiences (ACE) Study. *American Journal of Preventive Medicine, 14*(4), 245–258.

Eye Movement Desensitization and Reprocessing 473

Fernandez, I. (2007). EMDR as treatment of post-traumatic reactions: A field study on child victims of an earthquake. *Educational and Child Psychology, 24*(1), 65–72.

Francati, V., Vermetten, E., & Bremner, J. D. (2007). Functional neuroimaging studies in posttraumatic stress disorder: Review of current methods and findings. *Depression and Anxiety, 24*(3), 202–218. https://doi.org/10.1002/da.20208

Frigerio, A., Cattaneo, C., Cataldo, M., Schiatti, A., Molteni, M., & Battaglia, M. (2004). Behavioral and emotional problems among Italian children and adolescents aged 4 to 18 years as reported by parents and teachers. *European Journal of Psychological Assessment, 20*(2), 124–133. https://doi.org/10.1027/1015-5759.20.2.124

Frischholz, E. J., Braun, B. G., Sachs, R. G., & Hopkins, L. (1990). The Dissociative Experiences Scale: Further replication and validation. *Dissociation: Progress in the Dissociative Disorders, 3*(3), 151–153.

Goenjian, A. K., Pynoos, R. S., Steinberg, A. M., Najarian, L. M., Asarnow, J. R., Karayan, I., ... Fairbanks, L. A. (1995). Psychiatric comorbidity in children after the 1988 earthquake in Armenia. *Journal of the American Academy of Child and Adolescent Psychiatry, 34*(9), 1174–1184. https://doi.org/10.1097/00004583-199509000-00015

Green, B. L., Grace, M. C., Vary, M. G., Kramer, T. L., Gleser, G. C., & Leonard, A. C. (1994). Children of disaster in the second decade: A 17-year follow-up of Buffalo Creek survivors. *Journal of the American Academy of Child and Adolescent Psychiatry, 33*(1), 71–79. https://doi.org/10.1097/00004583-199401000-00011

Green, J. G., McLaughlin, K. A., Berglund, P. A., Gruber, M. J., Sampson, N. A., Zaslavsky, A. M., & Kessler, R. C. (2010). Childhood adversities and adult psychiatric disorders in the national comorbidity survey replication I: Associations with first onset of DSM-IV disorders. *Archives of General Psychiatry, 67*(2), 113–123.

Gunter, R. W., & Bodner, G. E. (2008). How eye movements affect unpleasant memories: Support for a working-memory account. *Behaviour Research and Therapy, 46*(8), 913–931. https://doi.org/10.1016/j.brat.2008.04.006

Harper, M. L., Rasolkhani-Kalhorn, T., & Drozd, J. F. (2009). On the neural basis of EMDR therapy: Insights from qEEG studies. *Traumatology, 15*(2), 81–95. https://doi.org/10.1177/1534765609338498

Hart, H., & Rubia, K. (2012). Neuroimaging of child abuse: A critical review. *Frontiers in Human Neuroscience, 6*, 52. https://doi.org/10.3389/fnhum.2012.00052

Hase, M., Balmaceda, U. M., Ostacoli, L., Liebermann, P., Hofmann, A. (2017). The AIP Model of EMDR therapy and pathogenic memories. *Frontiers in Psychology, 8*,1578. https://doi.org/10.3389/fpsyg.2017.01578

Hase, M., Plagge, J., Hase, A., Braas, R., Ostacoli, L., Hofmann, A., & Huchzermeier, C. (2018). Eye movement desensitization and reprocessing versus treatment as usual in the treatment of depression: A randomized-controlled trial. *Frontiers in Psychology, 9*, 1384. https://doi.org/10.3389/fpsyg.2018.01384

Hofmann, A., Hase, M., Liebermann, P., Ostacoli, L., Lehnung, M., Ebner, F., ... Tumani, V. (2016). DeprEnd©—EMDR therapy protocol for the treatment of depressive disorders. In M. Luber (ed.), *Eye movement desensitization and reprocessing (EMDR) therapy scripted protocols and summary sheets: Treating anxiety, obsessive-compulsive, and mood-related conditions* (pp. 289–311). New York: Springer Publishing Co.

474 Trentini, Carletto, and Pagani

Hughes, K., Bellis, M. A., Hardcastle, K. A., Sethi, D., Butchart, A., Mikton, C., … Dunne, M. P. (2017). The effect of multiple adverse childhood experiences on health: A systematic review and meta-analysis. *The Lancet Public Health*, *2*(8), e356–e366. https://doi.org/10.1016/S2468-2667(17)30118-4

Infurna, M. R., Reichl, C., Parzer, P., Schimmenti, A., Bifulco, A., & Kaess, M. (2016). Associations between depression and specific childhood experiences of abuse and neglect: A meta-analysis. *Journal of Affective Disorders*, *190*, 47–55. https://doi.org/10.1016/j.jad.2015.09.006

International Society for Traumatic Stress Studies. (2018). *PTSD prevention and treatment guidelines methodology and recommendations*. Oakbrook Terrace, IL: ISTSS. Retrieved from www.istss.org/treating-trauma/new-istss-prevention-and-treatment-guidelines.aspx

Ironson, G., Freund, B., Strauss, J. L., & Williams, J. (2002). Comparison of two treatments for traumatic stress: A community-based study of EMDR and prolonged exposure. *Journal of Clinical Psychology*, *58*(1), 113–128. https://doi.org/10.1002/jclp.1132

Jaberghaderi, N., Greenwald, R., Rubin, A., Zand, S. O., & Dolatabadi, S. (2004). A comparison of CBT and EMDR for sexually-abused Iranian girls. *Clinical Psychology and Psychotherapy*, *11*(5), 358–368. https://doi.org/10.1002/cpp.395

Jarero, I., & Artigas, L. (2012). The EMDR Integrative Group Treatment Protocol: EMDR group treatment for early intervention following critical incidents. *European Review of Applied Psychology / Revue Européenne de Psychologie Appliquée*, *62*(4), 219–222. https://doi.org/10.1016/j.erap.2012.04.004

Kar, N., & Bastia, B. K. (2006). Post-traumatic stress disorder, depression and generalised anxiety disorder in adolescents after a natural disaster: A study of comorbidity. *Clinical Practice and Epidemiology in Mental Health: CP & EMH*, *2*, 17. https://doi.org/10.1186/1745-0179-2-17

Karatzias, A., Power, K., McGoldrick, T., Brown, K., Buchanan, R., Sharp, D., & Swanson, V. (2007). Predicting treatment outcome on three measures for post-traumatic stress disorder. *European Archives of Psychiatry and Clinical Neuroscience*, *257*(1), 40–46. http://dx.doi.org/10.1007/s00406-006-0682-2.

Kendler, K. S., & Gardner, C. O. (2016). Depressive vulnerability, stressful life events and episode onset of major depression: A longitudinal model. *Psychological Medicine*, *46*(9), 1865–1874. https://doi.org/10.1017/S0033291716000349

Khan, A. M., Dar, S., Ahmed, R., Bachu, R., Adnan, M., & Kotapati, V. P. (2018). Cognitive behavioral therapy versus eye movement desensitization and reprocessing in patients with post-traumatic stress disorder: Systematic review and meta-analysis of randomized clinical trials. *Cureus*, *10*(9), e3250. https://doi.org/10.7759/cureus.3250

Kim, J. S., & Lee, S. H. (2016). Influence of interactions between genes and childhood trauma on refractoriness in psychiatric disorders. *Progress in Neuro-Psychopharmacology and Biological Psychiatry*, *70*, 162–169. https://doi.org/10.1016/j.pnpbp.2016.01.013

Lamprecht, F., Köhnke, C., Lempa, W., Sack, M., Matzke, M., & Münte, T. F. (2004). Event-related potentials and EMDR treatment of post-traumatic stress disorder. *Neuroscience Research*, *49*(2), 267–272. https://doi.org/10.1016/j.neures.2004.02.013

Landin-Romero, R., Moreno-Alcazar, A., Pagani, M., & Amann, B. L. (2018). How does eye movement desensitization and reprocessing therapy work? A systematic

Eye Movement Desensitization and Reprocessing 475

review on suggested mechanisms of action. *Frontiers in Psychology, 9*, 1395. https://doi.org/0.3389/fpsyg.2018.01395

Lanius, U. F., & Bergmann, U. (2014). Dissociation, EMDR, and adaptive information processing: The role of sensory stimulation and sensory awareness. In U. F. Lanius, S. L. Paulsen, & F. M. Corrigan (eds), *Neurobiology and treatment of traumatic dissociation: Toward an embodied self* (pp. 213–242). New York: Springer Publishing Co.

Lansing, K., Amen, D. G., Hanks, C., & Rudy, L. (2005). High-resolution brain SPECT imaging and eye movement desensitization and reprocessing in police officers with PTSD. *Journal of Neuropsychiatry and Clinical Neurosciences, 17*(4), 526–532. https://doi.org/10.1176/appi.neuropsych.17.4.526

Lee, C., Gavriel, H., Drummond, P., Richards, J., & Greenwald, R. (2002). Treatment of PTSD: Stress inoculation training with prolonged exposure compared to EMDR. *Clinical Psychology, 58*, 1071–1089. https://doi.org/10.1002/jclp.10039

Lee, C. W., & Cuijpers, P. (2013). A meta-analysis of the contribution of eye movements in processing emotional memories. *Journal of Behavior Therapy and Experimental Psychiatry, 44*(2), 231–239. https://doi.org/10.1016/j.jbtep.2012.11.001

Leeds, A. M. (2016). *A guide to the standard EMDR therapy protocols for clinicians, supervisors, and consultants.* New York: Springer Publishing Company, LLC.

Leist, T., & Dadds, M. R. (2009). Adolescents' ability to read different emotional faces relates to their history of maltreatment and type of psychopathology. *Clinical Child Psychology and Psychiatry, 14*(2), 237–250. https://doi.org/10.1177/1359104508100887

LeTendre, M. L., & Reed, M. B. (2017). The effect of adverse childhood experience on clinical diagnosis of a substance use disorder: Results of a nationally representative study. *Substance Use & Misuse, 52*(6), 689–697. https://doi.org/10.1080/10826084.2016.1253746

Liu, M., Wang, L., Shi, Z., Zhang, Z., Zhang, K., & Shen, J. (2011). Mental health problems among children one-year after Sichuan earthquake in China: A follow-up study. *PLoS One, 6*(2), e14706. https://doi.org/10.1371/journal.pone.0014706

Looi, J., Pagani, M., Nardo, D., Raphael, B., & Wahlund, L. (2010). Structural and functional neuroimaging in PTSD: A neurobiological update. In L. Sher & A. Vilens (eds), *Neurobiology of post–traumatic stress.* New York: Nova Science Publishers.

Lundqvist, D., Flykt, A., & Öhman, A. (1998). *The Karolinska Directed Emotional Faces – KDEF. CD-ROM from Department of Clinical Neuroscience.* Stockholm, Sweden: Psychology section, Karolinska Institutet.

Malandrone, F., Carletto, S., Hase, M., Hofmann, A., & Ostacoli, L. (2019). A brief narrative summary of randomized controlled trials investigating EMDR treatment of patients with depression. *Journal of EMDR Practice and Research, 13*(4), 302–306.

Markus, W., & Hornsveld, H. K. (2017). EMDR interventions in addiction. *Journal of EMDR Practice and Research, 11*(1), 3–29. https://doi.org/10.1891/1933-3196.11.1.3

Maslovaric, G., Zaccagnino, M., Mezzaluna, C., Perilli, S., Trivellato, D., Longo, V., & Civilotti, C. (2017). The effectiveness of eye movement desensitization and reprocessing integrative group protocol with adolescent survivors of the central Italy earthquake. *Frontiers in Psychology, 8*, 1826. https://doi.org/10.3389/fpsyg.2017.01826

476 Trentini, Carletto, and Pagani

Maxfield, L. (2008). Considering mechanisms of action in EMDR. *Journal of EMDR Practice and Research, 2*(4), 234–238. https://doi.org/10.1891/1933-3196.2.4.234

Minelli, A., Zampieri, E., Sacco, C., Bazzanella, R., Mezzetti, N., Tessari, E., ... & Bortolomasi, M. (2019). Clinical efficacy of trauma-focused psychotherapies in treatment-resistant depression (TRD) in-patients: A randomized, controlled pilot-study. *Psychiatry Research, 273*, 567–574. https://doi.org/10.1016/j.psychres.2019.01.070

Mitchell, A. J., Baker-Glenn, E. A., Granger, L., & Symonds, P. (2010). Can the distress thermometer be improved by additional mood domains? Part I. Initial validation of the Emotion Thermometers tool. *Psycho-Oncology, 19*(2), 125–133. https://doi.org/10.1002/pon.1523

Moreno-Alcázar, A., Treen, D., Valiente-Gómez, A., Sio-Eroles, A., Pérez, V., Amann, B. L., & Radua, J. (2017). Efficacy of eye movement desensitization and reprocessing in children and adolescent with post-traumatic stress disorder: A meta-analysis of randomized controlled trials. *Frontiers in Psychology, 8*, 1750. https://doi.org/10.3389/fpsyg.2017.01750

Morgan, L., Scourfield, J., Williams, D., Jasper, A., & Lewis, G. (2003). The Aberfan disaster: 33-year follow-up of survivors. *The British Journal of Psychiatry, 182*(6), 532–536. https://doi.org/10.1192/bjp.182.6.532

Murphy, B., Herrman, H., Hawthorne, G., Pinzone, T., & Evert, H. (2000). *Australian WHOQoL Instruments: User's Manual and Interpretation Guide.* Melbourne, Vic: Australian WHOQoL Field Study Centre.

Nardo, D., Högberg, G., Lanius, R., Jacobsson, H., Jonsson, C., Hällström, T., & Pagani, M. (2013). Gray matter volume alterations related to trait dissociation in PTSD and traumatized controls. *Acta Psychiatrica Scandinavica, 128*, 222–233.

Nardo, D., Högberg, G., Looi, J. C. L., Larsson, S., Hällström, T., & Pagani, M. (2010). Gray matter density in limbic and paralimbic cortices is associated with trauma load and EMDR outcome in PTSD patients. *Journal of Psychiatric Research, 44*(7), 477–485. https://doi.org/10.1016/j.jpsychires.2009.10.014

National Institute for Health and Clinical Excellence. (2018). Post-traumatic stress disorder. NICE guideline [NG116]. Retrieved from: www.nice.org.uk/guidance/ng116

National Institute of Mental Health. (2002). *Mental health and mass violence: Evidence-based early psychological intervention for victims/survivors of mass violence. A workshop to reach consensus on best practices.* NIH Publication No. 02-5138. Washington, DC: U.S. Government Printing Office.

Nemeroff, C. B. (2016). Paradise lost: The neurobiological and clinical consequences of child abuse and neglect. *Neuron, 89*(5), 892–909. https://doi.org/10.1016/j.neuron.2016.01.019

Nijdam, M. J., Gersons, B. P. R., Reitsma, J. B., De Jongh, A., & Olff, M. (2012). Brief eclectic psychotherapy v. eye movement desensitisation and reprocessing therapy for post-traumatic stress disorder: Randomised controlled trial. *British Journal of Psychiatry, 200*(3), 224–231. https://doi.org/10.1192/bjp.bp.111.099234

Norris, F. H., Foster, J. D., & Weishaar, D. L. (2002). The epidemiology of sex differences in PTSD across developmental, societal, and research context. In R. O. Kimerling, C. Paige, & J. Wolfe (eds), *Gender and PTSD* (pp. 3–42). New York: Guilford Press.

Eye Movement Desensitization and Reprocessing 477

Ostacoli, L., Carletto, S., Cavallo, M., Baldomir-Gago, P., Di Lorenzo, G., Fernandez, I., ... Hofmann, A. (2018). Comparison of eye movement desensitization reprocessing and cognitive behavioral therapy as adjunctive treatments for recurrent depression: The European Depression EMDR Network (EDEN) randomized controlled trial. *Frontiers in Psychology, 9*, 74. https://doi.org/10.3389/fpsyg.2018.00074

Oyama, M., Nakamura, K., Suda, Y., & Someya, T. (2012). Social network disruption as a major factor associated with psychological distress 3 years after the 2004 Niigata-Chuetsu earthquake in Japan. *Environmental Health and Preventive Medicine, 17*(2), 118–123. https://doi.org/10.1007/s12199-011-0225-y

Paauw, C., de Roos, C., Tummers, J., de Jongh, A., & Dingemans, A. (2019). Effectiveness of trauma-focused treatment for adolescents with major depressive disorder. *European Journal of Psychotraumatology, 10*(1), 1682931. Doi: 10.1080/20008198.2019.1682931

Pagani, M., Amann, B. L., Landin-Romero, R., & Carletto, S. (2017). Eye movement desensitization and reprocessing and slow wave sleep: A putative mechanism of action. *Frontiers in Psychology, 8*, 1935. https://doi.org/10.3389/fpsyg.2017.01935

Pagani, M., & Cavallo, M. (2014). Neuroimaging in PTSD-related psychotherapies. In *PET and SPECT in Psychiatry* (pp. 397–410). Berlin: Springer.

Pagani, M., Di Lorenzo, G., Monaco, L., Niolu, C., Siracusano, A., Verardo, A. R., ... Ammaniti, M. (2011). Pretreatment, intratreatment, and posttreatment EEG imaging of EMDR: Methodology and preliminary results from a single case. *Journal of EMDR Practice and Research, 5*(2), 42–56. https://doi.org/10.1891/1933-3196.5.2.42

Pagani, M., Di Lorenzo, G., Verardo, A. R., Nicolais, G., Monaco, L., Lauretti, G., ... Siracusano, A. (2012). Neurobiological correlates of EMDR monitoring – An EEG study. *PLoS One, 7*(9), e45753. https://doi.org/10.1371/journal.pone.0045753

Pagani, M., Högberg, G., Fernandez, I., & Siracusano, A. (2013). Correlates of EMDR therapy in functional and structural neuroimaging: A critical summary of recent findings. *Journal of EMDR Practice and Research, 7*(1), 29–38. https://doi.org/10.1891/1933-3196.7.1.29

Pagani, M., Högberg, G., Salmaso, D., Nardo, D., Sundin, Ö., Jonsson, C., ... Hällström, T. (2007). Effects of EMDR psychotherapy on 99mTc-HMPAO distribution in occupation-related post-traumatic stress disorder. *Nuclear Medicine Communications, 28*(10), 757–765. https://doi.org/10.1097/MNM.0b013e3282742035

Parikh, D., De Ieso, P., Garvey, G., Thachil, T., Ramamoorthi, R., Penniment, M., & Jayaraj, R. (2015). Post-traumatic stress disorder and post-traumatic growth in breast cancer patients – A systematic review. *Asian Pacific Journal of Cancer Prevention: APJCP, 16*(2), 641–646.

Paterniti, S., Sterner, I., Caldwell, C., & Bisserbe, J.-C. (2017). Childhood neglect predicts the course of major depression in a tertiary care sample: A follow-up study. *BMC Psychiatry, 17*(1), 113. https://doi.org/10.1186/s12888-017-1270-x

Perkonigg, A., Pfister, H., Stein, M. B., Höfler, M., Lieb, R., Maercker, A., & Wittchen, H.-U. (2005). Longitudinal course of posttraumatic stress disorder and posttraumatic stress disorder symptoms in a community sample of adolescents and young adults. *The American Journal of Psychiatry, 162*(7), 1320–1327. https://doi.org/10.1176/appi.ajp.162.7.1320

478   Trentini, Carletto, and Pagani

Perrin, S., Meiser-Stedman, R., & Smith, P. (2005). The Children's Revised Impact of Event Scale (CRIES): Validity as a screening instrument for PTSD. *Behavioural and Cognitive Psychotherapy*, *33*(4), 487. https://doi.org/10.1017/S1352465805002419

Pollak, S. D., Cicchetti, D., Hornung, K., & Reed, A. (2000). Recognizing emotion in faces: developmental effects of child abuse and neglect. *Developmental Psychology*, *36*(5), 679–688. https://doi.org/10.1037/0012-1649.36.5.679

Power, K., McGoldrick, T., Brown, K., Buchanan, R., Sharp, D., Swanson, V., & Karatzias, A. (2002). A controlled comparison of eye movement desensitization and reprocessing versus exposure plus cognitive restructuring versus waiting list in the treatment of post-traumatic stress disorder. *Clinical Psychology and Psychotherapy*, *9*, 299–318. https://doi.org/10.1002/cpp.341

Propper, R. E., & Christman, S. D. (2008). Interhemispheric interaction and saccadic horizontal eye movements: Implications for episodic memory, EMDR, and PTSD. *Journal of EMDR Practice and Research*, *2*(4), 269–281. https://doi.org/10.1891/1933-3196.2.4.269

Rodenburg, R., Benjamin, A., de Roos, C., Meijer, A. M., & Stams, G. J. (2009). Efficacy of EMDR in children: A meta-analysis. *Clinical Psychology Review*, *29*(7), 599–606. https://doi.org/10.1016/j.cpr.2009.06.008

Rogers, S., Silver, S. M., Goss, J., Obenschein, J., Willis, A., & Withney, R. L. (1999). A single session, group study of exposure and eye movement desensitization and reprocessing in the treatment of posttraumatic stress disorder among Vietnam War veterans: Preliminary data. *Journal of Anxiety Disorders*, *13*, 119–130. https://doi.org/10.1016/S0887-6185(98)00043-7

Scott, K. M., McLaughlin, K. A., Smith, D. A. R., & Ellis, P. M. (2012). Childhood maltreatment and DSM-IV adult mental disorders: Comparison of prospective and retrospective findings. *The British Journal of Psychiatry*, *200*(6), 469–475. https://doi.org/10.1192/bjp.bp.111.103267

Shapiro, E. (2012). EMDR and early psychological intervention following trauma. *European Review of Applied Psychology / Revue Européenne de Psychologie Appliquée*, *62*(4), 241–251. https://doi.org/10.1016/j.erap.2012.09.003

Shapiro, F. (1989). Eye movement desensitization: A new treatment for post-traumatic stress disorder. *Journal of Behavior Therapy and Experimental Psychiatry*, *20*(3), 211–217. https://doi.org/10.1016/0005-7916(89)90025-6

Shapiro, F. (1995). *Eye movement desensitization and reprocessing: Basic principles, protocols, and procedures*. New York: Guilford Press.

Shapiro, F. (2001). *Eye movement desensitization and reprocessing: Basic principles, protocols, and procedures* (2nd edn). New York: Guilford Press.

Shapiro, F. (2002). EMDR 12 years after its introduction: Past and future research. *Journal of Clinical Psychology*, *58*(1), 1–22. https://doi.org/10.1002/jclp.1126

Shapiro, F. (2014). The role of eye movement desensitization and reprocessing (EMDR) therapy in medicine: Addressing the psychological and physical symptoms stemming from adverse life experiences. *The Permanente Journal*, *18*(1), 71–77. http://dx.doi.org/10.7812/TPP/13-098

Shapiro, F., & Maxfield, L. (2002). Eye movement desensitization and reprocessing (EMDR): Information processing in the treatment of trauma. *Journal of Clinical Ppsychology*, *58*(8), 933–946.

Solomon, R. M., & Shapiro, F. (2008). EMDR and the adaptive information processing model: Potential mechanisms of change. *Journal of EMDR Practice and Research*, *2*(4), 315–325. https://doi.org/10.1891/1933-3196.2.4.315

Eye Movement Desensitization and Reprocessing 479

Spielberger, C. D. (1983). *State-trait anxiety inventory for adults.* APA PsycTests.

Stickgold, R. (2002). EMDR: A putative neurobiological mechanism of action. *Journal of Clinical Psychology, 58*(1), 61–75. https://doi.org/10.1002/jclp.1129

Stickgold, R. (2008). Sleep-dependent memory processing and EMDR action. *Journal of EMDR Practice and Research, 2*(4), 289–299. https://doi.org/10.1891/1933-3196.2.4.289

Tapia, G. (2019). Review of EMDR Interventions for individuals with substance use disorder with/without comorbid posttraumatic stress disorder. *Journal of EMDR Practice and Research, 13*(4), 345–353.

Te Brake, H., Dückers, M., De Vries, M., Van Duin, D., Rooze, M., & Spreeuwenberg, C. (2009). Early psychosocial interventions after disasters, terrorism, and other shocking events: Guideline development. *Nursing & Health Sciences, 11*(4), 336–343. https://doi.org/10.1111/j.1442-2018.2009.00491.x

Toyabe, S., Shioiri, T., Kuwabara, H., Endoh, T., Tanabe, N., Someya, T., & Akazawa, K. (2006). Impaired psychological recovery in the elderly after the Niigata-Chuetsu Earthquake in Japan: A population-based study. *BMC Public Health, 6*, 230. https://doi.org/10.1186/1471-2458-6-230

Trentini, C., Lauriola, M., Giuliani, A., Maslovaric, G., Tambelli, R., Fernandez, I., & Pagani, M. (2018). Dealing with the aftermath of mass disasters: A field study on the application of EMDR integrative group treatment protocol with child survivors of the 2016 Italy earthquakes. *Frontiers in Psychology, 9*, 862. https://doi.org/10.3389/fpsyg.2018.00862

Trentini, C., Pagani, M., Fania, P., Speranza, A. M., Nicolais, G., Sibilia, A., ... Ammaniti, M. (2015). Neural processing of emotions in traumatized children treated with eye movement desensitization and reprocessing therapy: A hdEEG study. *Frontiers in Psychology, 6*, 1662.

Tsai, K.-Y., Chou, P., Chou, F. H.-C., Su, T. T.-P., Lin, S.-C., Lu, M.-K., ... Chen, M.-C. (2007). Three-year follow-up study of the relationship between posttraumatic stress symptoms and quality of life among earthquake survivors in Yu-Chi, Taiwan. *Journal of Psychiatric Research, 41*(1–2), 90–96. https://doi.org/10.1016/j.jpsychires.2005.10.004

Tunnard, C., Rane, L. J., Wooderson, S. C., Markopoulou, K., Poon, L., Fekadu, A., ... & Cleare, A. J. (2014). The impact of childhood adversity on suicidality and clinical course in treatment-resistant depression. *Journal of Affective Disorders, 152*, 122–130.

Ularntinon, S., Piyasil, V., Ketumarn, P., Sitdhiraksa, N., Pityaratstian, N., Lerthattasilp, T., ... Pimratana, W. (2008). Assessment of psychopathological consequences in children at 3 years after tsunami disaster. *Journal of the Medical Association of Thailand = Chotmaihet Thangphaet, 91 Suppl. 3*, S69–75.

Valiente-Gómez, A., Moreno-Alcázar, A., Gardoki-Souto, I., Masferrer, C., Porta, S., Royuela, O., Hogg, B., Lupo, W., & Amann, B. L. (2019). Theoretical background and clinical aspects of the use of EMDR in patients with Bipolar Disorder. *Journal of EMDR Practice and Research, 13*(4), 307–312.

Valiente-Gómez, A., Moreno-Alcázar, A., Treen, D., Cedrón, C., Colom, F., Pérez, V., & Amann, B. L. (2017). EMDR beyond PTSD: A systematic literature review. *Frontiers in Psychology, 8*, 1668. https://doi.org/10.3389/fpsyg.2017.01668

van den Hout, M. A., & Engelhard, I. M. (2012). How does EMDR work? *Journal of Experimental Psychopathology, 3*(5), 724–738.

480 Trentini, Carletto, and Pagani

van der Kolk, B. A. (2007). The developmental impact of childhood trauma. In L. J. Kirmayer, R. Lemelson, & M. Barad (eds), *Understanding trauma* (pp. 224–241). Cambridge: Cambridge University Press.

van der Kolk, B. A., & d'Andrea, W. (2010). Towards a developmental trauma disorder diagnosis for childhood interpersonal trauma. In R. A. Lanius, E. Vermetten, & C. Pain (eds), *The impact of early life trauma on health and disease* (pp. 57–68). Cambridge: Cambridge University Press.

van der Kolk, B. A., Spinazzola, J., Blaustein, M. E., Hopper, J. W., Hopper, E. K., Korn, D. L., & Simpson, W. B. (2007). A randomized clinical trial of eye movement desensitization and reprocessing (EMDR), fluoxetine, and pill placebo in the treatment of posttraumatic stress disorder: Treatment effects and long-term maintenance. *Journal of Clinical Psychiatry, 68*(1), 37–46.

van Harmelen, A. L., van Tol, M. J., Demenescu, L. R., van der Wee, N. J. A., Veltman, D. J., Aleman, A., ... Elzinga, B. M. (2013). Enhanced amygdala reactivity to emotional faces in adults reporting childhood emotional maltreatment. *Social Cognitive and Affective Neuroscience, 8*(4), 362–369. https://doi.org/10.1093/scan/nss007

van Strien, N. M., Cappaert, N. L. M., & Witter, M. P. (2009). The anatomy of memory: An interactive overview of the parahippocampal–hippocampal network. *Nature Reviews Neuroscience, 10*(4), 272–282. https://doi.org/10.1038/nrn2614

Vanitallie, T. B. (2002). Stress: A risk factor for serious illness. *Metabolism, 51*(suppl. 1), 40–45. https://doi.org/10.1053/meta.2002.33191

Vaughan, K., Armstrong, M. S., Gold, R., O'Connor, N., Jenneke, W., & Tarrier, N. (1994). A trial of eye movement desensitization compared to image habituation training and applied muscle relaxation in posttraumatic stress disorder. *Journal of Behavior Therapy and Experimental Psychiatry, 25*, 283–290. https://doi.org/10.1016/0005-7916(94)90036-1

Wang, C. W., Chan, C. L. W., & Ho, R. T. H. (2013). Prevalence and trajectory of psychopathology among child and adolescent survivors of disasters: A systematic review of epidemiological studies across 1987–2011. *Social Psychiatry and Psychiatric Epidemiology, 48*(11), 1697–1720. https://doi.org/10.1007/s00127-013-0731-x

Weathers, F. W., Bovin, M. J., Lee, D. J., Sloan, D. M., Schnurr, P. P., Kaloupek, D. G., Keane, T.M., & Marx, B. P. (2018). The Clinician-Administered PTSD Scale for DSM–5 (CAPS-5): Development and initial psychometric evaluation in military veterans. *Psychological Assessment, 30*(3), 383.

Weiss, D. S., & Marmar, C. R. (1997). The impact of event scale-revised. In J. P. Wilson & T. M. Keane (eds), *Assessing psychological trauma and PTSD* (pp. 399–411) (New York: Guilford Press).

Wiersma, J. E., Hovens, J. G. F. M., van Oppen, P., Giltay, E. J., van Schaik, D. J. F., Beekman, A. T. F., & Penninx, B. W. J. H. (2009). The importance of childhood trauma and childhood life events for chronicity of depression in adults. *The Journal of Clinical Psychiatry, 70*(7), 983–989. https://doi.org/10.4088/JCP.08m04521

Wood, E., Ricketts, T., & Parry, G. (2018). EMDR as a treatment for long-term depression: A feasibility study. *Psychology and Psychotherapy: Theory, Research and Practice, 91*(1), 63–78.

World Health Organization. (2013). *Guidelines for the management of conditions specifically related to stress*. Geneva: WHO. Retrieved from: www.who.int/mental_health/emergencies/stress_guidelines/en/

Zhang, Z., Shi, Z., Wang, L., & Liu, M. (2011). One year later: Mental health problems among survivors in hard-hit areas of the Wenchuan earthquake. *Public Health*, *125*(5), 293–300. https://doi.org/10.1016/j.puhe.2010.12.008

Conclusion

Towards a Better Future

Alan Hall, Rosemary Ricciardelli,
Stephen Bornstein, and R. Nicholas Carleton

The psychological and social effects of exposures to potentially psychologically traumatic events have long plagued human societies. Over the last century, efforts to define and categorize the impacts of potentially psychologically traumatic events have developed with growing urgency as the severity, breadth, and costs of the problem are increasingly recognized. An ever-growing body of multidisciplinary clinical, biological, and social research has fuelled debates and changed understandings of how to define and diagnose mental health disorders such as posttraumatic stress disorder (PTSD), how exposures to different potentially psychologically traumatic events can compromise mental health, and how compromised mental health can impact individuals, family, communities, and organizations (Canadian Institute for Public Safety Research and Treatment (CIPSRT, 2019). The current collection reflects some of these debates and contributes to what we hope will be a growing consensus on what needs to be done to pursue effective strategies to support mental health. We also acknowledge that the wide range of research- and practice-based activities has produced a multitude of different approaches to mental health, as well as proposals for related government and organizational policies, many of which we start to address in the current collection. By bringing together a very diverse range of researchers and practitioners from various disciplines, the current text is intended to demonstrate the variability and complexity of current activities and to showcase convergence where available.

A central theme highlighted in the current collection is the variability in the manifestations and effects of potentially psychologically traumatic events across contexts. In Chapters 1 and 6, the authors unpack much of our early understanding of the impact of potentially psychologically traumatic events resulting from military service. Over the last several decades, the impact of potentially psychologically traumatic events outside of military service has increasingly been recognized; accordingly, the current text showcases the need for more research on the prevalence and impacts of potentially psychologically traumatic events across a wide range of occupations and life situations. For example, in Chapter 2, Weeks and colleagues provide up-to-date information about PTSD prevalence in

DOI: 10.4324/9781351134637-19

Conclusion: Towards a Better Future   483

diverse populations, recognizing the challenges involved in documenting general prevalence rates of, as well as the current challenges specific to, PTSD. Weeks and colleagues emphasize the need for higher quality studies, with more consistency and regularity as part of building the research foundation for more robust solutions for PTSD. Robust surveillance is argued as critical for effectively managing resources for remediating PTSD. Weeks and colleagues provide recommendations about next steps for research to inform policy, support people, and build solid foundations for the future.

In Chapter 5, Marrello and colleagues also underscore the sparsity of evidence documenting prevalence rates in Canada for PTSD among public safety personnel, military personnel, veterans, and other populations regularly exposed to potentially psychologically traumatic events. The authors note the critical gaps in our knowledge base, delineating the risks associated with such gaps, and discuss the opportunities that more robust prevalence data could provide. The chapter builds on the work by Weeks and colleagues by showcasing the diverse populations that appear disproportionately impacted by potentially psychologically traumatic event exposures and by unpacking the need for, and benefits of, improving the prevalence research for PTSD and potentially psychologically traumatic events for all Canadians.

Several of the current chapters document the significance of potentially psychologically traumatic events across a wide range of occupations and life circumstances, showcasing the variability and complexity of the sources of potentially psychologically traumatic events. The authors clarify that interventions need to be designed with a much better understanding of diverse contexts and situations that can produce potentially psychologically traumatic events while constraining help seeking and help provision. For example, in Chapter 9, Spencer and colleagues study the impact on police officers of investigating internet sex crimes perpetrated against children and women. The investigations done by police officers are framed within the concept of "dirty work", which describes the interactive impact of potentially psychologically traumatic event exposures, emotional labour, stigmatized work, and stigmatized communities. The researchers note a confluence of injurious factors potentially impacting police officers who work to manage internet sex crimes perpetrated against children in particular. In addition, the authors argue that the existence of these compounding stigmas warrants efforts by researchers, policy makers, and practitioners to better protect and support such officers. In Chapter 11, Ricciardelli and her colleagues describe the varied impacts of potentially psychologically traumatic event exposures on Canadian provincial and territorial correctional workers. The results provide nuanced delineations of the wide variety of potentially psychologically traumatic event-related and mental health injuries that can be experienced by correctional officers. Chapter 11 describes the multitude of challenges correctional workers can face in managing their emotions, accessing support, and engaging mental health care. Ricciardelli and colleagues conclude by providing specific

484   Hall, Ricciardelli, Bornstein, and Carleton

recommendations for opportunities to improve supports for the mental health of correctional workers more broadly.

The contributing authors also recognize that the impact of potentially psychologically traumatic events does not stop with the individual worker. Instead, there are social and psychological effects that radiate into the family and the community. In Chapter 7, for example, Cramm and colleagues describe the gaps in research and evidence-based practice regarding the impact of armed forces service and of PTSD on *families*. Most of the research currently available focuses on how military service, esposures to potentially psychologically traumatic event and PTSD impact the individual serving member; however, there is also growing evidence that families can experience intense changes in function, marital difficulties, parenting problems, and adjustment difficulties. Family members of persons who serve may also experience increased risks to their own mental health. The chapter emphasizes the need for more research and points to opportunities to provide effective proactive and reactive supports for family members of armed forces personnel, which can combine to provide better support for family members as well as for the persons who serve.

As detailed by contributors in several other chapters, exposures to potentially psychologically traumatic event exposures are not unique to work or occupational groups. Some life and social contexts involve greater risk of such exposures than others, as well as reduced access to mental health support services. For example, in Chapter 8, Waegermakers-Schiff and Lange provide guidance for understanding the interactive impacts of potentially psychologically traumatic events, PTSD, and homelessness. The authors report that persons who are homeless experience multiple potentially psychologically traumatic event exposures, which may explain disproportionate difficulties associated with PTSD symptoms. The challenges posed by repeated potentially psychologically traumatic event exposures are further complicated by barriers to accessing care and by high risks of burnout among workers trying to serve homeless populations. Chapter 8 provides compelling evidence for implementing trauma-informed care while underscoring the substantial challenges faced by persons who are homeless. Similarly, in Chapter 12, van Ginneken and Vanhooren provide information on the complex interactions between potentially psychologically traumatic events, PTSD, and imprisoned persons. Their work highlights how imprisonment can be a psychologically traumatic event and underscores that persons who are likely to become imprisoned are also likely to have experienced a significant history of potentially psychologically traumatic events exposures. Chapter 12 also contextualizes potentially psychologically traumatic events and posttraumatic growth experiences among correctional services as part of the processes involved with imprisonment. For some people, prison can provide much-needed stability and access to resources that may otherwise be unavailable to them. The authors help provide nuanced guidance that can improve care for imprisoned persons

Conclusion: Towards a Better Future 485

and for the correctional workers who serve them. The authors emphasize the opportunities to address what may be lifetimes of potentially psychologically traumatic event exposures while working towards posttraumatic growth.

Implicit in many of the chapters on potentially psychologically traumatic events related to occupations or life situations is the significance of culture, power, and social differentiation in shaping both vulnerability to mental health injuries and accessing help. However, some contributors were explicit in recognizing multiple causes of, and potential solutions for, PTSD that involve cultural, political, economic and social structures that constrain and define the social possibilities for different populations. For example, in Chapter 6, McCreary provides a clear and poignant description of how conceptualizations of masculinities interact with mental disorders, particularly PTSD, especially for persons regularly exposed to potentially psychologically traumatic events. McCreary's contribution showcases how gender roles directly and indirectly influence mental health through self-stigma, other-stigma, and barriers to help-seeking. McCreary also alludes to systemic challenges created by cultures involving gender role socializations that exacerbate self-stigma, other-stigma, and barriers to help-seeking; while also acknowledging that cultural changes regarding gender role socialization are likely to take time and must begin with recognizing and discussing the impacts of gender.

In Chapter 3, Szymanski and Hall highlight potential environmental, organizational, operational, and structural opportunities to help manage the challenges associated with PTSD, all of which might produce broad benefits for people exposed to potentially psychologically traumatic events. The authors detail how legislation can have rapid and significant positive impacts on the management of mental disorders, both directly and indirectly, by facilitating changes to organizations and even to individual stigma. Their work underscores the importance of collective, collaborative, evidence-informed actions when trying to make pervasive improvements to health care, while emphasizing the importance of political actors and action within and outside the workplace. Despite the legislative limitations Szymanski and Hall identify, they provide a hopeful message about progress grounded in the collective action of workers and labour unions.

In Chapter 4, Thompson and colleagues present other efforts to recognize the structural constraints and opportunities for managing PTSD. Thompson and colleagues highlight an under-used avenue for addressing the challenges of potentially psychologically traumatic event exposures and mental health injuries such as PTSD—primary medical care. For many Canadians, including public safety personnel, primary care physicians are among the first access points for all health care, including mental health care (Carleton et al., 2020). Primary care physicians might benefit from additional supports for identifying the highly varied mental and physical health challenges that might follow potentially psychologically traumatic

486   *Hall, Ricciardelli, Bornstein, and Carleton*

event exposures. Thompson and colleagues offer recommendations to improve trauma-informed activities in primary care practice. Front-line solutions for individual care providers and their patients to identify mental health challenges are critical for providing prompt and effective health care that can help mitigate the societal burden of PTSD. Not all populations have equal access to primary care physicians, but the implication is clear that various front-line health care and social workers can play a vital role if they are given the knowledge and the capacity to diagnose and intervene effectively and early.

The primary objective is typically mitigating the impact of potentially psychologically traumatic event exposures on people. That objective is best served with substantially more knowledge about the biopsychosocial manifestations, causes, and consequences of mental health injuries. By extension, having a variety of options and avenues for evidence-based mental health care increases flexibility, supports stepped-care approaches, and maximizes capacity for providing support. Accordingly, the chapters in the final section of our collection illustrate efforts to understand the biological, psychological, and social markers associated with PTSD and potentially psychologically traumatic events.

In Chapter 13, Eisenmann and colleagues provide data from animal modelling that can help develop our understanding of how humans experience PTSD. Their work clarifies the potential utility of animal models and the potential impacts of early life exposures to potentially psychologically traumatic events. The authors describe biopsychosocial interactions that can influence the experience of PTSD as part of a framework that leverages animal models. In Chapter 14, McCallum and colleagues address some potential benefits of animal modelling for understanding fear and PTSD. The authors showcase the potentially pervasive impact of even a single potentially psychologically traumatic event exposure and underscore the potential impacts of repeated exposures. Their work helps to describe the interactions between fear, memory, and PTSD, and clarifies the potential opportunities to employ pharmacological treatments to help mitigate PTSD.

In Chapter 15, Ewles and colleagues describe the important interaction between social support, potentially psychologically traumatic events, and PTSD for public safety personnel. There is growing evidence that personal support networks (e.g., spouses, family, friends, peers) play a critical role in supporting the mental health of people, including public safety personnel, managing the sequelae of exposures to potentially psychologically traumatic events. Results from the two research studies the authors summarize provide specific recommendations about how people might be helpful after someone experiences a potentially psychologically traumatic event and about several barriers that may impede help. The authors help to inform sustainable processes for supporting people who are regularly exposed to potentially psychologically traumatic events and emphasize possible socially focused opportunities for supporting

Conclusion: Towards a Better Future 487

PTSD. Specifically, the authors highlight opportunities that too often receive less attention than the biological and psychological avenues in biopsychosocial models.

In Chapter 16, Chalk and Bonar provide results from an evaluation of group-based cognitive processing therapy for PTSD. The results support using group-based cognitive processing therapy for PTSD as well as for other mental health conditions. The authors highlight recent developments regarding group-based interventions and offer suggestions for how research might further advance the effectiveness of such treatments. Their results may also be useful for informing proactive processes that can play a role in training and early intervention, in addition to treatment.

The collection closes with work by Trentini and colleagues who, in Chapter 17, provide an overview of historical and contemporary research supporting the use of Eye Movement Desensitization and Reprocessing for PTSD. The authors describe the phases of the Eye Movement Desensitization and Reprocessing protocol and analyse some proposed underlying mechanisms. The authors describe recent research on the neurobiology of Eye Movement Desensitization and Reprocessing and its potential uses for conditions other than PTSD.

What Is to Be Done?

Our collection illustrates the substantial progress being made in the study of potentially psychologically traumatic event-related disorders. The authors call for more research on diagnoses and symptoms, prevalence, causation, and treatment effectiveness. The work documents a consensus on the importance of PTSD and the related impact on a broad range of people. We also point to disagreements and uncertainties on several important issues that inform the path forward in both research and practice. In addressing such issues, questions are raised about: 1) how to identify the full range of events and contexts that can cause mental health injuries, including posttraumatic stress injuries; 2) how to better document potentially psychologically traumatic event exposures; and 3) how to understand what, if anything, can be done environmentally, organizationally, operationally, or structurally to proactively prevent or reduce potentially psychologically traumatic event exposures or their impacts. Questions have also been posed about the need to recognize that PTSD is only one of many mental health disorders that might result from being exposed to one or more potentially psychologically traumatic events. Our contributors speak to the importance of documenting the prevalence of each type of mental health injury that can follow exposure to one or more kinds or degrees of potentially psychologically traumatic event exposures. The collection also raises questions about 1) how to best remediate mental health injuries; 2) who is responsible for remediating mental health injuries and under what contexts; and 3) who is responsible for proactively mediating mental health injuries for persons exposed to

488 Hall, Ricciardelli, Bornstein, and Carleton

potentially psychologically traumatic events, particularly for people who endure repeated exposures.

The authors of several chapters describe the political and organizational challenges associated with leveraging the available resources to support people exposed to one or more potentially psychologically traumatic events. Organizations, occupations, and communities are structured in ways that disadvantage some subpopulations over others in terms of risk, supports, and access to treatment. The authors also describe the difficulties associated with managing the plethora of misinformation about mental health injuries that can lead to problems such as stigma and discrimination. Recognizing and resolving inequities, challenges, and misinformation are critical steps towards broader solutions for managing PTSD, and all of these begin with better communication. Several authors in the current collection emphasize the use of language that minimizes stigma and discrimination. There are many ways for potentiating more supportive language for mental health in general and PTSD in particular, but identifying best practices based on research evidence will be an ongoing challenge for all stakeholders.

Our contributors appear to share the view that an understanding of the breadth and depth of the challenges resulting from exposure to one or more potentially psychologically traumatic events is another critical step towards building better solutions. Evidence presented and reviewed in the collection suggests that there may be several multimodal biopsychosocial opportunities for mitigating PTSD. The opportunities include potential avenues for effective changes at several levels including environmental, systemic, structural, organizational, and familial, all of which can occur in addition to diverse efforts that may be described as focused more uniquely on the individual level. There is also increasing evidence that repeated potentially psychologically traumatic event exposures may require intense and ongoing mitigation strategies, many of which have yet to be fully developed and tested. In any case, the successful development and application of research depends on concerted advocacy efforts from occupational groups, labour unions, mental health experts, and community organizations committed to mitigating the experience of impact from potentially psychologically traumatic events for everyone.

Our contributors also appear to agree that researchers and practitioners can best support the development and applications of these solutions with broad, coordinated, collaborative multi-disciplinary efforts, which can reasonably be expected to have direct and indirect benefits for improving mental health. Accordingly, our next steps as researchers appear to involve coordinating proactive and reactive intervention efforts along with iterative evaluations to help build progressively more effective interventions. We hope readers have found the current collection to be a helpful contribution. We also emphatically thank our contributing authors and colleagues who continue to work towards a better future.

References

Canadian Institute for Public Safety Research and Treatment (CIPSRT). (2019). Glossary of terms: A shared understanding of the common terms used to describe psychological trauma (version 2.0). Regina, SK: Author.

Carleton, R. N., Afifi, T. O., Turner, S., Taillieu, T., Vaughan, A. D., Anderson, G. S., ... Camp, R. D. I. (2020). Mental health training, attitudes towards support, and screening positive for mental disorders. *Cognitive Behaviour Therapy*, *49*, 55–73. https://doi.org/10.1080/16506073.2019.1575900.

Index

Note: Page numbers in **bold** and *italics* refer to tables and figures, respectively.

Abdulmohsen, A. E. **95**
abnormal fear responses 359
abusive relationships 325
acoustic startle response (ASR) 355
acquisition 375, 377, 379
Adamec, R. E. 354, 380, 383
adaptive information processing 458
addictions 132, 221
Adeponle, A. B. **77**
adjunctive treatment for recurrent
  depressive disorder 466–467
adrenal hormones 30
adult PTSD **151–155**
adverse childhood experiences 131, **151**
Ahmad, K. **85**
Alberta 111
alcohol: and drug abuse 223; misuse
  co-morbidity 271
American Civil War 16–17
American Psychological Association
  (APA) 3, 17, 140, 192
amygdala hypertrophy 356
androgyny theory 180
anger 131, 141, **151**
anhedonia-like symptoms 353
animal models of PTSD 343–344, 378;
  chronic stress models 351–352; early
  life stressors 345–347; electric shock
  347–349; genetic models of PTSD-
  like symptoms 358–359; optogenetics
  359; physical stressors 347–352;
  psychosocial stressors 352–357;
  restraint stress 350–351; role, in
  research 344–345; single prolonged
  stress (SPS) 350–351; underwater
  trauma 351
anisomycin 381
anti-anxiety medication 309

antidepressants 309, 353
anti-femininity 183
anxiety 16, 18, 112–113, 132, 137, **152**,
  209, 309, 323; behavioural anxiety
  350; disorder 5, 157, 270; -like
  behaviour 350, 381; -like responses
  358; -like symptoms 353; men and
  masculinities 177; mood and anxiety
  disorders 132; PTSD-like anxiety 350
anxiolytic treatment 349
APA *see* American Psychological
  Association
Arksey, H. 198
Armour, C. **79, 98**
Army Alpha 21
Army Beta 21
Arvay, M. J. **79**
Asmundson, G. J. G. **82, 98**
ASR *see* acoustic startle response
associative learning 374, 376; *see also*
  non-associative learning
asthma 162, 221
asylum-seeking populations 163
Atkinson, R. C. 392n1
attention deficit disorder 209
Auger, C. **94**
avoidance behaviours 434
avoidant attachment 204

Bagheri, A. **77**
Bailey, M. R. 373
Baines, D. 309
Balsam, P. D. 373
battle fatigue 109
BDNF *see* brain-derived neurotrophic
  factor
BDNF receptor tyrosine receptor
  kinase B (TrkB) 377

BDNF transcription 377
Beal, A. L. **72**
Beard, G. 17
Beck Anxiety Inventory 466–467
Beck Depression Inventory-II 469
behavioural abnormalities 353
behavioural anxiety 350
behavioural independence 204
Beiser, M. **70**
Bell, V. **89**
Bem, S. L. **179**, 181
Bem Sex Role Inventory 181
Bench, P. J. 27
Benoit, A. C. **76**
Berdahl, J. L. **180**, 186
beyond-trauma approach 117
Biehn, T. L. **79**
Big Wheel, The (Brannon) 182
bilateral stimulation 462
Bill C-10 300
Bliss, T. V. 376
Boer War 16
Boolean operators 265
Bornstein, S. 297
Boulos, D. **79–80**, **97**
Boyer, R. **71**, **103**
brain activity investigation 461
brain-derived neurotrophic factor
   (BDNF) 354, 377
brain mechanisms 373
Brannon, R. **179**, 182–183, 187
breast cancer 416, 469–470
Brink, J. H. **66**, **77**
British Medical Association 18
Broca, P. 16, 22
Brown, R. 118
Brunet, A. **71**
brutalities 18
Bureau de normalisation du Québec
   125
burnout 223–225, 229; civilian version
   225; Professional Quality of Life
   (PROQoL) instrument 225; PTSD
   Check List 225; rates 237–238;
   regression analysis **230**
Burns, C. 250
Buzzard, E. F. 24

Caddick, N. 190
Calhoun, L. G. 321–322, 332
Canada, prevalence of PTSD 38–39,
   134; clinical 47; data extraction
   40–41; descriptive analyses *44–45*,
   46; discussion 48–50; economic
   burden of 38; eligibility criteria
40; *Federal Framework on Post-
   Traumatic Stress Disorder Act*
   39; indigenous populations 164;
   lifetime prevalence 48–49, **65–72**;
   methods 39–41; non-occupation
   related studies 48–49; PPTEs 157;
   PTSD prevalence 43–46; quality
   assessment 41, 46–48; search
   results 41–42; search strategy 40,
   63–64; self-reported 47; strengths
   and limitations 50–51; study
   characteristics 42–43; study selection
   40
Canadian Armed Forces (CAF) 198,
   431, 437
Canadian-born women-infant pairs
   163
*Canadian Charter of Rights and
   Freedoms* 114
Canadian Community Health Survey
   158; 2002 43, 49; 2012 43, 49
Canadian Community Health Survey-
   Canadian Forces Supplement
   (CCHS- CFS) 160–161
Canadian Forces Mental Health
   Survey (CFMHS) 161
Canadian HIV Women's Sexual
   Reproductive Health Cohort 166
Canadian immigrants 163
Canadian Institute for Public Safety
   Research and Treatment (CIPSRT)
   264, 300, 430
Canadian PTSD estimates 158–160;
   Canadian Armed Forces 160–161;
   careers with frequent PPTE
   exposures 161–162; homeless
   populations 163–164; indigenous
   populations 164; maternal PTSD
   164–165; medical comorbidity
   162–163; migrant populations 163;
   other population 165–166; youth
   samples 165; *see also* Canada,
   prevalence of PTSD
Canadian Standard Association 114
Canadian Standard for Psychological
   Health and Safety in the Workplace
   125
Canadian Standards Association 125
cancer 159; diagnosis and treatment
   468
cardio-pulmonary disabilities 221
cardiovascular arousal 17
cardiovascular diseases 159
Careful Workplace, The (Shain) 114
Carleton, R. N. 8, **100**, 134

492 *Index*

Caron, J. **87**
Cartesian dualism 16, 22
Catchpole, R. E. H. **89**
cerebral activity, abnormal 461
c-Fos staining 382
Charcot, J. M. 17–18
Charcot's hypnosis therapy 17–18
Chaulk, S. J. 10, 487
childhood: adversity 431; maltreatment 159; trauma 345
Childhood Trauma Questionnaire (CTQ) 159
child pornography 248, 254
Children's Impact of Traumatic Events Scale – II (CITES-II) 165
child sex crime: investigations 9; sexual victimization 248
child welfare system 221
cholecystokinin receptor-2 (CCK-2) 349
chronic: antidepressant administration 354; bronchitis 159; fatigue syndrome 159; mild stress 356; obstructive pulmonary disorder 221; pain 132, 154, 159; social instability 356; stress 111, 351–352; stressors 115, 139
chronic variable stress (CVS) 351
CINAHL 200, 265
civilian traumatisation 27
Clarke, D. E. **94**
Cleveland, J. **87**
Clinician-Administered PTSD Scale (CAPS) 139, 160
clinician–patient relationship 135
Cochrane 265
cognitive behavioural therapy 460, 467
cognitive processing therapy 433–437, 444; demographic variables **439–440**; effectiveness 447; individually and group therapy formats 436, 448–450; therapeutic benefits 435; trauma-focused psychological interventions 435
Cohen, H. **88**, 354
Cohen model 355
Collin-Vezina, D. **85**, **87**
Colquhoun, H. 198
combat neurosis 28–29; *see also* Shell Shock
combat trauma 8, 431
communicable diseases 221
comorbidity 281, 283
compassion fatigue 224
compensation for chronic stressors 115

compensation for mental disorder 114
Complex PTSD 139
Composite International Diagnostic Interview (CIDI) 159
conditioned stimulus 374
Conformity to Masculine Norms Inventory (CMNI) 183
consolidation 375–376
Copenhagen Psychosocial Questionnaire 122, 124
Corneil, W. **104**
correctional officers 296–298; burnout 300; contextualizing correctional services 298–301; critical incidents 302–309; environmental conditions 299, 302; health and well- being 299; help-seeking behaviour 309; interpersonal violence 302–309; mental health 302–309; methods 301; occupational stressors 300; part-time employees 301; personal and social life 309–312; PPTE 302–309, 311; presumptive legislation 312; results 302; self-reported health impacts 301; treatment 314; violence in prison 306–309
Correctional Service Canada (CSC) 298, 300
Corrigan, 255–256
Corrigan, P. W. 257
cortical function 457
cortisol levels, abnormal baseline 345
Covidence software 201
cowardice 24
Cramm, H. 9, 484
criminalized homeless 325
Critical Incident Stress Debriefing 240–241
Crohn's disease/ ulcerative colitis 159
Cronbach's alpha 229
Culpin, M. 23
cultural differences 155
Cunningham, I. 309
Curran, K. 326
cynicism 258

DaCosta's syndrome 17
Dallaire, Roméo 31
Davidson Trauma Scale (DTS) 162
depersonalization 223
depression 141, **152**, 209, 323
depressive disorders 112, 158
desensitization and reprocessing therapy 433
Desmarais, S. L. **87**

detachment 131
detoxification 325
diabetes 221
Diagnostic and Statistical Manual of Mental Disorders (DSM) 2, 50, 132–133; Clinician-Administered PTSD Scale-5 449; DSM-5 4–7, 138–139, 158, 167, 189, 226, 403, 438; DSM-III 5–6, 31, 343; DSM-III-R 6; DSM-IV 6, 157–158; DSM-IV-TR 6, 157, 159; gross stress reaction 29–30; pre-DSM-V 166
Diagnostic Interview Schedule for Children (DISC-4) 165
Dietrich, A. **90**
diminished feelings of personal accomplishment 223
dirty work 9, 248, 250, 254, 483; *see also* emotional labour and dirty work; sex crimes against children
dirty workers 249
disability 141
disagreements 2
discrepancy strain 184
distress on exposure 131
Dog-Eat-Dog 186
Doherty, C. E. 23–24
domestic violence calls 249
dose–response relationship 344, 353
drug dependence 159
Druss, B. G. 257
Du Fort, G. G. **69**
Dugal, N. **93**
Duranceau, S. **99**
dynamic nature of memory 374–375
dysfunctional fear modulation 349

Eadie, E. M. **93**
eating disorders 209
eclectic psychotherapy 460
effort syndrome 17
Eisenmann, E. D. 9, 486
Eisler, R. M. **180**, 185
electric shock 347–349
electroencephalogram (EEG) 350, 463, 469
electromyography (EMG) 350
electroshock therapy 22
elevated plus maze (EPM) 351, 388, 401
Elhai, J. D. **99**
Embase 200, 265
EMDR *see* eye movement desensitization and reprocessing;

eye movement desensitization and reprocessing (EMDR)
EMDR- Integrative Group Treatment Protocol 464
emotion(al) 253; contagion 278; detachment 304; distance 204; Emotion Thermometers 464; exhaustion 223; labour 253; numbing 415; regulation 211; support 409–411, 418
emotional labour and dirty work 247–248; data analysis 253; data collection 252–253; method 251–253; policing 248–251; QSR Nvivo qualitative research software 253; qualitative research project 251; results 253–258; Sex-crime investigators 247–258; sex crimes against children 248
engagement 133
enhanced negative feedback 345
environmental hazards 131
epidemiology of PTSD in Canada 157; DSM IV to 5 157–158; estimates 158–166
Erickson, J. **88**
etho-pharmacological exploration 389–392
Ewles, G. B. 10, 486
exposure freezing *388*
extreme behavioural response (EBR) 354
eye movement desensitization and reprocessing (EMDR) 457–460; as add-on treatment 466–467; adjunctive treatment for recurrent depressive disorder 466–467; applications beyond PTSD 463–469; on brain neurobiology in maltreated children 465–470; in child survivors of earthquakes 463–464; clinical and neurobiological effects 468–469; mechanisms of action 460–461; neurobiological correlates of trauma 461–463; in patients with substance use disorder 467–468; sequelae of PPTE 458; treatment **459**

Fallot, R. D. 135
familial disconnect 27
family- centred model of PTSD 214
Farley, M. **102**
fatigue 17
fear 18, 131, 374; cues 373; memories 374, 381; *see also* anxiety

494 *Index*

Federal Framework on Post- Traumatic Stress Disorder Act 39
feline predator stress model 387
female-typed traits (femininities) 181
femininity 17, 188
Fenta, H. **93**
Fetzner, M. G. **99**
fight-or-flight response 430
Fikretoglu, D. **71**, **95**
firefighters and PTSD 264–265; belonging and social supports 277–278; career firefighters 269; charting the data 266; collating, summarizing, and reporting the results 266; comorbidity 270–271; complex interplay of factors 271–273; critical incidents 268, 269; cumulative exposures 274; data charting 266; directed content analysis 266; early identification and critical incidents 276–277; individual personality traits 271; limitations 283; mental illness on productivity 264; occupational demands 264; occupational factors 272–273; organizational factors 276; panic and phobic disorders 271; person level factors 271–272; PPTE exposure 268–269, 274–275; prevalence, PTSD 270; primary prevention efforts 279; Prisma chart 267; psychological health 279; PTSD among 270–271, 276–280; relevant studies, identifying the 265; research question, identifying the 265; results 266–267; search terms 265; self-efficacy 272; social support 273; stress 274–276; study selection 266; suicidal behaviours, risk 266; trauma exposure among 267; volunteer firefighters 269
Firestone, M. **88**
first-responder occupations 111
First Responders Support Network 421
flashbacks 131, 462
Fleury, M.-J. **87**
Flynn, Kevin 112
foetal distress **151**
foot problems 221
foot-shock models 347–348
Ford-Gilboe, M. **95**
Forsyth, D. 19
forward psychiatry 22
Frankl, P. W. 324

Frewen, P. A. **90**
friend support 408
Frise, S. **70**
from molecule to memory 376–377

Garber, B. G. **101**
Garcia, H. 190
Garton, W. 22
gastrointestinal illnesses 159
gastrointestinal symptoms **151**
Gender Role Conflict (O'Neil) 185
gender role socialization 177–178
gender role strain 184
General Adaptation Syndrome 28
General Anxiety Disorder-7 442–443
genetics in susceptibility to stress 358
genome–environmental interactions 358
Gillis, K. **74**
Give'Em Hell (Brannon) 182–183
glucocorticoid responsiveness 347
Goodwin, R. D. **82**
Grenier, Stéphane 5
Gretton, H. M. **76**
Grigoriadis, S. **76**
gross stress reaction 29–30
Group Climate Questionnaire (GCQ) 440, 450
group cognitive processing therapy 429, 447; effectiveness 441–442; vs. individual cognitive processing therapy 448–450; psychological interventions for PTSD 433–437; psychological symptoms of distress, reduction 443–444; psychological trauma 430–432
group psychotherapy 434
Guglietti, C. **65**
Gulf War 109, 203
gut-brain axis **151**

habituation 374
Hall, A. 8, 485
Harris, M. E. 135
Harvard Trauma Questionnaire (HTQ) 163
Hausdorf, P. A. 411
Hawryluck, L. **78**
health and safety legislation 115
health care avoidance **153**
Health Sciences Association of British Columbia 115
Hebb, Donald O. 376
Hébert, M. **89**, 165
Heffren, C. D. J. 411

Index 495

Helmreich, R, L. **179**, 181
help-seeking behaviours 276, 416
Hensel, J. **65**, **81**
hepatitis 221
Hepatitis B/C 305
Hetherington, E. **83**
"Hierarchy of Controls" model 123
hippocampal volume 345
hippocampus 345–346
Hirschfeld, A. 415
HIV/AIDS 221, 305
Hochschild, A. 248
Holahan, C. K. 181
homelessness 163–164, 222
homicide 438
hormone balance, changes in 359
Horswill, S. C. 8
HPA axis 355
Hudson, D. **74**
human intelligence 21; *see also* Army
   Alpha; Army Beta
human psychiatric disorders 345
Human Rights Codes 125
Hwang, S. W. **83**
hyperactivation of the limbic system
   462
hyperarousal 359, 381, 462; memory
   391
hypermasculinity 276, 281
hypertension 159
hypervigilance 131, 141
hypothalamus-pituitaryadrenal (HPA)
   axis 345–346
hysteria 24–26; causal mechanisms of
   16–17; Charcot's hypnosis therapy
   17; social stigma 18; treatments 18

iatrogenic experiences 131
Impact of Event Scale (IES) 162
imprisonment 318; abusive
   relationships 325; adaptation to 323;
   benevolence 321; meaningfulness of
   world 321; negative consequences of
   318; positive re-interpretation 324;
   self-worth 321; substance abuse 325;
   victimization 325
incarceration 330–331
inflammatory markers 357
informational support 411
institutionalized personality traits
   331
instrumental support 411
Integrative Behavioural Couple
   Therapy 420–421
internal stress 185

International Association of Fire
   Fighters (IAFF) 264
International Classification of Diseases
   (ICD) 4–5, 163
International Prospective Register of
   Systematic Reviews (PROSPERO)
   39
inter-personal and community violence
   131
interpersonal conflict 420
interpersonal dysfunction 131
interpersonal traumatic events 431
intrusive involuntary memories 131
intrusive thoughts 462
Iraq and Afghanistan veterans 198
Iraq and Afghanistan Wars 109
irritability 28, 131
irritability and anger 131, 141
irritable heart 17

Jakupcak, M. 190–191
Janoff- Bulman, R. 321
Jetly, Rakesh 118
Jolliffe, E. 118

Kaiser normalization 229
Karaffa, K. M. 257
Kardiner, A. 28–29
Kaufmann cure 22
Keefe, A. 297
Kheirbek, M. A. 382
Khitab, A. **77**
Kierkegaard, S. 16
Koch, J. M. 257
Koltek, M. **73**
Korean and Vietnam wars 29–31
Kuksis, M. **93**

Lalonde, F. **88**
Lamoureux-Lamarche, C. **75**
Lancee, W. J. **67**, **81**
Lane, A. M. 9
Langendorff isolated heart system 357
Laposa, J. M. **104**
Law, R. **75**
learned helplessness 348
learning 375
learning disabilities 209
Lebanese Civil War 203
Ledgerwood, D. M. **65**
Lee, J. **81**
Levac, D. E. 198
Levant, R. F. **179**, 183, 187
Levine, R. E. **91**
LGBTQ+subpopulations 166

496   *Index*

life-threatening diagnosis **153**
life-threatening illness 160
lifetime PTSD prevalence 133
Lippel, K. 110–111
living on the streets 221
Lømo, T. 376
long-term memory 375
long-term potentiation 376
loss of loved one, sudden 431
Lotze, H. 16
Loughlin, J. O. 191

MacCallum, P. 10, 486
Mahalik, J. R. **180**, 183, 187
maladaptive beliefs act 434
maladaptive developmental changes 345
Malat, J. **78**
male-valued personality traits 179
malingering 24–25
manhood 185–186
Manitoba's law 111
Marrello, D. 9, 483
Martin, C. E. 299
Martin, N. **67**
Maruna, S. 326
masculine gender role: norms 132; stress 185
Masculine Gender Role Stress (Eisler & Skidmore) 1885
Masculinity Contest Culture (MCC) 186
masculinity ideology 179, 181
Maunder, R. **103**, 118
Maxfield, L. 458
MAXQDA 202, 266
McCreary, D. R. 9, 485
McIntyre-Smith, A. M. **82**
McLean, L. M. **70**
mechanistic Target of Rapamycin (mTOR) kinase 377
medically unexplained symptoms 132
Medline 265
memory: defined 375; dynamic nature of 374–375; from molecule to 376–377; trace 375; traumatic fear memories 373
men and masculinities 9, 177–180; depression 177; gender role strain, stress, confl ict, and precarious manhood 184–187; generalized anxiety 177; ideology 181–182; importance of 191; male role norms 182–184; masculine-typed personality traits 180–181; mental

disorders 177; mental health 9, 178, 187–188; mental health treatment experiences 188–189; PTSD, application to 189–191; reviewed constructs **179–180**; self-perceptions of 190; substance abuse issues 177
mental disorders 112, 221; defined 3–4, 38; diagnostic discourse 4; distress or impairment 4; health services for 39; inherent labelling 4; prevalence rates in public safety 403
mental health: benefits 319; disorders 323; injuries 7, 486; professionals 212, 223; related disability 31; related experiences 50; stigma 132, 187; strategy 118
Mental Health Commission of Canada 125
mental illness: defined 3; hereditary 24
Mental Injury Tool Group 121–126
mental stress 110
mesolimbic dopamine pathway 354
Meta-analysis of Observational Studies in Epidemiology (MOOSE) guidelines 39
migraine headaches 159
military combat 131
Military Family Resource Centres 212
Military Masculinity 190
military veteran families 198–199, 484; changes in relationships 203–204; charting the data 202; child development 207; children and civilian spouses 203; communication patterns 204–205; directionality of transmission 210; emotional demands 208; ex-POW 210; family adaptation to military veteran PTSD 210–212; family-centred care 211; family environment and communication styles 208; family's emotional and psychological distress 208; female civilian spouse 202; partner's withdrawal 204; PTSD disrupts family functioning and well-being 203–207; relevant studies, identifying 199–202; research question, identifying 199; resilience, enhancing 211; results 202–203; roles and responsibilities 205–207; secondary trauma in children 209–210; secondary trauma in spouses 208–209; spousal cohabitation, separation, and divorce 203; spousal mental health and

well-being 208; spouse's desire for intimacy and closeness 204; spouses of prisoners of war (POW) 209; trauma and family systems 207–210; treatment and support programs 211–212
Milliard, B. 118
Mini International Neuropsychiatric Interview (MINI) 159
Mini International Neuropsychiatric Interview-Plus 164
minimal behavioural response (MBR) 354
Ministry of Community Safety and Correctional Services 124
misconduct 323
mistrust 131
modified PTSD Symptom Scale (MPSS-SR) 164–165
Monson, E. **68, 85**
Montgomery, Adam 31
mood and anxiety disorders 132–133
Moran, C. M. W. 24
Morrison, A. R. 191
motor vehicle accidents 131
mTOR 377–378; activation by subregion *385*; activation in control and stressed groups *384–385*; hyperarousal memory 391; pavlovian fear conditioning 379–380; pharmacological treatments 377–378; phospho mTOR 382, 384; in predator stress 381; predator stress-induced fear memories 382; and Rapamycin 373–392
multiple chemical sensitivities 159
muscle cramps 19
Myers, C. S. 19
myocardial infarction (MI) 162

National Institute of Mental Health 240
natural disasters 131
negative attitudes towards sexual minorities 183
negative moods, even related 131
negative self-perspectives 4
Neis, B. 297
Nelson, C. **83, 95**
neuroanatomical distribution of mTOR activation 382–386
neurochemistry 359
neurodevelopmental changes 345
neuropeptide Y 355
neurotic disturbances 28

Newcastle–Ottawa Quality Assessment **105–108**
Newcastle–Ottawa Scale scoring guide 64
Newman, S. C. **69**
nightmares 131, **152**, 462
N- methyl- D- aspartate (NMDA) glutamate 376–377
nociception 350
non-associative learning 374–376
non-associative memory testing 388; acoustic startle testing 402; behavioural testing 401; drug administration 401; light/dark box 402; open field 401
non-genomic intergeneration transmission 358
non-trauma- focused psychotherapies 450
norepinephrine levels 357
No Sissy Stuff (Brannon) 182

O'Brien, K. K. 198
occupational demands 418
Occupational Health and Safety Act 118–121, 123
Occupational Health Clinics 122, 124
occupational potentially psychologically traumatic event exposure 273
occupational PTSD 154
occupational stress injuries 2, 124
occupational stressors 276, 296, 300
Ohayon, M. M. **92**, 158
O'Malley, L. 198
O'Neil, J. M. **180**, 185
Ontario: Bill 127 115; Bill 163 119, 121–123; firefighters and paramedics 116; *Occupational Health and Safety Act* 118–121, 123; Occupational Health Clinics 121–122
Ontario Federation of Labour (OFL) 117, 119
Ontario Ministry of Safety and Correctional Services 116
Ontario Nurses' Association (ONA) 119
Ontario Public Service Employees Union 113, 117, 119, 124–125
Ontario unions 124
Ontario Workplace Safety and Insurance Board (WSIB) 115
operational exhaustion 109
operational stress injuries (OSI) 2, 5, 40, 437–438

498 *Index*

Oppenheim, H. 17, 19
Oppenheim's concept of traumatic neurosis 26
optogenetic modelling 359
orexin system 355
organizational emotional labour 249
organizational social support 407
organizational stress injuries 5
Ottawa Police Association in Ontario 408
Ovid MEDLINE 200

Pagani, M. 463
paralleling associative fear memories 381
parent–child tumult 255
partial behavioural response (PBR) 354
pathological hyperarousal 141
Patient Health Questionnaire 44
Patterson, B. 9, **84**
pavlovian fear conditioning 374, 378–379; limitations 380; mTOR 379–380
Pavlovian model 374
PCL-C 225–226, 229
PC-PTSD (Primary Care PTSD) screening tool 138
peer support programs 407–408
pension hysterics 25
pension-seeking Canadian war vetrans 160
Pepys, S. 16
Perlick, D. A. 257
Personal Attributes Questionnaire 181
personal limitations 421
personal support networks 486
personal transformation 324
person-by-situation interaction 178
pharmacological treatments: animal models of PTSD 378; consolidation 375–376; dynamic nature of memory 374–375; from molecule to memory 376–377; mTOR 377–378; mTOR and pavlovian fear conditioning 379–380; pavlovian fear conditioning 378–379; predator stress 380–392; PTSD 373; rapamycin 377–378
pharmacotherapy 141
phobic avoidance 141
Phoenix, C. 190
phone interviews 158
phospho mTOR 382
Phosphorylated cAMP response element binding protein (pCREB) 383
physical and sexual abuse 460

physical health conditions 132
physical health problems 159
physical injury 131
"physical- mental" claims 110
physical stressors 347; chronic stress models 351–352; electric shock 347–349; restraint stress 350–351; single prolonged stress (SPS) 350–351; underwater trauma 351
physical traumas 7
physical violence 326
physiological hypersensitivity 28
Pleck, J. H. **179**, 181, 183–184
Plesner v. British Columbia Hydro and Power Authority 114
Podnar, D. J. 10
Pogrebin, M. R. 253
policing: challenges 247–248; child exploitation online 248; cynicism 258; digital communication technologies 247; Internet Child Exploitation (ICE) units 247–248; mental health service 258; of online environments 247; online luring and the production 248; sex crimes against children 253; sexual violence-related units 249; vicarious traumatization 258; videos, examining 254–255
Poole, E. D. 253
population, interventions, comparisons, outcomes, and study design framework (PICO) 39
positive illusion *see* posttraumatic growth
positive screenings for PTSD 163
positive therapeutic alliance 446
post-incarceration syndrome 331
postnatal stress 346
posttraumatic growth 139, 321–322; appreciation of life 321; defined 330; new possibilities in life 321; personal growth and a strengthening 329; personal strength 321; positive changes 322; relational dimension 329; relationships with others 321; spiritual change 321
posttraumatic stress 5
posttraumatic stress disorder (PTSD) 1, 15, 31–32, 109–110, 482; avoidance of stimuli associated with traumatic event 6; in Canada 8; checklist for DSM-5 440; defined 4–5, 131, 143, 198; diagnosis 133, 403; distress on exposure 131;

DSM-III diagnosis of 6; emotional numbing 415; flashbacks 131; heterosexual relationships, impact on 204; hyper-arousal symptoms 6; interpersonal dysfunction 131; intrusions related to the traumatic event 6; intrusive involuntary memories 131; lifetime prevalence 161; manifestations of 131; negative cognitions and mood 6; negative moods, even related 131; nightmares 131; PCL-C 225–226; presumptive injury 33; prevalence rates 157; in primary care 143; rate of 198; screening 144; secondary trauma **200–201**; self-report questionnaires 440; significant dissociation 131; susceptibility 32, 345; symptoms transmission 213; syndrome 140; trauma-and stress-related disorders 6; traumatizing event, avoidance of reminders of 131

posttraumatic stress injuries (PTSI) 2, 4–5, 40, 248

posttraumatic stress symptom (PTSS) 2, 4

post-war mental health challenges 20

potentially psychologically traumatic events (PPTE) 7, 15, 29, 112, 132, 134, 139, 177, 198, 430, 482; careers with frequent PPTE exposures 161–162; exposure to 15, 134; historical context 16–18; memory 375; *see also* posttraumatic stress disorder (PTSD)

potentially traumatic exposures **152**

potentiation 376

Poundja, J. **103**

predator-based psychosocial stress model 355–357, 359–360

predator odour 354–355

predator stress 354, 380–392; cat exposure 380–381; consolidation, and protein synthesis 381–382; experimental approaches 382–392; mTOR in 381; protein synthesis 381

predator stress-induced fear memories 382–386

predator stress-induced memory formation 392

Preferred Reporting Items for Systematic Reviews and Meta-Analyses (PRISMA) 39, *42*

prenatal stress 345

presumptive legislation 109

presumptive legislation in Canada and PTSD 109–113; exclusion of chronic stress 114–116; *Five-Year Plan for Workplace Injury and Illness Prevention* initiative 112; health and safety legislation 115; mental injury tool model 123–126; New Brunswick 113; Ombudsman's report 116; Ontario's focus on PTSD and first responders 116–121; Ontario workers 112; police officers' complaints 116; Prince Edward Island 113; Saskatchewan 113; Union Response to Bill 163 121–123

pretrauma personality traits 272

Prevatt, B.S. **93**

primary care, PTSD in 131–133; adult PTSD in primary care 142; brriers and facilitators to recognition and diagnosis 136–137; clinicians 135–136; delay in treatment 133; diagnosis 139–140; documented detection 134; knowledge transfer tool 143; psychiatric disorder 3, 132–134, 158; psychologically traumatic events 143; psychological trauma 134–135; reattribution 136; reframing 136; screening 137–139, 144; "trauma-informed" primary care 135–142; treatment 140–142, 144

primary care clinicians 133, 136, 140–141; adult PTSD 142; Clinician-Administered PTSD Scale (CAPS) 139; clinician–patient relationship 135; detection or documentation 134; pharmacotherapy by 141; psychotherapy by 141; PTSD treatment 140

primary care physicians 485

Primary Care PTSD DSM-5 137–138

primary traumatic events 241

prisoner assault 300

prisoner-on-prisoner violence 304

prisoners, posttraumatic growth 318–320; financial problems 319; homelessness 319; in-prison activities 330; low educational attainment 319; manifestation of posttraumatic growth among 322–328; mental health problems 319; methodological note 320; need for meaning 324–326; need for survival 322–324; negative consequences 330; positive illusion 329–331; posttraumatic

500 *Index*

growth 318, 320–322; posttraumatic growth in ex-prisoners 322; PPTE 318; psychological suffering 324; religion and redemption 326–328; self-improvement and strengthening relationships 328–329; self-reported transformation 330; substance abuse 319; unemployment 319; victimization 319

prisoners of war (POW) 209, 213
Prison Health Policy Unit 325
Prison Health Task Force, 2002 325
prison work 302; everyday violence 306–309; *see also* correctional officers
Professional Quality of Life (PROQoL) instrument 225
professional use of self 242n1
prolonged exposure therapy 433
PROSPERO 50
protein synthesis 376, 381
protein synthesis inhibitors 375, 381; *see also* anisomycin
protracted traumatic events 322
provider–patient relationship 140
provincial jurisdictions in Canada 110; mental health claims 110
psychiatric disorders 3, 132–134, 158
psychiatric illness 3
psychiatry 16
psychodynamic interventi 23
psychodynamic therapies 21
psychoeducation on PTSD 434
psychological androgyny 180
psychological disorder 3
psychological first aid 140
psychological gender 178
Psychological Health and Safety in the Workplace 114
psychological injuries 110
psychologically traumatic birth experiences **151**
psychologically traumatic events 7, 110, 143, 145; at work 403
psychological maltreatment 460
psychological stress 346
psychological stressors 7
psychological traumas 5, 7, 17, 131, 136, 143, **152**, 429
psychoneurosis 28
psychosocial stressors 352; predator-based psychosocial stress 355–357; predator odour 354–355; predator stress 354; social defeat stress 352–354

psychotherapy 18, 22, 141, 433
PsycINFO 200, 265
PTSD-like anxiety 350
PTSD-like symptoms, genetic models of 358–359
PTSD models 354
public safety personnel (PSP) 6, 160
Puri, N. **66**
Put Work First 186

randomized controlled trial of civilians 436
rapamycin 377–378, 381, 389, 392, 401
rapid eye movement theory 461
rat-exposure test: and fear memory 387–389; and rapamycin 389–392
Red Cross training case workers 27
Redwood-Campbell, L. **92**
Re-Engineering Systems of Primary Care Treatment in the Military (RESPECT-Mil) 138
refugee 163
RefWorks version 2.0 40
Regambal, M. J. **104**
Regehr, R. **103**
religious conversion 326–327
Resick, P. A. 436
resilience-enhancing cultural interventions 282
respiratory diseases 159
restraint stress 350–351
Reynolds, J. J. **151**
Ricciardelli, R. 9, 483
Richardson, J. D. **67**, **99–100**, **102**
Richmond, K. 187
Rivers, W. H. 23
Robinson, D. **101**
Rodin, G. **84**
Ross, L. E. **92**
Roth, M. L. **90**
Roundtable on Traumatic Mental Stress 117
Rousseau, C. **75**
Royal Canadian Mounted Police (RCMP) 162, 431, 437

Safe Streets and Communities Act 300
Samuels-Dennis, J. A. **93**
Santiago, P. N. 430
Sareen, J. **83**, **96**, 158
Scheibe, S. **81**
Schiffrin, R. M. 392n1
screening 133
secondary traumatic stress 223–225, 229; regression analysis **230**

secondary traumatization 213
Seidler, Z. E. 188–189
selective serotonin reuptake inhibitors (SSRIs) 141, 348
self-forgiveness 326–327
self-identified men 177
self-monitoring 248
self-report questionnaires 440
self-report symptom 438
self-stigma 187, 485
self-sufficiency 204
Selye, Hans 28
sensitization 374
serotonin 357
serotonin-norepinephrine reuptake inhibitors (SNRIs) 141
sertraline 357
session rating scale (SRS) 440
sex-crime investigators 247–258
sex crimes against children 247–248, 483; digital innovations 247; dirty work involve 250; investigation 249; policing 247; PTSD and 247, 250; vicarious traumatization 258
sex offender 255–256
sexual abuse 326
sexual assault 153, 431; survivors 435; victims of 416
sexual exploitation 247
sexual harassment 432
sexual orientation 181
sexual violence 131, 139, 141, 249
Shain, M. 114, 119, 121, 296
Shallow, T. 380
shame 131
Shapiro, C. M. 158
Shapiro, F. 458
Shell Shock 19–26, 109, 429; childishness 26; electroshock therapy 22; familial disconnect 27; femininity 26; S 20; W 20
shock-induced Pavlovian fear memories 382
short-term memory 375
Show No Weakness 186
significant dissociation 131
Sikka, A. 110–111
"Silence to Violence" program 331
single photon emission computed tomography studies 462
single prolonged stress (SPS) 350–351
sinking 323
Skidmore, J. **180**, 185
skills-based training 420
sleep deprivation study 355

sleep disturbances 58, 131, 462
sleep pathology 154
Smith, B. 190
social debilitation 4
social defeat stress 352–354
Social Epidemiological Model 122–123
social identity 327
socially desirable personality traits 181
social phobia 158–159
Social Sciences and Humanities Research Council (SSHRC) 259n1
social-sensory deprivation syndrome 331
social support and public safety personnel 403–405; alignment 419; availability 419; barriers to seeking and providing support 412–416; challenges providing effective support 416–419; emotional support 409–410; formal organizational supports, role of 406–408; friend support 408; improving social support 419–421; organizational and community supports 422; personal support networks, role of 408–410; quality 419; role of 405–406; spousal support 408–409; support providers 421–422; support seekers 421; traumatic event exposures, support following 411–412
social withdrawal 154
Sociological Abstracts 200
Sockalingam, S. **66**
soldier's heart 17
soldier suicides 17
Soyer, M. 330
Spence, J. T. **179**, 181, 483
Spencer, D. 9
spouses/romantic partners: needs 421; resource mobilization 413; spouses of prisoners of war (POW) 209; support 408–409
stabilization 133
Stamm, B. H. 223
Stapleton, J. A. **100**
startle response 131
State-Trait Anxiety Inventory 468
Stein, M. B. **91**, 145
Stewart, D. E. **91**
stigma 407, 413
stoicism 190, 276
Strehlau, V. **86**
Strength and Stamina 186
stress from the war 29

502 *Index*

stressors 4–5; chronic 115, 139; early life 345–347; occupational 276, 300; physical 347–352; psychological 7; psychosocial 352–357; work-related 405
stressor–strain relationship 405
stress prevention 121
Stretch, R. H. **71**
Structured Clinical Interview (SCID) 162, 165
Stuber, M. L. **94**
Sturdy Oak, The (Brannon) 182
sub cortical amygdala 377
substance abuse 325
substance-use disorder (SUD) 132, 163
suicides **152**, 438; attempted 323; behaviours, risk 266; ideation 184; soldier 17
support for self-esteem 411
Supporting Ontario's First Responders Act 112
susceptibility 359
sychological trauma 8
symptom- based questionnaire 50
synapse 376
Szymanski, T. 8, 485

talk therapy 23, 420
Taylor, S. E. **87**
Tedeschi, R. G. 321–322, 332
thalamocortical binding model 461
therapeutic alliance of psychotherapy 450
Thompson, E. H., Jr. 183, 485–486
Thompson, J. M. 8, **179**
tianeptine 356
Tibbo, P. **74**
Torchalla, I. **94**
total warfare 18
toughness 183
traditional male role norms 179
transgenic manipulations 349
translational utility of foot-shock 349
trauma-and stressor-related disorders 6, 132, 157, 189
trauma-aware primary care 143
trauma-focused Cognitive Behavioural Therapy 457
trauma-focused psychotherapy 431, 434, 450
trauma-informed care 133, 135–136, 142, 155, 240, 484; barriers and facilitators 136–137; diagnosis 139–140; screening 137–139, 144; treatment 140–142

trauma-informed clinicians 145
trauma-informed supportive mental health care **151**
trauma-related mental illness 113
trauma survivors 223
trauma symptoms, regression analysis **230**
traumatic events 6; accumulation of 404
traumatic fear memories 373
Traumatic Mental Health Summit 118
traumatic neurosis 17, 19–21, 30
traumatizing event, avoidance of reminders of 131
treatment dropout 142
tremors 17, 19
trench warfare 18
Trentini, C. 10
tuberculosis 221
Turna, J. 9

unconditioned stimulus 374
underwater trauma 351
unexpected death 131

Van Ameringen, M 9, 49–50, **69, 86**
Vandello, J. A. **180**
van Ginneken, E. F. J. C. 9, 484
Vanhooren, S. 9, 484
Varimax rotation 229
Vedantham, K. **72**
Verreault, N. 165
Veterans Affairs Canada: survey 160; technical report 45
vicarious traumatization 415–416
victimization 325
victim–offender relationships 249
victim-sensitive crimes 249
victims of sexual assault 416
victim support 253
Vietnam War 30–31, 132, 203
violent deaths, sudden 431
Vogel, D. L. **73**
Volk, J. S. **83**

Waegemakers Schiff, J. 9
war captivity 322
war neurasthenia 17–18, 21, 24, 26
war neurosis 26
war-related distress 16–17
war-related memories of trauma 23
Weeks, M. 8, **71, 97**
Wilberforce, K. **104**
Wilson, L. 326
Wolfe, J. **91**

Index 503

Woo, W. L. **91**
Woodworth test 20; *see also* Army Alpha; Army Beta
Workers Compensation Act 114
Workers' Compensation Appeals Tribunal decision 114
Workers' Compensation Board (WCB) 111
working within homeless serving sector 221–224; burnout in homelessness services 223–225; coping mechanism 224–226; debriefing protocols 238; demographics 226–229; educational background 228; healthy coping methods 235; homelessness 222; inadequate salaries 239; negative outcome 235–237; organizational acknowledgment, lack of 234; organizational factors 222, 229–233; participant demographics **227**; PPTE 221, 238, 240; PTSD, incidence of 223; qualitative responses 233–237; re-traumatized at work 234; salaries 222; study design and methodology 224–226; trauma-informed care 240; traumatic stress 237; workers, challenges 222–223; workplace and job 237

workplace violence and harassment 115
work-related stressors 405
World Health Organization World Mental Health Composite International Diagnostic Interview (WHO WMH-CIDI) 160
World Trade Center 9/11 terrorist attacks 269
World War I (WWI) 15, 32; beyond the 27–32; end of 26–27; mental health, discourse on 15; neuroses and mental disorders 17; psychological consequences and 18–25
World War II (WWII) 28, 32, 203; psychiatric treatment centres 29
Wright, M. **88**
Wundt, W. 17

Yarvis, J. S. **100**
Yealland, L. R. 24
Yehuda, R. 358
Yom Kippur War 203

Zabkiewicz, D. M. **73**
Zamorski, M. A. **96–98, 101**
Zhang, J. 9

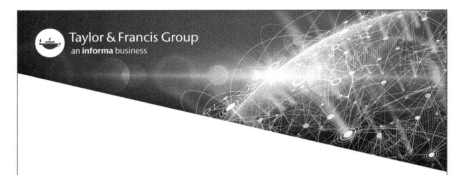

Milton Keynes UK
Ingram Content Group UK Ltd.
UKHW020345270524
443136UK00003B/25